# PAUL V. McNUTT AND THE AGE OF FDR

# PAUL V. McNUTT
## and the Age of
# FDR

DEAN J. KOTLOWSKI

INDIANA UNIVERSITY PRESS   *Bloomington and Indianapolis*

*This book is a publication of*

Indiana University Press
Office of Scholarly Publishing
Herman B Wells Library 350
1320 East 10th Street
Bloomington, Indiana
47405 USA

iupress.indiana.edu

*Telephone* 800-842-6796
*Fax* 812-855-7931

*Manufactured in the United States of America*

Library of Congress Cataloging-in-Publication Data

Kotlowski, Dean J.
Paul V. McNutt and the age of FDR / Dean J. Kotlowski.
pages cm
Includes bibliographical references and index.
ISBN 978-0-253-01468-9 (cl : alk. paper) — ISBN 978-0-253-01473-3 (eb) 1. McNutt, Paul V. (Paul
Vories), 1891–1955. 2. United States—History—1933–1945. 3. Ambassadors—United States—Biography.
4. Governors—Indiana—Biography. 5. Roosevelt, Franklin D. (Franklin Delano), 1882–1945—
Friends and associates. 6. McNutt, Paul V. (Paul Vories), 1891–1955—Travel—Philippines. I. Title.
E748.M157K67 2015
327.2092—dc23
[B]
2014027037

1 2 3 4 5    19 18 17 16 15

*For*
*Darin and Donna*

# Contents

# Acknowledgments

OVER THE PAST TEN YEARS of researching and writing this book, I have had the privilege of visiting approximately three hundred different manuscript collections in seventy-five separate archives across the United States, Canada, and the Philippines. An extraordinary group of individuals and institutions facilitated and invigorated my work, and I am honored to thank them here.

Financial support for this project came early on from Indiana University in Bloomington, particularly the Louise McNutt Endowment; the College of Arts and Sciences, headed by Dean Kumble Subbaswamy at the beginning of this project; and the Department of History, chaired successively by John E. Bodnar, Claude A. Clegg III, and Peter Guardino. Grants-in-aid of research from the following libraries and organizations helped build the archival foundation for this study: the Arthur and Elizabeth Schlesinger Library, Harvard University; the Bentley Historical Library, University of Michigan; the Franklin and Eleanor Roosevelt Institute, Hyde Park, New York; the Harry S. Truman Library Institute, Independence, Missouri; the Herbert Hoover Presidential Library Association, West Branch, Iowa; the Philippine-American Educational Foundation, Makati City, Philippines; and the Fulbright Board, Washington, D.C.

Salisbury University provided assistance in numerous ways, including two semester-long sabbaticals; a year-long leave, during which I served as Paul V. McNutt Visiting Professor of History at Indiana University; and grants to visit archives, give lectures, and present conference papers. I thank the Office of the Provost, headed by Provost Diane D. Allen and the former provosts, David Buchanan and Thomas Jones; the Fulton School of Liberal Arts, led by Dean Maarten L. Pereboom and the former dean, Timothy G. O'Rourke; and the Department of History, including the chair, Creston S. Long, and former chairs Melanie Perreault and Maarten L. Pereboom, who was an early enthusiast of this project, as was our departmental administrator, the late Mia Vye. In addition, I am grateful for support from the Salisbury University Foundation and the Faculty Development fund.

As my research led me in new directions, a dedicated group of librarians and archivists provided valuable expertise and unflagging assistance. I would like in particular to thank the staff at the Lilly Library at Indiana University, especially

Saundra Taylor and David Frasier; the Indiana University Archives, especially Bradley Cook; the Indiana State Library, the Indiana Historical Society, and the Indiana State Archives, especially Rick Applegate; the National Archives at College Park, Maryland; the Franklin D. Roosevelt and Harry S. Truman presidential libraries, especially Robert Clark, William Baehr, Randy Sowell, and the late Elizabeth Safly; the National Library in Manila; and the Library of Congress in Washington, D.C. The Library of Congress is a treasure-house of unpublished materials on the era of the New Deal and World War II, and I especially wish to thank Bryan E. Cornell at the Recorded Sound Reference Center and the staff at the Manuscripts Division: Jeffrey N. Flannery, Frederick Augustyn, Jennifer Brathovde, John Haynes, Joseph Jackson, Patrick Kerwin, Bruce Kirby, and Lewis Wyman.

John L. Krauss and his late wife, Eleanor ("Nonie") Werbe Krauss, generously opened their collection of McNutt family materials, shared memories, and encouraged people who knew McNutt, including Howard and Shirley Krauss, John Hurt, and Anne Veihmeyer, to speak with me. Joanne Raetz Stuttgen gave me a fascinating tour of McNutt's hometown of Martinsville, Indiana. And the late Colleen Kristal Pauwels encouraged me to examine McNutt's files from when he was dean of the Indiana University School of Law.

I am humbled to have had many colleagues and friends read this work in whole or in part, comment on conference papers or journal articles related to it, suggest sources, offer advice, and provide encouragement. I thank Stephen B. Adams, Edward D. Berkowitz, John E. Bodnar, Alexia Bock, Donald T. Critchlow, Nick Cullather, Esmeralda Cunanan, Susan Curtis, Sharon Delmendo, Larry DeWitt, James M. Diehl, Bruce J. Dierenfield, Rene R. Escalante, Jo Ellen Fitzgerald, Anne Foster, Jonathan Goldstein, Victoria González-Rivera, Joan Hoff, Manfred Hutter, Glen Jeansonne, Katherine Jellison, Paul A. Kramer, William Roger Louis, Glenn May, Michael E. McGerr, Barry Mehler, Iwan Morgan, Heiko Muehr, Paul V. Murphy, Jeppe Nevers, Ricky Earl Newport, Lino Nicasio, Henry Oinas-Kukkonen, Keith W. Olson, Klaus Peterson, Nicole Sackley, Eric Sandweiss, Melissa Schock, Tracy Uebelhor, and Allan Winkler. I thank my students at Salisbury University for sharing my enthusiasm for McNutt in my course on America in the Great Depression. I regret that Robert A. Berry, my good friend and mentor in the Department of History at Salisbury University, did not live to see the completion of this book.

Four people made special contributions. James H. Madison, whose immense knowledge of Indiana history is coupled with the elegance of his prose, pointed me toward sources and gave each chapter a close reading. Dean J. Fafoutis was an unstinting supporter of this work from its inception. Friend, colleague, and former editor of *International Social Science Review*, Dean shared his knowledge of political and diplomatic history, listened to my ideas, applauded my discoveries, and edited the entire manuscript with his trademark red pen. As this project neared completion, Manav Ratti generously undertook close readings and offered astute advice for the introductory and concluding chapters. Jim Welsh did not live to see the book's publication, but he remained a steadfast friend, patient listener, champion of my work, and source of inspiration and joy, as is his wife, Anne Welsh.

In preparing this book for the publication, I was fortunate to receive the superb guidance and assistance of a number of talented people. My special thanks go to Robert J. Sloan, editor in chief of Indiana University Press, for his professionalism, flexibility, and wise counsel. Also at Indiana University Press, Jenna Whittaker and Darja Malcolm-Clarke helped transform the manuscript into a book, and Susanna J. Sturgis was an outstanding copyeditor. Rebecca A. Bryant and Blake A. Harvey at the Department of History at Indiana University graciously assisted me during the final phase of research and as the book neared publication. I am grateful to *Diplomatic History, Indiana Magazine of History, International History Review,* and *Journal of Policy History* for permission to reprint material from articles I have published with them. Full citations of these articles appear in the bibliography.

My family provided love, generosity, and welcome diversions throughout my work on this project. I must begin by thanking my mother, Gail Belcher, and my father, Roger Kotlowski, for all that they have given, and by paying tribute to the example and wisdom of my late stepfather, Ronald C. Belcher. As I researched and wrote this book, I drew inspiration from my late grandparents, George K. Kari and Grace R. Kari, who came of age during the Great Depression and World War II, and who gave me my first lessons on Franklin D. Roosevelt. My aunt, Donna Manuele, and my uncle, Salvatore Manuele, have long encouraged my academic endeavors, as have their sons, Jamie and Justin, and their families. My nephews Michael Slater, Nathan Slater, Ryan Slater, and Matthew Kotlowski are all fine young men who continue to inspire me in many ways. My brother, Darin Kotlowski, and my sister, Donna Slater, have been sources of strength, as has my sister-in-law, Amy Kotlowski. It is to Darin and Donna that I dedicate this book.

# Abbreviations

| | |
|---|---|
| ACHS | Allen County–Fort Wayne Historical Society, Fort Wayne, Indiana |
| ALL | National Headquarters of the American Legion Library, Indianapolis, Indiana |
| BHL | Bentley Historical Library, University of Michigan, Ann Arbor |
| *BWS* | *Bloomington Weekly Star* |
| CB | Carlisle Barracks, Pennsylvania |
| CBW | Committees on Biological Warfare |
| CSHM | Center for the Study of History and Memory, Indiana University, Bloomington |
| *CT* | *Chicago Tribune* |
| DDEL | Dwight D. Eisenhower Library, Abilene, Kansas |
| *DMR* | *Des Moines Register* |
| DNC | Democratic National Committee |
| FDRL | Franklin D. Roosevelt Library, Hyde Park, New York |
| FERA | Federal Emergency Relief Administration |
| *FRUS* | *Foreign Relations of the United States* |
| FSA | Federal Security Agency |
| FSU | Florida State University, Tallahassee |
| GMMA | George Meany Memorial Archives, Silver Spring, Maryland |
| GU | Georgetown University, Washington, D.C. |
| HHPL | Herbert Hoover Presidential Library, West Branch, Iowa |
| HL | Houghton Library, Harvard University, Cambridge, Massachusetts |
| HSTL | Harry S. Truman Library, Independence, Missouri |
| *IDS* | *Indiana Daily Student* |

| | |
|---|---|
| IFWPP | Indiana Federal Writers' Project Papers, Indiana State University Library, Terre Haute |
| IHS | Indiana Historical Society, Indianapolis |
| *IN* | *Indianapolis News* |
| *IS* | *Indianapolis Star* |
| ISA | Indiana State Archives, Indianapolis |
| ISL | Indiana State Library, Indianapolis |
| *IT* | *Indianapolis Times* |
| IU | Indiana University |
| IUA | Indiana University Archives, Bloomington |
| *LAT* | *Los Angeles Times* |
| LC | Library of Congress, Washington, D.C. |
| LL | Lilly Library, Indiana University, Bloomington |
| *MB* | *Manila Bulletin* |
| MCPL | Monroe County Public Library, Bloomington, Indiana |
| *MDN* | *Manila Daily News* |
| *MD* | *Martinsville Democrat*, Indiana |
| MMA | MacArthur Memorial Archives, Norfolk, Virginia |
| *MP* | *Manila Post* |
| *MT* | *Manila Times* |
| *MTLM* | *Manila Times* Library and Morgue |
| NACP | National Archives, College Park, Maryland |
| NAS | National Academy of Sciences |
| NLP | National Library of the Philippines, Manila |
| *NYT* | *New York Times* |
| *NYHT* | *New York Herald Tribune* |
| OF | Official File |
| OHRO-CU | Oral History Research Office, Columbia University, New York |
| OHS | Oral History Series, Monroe County Public Library, Bloomington, Indiana |
| *PFP* | *Philippines Free Press* |

| | |
|---|---|
| *PH* | *Philippines Herald* |
| PPF | President's Personal File |
| PVMP | Paul V. McNutt Papers, Lilly Library, Indiana University, Bloomington |
| PU | Princeton University, Princeton, New Jersey |
| RG | Record Group |
| SL | Schlesinger Library, Harvard University, Cambridge, Massachusetts |
| SSAA | Social Security Administration Archives, Baltimore |
| SVPP | Senatorial and Vice Presidential Papers |
| UIL | University of Iowa Libraries, Iowa City |
| UP | University of the Philippines |
| USHMM | United States Holocaust Memorial Museum, Washington, D.C. |
| UVA | University of Virginia, Charlottesville |
| *WDN* | *Washington Daily News* |
| *WES* | *Washington Evening Star* |
| WHCF | White House Central Files |
| WHMC | Western Historical Manuscripts Collection, University of Missouri Library, Columbia, Missouri |
| WL | Herman B Wells Library, Indiana University, Bloomington |
| WMC | War Manpower Commission |
| *WP* | *Washington Post* |
| WRS | War Research Service |
| WSU | Wayne State University, Detroit, Michigan |
| YUL | Yale University Library, New Haven, Connecticut |

# PAUL V. McNUTT AND THE AGE OF FDR

# INTRODUCTION

## *A Man, an Era, and a President*

THE TALL, TANNED, AND STRIKINGLY HANDSOME man at the podium had perspiration on his face, and his mouth was tightly drawn, almost in a frown. His seriousness contrasted with the animation of his audience, who cheered him on. He appealed for calm, but the crowd would not allow him to speak. When at last he articulated his words, his brief remarks disappointed his supporters. Paul V. McNutt was withdrawing his name from consideration for vice president. It was the most dramatic moment of McNutt's political life. The date was July 18, 1940, and the setting was America's second-largest city—Chicago, site of many political gatherings. McNutt was standing before delegates to the national convention of the Democratic Party. The significance of that moment in 1940 would not emerge for some time. McNutt never became vice president of the United States. And the chief object of his soaring ambition— the White House—would elude him forever.

Although McNutt never became president, he was a presence on the national political stage from the late 1920s until his death in 1955. In fact, over the first half of the twentieth century, few politicians possessed a more diverse résumé. In the 1920s McNutt became a state and national commander of the American Legion. As governor of Indiana (1933–1937), he backed the New Deal

1

and emerged as one of the nation's strongest governors. He served Presidents Franklin D. Roosevelt and Harry S. Truman as federal security administrator (1939–1945), high commissioner to the Philippines (1937–1939 and 1945–1946), chair of the War Manpower Commission (1942–1945), and ambassador to the Philippines (1946–1947). His hope to be the Democratic nominee for president in 1940 vanished with FDR's nomination for a third term. He next sought the nomination for vice president, until Roosevelt indicated his preference for Secretary of Agriculture Henry A. Wallace and McNutt acceded to the president's wishes. A possible candidate for president and a viable candidate for vice president in 1940, McNutt showed what was and what might have been in American politics in the mid-twentieth century.

Despite such a career, McNutt has become a forgotten figure, which is often the fate of politicians who never attain the presidency. As a result, his various activities have received only passing mention, in a spate of specialized studies.[1] The sole biography of McNutt is an episodic, uncritical work published by a small Indiana press in the 1960s.[2] Writing on Indiana politics, the historian James H. Madison observed: "Paul McNutt towers over the 1930s, yet there exists no satisfactory biography."[3] This oversight is surprising, since biographies and autobiographies of other New Deal–era figures such as Benjamin V. Cohen, Robert H. Jackson, and James A. Farley have been published in the past decade. As a result, McNutt's relationship with Roosevelt and his role in the transformative policies wrought by FDR have been lost to later generations.

Part biography, part history, *Paul V. McNutt and the Age of FDR* addresses three interrelated subjects. First, the book examines the life of Paul McNutt, including his early years, characteristics, personal life, and political rise, as well as his accomplishments, shortcomings, struggles, and descent from prominence. Second, the book concentrates on the era in which McNutt operated as politician and policymaker. McNutt's career sheds light on the history of Indiana (and of Indiana University, his alma mater, where he also served as dean of the law school); veterans' politics following World War I; the expansion of executive power at the state level during the Great Depression; the theory and practice of liberalism during the 1930s and 1940s as federal administrators understood it; the internal dynamics of the Roosevelt and Truman presidencies; and the transition from colonial administration to independence in the Philippines. In so doing, this book underscores the challenges that the United States faced during a period of economic depression, domestic reform, global conflict, cold war, and decolonization. The final topic is Franklin Roosevelt himself. The ways in which the careers of McNutt and FDR paralleled, intersected with, and diverged from one another enhances understanding of Roosevelt as a person and a leader. FDR's dealings with McNutt illuminate the president's skill at side-tracking political rivals, his drive for an unprecedented third term, the reach and durability of his New Deal, and his tactics for mobilizing the American home front during the Second World War.

McNutt, the centerpiece of this book, possessed a complicated persona, one that both matched and departed from his public image. During the 1930s and 1940s, politicians, reporters, and other writers emphasized two of McNutt's qualities: his ambition and his appearance. They were right to do so. McNutt longed to be president, although, as this book argues, he did not from boyhood have his eyes fixed on the White House. As a man, he cut an impressive figure, with his tall frame, well-proportioned body, thick silvery hair, black eyebrows, angular facial features, and well-tailored suits. "Paul McNutt was a symphony in blue," wrote Inga Arvad, a reporter for the *Washington Times-Herald* and an early lover of John F. Kennedy. "McNutt's clothes do not look as if they were made to order, but as if they had grown out like the plumage of a bird." Men as well as women commented on his good looks. The sculptor E. H. Daniels, who did a pair of portrait busts of McNutt, thought he had the "head of a scholar" and a face that radiated "purpose and intellectual strength." "You could imagine what he would do today with television," Senator Birch E. Bayh of Indiana once speculated.[4] To borrow a commonplace expression conferred upon one occupant of the White House—Warren G. Harding—McNutt looked like a president even if he never became one.

Alongside the good looks were less attractive qualities. McNutt was quite vain. Indeed, the photograph on his "McNutt for Governor" buttons, in 1932, had been snapped seven years earlier, and the likeness on his "McNutt for President" buttons in 1939 was from his first year as governor—1933. By drawing attention to himself, he excited awe and envy from onlookers. Yet the distinguished exterior masked inner doubts. In his interactions with others, McNutt was shy and insecure. As a young man, he had sought a place both among and above his peers but when forced to choose, he pursued the lonelier course of accomplishment and ambition rather than the favor and friendship of colleagues. McNutt's reticence, combined with his rapid political rise, earned him a reputation for arrogance that was not entirely undeserved. The more routine aspects of politics, such as making small talk or pressing the flesh with voters, and the daily grind of public administration never became his forte. McNutt competed in—and won—just one election during his career, and he generally found capable assistants to perform the mundane chores associated with policymaking. His preference was for the limelight—the public stage—and he spoke forcefully and tirelessly on the stump and over the airwaves. Simply stated, McNutt was more at home standing at a podium than conversing around a dinner table; his wife, Kathleen, once quipped: "Paul spoke better on his feet than he did on his seat."[5]

A number of contradictions marked McNutt's life. As a young man, he balanced duty to his parents with a desire to escape small-town Indiana. Yet after studying English literature at Indiana University (IU), and then law at Harvard University, he returned to IU as a professor and became dean of its law school in 1925. McNutt patriotically volunteered for service in World War I but then pragmatically used his experience to attain the leadership of the American Legion and, eventually, the Indiana governorship. He remained devoted to Kathleen and their child, Louise, without allowing either Kathleen's distaste for politics or Louise's ill health to disrupt his career path. While he sought ever higher offices, McNutt's ambition was confined within the existing institutions, patterns, and ethics of American political life. He thus embodied change and continuity. He won renown as a reform governor, besting nearly every other state executive in his support of the New Deal, but he then upset liberals by using National Guard troops to end strikes and by establishing a political machine under his direct control. Eager for national office, McNutt initially opposed Roosevelt's first nomination for president in 1932, when he angled to become the Democratic standard-bearer. Then, in 1940, he deferred to FDR as the president sought a third term and selected Wallace to be his running mate, even though McNutt appeared to have enough support to gain the vice-presidential nomination.

There were other contradictions as well. McNutt began his public career as a staunch Legionnaire, assailing pacifists, radicals, and Communists at a time when the first Red Scare, in the late 1910s, was a faded memory. But, near the end of his public life, he opposed the excesses of the second Red Scare of the 1940s and 1950s. Although a partisan Democrat, he worked with Republicans who could advance his ends. As the product of a white, middle-class upbringing, he was nowhere near the forefront of the movement for African-American rights. Yet, in a most humanitarian act, McNutt, as high commissioner to the Philippines, helped 1,300 Jews flee Nazi Germany and emigrate to the Philippines during the late 1930s. Lastly, although he seemed consumed by political ambition, his talents extended beyond politics, and he voluntarily exited public life.

Such disparities must not be exaggerated. McNutt's willingness to work alongside Republicans partly reflected the political culture of his native state; Hoosiers of opposite parties had a habit of cursing one another during election campaigns and then locking arms afterward. Some of the shifts in McNutt's positions—and tactics—derived from his maturation. The verbal salvos he lobbed at radicals during the 1920s, when he was a young Legionnaire, had given way by the 1940s to a nuanced understanding of how to fight Communism and protect civil liberties. And after initially defying—and offending—the Roosevelt campaign in 1932, McNutt understandably was reluctant to challenge FDR for the presidency or Wallace for the vice presidency in 1940. His career displayed as much consistency as contradiction. While McNutt at times amplified or muffled his stand on issues in accordance with shifting political circumstances, he seldom repudiated old positions in favor of new ones. His support for Social Security, and nearly every other New Deal program, proved unwavering. With respect to foreign policy, McNutt, beginning in the 1920s, was a staunch internationalist who was determined to defend American interests abroad. Finally, McNutt's personal and public lives often intersected in fascinating ways. As he struggled with his own insecurities, he simultaneously championed security for Americans from economic hardship, foreign threats, and subversives at home.

McNutt's philosophy rested on the idea of security, a theme emphasized by recent scholars of the New Deal, Second World War, and early Cold War. In 1935, McNutt defined security as government-sponsored protection "against the major hazards and vicissitudes of life," a phrase also used by FDR.[6] To promote economic security, McNutt, during his years as governor of Indiana, supported old-age pensions, relief for unemployed people, and Roosevelt's signature reform, Social Security. His actions were not entirely unique, and he was neither a profound nor original thinker. Rather, he emerged as a pragmatic leader, attuned to the challenges of his times and the needs of his constituents, as well as a quintessential New Dealer, notwithstanding the reservations expressed about him by liberal members of President Roosevelt's circle. As the historian David M. Kennedy has stressed, "Job security, life-cycle security, financial security, market security—however it might be defined, achieving security was the leitmotif of virtually everything the New Deal attempted."[7] Such words—even their rhythmic cadence—echoed a speech given by McNutt in Louisville in 1939, after he had become administrator of the Federal Security Agency (FSA), with responsibility for the myriad of federal welfare programs. "It is difficult to find a single word which more nearly epitomizes the longings of the human

spirit than the word 'security,'" McNutt declared. "Implied here are those decencies of civilization which we regard as essential to the good life—economic
security, political security, intellectual and spiritual security."[8]

A biography of McNutt adds weight to the argument that security was the
leitmotif of the New Deal and, indeed, of related federal policies, foreign and
domestic, in the years immediately following the Great Depression. Scholars
such as Kennedy have begun to rescue the New Deal from the charge of critics—and cynics—that it lacked focus and consistency. "Roosevelt's enemies,"
the newspaper publisher Roy W. Howard wrote in 1935, "have long contended
that he had no complete plan and no terminal facilities for his program."[9] Yet
Roosevelt in 1936 summarized the aim of his first term as removing some of
the "chances" from American life and substituting in their place "security for
people so that they would not individually worry, security for their families,
security for their homes, a greater security for their jobs, and, incidentally, a
greater security for people who employ them."[10] Although McNutt's embrace
of security derived from several influences, his experience as governor, having
charge over a specific geographic area with a sizeable population, helped him to
see security as central to liberal thought and practice as early as the president.
Then as war loomed in Asia and Europe, national security moved to the forefront of Roosevelt's agenda and McNutt's speeches. In 1939, McNutt envisioned
a world in which the individual was protected not only from "poverty and want"
and "disease and ill-health" but also from international aggression and "the
violent disruption of the ethical ideals incorporated in his cultural heritage."[11]

World War II expanded and reshaped the concept of security, for the federal
government and for McNutt. As the war approached, McNutt pegged the Federal Security Agency's health, welfare, and job-training programs to efforts to
strengthen the nation's defenses. During the war, he headed, along with the
FSA, the Office of Defense Health and Welfare Services (ODHWS), which
helped communities fight prostitution and venereal disease, boost "health,
welfare, and morale," improve nutrition and physical fitness, and provide child
care for workers and recreation for servicemen (with McNutt's support, the
United Service Organizations came into existence).[12] The work of the ODHWS
reflected the belief of McNutt and his staff that healthy people made better
workers and soldiers and that "social and economic security . . . is related to
national defense."[13] Roosevelt and members of his administration concurred.
Indeed, when the White House sought a home for its top-secret biological weapons program, Secretary of War Henry Stimson proposed the Federal Security

Agency because it oversaw the Public Health Service.[14] As a result, the so-called War Research Service, which studied the defensive and offensive aspects of biological warfare, came under McNutt's domain. He thus entered a field which Americans living in the twenty-first century know as homeland security. The activities of the Federal Security Agency, War Research Service, and ODHWS also embody what the historian Elizabeth Borgwardt has called the "core idea" to emerge during World War II: an "integrated vision of 'security'" revolving around FDR's devotion to freedom of speech and religion and freedom from want and fear. According to Borgwardt, "Roosevelt's Four Freedoms elegantly expressed the assumption that economic security supported political stability, in an international projection of the ideology and values that underpinned the domestic New Deal." Simply stated, Americans, after securing a more decent society at home, would fight to protect and then to extend that society abroad.[15]

McNutt's thoughts on security were holistic, encompassing foreign as well as domestic policy. Earlier than most Americans, he sensed the threat posed by dictatorships and urged making "adequate provision for our national security" via continued military training on college campuses and increased expenditures on arms.[16] Although such proposals, along with an antipathy toward pacifism and Communism, made up the agenda of the American Legion, Mc-Nutt maintained a realistic perspective on international relations throughout his public career. He deemed disarmament treaties and efforts to promote peace by outlawing war to be misguided at best and dangerous at worst, for they underestimated the determination of nations to pursue their own self-interest. Faced with such realities, America had to be engaged in, rather than isolated from, international politics. As the high commissioner in Manila during the late 1930s, McNutt urged the U.S. government to retain the colony as an outpost of American power rather than grant it independence and leave it vulnerable to Japan. During his second tenure as high commissioner in the mid-1940s, McNutt worked to tie the newly independent Philippines to the economic, diplomatic, and military agenda of the United States during the early Cold War. The seemingly aggressive designs of the Soviet Union in the 1940s and 1950s, along with earlier aggression by Germany, Italy, and Japan, confirmed in McNutt's mind the need for the United States to maintain its defenses and check the ambitions of dictators.[17] The idea that America's national security had to be collective, that is, entwined with that of its allies and other friendly states, became the consensus among U.S. policymakers following Pearl Harbor, although it had been McNutt's view before that, when he had recommended retention of the Philippines.

McNutt's cynicism about human nature and idealism about the capacities of a well-led democratic state underlay his approach to security. He understood that the avarice, aggression, deception, and dishonesty exhibited by governments originated with individuals and filtered upward. To use his words, McNutt lived through such "violent disruptions" as two world wars, the Russian Revolution, and the Holocaust, in addition to the reemergence of the Ku Klux Klan in the 1920s, the onset of the Great Depression, and the beginning of the Cold War. On a personal level, he endured harassment by bullies during his boyhood, attacks from Republican opponents, and the jealousy of FDR's intimates. McNutt thus recognized—and remembered—that humans were prone to act irrationally, irresponsibly, maliciously, and aggressively. But he also knew that a democratic government that was wisely led, skillfully administered, and attuned to the needs of average people could dampen the appeal of radicalism, revolution, and war. Put another way, a benevolent state would make human existence, rather than humans themselves, less harsh. Like Roosevelt, McNutt believed that "government may be a great instrument of human progress."[18] Using its powers to afford people a greater sense of security was the key for him and for FDR.

McNutt's relationship to policymaking on security-related issues proved bifurcated. At one level, his impact was direct but sporadic. McNutt fashioned Indiana's welfare state, helped Jewish refugees reach the Philippines, headed the ODHWS, and oversaw the Philippines' transition from colony to client. He also presented policy alternatives to FDR on expanding Social Security and retaining the Philippines (here, he was more a policy advocate than a policymaker). At another level, however, his connection to national policymaking was indirect. McNutt's conception of security offered a window into the mindset that underlay such policies as Social Security, American intervention in World War II, and Cold War–era containment which other, larger figures would inaugurate. The liberalism that had emerged by the 1940s was "tough-minded"—a "fighting faith"—and the hard-headed and ever practical McNutt fit within that milieu.[19] After 1945, for example, his speeches openly disdained pacifistic talk about the "brotherhood of man" and "one world"—a phrase popularized by the late Wendell Willkie, his fellow Hoosier and a former fraternity brother.[20] To the contrary, McNutt reminded Americans of the imperatives of the Cold War, that "the bloody ordeal of this century is not over and we have a job to do."[21]

McNutt was notable for what he might have been as well as for what he did and said. For example, he might have become the leader of postwar liberalism. With his anti-Communism, support for New Deal programs, realistic approach to international affairs, advocacy of military preparedness, and grasp of the underside of human nature, McNutt was an archetypical Cold War liberal who was "unusually concerned with security."[22] He strongly believed that the so-called welfare-warfare state was the means to provide economic and social security for Americans at home and national security for America abroad. Following the Second World War, McNutt backed President Harry Truman's major foreign policy initiatives, including the Marshall Plan, to contain Soviet power in Europe, and the United Nations–approved intervention in Korea, to repel Communist advances in Asia. His own contribution to containment and to America's emerging defense perimeter in the Pacific came at the close of his public career. While serving as ambassador to the Philippines from 1946 to 1947, McNutt negotiated a treaty under which the United States gained access to military bases in its former colony.[23] In Truman, McNutt found a kindred spirit: a fellow Legionnaire, anti-Communist, and proponent of security who became the nation's leading Cold War liberal. But a succession of events, some of them beyond McNutt's control, prevented the Hoosier from occupying the office to which Truman ascended in 1945.

FDR was the biggest obstacle to McNutt's presidential ambitions. McNutt looked forward to 1940, expecting the president to observe tradition and retire after two terms. Yet the approach of war, and Roosevelt's desire to keep the Democratic Party sailing on a liberal track, encouraged the president's supporters to push for a third term. The McNutt forces answered with a presidential boom of their own. But FDR handled McNutt—and other ambitious subordinates—deftly, via a blend of flattery, favors, and deception. During the mid-1930s, Roosevelt tapped McNutt to defend the national administration in several speeches. In 1937 the president dispatched him to Manila, partly to placate him with a government job, partly to prevent him from pressing for a position in the cabinet, and partly to get this rising political star out of the country. In 1939 Roosevelt next appointed McNutt as federal security administrator, again for a variety of reasons, though he certainly wanted the Hoosier to remain inside the administration as 1940 approached. With respect to the election, the president kept quiet about his plans, allowed loyal lieutenants and party bosses to organize support for a third term, and preempted other Democratic liberals from challenging him for the nomination. Ever a realist, McNutt declared that he was a candidate for president only if FDR was not. In the end, Roosevelt secured renomination and the vice president of his choosing. McNutt's ambition was frustrated, and his appeal waned. He continued to oversee the Federal

Security Agency. Later, in addition to the ODHWS, McNutt secured another wartime posting, as chair of the War Manpower Commission, albeit without the sustained presidential support that this assignment required. McNutt faltered, and he received almost no consideration for his party's nomination for vice president in 1944. A year later, he was back in the Philippines, where his past experience had become valuable expertise to a new president. Thereafter, he went into private business. After 1947, his public life was limited to making speeches.

McNutt's relations with Roosevelt illustrate aspects of FDR's character, some of which were less than admirable. These include the president's pettiness, his jealousy (of a younger man), his willingness to pit subordinates against each other (such as McNutt and the Democratic National Committee chair Jim Farley), and his ruthlessness—a probe by FDR's Treasury Department of McNutt's political machine helped to undermine his presidential and vice-presidential prospects. Moreover, McNutt and FDR were too alike to become close. The Indiana novelist and political observer Meredith Nicholson noted that "Paul has more of the President's own qualities—personality and mentality, courage, initiative, etc. than any other man who could possibly be a contender."[24] No less than McNutt, FDR was vain—at times in a "childish" manner, accordingly to his ally Frances Perkins.[25] And, like McNutt, he had to occupy center stage to the point that his daughter, Anna, would remind her children to refrain from waving to crowds at public events because the cheering was for the president.[26] Not surprisingly, McNutt never become one of FDR's intimates. "Roosevelt disliked ambitious people," the historian Robert H. Ferrell said, and McNutt fit that description.[27] "The only people who repelled [FDR]," said Perkins, "were pompous bores."[28] Again, McNutt gave the impression of being such a person.

The relationship between McNutt and Roosevelt also underscored the president's guile as he navigated between a conservative reaction at home and fascist aggression abroad to win an unprecedented third term in the White House. By examining McNutt's quest for the presidency, FDR's ambitions are illuminated. *Paul V. McNutt and the Age of FDR* argues that Roosevelt's decision to seek a third term came around the end of 1939, earlier than many popular writers and scholars have conjectured. It was motivated as much by domestic politics—FDR's desire to keep his party moving in a liberal direction—as by the need to retain an experienced leader in the White House while war escalated in Europe. Roosevelt's interest in a third term thus emerges as less statesmanlike and improvised and more devious and intentional than is usually thought.[29]

McNutt's failure to win national office can only partly be attributed to FDR. McNutt's string of early successes came so easily that when he was forced to choose between challenging Wallace for the vice presidency or acceding to Roosevelt's wishes, he chose the latter, confident that his turn would come again. It never did. McNutt remained overshadowed by FDR. Roosevelt commanded the national Democratic Party between 1933 and 1945, at a time when McNutt was a state-level leader, presidential appointee, and instrument of White House policy. After failing to secure the vice presidency in 1940, McNutt sank into obscurity as a presidential might-have-been. Had he fought Wallace for the vice presidency, the story goes, McNutt would have won the nomination and held on to it for he had support within the party. As the nominee for vice president in 1944, McNutt would have become president when FDR died in 1945. "How he would have fared as president is a fascinating speculation," the historian Lewis E. Gleeck Jr. has reckoned. "He was better qualified than Harry Truman and would probably not have made Truman's early mistakes, but whether he would have risen so magnificently to the challenges the way Truman did after the latter's quick maturing in office is equally speculative."[30]

Such conjecture is beyond the scope of this book. *Paul V. McNutt and the Age of FDR* considers who McNutt was, what he did and did not accomplish, where he fit within the pattern of American politics and diplomacy over the first half of the twentieth century, and how he served—and interacted with—Franklin Roosevelt and, to a lesser extent, Harry Truman. In the end, McNutt became a supporting actor in two of the most compelling dramas in American history: the origins and development of the New Deal and the emergence of the United States as a global superpower. While he remained a secondary political figure, that is, someone above the grunts and below the greats, there is one compelling caveat in his biography: McNutt was that rare public official who had positioned himself to reach the top of the political pyramid.

The city was Philadelphia, the event was the Democratic National Convention, and the date was July 14, 1948—nearly eight years after the nomination of the Roosevelt-Wallace ticket. The president, Truman, was seeking the party's nomination although he was less than popular, particularly among conservative white southerners who resented his advocacy of civil rights for African Americans. After the balloting commenced, a delegate from Florida rose to nominate a man who, he insisted, could unite the fractured Democrats and then vanquish the nominee of the Republican Party. The candidate, he reminded the delegates, had stood before this convention in 1940, pleading for the opportunity to speak and then requesting that his name be withdrawn from consideration for vice president. This sudden, impromptu nomination of McNutt for president in 1948 was unexpected by the delegates and was a faint echo of what might have been in 1940. When the balloting was completed, Truman had won the party's nomination with 947½ votes. Senator Richard B. Russell of Georgia, the favorite of the white southerners, came in second place with 263 votes. McNutt, who finished third, received one half of one vote.

# 1

## "I SEE . . . A GREAT FUTURE"
## (1891–1913)

PAUL VORIES MCNUTT was born on July 19, 1891, and he was running for the White House the second "his umbilical cord was severed."[1] That was what his critics alleged later on. The truth was much more complicated. "He was a smart boy," John Crittenden McNutt, his father, remembered, "but we never thought he might be President."[2] Ruth Neely McNutt, Paul's mother, saw her first and only offspring as a "child of destiny," although not necessarily bound for the White House.[3] Indeed, as her son launched his campaign to succeed President Franklin D. Roosevelt, Ruth had trouble remembering the precise time of Paul's birth. It had occurred around four o'clock in the afternoon, but the difficulty of the labor seemingly had clouded her memory. "Too bad," Ruth related, "we did not foresee the possibility of sometime needing to know the exact time."[4]

On one level, there was something commonplace about the young McNutt. Paul was the scion of a middle-income family residing in the middle section of a midwestern state. As a boy and young man, he sought to be part of a group. At the same time, he was well aware of the extraordinary gifts, intellectual and physical, that placed him ahead of the pack. And from an early age, he learned to value diligence, ambition, and success. McNutt's upbringing shaped his character; he derived a good deal of his nature from his mother and a considerable amount of nurturing from his father.

McNutt's early years were not idyllic. Like many young people, he wrestled with social awkwardness, personal insecurity, and tensions with his parents. Through his father, McNutt became acquainted with partisan politics. And while studying at Indiana University, he became involved in campus politics and associated with a vague notion of public service. Yet, he showed little interest in the larger social and economic questions debated by Americans early in the twentieth century. If McNutt did not experience all the great causes of that era, his parents, teachers, and classmates nevertheless foresaw a great future for him. What exactly he might do with his many talents remained uncertain at the time he graduated from university in 1913. McNutt's youth thus revealed that his much-discussed ambition to be president of the United States was not a lifelong endeavor.

By Paul's own admission, his family was not obsessed with its genealogy. "None of us has made the effort to put all the parts of the family tree together," he later wrote.[5] His ancestors most likely descended from a clan named Mac-Naught or MacNaughten which lived in Kilquhanitie, County Kirkcudbright, Scotland, as early as 1448. Although the family owned land, it had experienced hard times by the end of the seventeenth century. Around 1696, John Mac-Naught and his four sons resettled in the northern part of Ireland. There, the family's name became "MacNutt" and then "McNutt."[6] In the 1700s, McNutts began migrating to North America, first to Maryland and Virginia and later to areas west.[7] The motto beneath their coat of arms—*Omnia fortunae committo*, meaning "I commit all things to fortune"—signified the boldness (or the desperation) that had pushed McNutts to Ireland and then to America.[8]

The history of John C. McNutt's family dated to the close of the eighteenth century. Around 1796, his great-grandfather, Alexander McNutt, who may have descended from John MacNaught, migrated from either Scotland or the northern counties of Ireland to present-day Ohio. One of his sons, also named John, moved west, to Johnson County, Indiana, some twenty miles south of Indianapolis. He married and sired several children, including a son, James McNutt, who was Paul McNutt's paternal grandfather. James and his wife, Cynthia, became the parents of John C. McNutt—Paul's father—who was born on May 25, 1863. Unfortunately, James McNutt died four years after John's birth, leaving behind a pregnant wife and three children. Although John's mother eventually remarried, her second husband also died, just two years after their wedding.[9]

Overcoming these setbacks required hard work, and John was up to the challenge. His diligence might be attributed to a pioneer spirit, a sort of roughhewn individualism. He was proud that two of his great-grandfathers were among the earliest settlers in Johnson County. John began life as a "poor country boy" who put himself through primary school by hauling logs in winter and working as a farmhand in summer.[10] But tilling the soil of southern Indiana, most of it already cultivated and inferior to the farmland farther north, did not satisfy his widening ambitions. After graduating from high school, John decided to become a teacher. He attended a normal school in Morgantown, Indiana, for a year and then completed a six-week course at a teacher's institute. After the institute's director—a man named Vories—allowed him to enroll without charge, John promised to name his first son after him. For five years, the future father of Paul Vories McNutt taught school in Brown, Johnson, and Morgan counties, earning twenty dollars a month.[11]

But John was not content. At that time, "school-teaching was the country boy's most reliable stepping-stone to another career."[12] For John, that career would be law. His decision stemmed from two considerations. First, the expansion of democracy in America during the nineteenth century had led to fewer standards for the training of lawyers and to more men of lower station studying for admission to the bar. As late as 1932, when the state of Indiana mandated a written examination, aspiring lawyers needed only to be citizens of the state and at least twenty-one years old and to have secured affidavits testifying to the candidate's "good moral character." According to John Hurt, a law partner of John C. McNutt, lawyers "might have had experience as clerks in law firms or working in the courts, but they had not necessarily gone to law school."[13] A few managed to avoid any course of study. One lawyer, a college classmate of Paul McNutt's, recalled how his cousin, a loquacious barber, decided to embark on a new career. "He just went out and got a few affidavits and started practicing law."[14] In this hit-or-miss setup, John C. McNutt never went to law school, but his son did—and his uncle directed the law program at Indiana University.

In pursuing a career in law, John also drew inspiration from his uncle, Cyrus Finley McNutt, who had raised him following his father's death. Cyrus McNutt graduated from Franklin College and then practiced law in Franklin, the seat of Johnson County. He later became a professor at Indiana University in Bloomington, where he eventually headed the department of law, a position that his grandnephew, Paul, would later occupy. But after the state legislature slashed funding for the law department, the university suspended the program. Cyrus then opened a law practice in Terre Haute, sixty miles west, and became judge of the city's superior court. Beginning in 1883, and while still teaching, John read law under his uncle's tutelage. He also studied at a law office in Franklin and won admission to the Indiana bar in 1884, at the age of twenty-one. Two years later, he opened a law partnership in Franklin.[15]

The year 1886 marked another milestone for John. On July 7, he married Ruth Neely of Morgantown. "I have always adored her," John later said of Ruth.[16] Besides being teachers, the couple were descended from the earliest Europeans in central Indiana, and shared a respect for hard work and social success. Ruth traced her family to Daniel Prosser, a soldier who attained the rank of captain during the American Revolution. After the war's end, Prosser and his family eventually settled in Ohio, where he acquired a farm. Prosser's oldest son, John, followed in his father's footsteps. He and his family migrated to Cass County, Michigan, and then, in 1836, to Brown County, Indiana, where John prospected for gold, cleared trees, and farmed. The work was onerous and the nearest village was "a miserable little hamlet" encompassing "a few log cabins" overlooking "a narrow muddy road."[17] Yet John remained in Brown County, as did his son, James, and granddaughter, Sarah Prosser. In 1863 Sarah married Jacob Meyer Neely. She gave birth to Ruth, her first child, two years later.[18]

Ruth's father was an exemplar of the successful, self-made community leader. Born in Brown County and educated in township schools, Jacob Neely was a tanner who eventually became a local postmaster. A veteran of the Civil War, Neely was an assistant adjutant general of the Grand Army of the Republic, and he headed that organization's Indiana branch—as his famous grandson would later head the Indiana Department of the American Legion. A lifelong Mason, Neely held leadership offices in the order in both Morgantown and Martinsville, the seat of Morgan County, where he was appointed deputy county clerk in 1891. Voters later elected him deputy county auditor and county clerk. Residents of Martinsville regarded him as loyal, kindly, and genial as well as capable and efficient; they later eulogized him as one of their best-known citizens. Neely was one of those late-nineteenth-century men who had voted as they "had shot."[19] "He was very much a Republican, having been a Union soldier," Paul McNutt explained in 1940, "and if he were living today I doubt if he would vote for me, a Democrat."[20]

Paul's prediction was believable. The late nineteenth century marked a period of intense partisanship, involving fierce loyalty to the major political parties and wide voter participation among the white men who enjoyed access to the ballot box. Newspapers typically cheered the successes of the party with which they were affiliated and hissed at the opposition. Although partisanship waned during the first decade of the twentieth century as issues and a candidate's personality competed with party allegiance to define campaigns, this change proved more gradual among Hoosiers. Indiana, an evenly split swing state throughout the late nineteenth century and the early twentieth, retained a competitive brand of politics characterized by strong party identification, high turnout, and an unrepentant system of patronage—something which Paul McNutt later exploited during his governorship. To even consider switching parties was tantamount to sin.[21]

Interestingly, partisanship served to unite as much as divide Democrats and Republicans in Indiana and, no doubt, in the McNutt family as well. Loyalty to a political party was, after all, something nearly all Hoosiers could recognize and respect.[22] When asked about "independence" among Indiana voters, Jack New, a longtime operative in the state's Democratic Party, doubted whether such a tradition existed.[23] Herman B Wells, a protégé of Governor McNutt's and later the president of Indiana University, agreed: "Hoosiers always can understand bi-partisanship; they can't understand non-partisanship. They don't believe there is any such thing."[24] In fact, it was not unusual for community leaders of one party to number prominent citizens of the other party among their closest friends. "We might not have agreed on politics, but we agreed on a number of human issues," John Hurt, John C.'s law partner and a lifelong Democrat, wrote of one Republican.[25] In this setting, one can only imagine the sort of political discussions that Paul McNutt must have had with his maternal grandfather.

Paul took pride in his ancestry and his family. To be sure, the mature McNutt was "a whirlwind of activity," a body in forward, not backward, motion.[26] His lowest grade in college, a B-, came in history. And what he knew of his lineage was at times wrong.[27] Yet Paul, born following the closing of the frontier in 1890, remained the product of a regional culture that, according to the historians Andrew R. L. Cayton and Peter S. Onuf, "expressed itself in the making of myth, imagining a frontier era in which people—middle class, midwestern people—had once been the powerful progenitors of a new civilization."[28] As governor, McNutt saluted the "pioneer vision and courage" of Indiana's earliest settlers.[29] More important, family members, and the places associated with them, imbued in Paul a sense of his niche in an upwardly mobile clan. In 1932, during celebrations honoring the Bethlehem Primitive Baptist Church, "one of the oldest religious societies" in Johnson County, he spoke twenty paces from the graves of his McNutt ancestors—grandfather, great-grandfather, and great-great-grandfather.[30] With his father and daughter attending, Paul was moved by being in the presence of six generations of McNutts.[31] Regarding his mother's family, he once boasted that he had been the favorite grandchild of Jacob Neely, their political differences notwithstanding. "He must have thought something of me," Paul added, "for he remembered me in his will."[32]

In John McNutt, Ruth married a man somewhat similar to her father. John experienced his share of successes. He won election and then reelection as prosecuting attorney for Johnson and Shelby counties in 1888 and 1890, respectively. Indeed, the McNutts were living in Franklin when their son, Paul, was born in 1891. Beginning in 1893 they lived in Indianapolis, where John served six years as librarian for the law library of the Supreme Court of Indiana. Thereafter, he moved his family twenty-five miles south, to Martinsville, where he formed a law partnership. Unlike his father-in-law, however, John was not universally acclaimed as a pillar of this community. That may have been because Neely already occupied such an honored place. It also reflected John's open affiliation with the Democratic Party in Republican-leaning Morgan County. Throughout his life, he was one of the few Democratic lawyers in Martinsville and a "persistent politician."[33] During the elections of 1914, for example, John addressed a packed schoolhouse, where he skewered former president William Howard Taft while extolling the accomplishments of President Woodrow Wilson.[34]

John McNutt, moreover, was not one to hide his family's success. His law clients included railroads, and John "proudly wore in his lapel" a fifty-year service pin from the Illinois Central.[35] He owned "one of the nicest homes" in Martinsville, a two-story Dutch colonial house near the courthouse square.[36] A college classmate of Paul thought that John had made "a good practice" but was not "rolling in money."[37] Few in Morgan County were. The hill people of the county's southern tier were prone to "overproduce children and underproduce crops."[38] Although Morgan County had fertile farmland and abundant springs, Martinsville, a town of about five thousand, boasted little industry, save for a few factories that made buckets and furniture. The principal attraction was the artesian waters provided by sanitariums, the largest of which was a few blocks from the McNutt home.[39] A survey, conducted during the 1930s, affirmed that the "inhabitants of Morgan County are homogeneous [r]acially, socially and culturally."[40] Martinsville became economically stagnant as the sanitariums declined. In 1948, while driving through the city, McNutt told Hurt: "John, this downtown looks like it did fifty years ago." Nearly a half century later, Hurt's daughter made a similar observation.[41]

Such a climate could be daunting to newcomers, particularly those who achieved a modicum of success. John Hurt noticed "a lot of jealousy among the old-line families" of Martinsville toward the McNutts.[42] One wonders what some residents of Morgan County thought of a Christmas message from Ruth which ended "Greetings from the House of McNutt."[43] In the face of envy, real and imagined, John McNutt was stoic. He once admonished one of his law partners never to express hatred for "anybody or anything" because "hatred will destroy YOU."[44] His own poise drew mixed responses. To admirers, John McNutt was "straight and sure of step," a "well-known lawyer" who exhibited thrift, precision, and command of his profession.[45] To detractors, such as Claude G. Bowers—Hoosier author, diplomat, and, although a Democrat, a foe of Paul's—the elder McNutt was "something of a pompous ass."[46]

Ruth McNutt was something of a paradox. Ruth's niece, Grace Woody, remembered her as a "beautiful, reserved, proud woman who always bore herself with unrelenting dignity."[47] Yet she lacked a suitable outlet for her talents and an inner resolve. A teacher no more, Ruth, like many middle-class housewives, devoted herself to church activities—she was Methodist—and participated in the projects of various clubs.[48] She compared members of the Women's Club of Martinsville to pioneers, those souls who "always travel a rough road—whether it is the grass grown road of the covered wagon or the ridicule strewn of a new idea."[49] By expressing this view, she simultaneously celebrated her family lineage, suggested that unexplored paths lay before women, and hinted at the ridicule visited on those in the public arena. Ruth braced herself for such abuse, targeted at her husband or, later on, her son. While going through her late aunt's possessions during the 1940s, Grace discovered a "scrap of paper, crumpled and worn," bearing these words: "This House will admit of no defeat. Queen Victoria."[50]

Ruth buried herself in activity. "I'm rushed to death—most of the time! Oh you know how it goes!" began one of her Christmas greetings. To friends, she lent a hand and revealed a "delightful sense of humor."[51] But to family members, such as Grace, who was like a sister to Paul, she might forget to give a Christmas gift or even to bid good-bye. There were other paradoxes as well. Although Ruth saved the envelopes on which her husband recorded the sums of his "accumulating fortune," she found comfort in the "plain and simple home" of a nearby seamstress. "I always feel I can be myself here," she said. Above all else, Ruth valued education, books, and ideas.[52] She collected clippings from newspapers and from poems—romantic as well as prayerful—and even copied by hand or composed herself rhyming couplets: "The world is wide—; But books are like the famous boots; With seeing eyes and lengthy stride; You may view the earth with love and pride; While sitting by your own fireside."[53] Some of Ruth's verses appeared to be self-reflective, perhaps even self-critical:

> Why was it that her charm revealed
> Somehow the surface of a shield?
> What was it that we never caught?
> What was she, and what was she not?[54]

The elusiveness of the woman in the poem is the elusiveness that Grace would perceive. "Sensitive, romantic, expansive," Grace wrote to Paul after reading Ruth's hidden treasures. "Why, we did not even know her!"[55]

The mother and father that young Paul knew were attentive, albeit somewhat controlling, parents. Ruth, a conscientious mother, saved mementos of Paul, including his baby shoes and locks of his hair, as she strove to "guide his footsteps."[56] Strict about neatness, she made her son lay newspapers in the kitchen when he ate crackers so as to prevent any crumbs from reaching the floor.[57] Ruth also reproached Paul for displays of anger, such as when he resisted eating some soup because "it was too damned hot."[58] When Paul, no older than seven, wrote Santa Claus to ask for a watch, "Santa" answered the wish and left a note telling him: "You are a tolerably good boy but you must keep your temper better and do just as your Papa and Mamma say, for they are your best friends. Don't get mad and it will be easier to be a good boy—."[59]

More than his temperament, Paul's health caused the greater worry. It was of special concern to Ruth, who had almost died in childbirth. Her son contracted scarlet fever and Bright's disease, and he suffered from bronchial ailments. The worst was diphtheria, which Ruth caught and which nearly killed Paul when he was eight. John's decision to dismiss the family physician, who had scoffed at prescribing the latest antitoxin, may have saved their son's life. After the crisis had passed, the McNutts moved from Indianapolis to Martinsville, to be near Ruth's parents. There, Paul remained "a delicate child," and partly for that reason his mother forbade him to fight with other boys.[60]

A combination of pretense and puniness made Paul's introduction to Martinsville's schools particularly jarring. The new arrivals were city folk, and Ruth dressed her son in the latest fashion for aristocratic young men. "The Fauntleroy period had set in," as the novelist Booth Tarkington expressed it in *The Magnificent Ambersons,* a novel that took place in Indianapolis. Not unlike Tarkington's Georgie Amberson Minafer, Paul Vories McNutt sported, on his first day, "a silk sash, and silk stockings, and a broad lace collar, with his little black velvet suit."[61] The attire, and the airs it connoted, provoked his male schoolmates into dunking him into a mudhole. Afterward, Paul pleaded with his mother to allow him to defend himself, and she relented. The next day, he fought back, taking on the entire class and then returning home with "shredded clothes and a broken umbrella."[62] According to one account, "weeks passed before Paul shed his last ruffle."[63] Court Asher, a schoolmate from a poor family and later the editor of an anti-Communist, anti-Semitic rag, remembered that young Paul wore a derby hat—"the first derby hat in town." The other kids, again, registered their disapproval, this time by pelting his bowler with rocks. "We use[d] to rock him home from school ever' noon," Asher boasted.[64]

At one level, this bullying marked Paul's first encounter with class differences, whether or not he understood it as such. The northern section of Martinsville, known as Bucktown, was a rough area of shabby cottages inhabited by manual laborers and their rowdy sons. To the south, near the courthouse square, lived the professional classes, such as the McNutts, often in imposing Victorian homes. North School, which Paul attended, was approximately a mile from his home and located in Bucktown, on the border of the two districts. That meant that Paul's classmates included both ruffians and the refined, with the former unlikely to cotton to an outsider masquerading as a Lord Fauntleroy. Years later, when Paul was in high school (and more popular with his peers), he walked a single block to school. While at North School, however, the long walk home—every afternoon and in the face of his tormentors—must have seemed an endless ordeal.[65]

What was the impact of this bullying? One correspondent, who was unfriendly to Paul McNutt's presidential campaign, cited sociological evidence claiming that "the Lord Fauntleroys" of the 1890s, "because of the persecution experienced at a tender age," were more apt than other youngsters to become hard, suspicious, pugnacious, and vindictive as adults.[66] McNutt, the man, exhibited those traits in varying degrees, but it is impossible to trace all of them to any single cause. In the short run, the bullying showed Paul that it was possible to obey and then to repeal parental strictures. The family scrapbook contained a photograph of a transformed Paul, aged eight or nine, clad in knickers, a black sweater, and a dark cap. He holds a football in one hand and places the other hand on his waist. His feet are set apart, and he scowls—more likely, from his expression, to pummel a Lord Fauntleroy than to dress as one. To recast his wardrobe, and to reinvent himself, Paul must have stood up to someone besides schoolyard bullies, probably his mother. In the long run, Paul's ordeal taught him a lesson about the more negative dimensions of human nature. Throughout his public life McNutt perceived sundry opponents—Republicans, Communists, Nazis—as bullies to be mastered only through steely resolution.[67] At the same time, McNutt's experience with bullying shaped the sensitivity and respect he would show toward other victims of abuse, such as Jewish refugees during the 1930s, whom he would seek to protect by bringing them to the Philippines, the topic of chapter 9.

It is striking that many aspects of McNutt's boyhood can find echoes in the early life of Franklin D. Roosevelt. Roosevelt, like McNutt, was an only child, dressed by his mother, Sara, in ruffled garments that she carefully preserved. Alice Roosevelt Longworth, Theodore Roosevelt's acid-tongued daughter, recalled the young FDR, her distant cousin, as "slender and delicate"—a real mama's boy—adding: "When Franklin wants to get tough with me I think of little Lord Fauntleroy."[68] Yet Sara Roosevelt showered more affection on "her boy Franklin," to paraphrase the title of her memoir, than Ruth McNutt provided her son.[69]

Paul's struggles also resembled those of another Roosevelt, the introverted Theodore, more than those of the gregarious Franklin. "TR," not unlike McNutt, began life as a "little lad . . . in stiff white petticoats, with a curl right on the top of his head." A "sickly and awkward boy," Theodore made an inviting target for bullies, until he embarked on a regimen of bodybuilding. Partly, perhaps, as a result of challenges to their masculinity, both TR and McNutt became closer to their fathers than to their mothers. McNutt, as will be shown, was wary about developing relationships with women. The same was true for Theodore Roosevelt who, according to the historian Sarah Watts, held in check his "emotional and sexual desire" because he saw "women's attentions as an alluring but deadly manifestation of his own weakness, one that had to be overcome before he could consider himself a real man." Parallels between TR and McNutt should not be pressed too far. Theodore overcame his shyness earlier in life than did Paul.[70]

"Shy" and possessing "something of an inferiority complex"—characterizations of the mature McNutt by a member of FDR's inner circle—also would have described him as a boy.[71] Paul's difficulty in adjusting to a new home led him to retreat into a restricted world uniquely his own. Like his father, he worked, delivering the *Indianapolis Star* and the *Martinsville Reporter,* a rather solitary task. Like his mother, he hid favorite letters and documents in his room, in a box marked "P.V.M.—Private Papers."[72] Yet Paul was too active, too determined, and, perhaps, too needy to remain a loner forever. Less than popular with his peers, at least initially, he instead "tagged after" a trio of older boys who insisted that their young protégés perform errands for the privilege of their company. Paul chased after tennis balls but bore the boys no grudge. "Those days," he reminisced, "gave me my first real insight into the joy and satisfaction of social contacts."[73]

Success at school provided further satisfaction. Paul led his class at spelling bees and in mastering the multiplication table. One teacher called him "the most nearly perfect student I ever had."[74] He was almost too perfect. Embarrassed over repeatedly winning a drawing contest, he asked his cousin Grace to accept the one-dollar prize in his place. "Everybody praised Paul," Grace said, "and the family expected him to make great achievements."[75] His accomplishments grew, which doubtless impressed his schoolmates, and so did he, which almost certainly deterred bullies. Robert Phelps, a member of the gang that had given the former Lord Fauntleroy his mud-splattered initiation, became one of Paul's friends and described him as "a master mind . . . in almost everything we did in schoolrooms and out."[76] Paul and his cohorts participated in Halloween mischief, ball games of all types, and meets at the swimming hole. Even at play, Paul challenged himself and stood apart from the pack. An avid skater, he often tried to find the breaking point of the ice. Once it cracked beneath him and Paul's friends struggled to fish his shivering body from the water. Overall, however, the son of Ruth McNutt remained "grave-faced" and driven.[77] "Often we'd pass his home and whistle for him," Phelps said, "and he'd ignore our whistle and keep on studying instead of coming out to play catch."[78] "I think," Phelps reflected, "he himself would give his mother credit for much of this industry."[79]

Ruth had her share of help. In grade school, Paul no doubt learned the Mc-Guffey code, a loose set of bourgeois ideals embedded in the famed readers used in schools across the United States between 1850 and 1900. With an optimism that was more attuned to America's rural past than its industrializing present, these books heralded such values as diligence, perseverance, obedience to parental authority, and the pursuit of goals. The press reinforced the McGuffey code by arguing that parents could render no greater service to their children than to educate them. Ruth and John McNutt, both former teachers, needed little persuading. Fortunately for them, they had institutions of support. Whatever its limitations, Martinsville was a county seat, with a courthouse, churches, and a modern high school, completed in 1901 and boasting 180 students and eight faculty members.[80]

Yet it was Ruth who kept her son on the right track. Sometimes her discipline was overt, and sometimes it was not. When Paul went to the circus instead of sweeping the hallway, as he had been told to do, Ruth made him clean the hall five times after he returned. After discovering a pipe and some tobacco hidden near the furnace, which Paul tended, she took them and kept quiet. Having made her point, his furtive smoking came to an end. Paul remembered his mother as being strict with him, but he also mustered the nerve to challenge her authority. "When she reproved him for some infraction," one journalist later noted, "he coolly informed her that if she cut across his will less they would get along better." Ruth drew back, perhaps impressed by her son's independence and perhaps knowing that he was well on his way to making something of himself.[81]

Ruth's impact on Paul cannot be underestimated. McNutt's political outlook, at its most idealistic, involved a desire to offset selfishness through service to a larger cause. Such thinking probably originated with his mother. Ruth, for example, openly adored Christmas: "The air softens animosities, forgives injuries, overcomes selfishness, awakens hallowed memories and makes Christmas the best time in the year, because it is the kindest time."[82] In other words, people, under the right conditions, were capable of rising above their faults and self-interests to behave grandly and generously toward one another. Yet Ruth herself lacked warmth, and that lack of maternal love may have been the source of Paul's insecurities, shyness, and aloof personality. "Her tender thoughts, romantic dreams and lovingness were bound by her restraint," Grace Woody noted. As a result, Paul "may never have known the depth of her affection."[83]

John, in contrast, coddled his son, and the McNutt men remained close. When John served as librarian for Indiana's supreme court, Paul accompanied his father to the library. John introduced his son into the male-driven world of partisan politics. Parades, drilling companies, and similar spectacles were common, and during the election of 1900, Paul marched in a boys' fife and drum corps in support of William Jennings Bryan's campaign. When a formation of Democrats passed before his window, Paul cheered—as did a friend, the son of a Republican whom he had paid ten cents to applaud. Paul seemed to confirm the oft-repeated adage that "every Hoosier baby is born with a ballot in his hand."[84] Before he graduated from eighth grade, the office of secretary of the Epworth League, a Sunday school organization at his Methodist church, became open. Paul broke with traditions by nominating himself for the position and then buttonholing voters. He won. It would be a stretch to trace his political ambition to this episode. As governor, McNutt privately affirmed: "I had no thought of entering political life when a boy."[85] It would not be an exaggeration, however, to say that interest in politics and a devotion to the Democratic Party were visible threads tying Paul to his father.

The relationship between John and Paul said something important about the family culture of the McNutts. Even if Paul had not been groomed from birth for the presidency, this family took its politics seriously and celebrated its partisan ties. The McNutts also valued professional success. Paul's father, as we will see, had the means to send him to college, which opened a range of possibilities to young McNutt. And yet Paul always managed to get his way on whatever path he set out on. That was because his parents guided, rather than dictated to, their son. He thus saw no reason to rebel openly against them.

It was John, not Ruth, who guided their son on one important matter: sex. By his teen years, Paul was a tall, handsome youth, possessing both chiseled features and thick raven hair that caused women to swoon. He "liked girls" but had "no steadies."[86] Paul socialized with girls during hay rides and, especially, at dances, some of them in nearby towns. Edith Wilk, future wife of Wendell L. Willkie, Paul's future college classmate, recalled seeing him at dances in her hometown of Rushville. John noticed these goings-on and decided to have a talk with his son. During their conversation, the elder McNutt pounded his fist on a desk and "told Paul that he would rather kill him than see him get into trouble." The display of anger worked, or so John later bragged: "There's not a cleaner man in the world today than Paul."[87] A rumor that Paul once was engaged to a woman who dumped him to marry a doctor lacked corroboration and credibility—this "fiancée" purportedly ended the engagement because she did not think he "was going anyplace."[88] In truth, Paul was too shrewd to surrender his future prospects for a passing fancy or on a sexual tryst, and some budding romances may have been nipped by his competitive instincts. "We all liked him," one high school classmate recalled. But, she added: "You had to go some to beat him in his classes."[89]

It was at Martinsville High School that Paul began to blossom as a leader. His gang engaged in their share of horseplay, tying cows to doorknobs and sneaking into classrooms at night to switch books in their schoolmates' desks. Over time, however, they used pranks to buck school policy. When Paul's class donated a drinking fountain to the school, the trustees accepted it but, in order to save money, kept the pressure so low that "just a thin stream of water would come through it." Paul was among a group of kids who slipped into the building one night and adjusted the water valve. Their endeavor went awry when water spouted "geyser-like," striking walls and leaving the school "sole-deep in water." When, years later, the Latin teacher learned that Paul had been among the ringleaders of the misadventure, she was shocked. As Phelps recalled, "She always thought Paul was the smartest, finest boy in the class."[90]

That teacher was correct, for Paul was the standout at Martinsville High. He made straight As, finished first in his graduating class, and seldom missed school—a sign that his health had improved.[91] He pitched for the baseball team, participated in debates, and was elected president of the senior class. More important, Paul strove to better his school. He founded a dramatic society and took the leading part in Charles Dickens's *The Cricket on the Hearth,* beginning a lifelong love of the theater. In his senior year, he persuaded school officials to allow his class to publish a newspaper. Thereafter he became editor in chief of *The Nuisance,* a name that he himself selected "after an epithet the principal had used in expressing his distaste for the venture."[92]

Paul envisioned *The Nuisance,* despite its title, as a boon, not a bother, to the school. It began as a newspaper and evolved into an annual publication, "a remembrance of school life." Its publication revealed a nascent reform impulse in Paul. Understanding that his school was beset by cliques—a "rampant class spirit"—he dismissed the argument that a paper would intensify such divisions. Paul was confident that, under his guidance, this broadsheet would "make the school better" and bolster student pride in Martinsville High. "We have endeavored to make a paper for, and by students," the editor proclaimed in the yearbook edition of *The Nuisance,* "something that would stimulate their interest in the school and school work."[93] Whether he achieved those idealistic ends remains unclear. But writing for *The Nuisance* enabled the young McNutt to refine his literary voice.

Paul's contribution to the yearbook displayed his gift for expression, his sense of place, his longing for greener pastures, and his superficial understanding of the economic challenges facing many Hoosiers. Entitled "Brown County Gold, That's All," it told the story of Jake, a farmer in the county where Paul's mother had been born. The seventeen-year-old author portrayed this scenic region mystically, as "a picture more perfect than any artist had ever painted." Jake's parents, like Paul's forefathers, had come to Brown County in search of gold and then had cultivated land that was less than fertile. Still, Jake loved his farm and resisted encroachments by surveyors working for a railroad. If Paul's talk about the "avariciousness" of this railroad was emblematic of the Progressive Era, his short story was neither an exercise in exposé nor a meditation on class struggle. In fact, its ending resembled rags-to-riches optimism. After being arrested by railroad police, Jake saw the light, sold his land, and then headed home—joyful. "All the way he painted in his imagination the new house he would build, the new clothes his wife should have, and above these the picture of the boy in school." This piece integrated a number of themes—bucolic beginnings, daily struggles, the value of an education, and the hope for a better life—without considering the fate of the family. After disposing of their property, they presumably prospered, or so the author suggested. When Jake returned with sacks of newly bought goods, his wife inquired what they held. "The gold of our dreams, dear," he replied, "Brown county gold, that's all."[94]

"Brown County Gold, That's All" was not Paul's first stab at writing fiction. At the close of his sophomore year of high school, he composed, for an English class, a short story that revealed aspects of his personality: ambition, competitiveness, perseverance, and defiance—of odds and critics. "Jack Dorste, Varsity Man" told of a college student, at fictional "Melville University," who was determined to win a coveted letter in track. The piece appeared to be semi-autobiographical for Paul played sports, although he was not a notably gifted athlete. Jack Dorste, moreover, resembled the author physically: "He was a long, slim, angular fellow with . . . most of his lank body in his lower appendages, hence his appellation, 'Legs.'" After repeatedly failing to make the track team, Jack, in his final semester, decided to brave "the jeers and taunts" and "try and try as he never had before." "How often he had pictured himself strutting up the street with a great white 'M' on his sweater," Paul narrated, of his alter ego's vanity. In the end, at a track meet against archrival Stahlman College, with the score tied, a member of Melville's team went down to injury just as the final event, the one-mile race, was to start. The coach substituted Jack, who, energized by the "frenzied shouts" of "Rah! Rah! Rah! Melville," ran the race and fell across the finish line—victorious. But was that enough to earn a letter? Weeks later, at commencement, a professor read the list of lettermen, saving the name of the track team's most recent hero for the end. "Jack Dorste, Varsity man at last," the author concluded, with relief and relish.[95]

"Jack Dorste, Varsity Man" is full of insights into the young McNutt. The piece may have been inspired by some event in Paul's life, for it showed an understanding of track. And it also looked to his future, for Paul himself would attend college one day. The story was, significantly, masculine in its characters, subject, and scenes; Paul described the "high pitch of excitement" of the boys' locker room before the meet but simply noted the "laughing, chattering co-eds"—who looked on from the stands. Dramatic, colored with spectacle, the plot featured an audience (the fans), a stage (the track), a solitary hero (Jack Dorste), and a climatic triumph. Its McNutt-like protagonist, through sheer will, managed to become part of a team—and to race into the long-coveted spotlight.

Paul's graduation from high school in 1909 marked a real-life triumph for him and for his family. The former schoolyard patsy had emerged as the "biggest gun" in his class, and the onetime newcomers to Martinsville were parents of a class president.[96] Bob Phelps attributed his friend's ascent to "resolution plus horse sense and energy."[97] In the process, Paul won a spot both among his peers and on a perch overlooking them. In the yearbook, one classmate joshed him as "a villain, a liar, a mean horse thief," adding: "All these and more make an editor-in-chief."[98] At the same time, Paul's accomplishments begot ever higher expectations, even from fellow students. The senior-class "prophetess" foresaw "Paul the Wise Man" poring over law books and earning, ultimately, "a great name in the annals of the world." "I see for thee a great future," she predicted.[99]

For Paul, the road ahead was simultaneously clear and uncertain. He elected to attend Indiana University (IU) in the fall to prepare for a career in law. That decision was natural enough, for his father was a lawyer and both his great-uncle Cyrus and one of Cyrus's sons had been law professors at IU. In deference to pleas from his mother, a "staunch Methodist," Paul briefly attended classes at DePauw University in Greencastle, Indiana, but decided that Indiana University, the flagship of higher education in the state, had more to offer.[100] Besides, the university lay just twenty miles south of Martinsville, and Paul seemed to have dreamed about attending IU. In "Jack Dorste, Varsity Man," the track hero attended Melville University, whose school colors were red and white—just like Indiana's. Not coincidentally, the colors of Melville's foe, Stahlman College, were gold and black, identical to those of IU's archrival, Purdue University.

John McNutt was happy about Paul's plans. The elder McNutt "had always had the hope that his son would study law and become his partner in practice."[101] So Paul, ambitious as well as obliging—one classmate tagged him "his father's son"—went off to Bloomington.[102] Standing out among the 180 students at Martinsville High School was one thing. Excelling at IU, with a student body of 1,300, would prove quite another.[103]

The Indiana University that McNutt entered was far from the world-renowned institution it was to become after World War II. The campus consisted of approximately ten buildings, red brick as well as limestone, arranged in an "L" and set amidst maple, poplar, and oak trees. Wooden walkways, along with a narrow, shallow river—the Jordan—snaked through the campus's dense forest.[104] IU's verdant scenery emblemized the rusticity of its location, populace, and leadership. Getting to and from Bloomington, seat of Monroe County, required a "patient disposition" since travelers endured muddy roads and a local railroad whose train stopped "at the least provocation."[105] The town's size attracted few traveling shows. In fact, Bloomington might have been christened the backwater that lacked water, for many residents rightly deplored its unsteady supply of water. "Provincial and restrained" was how one newcomer, just two years older than McNutt, described the townsfolk.[106] Likewise, the student body was homogeneous—Hoosier, white, and largely rural.[107]

The students' background, if not their outlook, meshed with that of Indiana University's tenth president, William Lowe Bryan. Born on a farm in Monroe County, a graduate of IU who had also studied philosophy at Clark University in Massachusetts, Bryan became president in 1902. Dignified and aloof, he shunned tobacco, alcohol, and card games and lectured male students on the virtue of chastity.[108] "Gentleman," he used to say, "every time I find myself thinking of a woman's body I go and take a cold shower."[109] He was old-fashioned in other ways. Well into the 1930s, Bryan rode to campus in a horse and buggy.[110] Members of his Presbyterian church thought Bryan "grandfatherly."[111] To young members of the faculty, Bryan, by his final years, was a "fuddy-duddy."[112] To McNutt, however, he remained worthy of admiration as an educational statesman, one who "personified Indiana University" throughout McNutt's years as a student, teacher, and dean.[113] In the words of one alumnus, Bryan's "very presence" reminded students that they were at IU "primarily to develop their intellectual powers."[114]

McNutt had cause to be in awe of Bryan and of the university he was trying to build. If conservative in habits, Bryan proved "liberal in intellectual outlook." He was a pioneer in the field of psychology, which was emerging from philosophy; a follower of William James's ideas about pragmatism; and a believer in the Progressive Era gospel of professionalism. Bryan wanted academic departments to do more than offer courses toward completing a major: they must prepare students for occupations, in fields such as law, medicine, or business. Yet the institution he inherited in 1902 was little more than a normal school, for the vast majority of its graduates became teachers, and it had only one small professional school, the faculty of law. Over his thirty-five-year presidency,

Bryan established additional schools, from medicine to music, and in so doing directed Indiana toward becoming a true university. He tethered nineteenth-century ends—the expansion of economic opportunity—to twentieth-century means, such as equipping individuals with expertise.[115] Giving the "poorest" students the means to improve their station was, for him, "the mission of democracy."[116] One classmate of McNutt's, who was also a first-generation college student, found Indiana University to be "quite wonderful."[117]

Yet, the adjustment to university life revived McNutt's insecurities. He was, after all, entering a larger academic and social arena as well as living in a new location. The only other such change had occurred a decade earlier, when the McNutt family moved to Martinsville, a move which, initially, was difficult for Paul. At IU, he quickly achieved membership in Beta Theta Pi, "the oldest and most exclusive fraternity at the university." (In later years, the IU chapter of Beta Theta Pi was often referred to as "Paul McNutt's fraternity.")[118] His lodgings must have seemed strange. McNutt lived with twenty-five or so fraternity brothers in a small house with a large front porch, common sleeping quarters, a living room, and a large bathroom used by all.[119] Clearly, he was no longer an only child occupying a space of his own. He even appeared jolted when a posse of Betas greeted him at Bloomington's railway station, "hallooing": "McNutt! Are you McNutt from Martinsville?" "Yes," he replied. Thereupon the crew grabbed their newest recruit and deposited him and his belongings in a carriage.[120]

McNutt had another reason for feeling a bit overwhelmed. The Betas were known across the campus as a "bunch of 'smoothies'" having "aspirations to social pre-eminence" and exuding a sense of entitlement.[121] According to Ralph V. Sollitt, an older Beta and a "big man on campus," McNutt was a "high-grade boy" and "very intelligent," but "quite shy" and, as a freshman, uninterested in student politics.[122]

As in his boyhood, McNutt studied—and studied hard. At IU, he was no "social light" but one of the "grinds," a tag hung on him by less diligent classmates.[123] "He flung it back at them," one journalist noted, "by trying out for the freshman baseball squad."[124] During his first year at Indiana University, McNutt achieved more than just making the baseball team. He earned five As and one B on the way to compiling another stellar scholastic record. In his four years at IU, he scored straight As in English, his major, and won admission to Phi Beta Kappa. McNutt's accomplishments earned praise from professors and "acclaim from the university's intellectuals."[125]

It was onstage that McNutt first made his mark at Indiana University. In the fall semester of his freshman year, he joined Strut and Fret, IU's theatrical company, whose name derived from a line in Shakespeare's *Macbeth,* and landed a leading part in Arthur W. Pinero's farce *The Magistrate.* The *Indiana Daily Student* graded McNutt "especially good" in his debut.[126] The next semester, McNutt, "before a crowded house," triumphed as Mr. Lofty, "a pompous, conceited, self-important whelp," in Oliver Goldsmith's *The Good Natured Man.*[127] Thereafter, his range as an actor expanded. As the romantic lead in *Sweet Lavender,* another Pinero farce, McNutt, the *Daily Student* opined, conveyed "manliness and tenderness in rare combination."[128] In J. M. Barrie's *The Admirable Crichton,* however, he supported his fellow Beta, Ralph Sollitt, with an "intelligent interpretation" of Lord Loam, the "owner of queer ideas" and father to three headstrong daughters.[129] By his junior year, McNutt, in the premiere of the anonymously written *The Leopard,* was once again in the starring role, this time as a senator's son who empathizes with strikers in his father's mill—an ironic foretaste of the labor unrest that he later experienced as governor of Indiana. Comfortable as both a leading man and a character actor, McNutt, some classmates predicted, might forsake the courtroom for the stage.[130]

Although pursuing a career in acting was never among his goals, it offered many things to McNutt. It remained a source of enduring pleasure, a diversion in which he delighted from high school to retirement. This taciturn man, one of his protégés recalled, came to life at the mention of the latest play; a group of associates once listened, enthralled, as McNutt recounted the plot of *Harvey,* which he had seen in New York. Moreover, acting may have fulfilled some hidden need for belonging to a group (in this case, a troupe) and for occupying center stage. "Although he became a public servant . . . ," a former classmate at Indiana University stressed, "in those days he was more interested in dramatics than anything else."[131] The *Arbutus,* IU's student yearbook, summarized McNutt's junior year in two words: "Stage presence."[132]

At IU, theater became an outlet for McNutt's reform instincts and personal ambitions. In January 1912, the middle of his junior year, McNutt was elected president of Strut and Fret. It proved a trying time, when students were grumbling that membership in the club was the product of "political maneuvering" rather than dramatic promise.[133] McNutt reorganized Strut and Fret, enlarged its membership, and energized it with a vow "to produce the best for Indiana."[134] A year later, however, the *Daily Student* complained that "Strut and Fret has not produced a single play on a lofty subject" involving "the social questions of the day."[135] The president's landing of the leading roles in both *The Leopard* and *Billy*, along with his senior-year editorial in the *Daily Student* commending the club "as one of the best college theatrical organizations in the country," did little to quiet criticism.[136] "Strut and Fret is a political organization with dramatics as a side issue," *The Arbutus* sneered. In a standard performance, "the players strut while the audience frets."[137] To what extent this criticism was aimed at the club's president remains unclear. Throughout McNutt's career, his personality often overwhelmed the institution he was heading and overshadowed the reform program he sought to push.

McNutt slowly moved from stage actor to political actor. Although Sollitt claimed that he had to force McNutt to become active in campus politics, once he entered that arena, it was with gusto. In 1911 the prize that McNutt coveted was the presidency of the Indiana University Union, the agency that governed campus recreation and student activities, and the obstacles before it were formidable—the president was by precedent a senior endorsed by the various fraternities. McNutt, in his sophomore year, used strategic alliances and machine-style tactics to achieve his end. After he won unanimous backing from the union's board, a pair of rival tickets surfaced to contest the election. For help, McNutt turned to a campus radical, Wendell L. Willkie of Elwood, Indiana. Willkie and his two older brothers had proven "too idealistic, too self-sufficient, [and] too argumentative" for campus life.[138] As such, they happily rallied non-fraternity students—the "Barbarians"—on behalf of the McNutt-led slate, which prevailed.[139] Had Strut and Fret honored the origins of its name with a production of *Macbeth*, McNutt might have made a fine Malcolm, the fair-haired prince who persuades others to fight his battles, and Willkie a convincing MacDuff, Malcolm's stout-hearted, if tractable, field general.

McNutt's victory illustrated his emerging political guile. After all, a member of IU's "most aristocratic fraternity" had gained the presidency of the Indiana Union by winning the non-fraternity vote.[140] And McNutt did so without soiling his own hands. When President Bryan probed charges of manipulation by the union's nominating committee, McNutt was able to deny, straight-faced, any involvement by either himself or his fraternity. He was learning how to win office as IU students before, during, and after him had. "Campus politics was a sport," C. Leonard Lundin, a professor of history at Indiana University between 1937 and 1977, recalled. A coalition would form "by various manipulations" and then win the election. Lundin noticed an absence of "real issues" in these struggles and a fault line dividing "the organized and the unorganized students."[141] Operating in this setting, McNutt was gaining experience in the art of "making deals" as a "preparation for practical Indiana politics."[142] He also was showing an aptitude for securing an end with little concern as to the means.

At the same time, McNutt believed strongly in the work of the Indiana Union. He assumed his new office gracefully, dubbing it "more of a responsibility than an honor," and reached out to the student body as a whole, proclaiming: "The Union needs you and the University needs the Union."[143] McNutt rewarded his supporters—Willkie obtained a seat on a committee assigned to rewrite the union's constitution—and thus demonstrated that good governance often makes the best politics. He kicked off his presidency with a membership drive at an open house featuring President Bryan and IU's football coach as the principal speakers. The union, on McNutt's watch, inaugurated a fund to cover the hospital expenses of needy students and increased its membership rolls. McNutt closed his presidency by advocating a separate building for the union, an idea that became a reality in the 1930s. In the interim, he advocated tirelessly for the union.[144]

Stewardship of the Indiana Union enabled McNutt to become what he had been in high school: a force as well as a presence on campus. The *Daily Student* applauded the union for furnishing "wholesome recreation," enjoyable meetings, and a place where students can socialize.[145] Such accolades earned McNutt a spot on the *Daily Student*'s list of "Indiana's Ten Biggest Men" as well as a close association with President Bryan, whom he knew how to cultivate.[146] After McNutt won unanimous union approval for Bryan's "very liberal hospital fee offer," he vowed to confer with him "during the first week of fall term as to the means of regulating the scheme." McNutt also lauded the president's "invaluable service" to the union.[147] Bryan, in turn, praised McNutt for maintaining the "highest standard of scholarship" and emerging as "a natural-born leader."[148]

In the fall of 1912, McNutt secured yet another honor, the presidency of the senior class. The margin of victory was somewhat modest—115 votes to 91 for his opponent—suggesting that he had made more than a few enemies. Some IU students thought McNutt a "blue blood" and "on the snobbish side"—manifestations of his membership in Beta Theta Pi, his shyness, and his successes. But he was becoming an adept leader who knew how to get "what he went after."[149] Devoted followers helped. Both Willkie, the president of the campus Democratic organization, and George W. Henley, the president of the Republican outfit, campaigned for him. "We ran around with a tobacco-chewing crowd that didn't think much of Paul," Henley recollected, "and we had to work hard to get the votes to make him president."[150] The election demonstrated that McNutt commanded the respect of a majority of his classmates. One alumnus of Indiana University expressed it cynically: "When you can't buck a man you might as well go along with him."[151]

If politics appealed to McNutt's ambitions and his cunning, the pursuit of writing showcased his ideals and stemmed from his heart. "Journalism was my first love," he told one confidant.[152] In Bloomington, he served as a reporter for an Indianapolis paper, and he wrote for the *Indiana Daily Student*. When, in his last semester, McNutt became editor of the *Daily Student*, he gained a pulpit from which to sermonize on journalism, the university, and human nature itself. His opening editorial pledged "to further the interests of the entire student body and of the University" by printing stories "of vital interest" and commentary "free from control by any faction."[153] Wounds sustained in campus political battles—of which McNutt was now a veteran—throbbed, and he could have been speaking to himself as much as to his readers in decrying "selfishness" as the "one great fault of the average Indiana University student."[154] McNutt's solution was as sincere as it was self-serving. He believed students must become involved in the work of the school, particularly the Indiana Union, as he had done, and they might even engage in "various sorts of public service," as he would do. "The man who is proud of an education simply because it is something that but few of his associates have, defeats the purpose of his University training," he wrote.[155] If his thoughts about public service were still forming, McNutt was beginning to see such work as both personally fulfilling and a fulfillment of the mission of a state-run university.

The editorial pages of the *Daily Student* chronicled McNutt's attachment to Indiana University, which he boosted. He extolled contributions made by Strut and Fret, the Indiana Union, the glee club, the debate team, and, of course, President Bryan—"one of the leaders in the educational world."[156] To lift school spirit, McNutt preached the importance of having "traditions," customs which, at other schools, instilled a sense of loyalty in both students and alumni. "Many of the world's best things are based upon sentiment," he asserted. Yet McNutt did not want emotion to outdistance reason or progress to be sacrificed for nostalgia: "The traditions of Indiana University should be such that [it] will make its students true citizens of the state, backers of every worthy enterprise, [and] the substantial, public spirited people that form the backbone of this nation."[157] Although *The Arbutus* chided the *Daily Student* as "seldom interesting, always dull, [and] frequently hopeless" and its "present editor" as no "Horace Greeley,"

McNutt probably paid no heed.[158] To him, journalism was a respite, an oasis where inspiring prose could soar above the daily grind and fray of political alliances and electioneering.

Did McNutt ever relax and have fun? Yes, sometimes. Over six feet tall, dark-haired, and handsome—the "coeds' 'matinee idol'"—he enjoyed female companionship but no lasting romances.[159] "Women are nice," he told his mother, "but why do they always want [you] to go with one girl?"[160] His boyish charm could be irresistible. Once, while showing some sorority sisters the dance steps for a play by Strut and Fret, McNutt smelled apple pie in the kitchen of their house. He crept in and asked the cook for a piece. She happily surrendered a huge slice.[161] Among the self-proclaimed "Don Juans" of the Beta house, stories about women were far less chaste. The brothers' bravado and banter allowed "even the most sheltered little lamb" to feel like "a veritable roué."[162] Judging from his upbringing, behavior, and temperament, McNutt was more lamb than roué.

Indeed, McNutt was more at ease in the company of men and alcohol, a product of fraternity life and a desire to be "one of the boys." Once, while in Chicago, McNutt tried to outdrink a fellow Beta but experienced a "down-fall" after he departed the city on the wrong train and later awoke in an entirely unexpected destination.[163] If McNutt had his drinking buddies, he also had protégés such as Sherman Minton—football player, president of the Indiana Union, and later, with the backing of Governor McNutt, a U.S. senator—and cohorts such as Oscar R. Ewing, a fellow Beta who helped run McNutt's presidential campaign in 1940 and who later served President Harry S. Truman as federal security administrator.[164] McNutt valued these relationships for their own sake, and they would prove valuable for his future plans. In one of his last editorials, he even waxed nostalgic about how friendships from college days often proved the "most steadfast" of ties. He closed with an expression of guilt, longing, and opportunism so typical of him: "Each Senior feels ashamed that he has not made more friends . . . One month remains. In that time he may be able to increase his circle of friends."[165]

McNutt's most noteworthy chum was Willkie. As Democrats and sons of small-town lawyers, the pair became, in Willkie's words, "exceedingly friendly."[166] According to Willkie's wife, Wendell and Paul "got along well" at IU.[167] But one member of Beta Theta Pi questioned how close the two men really were.[168] They seemed, if anything, political allies more than best friends, and, when seen side by side, must have seemed the odd couple of campus. Willkie's rough appearance and uncombed hair concealed an open, maturing mind that absorbed Karl Marx and other unorthodox authors. McNutt, in contrast, was neatly attired in "finely tailored" suits and conventional in thought.[169] Classmates joked that in college Paul was the conservative and Wendell the liberal. Indeed, James Albert Woodburn, a professor of history at IU, remembered Willkie as a "pretty good progressive," but significantly he could not recollect which "progressive"—Woodrow Wilson or Theodore Roosevelt—Willkie had backed in the presidential election of 1912.[170] In that contest, McNutt, an unswerving partisan, voted the straight Democratic ticket.[171] During the campaign, in fact, McNutt delivered his maiden political speech, on Wilson's behalf, at the Morgan County Courthouse in Martinsville.[172] Overall, McNutt was less adventurous, politically and intellectually, than Willkie.

George Henley, who knew both McNutt and Willkie, summarized the contrast between them: McNutt was "white collar" while Willkie was one of the "rough necks," that is, the students who "didn't necessarily shave every day."[173] As might be expected, Willkie and McNutt held divergent views about fraternities. Willkie assailed them as "a sort of caste system" and joined McNutt's Betas only after receiving an ultimatum from his girlfriend. At one point, Willkie paced and fretted: "If I don't join a fraternity, I'll lose my girl, and if I do, I'll lose my soul." According to one source, McNutt and two other Betas persuaded Willkie's girlfriend to demand that Wendell join the fraternity.[174] In the end, the heart—or the threat—prevailed and Willkie became a member of Beta Theta Pi just before graduation.

That decision magnified the disparate personas of Willkie and McNutt. Willkie seemed warmer and more "*genuinely* friendly" than McNutt, "who always had his eye on the main chance."[175] Indeed, classmates called Paul "Venus McNutt," a play on his good looks and Olympian ambition. The nickname, and the reputation, stuck. A year after McNutt's graduation, *The Arbutus,* in a pantheistic feature entitled "Ye Gods," sculpted a classical bust from Paul's senior-year portrait and, beneath it, dubbed Venus McNutt "the God of Politics, adored by the ambitious and those who hunger and thirst after college honors."[176]

Such commentary revealed an essential point: McNutt graduated from Indiana University with "high distinction" in 1913.[177] As her son accepted his diploma, Ruth exuded pride. "I can think of no greater joy . . . than that of a mother realizing her fond expectations regarding her son," a friend wrote to her. "You are only reaping what you have sown."[178] John McNutt, in contrast, might have harbored some disappointment. After all, Paul had majored in English, not law, and his interests lay in journalism, drama, and politics. But John's pressure on his son was never insistent, and since the family was secure financially, Paul did not have to become a lawyer. The young McNutt was diligent, talented, and more than likely to succeed. "We realized the potentialities of Paul," Henley recollected.[179] But where, ultimately, would such potential lead?

# 2

---

## NEW DEPARTURES, OLD HAUNTS
## (1913–1925)

---

FRESHLY GRADUATED FROM INDIANA UNIVERSITY, Paul V. McNutt was ready to leave the Hoosier State, though not permanently. In the half-dozen years following graduation, McNutt left his native state for two extended periods, first to attend Harvard Law School and second to join the army in World War I. From those two pivotal experiences, McNutt began to emerge as a man of the nation, if not the world. He entered that exclusive club of Americans who has not only a college education, but a degree from Harvard as well. Association with that school's name helped to launch McNutt's career as a law professor and a dean. The Great War had an even greater impact. It focused and kept McNutt's attention on issues of international relations, national defense, and patriotic service, even though, as fate would have it, he never saw combat overseas. On a more personal level, the war, in an unexpected way, allowed McNutt to "grow up"—that is, to meet his future wife and to begin a family of his own.

At the same time, there were powerful forces, mainly familial, that pulled him back to Indiana. The life to which McNutt returned was less than interesting. While his own horizons had broadened, the landscape in Martinsville and Bloomington remained all too familiar, personally and professionally. The McNutt who graduated from Indiana University was uncertain and searching. Twelve years later, he was more settled but still restless. That restlessness intensified McNutt's ambition.

During his senior year at IU, McNutt began exploring what he would do with his life. Two roads lay ahead: he could assist the political career of his father, who in 1912 was aiming for a spot on Indiana's supreme court, or he could study for a bachelor's degree in law (LLB) at Harvard Law School. Both paths merged, since securing a seat on the court would enable John C. McNutt to pay his son's tuition at law school. Like many ambitious young people of this era, Paul was prepared to forsake small-town life in the Midwest for better opportunities, both intellectual and financial, in the great cities of the East Coast.[1] Indiana Democrats, however, passed over John as their candidate for the state supreme court. Undaunted, John took out a $4,000 mortgage on his house and used the money to send Paul to Harvard.[2]

Harvard has earned a royal reputation in the annals of higher education. By the time the oldest university in the United States celebrated its 350th anniversary in 1986, it claimed "six American Presidents, thirty Nobel laureates, two dozen Pulitzer Prize winners, over two hundred Rhodes Scholars, and numerous Supreme Court justices, congressmen, Cabinet officers, [and] governors."[3] Associated with letters and learning, bluebloods and Boston Brahmins, Harvard was a sort of a training camp for the sons of the well-off. "The evil development of Harvard is the snob," Theodore Roosevelt, a graduate of Harvard, once sneered.[4] Yet, Harvard was sufficiently strong and confident to maintain "a normal state of self-dissatisfaction," a constant striving for improvement.[5] More than anyone else, Charles William Eliot, president of Harvard from 1869 to 1909, made the university "into an instrument of national purpose."[6] Among other things, Eliot modernized Harvard's professional schools, such as law and medicine. McNutt, who had watched Indiana University struggle to establish a core of professional schools, now had the privilege of studying at an institution that was what IU aspired to be, a truly modern university.

For a green law student from the heartland of America, Harvard could be overwhelming. During the final three decades of the nineteenth century, the school of law, under the deanship of Christopher Columbus Langdell, expanded and professionalized its faculty, replacing retired judges and lawyers with "men who had chosen law teaching and legal scholarship as their life-work."[7] In so doing, Langdell transformed a master-apprentice system, whereby students at Harvard read law under a member of the legal community, into a professional school with written examinations and a three-year course of study.[8] Langdell introduced the use of casebooks, rather than textbooks, from which students mastered the law by analyzing original sources instead of memorizing data from lectures. Students formed a "habit of intellectual self-reliance" by dissecting a case, evaluating the court's decision, and then studying other related cases to observe the law's principles in "full development."[9] Such dramatic changes in instruction raised both academic standards and the reputation of the law school.

With its growth, Harvard Law School demanded grander buildings to serve its students and to emblemize its progress. McNutt would have taken classes in Austin Hall and Langdell Hall. Austin Hall housed a large lecture hall that featured a podium enveloped by a crescent of tiered seating. The layout enhanced classroom interaction and the case method by allowing the students to face each other and by enabling the instructor to call on any class member merely by pivoting his body. As the law school grew, Langdell Hall went up. With its "sequence of pavilions, colonnades, and wings" made of white limestone, Langdell Hall invoked an "imperial image" more attuned to the architecture of the United States capital, or that of Ancient Rome, than to that of the Harvard campus.[10] Such imposing buildings, and the excellence for which they stood, left a mark on McNutt. Years later, after returning to Indiana, he liked to visit the office of a lawyer friend in Indianapolis. There, he would seat himself in a chair and survey Indiana's capital city. According to one journalist, "It seemed to please him to identify some of the buildings in his line of vision with structures on the Harvard campus."[11]

Harvard Law School proved a unique experience for McNutt. To be sure, he maintained old ties and old habits. He lived at the Beta Theta Pi house in Cambridge, studied diligently, and easily passed his annual examinations. In fact, by the end of his first year, he had won a $150 scholarship to continue his studies. Yet the financial strain of attending an Ivy League school meant that McNutt had to work to meet expenses. He landed the presidency of Harvard's legal aid society, an office that paid a salary, and he became a correspondent in Boston for the United Press. McNutt loved journalism, and sports became his beat as he covered both the Boston Braves, 1914 World Series champions, and the Red Sox, who prevailed in the fall classic in 1915 and 1916. Along with providing enjoyment, such work brought hidden benefits: "News writing," another journalist later observed, "[and the] slangy jargon of the sports writer, humanized his academic papers at law school."[12]

News reporting also represented an escape from law school, where the pressure could be intense. In his freshman year, McNutt took Property I with Professor Edward Henry Warren, whom the students tagged "Bull" for he had "a great thick neck" and a knack for scaring his charges to death. Warren greeted the first-year students with an invitation to turn and look at the man on their right and then to turn and look at the man on their left. After they completed this exercise, he admonished: "One of you three will not be here next year." As McNutt himself related, one student who failed to make the grade was a fellow Hoosier and future composer: Cole Porter. During one class, Warren asked Porter to recite the facts of a case they were studying. In a scene that might have come from the pages of John Jay Osborn Jr.'s novel *The Paper Chase*, Porter, unprepared, fumbled his answer. An angry Warren "leaned over his desk and very superciliously said, 'Mr. Porter, why don't you learn to play the fiddle?'" Porter, in an act of rebellion that would have been alien to McNutt, walked out of the class and withdrew from the law school.[13] This tale may have been an apocryphal piece about the early struggles of an American musical genius.[14] Nevertheless, McNutt's retelling of it revealed something about the pressures he himself must have endured at Harvard.

Despite the stress, McNutt gained enormously from law school, and he was proud of his ties to Harvard. Living in Cambridge encouraged him to think in a national context. In 1916, as president of Harvard Legal Aid, he invited two well-known leaders, Thomas R. Marshall, vice president of the United States and a former governor of Indiana, and Alton B. Parker, the Democratic Party's nominee for president in 1904, to address his graduating class at law school. Although both men declined the offer, McNutt understood that Harvard was prestigious enough to command such speakers. Equally important was what McNutt took away from Harvard. He later used the case method when he became a professor of law at Indiana University. And for him, Harvard remained the model of all that a law school should be. During the 1920s, McNutt kept in contact with his former professors, and he revisited Cambridge. On two occasions, he tried to return to Harvard Law School as a teaching fellow, and he harbored dreams of becoming its dean.[15] McNutt must have been reluctant to leave Boston when he graduated in 1916.

Yet familial pressures were never far from McNutt's thoughts. Paul's future wife would remember John McNutt as both "possessive" of his son and "fervently" hopeful of having him as a law partner.[16] That John had helped pay Paul's way through law school only added to the son's sense of obligation. In 1914, while still a law student, Paul won admission to the Indiana bar and formally joined the Martinsville firm of McNutt and McNutt. But he was determined to search for an alternative career path acceptable to both him and his father. Politics appeared the safest bet. When asked at Harvard whether he intended to be a lawyer, he allegedly responded: "I intend to be President of the United States."[17] In truth, back then, he set his sights on an office less grand. In March 1916, McNutt ran for the Democratic Party's nomination as prosecutor of Morgan County. It was a bold move for a law student. McNutt compounded his audacity by informing the party faithful that his responsibilities in Cambridge prevented him from canvassing in person. Amazingly, he lost the nomination by a scant four votes.[18]

After graduating from law school, McNutt returned to Martinsville and practiced law with his father. Following his successes at IU and at Harvard, it was a less-than-exciting experience. Although he won his first case, involving a divorce, McNutt grew restless.[19] He returned to familiar haunts, serving as secretary for his graduating class at IU and organizing the class's first reunion. He did new things as well. When in 1916 the mayor of Martinsville departed for a two-week trip, he named McNutt acting mayor. The local Democratic newspaper described the younger McNutt as eager for action, even though the temporary mayor heard nothing more momentous than the case of a motorist who had violated the speed limit.[20] The appointment no doubt came about at the instigation of the elder McNutt, who was respected by Martinsville's Democrats.[21]

That same year, another political cause captured Paul's attention: John McNutt sought the Democratic nomination for a seat on the state's appellate court. Paul aided his father's campaign by rallying old IU classmates. They, in turn, asked their fathers to back his father, who prevailed by a razor-thin margin at the state convention. After a clerk read the final tally, Paul "grabbed his father around the neck and gave him a good hug."[22] "We had a stiff fight," young McNutt crowed, "but that fact [made] the victory sweet."[23]

The fall campaign showed how easily Paul McNutt could steal the spotlight. Speaking in Bloomington, he portrayed the Democratic nominee for governor, John A. M. Adair, as a "poor man" who had worked his way up the political ladder, and he skewered the Republican candidate, James P. Goodrich, as a stand-patter, "one of the richest men in the state," and "Jim Good-and-rich."[24] (Goodrich, a self-made businessman, accepted no campaign contributions and instead financed his bid for the governorship out of his own pocket.)[25] Meredith Nicholson, a well-known Hoosier novelist, shared the stage with McNutt and left town impressed: "Paul skinned Jim Goodrich to a turn . . . and the crowd so enjoyed Paul that my much more academic discussion of the great principles of Plato and A. Jackson went flat."[26] That November, the Democratic slate in Indiana also "went flat." Narrowly reelected, Woodrow Wilson lost the Hoosier State; Republicans won both of its seats in the U.S. Senate, Goodrich beat Adair, and John McNutt failed in his bid for the appellate court.

As 1916 turned into 1917, the aftermath of John's defeat at the polls and Paul's restless ambition must have caused unease at the McNutt home. Paul's solution was to enroll in Indiana University's school of law to study for his doctorate in jurisprudence. Two unrelated occurrences changed his plans. First, a month after Paul decided to return to school, an unexpected faculty retirement led President William Lowe Bryan to appoint him an instructor of law.[27] Bryan held McNutt in high regard, and he had heard "very good reports" of his work in law school.[28] After accepting the appointment, McNutt explained his decision to his parents: "We'll be going to war soon and I'll go. This will be good experience when I come back."[29] John and Ruth acceded. While teaching at IU, Paul remained nominally a partner in John's firm.

The second crucial event for McNutt came in April, when Congress declared war on Germany. McNutt's remarks to his parents were portentous, for he would soon join the army. But even he could not have foreseen the extent to which the war would change him. Until this point in his life, McNutt had been a mass of contradictions, multifaceted in his talent—with aptitude in art, letters, theater, journalism, electioneering, and public speaking—but constricted in his personal life, enjoying few close relationships and remaining captive to family expectations. The war broadened McNutt's perspective to encompass happenings overseas, and focused his energies on a specific task, the training of soldiers to vanquish an enemy on a distant battlefield. Participation in World War I was a "great departure," for both the United States and Paul McNutt.

When the United States entered World War I on the side of Great Britain and France, it changed the nation's foreign policy and its assumptions about foreign affairs. For over a century, America had adhered to its tradition of isolation, that is, "abstention from foreign wars and an adamant refusal to enter into alliances with other states." It looked outward on a mostly peaceful world, and inward at its own prosperity, and judged isolation to be the correct course. Americans were reluctant to recognize that the absence of a major European war between 1815 and 1914 was an unnatural phenomenon or that their own safety during this period rested precariously on the continuation of British sea power.

When in 1914 Great Britain, France, and Russia went to war against Germany and Austria-Hungary, this "Age of Free Security" for the United States quickly passed.[30] Americans watched as British and French troops struggled to stop a German advance on Paris. They saw their nation's rights as a neutral violated and its citizens slaughtered as German submarines sank unarmed passenger ships without warning. By April 1917, an array of factors—submarine attacks, Germany's pursuit of an alliance with Mexico, and a growing sense that the New World's arms and ideals could save the Old World from itself—led President Wilson to ask Congress to declare war against the government in Berlin. After the House and Senate complied, the journalist Frank Cobb proclaimed that "the old isolation is finished."[31] The debate over America's role in the world was not finished, of course, and McNutt would participate in it throughout his public life.

At the time America entered World War I, McNutt was an instructor of law at Indiana University, a school that was just beginning to mobilize for war. Generally speaking, Hoosiers and midwesterners embraced "more slowly" than citizens in the East the program of "reasonable preparedness" launched by Woodrow Wilson's administration in 1915.[32] By 1916, Indiana University required only freshman male students to drill regularly. Not until Germany resumed unrestricted submarine warfare on February 1, 1917, did patriotic fervor, and the demand for "some form of military organization," engulf the campus.[33] In March 1917, the university established a Reserve Officers' Training Corps (ROTC), an organization that Bryan and McNutt came to cherish and defend in coming years against criticism by pacifists. Following Congress's declaration of war, in April 1917, Bloomington came to resemble a military depot, as volunteers and draftees left for the army while other recruits arrived to be sheltered and trained. All able-bodied freshmen and sophomore males, moreover, were now required to drill, at sunup and at dusk. Fourteen members of the IU faculty did their part by entering the service.[34]

McNutt wasted little time before enlisting. Although up to this point in his life he had showed almost no interest in foreign and military affairs, McNutt, like most Americans, suffered no want of patriotism. He was too active and too driven to remain aloof during what promised to be the defining drama of his youth. Like many professors who joined the army, he surrendered to a "yearning for the battleground, a desire for excitement, patriotism, and an instinct to serve." He may have been influenced by "a kind of masculine mystique, an indefinable dissatisfaction with a life of scholarship and teaching while an ex-

citing war was raging in Europe."[35] Whatever his motivations, a month following the declaration of war, McNutt decided to train as an officer. In a letter of
recommendation, Bryan praised McNutt's "honest[y], sobriety, and morality"
and his "natural-born" leadership skills.[36] Since McNutt held both college and
advanced degrees at a time when few enlisted men had progressed beyond the
seventh grade, his move into the officer corps was swift. One of the so-called
ninety-day wonders, the tall, thin-faced, and recently promoted assistant professor entered the officers' training camp at Fort Benjamin Harrison, near Indianapolis, in August 1917. He left camp exactly three months later.[37]

Officer training was an exhausting grind, one which began at five o'clock in
the morning, ended at ten in the evening, and filled every hour in between.
Aspiring officers performed their share of menial tasks—at Fort Benjamin
Harrison, McNutt dug trenches alongside other men.[38] Mainly, they mastered
fundamentals of marksmanship, scouting, patrolling, drilling, route marches,
and, in cavalry and artillery units, horsemanship. One officer at Fort Sheridan,
Illinois, compared the monotony of training to "hoeing a garden on a rainy day"
and the chore of absorbing the drill instruction manual to reading column after
column in *Webster's Dictionary*. Through it all, the camps struggled to provide
for the recruits. One soldier at Fort Benjamin Harrison had to make an hour-
and-a-half journey to Indianapolis just "to get oil and rags to clean his rifle." At
the same time, he crowed, "They are feeding us here like lords."[39]

On the outside, at least, McNutt emerged from officer training a changed
man. "Army beans put weight on him," a journalist later remarked. "Army officers put captain's bars on him."[40] McNutt and Sherman Minton—a fellow
captain, a former fraternity buddy, and a future United States senator—showed
off their new uniforms, and their élan, during an address at IU. These "splendid
young men," the *Indiana Daily Student* beamed, exemplified the "hundreds
who have gone out from our college to do their part." The "crowd of friends"
applauded them heartily and "thronged the platform."[41]

What followed might have seemed, to Captain McNutt, somewhat familiar:
The "Hoosier schoolmaster," as one journalist called him, became an instructor of soldiers. Between December 1917 and the end of the war eleven months
later, McNutt was sent from one military base to another, first to Texas—Camp
Travis, Kelly Field, and Camp Stanley, near San Antonio—and later to Camp
Jackson in South Carolina. At Camp Jackson, where seven thousand officers
and nearly eighty thousand enlisted men prepared themselves for the field artillery service, McNutt instructed soldiers and wrote training manuals.[42] At

this massive university of sorts, he saw shadows of his past and glimpses of his immediate future—teaching young people and exercising leadership at a place of instruction.

One part of training reminded McNutt of his own upbringing. During World War I, the U.S. Army moved to stamp out "sexual vice." To fight venereal disease, the army enlisted the Commission on Training Camp Activities (CTCA), an umbrella organization which drew on the resources of the Young Men's Christian Association (YMCA), the Jewish Welfare Board, and the Knights of Columbus. Placing results ahead of reticence, the CTCA's pamphlets argued that such previously taboo practices as masturbation were "preferable to potentially infectious liaisons."[43] The commission also parroted conventional thoughts about the virtues of abstinence as a way for men to keep their "bodies clean" and "hearts pure."[44] One CTCA poster exhorted: "Remember the Folks at Home. Go back to them physically fit and morally clean. Don't allow a whore to smirch your record."[45] For many recruits, this campaign represented "the first thorough sex education they had received."[46]

McNutt himself must have wondered just how many of his men had been told by their fathers of the need to remain sexually "clean," as he had been by his.[47] Speaking before a church group in his hometown of Martinsville, McNutt later related that at one training camp more than half of the recruits were physically unfit because, as he euphemistically put it, they had not taken care of the "masterpiece entrusted to them by their Maker," meaning their body. That McNutt was referring to venereal disease there is no doubt, for he cited "army regulations" that helped men to guard "against evil in all its forms" and praised the YMCA "for the noble work it has done, is doing and will continue to do" in this area.[48] Wholesome and handsome, McNutt embodied the "male sex role" promoted by social hygienists during the war—someone "powerful but pure, virile yet virginal."[49]

McNutt made a fine officer. He was energetic and diligent. "I have no time of my own when I am at camp," he reported from South Carolina.[50] More important, whether it was due to his intelligence, erudition, presence, or some other trait, he was capable of commanding, if not inspiring, men who were not always of his background. After the war, he received a pair of fawning letters from one of his charges—Sam Catanzarito from Pennsylvania—whose misspellings and grammatical lapses hinted at his working-class origins. This soldier had become so attached to McNutt that he sent him a personal photograph and confided that he liked army life better than living at home.[51] McNutt also earned rave reviews from his own superiors. At the close of the war, the adjutant at Camp Jackson commended McNutt for being a "very capable officer" who had performed all his duties in an "excellent manner" and with "fine results." "I have written many letters of commendation on the services of officers," he emphasized, "but have never written one with as much pleasure, or one more deserving, than this one."[52]

For McNutt, army life opened new opportunities—to a point. Although he had entered Fort Benjamin Harrison with no military experience, he left a captain, at a time when the majority of men who went through officer training emerged with the rank of lieutenant. In August 1918, McNutt was promoted to major in the field artillery and a year later, after the war's end, he became a lieutenant colonel in the artillery reserve. "Starting from the very bottom in the country's wartime military machine and rising to the rank of lieutenant colonel," a reporter for *American Legion Monthly* noted, "is a record which, even without amplification, would tell much about the sort of man he is."[53] Indeed, McNutt thrived on the discipline and structure as well as on the hard work and recognition associated with army life.

Something was missing, however. McNutt longed to be sent overseas. Like other Americans, he could not help seeing propaganda, circulated by the U.S. government's Committee on Public Information (CPI), accusing Germany of rank depravity.[54] Not unlike Captain Harry S. Truman, a fellow officer in World War I, McNutt, it seems safe to say, must have been eager "to fire at least one volley at the Hun."[55] "He had visions of the Argonne, Chateau Thierry and newer fronts," a reporter noted of McNutt. Alas, when the German home-front collapsed, so did his hope of seeing combat.[56] The war came to an end on November 11, 1918, while McNutt was still an instructor at Camp Jackson. Unlike Truman, who had commanded troops on the battlefield and, in so doing, had learned about his capacity to lead under the greatest of pressures, McNutt could claim no comparable feat.[57]

McNutt's experience in World War I was, in key respects, Rooseveltian. Like Theodore Roosevelt, who had volunteered for combat during the Spanish-American War, McNutt eagerly donned a military uniform in the service of his country. Like Franklin D. Roosevelt, who was assistant secretary of the navy in Wilson's administration and never saw fighting firsthand, McNutt's contribution to the war effort was more humdrum than heroic. They made up for that fact in parallel ways. Just as FDR had long favored a big navy, McNutt, during the 1920s, backed higher appropriations for the military as a way to bolster

America's defenses. At the same time, like TR, he never lost the desire to see combat. After the United States entered the First World War, Theodore Roosevelt, at the age of fifty-eight, asked President Wilson for permission to raise a cavalry unit. A quarter century later, after the United States entered the Second World War, McNutt, who was fifty years old, went before General George C. Marshall, the army's chief of staff, to volunteer for active service in the United States Army.[58] Neither offer was accepted.

Although or perhaps because he never saw combat, McNutt loved the U.S. Army—its trappings as well as the ideal of patriotic sacrifice for which it stood. World War I brought him into the service, trained him, and gave him the chance to mold other men. Yet circumstances shielded him from the horrors of mechanized warfare. For McNutt, then, there was no searing specter of death to wash away the idea of combat as "glorious, adventurous" sacrifice and a "virile antidote to the effete routine of modern life."[59] Unlike some of his fellow citizens, he never questioned the cause, of democracy and security for all nations, for which Americans fought during the Great War. In 1923 McNutt told a group of war mothers that "a war to overcome false principles," that is, selfish, national ambitions, was "a war of eternal glory." So it was with World War I. McNutt praised his fallen comrades in that war for "heroic" sacrifice, for answering the "call of highest duty," and for "unselfish devotion to the common cause" of defending America and extending its ideals.[60] Generally speaking, he retained a gallant, unsullied view of military service.[61]

McNutt fell in love with more than the army during World War I. On Christmas Eve 1917, while McNutt was still in Texas, he and a friend, Captain L. Kemper Williams of New Orleans, went to a dance at a country club in San Antonio. The city was "alive with soldiers then" and the women had a saying: "Fox-trot with a soldier, leave him with a smile, for tomorrow he may be cannon fodder."[62] San Antonio became known as the "mother-in-law of the army" because "so many soldiers met their wives there."[63] At the dance, McNutt spied an attractive young woman who was "swirling around the dance floor with another officer." "Come along," Williams gestured, after noticing McNutt's interest. They cut in, and Williams introduced his friend as "Captain McNutt," which caused the woman to burst into laughter.[64]

The bemused woman, who would soon share the McNutt surname, was Kathleen Timolat. She came from a family of means. Kathleen's mother, Sarah Louise Merriam, was the daughter of a prominent druggist who had founded the National Wholesale Drug Association. Her father, Harry N. Timolat, was a wax chemist and entrepreneur. Kathleen, their only child, was born in Minneapolis on May 26, 1894. Shortly thereafter, Timolat moved his family to Chicago, where he worked for a chemical company.[65] But he longed for financial independence, and he believed that a fortune could be made from the wax of the candelia cactus that grows in the northern states of Mexico. In 1910, Timolat leased 400,000 acres in Mexico, opened a wax mill, and became friends with Francisco I. Madero, a leading opponent of the dictatorship of Porfirio Diaz and president of Mexico from 1911 to 1913. Mexico's descent into revolution and civil war cost Madero his life and Timolat his business. Revolutionaries burned Timolat's mill and home, forcing him and his wife to flee Mexico "through wild mountain passes."[66] Thereafter, Timolat quit Mexico and relocated his wax enterprise to San Antonio.[67]

Like her father, Kathleen was adventurous and independent, qualities that must have excited Paul. On the trip from Chicago to Mexico, Timolat had stopped off in San Antonio to enroll Kathleen in the Mulholland School, a finishing institution for "girls of good families." Mulholland taught "Miss Timolat" about languages, art, music appreciation, and that facility, associated with many upper-crust women, "of how to balance a tea cup while engaging conversational pleasantries."[68] Yet she was no typical debutante. Kathleen vacationed with her parents when they lived in Mexico. There, she rode her pet pony and shot a revolver—at tomato cans during target practice and at rattlesnakes from her saddle. "Neighboring Spanish dons," one journalist reported, "shook their heads at the brazenness of the senorita who rode alone through the wilds." For protection, Timolat told Kathleen to "shoot if any one gets near your horse's head," and he had no doubt that, if threatened, she would have fired.[69] The example of her mother perhaps reinforced Kathleen's sense of autonomy. Although Sarah Timolat's father had been in the pharmaceutical trade, she was a Christian Scientist, meaning she used prayer, not medical care, to cope with sickness.[70] Kathleen herself was a lifelong Christian Scientist, and differences over her religious practices later caused tension during her marriage to Paul.

It was no surprise that Kathleen captured Paul's attention. Tall, slim, and radiant, with blue eyes offset by reddish brown locks, she had grace and warmth—expressions of her comfortable upbringing, polished by finishing school. Kathleen's correspondence from the latter part of her marriage to Paul betrayed as much, for she conveyed that recipients of her missives were special people indeed. To confidants, she punctuated the addressee's first name with the word "darling."[71] She thanked generously and genuinely, for the "perfectly beautiful lilies!" and for a "lovely weekend with you and your sweet children!"[72] She could transform the mundane into the "wonderful," such as when friends sent some farm-grown produce: "Besides their goodness there was a sentimental interest that made everything taste better—and we all send our gratitude."[73]

Kathleen was completely natural and "entirely unimpressed with her own importance," traits that tended to put others, like Captain McNutt, at ease. She spoke "pretty freely" and proved an "exceptionally clever conversationalist."[74] One member of the McNutt family remembered Kathleen as having a "parlor wit" matched by a risqué side either belied or abetted by her refined education. After this relative commented on how the hemlines of women's dresses had been migrating northward, Kathleen, feigning the outrage of a red-blooded male, wondered what was so wrong with that! "She has a rich voice," a female journalist once observed, "and a delicious sense of humor that curves her lips in a smile and dimples her cheeks at the slightest provocation."[75] Kathleen at times used humor and candor to check Paul's ego. When, years later, he teased that "she never lived until she married me," her reply was "I had 24 perfectly good years before that."[76]

Whether it was by wit or warmth, Kathleen bewitched Paul. Theirs was a match in which opposites attracted. She was outgoing and outdoorsy. He was reserved and a reader of books. If she proved friendly, he could appear frosty. Those who knew the McNutts later in their marriage stress how Kathleen helped to make Paul conscious of people. The couple also had things in common. Like Paul, Kathleen enjoyed golf, theater, and dancing. They parted when it came to music, which was one of Kathleen's passions. She sang and played an instrument, although not very well, and he not at all.[77] They shared similar backgrounds as only children from families that valued hard work and success. Like most people, they had their insecurities. Paul expressed his by hiding behind a protective wall while Kathleen dealt with hers by letting down her guard. Years later, during Paul's campaign for the White House, Kathleen would describe the difference between them. She was, she told one reporter, "the extrovert in the family." "Beneath all the glamour, brilliance and sometimes brittle exterior," Kathleen explained, "Paul really is a sensitive soul. All his life he has had to fight off being somewhat shy."[78]

The romance rapidly progressed toward engagement and marriage. The speed of the courtship was in part the product of a time "when soldiers got moving orders at a moment's notice."[79] Paul knew that, and he knew who would make him happy. So he stated his intentions to Harry Timolat. "Now, what could you do?" Timolat laughed, years later, while recalling this declaration. "He was a handsome chap. He had a good handshake and so I said, 'Yes.'"[80] But Paul had doubts that Kathleen would have him; when he proposed, he had not yet invested in an engagement ring. Kathleen said "yes," and the couple wed on April 20, 1918, at St. Paul's Episcopal Church, across from the entrance to Fort Sam Houston. The bride, wearing a "tailored suit of midnight blue," was given by her father to the groom, who was attired in his captain's uniform. Kemper Williams, who had introduced the couple nearly four months earlier, was best man. After the ceremony, the newlyweds departed for a getaway to New Orleans and then Martinsville before settling in South Carolina, where Paul assumed his duties at Camp Jackson.[81]

Paul's love for Kathleen deepened over the next year. Eager to be a "dutiful son" to a new set of parents, Paul wrote his mother-in-law a month after the wedding to express gratitude "for letting me have her." He confessed a powerful aversion to surrendering any time with his new wife, who continued to surprise, even to amaze, him. Kathleen also won over her new in-laws. "You should have seen her in Martinsville," Paul reported to Sarah Timolat. "My Father and Mother are just as much in love with their daughter as I am."[82] On St. Valentine's Day 1919, as his first wedding anniversary neared, Paul sent Kathleen a spray of flowers and a note that read "A year ago today I thought I knew what love was. Today I am sure. Your love has given me more joy than anything in the world. It is my most valuable possession and I shall try each day to cherish and protect it." Paul's comment, about not knowing what love was until he was nearly twenty-eight, hinted at his past loneliness. And he kept his vow of fidelity. Kathleen was the only woman with whom he ever had a romantic relationship.[83]

Paul and Kathleen spent the rest of the war in South Carolina. While he was at Camp Jackson, she lived in a boardinghouse in Columbia. The young tenants impressed the Aughtrys, the couple who owned the boardinghouse. To Mr. Aughtry, Paul was "a fine man" without "bad habits" and "sort of quiet." Mrs. Aughtry, like many women, thought him "very handsome," and she also managed to penetrate his shyness to uncover "a wonderful personality" who was "full of fun." They both found Kathleen "lovely and charming." Kathleen amused the Aughtrys when, at war's end, she joshed that she never had seen her husband wear anything except an army uniform. Then, following the armistice, Paul went into a shop to buy a suit, and Kathleen was "biting her finger nails" as she wondered if he "would look as handsome in a suit as in a uniform."[84]

McNutt's active military service ended on March 14, 1919, when he was honorably discharged from the army. He then accepted a commission in the field artillery section of the reserve officers' corps rather than remain in the regular army. The decision made sense, for it allowed McNutt to continue to participate in the military through the reserves, in which he later became a leader, while also holding a civilian job. But the choice was not inevitable. One of McNutt's superior officers had recommended him for promotion to lieutenant colonel. Had the war not ended when it did, the promotion would have gone through and McNutt might have stayed in the army.[85]

Choices, of course, were no longer exclusively Paul's to make. Kathleen wanted to settle down in a "white house with a picket fence," where she would greet her spouse "when he comes home from the day's work."[86] But where would that house be—and where was he to work? Paul's parents had a definite answer. John dreamed that his son would become an active partner in his law firm, and Ruth no doubt shared his vision. When the newlyweds came to Indiana in 1918, John and Ruth threw a reception to introduce Kathleen to their friends and to showcase their community for the new bride. "Everyone liked her," Paul wrote his mother-in-law, about Kathleen's visit. "Mother writes me that when people call they always say—you must see to it that she comes back to Martinsville to live."[87]

Indiana University, in the person of President Bryan, ultimately resolved Paul's dilemma. With an assistant professorship waiting for him, a return to IU was the likeliest path. But because his discharge from the army came during the spring semester of 1919, the earliest he could resume teaching was the following autumn. In the interim, Paul and Kathleen lived with his parents in Martinsville while he worked at his father's law firm. It was not the best year of their lives. Kathleen may have loved Paul, but she only tolerated his native state. And she was, at best, ambivalent toward her in-laws. Paul's mother remained stringent about neatness, insisting that her nieces, when washing dishes at her home, eliminate all traces of food and water from the prongs of forks. Kathleen must have found such priorities maddening. Ruth, in turn, was almost speechless when, one day, she saw her daughter-in-law go into the living room, put some music on the phonograph, and dance about. Kathleen was largely responsible for dissuading her husband from settling in Martinsville and practicing in his father's firm.[88]

Other options surfaced in the summer of 1919. President Ernest H. Lindley of the University of Idaho offered McNutt the deanship of his law school. The details as to how all this came about remain sketchy. Lindley was a native of Bloomington and had been a professor of philosophy at Indiana University when McNutt was an undergraduate.[89] In 1919, Lindley was traveling east to interview candidates for the deanship, and he probably visited Bloomington and met McNutt. (He also was trying to hire, for his law school's faculty, Wendell L. Willkie, Paul's college classmate.) Although McNutt rejected the offer, he no doubt felt buoyed as he waited for something closer to home. His patience was rewarded when Bryan, eager to keep McNutt on staff, promoted him to full professor at a salary of $4,000 for the academic year 1919–1920. The salary was a princely amount—the deanship at Idaho paid $3,500.[90] McNutt accepted the appointment, which made him the youngest full professor on campus. For the rest of his life, he remained a professor of law at IU.[91]

After McNutt returned to Bloomington, his domestic and professional life became clearer, though not entirely so. Paul and Kathleen at first rented a room, across from the Indiana University Union, that Kathleen found simply "beautiful."[92] They later moved into a house a few blocks from campus. If that made Kathleen happier, she was even more joyful in 1920, when her father transferred his business, renamed the Cantol Wax Company, to Bloomington. Her parents would be closer to them than Paul's parents would—quite close in fact. For at least a year, the Timolats lived with the McNutts. Paul accepted the arrangement out of love for Kathleen and because he liked Harry Timolat, who regarded him as a son. In 1922, Paul and his father-in-law purchased separate homes in University Courts, which was destined to become something of a faculty ghetto.[93] McNutt was now a husband, an academic, and a homeowner. But, after the stimulation of Harvard, the challenges of the army, and the excitement of love and courtship, would he be content as a professor in a small university town in the Midwest?

For a time, McNutt enjoyed teaching at Indiana University. He was returning to his alma mater, where he had stood out, and he was assuming center stage once again, as a professor. He also faced new challenges. Since the law school had just five full-time faculty members, McNutt had to teach a variety of courses, including Contracts, Equity, Evidence, Legal Ethics, and the Legal System in Indiana, as well as Taxation, Torts, and Trusts.[94] He used his notes from law school to write his lectures. But Harvard remained on his mind. McNutt regaled his students about how the case method had originated under Dean Langdell, how its adoption had spread beyond Harvard, and how it had become standard practice in "the leading law schools of the country."[95] In so doing, McNutt associated himself with the honored name of Harvard, and all that school's innovations, while standing among (and above) his fellow Hoosiers.

When McNutt spoke, students listened and jotted notes. He was an effective teacher chiefly because he was an excellent speaker.[96] "He has the unusual faculty," one former student remarked, "of making the dullest subject seem interesting."[97] McNutt typed out his thoughts beforehand, and relayed them to the class without reading them in an overt way. According to one law student, the future songwriter Hoagy Carmichael, "he had the faculty of scanning his notes from right to left with a broad sweep of the head and eyes as though he was trying to recall his vast store of knowledge." Carmichael was impressed, but then a bit dismayed, when he happened to notice that every word uttered by McNutt was "lying face up on his desk."[98] Like Harvard's law professors, McNutt was "all business" in the classroom. In a "booming voice," he addressed his students as "mister" or "miss." He reserved little time for their questions, but he expected answers when he pressed them. "You'd be shaking in your boots," one former student explained, as he and his classmates awaited a query. McNutt called so frequently on one squeaky-voiced first-year student that the self-conscious chap withdrew from the law school. In the classroom, McNutt had "a perfect sense of timing," knowing "exactly when the bell was going to ring." When he was running for governor in 1932, Professor McNutt, with nary a glance at his watch, could gather his materials and be at the door—and off to some campaign event—just as the class period ended.[99] Overall, he employed a confident, if somewhat detached, manner of lecturing that foreshadowed his later stump speeches.

In less formal settings, students, particularly the high achievers, found McNutt engaging. Charles A. Halleck, a law student at IU and later a congressman from Indiana and Republican leader of the U.S. House of Representatives, became a big fan of McNutt's: "I used to walk into his office . . . and sit around and chew the fat with him."[100] McNutt always had time for serious conversation. He chatted with law students when he encountered them on the street, and he often visited a house where a number of them lived to discuss the law school.[101] Such interactions may have had a political purpose. At the end of the school year in 1922, 1923, and 1924, the law students unanimously, and prophetically, identified McNutt as the professor most likely to succeed Charles Hepburn as dean of the law school. At the same time, McNutt could be very down-to-earth with those who knew him well.[102] One student remembered him as a "personality" not just a "prof." McNutt's classes and his style of instruction, he went on, earned the professor lots of "friends amongst the undergraduates."[103]

McNutt expected much of his students, at least at first. The purpose of education, he once reflected, was not to spoon-feed facts but "to teach the student how to study." McNutt insisted that his charges "do the work" themselves, a perspective in tune with the case method. But many students, he lamented, "do not come with this in mind."[104] A great number of them appreciated McNutt's rigor and his detailed, "well prepared" presentations.[105] A few, however, were less impressed. Walter E. Treanor, who later joined the faculty at the IU law school before becoming chief judge of the Indiana Supreme Court, took Mc-Nutt's Damages course and wrote an examination that was not "difficult," just "long" and "tedious."[106] As McNutt spent more time on politics and less time on teaching, he used the same test questions each year. Predictably, students procured copies of McNutt's past questions before preparing for his exams.[107]

Over time, McNutt tired of teaching. Part of the problem was the student culture at Indiana University, which remained "a decent, if provincial, university."[108] In the 1920s, young people entered IU in greater numbers than ever before, coming more often from urban rather than rural areas.[109] They were mainly native Hoosiers, friendly and unaffected, for as Hoagy Carmichael put it, "the snobs, some of the rich, and the deeper students went East to the hallowed halls of learning."[110] Herman B Wells, a classmate of Carmichael's and later president of IU, remembered the student body as "a mixture of youngsters just out of high school and returning veterans from World War I" who had "enough in common to be collegial."[111] While some students studied hard, others reveled in the "heedless and headless Twenties."[112] This was the age of jazz and bathtub gin, a time when America's youth danced the Charleston in speakeasies.[113] Wells found the atmosphere at IU to be "friendly and relaxed," campus life "informal and unstructured," and the intellectual climate "simple," "unsophisticated," and "tolerant."[114] Law students and medical students delighted in their own form of merriment: in 1920, they began contesting an annual football game that always went in the books as a scoreless tie.[115]

Most of these goings-on would have been foreign to McNutt. He had spent his undergraduate days putting on plays, running for office, editing the *Daily Student,* and boosting, not lampooning, the university and its administration. To be sure, McNutt had some things in common with the kids. He drank alcohol, and both he and Kathleen were superb dancers, meaning that they frequently chaperoned campus socials.[116] But Paul was too serious—and driven—to be a "party boy."[117] The way he carried himself in Bloomington suggested as much. "He was always going places swiftly when in the business district of the town," one journalist stressed. "No small-town loitering over a cigar at a drugstore." Some folks thought him "uppish" for too often failing to greet them. But his friends just shrugged, reasoning that he had "something on his mind."[118] Mc-

Nutt wished he could have said likewise about many students in his classes. He once lamented that the IU law school did not attract the best law students in the state.[119]

The law school's deficiencies no doubt dispirited McNutt as well. To be sure, IU had used the case method since the turn of the century. Between 1906 and 1918, the law school expanded its offerings to include a joint arts-law degree, in which students could receive an AB and LLB in five years, and it also offered a doctorate of jurisprudence. In 1908 the law school moved into an enlarged home, Maxwell Hall. But the school lacked national eminence. While the law school at the University of Chicago had a number of "leaders in their respective fields," IU had a law professor who had begun life as a carpenter and made frequent references to woodworking in his lectures. A new day appeared to dawn in 1918, when Charles Hepburn became dean of the law school. Hepburn, a descendant of the author of the famed McGuffey readers, had a reputation as an outstanding legal scholar.[120] Nevertheless, IU's law school remained primarily "an institution for training lawyers for the Indiana bar."[121]

McNutt's professional disappointments were matched by personal frustrations. His health problems resurfaced in February 1920, when he contracted influenza. That same year, Kathleen lost a son. Paul referred to this misfortune years later when he consoled a cousin whose baby boy had lived only a few hours: "We had a like experience in 1920 and know what it means," he wrote.[122] Kathleen's Christian Science faith, which prevented her from accepting medical treatment, did not help matters. In 1921, when Kathleen again went into labor, she refused medical care, despite suffering excruciating pain. The birth was "so terrible" that Paul finally said, "I can't stand this," and went to fetch a doctor.[123] Kathleen delivered a girl, Louise, on June 27, 1921. Yet the new mother's health was frail and her recovery took weeks.

While Kathleen recuperated, Paul entertained an offer to become dean of the law school at the University of Kansas. The salary was appealing and the school's chancellor, Ernest H. Lindley, was persistent. After serving as president of the University of Idaho and offering McNutt the deanship of that university's law school, Lindley had gone to Kansas as chancellor. Lindley pressed for an answer to his latest offer, but Paul, citing Kathleen's health, delayed. Ultimately, he decided that there were too many ties binding him to Indiana.[124]

The newest of these ties involved McNutt's in-laws, now resettled, along with their wax business, in Bloomington. Harry Timolat, the company's president, put "every cent he had" into making the Cantol Wax Company successful, and

Paul felt obliged to help by serving as treasurer.[125] A nationwide recession and relocation costs kept Cantol in the red during 1921, its first year in Bloomington, but prospects brightened the following year when some of Cantol's preferred stock went up for sale. John C. McNutt bought stock and joined the board of directors, as did Kathleen, who had been her father's secretary before she was married. Another investor was Thomas Taggart, the Democratic Party boss in Indiana and former mayor of Indianapolis. As the economy recovered, Cantol's second year was better—"very satisfactory" in the view of Paul and his father.[126] Between 1921 and 1923, the firm's annual deficits steadily shrank.[127]

Yet the Cantol Wax Company was neither exceptionally profitable to Timolat nor especially interesting to McNutt. Under Timolat, the company branched off into other areas, producing a wax to waterproof stone and other building materials, a sensible move in a state blessed with limestone.[128] Yet it is difficult to see how Cantol competed against better-known brands of wax products, such as Johnson's and Old English. To finance Cantol's operations and ventures, Timolat sold quantities of its preferred stock and mortgaged its assets.[129] Over time, such matters became increasingly remote to McNutt. Like Franklin D. Roosevelt, who plunged into various investments during the twenties, Paul was neither a successful nor a devoted businessman.[130] When Cantol took out a second mortgage in order to gain a loan of $10,000, Paul's father had to prod him to close the deal.[131] Over the years, John McNutt often handled the nuts and bolts of his son's finances.

When McNutt's mind wandered, it was toward politics, not business. He considered making a race for Congress in 1920 but decided against it, dismayed, he claimed, by the low "grade of company" that he would have to keep on Capitol Hill.[132] He also understood that voters were fed up with the wartime administration of Woodrow Wilson and that Democratic candidates would have a tough time getting elected. McNutt found other outlets for his restlessness. He became active in the reserves, advancing from the rank of lieutenant colonel, to which he was appointed in 1919, to colonel in 1923. As colonel, he commanded the 326th Field Artillery Reserves from 1924 to 1937.[133] The reserves, like the army, allowed McNutt to organize, lead, and travel. At the end of World War I, he became an early member of the Reserve Officers Association (ROA) and served as commander of its Indiana department between 1923 and 1924 and as its national vice president in 1927.

The ROA promoted the interests of the reserve and the well-being of reservists via its state and district chapters. As state commander, McNutt urged the local chapters to do "their utmost in enrolling all officers in the State Association" and he dispensed funds to achieve that end.[134] By 1924, the ROA's national office was praising Indiana as "one of the best organized states in our Association."[135] McNutt's tirelessly enthusiastic speaking at numerous district meetings surely helped. "We shall not lack for Pep if you are here to deliver the Punch," a leader of one Indiana ROA chapter wrote him.[136] In the future, such organizational prodding and speechifying would characterize McNutt's leadership of the Indiana American Legion. In the present, such efforts reconnected him to army life and gave him the opportunity to leave Bloomington, mentally and physically.

McNutt also took to the road on behalf of Indiana University. In 1922, he worked on the Memorial Fund Campaign, a drive to raise money for a stadium, auditorium, women's dormitory, and new home for the union.[137] During the campaign, Paul and Kathleen spent time in New York, where McNutt organized the IU alumni and raised the targeted amount of $15,000.[138] "We hear good reports [of] your work at New York City," the bursar at IU wrote him.[139] This campaign took McNutt to Chicago and to points within Indiana, from Evansville in the south to the Calumet region in the north. Eugene Von Tress, IU's alumni secretary, thought McNutt "a magnetic personality" and "a very forceful speaker."[140] Edith Schuman, an undergraduate at IU during the 1920s, remembered McNutt as "one of the prime movers" in the Memorial Fund Campaign, a "marvelous" speaker, and "the best looking man you ever saw."[141] President Bryan fittingly named him chair of a committee to find a location for the new Memorial Union, which was eventually built on the south bank of the Jordan River and dedicated in 1932.[142]

McNutt gained a great deal from the Memorial Fund Campaign. He was, after all, participating in a worthwhile endeavor in the name of both his alma mater and those who had fallen in World War I. "Memorial" appeared in the name of all the buildings funded by the campaign, and a marker, bearing the words "in memory," was placed in the floor of the new union. In pushing the campaign, Bryan himself resorted to wartime appeals, with talk of planning "every line of attack," converting alumni to an "I.U. of sacrifice," and achieving "a successful finish just as we did in the Great War."[143] The project belied the stereotype of the 1920s as a "slap-happy age."[144] Such work only strengthened McNutt's ties to his alma mater. He went on to organize his graduating class's ten-year reunion in 1923, and he served as secretary of the IU Alumni Association from 1923 to 1924.[145]

McNutt's service won kudos. W. A. Alexander, secretary of the Memorial Fund Campaign, was "pleased" with McNutt's fundraising in New York.[146]

Ralph V. Sollitt, a fraternity buddy and the head of the United States Shipping Board, congratulated McNutt on a "magnificent piece of work for the University," which would, he predicted, "do you a lot of good later on."[147] Bryan had taken notice and was grateful for McNutt's "splendid work."[148] Von Tress was even more fulsome in his praise: "Indiana University never had a more sincere supporter than Paul McNutt."[149]

It was not enough for McNutt. He longed to return to Harvard, and in 1924 he seemed to get his chance. Roscoe Pound, dean of Harvard Law School, appointed him Ezra Ripley Thayer Teaching Fellow for one year, starting in September 1924.[150] The board of trustees at IU thereupon granted McNutt a year's leave of absence in order to study at Harvard for a doctorate in juridical science.[151] But as Paul began looking for accommodations in Cambridge, Kathleen's mother died unexpectedly. Ever dutiful, he comforted his wife and father-in-law and pledged to make a home for them. In fact, Paul, Kathleen, and Louise all moved into Timolat's house. Although McNutt was able to defer his fellowship for one year, family ties once again kept him in Indiana.[152]

Kathleen did not share Paul's urge to roam. Whatever her impressions of Indiana as a whole, she enjoyed Bloomington. For the first time in her marriage, she had a home of her own, which she furnished with family heirlooms. Life in this college town suited her. Kathleen found IU's faculty "cultured and broadminded." "We all had such grand times," she remembered, "sitting about the fire and exchanging ideas on just anything and everything." It was, one professor later admitted, a time of "low living and high thinking"—a point with which Kathleen agreed: "None of us made much money" during those "carefree and happy" days.[153] To be sure, Kathleen enjoyed travel, and she would follow her husband as his career took him to distant locales. But in the 1920s, only Paul's restless spirit appeared to stand between Kathleen and a relaxed life in Bloomington.

As 1925 opened, McNutt was quite restless. The range of talents that had allowed him to stand out as a youth had been channeled into a specific career as an academic, augmented by service in the army and reserves. Yet, by the mid-1920s, he was no longer young. Touches of the gray that soon would overwhelm his thick, dark hair had started to show. His opportunities for distinction and fulfillment in a small midwestern city seemed to lessen as his familial commitments and his appetite for new experiences—the deanship of a law school, a fresh venue in which to live and to study, and the chance to travel—were heightening. Harvard Law School and World War I had unveiled a world outside of Indiana. By 1925 McNutt felt himself trapped in Indiana.

# 3

## TRIUMPH AND TRAGEDY
## (1925–1926)

AS PAUL McNUTT'S FRUSTRATION in Bloomington grew, so too did his dreams of escape. He found some diversion playing cards with a few acquaintances in a loft above Bloomington's Princess Theater. The players all belonged to the local American Legion, which McNutt joined in 1919. As his friends bantered, McNutt drifted off. He would at times emerge from his daydreaming to comment, offhandedly: "It would be kind of nice to be president of the United States, wouldn't it?"[1] That remark was surely more illustrative of his itch to do something—anything—important than indicative of any pending campaign for the White House.

In the 1920s, McNutt could only dream about occupying elected office, the presidency or otherwise. He was, after all, a Democrat during a time of Republican dominance. The reformist energies associated with the Progressive Era had exhausted themselves by 1920, allowing Warren G. Harding, an orthodox, conservative Republican, to win the presidency. Braced by a generally booming economy, the Grand Old Party (GOP) retained control of the White House in the elections of 1924 and 1928. A similar trend prevailed in Indiana, where Republicans wrested the governorship from Democrats in 1916 and kept it for sixteen years, despite a succession of scandals. Warren T. McCray, governor from 1921 to 1924, emerged as a Hoosier Harding, for he advocated "a season of government economy and a period of legislative inaction" and later became

tainted by corruption. Nevertheless, voters in Indiana, content with the decade's prosperity, elected Republicans Edward L. Jackson and Harry G. Leslie
to the governorship in 1924 and in 1928, respectively.[2]

Understanding the political realities, McNutt found other outlets for his
growing ambition. Starting in 1925, his goals became more tangible and focused, and his pursuit of them more aggressive. The "young man in a hurry,"
so despised later on by members of Franklin D. Roosevelt's inner circle, was
coming into full view. McNutt would never follow a long-term, Machiavellian
strategy to reach the White House. Instead, he pursued opportunities closer to
home, pragmatically, as they cropped up. At some point during the 1920s, Mc-
Nutt decided that he wanted to be dean of the law school at Indiana University.
Offers of deanships at the University of Idaho and at the University of Kansas
may have led him to consider an administrative position at his home institution.
Or he might have been pursuing a larger aim, to return to Cambridge as dean
of the Harvard Law School. McNutt had confided to his wife, and to a friend in
Indianapolis, that that was his goal, and, if so, then holding the deanship at IU
was a sensible first step.[3]

McNutt would claim his prize and begin an important transition in his life.
As dean of the IU law school, he moved beyond seeking "distinction," that is,
a form of success—scholastic or professional—that commanded attention,
and toward exercising "leadership"—heading a unit of some size, presenting
ideas before its membership, and then shaping and pressing an agenda. Being dean allowed McNutt to think deeply about larger issues of education, of
the public's responsibilities to learning and research, and of the state's role in
financing universities. At the same time, the twenties were not a happy time in
McNutt's life. Illness struck his daughter, Louise, and cast a shadow over his
accomplishments. At a time when this increasingly public man tasted his first
real professional triumphs, the private McNutt dealt with a family tragedy.[4]

McNutt's interest in the deanship of the IU law school reflected the sort of
academic he was—a "front runner," that is, a professor who thinks he must
"bear the burdens of the whole institutional responsibility."[5] Apart from their
teaching duties, front-runners are known more for their service on university
committees, or other such assignments, than for their scholarly productivity.
McNutt was active in the Memorial Fund Campaign and the Indiana University
Alumni Association. He served on the university's Alumni Council, and he
chaired the Activities Fees Committee, which granted exemptions for students

from university fees, and the Faculty Athletic Committee, which scheduled IU's intercollegiate sports. At the same time, articles and casebooks solicited by law journals and publishers were never written, largely because university fundraising campaigns and, later, the administrative work of running the law school consumed McNutt's time.[6] Front-runners often sacrifice scholarly renown for the opportunity to serve their university and move into its administration. By the mid-1920s, McNutt, despite his lack of seniority, had been doing yeoman work for IU, and President William Lowe Bryan knew as much.

In the meantime, the Indiana University School of Law was in weak hands. Charles McGuffey Hepburn, the dean since 1918, was sixty-seven years old in 1925. A native of Virginia, Hepburn had received his LLB from the University of Virginia and had been a professor of law at Indiana since 1903. More scholar than administrator, he published several books, including a casebook on torts. But, as dean, Hepburn seldom initiated major changes. He had a soft spot for men of his generation who, like himself, had practiced law and then taught the law. The law faculty at Indiana University included many professors of this sort who were neither progressive in outlook nor active in scholarship. Partly as a result, the reputation of the law school continued to lag behind its institutional peers.[7] One Indiana congressman asserted that IU's law school required a "militant vigor" to put it "on the Map."[8] Instead, Hepburn stooped to making "caustic criticisms" about the lowly state of legal ethics in Indiana. Such remarks only angered members of the Indiana State Bar Association, who in turn complained about the dean to the board of trustees at Indiana University.[9] By the 1920s, Hepburn had become a lion in winter, roaring about whatever pleased him and pouncing on anything that did not. He supported scholarly research by his faculty, and he backed McNutt's plan to return to Harvard as a teaching fellow in 1924–1925. But the changes associated with modern life ignited his eccentric side. Uncomfortable with liberated young women smoking in public, Hepburn complained to Bryan that the "careless cigarette," in league with blowing leaves and the wooden walkways on the IU campus, threatened to ignite a conflagration.[10] On a more serious note, Hepburn had trouble relating to students. One IU alumnus who liked Hepburn personally found him "too deep for most of us."[11]

Hepburn's great cause, to bring the state bar association's journal to campus, proved to be his downfall. He believed that acquiring and then revamping this journal would raise the profile of the IU school of law and improve its relationship with the state bar association. Yet his vision for the journal was as narrow as his plans for editing it were controversial. Hepburn disparaged the sort of law review put out by other law schools which published "long, critical articles on questions of general law." Instead, he wanted his journal to explore issues related to state law and enhance the legal profession in Indiana. Hepburn proposed that an editor in chief be installed in Bloomington to oversee the journal and that members of the IU law faculty devote one hour each day to helping with editorial tasks. He also proposed that each faculty member write at least one "full size critically scholarly article" for the law review every year.[12] A majority of the law school's six-member faculty voted to reject Hepburn's plan on grounds that the proposed journal belonged more to the bar association than to the university and that the task of producing a journal, would tax an overextended faculty. Yet Hepburn remained firm, and the IU board of trustees backed him and his proposed journal.[13] If the dean and the trustees were to be resisted, the faculty would need a leader to appeal directly to President Bryan.

McNutt took the lead in ousting Hepburn as dean. In March 1925, just days after the trustees approved Hepburn's plan for a law journal, McNutt wrote Bryan a missive on "problems which have arisen in connection with the law school." The memorandum detailed professors' complaints over low salaries, insufficient time for research, faculty departures, poor students, and an inadequate law library. McNutt's solution was a greater financial commitment by the university to upgrade faculty salaries and the library, and he outlined a three-year budget to accomplish that. In so doing—and in giving "McNutt" the highest salary of any faculty member—he clearly anticipated being dean when classes commenced in the fall. McNutt never once mentioned the fellowship at Harvard, which, after a year's delay—and with Hepburn's generous support— he was to assume in academic year 1925–1926.[14] His eye had become fixed on a more exalted position, at IU.

Any doubt that McNutt's letter was a campaign manifesto for the deanship vanishes when one reads his comments about Hepburn's pet project. "The publication of . . . a journal by this faculty seems inadvisable at this time," McNutt asserted. He reiterated the faculty's reservations about publishing a law journal and stressed that only after the "reorganization of the law school," with a "full faculty in residence," could such a journal be published successfully.[15] McNutt thus suggested that Hepburn had become an obstacle not only to academic distinction and democratic governance at the law school, but to the very aim, a law journal, that he had striven to achieve.

Bryan responded swiftly and shrewdly to the McNutt memorandum. Citing the tight budgets facing the university over the next two years, Bryan told McNutt that little could be done about faculty salaries or the library at the law school. However, he and the board of trustees took a fiscally neutral step when, in April 1925, the trustees elected Hepburn "Research Professor of Law" and named McNutt to succeed him as dean.[16] IU's president achieved a masterstroke, replacing an aging administrator with a youthful go-getter and recharting the course of McNutt's ambition by pulling it within IU's walls.

What can be said about McNutt's actions? To start with, Hepburn had made his own troubles by pushing an agenda against the will of his faculty. That opened the door for McNutt, who placed himself at the forefront of an effort to change the law school. If his ends were justifiable, his means showed a streak of ruthlessness. By writing to Bryan and the trustees, McNutt had undermined his dean and then claimed his position. While Hepburn displayed no hard feelings toward his successor, McNutt "was resented by all members of the Hepburn family."[17] Hepburn's son, Andrew, called his actions "cowardly and traitorous." He accused McNutt of fomenting a situation "intolerable to a man who had been your friend," and then executing his "dastardly betrayal." He compared McNutt to Judas and to Cesare Borgia, the notorious plotter in the serpentine politics of fifteenth-century Italy and the alleged inspiration for Machiavelli's Prince.[18] It was the first of many epithets hung on McNutt.

Such criticism was more than offset by praise for McNutt's appointment. Former students and Indiana lawyers lauded McNutt's youth, brains, and energy as being exactly what the law school needed. After learning of McNutt's appointment, a law professor who had left IU for George Washington University wrote that he at last saw a "future ahead" for Indiana's law school.[19] Another man thought that the law school was bound to flourish under McNutt's "enthusiasm and direction."[20] Two old fraternity buddies lauded McNutt's success. Wendell L. Willkie, now a lawyer at the Goodyear Tire Company, predicted that "it was but a question of time" before McNutt succeeded William Lowe Bryan.[21] C. M. Piper, also at Goodyear, agreed, asserting that he would make "a much better president" than Bryan.[22] Such praise encouraged McNutt to think of bigger things. At the time, however, he simply delighted in his triumph in becoming the youngest dean at Indiana University and the youngest dean at any accredited law school in America.[23]

After the cheering stopped, McNutt settled into the business of the law school. His office was in Maxwell Hall, a limestone building adorned with menacing gargoyles, which had opened in 1890 as the university's library. By

1925, the law school occupied all of Maxwell Hall, save for a few offices used by the highest officers of the university's administration, including Bryan. The law school had a moot court in the nearby Student Building, and a library and classrooms in Maxwell Hall. Law students at IU followed a set curriculum in their first year before taking electives in their second and third years.[24] The "oldest law school west of the Allegheny mountains," as McNutt liked to style it, used the most modern technique—the case method—for teaching law. Nevertheless the IU law school faced intense competition from other schools. In his first annual report as dean, McNutt stressed that the school "cannot cease to go forward without going backward."[25] It was a signal that changes, and an energetic leader, were at hand. "As he had reorganized the college dramatic society 15 years earlier," one journalist later noted, "he now put the law school on a new and more efficient footing."[26]

The priorities of the new dean were plain. Like Herman B Wells, later a protégé of McNutt's and president of Indiana University between 1938 and 1962, McNutt knew that his chief objective was "the recruitment and retention of superior faculty members."[27] He cultivated a collection of dynamic teacher-scholars, who had been trained to instruct students and conduct original research in their fields of specialization, rather than former lawyers and judges. Among his faculty, McNutt especially liked Paul L. Sayre, who had two degrees from Harvard. In 1929, McNutt hired a pair of law professors from the University of Oregon: Bernard C. Gavit, a specialist in civil and criminal procedures; and Fowler V. Harper, an expert on torts, who replaced the recently deceased Hepburn. Both Gavit and Fowler made strong impressions on the law faculty and went on to bigger things. Gavit succeeded McNutt as dean, and Harper, who remained on the law school faculty until 1947, advised McNutt during his campaign for the White House and served under him at the Federal Security Agency and War Manpower Commission.[28] McNutt's knack for recruiting talented subordinates began at IU.

McNutt did a number of things to retain faculty members. Despite publishing little scholarship himself, he pressed Bryan and the board of trustees to underwrite faculty research. McNutt championed professional development opportunities for faculty, and he helped two professors complete their graduate studies. He requested generous, but not uniform, raises, meaning that he was making hard choices about the value of each professor. The results were mixed. By 1930, the average full professor of law at IU was earning over $5,100 annually—$2,000 less than what law professors made elsewhere in the Midwest.[29]

To increase salaries further, the dean proposed a fixed scale, "comparable with that of schools of equal rank and based upon teaching ability, length of service, productive scholarship, and service to the law school." If the money to finance such a scale was unavailable, McNutt was willing to forgo the entire budget of the law library in order to increase faculty salaries.[30]

That McNutt would even consider such an exchange spoke to the depth of IU's financial woes. Herman Wells, in his memoirs, summarized the university's dilemma as one of "money, money, but never enough." Those associated with IU, Wells emphasized, "repeatedly lamented the inadequacy of the state's support for higher education."[31] In 1926, a survey of higher education in the states of the Midwest (Ohio, Michigan, Indiana, Illinois, Wisconsin, Minnesota, and Iowa) found only Indiana trailing the regional average in its support of both private and public colleges. Studies done in the 1920s showed that among these states the share of taxpayer dollars going to higher education was lowest in Indiana.[32] Part of the trouble was President Bryan, who found it demeaning to ask the state legislature for increased funding. Bryan tried other ways to raise money, through the Memorial Fund Campaign and through subordinates such as McNutt—who was tireless, a fine orator, and increasingly visible statewide because of his position as dean and his work with the American Legion. McNutt served on the IU legislative committee, and in that capacity, he met with Republican governor Jackson in 1926 to press IU's case for increased funding.[33]

The law school gained little from such efforts.[34] In 1930, the annual budget at law schools in the Midwest averaged $114,000 while McNutt had to make ends meet with just $54,000. He even asked Bryan for money for routine supplies. The onset of the Great Depression destroyed McNutt's dream of achieving parity in faculty salaries with other accredited law schools. Partly as a result, the law school lost several professors to other institutions. To highlight the ongoing problem of funding, McNutt changed the title of his annual report from "Progress of the Indiana University School of Law" to "The Needs of the Law School."[35]

Even with a tight budget, McNutt made headway in some areas. He doubled the holdings of the law library and secured money for a librarian. The number of full-time professors at the law school increased from six to eight between 1925 and 1933, and, in McNutt's first six years as dean, student enrollment jumped fifty percent. Many of these students were quite able. Walter E. Treanor, a professor of law and later chief judge of the Indiana Supreme Court, noticed that several new law students either already held BA degrees or had transferred to Indiana University from other law schools. Treanor found these students to be either "average or above," expected a "higher quality of work" from them, and thus thought it time for a "tightening up" of academic standards at the IU law school.[36] By then, however, McNutt was so absorbed in other pursuits that the idea of raising requirements at the school apparently escaped him.

McNutt's greatest achievement as dean was the publication of the *Indiana Law Journal*. Although the brainchild of Hepburn, McNutt was opportunistic enough to push the idea. The new dean, however, insisted that the law journal be something more than the organ of the Indiana State Bar Association. It must publish "first-class" scholarship.[37] A few members of the association resisted the idea, but McNutt won them over—he frequently complimented the association and spoke before its membership, on topics of their choosing. And after the first issue of the journal appeared in 1925, McNutt and Sayre, the journal's editor, solicited articles from lawyers and judges across Indiana. In April 1926, the dean reported that that the law journal was "firmly established" and making "a most favorable impression among members of the bar."[38] After the university gained complete control over the *Indiana Law Journal* in 1948, the faculty of the law school voted to allow students to edit it under faculty supervision. McNutt thus played a role in establishing a student-edited law journal, something that Chief Justice Earl Warren once hailed as "the most remarkable institution in the Law School world."[39]

McNutt's program for Indiana's law school could be summarized in one word: "Harvardization." The changes he pushed for—a faculty of teacher-scholars, competitive salaries, scholarly research and professional development, and a first-rate law journal—he had seen at Harvard, which was his ideal of all that a school of law should be. McNutt was fond of pointing out that Harvard was not only the oldest law school in the nation but the one that enjoyed "unquestioned leadership in the field of legal education."[40] He went to great lengths to recruit and retain professors with ties to Harvard. On the advice of Roscoe Pound, dean of Harvard Law School, McNutt hired Robert C. Brown as assistant professor of law at IU and then helped him locate suitable housing in Bloomington. The Indiana-Harvard "exchange" worked both ways. Under McNutt, four members of the law faculty spent a year of study at Harvard.[41] To be sure, this traffic between Bloomington and Cambridge might have been part of effort to pave the way for McNutt's own triumphant return as Harvard's dean. Yet he remained proud of Harvard Law School's leadership and "outstanding service" to the wider nation, and he wanted his faculty to get a taste of that.[42] McNutt hoped that he and his professors, working together, might even lift IU to a similar level of excellence.

McNutt never realized that goal. In fact, it was under his successor, Bernard Gavit, that the IU law school enhanced its national reputation. Gavit, dean from 1933 to 1952, tightened admissions to the school. He also backed the state legislature when, in 1936, it required aspiring lawyers to have a law degree before taking the bar examination. This measure ended the long era of almost nonexistent standards for practicing law in Indiana. Following World War II, with enrollment rising to record levels, Gavit would add several distinguished faculty members, and he made plans for the law school to leave Maxwell Hall for a more spacious building.[43] Gavit benefited from favorable circumstances unavailable to McNutt, including statewide support for higher standards of legal instruction, a postwar boom in university enrollment and tuition dollars, and the presidency of Herman B Wells, who was far better at raising money than was Bryan. In addition, because Gavit also lacked McNutt's political ambitions, he was free to concentrate his attention and energy on building the school in ways that his predecessor, as we will see, could not.

This analysis is important because a university's renown derives not only from its top leadership but also from its lower-level builders—deans, chairs, and program heads. At IU, several names stand out. Alfred C. Kinsey founded the Institute for Sex Research which produced a succession of volumes on human sexual behavior. During the 1960s, Robert F. Byrnes helped to transform the department of history into a nationally ranked PhD-granting program. Coach Jerry Yeagley took the men's team in soccer, initially a club sport, into the National Collegiate Athletic Association and won six national championships between 1982 and 2003. And Wilfred C. Bain, dean of IU's school of music between 1947 and 1973, founded its opera theater and retired as head of the nation's highest-ranked music school.[44] McNutt's accomplishments as dean were not monumental enough to earn him a place among Indiana University's great builders.

McNutt would have defended his record as dean by citing the fiscal restraints under which he operated. In speeches, he struggled to comprehend the public's reluctance to fund state universities since education was to him the swiftest and surest route out of "humble surroundings." McNutt's advocacy of college-level education enabled him to see "democracy" in social and economic, as well as political, terms. "Democracy does not come merely with the granting of suffrage," he declared. "Democracy comes when every man has the right to enjoy, in accordance with his capacity, the opportunities which science and nature offer."[45] Yet McNutt deplored the low rate of investment in higher education. In a speech written in 1924, he relayed the dreary details about spending on higher education in Indiana. At IU, the bitter harvest included overcrowded classrooms, an inadequate library, creaky buildings, faculty departures, and a university sinking into mediocrity. Yet, each year, Hoosiers spent far more on such luxury items than they did on universities. In pointing this out, McNutt decried his fellow citizens for reaping benefits from past scientific discoveries and then denying funds for future research. "Have we become like misers?" he asked. "Have we come to the place in life where luxuries for private consumption are of greater social importance than governmental expenditures for necessities?"[46]

McNutt's answer to such questions was no, for he was not at all conservative on the matter of public education. In his 1924 speech, he advocated a tax increase to fund state universities, even though the idea was anathema to politicians. According to McNutt, the state had a "duty" to promote education, which he dubbed a "birthright" of every child. He went on to praise Walter Hines Page, former U.S. ambassador to Great Britain, who had observed that education opened new opportunities for the "Forgotten Man."[47] Such priorities—and rhetoric—foreshadowed the New Deal, and McNutt was serious about pushing them. During his years as governor, he recycled parts of his speech on education to promote his own agenda for political, economic, and social reform.[48]

The struggle over state financing of higher education profoundly affected McNutt. The issue strengthened his suspicion about the selfish, shortsighted side of human nature. Yet, paradoxically, it revealed his faith in the ability of government, energetically led, to overcome private desires and to promote a public good. Though unable to convince Hoosiers to improve higher education through higher taxes at this time, McNutt understood that the conservative temper of the twenties, exemplified by Republican rule in the White House and at the Indiana statehouse, was not permanent; that his arguments were sound and his cause just; and that "the people of Indiana . . . will find themselves ultimately."[49] Perhaps McNutt had even started to think that he would be the one to lead them to their senses. His advocacy of public education certainly did his reputation no harm. "He had a starring vehicle," a reporter later observed, "and he played his role for all it was worth."[50]

Day to day, however, the effect of meager funding at the law school discouraged McNutt. "The failure of our people to give adequate support to education," he wrote a friend, "has caused me to consider the possibility of moving."[51]

Accordingly, when, in 1926, McNutt weighed an invitation to become dean of the law school at Washington University in St. Louis, he insisted that the university's chancellor commit sufficient resources to making his law school nationally eminent, and he offered suggestions on how to do just that. In the end, Washington University's chancellor decided that McNutt's ideas (or demands) were too radical and instead named an internal candidate. By standing on principle, McNutt passed up the chance to earn $10,000 a year at Washington University, more than twice his annual salary at IU.[52]

There were two other reasons why McNutt chose to remain in Indiana. The first was political. By 1926, McNutt, as we will see, was becoming active in the American Legion and was eyeballing a new office, commander of the Legion's Indiana Department. McNutt claimed that he wanted to remain at IU where he could be of "more value" than to "any other" school.[53] Perhaps, but he also could not command the Indiana Legion from St. Louis, and building comparable connections out in Missouri would have required years of effort. The second reason was personal and tragic, involving a long-term illness that had struck McNutt's daughter. John C. McNutt alluded to "dear Louise's situation" in voicing concern about his son possibly leaving IU.[54] For the remainder of the twenties, Louise was the principal focus of McNutt's private life.

Louise McNutt's period of "child-martyrdom," as the Indiana novelist Booth Tarkington, a casual acquaintance of the McNutts, described it, began on a warm day in 1925, around the time that Paul was named dean of the Indiana University law school.[55] Louise, not yet four years old, and some neighborhood children were playing with a hose, splashing about in their bathing suits near the McNutt home. As Paul watched, he noticed an odd curvature in Louise's back. He went inside and asked his wife, "Have you looked at Louise's back?" Kathleen said no. Paul then described what he had seen. "Oh, that's nothing," Kathleen answered. "It'll go away."[56]

Kathleen's response partly reflected the teachings of her church. The Church of Christ, Scientist, professed that one gained salvation and health by accepting the "innate imperfection of all people and the unreality of the material world."[57] "Sin, pain, and disease" were but illusions arising from "the errors and fears" of the mind.[58] Christian Scientists sought healing, not through medicine and doctors, but through "prayer, study, and introspection" assisted by special practitioners, members of the church who helped them cope with the "mental roots" of the disease.[59] At the same time, Christian Science exhibited intolerance "of medical and pharmaceutical science of many public health measures, and hence of a scientific search for knowledge."[60] That attitude was at odds with McNutt's own habit of thinking, his academic training, and his advocacy of funding for universities as a way to further scientific research. On this issue, Paul and Kathleen inhabited different worlds.

How and why Kathleen embraced Christian Science is unknown. Although her faith almost certainly originated with her mother, a Christian Scientist, it may have been reinforced by some desire for self-fulfillment. Although Kathleen was smart, energetic, and independent-minded, she had neither a college degree nor professional training nor gainful employment, aside from a minor post in her father's wax business. She was a housewife, assigned by traditional gender roles to care for the home, rear children, and oversee the religious life of her family. Christian Science may have provided Kathleen with a sense of personal satisfaction or importance. At a time when many Christian denominations required extensive training for their clergy and excluded women from their leadership, Christian Science welcomed both female and male healers. The founder of Christian Science and the author of its principal tract, *Science and Health with Key to the Scriptures* (1875), was a woman, Mary Baker Eddy. Just as women in older and larger Protestant denominations had participated in a range of reform movements throughout the nineteenth century, from abolition to temperance, women of the Christian Science church also performed a multitude of duties—developing doctrine, organizing churches, and healing. Even if Kathleen engaged in none of these tasks, she may have insisted on her maternal prerogative to oversee her daughter's health and spiritual development. She was not reluctant to express herself. "Mother says you should stand up for what you think is right," Louise wrote in her diary, "but that often involves a great deal of trouble."[61]

A personal experience would have deepened Kathleen's adherence to Christian Science. For example, when Kathleen became ill, as she did near the end of World War I, she would have forsaken medicine for prayer and no doubt emerged, after her recovery, even more firm in her faith. Testimonials of such healing formed an important part of the Christian Science service.[62] Kathleen would have heard these accounts and become fortified in her beliefs. This much is certain: She remained a Christian Scientist throughout her life, and following Paul's death in 1955, she married an official in her church.

Whatever the reasons behind Kathleen's faith, her response to Louise's ailment bothered Paul terribly. The result was considerable tension between them.[63] The dispute became a personal one for Paul, since he had been a "delicate" boy who at age eight had survived diphtheria only after a physician's intervention.[64] Moreover, he had spent much of his youth in Martinsville, whose claim to fame was health care, and where a spate of mineral wells and sanitariums, dietitians and doctors, offered artesian waters to cure the ill. "Health Comes First" was the motto of Home Lawn Sanitarium, located just blocks from where Paul's parents lived.[65] Yet he had married a woman who "cleaned out the medicine cabinet." Equally disturbing was the manner in which Kathleen cared for herself. She resisted any medical treatment during her two pregnancies, delivering Louise only after a difficult labor and after Paul had fetched a doctor. Some members of the McNutt family attributed Louise's illness to the difficulty of her mother's labor.[66] Like many people in her church, Kathleen apparently believed that Christian Science healing and medical treatment were so distinctive "that to combine the methods would be unfair to both of them."[67] In the end, Paul resolved that his health and that of his wife was one thing. His daughter's was quite another. So he insisted on getting Louise to a doctor.[68]

Paul's parents became valued advisers throughout Louise's illness. After doctors x-rayed Louise's back, Paul informed his father and mother. John and Ruth McNutt were worried but not surprised, for they had seen "that Louise has been ailing for some time." John told the Martinsville physician who had delivered Louise of the child's symptoms, and he said that it sounded like tuberculosis. Paul's father, ever the careful lawyer, then made his case to his son. The doctor "says that T.B. in children is readily cured by proper treatment, diet and watchful care," John wrote Paul. Then, in a "closing argument," John reminded Paul of his near-death experience as a boy and how he had been saved by a doctor and his mother's care. "Louise inherits your early constitutional weakness," John McNutt emphasized, "and needs the same treatment."[69]

Paul, like most Americans, understood the threat posed by tuberculosis. The disease had a long history and was known by multiple names, including consumption and the "Great White Plague." Louise seemed an unlikely victim, for the tubercle bacillus spread quickest in areas beset by overcrowding, substandard housing, and impure food or water. Nevertheless, public health campaigns had targeted all Americans, regardless of location, class, or race, to take preventive steps. Treatment for tuberculosis consisted of "rest, fresh air, sunlight, and good nutrition," often in a sanitarium. Although the number of deaths from tuberculosis in Indiana dropped dramatically during the 1920s and 1930s, the disease remained serious enough to command popular attention and to cause members of McNutt's family to act when it appeared in Louise.[70]

Louise received medical care and began a long road to recovery. She saw a specialist in Indianapolis and underwent repeated x-rays. For more than a year, she managed to move about, write letters, and read books. But she also suffered feverish relapses. "Louise has been sick for the past week," Paul told a cousin, as he postponed a trip.[71] Around June 1926, doctors confirmed that Louise had tuberculosis of the spine. A bone specialist in Indianapolis examined Louise's back, shook his head, and said: "It's a shame. She should have been in a brace after she was born."[72]

Under the circumstances, doctors prescribed bed rest for Louise. As it turned out, she would lie flat down and immobilized—for the next three years and eight months. At first Louise accepted what she called her "predicament" with "the best of grace."[73] But the tedium, if not the pain, must have been unbearable. Paul's parents often found her to be nervous.[74] Neighbors could hear Louise scream through open windows during the summertime. These families—old-line and Republican—sneered that McNutt was not taking proper care of his daughter. Suspecting that Kathleen's religion was the culprit, they gossiped: "Isn't it a shame the way they treat that girl?"[75] Paul, in fact, tried to ease Louise's suffering by hiring a nurse to care for her. He also bought a Bradford frame, a wooden board fifty-three inches long and fifteen inches wide, and ordered a large baby carriage. Paul would strap Louise in the frame, place it on top of the carriage, and then push his daughter around the neighborhood. Louise's second cousin, Shirley, who was around the same age, also pushed the carriage. But these excursions into the fresh air offered scant relief for what became a "terrific ordeal" for Louise and her parents.[76]

The cost of the Bradford frame and carriage, not to mention the doctors and nurses, taxed McNutt's resources. By 1927, he was not at all wealthy. He owned no real estate; in 1924 he had apparently sold his house in the University Courts area of Bloomington when he and his family moved into the home of his father-in-law, Harry N. Timolat, following the death of Timolat's wife. After Timolat remarried and moved out, Paul and Kathleen remained in the house, a six-room, red-brick bungalow with a porch and a second-story loft. In 1927, the place had no refrigerator, no radio, no phonograph, no electric iron, no silver-plated flatware, and only a scattering of household conveniences: an electric washer, a vacuum cleaner, and a sewing machine. Paul and Kathleen possessed a few symbols of a middle-class lifestyle—a piano, an Oriental rug, and a 1926 Chrysler valued at $800—and, for a time at least, they employed domestic help, suggesting they lived beyond their means. By 1927, Paul had saved $537, but he owed

$2,300 in notes. When his fraternity solicited a contribution toward building a new house, Paul demurred, citing "the heavy expense" imposed by his daughter's illness.[77] John McNutt helped out by paying off his son's automobile note.[78] Paul McNutt no doubt had pressed so ardently for higher salaries at the IU law school because he needed money—badly.

Louise's illness showed two sides of Paul's character. On the one hand, there was the private man, the loving father who referred to Louise tenderly as "my little girl."[79] A bond developed between father and daughter for they were a lot alike, smart and bookish. John E. Hurt, a law partner of John McNutt, remembered Louise as "very intelligent" and someone who "thought along the lines that her father thought," a reference to their shared interest in politics, which surfaced later on.[80] During Louise's illness, Paul may have encouraged his daughter to dream about pursuing a career someday, either because he perceived her talent or because he wanted to distract her from her suffering. The dean of the IU law school was open to the idea of women becoming lawyers. In 1927, he wrote one man: "I should have no hesitancy in permitting my own daughter to study law if she desired to do it."[81] Comments such as those evoke another side of McNutt: his belief in pursuing—and succeeding—in a profession. In 1926, when Louise's illness was serious, Paul stayed close to home.[82] As her condition stabilized, however, McNutt's speaking engagements resumed, especially, as we will see, before American Legion audiences. He even made two extended visits to Europe with the Legion, in 1927 and 1929.[83] Louise's illness would not be allowed to sidetrack Paul's ambitions.

When her father was away, who cared for Louise? It was not always Kathleen, who often traveled with Paul. Louise may have resented her mother's absences. In her diary, Louise jotted "love" after each mention of her father and mother. Nevertheless, she referred to Kathleen formally, as "Mother," and to Paul affectionately, as "Daddy."[84] And, decades later, when Louise was ill and dying, she cried out for her daddy, not her mother. During the 1920s, the family member who became Louise's caregiver when her parents were gone was her grandfather, Harry Timolat. Louise called him "Bappa," and the pair became close. Years later, when "Bappa" was ill and near death, Louise wrote almost prayerfully: "I do love him *so much*. Please help me to know the truth about him. He is such a dear.[85] McNutt's own parents, in contrast, lived over twenty miles away, and were less able to offer assistance. "We were at Bloomington Friday night . . . ," John McNutt wrote his son, who was then in Europe, "and found everybody well, but all pretty nervous. The strain on the nurse and Mr. Timolat has been great."[86] In so writing, John may have been either exorcising his own guilt or perhaps trying to instill some of it in Paul.

Rather than hide Louise's illness, Paul put the best face on it. He often wrote acquaintances that his daughter was improving.[87] "We have a long fight ahead of us, which requires courage and patience," Paul informed one friend, "but I am confident that she will completely recover."[88] As a result, his associates were under the impression that Louise was coping "like a good little sport."[89] She did get better, following years of rest and some dashed hopes. After more than three years on the Bradford frame, Louise looked forward to her liberation, on Christmas Day 1929. Alas, as that date drew near, a physician counseled delay and Paul agreed, for he did not want his little girl "subjected to the tragedy of going back on the frame."[90] Finally, in February 1930, Louise lost the Bradford frame and could sit up—for ten minutes, every two hours.[91] Within a month, she was spending three hours a day in a wheelchair, getting "the greatest pleasure out of moving herself around."[92] Over the next year, she progressed from wheelchair to steel brace to corset to jacket. Paul was happy with Louise's "marked improvement" and proud of her pluck.[93] After detailing to a sick friend the history of his daughter's long recovery, Paul employed a masculine and soldierly metaphor: "I know just how much of a fight it takes to win the battle."[94]

Did he know? Paul had cast his daughter's illness as "our trouble."[95] Yet, it was Louise who had been confined to bed and would remain self-conscious about her appearance thereafter. By 1932 she had returned to school and was "very much interested in her work" but she worried about "reducing her weight" after years of immobility.[96] Around that time, Louise left home for the first time to visit her cousins in New Jersey. Her closest cousin, Shirley, recalled how much fun they all had, especially during an excursion out to Sea Girt, where Louise waded into the ocean. But wearing a bathing suit, which scarcely covered her somewhat humped back, was unpleasant, and Shirley's father advised the kids to play in the less crowded areas of the beach, lest people stare. After Louise had been there a month, Kathleen made her come home. "She cried," Shirley remembered. "She didn't want to go." Such memories, along with the physical scars of tuberculosis, remained with Louise. She often wore capes so as to conceal her back. And when, just two years before her death, Louise became ill with what doctors thought was cancer, x-rays showed that the growth in her lungs was scar tissue left by tuberculosis.[97]

As Louise healed, so did the McNutt marriage. That was not surprising, for its foundations proved solid, if conventional. Kathleen was a loyal and dutiful wife, that is, supportive of her husband and his aspirations. "When you have a husband with so much vitality and enthusiasm," she later told a reporter, "the wife must abandon a life of her own. I didn't want a career."[98] Although she had no interest in the nuts and bolts of politics, whether academic, American Legion, or electoral, she enjoyed going places and meeting people, and she excelled socially. "Mrs. McNutt," a journalist noted, "had a metropolitan charm that fascinated academic Bloomington."[99] As Paul became increasingly active in the American Legion, Kathleen's gregarious personality proved "a real help" as he made contacts around the state.[100] Kathleen welcomed these respites from Louise's illness; Paul remembered that his wife was "bitterly disappointed" when she was unable to make one particular trip.[101] Paul, for his part, felt a strong need to have Kathleen close by. In planning one excursion, he hoped "that she will be with me a good share of the time."[102] Kathleen was, in her husband's words, a "wonderful helpmate."[103]

Paul, in turn, remained faithful to Kathleen. During the troubled period of Louise's illness—and afterward, for that matter—McNutt never strayed from his wife. Several things worked against any extramarital romances. There was President Bryan's insistence that members of the IU community observe the strictest propriety, as well as Paul's own sense of right and wrong. McNutt abhorred divorce, which he described in lawyer-like and soldierly terms as a "failure of the contracting parties to recognize and practice the principles of sacrifice and service."[104] McNutt, for his part, remained devoted to Kathleen. Paul's last surviving letter to her, written in 1945, is most tender, from its salutation ("Darling") to its closing ("entirely yours") to its final sentence: "I love you more than anyone in the world." With respect to her health, the couple had reached a truce of sorts in which Paul could cajole and coax, but not command, his wife to seek professional medical care. "I am greatly disturbed by the news that you are not feeling well enough to go out," he wrote Kathleen in 1945. "What is the trouble? Take care of yourself, Darling."[105] Throughout her life, Kathleen McNutt often suffered aliments of one sort or another. Yet she remained a Christian Scientist, committed to her own version of health care. Paul, in turn, continued to see doctors and dentists on his own and to respect her wishes.[106]

The dynamics of the McNutt family during the 1920s resembled, to some extent, those of the Roosevelts during the same period. Out of political office and dabbling in business ventures—a few successful, but many not—Franklin D.

Roosevelt leaned on his surviving parent, Sara Delano Roosevelt, in ways that Paul and Kathleen McNutt relied on their parents. Sara controlled the purse and, not unlike John McNutt, she often paid the bills of a son who spent beyond his means. Sara, like Harry Timolat, also cared for and doted on her grandchildren, becoming the adult they appeared to love the most. The biggest difference between the two families, aside from wealth, involved the respective marriages. By the 1920s, Franklin and Eleanor were leading almost separate lives in separate homes with separate clusters of friends. This unconventional arrangement was partly the product of FDR's liaison with his wife's social secretary, Lucy Mercer, and partly the desire of Eleanor to seek independence outside of a home run by her husband and mother-in-law. The McNutts, in contrast, never experienced the betrayal and sorrow of an extramarital affair, and Kathleen, unlike Eleanor, remained content playing a largely subordinate role to her husband.[107]

During the 1920s, the Roosevelt and McNutt families had to cope with serious illnesses. Infantile paralysis struck FDR in 1921, four years before tuberculosis appeared in Louise McNutt. Like TB, "polio" was not then an uncommon disease, and there was no remedy for it, save for rest. FDR and Louise McNutt both lost physical mobility, Roosevelt permanently, as a legacy of his disease, and Louise temporarily, as a part of her recovery. Paul, who was not sick, and FDR, who was, responded to these challenges much as they would to the national crisis of the 1930s—with a surface optimism. Not unlike Paul's hopeful dispatches of Louise's progress, and Louise's own grit, Roosevelt retained much of his "relentless cheer" as he struggled to regain use of his legs.[108] Nevertheless, the daily strain often tested each man's patience. FDR once drove his daughter, Anna, to tears when he hollered at her for dropping an armload of books.[109] McNutt, wrought up over his daughter's health, would become "snappish" at a "facetious" remark uttered by one of his students in class.[110] Interestingly, these afflictions interrupted the predominant pattern in each man's marriage. The Roosevelts became closer, during 1921 and 1922, as Eleanor nursed her husband and parried her mother-in-law's pressure for him to retire to their family's estate.[111] The McNutts, in contrast, grew apart as they disagreed over how to handle Louise's illness in light of Kathleen's religion. As these illnesses receded, however, both marriages resumed their prevailing dynamics.

The illnesses affected Roosevelt and McNutt politically. FDR, nine years older than McNutt and nationally known, found his political career sidetracked by his bout with polio and the ensuing paralysis. Roosevelt, whom the Democrats had nominated for vice president in 1920, was determined to walk without crutches before again seeking public office. Meanwhile, McNutt gradually became known across Indiana. But, in the 1920s, he turned aside feelers to seek statewide office, citing the "financial obligations" engendered by Louise's illness.[112] Politically, the result may have been "something of a blessing" for the years following the 1920s were auspicious ones for Democrats.[113] How the illnesses influenced the political outlooks of FDR and McNutt as the country headed into the depression is less certain. Although Eleanor Roosevelt believed that polio had given her husband "a deeper empathy for other people," the political scientist James MacGregor Burns disagreed: "Those who see a new humanitarian rising from the sickbed ignore Roosevelt's decade of immersion in Wilsonian progressivism."[114] After becoming governor of Indiana, in 1933, McNutt interestingly championed economic "rehabilitation" for his state.[115] While it is tempting to attribute that therapeutic term to Louise's affliction, McNutt, as will be shown, had other reasons for employing it. Nevertheless, proximity to two of the nation's most dreaded diseases enabled both McNutt and Roosevelt to learn a valuable lesson about what it meant for people to struggle against powerful forces beyond their control.

By the mid-1920s, Paul McNutt was rapidly maturing as a professional and as a person. He dealt with his restlessness and frustrations, as well as life's sharp corners, by meeting them directly and making the best of them. He also accepted certain realities. A career in elective office, during an age of Republican dominance, was out of the question. So, too, despite some flirtations, were any plans of leaving his native state. "Indiana is my home," he wrote one associate, "and my best friends are here."[116] Instead, McNutt tried his hand at leadership, as dean, and he became the face of IU's law school. At the same time, he kept his domestic life intact. McNutt loved his wife, but was willing to intervene in her sphere if he thought it necessary, such as during their daughter's health crisis. Rather than shirk—or evade—his duties, McNutt led, at the office and at home.

Maturity did not mean complacency. McNutt could prepare yearly budgets for the law school, and battle with Indiana University's administration, for only so long. And he never seemed to tire of giving speeches. For McNutt, the position of dean had become, successively, a prize to be won, a job to be done, a platform to expound his ideas, and a pathway to something better. This pattern would repeat itself over the course of his public career for "no one who knew Dean McNutt expected him to stop rising."[117]

# 4

## THE LEGION AND LEADERSHIP
## (1926–1928)

DURING THE 1920S, PAUL McNUTT was involved in politics of almost every sort—except the electoral variety. He played academic politics when he wrested the deanship of the Indiana University law school from Charles M. Hepburn. He coped with family politics, navigating between his wife's Christian Science faith and his daughter's illness while accepting assistance, financial and otherwise, from both his parents and his father-in-law. In addition, McNutt became engaged in veterans' and interest-group politics via the American Legion. Before winning elected office in 1932, he had seen how power could be secured, exercised, and used in a variety of relationships and settings.

The American Legion was special to McNutt. In terms of self-fulfillment, Mc-Nutt's service as a dean at IU never matched his experience in the Legion. The Legion embodied McNutt's ideals, honored his past as a soldier, and pointed toward a future beyond Bloomington. It allowed veterans of World War I to continue their soldierly associations and to celebrate their patriotism without the racial, religious, and ethnic exclusivity of the Ku Klux Klan, which had reemerged a force during the 1920s. The American Legion was also thoroughly of, although not limited to, Indiana, where the organization enjoyed widespread support and built its national headquarters. For many men, it was a fraternity—a male-only space where the many convened, discussed, and socialized while the few delivered speeches and ran for the organization's offices. The Legion enabled McNutt to be a part of a crowd and to stand above his peers.

McNutt's rise in the American Legion exemplified much of his life's pattern. Offices in the Legion became objects of his ambition, the prizes he competed for. After gaining them, McNutt labored to promote the Legion's agenda. His speeches expounded on the virtues of patriotic service, the duties of citizens, the need for a muscular program of national defense, the alleged threat to the American republic by Communists and pacifists, and the entitlement of veterans to social services. And yet, while believing in, and promoting, the Legion's message, McNutt would advance beyond the organization. Through the American Legion, he came to occupy larger stages, first as commander of its Indiana Department and later as its national commander. To gain those offices, McNutt had to disclose his intentions, line up supporters, and prevail at conventions, both state and national. The Legion thus provided McNutt with experience expressing his ambition and mobilizing his supporters. It also gave him state and national renown, just as the Grand Old Party's grip on power in Indianapolis and Washington, D.C., was weakening. McNutt did not exactly plan his entry into electoral politics in such a calculated manner. But his political ascent could not have been mapped out any better.

The American Legion that McNutt joined, and would one day lead, began as a grassroots movement whose founders were "nobody, and everybody."[1] World War I had given American soldiers a common experience and a sense of brotherhood toward one another, and it was almost inevitable that, as veterans, they would organize. Following the end of hostilities, a group of officers led by Lieutenant Colonel Theodore Roosevelt Jr., son of the former president, met in Paris in 1919 to form what became the American Legion. These officers were a highly pragmatic group and founded the Legion out of the fear that "left-wing doctrines might infect the restless troops" who "might link hands with dangerous 'bolshevik' elements at home."[2] That did not happen. Instead, over the next two decades, Legionnaires founded twelve thousand posts, of varying sizes, in locales across America.[3] Each state had its own department and each department had its own commander, while an executive committee and a national commander, elected for a one-year term, oversaw the Legion.[4] By the eve of World War II, membership had swelled to over one million, meaning that more than one in four veterans of World War I had joined the organization.[5] The

Legion was open to all who had served in the armed forces in the First World War, whether or not they had experienced combat. It sometimes accepted non-soldiers, such as Franklin D. Roosevelt, who had served as assistant secretary of the navy, a civilian administrative post, during the war.[6] This openness proved crucial for McNutt, who had remained stateside during the First World War. The refrain that McNutt was "the teacher who never taught, the soldier who never fought, the lawyer who never tried a case" would be hummed later on by political opponents, not by rivals in the Legion.[7]

As an institution, the American Legion managed to look backward, sideways, and ahead all at the same time. Veterans' organizations had deep roots in American history. The Legion, like the Grand Army of the Republic (GAR), which had been formed by Union soldiers following the Civil War, strove to maintain and promote bonds between its members. Social functions tied Legionnaires together; despite the advent of Prohibition, alcohol flowed freely at local, state, and national meetings during the 1920s.

The culture of the Legion, with its mixture of spirits, revelry, and hijinks, steeled by war stories and masculine bravado, enabled men of middle age to revisit their youth and to escape "the routine of everyday work and the constraints of community life."[8] The organization was populated by youthful veterans who mirrored the temper and aims of the newly founded Legion itself—"a good, game scrapper, ready to fight for a cause."[9]

A principal cause of the American Legion, as it had been for the GAR, was to secure benefits for veterans. In this area, the Legion's greatest victory came in 1924 when, over the objections of business leaders, who feared inflation, and over the veto of President Calvin Coolidge, who was determined to balance the federal budget, Congress passed a bonus for those who had served in World War I. The bonus was really a life insurance policy to be paid to the heirs of each veteran upon his death, or to the veteran himself after twenty years. Although the bonus did not foreshadow the social concern and federal activism of the New Deal, it did signal a major financial commitment by Congress to a specific group during a period of conservative governance.[10]

Veterans' benefits in general and the bonus in particular exemplified a statist aspect of the American Legion. According to the sociologist Theda Skocpol, veterans' benefits cannot be heralded as the beginnings of a national welfare state because they provide federal dollars only to a small section of the population "who by their own choices and efforts as young men had *earned aid*."[11] In any case, the Legion successfully lobbied Congress to fund allowances and hospital care for veterans and to establish a Veterans' Bureau in the executive branch. In the late 1930s, Congress expanded and liberalized pensions for World War I veterans, creating a national system that was comparable to the benefits available to Union veterans of the Civil War. Moreover, the Legion's concern for the well-being of veterans led it to espouse some progressive causes. The organization established an endowment to support veterans' children, and it endorsed a constitutional amendment to outlaw child labor so that no youngster who have "to spend long, hard hours in a shop." The Legion dismissed critics who called the amendment "Communistic" by reminding audiences of its long record as "Communism's most implacable and powerful foe in America."[12]

The Legion gained its anti-Communist credentials early on, when it campaigned for "100 percent Americanism."[13] This effort operated at three levels. First, the Legion strove "to inculcate a sense of individual obligation to the community, state and nation" by promoting public remembrance of patriotic sacrifice. The organization encouraged the construction of war memorials and persuaded Congress to designate "The Star-Spangled Banner" the national anthem and Armistice Day—November 11—a national holiday.[14] Second, Legionnaires worked to protect the United States from external enemies through a program of military preparedness. Third, the organization worked to safeguard America "from foes within."[15] To assure the loyalty of the next generation, it favored displaying the Stars and Stripes on school grounds, teaching upbeat interpretations of American history—not fault-finding revisionism—and offering military training in high schools and colleges. The preamble to the American Legion's constitution pledged to defend the Constitution of the United States in the name of "God and Country."[16]

The Legion was unable to speak of American ideals without citing the need to defend them. In the shadow of the Russian Revolution, strikes at home, and the Red Scare of 1919–1920 (when the U.S. attorney general deported alien radicals), the Legion attempted to silence the views of people whom it deemed subversive. The organization was not opposed to freedom of speech, just "un-American free speech."[17] Hanford MacNider, the Legion's national commander from 1921 to 1922, attempted to set those boundaries by defining as un-American anyone who "sows discord" about the U.S. government, "attempts to create class enmity," and "says that as a nation we are unfair."[18] The title of a speech reprinted and distributed by the Legion stressed that Americans must choose between being "Red, White and Blue" or "Red, Pink and White."[19]

Communists emerged as targets for the American Legion, as did pacifists, who enjoyed popular sympathy following World War I. Many Americans, disillusioned because their nation had not achieved its wartime aims to promote democracy and a lasting peace, turned toward isolationism and against war during the 1920s. The peace movement was strong and diverse. It consisted of such organizations as the Carnegie Endowment for International Peace, which backed U.S. entrance into the League of Nations, and the Federal Council of Churches, which pushed disarmament. Prominent individuals became involved; the attorney Salmon Levinson urged the outlawing of war. Women remained at the forefront of the movement—Carrie Chapman Catt headed the National Conference for the Cause and the Cure of War, which espoused peace in a general manner, while Jane Addams's Women's International League for Peace and Freedom attacked imperialism and militarism specifically. By the 1920s, the historian Robert David Johnson has written, the peace movement had transformed itself "into a bloc more radical, unified, antimilitarist, anti-imperialist than during the years before American entry into the European war."[20] The National Council for the Prevention of War acted as a "clearing-house" and sustained the peace movement.[21] This organization earned a reputation for radicalism, as did its executive secretary, Frederick J. Libby, a Quaker, who denounced all forms of militarism, including the presence of the Reserve Officers' Training Corps (ROTC) on college campuses.[22]

The Legion assailed Libby as an "arch slacker" and strove to counter his appeals.[23] It denied that a program of military training in schools and colleges promoted militarism by citing its roots in American education, its impact on strengthening the bodies of American youth, and its benefits in keeping the United States strong enough to deter aggression by other nations. The Legion also cast the debate over training in terms of patriotism. The organization attacked "professional" pacifists for being either "secret Communists" or "unwitting dupes" for advocating disarmament in the face of external threats.[24] "There is room in this country for only one 'ism,'" declared National Commander Frank N. Belgrano Jr. in 1934. "That is Americanism."[25]

There was another powerful movement of the 1920s that promoted "100 percent Americanism": the Ku Klux Klan. Both organizations gained footholds across the nation and drew members from among middle-class professionals, merchants, and farmers. Around 300,000 Hoosiers joined the Ku Klux Klan. According to estimates, between twenty and fifty percent of Hoosier Legionnaires were Klansmen. The Klan and the Legion offered their memberships "a sense of group solidarity."[26] Both organizations were avowedly patriotic, anti-radical, and unfriendly toward immigrants. The Klan attacked as un-American those born overseas as well as Catholics, Jews, or African Americans. The Legion, if less vitriolic, still lobbied Congress to restrict immigration. Both the Klan and the Legion sponsored programs to assimilate the children of immigrants into the English-speaking mainstream. But the Legion, which stressed military service, focused its ire on non-naturalized immigrants, which it suspected of being slackers since, as non-citizens, they were ineligible to be drafted during wartime.[27]

That concern marked one of many differences between the Klan and the Legion. Nativism was far more central to the Klan's efforts and ideology than it was to those of the Legion. The Klan, unlike the Legion, linked immigrants to a wide range of problems, including alcohol abuse—in which Legionnaires often indulged. More important, the Klan based its "Americanism" on one's origins, asserting that native-born white Protestants were the loyal and true Americans. The Legion, in contrast, accepted into its ranks African Americans, Jews, Catholics, and foreign-born citizens who had participated in the Great War. U.S. citizenship by either birth or naturalization, service in the military, and adherence to the nation's founding principles and the Constitution defined the Legion's "Americanism." Moreover, although both organizations had their rituals, Klansmen, shrouded in white hoods and robes, became steeped in secrecy while Legionnaires, attired in blue suits and caps, appeared neither mysterious nor mystical. Lastly, the Klan sometimes resorted to violence and vandalism to intimidate opponents, while the Legion seldom took such extralegal steps.[28]

The emergence of the Legion and the Klan emblemized the anxiety that had gripped many Americans. Together, World War I, strikes, race riots, the Red Scare, and a fierce debate over the Versailles Treaty and its League of Nations unsettled the country and revealed a deeper crisis of national identity. By the twenties, the United States was an urban, industrialized nation with a not-so-distant rural, agricultural past; an isolationist republic that had briefly shed its century-long policy of non-participation in European wars; a nation victorious in its most recent conflict, but disillusioned over the ensuing peace; and a multiethnic, multiracial country in which native-born, white Anglo-Saxon Protestants continued to rule and assert their legitimacy to rule. In this era of uncertainty, the Klan and the Legion defended what they deemed Americanism, whether it was the race-based message of the Klan or the Legion's veneration of patriotic service.

The Legion quickly became a venue for veterans to distinguish themselves and to become active politically. To be sure, the Legion's constitution defined the organization as "non-political," and it forbade local posts from endorsing candidates for elected office. Nevertheless, individual members were involved in partisan activities. In 1920, Theodore Roosevelt Jr. and other Legion founders promoted the candidacy of General Leonard Wood for the Republican Party's presidential nomination. Moreover, the list of national commanders who attained public office was long. It included Theodore Roosevelt Jr., who was assistant secretary of the navy under President Warren G. Harding and who ran unsuccessfully for governor of New York in 1924; Hanford MacNider, who served as assistant secretary of war under President Calvin Coolidge and, later, as U.S. minister to Canada; and Louis A. Johnson, assistant secretary of war under FDR and secretary of defense under Harry S. Truman. The number of departmental commanders who went on to be elected governor or U.S. senator from their home states was, if anything, even greater.[29]

McNutt became attracted to the Legion for obvious reasons. The Legion was a masculine organization, and McNutt had long been more at ease in the company of men than of women. As an undergraduate at Indiana University, he had joined a fraternity and had become part of its subculture, where he had his first experiences with alcohol. He had volunteered for service in World War I, become an officer, and exuded pride in his contribution. After the war, he kept up his soldierly ties. McNutt accepted a commission in the field artillery section of the Officers' Reserve Corps, where he rose to the rank of colonel, and entered the Reserve Officers Association, leading the organization's Indiana branch from 1923 to 1924. He also was a joiner in this "nation of joiners."[30] A political profile from 1938 described him as "a Methodist, a Mason, an Elk, a Kiwanian, a Rotarian, a dean, a professor, [and] a colonel."[31] It was only natural, then, that he would become part of the leading veterans' organization from the Great War, just as his favorite grandfather had become part of the leading veterans' organization from the Civil War.

The American Legion also had strong ties to McNutt's native state. Indiana's capital city was home to the leadership of the Legion; at the organization's first national convention in 1919, Hoosiers, aligned with delegates from the South and West, were able to get Indianapolis, not Washington, D.C., selected as the location of the Legion's national headquarters. This success enabled the Legion to become highly visible in Indiana and its members to become a political force in the state. During the 1920s, the Legion had sufficient political muscle in Indiana to secure public funding for a state headquarters, a building to house the national headquarters, and a monument to honor veterans of the Great War—all in Indianapolis.[32]

Did McNutt join the Legion simply to advance his political aspirations? Not quite. When McNutt became a member of Bloomington's post in 1919, he had behind him just one race—his unsuccessful campaign for Morgan County prosecutor in 1916—and only thoughts about running for Congress in 1920. At that point, a political career was hardly inevitable. Nevertheless, later reporters, seeking to understand McNutt's rise, correctly pointed out that the Indiana Legion had emerged as a "training ground and springboard" into public office for ambitious young Democrats and Republicans.[33] "They started in organizing Legion posts and learning the ethics and primary purpose of politics," Harold Feightner, a journalist in Indiana, observed. "There [were] quite a few fellows who grew up and learned their P's and Q's through the American Legion."[34]

For McNutt, the American Legion was, at first, a refuge and only later on a springboard to statewide office. He joined the organization following World War I, when his future was unsettled. And he began to socialize with Legionnaires, over games of cards in Bloomington, as he grew restless with academic life. Then, in the mid-1920s, as McNutt clarified his professional goals, acted on his ambitions, and secured the deanship of the IU law school, he, not coincidentally, showed greater interest in the Legion. For Hoosier veterans, Feightner recalled, the local post was "a place to be active."[35] By 1925, McNutt had become involved in his post in Bloomington. After 1925, as the health of his daughter worsened and then improved, McNutt acquired a fresh set of motives to get out of Bloomington, at least temporarily, and to seek new opportunities via the Legion. Although participation in the American Legion turned out to be a superb apprenticeship for running for governor, personal as well as political needs led McNutt to embrace this organization during the early and middle 1920s.

Ideals as well as ambition fed McNutt's interest in the Legion. He shared the Legion's core values, especially with respect to patriotic service. Regarding the Officers' Reserve Corps, of which he was a member, McNutt wrote: "I want to see it live and prosper and I intend to do everything in my power to help." As a former soldier and a current reservist, he deemed military service "a patriotic duty." "Every man, who is capable of holding a commission, owes it to his country to achieve and hold a reserve commission," McNutt declared, in exhorting students at Indiana University to join the reserves. Yet, cynical about human nature, and the desire of Americans for comfortable lives, on the one hand, or personal glory, on the other, he reckoned that students would ask: "What is there in it for me?"[36] Like many Legionnaires, McNutt recognized that selfish pursuits posed a serious threat to both patriotic service and military readiness.

McNutt found himself in a tug-of-war to prevent students from shirking what he deemed their duty. In 1926, a debate erupted at Indiana University over military training. Some students asserted that such training should remain compulsory, at least for male freshmen and sophomores—an outgrowth of the campus's mobilization during World War I—while others, citing the policies of Harvard, Yale, and Princeton, wanted it to be voluntary. The latter group drew inspiration from the pacifist leader Frederick Libby, who was on a nationwide speaking tour. But the former group collected six hundred student signatures in favor of continuing compulsory military training. Their chief supporter was President William Lowe Bryan. U.S. participation in the Great War had convinced Bryan, a onetime pacifist, that "it is sometimes right and necessary to use force in defense of life." He insisted that all male underclassmen at IU, except for conscientious objectors and "others with reasonable excuses," enroll in ROTC.[37]

The debate escalated in March 1926 when Libby addressed the Indiana University community at its convocation. Bryan did not attend the event, and neither did McNutt. A few days afterward, McNutt publicly registered his disapproval of Libby during a speech on "character education" before the Parent-Teacher Association of Indianapolis. McNutt reiterated that it was the duty of every American citizen "to serve this nation in time of war" and that military training in colleges was essential to maintaining "an adequate national defense." McNutt's vehemence descended into an attack on Libby that the pacifist leader took as an affront. McNutt charged Libby and his ally, Thomas Que Harrison of the Fellowship of Youth for Peace, with undermining America's national defense by "seeking to abolish military training in the schools."[38]

Convinced that peace activists "threaten the safety of our government," McNutt vowed to thwart them.[39] He began to solicit data on Libby and Harrison so that he might go after them "hammer and tongs."[40] After Harrison urged students at the University of Chicago "to bring discredit and ridicule on the military" by resisting mandatory training, McNutt escalated his attacks.[41] In the fall of 1926, he accused leaders of "so-called peace organizations" with being Communists—"Reds"—who "work for the abolition of all means of defense in order to make way for the revolution." To be sure, McNutt tempered his Red-baiting by distinguishing between the subversive pacifists, those who wanted to end ROTC, from a small number of "honest, well-meaning conscientious objectors." Nevertheless, a half decade after the first Red Scare, and two decades before the second one, McNutt called for the "the exposure and deportation" of Communists.[42] The leaders of the peace movement clearly had gotten under his skin. After McNutt addressed the Indianapolis Council of Women, a member of the audience remarked that the speaker had spent "half his time" berating Libby.[43] A few months later, McNutt privately boasted of having been "on the trail of the pacifists in this State for six years."[44]

That claim, exaggerated or not, betrayed something important about McNutt at this point of his life: he was spoiling for a fight and aching to engage in public debate. He described this task of "fighting subversive movements" as a "labor of love."[45] "I am thoroughly aroused," McNutt informed a friend in Indianapolis, "and intend to wield the cudgel whenever the opportunity presents itself."[46] Denied the chance to serve in Europe during World War I and seeing a political career as out of reach, at least for the time being, McNutt lashed out on an issue and against an enemy about which he felt viscerally.

On the whole, the crusade against pacifists, and "Reds," helped McNutt's career. To be sure, McNutt distaste for these groups was genuine. He privately denounced the "professional pacifist" as a peddler of "subversive" propaganda.[47] And he pressed this point in public, even though it was less than popular. At a time when most Americans sought a lasting peace, without accepting major international commitments, the public was unlikely to insist upon military training. Indeed, women, who had just won the right to vote and who were active in the peace movement, wrote to McNutt to protest his attacks on pacifists.[48] Furthermore, the first Red Scare, into which much of McNutt's rhetoric sought to tap, was a fading memory. The *Kokomo* (Indiana) *Dispatch* chided him for being out of step with the times:

> Mr. McNutt might find more wicked foes for his thrusts than those he pleases to brand as pacifists. We need more of their class of clear sighted citizens of the world. As for the "reds"—well, we haven't seen one for a long time, though perhaps Mr. McNutt sees them lurking in Indiana cornfields and briar patches.[49]

Nevertheless, McNutt's strong defense of military training would have strengthened his relationship with President Bryan, a firm supporter of ROTC, and his anti-pacifism and anti-Communism squared with mainstream thinking in the Legion. McNutt's ideas and rhetoric, as well as his rising visibility on the stump, would prove useful as he energized his local post and looked to win election as commander of the Indiana Legion.

McNutt's ascent in the Legion began locally. In Bloomington, Legionnaires had founded the Burton Woolery Post No. 18, named to honor a local boy and an IU student, Henry Burton Woolery, killed in action near Esperance Ferme, France, in 1918. As the post set out to elect a new commander, in October 1925, McNutt disclosed that friends were urging him to be a candidate. Although he professed uncertainty about entering the race, he allowed his devotees to "make a quiet canvass" of the membership about a possible bid.[50] Such thinly veiled ambition and maneuvering would be repeated in McNutt's later campaigns for office. And it worked. The Bloomington post had endured fluctuations in its membership, and McNutt—young, dynamic, attractive, and smart—appeared to be the person to shake it from its doldrums.[51] Legionnaires in Bloomington were flattered that such "a big man like the dean of the law school was willing to accept the command," and they elected him their leader.[52]

With the prize won, McNutt launched a recruitment drive by distributing lists of veterans to each of the post's eighty-seven members. Each member then "had to sell the Legion to as many on his list as humanely possible."[53] McNutt exceeded his goal of recruiting 250 new members; by the end of his term, the Burton Woolery Post had 502 members. The jump had made Bloomington the second-largest post in the district and third-largest in the state—and McNutt's stature in the Indiana Legion rose.[54] Clarence A. Jackson, commander of the Department of Indiana, spread word of McNutt's accomplishments, and the *American Legion Weekly* "carried stories of the feat." The acclaim added to the contacts McNutt had made in the Reserve Officers Association. The result was "more dinner engagements, a widening of his range of friends, more speeches [and] train jumps to make classes at the law school."[55]

The cheering boosted McNutt's confidence as he eyed a higher office: commander of the Indiana Legion. The state commander would be elected to a one-year term in much the same way that political parties nominated candidates, at a convention to be held at Marion in August 1926. In launching his campaign, McNutt sounded like an American politician of the previous century, bashful about seeking office and insistent that friends were pushing his candidacy. "I have been strongly urged to become a candidate for State Commander of the American Legion," McNutt told one associate. "I have no intention of entering any general scramble for the place because I feel that, at this stage of the Legion's development, the office should seek the man rather than the man the office." Then he added: "I am willing to serve if the members of the Legion want me."[56] Such false modesty confirmed an old adage about Indiana, that "every Hoosier baby's first words are: 'Although I am not a candidate for any public office, if nominated by the people of my party and elected by the sovereign vot-ers of the great State of Indiana, I will serve to the best of my ability.'"[57] Before the Department of Indiana convened, McNutt was encouraging supporters to canvass on his behalf. He also suggested that other candidates might consider withdrawing and, when that failed, he communicated with Legionnaires in the districts of his rivals in order to cut into their support.[58] McNutt also prepared well for the convention; his local post nominated him for state commander and endorsements came from other posts as well.[59]

McNutt was no shoe-in for the top spot in the Indiana Legion. He was, after all, an "ivory tower" type, sneered more "earthy" veterans.[60] Moreover, many former enlisted men disliked having too many former officers like McNutt "in prominent places in the Legion."[61] And Republican Legionnaires were not fond of this enthusiastic Democrat.[62] McNutt's rather recent embrace of the Legion led others to question his commitment. McNutt overcame these ob-stacles through hard work, shrewdness, and luck. He arrived early in Marion and conferred with his managers—Bloomington Legionnaires, all of them Republicans. On their advice, McNutt addressed as many district caucuses as possible, even on short notice. This strategy showcased McNutt's magnetism and "ability to transfix any audience." While McNutt pressed the flesh and made speeches, his aides searched for delegates to buttonhole. More than a few Legionnaires protested such overt campaigning as being at odds with their organization's practices.[63]

McNutt benefited from perceived flaws in his opponent, Eugene O'Shaughnessy of Lawrenceburg, Indiana. On the surface, O'Shaughnessy was a strong candidate, better known than McNutt and part of a circle within the Indiana Legion that saw the office as "an honor to be conferred, not a prize to be contested."[64] Yet he was Roman Catholic and the owner of a distillery. To make matters worse, he had placed in his headquarters a large punch bowl filled with whiskey. The reputation of the organization was at stake, for many resi-dents of Marion had refused to rent rooms to Legionnaires, being fearful that the convention would descend into a "big drunken orgy."[65] Members of the Ku Klux Klan, who hated alcohol as much as they hated Catholics and who saw the one inextricably linked to the other, opposed O'Shaughnessy's candidacy. "We must admit, however distasteful to us it is," one of McNutt's supporters wrote, "that there is some very strong Klan sentiment in the American Legion."[66]

The Klan held no appeal for McNutt. Although McNutt was a white Anglo-Saxon Protestant and thus eligible to join the Klan, he never identified with that organization's unapologetic exclusivity, having been labeled—and bullied as—an outsider during his youth. McNutt was also an educated man and an educator who no doubt took offense at Klan efforts to intervene in education. The organization pressed schools to fire teachers who discussed international-ism and advocated U.S. membership in the League of Nations, which McNutt, a Wilsonian Democrat, backed, at least nominally.[67] As partisan Democrats, McNutt and his father knew that the KKK had become entwined with Indiana's Republican Party during the 1920s.[68] John C. McNutt dismissed a measure to reform the state's education system as a "Klan bill," and he hoped for its defeat in the General Assembly.[69] Paul McNutt privately denounced the "activities" of the KKK as "pernicious."[70] Yet, sagacity prevented him from attacking an organization whose members marched in Bloomington and also joined the Legion.[71]

In the contest for state commander of the Legion, McNutt publicly kept mum on the Klan. After eight ballots, the professor from Bloomington prevailed over the distiller from Lawrenceburg with a final vote of 206 to 176. A "howling" crowd carried the victor to the stage, where McNutt, sounding like a veteran politician, proclaimed that "the heart of the Legion is in the local posts."[72] McNutt's post, of course, had been the heart of his campaign. He won for other reasons as well, including his patriotic rhetoric and defense of military train-ing. "I like your platform, of going after pacifism," one supporter told the state commander-elect.[73] At the same time, O'Shaughnessy's religion—and ties to alcohol—had alienated delegates. "I was not for you when I arrived in Marion because of what I felt was your lack of interest in Legion affairs prior to this year," one man wrote McNutt, "but after learning all that I could about your opponent I was convinced that the interests of the department would be best served by your election."[74]

As commander, McNutt served the Indiana Legion with relentless energy. He stepped up his speaking; during one period in 1927, he spoke sixty-one times in fifty-seven days. Indiana's many unpaved roads made such a schedule strenuous. Sudden downpours turned roads into muddy swamps that snagged automobiles, including McNutt's. He also traveled via Indiana's network of interurban trains, a long-standing method of transportation, and by airplane, a newer mode shunned by the fainthearted.[75] No one, a friend warned McNutt, "could pay me to take a flying machine!!!"[76] McNutt juggled this speaking and his regular teaching at the law school by making addresses at night, on holidays, and after his classes had let out. He might travel all day to reach Fort Wayne, or some other point in northern Indiana. After speaking, he departed by train, at night, for Indianapolis, sleeping along the way and arriving in time to catch the 6:30 AM train for Bloomington. By midmorning, he was home in time to teach his classes.[77]

In addition to his teaching, McNutt spoke to civic groups and at graduation exercises, usually for a small honorarium. McNutt's finances, limited by his daughter's illness, made charging such fees necessary. Moreover, he had to raise money to support his extensive speaking schedule, for he exhausted his annual travel allowance as state commander after just two months in office. The "best index to his speaking ability" was the large number of invitations that McNutt received to speak outside Indiana.[78] He traveled forty thousand miles across eighteen states during his year as state commander.[79]

On these trips, McNutt made new friends and impressed new audiences. In March 1927, before addressing the Department of Iowa in Mason City, he stayed with the parents of Hanford MacNider, a past national commander. Following the visit, the house guest praised MacNider's family, hospitality, and leadership for cultivating in Iowa a "Legion spirit" as tall as the state's corn.[80] McNutt had reason to sound upbeat. The editor of the Mason City *Globe-Gazette* had pronounced his address "the finest thing" he had heard in three years of such gatherings, and he predicted that one day Iowa Legionnaires would "cast a unanimous vote for Paul McNutt for national commander."[81] Indeed, a member of the Department of Iowa noted that "many Legionnaires" in his state felt "much closer to the Department of Indiana" after hearing McNutt speak.[82]

McNutt's energy seemed endless. Even his pastimes involved activity and competition. McNutt golfed and joshed about his score. College football was another passion. An Army-Navy game that McNutt and his wife attended in Chicago, in 1926, thrilled him. Predictably, he rooted for Army—which lost.[83] McNutt was acquainted with futility on the gridiron for his favorite team, that of Indiana University, was often inept; when IU managed to upend its archrival Purdue, McNutt expressed his "surprise and joy."[84] Yet, such diversions proved less frequent after he became state commander. Partly to catch up on work, McNutt in 1926 passed on a trip up to South Bend to watch Indiana play Notre Dame.[85] Friends urged him to relax. A fraternity brother told him "to cut out some of this speech-making" and "sit down in an easy chair" or "we will be patting you in the face with a shovel."[86] Signs of fatigue became evident. After one "strenuous trip," McNutt wondered "whether it was worth the energy and effort." But the applause erased his doubts. "The response has been so gratifying," he admitted, "that I have definitely concluded that the game is worthwhile."[87]

The Indiana Legion thrived under McNutt. To be sure, not all of its accomplishments could be attributed to the new commander. The revival of *The Hoosier Legionnaire,* the department's organ, took place on McNutt's watch but was due to the work of its editor, John H. Klinger.[88] Nevertheless, it was McNutt who oversaw a successful fight to boost state funding for an orphanage to care for the offspring of deceased soldiers.[89] More important, McNutt did statewide what he had done locally: increase membership in the Legion. He set quotas for membership drives, called meetings to revive dormant posts, chided the ones that lagged in finding new members, and congratulated those that produced results.[90] During McNutt's year as state commander, membership in the Department of Indiana climbed from 18,336 to 25,505.[91] One Legionnaire praised him for placing himself at "the beck and call of every post."[92] Even a critic of McNutt's rapid ascent in the organization conceded that his speeches had done much to sell the Legion to Hoosiers.[93] McNutt, his earliest biographer asserted, was "one of the most active and successful Legion commanders the state ever had."[94]

If McNutt was good for the Indiana Legion, the Indiana Legion was also good for McNutt in three respects. First, his leadership position allowed him to travel to distant places. Late in 1927, McNutt ventured beyond the American heartland when he and his wife attended the Legion's national convention in Paris. The organization stretched its four-day gathering there into a two-month excursion that allowed members to explore the sites, cities, and cemeteries associated with soldiers of the American Expeditionary Force in the Great War.[95] Second, the office of state commander temporarily removed McNutt from party politics. After his election, he brushed aside pressure from Indiana Democrats to campaign for the state ticket in 1926.[96] "Any partisan speeches," he warned, could have "an unfortunate reaction" by turning Legionnaires "against our candidates."[97]

Third, the Indiana Legion provided McNutt with valuable political contacts, and none proved more precious than that of Frank M. McHale. At the time of McHale's death in 1975, Democrats and Republicans alike praised him as a giant in Indiana politics.[98] Born to Irish immigrants, McHale graduated from the University of Michigan, where he earned All-American honors in football. After graduation, he became a lawyer in his hometown of Logansport. McHale served in World War I, organized his local American Legion post, and won election as its commander. He rose in the Legion's Indiana Department, becoming a member of the Department's Legislative Committee from 1919 to 1929. Along the way, he emerged as a successful banker and a loyal servant of the Democratic Party. As McHale aged, he came to resemble a stereotypical political boss— bald, fleshy-faced, and large, weighing 300 pounds.[99]

McHale was an impressive person. As a Catholic, he opposed bigotry and challenged the Klan. Once, as Klansmen prepared to parade through Logansport, McHale went into the middle of the street and planted a baseball bat on the ground. He remained in place, defiant, forcing the hooded knights to "part around him as they marched by."[100] The Klan's infiltration of the Indiana GOP only strengthened his devotion to the Hoosier Democracy. McHale was a delegate to every Democratic National Convention between 1928 and 1972, and he also served as a Democratic National Committeeman from 1937 to 1952.[101] In keeping with the political culture of his native state, McHale cherished his party, cursed the opposition, denounced extremists of all stripes, and reached out to fallen foes after elections. "He could be a formidable adversary," one reporter observed. "Yet he was always forthright."[102] In 1975 Eugene C. Pulliam, publisher of the Republican *Indianapolis Star,* eulogized McHale as "the outstanding leader of the Democratic Party in Indiana" for nearly a half century.[103]

Although McHale's achievements were substantial, his name would forever be tied to McNutt's star. Their association began in the Indiana Legion, when McNutt solicited McHale's support in his campaign to be state commander.[104] Although in that contest McHale backed O'Shaughnessy, his fellow Irish Catholic, the paths of the two men continued to cross.[105] In 1927, Hoosier Legionnaires, with McNutt's blessing, elected McHale as state commander. The outgoing commander had persuaded four other aspirants for his office—all Protestant—to withdraw so that McHale could be elected, unopposed, in a "strike against the Klan."[106] In so acting, McNutt may have been trying to atone for his victory over O'Shaughnessy while also reaching out to Indiana Catholics.

In McHale, McNutt found a friend as well as an ally. The two men shared many values, including a love of party, public service, and country. McHale, like McNutt, had no use for those who sat on the sidelines, thinking them either "selfish" or "cowardly."[107] The two men complemented each other very well. McNutt was a show horse, the political candidate as matinee idol, while McHale was a work horse, the unseen strategist.[108] It was McHale, as legislative leader of the Indiana Legion, who had helped persuade the state legislature to build the War Memorial Plaza in Indianapolis, a pyramidal limestone monument to veterans of the First World War.[109] Yet it was McNutt, as commander of the Indiana Department, who presided over the dedication of that monument, flanked by General John J. Pershing, commander of the American Expeditionary Force in the Great War.[110] Such a contrast recalled a scene from a play by the Hoosier author George Ade, in which a county chairman tells his doe-eyed candidate: "All right boy, you get along out there with your Galahad speech while I put on the gum shoes and go get the votes."[111] McHale understood his role with respect to McNutt's career, and he performed it loyally. "Once you pledge yourself to support a candidate . . . ," he later counseled young people, "don't desert that candidate, unless he gives his permission."[112] Between 1928 and 1940, McHale's skills as a political organizer, his wisdom, and his occasional misjudgments would be the exclusive property of Paul McNutt.

For much of 1928, McNutt and McHale remained apart. As McHale assumed his duties as state commander of the Legion, McNutt undertook a new task, that of civilian aide for Indiana to the secretary of war. Appointed to the post late in 1927, McNutt was responsible for Indiana's Civilian Military Training Camps (CMTC).[113] This program had originated before America's entrance in World War I, with the famed Plattsburg Camps, once described as "summer séances of well-to-do businessmen and college boys training at their own expense to be military officers."[114] Under CMTC, the Department of War furnished camps, instructors, and equipment while the general population provided able-bodied volunteers.[115] The problem for McNutt was that Indiana had lagged behind other states in providing its share of men. He went to work setting enrollment quotas, replacing chairman in counties with low participation, and launching a statewide publicity blitz in cooperation with the Indiana Legion—headed by McHale.[116] Under McNutt's leadership, Indiana exceeded its CMTC quota for the first time.[117] He deemed this latest patriotic enterprise to be another "labor of love."[118]

McNutt was acquainting himself with another love—higher office—and, in 1928, the post of national commander of the American Legion beckoned to him. He began his campaign with professions of modesty coupled with some behind-the-scenes maneuvering. "If the Indiana Department wants me to make the race (and it looks as if this were the case)," McNutt wrote a supporter in mid-1928, "I shall get in 'with both feet.'"[119] By that time, he was already in. Four months earlier, John W. Wheeler, a McNutt confidant, had quietly organized a

campaign committee—after McNutt had prodded him to do so.[120] When two
posts unanimously endorsed him for national commander, McNutt, somewhat
less than truthfully, claimed that they had done so "without any solicitation on
my part." "Naturally," he then explained, "I cannot disregard such an expression
of confidence."[121] Eventually, with McHale's support, Indiana Legionnaires
unanimously endorsed McNutt for national commander.[122]

If lining up the Indiana Legion was the first phase of McNutt's campaign,
then introducing the Hoosier to other departments marked its second part.
McNutt was already known in the surrounding states, particularly Illinois, Wisconsin, and Ohio, where he had given well-received speeches and was benefiting
from a widening circle of contacts. For example, Wendell L. Willkie, who was
living in Akron, Ohio, urged the commander of his post to endorse his college
chum.[123] Others engaged in lobbying. McHale "did some very effective work"
on McNutt's behalf at the Department of Michigan's annual convention.[124]
McNutt's own travels to Iowa, Missouri, Kansas, and Nebraska did him considerable good.[125] "The enthusiasm over the speech you delivered at Grand Island,"
one Nebraskan told him, "has not yet subsided."[126] Such praise encouraged
McNutt to solicit support from Legionnaires in Pennsylvania and Florida.[127]

While all that went on, a scent of scandal threatened the McNutt campaign.
In 1927, while serving as commander of the Indiana Department, McNutt had
negotiated an arrangement with a Boston-based company named Temple Tours
to conduct tours of battlefields for Indiana Legionnaires attending the national
convention in Paris. In exchange, he allegedly was to receive a five percent commission on each fee paid by a Legionnaire who signed up for a tour. The author
of these allegations was Andrew Hepburn, son of the man whom McNutt had
replaced as dean of the IU school of law and an agent for Temple Tours.[128] But
the president of Temple Tours affirmed that McNutt "never asked nor accepted
commission on behalf of the American Legion or the Indiana Department for
these tours."[129] Hepburn, however, had charged McNutt with making a separate, personal deal with the touring company outside the purview of the Legion.
Whether this charge was true remains unclear. In the end, an investigation by
the Indiana Legion exonerated its former commander of any wrongdoing.[130]

The affair said some important things about McNutt. It revealed that his
ambition had consequences, for Hepburn surely wanted revenge on the man
who had dethroned his father.[131] In a letter to McHale, McNutt dismissed the
charges as "dastardly."[132] He went further, perceiving a "nefarious scheme" on
the part of his "enemies" to use "Hepburn's lie" to remove him from "the Legion

picture."[133] Indeed, during the 1932 gubernatorial race, Indiana Republicans "pilfered" the records of the probe but did not use them against McNutt to any significant effect.[134] Nevertheless, even if McNutt needed the money from these tours—as, with the illness of his daughter, he doubtless did—he should have been more sensitive to the appearance of impropriety, of using his position in the Legion for personal profit. It was not the last time that questions about McNutt's finances threatened to derail him politically nor was it the last time that McNutt would confide in McHale.

McHale was instrumental in managing the final phase of McNutt's campaign, the period leading up to the Legion's convention in San Antonio. He and McNutt had their work cut out for themselves. Not unlike the Department of Indiana before McNutt's election as commander, a clique within the Legion had secured the election of the past two national commanders. In 1928, this "machine" rallied around the candidacy of John H. Ewing of Louisiana. In response, seven "independent candidates," including McNutt, surfaced to challenge Ewing.[135] The array of candidates did not bode well for McNutt, who was still a newcomer to the Legion. As one Hoosier warned, "I do not think this is a McNutt year for National Commander."[136] As he had before his election as state commander, McNutt took a stab at some preconvention maneuvering, proposing to meet with two of his rivals before the convention opened.[137] This effort failed and the field remained crowded.[138] McNutt thus braced for a "dog fight" in San Antonio.[139] "The action of a national convention is a most uncertain thing," McNutt sighed—a prophetic comment from a man whose political fate would later be decided at two Democratic National Conventions, those of 1932 and 1940.[140]

McNutt overcame his status as an underdog with preparation, organization, and tireless speaking. Not unlike the Marion convention in 1926, McNutt and his advisers arrived in San Antonio a few days early to survey the landscape. The plan was for the candidate to replicate his feat at Marion by addressing as many delegates as possible. In the meantime, McHale, who already had introduced McNutt to state commanders via letters, lobbied them in San Antonio. He knew that, even if McNutt did not place among the top three contenders on the early ballots, the Hoosier might triumph later on, if he could emerge as the second choice of enough delegates. During McNutt's campaign for the White House, McHale employed these same tactics, sending letters to disclose his candidate's intention and attributes, and a similar strategy, presenting the Hoosier as an alternative to the other leading Democrats. Thus, in San Antonio,

McNutt made the speeches, Galahad-like or otherwise, while McHale rounded up the votes.[141]

Yet, doubts about McNutt's prospects lingered in a rather unexpected quarter. Kathleen McNutt accompanied her husband to San Antonio, and she was not confident about her husband's chances.[142] Paul, meanwhile, spoke relentlessly before state caucuses throughout October 10 and into the small hours of October 11, the day of the balloting. Returning to his hotel room, exhausted, he raised a finger "in a characteristic gesture" and announced to Kathleen: "I'm the next National Commander." Paul explained his campaign's strategy, how New York had promised him its seventy-five votes following the second ballot, and how he would probably prevail by the fourth ballot.[143]

On October 11, Legionnaires got down to the business of selecting their next commander. Every Legion convention had been "at once a parliament and a pageant," and this one was no different. It opened with a parade featuring U.S. cavalrymen, cowboys, and Californians riding in a covered wagon.[144] Inside the auditorium, the nominations for national commander went forward. McHale rose to present McNutt's name. He praised the Hoosier's service in the army, emphasized his record as state commander, and then credited McNutt, rather than himself, with securing the funds to build the War Memorial Plaza in Indianapolis.[145]

What occurred afterward stunned many observers. The press in San Antonio had slighted McNutt's chances. But the first round of balloting put him in third place with 189 votes. Roy Hoffman of Oklahoma was first with 245 votes, followed by Ewing with 231, with the remaining votes distributed among four other candidates. On the second ballot, McHale's "second choice" strategy appeared to pay off as McNutt surged into second place with 213 votes, behind Ewing's 245.[146] At that point, Ewing, the machine's candidate, realized that he had peaked, and he decided to play kingmaker. On the advice of a fellow Louisianan, L. Kemper Williams, McNutt's "old army buddy" and the best man at Paul's wedding, Ewing withdrew from the race and cast Louisiana's fifteen votes for McNutt. Delegations from the large states followed suit. Hoffman performed the final act, announcing Oklahoma's seventeen votes for the Hoosier and then urging that the vote be made unanimous, which it was.[147] A jubilant Indiana delegation then paraded to the stage.[148] "It was a great fight and a great victory," the *Bloomington Star* reported.[149] Yet lurking beneath the congratulations was something worrisome, a mounting confidence—even arrogance—that, having mastered this convention, McNutt's followers could prevail at other, later conventions. "My Hoosier supporters," McNutt wrote a friend a month after his election, "are not lacking in the rudiments of political strategy."[150]

The San Antonio convention marked McNutt's greatest personal victory to date. Despite doubts and talk of defeat, even from his wife, he triumphed, and letters of congratulations poured in.[151] The most precious message was from his daughter: "I am so happy for you daddy love to you and mother."[152] McNutt himself returned to "the greatest welcome ever given a citizen of Bloomington."[153] Automobiles lined Kirkwood Avenue, the city's main artery, and thousands greeted his train at the station.[154] "It's good to be home where the ties are strongest," McNutt declared.[155] Then, escorted by an ROTC regiment, a university band, and dignitaries of the Legion, McNutt's well-wishers paraded to Assembly Hall, where President Bryan was waiting.[156] "You belong in a special sense to your home people," he told McNutt. "You belong to Martinsville. You belong to Bloomington. You belong to the State of Indiana. You belong to Indiana University."[157] But Bryan must have wondered whether this victory was a calculated stepping stone, and McNutt a "bird of political passage."[158]

# 5

## NATIONAL VISTAS, STATE ELECTIONS
## (1929–1932)

AS NATIONAL COMMANDER OF the American Legion, Paul V. McNutt saw his life change, dramatically and permanently. Holding this office, as one of McNutt's staunchest supporters in the Legion emphasized, transformed one into a national figure.[1] Kathleen McNutt noticed this change at once, and she disliked it. As reporters and photographers gathered around the newly elected commander, Kathleen walked past the correspondents, approached Paul, and then asked him: "Honey, can't I even kiss you anymore?"[2]

Commanding the American Legion in the late 1920s, like serving in the army a decade earlier, widened McNutt's vistas. His speechmaking continued, but his audiences were larger. The raised platform on which McNutt now stood allowed him to refine his thinking on topics from patriotic service to veterans' benefits to national defense. On that last issue, he would challenge a president of the United States. In fact, it was during the late 1920s and early 1930s that McNutt began to think seriously about occupying the White House himself. After the Legion's convention in San Antonio, one man, sensing "no limit" to McNutt's success, said he expected to vote for him for president "in the future."[3] In time, McNutt proved willing to entertain the idea, for his restless ambition had not subsided. Just a month after his election as commander, he told a former classmate that his life since law school had been "uneventful."[4] That was about to change.

Just as leadership of the American Legion was opening new horizons to him, events in Indiana gave McNutt the opportunity to win elected office. The Republican Party, weakened in Indiana by scandals during the 1920s, was blamed for the stock market crash of 1929 and the ensuing economic depression. Hoosier Democrats stood to benefit, none more than McNutt. As dean of the law school at Indiana's largest public university, and as past commander of the Indiana Legion, McNutt had statewide appeal, and he had been mentioned as a possible governor. By 1932, the Democratic nomination for governor was McNutt's for the taking.[5]

Yet the prospect of such a bounty only heightened McNutt's ambitions. If the governorship was probable, then the vice presidency—or even the presidency—in 1932 was in the realm of possibility. With the Grand Old Party (GOP) as damaged nationally as it was locally, the Democratic nomination for president became a guaranteed ticket to the White House. The race for the nomination spawned a host of aspirants, including Franklin D. Roosevelt, and a divided convention, not unlike the Legion's annual meeting at San Antonio in 1929. By the summer of 1932, McNutt had secured the Democratic nomination for governor and was seeking something more, the party's nomination for president. Alas, in so seeking, he challenged FDR and made what may have been the greatest miscalculation of his political life.

As commander of the American Legion, McNutt entered the national stage, speaking widely on issues of public importance. Looking at his nation in the 1920s, he denounced the freewheeling frivolity and a "sordid scramble for gain."[6] Who should be blamed? Not American institutions, McNutt explained to one audience. "The fault lies with our people," whose problem was selfishness.[7] As a former soldier, McNutt looked back fondly on the "great wave of patriotic fervor" that had swept the United States during the Great War. As a Legionnaire during the Roaring Twenties, he saw a nation uninterested in sacrifice.[8] In response, McNutt continued to extol the virtues of America, the nobility of military service, and the need to fight pacifists and to fund a strong national defense.

These were well-worn themes in McNutt's speeches, yet two things had changed by this time. First, McNutt had honed his skills and was emerging as a particularly fine speaker. His oratory drew upon his years as an undergraduate at Indiana University, where he had majored in English and acted in plays, and from his training as a lawyer, where he had been taught to be mindful of the facts. In making his points, McNutt was "clear, forceful, and convincing, and yet so simple and direct that all could understand."[9] He worked hard at drafting and revising speeches. Once it was polished, he delivered the same address, again and again. Allen Drury, a United States Senate aide and later a novelist, heard McNutt speak in 1944 and described him as "the sort of speaker who swoops down on his sentences, lowering his head on the first half and then giving 'em the old chin on the last half."[10] McNutt's words were his script. The orator became an actor, of sorts; the platform was his stage; the podium, his prop; and the crowd, his audience.

The second change was that as national commander McNutt had integrated his ideas into a coherent train of thought. McNutt urged what he called "preparedness for peace."[11] "The burden of war," he explained, "falls upon the citizen soldier." He thus pressed for a vigorous policy of preparedness to ensure that soldiers had proper training and modern weapons. Such a program promised to reduce casualties during wartime and ward off aggressors during peacetime. "Adequate national defense is necessary to command respect," McNutt asserted.[12] To keep America fit and ready, McNutt pushed the Legion's campaign to promote civic education and praised the work of the Reserve Officers' Training Corps (ROTC) and the Civilian Military Training Camps (CMTCs). He cast preparedness as a moral struggle, with the heroes being those who had served, were serving, and would one day serve their nation. The enemies were the agitators who, under "the banner of peace," sought to destroy the "loyalty" of Americans to their armed forces. "We are not paid propagandists," McNutt affirmed, referring to his fellow Legionnaires and chiding pacifist organizations, "and we have no selfish interest."[13]

The conflicts between selfishness and service, pessimism and optimism, evil and good, were personal ones for McNutt. His speeches displayed thoughtfulness, occasional introspection, and a hint of spirituality. In one commencement address, "Service and Sacrifice," McNutt warned graduates that they would experience hardships in life—they would "reach to pluck the flower and find a thistle." Literature as well as life was replete with pessimists—Moliere, Schopenhauer, Swift, Nietzsche, and Shakespeare, who, McNutt later explained, wrote plays devoid of heroes. With respect to daily life, many graduates would find themselves forced into jobs not of their choosing and then grow "intolerably weary" with them. McNutt's answer to despair was to soldier on, in service to home, occupation, church, community, state, and nation. Almost presaging the presidential inaugural address of another former soldier—John F. Kennedy—McNutt declared: "Your question is what can I do, not what is to be done for me."[14]

The most remarkable part of this address was its religious references and literary flair. McNutt pulled from the gospel of Luke the saga of two sisters, Mary, who was content to sit at the feet of Jesus and hear his teachings, and Martha, who spent her time engaged in housework. With the help of his favorite poet, Rudyard Kipling, McNutt turned this story around by celebrating the labors of Martha over the faith of Mary. He read excerpts from an early version of Kipling's "Sons of Martha," an unabashed ode to those who toil in the world of man instead of revere the word of God:

> To these from birth is Belief forbidden;
> From these till death is relief afar,—-
> They are concerned with matters hidden;
> Under the earth line their altars are
> Lift ye the stone, or cleave the wood,
> To make a path more fair or flat,—
> So! It is black already with blood
> Some sons of Martha spilled for that!
> Meanwhile, he says, the Sons of Mary
> . . . sit at the feet, and they hear the Word—
> They know how truly the Promise runs
> They have cast their burden upon the Lord
> And—the Lord
> He lays it on Martha's Sons.

McNutt surely saw himself as a son of Martha—realistic, not overtly faithful, consumed by service, and at times underappreciated. The speaker, however, offset the subversively secular message of this verse by comparing the soldier's "unselfish service" to his nation to Christ's "divine sacrifice" at Calvary.[15]

This address highlighted the many complexities and paradoxes of Paul McNutt. McNutt, who was often distant from his mother, clearly had been influenced by her love of poetry and by her piety. Although close to his father, McNutt jabbed at him indirectly, commenting on the unhappiness of young people "forced," perhaps by their parents, into specific trades. And McNutt continued to see the world in pessimistic terms. Left to their own devices, people too often were selfish, pleasure-seeking, or just plain evil. McNutt's veneration of service proved convenient, for it allowed him to justify his past and current endeavors—student leader, soldier, professor, dean, and Legionnaire—and to point himself toward a future in politics. Labeling others as selfish also allowed

McNutt to avoid any examination of his own selfishness, that is, his pursuit of honors and offices. McNutt's configuration of the wider world left ample room for his own ambitions.

McNutt's low regard for human nature shaped his hard-headed views on foreign and defense policy. One reason he disdained pacifists was that he doubted that humans possessed sufficient goodness to achieve peace. The reality to be coped with was that "hate, fear, lust, greed and envy" in individuals filtered up to nations and their foreign policies.[16] Wary of European nations beset by hunger, bankruptcy, and jealousy of the United States, McNutt foresaw the emergence of aggressive dictatorships and urged necessary preparations. Anticipating the global crisis of the 1930s, he asked, in 1925: "Would you clean up a gang of thugs and murderers by sending peaceful citizens, unarmed, into their midst?"[17] As national commander, he stressed "the importance of making adequate provision for our national security."[18] With respect to achieving a lasting peace, McNutt saw a glimmer of hope in America's "institutions and ideals," which, if protected and preserved, could abet the "development of civilization" around the world—words that foreshadowed his imperialistic perspective about U.S. policy in the Philippines. But that was in the long term. In the short term, McNutt doubted that the American experiment could be peacefully replicated elsewhere. "We cannot reform the rest of the world by example," he wrote in 1929.[19]

Rather than reform the world, National Commander McNutt would defend America with arms. To be sure, he did not oppose international commitments and collective security arrangements for the United States. As a Democrat and a Wilsonian, he backed U.S. entrance into the League of Nations and the World Court. But by the late 1920s McNutt was not campaigning for these causes, to which the public was at best indifferent.[20] He held an even lower opinion of the Kellogg-Briand Pact, under which fifteen nations, including the United States, agreed to renounce war as an instrument of national policy except in cases of self-defense. McNutt dismissed the treaty as a "gesture."[21] "As long as individuals break promises, so will nations," he stressed. "It is a sad commentary on human nature."[22] In contrast to the toothless Kellogg-Briand Pact, he favored "any practical method," meaning an enforceable agreement, to bring about peace.[23]

In McNutt's opinion, the strengths of such agreements rested on having adequate stockpiles of weapons. In 1929, he prodded Congress to fund a set of new navy cruisers and attacked past disarmament efforts, particularly the Five Power Pact of 1922, which limited the tonnage of capital ships for the United States, Great Britain, France, Italy, and Japan. And when President Herbert

Hoover suspended the construction of three cruisers authorized by Congress, McNutt wired the president to protest. Hoover defended his decision by asserting that negotiation was the best way to reduce armaments and restore parity at sea. A small-government Republican and a Quaker, Hoover believed that more arms would lead neither to security and peace but to "burdensome expenditure" at home and suspicion and misunderstanding abroad.[24]

McNutt, in his exchange with Hoover, was offering a policy option to the president. It was a role he later would play at times with FDR, although as a member of the administration and its party. Not surprisingly, Hoover ignored McNutt, an outsider and a critic of the administration's defense policy, and went ahead with his plans for disarmament by sending a delegation to a naval conference in London in 1930. In this instance, public opinion was with the president.[25] McNutt understood as much. "It is amazing and distressing," he complained, "to discover how little the people generally know or think about matters of national defense." Too many Americans, McNutt lamented, view military policy only "in terms of the tax dollar."[26]

The debate over national defense suggested that McNutt was envisioning a larger role for the federal government in American life. He certainly was willing to use federal dollars to fund projects he deemed worthwhile, such as the rehabilitation of veterans and provisioning of their orphans and dependents. This was a major cause of the Legion, and it became McNutt's as well. The Legion's commander pressed Congress to build more hospitals for veterans. The plight of disabled veterans touched McNutt, the grandson of a Civil War veteran and the father of a sick daughter, in a most personal way.[27] In 1928 he scribbled a Christmas message to former soldiers at hospitals, praising their courage and pledging to work for them "every day of the year."[28] The note might have sounded trite, but McNutt repeatedly emphasized the needs of those who had been wounded and vowed not to rest until "every veteran disabled in the World War receives the care and award to which he is entitled."[29] One veteran who had heard McNutt speak came away impressed that he was "on the right side" of this issue.[30]

After leaving the post of national commander, McNutt continued to think about veterans, especially with respect to immediate payment of the World War I bonus. Passed in 1924, the bonus was to be paid to the heirs of each veteran upon his death or to the veteran directly after twenty years. In 1932, during the depth of the Great Depression, veterans descended upon Washington, D.C., to demand payment of the bonus at once—a position rejected by both Hoover and Roosevelt. In making his case against the bonus (and for a more extensive welfare state), FDR stated that "no person, because he wore a uniform, must thereafter be placed in a special class of beneficiaries over and above all other citizens."[31] McNutt, however, favored immediate payment of the bonus. The money, he stressed, was due to the veterans for their service, and its swift dispersal would provide relief and pump badly needed dollars into the depression-era economy.[32]

In McNutt's speeches on behalf of veterans' issues, one senses the beginnings of his embrace of the welfare state. To be certain, McNutt, as national commander, did not seek a federal answer to most problems.[33] And, as mentioned earlier, the enactment of veterans' benefits did not portend the establishment of a welfare state. Nevertheless, McNutt's concern for disabled veterans led him to back what he termed "welfare measures" to provide "adequate care and protection " for those who were "the unfortunate products of modern civilization." He praised the Massachusetts government for adopting policies to provide greater security for its poorer citizens. "The answer to the question, 'Am I my brother's keeper?'" McNutt averred, "is 'Yes.'"[34] He never forgot the contributions of the American Legion on behalf of war orphans and widows, and he lauded the organization for its "outstanding welfare accomplishments."[35] McNutt's vision was steadily widening to encompass social and economic, as well foreign and military, issues.

As national commander, McNutt was able to convey his thoughts to more people than ever before. While visiting New York, he spoke on the Kellogg-Briand Pact to a nationwide radio audience. And a newsreel carried his comments about Hoover's suspension of the cruisers. In fact, when Louise McNutt heard that her father was about to appear on film, she insisted on being wheeled to a local theater to see for herself. "She was thrilled to death clear through the show," her mother told the press.[36]

Louise could not have been happy, however, when in the spring of 1929 her parents departed for a six-week tour of the South and West, leaving her in the care of a nurse and her grandfather Timolat. On that trip, McNutt made an average of three speeches a day, in person and over the radio. McNutt's western swing was so long that the *Indiana Daily Student* heralded his return with a headline beginning "Dean McNutt Spends Quiet Day at Home."[37] It was a fleeting respite. By the end of September 1929, after the McNutts had completed another tour of Europe, Paul had traveled almost ninety-five thousand miles as national commander, much of it via airplane.[38]

The McNutts' trip to Europe in 1929 was a much bigger affair than the one they had taken two years earlier. McNutt led the delegation of Legionnaires to

Paris to dedicate the headquarters of the organization's Department of France and attend the congress of the nine-nation Allied Veterans Federation, widely known as FIDAC, Fédération Interallié des Anciens Combattants. Their itinerary also covered a large expanse of the continent—England, the Netherlands, Yugoslavia, Hungary, Austria, Italy, France, Belgium, and Germany. The ceremonial nature of this excursion, along with the leadership position occupied by McNutt, enabled the Hoosier to represent his country. "Salutes were fired in his behalf," one journalist observed. "Flags dipped for him. He knelt for his nation before the Unknown Soldiers of France and Italy."[39]

McNutt also got the chance to meet heads of government. This was not exactly a new experience for him. As state commander, he had had an audience with President Calvin Coolidge.[40] While in Europe, McNutt met with foreign leaders, including the pope and the man with whom he would one day be compared, Benito Mussolini of Italy. The encounter with Mussolini was intriguing, for Americans held contradictory views of him, as a menacing autocrat, as a competent manager of a long-divided nation, or as a tinhorn dictator with his jutting jaw and strutting strides.[41] Il Duce tested the diplomatic skill of McNutt, who earlier had attacked the Italian leader as a military threat to America and as a showoff. Meeting with Mussolini seemed to change McNutt's opinion, for he found the Italian leader to be "a very interesting man" and remembered their tête-à-tête as "one of the high lights" of his trip to Europe.[42] While in Italy, McNutt also worked to avert embarrassment when a fellow Legionnaire published an article critical of Mussolini. But in so doing, he bent quite far in the opposite direction. McNutt wrote the leader of FIDAC in Italy to express the Legion's "high regard" for Il Duce, praising his "outstanding contribution to civilization" and his "splendid accomplishments" in the area of "good government."[43]

McNutt would have been unable to travel, speak, and lead the Legion without the blessing of Indiana University. President William Lowe Bryan allowed McNutt to retain his university post and his deanship. Bryan wanted to keep McNutt happy, for he hoped to use the dean—and his influence with the Legion and with the press—to mobilize public support for IU as the state legislature reviewed its annual budget request.[44] Only after that effort came to nothing, and after McNutt had relinquished the office of national commander, did Bryan criticize his gallivanting.[45] Similar resentments had surfaced in the law school. Law professor Walter E. Treanor complained that, during McNutt's first few months leading the Legion, the dean was seldom seen around Maxwell Hall and that the law faculty had to convene on its own to handle pressing matters.[46]

McNutt also received support at home and within the Legion. To be sure, Kathleen chaffed about her oft-absent spouse. "Kathleen assures me," Paul joked, "that my next job will be that of being a good husband."[47] To mollify his wife, McNutt brought her along on many of his trips. She, in turn, remained ever dutiful, clipping from papers articles about and photographs of her husband. McNutt also enjoyed the backing of a competent staff at the Legion's headquarters, led by James F. Barton, the organization's national adjutant. At their first meeting, McNutt told Barton: "Jim, you stay here and run things and I'll go out and put on the medicine show."[48] This division of duties somewhat paralleled McNutt's relationship with Frank McHale.

With respect to the Legion as an institution, McNutt simply adapted to the organization's existing bureaucracy, traditions, and agenda rather than try to reform it. Elected without the support of the Legion's established leadership, McNutt might have tried to change the manner in which the organization selected its national commanders. But there is no reason to think that he did so. In 1933, former national commander Hanford MacNider complained to Theodore Roosevelt Jr., another former national commander, about how the Legion remained in the hands of a few "politicos" who "dictate absolutely every job in the outfit."[49] To be sure, such laments—from one Republican to another—reflect the fact that a number of Democrats, including McNutt and Louis Johnson, who served as national commander from 1932 to 1933, were rising to leadership offices within the organization.[50] Nevertheless, there was an obvious pattern to McNutt's leadership, for he preferred to work within the system. As governor of Indiana in the 1930s, he would practice the prevailing ethics of his state by forming a political machine of his own and by unapologetically utilizing a system of patronage.

Although not a reformer, McNutt was a successful national commander. According to Harry H. Woodring, a Legionnaire from Kansas and later secretary of war under FDR, McNutt's speeches made a great contribution to the organization by spreading its message and energizing its membership.[51] By the end of McNutt's term, the Legion's membership had grown by over thirty-six thousand—the largest annual increase since 1921. Meanwhile, the Legion's lobbyists, no doubt directed by Barton, had pushed some valuable legislation through Congress, including a nine-million-dollar bill to improve veterans' hospitals. As the face of the Legion, McNutt received credit for such breakthroughs. If McNutt used the organization to propel himself into a political career, as some critics later asserted, "he certainly did the Legion no harm." That was the view of Clarence A. Jackson, a former commander of the Department of Indiana, and many members agreed.[52] An Ohio Legionnaire vowed to support McNutt in any enterprise.[53] In Bloomington, Legionnaires and Rotarians had an idea of what that enterprise should be. At a meeting of both organizations held in November 1929, they nominated McNutt for president of the United States.[54]

After relinquishing his duties as national commander in October 1929, McNutt was unsure about his future. He remained sentimentally attached to Indiana University, and he often opened his home to visitors during the weekend when Indiana's football team played Purdue for the "Old Oaken Bucket."[55] Yet, he also considered a life beyond his native state. McNutt confided to a friend that he would stay at IU until the close of the spring term in 1930 but would promise nothing beyond then. "My desire is to stay in Indiana," he informed another associate. "My judgment is that I should leave."[56]

McNutt weighed a range of options. He thought about going into journalism—his "first love" as an undergraduate.[57] But he saw no opportunity to edit or run a newspaper. McNutt's old ambition, of returning to Harvard Law School as dean, was also dead, a casualty of his association with the Legion, an organization not readily allied with the Ivy League. McNutt considered going to another college, but he found few appealing offers. Kathryn McHale, the sister of Frank McHale and acting director of the American Association of University Women, had recommended him for the presidency of Goucher College, in Baltimore. But McNutt doubted that he could be happy at a women's college, since his experience had been in coeducation.[58] Thinking that McNutt might fit in at Ann Arbor, Frank McHale floated his name for the presidency at the University of Michigan. Alas, McHale's ties to the board of regents there were weak.[59] Furthermore, one regent dismissed McNutt as unfit for the position because his "principal occupation" had been leading the American Legion.[60] Michigan's board of regents never considered him as a serious candidate. Reports of McNutt forsaking Bloomington for Ann Arbor, Walter Treanor sneered, "outran the actual developments."[61]

At the same time, events within Indiana allowed McNutt to consider a career in politics. Put simply, by the middle of the 1920s, the ruling Republican Party was in a state of distress. The party had long endured a personalized form of factionalism, one seldom blemished by ideological debate. Yet it was the fire of scandal that really singed the state GOP. Warren T. McCray, governor between 1921 and 1924, resigned his office after a federal court found him guilty of mail fraud. McCray then spent three years in a federal penitentiary in Atlanta before President Hoover pardoned him in 1930. Fellow Republican Edward L. Jackson, elected governor in 1924 with the support of the Ku Klux Klan, fared little better. In 1928 he faced charges of bribery—relating to $10,000 he had once offered McCray at the behest of the Klan—and escaped conviction only because the statute of limitations had expired.[62] The journalist Harold Feightner called the 1920s the "Tragic Era" in Indiana politics, and former governor James P. Goodrich, a Republican, dismissed Jackson's administration as "a sorry mess."[63] McNutt remembered Jackson as a brainless man who spoke gibberish on the stump.[64]

Indiana Republicans groaned over the state of their party. One man proposed a housecleaning of all the "nauseating, disreputable slime" that had "besmirched" the party.[65] To that end, in 1927 an Indianapolis group launched the "New Deal Republican Movement" to end boss rule in the GOP, "cleanse" the party, and "lash the money changers from its temple."[66] The group's name, "New Deal," and some of its rhetoric, about expelling "money changers," presaged the words, if not the program, of FDR. Such talk was heard elsewhere. A minister in Indianapolis, upset over the hard times plaguing farmers as well as the shenanigans of the GOP, warned in 1928: "We mean to have this 'new deal' even if we have to turn to the Democratic Party for it."[67] As that year's election neared, other Republicans looked for a different kind of salvation from the Democrats. Harry S. New, a U.S. senator from Indiana, and Goodrich hoped that Democrats would nominate New York governor Alfred E. Smith for president. A Democratic ticket headed by Smith, a Catholic, would deliver largely Protestant Indiana into the hands of the Republicans once again.[68]

McNutt, for his part, had been tempted to run for governor in 1928. He wrote that things were so "rotten" in state government that he "prayed" for a Democratic triumph that November.[69] Hoosiers had been hearing for some time that McNutt was a possible "savior" for the Democrats. "We're going to need a Grover Cleveland awful bad in a few years," Meredith Nicholson, an Indiana author, once wrote McNutt, invoking the name of one of the Democrats' most publicly upstanding and fiscally conservative presidents, "and, you, son, are the boy I've picked to stand for things as he stood for them."[70] By the time that McNutt had completed his term as state commander of the Legion, in 1927, a boom for him to run for governor was under way. McNutt, however, begged off, citing the illness of his daughter, which had drained him of the financial means to wage a campaign. His association with the avowedly nonpartisan American Legion also precluded a run, as did the candidacy of fellow Democrat Frank C. Dailey, whom McNutt considered a "close personal" friend.[71]

McNutt had a more important reason for shunning the governorship. His father advised him to ignore the boom for governor and run instead for national commander, since Smith's candidacy "would make [it] next to impossible" to elect a Democrat to the Indiana statehouse.[72] Paul agreed. After the Democrats nominated Smith, McNutt calculated that the "strong prejudices" of "our people" meant that Smith had "little or no chance to carry Indiana" and he would drag the entire ticket down to defeat if he lost the state by more than 100,000 votes.[73] Smith did indeed lose Indiana to Hoover, by 283,000 votes. And Dailey lost the governorship to his Republican opponent, Harry G. Leslie, speaker of the Indiana House, by 44,000 votes. McNutt, meanwhile, had won the post of national commander and then cited the Legion's avoidance of electoral politics to explain why he could not campaign for Dailey that fall.[74] McNutt thus exhibited caution, guile, and selfishness, for he did nothing to help the political fortunes of a "close" friend.

The Democratic Party in Indiana was, in truth, ill positioned to take advantage of GOP woes for most of the 1920s. To be sure, during the late nineteenth and early twentieth centuries Indiana's competitive two-party system had placed the state at the center of presidential politics. Even in the Republican-dominated 1920s, Democrats scored well in local elections at the start of the decade, before economic good times set in, and in farm areas left out of the decade-long prosperity. Yet the party in Indiana, like its national counterpart, was divided over Prohibition, between the urban "wets" and rural "drys," and over whether or not to condemn the Klan, which Indiana Democrats eventually did. To make matters worse, the party's most able leaders, former Indianapolis mayor Thomas Taggart and former governor Samuel M. Ralston, were ill and aging. Rudderless, Indiana Democrats grew negative in rhetoric, denouncing high taxes and fiscal extravagance at the Republican-led statehouse; rigid in outlook, defending the party's traditional beliefs in local authority and limited government; and nostalgic in tone, as Nicholson's invocation of Cleveland suggested.[75] Claude G. Bowers, a Hoosier Democrat, journalist, and author, complained of his party's lack of "great leaders" and "fighting speeches" and of its "apologetic attitude toward the enemy" that together had led to an electoral "inferiority complex."[76]

The Great Depression changed things for Indiana Democrats in general and for McNutt in particular. After the stock market crash, as the economy sank into stagnation and widespread unemployment, the standing of the ruling Republican Party nosedived. The fortunes of Indiana's long-exiled Democrats revived in 1929, a few weeks after the crash, when the party scored well in municipal elections, especially in Indianapolis, where it elected Reginald Sullivan as mayor. Then, in the years that followed, the GOP grew bewildered over the economic slide and seemed devoid of fresh ideas to reverse it. In 1930 James E. Watson, Republican of Indiana and majority leader of the U.S. Senate, fretted that his constituents would hold him responsible for economic trends over which, he lamented, "I have no more control than I have over the tides."[77] That same year, Senator Arthur Capper of Kansas bemoaned the fact that he had "never known such gloomy prospects" for Republicans in his region, which had long been friendly toward the GOP.[78]

In this setting, McNutt showed growing interest in a political career. Early in 1930, McNutt was torn between reports that he could "get the nomination for governor or senator without much trouble," concern about the cost of any campaign, and a desire to leave academe, "forget politics," and start earning enough money to provide security for his family.[79] By April, however, he had made himself available: "If I am called upon to represent my party at the polls, I shall consider such a call."[80] A year later, McNutt was in with both feet. "I have no political aspirations except as a part of a desire to witness the regeneration of the State of Indiana," he told a supporter in 1931 before affirming that he was "anxious to do anything" in his power "to bring this about."[81]

Why enter politics? Personal ambition played a large role, of course. McNutt also came from a political family and had long found politics intriguing. Yet he was not going to run for office under unfavorable circumstances, as he revealed in 1928. And McNutt's thoughts about forgoing politics in order to earn money to support his family were not passing ones, for he would do just that near the end of his life. Thus, a career in politics had not been inevitable. What changed was the onset of the depression. McNutt, ever the realist, grasped that America was on the brink of a great crisis. "[I] have a very definite notion that the present depression may be of some years' duration," he wrote as 1929 came to a close. In the short run, McNutt, a former national commander of the Legion, worried about the effect of unemployment on "ex-service men."[82] In the long run, McNutt, the soldier who had missed the opportunity to see combat in World War I, did not want to remain on the sidelines again during a national emergency.

Which office should McNutt seek? Something statewide was the obvious choice. In 1930 Hoosiers would elect a secretary of state, a position which oversaw a fair amount of patronage, especially with respect to local branches of the state motor vehicle licensing bureau. Yet one Republican newspaper correctly predicted that the post would prove too small for McNutt, whose eye was most likely on 1932, when he might run for governor or the U.S. Senate. Moreover, with his daughter still sick, the secretary of state's salary was insufficient to maintain his household.[83] By July 1930 McNutt was inclined to wait and run for governor in 1932. Nevertheless, he faced pressure to make the 1930 race. McNutt's answer was to insist that he would perform "greater service [to the party] off the ticket," as a speaker.[84]

McNutt's best-known speech in 1930 was the keynote address he made to the Democratic state convention at Cadle Tabernacle in Indianapolis. Over the years, he had spoken before law students, civic groups, and Legion audiences but seldom at partisan gatherings. With that in mind, R. Earl Peters, chair of the Indiana Democratic Party, arranged for McNutt's debut at the state convention, and he made the most of the opportunity. "We have met to prepare for a change of government," McNutt told his fellow Democrats, "and for its restoration to the people." He thundered against "the revelry and evil of the Harding regime, the inaction of the Coolidge administration and the vacillation and ineffectiveness of the Hoover experiment," which had left America in a state of "leaderless uncertainty" and "economic chaos." Indiana Republicans caught his wrath as well. McNutt observed that the poet William Herschell had written "Ain't God Good to Indiana" in 1919, before McCray, Jackson, and the disgraced Klan leader D. C. Stephenson had "appeared on the scene." He contrasted such leadership with that of his party, which bore "the impregnable armor of Thomas Jefferson," "the efficient sword of Andrew Jackson," "the rugged honesty of Grover Cleveland," and "the ideals of Woodrow Wilson." Under the banner of these leaders, the Democratic Party, he closed, "moves on to victory."[85]

The audience was enthralled. "Cadle Tabernacle reverberated with noise," the *Goshen* (IN) *Democrat* reported, "as delegates cheered McNutt to echo."[86] "A wonder," "splendid," and "excellent" were among the accolades the address received.[87] Fellow Democrat Wendell L. Willkie, McNutt's IU classmate who was practicing law in New York City, sent along his congratulations.[88] In one speech, McNutt had begun to reverse the "inferiority complex" that had afflicted Hoosier Democrats. "I have seen strong men weep," one journalist recalled, "from the mere memory of that keynote address."[89] Even Republicans conceded that

McNutt had triumphed. One of McNutt's Republican friends read the address and joshed: "I am glad I did not hear you deliver it, for I fear you would have converted me on the spot."[90] That compliment revealed much about Indiana politics, for partisanship did not preclude rapport across party lines.

The keynote address underscored the fact that McNutt was no ordinary speaker—and no typical Democrat. To be sure, he had paid homage to the Democratic Party for adhering to traditional ideals—respecting the limitations of government power, lodging authority closest to those governed, and curtailing special privileges. But, as will be shown, Paul McNutt, like FDR, was no hidebound Democrat, fearful of employing the instruments of government to effect reform at home and a safer world abroad. Both men often annoyed conservatives within their party by promoting an active state and courting voters across party lines. Indeed, near the end of his speech to the state convention, McNutt invited "independent voters," "Lincoln Republicans," and "[Theodore] Roosevelt Republicans" to link arms with Democrats "to preserve free institutions and popular government."[91]

Such an appeal doubtless stemmed from McNutt's service in the Legion, where he had become familiar with members of both political parties, and it had a powerful effect. The journalist Harold Feightner conjectured that the typical Indiana Legionnaire, regardless of party, studied McNutt, dubbed him a "spectacular" political talent, and then decided that "we got something to fight for," meaning the election of their fellow Legionnaire to office.[92] "Few men, Paul," a Republican friend of McNutt's told him, "are able to command the respect of the opposition . . . as you do."[93] McNutt thus sought a place among his fellow Democrats and one above—or beyond—them as well.

All this signaled that McNutt was no run-of-the-mill politician. He certainly did not look like one, with his lean, lanky frame, chiseled face, dark eyes, and graying hair. And yet, he had mastered the basics as well as any seasoned politician, particularly the importance of good timing, strategic alliances, and able lieutenants. McNutt earlier had backed Earl Peters to chair the state Democratic Party, and after Peters won, by one vote, he asked McNutt to keynote the party's 1930 convention. Facing a factionalized party with a host of aspirants for secretary of state, McNutt surveyed the field and endorsed the eventual nominee, Frank Mayr Jr. of South Bend. His alliances with Peters and Mayr, as we will see, did not last. But he made up for that by building a loyal following among young Democrats, most of them Legionnaires. They included Frank McHale; Pleas E. Greenlee, a newspaper manager who was state adjutant for the Legion; and Bowman Elder, treasurer of the Indiana Legion. McNutt also had the support of John W. Wheeler, a Republican who had boosted his bid for national commander; Douglas I. McKay of New York, a railroad car executive and McNutt's closest confidant outside of Indiana; and Virgil Simmons, an ally of Earl Peters and the only non-Legionnaire in McNutt's circle. These men advised McNutt, worked to advance his fortunes, and, along the way, annoyed older Democrats in Indiana, who had been in the political wilderness for a long time and were becoming uneasy with McNutt's rapid ascent.[94]

McNutt was fast becoming his state's most impressive leader. Peters named him to the advisory committee of the Indiana Democratic Party, welcomed his advice, and booked him as a speaker for the home stretch of the 1930 fall campaign. Late in October, a large, animated crowd in Fort Wayne greeted McNutt's remarks and his forecast of a Democratic victory with a "prolonged applause."[95] One man, who claimed to have heard some of the greatest political orators of the recent past, from William Jennings Bryan to Robert M. La Follette to Al Smith, beamed that McNutt had given "the best campaign speech I ever heard."[96] Looking back later, former mayor Reginald Sullivan of Indianapolis remembered McNutt as "the leading orator of Indiana."[97]

The more McNutt excelled on the stump, the more the opposition tried to knock him off it. For example, after McNutt lambasted the high taxes under Republican rule, a member of the GOP's state committee traveled to Bloomington to pay the final installment on his own annual tax bill.[98] (One newspaper dismissed this stunt as "peanut politics" designed to shift attention from "the real issues of the campaign."[99]) Another Republican protest, that McNutt had been using his position at IU for partisan purposes, carried a bit more bite. "Is Indiana University to be sacrificed to the burning ambition of Prof. Paul McNutt?" asked the *Oxford Gazette,* a GOP paper.[100] Governor Leslie, sensing an opening, talked about withholding funding from IU if these speeches continued. Unaccustomed to this type of criticism, McNutt fumed about "a few blind, unfair partisans" who questioned his integrity. In the end, he asserted his right to discuss the "official" record of the state government, and the matter dropped.[101]

McNutt, who saw and heard the crowds, expected a "sweeping Democratic victory."[102] That happened. The Democrats regained the Indiana House with a margin of 75 seats to 25 for the GOP, and they carried ten of the Hoosier State's thirteen congressional districts, reversing the distribution of seats from before the election. Mayr prevailed in his race for secretary of state.[103] McHale credited McNutt with the "great landslide," and many people agreed.[104] "Congratulations on the 'clean sweep,'" one man wrote him. "It must be nice to win and also have your taxes paid!"[105] A resident of Logansport, Indiana, went even further: because of his part in the victory, he told McNutt, "You are entitled to anything you want within the gift of the Democrats in Indiana."[106]

What McNutt wanted was the sure thing and a shot at something bigger. The sure thing was nomination to statewide office in 1932, and his preference was for the governorship. He reached his decision after consulting with his advisers, all of whom save Greenlee favored a race for governor.[107] McKay insisted the Senate was "a hotbed of feuds" while the governorship was the place to demonstrate "executive talent," solve problems, gain experience working with a legislature, and become both "efficient and popular"—as Al Smith had done. McKay had another reason for invoking the name of the former governor of New York. He believed that McNutt, a Protestant, was better positioned than Smith, a Catholic, to claim the White House for the Democrats.[108]

Discussions of the presidency extended beyond the McNutt circle. A number of Hoosiers complimented McNutt for his success in 1930 campaign by predicting his ascent beyond Indiana. Yet they wanted McNutt to serve first as governor, so that he might "clean up" the state's government and "redeem Indiana from sixteen years of gross mis-rule."[109] Outside Indiana, his boosters were very often Legionnaires.[110] The most serious offer of support for a presidential bid came from Charles L. Wilson, an old army buddy of McNutt's and a member of the Oklahoma state highway commission. Wilson claimed to represent a group of "influential Democrats in Oklahoma" who wanted McNutt to be the party's standard-bearer in 1932. He asked McNutt for permission "to start a boom at the proper time" and pledged "a considerable amount of money" toward any campaign for the presidential nomination.[111] Such encouragement, originating in another state's party, intrigued McNutt, who sent Wilson's letters to McKay for consideration.[112]

McNutt was open to a spot on the national ticket in 1932. The 1930 elections, McHale told him, had made Governor Franklin D. Roosevelt, reelected by a landslide in New York, the "undisputed" front-runner among Democrats— with McNutt occupying "second place." McHale advised his friend to start "making your connections along that line, as destiny seems to have picked you for this place."[113] It was not clear, however, whether McHale was thinking of the party's presidential or vice-presidential nomination. In any case, McNutt was determined to keep his options open. When his brain trust convened in Indianapolis late in 1930, its members recommended that McNutt curtail his out-of-state speaking, concentrate on winning office in Indiana, and play down talk about a place on the national ticket, lest he become a target for rival presidential campaigns. McNutt agreed. The strategy thus became one of watchful waiting.[114] McNutt continued to monitor political developments within and without Indiana.[115] Although he declined an invitation to visit Oklahoma, he encouraged Wilson to share intelligence, on a "confidential" basis, regarding presidential politics in the Sooner State.[116]

Why, one might ask, did McNutt and his followers think that they could play in the big leagues of presidential politics when their man had never won elected office? In part, they were overconfident. McNutt had immense talents, and he had never failed to gain whatever he sought. He won the Legion post against large odds, and it had turned him into a national figure and his aides into kingmakers of a sort. The 1930 elections had helped to revive the Hoosier Democratic Party and make McNutt its face. Indiana's long history of competitive politics and national party candidates was another factor. If Virginia, Ohio, and New York vied for the title "mother of presidents," Indiana alone was known as the "mother of vice presidents."[117] Between 1868 and 1916, the two major parties had nominated a Hoosier for vice president on nine separate occasions.[118] Of course, McHale's comment, about McNutt running just behind FDR, was exaggerated. Yet McNutt and his team could reason that their man was doing little more than wait, watch, and dream about a place on the ticket—for the time being.

In 1931 McNutt kept to his script. He tended his campaign for governor, which began "very well" and unfolded, in his view, in an "entirely satisfactory" fashion.[119] The opposition to McNutt's nomination was weak. It originated in the office of the secretary of state, Mayr, and it included the remnants of the Democratic Party machine in South Bend, Mayr's hometown. McHale worried about this clique and pressed McNutt to quash it.[120] Yet McNutt saw no threat from Mayr, an erratic candidate who sometimes spoke well and at other times was "a complete flop."[121] McNutt, in contrast, enjoyed the backing of nine out of thirteen district party chairs in the state, and he ran well in the polls, however rudimentary. The news on the gubernatorial front was good, so much so that McNutt thought that he could be nominated by acclamation.[122]

For McNutt, developments at the national level during 1931 proved equally "satisfactory." To be sure, FDR was the favorite for the Democratic presidential nod, and his campaign was run by two shrewd strategists, Louis McHenry

Howe, who managed it from New York, and James Aloysius Farley, who traveled about the country hunting for convention delegates. But the bad news came in threes for Roosevelt's forces. First, the rules of the Democratic Party stipulated that a nominee for president had to gain the votes of two-thirds of the delegates to the national convention, and FDR was short of that number. Second, Roosevelt did not have the undivided support of his own state delegation, since former governor Smith remained popular in New York. Lastly, FDR faced competition for the nomination. Besides Smith, other candidates included Governor Albert C. Ritchie of Maryland; Speaker of the House James Nance Garner of Texas; Governor William H. "Alfalfa Bill" Murray of Oklahoma; the industrialist Owen D. Young; Melvin A. Traylor, a banker from Chicago; and former secretary of war Newton D. Baker, who was available as a compromise choice. There also were several state-level leaders—or "favorite sons"—such as Governors Harry F. Byrd of Virginia and George H. White of Ohio, and a few dark horses, including former secretary of the treasury William Gibbs McAdoo—and McNutt. The field made for a fluid contest that seemed headed for a deadlocked, multi-ballot convention, something endured by the Democrats in 1912, 1920, and 1924—and by the American Legion in 1928.[123]

On the surface, McNutt remained aloof from presidential politics. Peters and McKay kept him abreast of developments surrounding Roosevelt's campaign.[124] In June 1931, when FDR visited Indiana to attend the national governors' conference, he met McNutt by chance, and the two men engaged in a rather "lengthy discussion." Yet, when quizzed by reporters on "the feeling in Indiana toward Roosevelt," McNutt replied, circumspectly, that the New York governor "had many friends in this state" but that it was "too early to say" whom Indiana would support next year.[125]

Thereafter, the McNutt forces reckoned that FDR might be faltering. After the governors' conference, Roosevelt, Ritchie, and other Democratic governors visited the resort town of French Lick, a traditional getaway for Hoosier Democrats. McNutt was more impressed by Roosevelt, whose rooms were "crowded," than by Ritchie, whom the press and the other politicians ignored.[126] But Earl Peters spoke with FDR and learned of his weaknesses—his resentment of "persistent talk about his physical infirmities," the opposition of John J. Raskob, chair of the Democratic National Committee, to his candidacy, and the "deep seated" divisions in the Democratic Party of New York. Peters saw an opening for "some Democrat, not now prominently mentioned," to emerge as a "strong contender for the presidential nomination." Believing McNutt to be that Democrat, Peters wanted him to keynote the following year's national convention. Given the chance to address the party, McNutt, he predicted, might be able to replicate the feat of William Jennings Bryan at the 1896 convention, that is, to electrify delegates with a "Cross of Gold"–style speech and stampede his way to the nomination.[127]

Meanwhile, Roosevelt's campaign, strong in the South and West but needing delegates in the Midwest, courted Indiana. In August 1931, James Farley came to Indianapolis to meet with state Democrats, including McNutt. But nothing of note came of the visit, for Farley knew little of McNutt (he had referred to him as "Colonel McNaught") and the two men did not speak directly.[128] Nevertheless, McNutt had friends—Legionnaires, presumably—in Georgia, where FDR lived for part of the year, who were talking him up to Roosevelt and Farley. These Georgians pressed McNutt to accept the vice presidency on a ticket headed by FDR. The Hoosier seemed unimpressed, replying that "the situation would take care of itself."[129] To get a better measure of McNutt, Roosevelt invited him to his home at Hyde Park, New York, where the two men had a "three hour interview" in December 1931. What they discussed is unknown, and McNutt would not bargain until "the question of leadership in Indiana" was settled.[130] Such coyness may have been designed to force Roosevelt to endorse McNutt's nomination for governor, while simultaneously keeping alive the Hoosier's hopes for a spot on the national ticket.

With so much going their way, the McNutt forces grew confident about events inside and outside of Indiana. After McNutt declared his candidacy for governor early in 1932, Frank McHale and Pleas Greenlee worked to form McNutt for Governor clubs. Gradually, Mayr's campaign petered out. In the May primary, delegates loyal to McNutt captured 1,181 out of 1,559 seats at the convention. Willkie, meanwhile, advised McNutt to cultivate Governor White of Ohio, whom he had known from living in Akron. Willkie suggested a tethering of some sort—McNutt's ambition and White's wealth—as the convention approached.[131] Rumors of other alliances circulated. McNutt's association with Charles Wilson of Oklahoma, along with the visit of Alfalfa Bill Murray to Indianapolis, sparked talk of a Murray-McNutt ticket.[132] Furthermore, after dropping his presidential bid, Melvin Traylor invited McNutt and Peters to come to Chicago so that they might search "the middle west for possibilities" at the convention.[133] Meanwhile, FDR remained short of the number of delegates required to win the nomination. Partly for that reason, Mary W. Dewson, head of the women's division of New York's Democratic Party, wrote to remind Mc-

Nutt that "sentiment in Indiana is very strong" for Roosevelt and to urge him to send to Chicago a delegation instructed to back FDR.[134]

Dewson was more deferential to the will of rank-and-file Democrats in Indiana than was McNutt. Polls hinted that a majority of the state's Democrats supported FDR for the nomination. Earl Peters, more than other McNutt boosters, saw the handwriting on the wall and discreetly joined the Roosevelt forces in Indiana.[135] But McNutt was defiant. Farley, on the eve of the Indiana state convention, wrote him to express the "hope" that Indiana would instruct its delegates to vote for Roosevelt.[136] To make that a reality, Farley dangled carrots before McNutt, including the vice-presidential nomination. (Roosevelt's team, it should be stressed, had made "at least a half a dozen" such offers to other Democrats.)[137] McNutt declined, for he regarded these overtures as acts of desperation by Roosevelt's managers. "Indiana is very important to them," McNutt wrote McKay. "All of this makes our position stronger."[138] Frank McHale and Bowman Elder concurred, prompting Robert E. Proctor of Elkhart, the leader of FDR's campaign in Indiana, to ask them: "What kind of meat do you fellows eat that makes you so strong?"[139]

McNutt's team subsisted on youthful energy, momentum, deals, and even threats. McNutt, McHale, Elder, and Greenlee ran, for Indiana, a new type of gubernatorial campaign revolving around McNutt for Governor clubs, established outside of the party, to mobilize independents, Republicans, and Democrats. Such a strategy, which did not discount the work of party committees, still irritated older Democrats.[140] Long-serving Democratic chieftains held a bifurcated view of these newcomers, seeing them as "engines of party victory" on the one hand and as "politically ambitious veterans" challenging "the party's established order" on the other.[141] In time, the Legionnaires who had infiltrated the party became known disdainfully as the "Boy Scouts."[142] Nevertheless, at the state convention in June 1932, McHale and company had the organization and votes to nominate McNutt for governor. The boy scouts then performed "good deeds" toward party harmony by accepting Frederick Van Nuys, an older Democrat, as their nominee for the U.S. Senate and Mayr for another term as secretary of state. (Later on they settled scores with those who had fraternized with Mayr.)[143] With respect to the national convention, however, they brooked no compromise. When Proctor pushed for a delegation instructed to vote for FDR, McHale warned that he had the votes to block him. In the end, the thirty-vote Indiana delegation headed to Chicago uninstructed.[144]

The McNutt forces arrived in Chicago filled with anticipation. McHale and Elder hoped to deadlock the convention and secure the presidential nomination for McNutt on a later ballot, in an encore of the Legion's convention three years earlier. According to Claude R. Wickard, another Hoosier Democrat, McHale was "undoubtedly planning all the time to elect Paul McNutt President of the United States, way back [in 1932]."[145] To that end, the McNutt forces rallied behind a stalking horse, Newton Baker, whom McNutt could support earnestly as a fellow internationalist and supporter of the League of Nations and World Court. Supporting Baker carried another reward, an endorsement of McNutt's gubernatorial bid by the *Indianapolis Times*. Roy W. Howard, co-owner of the Scripps-Howard chain of newspapers and publisher of the *Times*, had settled on Baker as his candidate, and he vowed to back McNutt for governor if the Indiana delegation fell in behind Baker.[146] As the deal fell into place, McHale observed that Indiana was now in a good "strategic position."[147] To maintain it, he exhorted every Hoosier delegate to be a "ball player" and to stick with his plan. Those who resisted were branded "enemies."[148]

At the convention, McNutt, McHale, and company opposed Roosevelt at almost every turn. They held the Hoosier delegation together to cast three votes against FDR-backed motions: the election of Senator Thomas J. Walsh as the convention's permanent chairman and the seating of two contested pro-Roosevelt delegations, one from Minnesota and the other from Louisiana. Alas, to the Hoosiers' chagrin, the Roosevelt forces prevailed on each vote. Still, the FDR campaign remained short of the two-thirds majority (770 votes) needed to claim the presidential nomination. In the balloting for president, Roosevelt started out well, with 667¾ votes on the first ballot. But his total increased only slightly, to 677¾ and 685¾ votes on the second and third ballots, respectively. The thirty-vote Indiana delegation held firm, giving New York's governor just fourteen votes on the first ballot and sixteen votes on both the second and third ballots. Whenever Proctor tried to scare up added votes for FDR among the Hoosiers, "he found that the leaders of Paul V. McNutt's group had preceded him."[149] With respect to Roosevelt, one of McNutt's allies told Proctor flat out: "We have him stopped."[150] McNutt himself called FDR's showing on the third ballot "disappointing."[151] "The Indiana delegation is performing very well," Roy Howard wrote a friend, as he anticipated "Baker's ultimate nomination."[152] After the third ballot, Roosevelt telephoned Baker to declare the convention "a jam" and to predict that it eventually "will turn to you."[153]

That never happened, thanks to a dramatic switch. The prospect of Baker's nomination alarmed both the newspaper magnate William Randolph Hearst, who hated Baker for his past embrace of internationalism and who had influence over the California delegation, and Speaker of the House Garner, Hearst's ally and the head of the Texas contingent. To stop Baker, Hearst and Garner agreed to swing their states behind FDR on the fourth ballot. After California announced its shift, Illinois and Indiana also switched to Roosevelt on the fourth ballot. Mayor Anton Cermak of Chicago, a leader of the "stop Roosevelt" movement rose to announce that the combined eighty-eight votes of his state and Indiana were now for FDR.[154]As Cermak addressed the convention, McHale stood "on a chair with a spotlight on him, holding the Indiana banner." Afterward, McHale approached a microphone and proclaimed: "Indiana, thirty votes for Roosevelt."[155] He and Cermak apparently had come to an understanding, to climb aboard the New York governor's bandwagon if his nomination looked certain.

For the Roosevelt forces, California and Texas had saved the day and, for Farley, the shift of Illinois and Indiana was a case of too little, too late. Partly as a result, Garner gained the nomination for vice president while McNutt earned nothing, save "a lifetime's animosity from Farley for his refusal to cooperate."[156] With respect to Indiana, Farley had predicted, publicly, that the Hoosier State would give FDR twenty of its votes.[157] That did not happen until the fourth ballot. Farley's frustration would harden into contempt for McNutt, whom he privately assailed as "the 'platinum blond' S.O.B. from Indiana."[158] By the late 1930s, knowledge of the Farley-McNutt antagonism became so widespread within the Democratic Party that it threatened to undermine McNutt's bid for the White House in 1940. Farley by that point had numerous friends nationwide for he had served as chair of the Democratic National Committee and as FDR's postmaster general between 1933 and 1940.[159]

Partly to end the feud, and to bolster his friend's prospects for 1940, McHale later tried to rearrange the events of the 1932 convention so as to lessen Indiana's resistance to FDR's nomination. In 1939 McHale spread the word that, seven years earlier, Illinois and Indiana had agreed to shift to Roosevelt on the third, not the fourth, ballot—before Texas and California had done so. But the roll call on the third ballot had occurred in a near-empty gallery, early in the morning, and as a result, delegates from Illinois and Indiana delayed their change until the next ballot, when a packed house would be on hand to cheer the party's nominee.[160] Although intriguing, this story ignored the fact that Cermak had decided to embrace FDR *following* the third ballot, *after* he learned that California and Texas were switching to Roosevelt. Even as the fourth ballot began, the mayor continued to thwart FDR, including packing the galleries with Smith supporters who initiated a "prolonged booing" of pro-Roosevelt delegates.[161]

If McHale was telling the truth and Indiana had wanted to switch to FDR on the third ballot, then the only way to reconcile that claim with the actions of Chicago's mayor is to say that Cermak had double-crossed McHale.

The 1932 Democratic National Convention showed that, while McNutt was starting to emerge as a prominent figure within his party, he still had a lot to learn about national politics. To be sure, McNutt showed some guile, such as when he declined to be a delegate to the convention so that he might remain aloof from any compromises, deals, or hurt feelings that might emerge from the proceedings. Yet he made two large mistakes. First, he put too much trust in the judgment of McHale, who had no experience running a presidential campaign during a national party convention. Second, McNutt participated overtly in the "Stop Roosevelt" effort.[162] Frank C. Walker, the chair of the Democratic National Committee during the early 1940s, recalled McNutt as being "strong and firm" in his allegiance to the anti-Roosevelt movement in 1932.[163] FDR remembered such intransigence as well. "Years later," the historian Donald A. Ritchie has written, "Franklin Roosevelt had a sure measure for judging a politician's reliability: 'Was he with us B.C.?' he would ask, meaning 'before Chicago.'"[164] In 1944 the president told Vice President Henry A. Wallace that in 1932 "he had to make a deal either with McNutt or Garner."[165] It was no choice. Garner and Hearst commanded more votes and were moving toward FDR for reasons of their own.

After Roosevelt won the presidency, McNutt was not entirely left in the cold. But he had to work hard to win Roosevelt's confidence and to counteract the impression, fanned by Farley, that he was an arrogant, selfish young man. He never fully succeeded on either count. The most troubling trait that the 1932 convention revealed about McNutt was his reluctance to accept responsibility for his own mistakes. To one booster, he wrote, cryptically and somewhat conspiratorially, that at Chicago "the die was cast before the convention assembled."[166]

As 1932 came to an end, McNutt had more reason to look forward than backward. The Democratic nomination for governor was his, and as the depression worsened in Indiana, his election prospects brightened. In describing the economic crisis, one Hoosier paraphrased James Whitcomb Riley, Indiana's most famous poet: "The frost is on the Pumpkins; And the corn is in the shock; The farmer is on forced vacation; And his farm is in the hock."[167] As the state's revenues plummeted and the slashing of workers' wages became drastic, former governor Goodrich worried about the "immediate future" of his GOP.[168] Senator Watson, a Republican facing reelection in 1932, wrote pessimistically about a "muddled and tumultuous situation in Indiana."[169] The fortunes of the Hoosier Democratic Party were exactly the opposite. In August 1932, one Democratic newspaper ran a mock advertisement making fun of the Republicans' decline: "Public sale—closing out sale of the Grand Old Party." Scheduled for election day, this auction featured such GOP "stock" as "one moss-grown platform," "fourteen million moonshine stills," and "eleven million Dinner Pails. All Empty."[170] McNutt's hometown newspaper got into the act, lampooning "Hoo-Hoo-Hoo" Hoover as the "rich old Daddy" of a million hungry men.[171]

McNutt ran a spirited campaign. In his first radio address, McNutt paid respects to his party's traditional ideals of "frugality in government." Yet he also vowed to run an active administration in Indianapolis, to "reestablish confidence in government" and "to make it a useful instrument rather than a burden" to citizens. He pledged tax reform—limitations on property taxes and passage of a state income tax—"the strictest economy consistent with proper transaction of public business," tighter regulation of utilities, revision of banking laws, relief for farmers and wage earners, and proper care of the aged. To knit together his agenda, McNutt adopted the mantle of change à la FDR: "I pledge myself to a new deal for the people of Indiana."[172]

During the fall campaign, McNutt used his varied talents, and his talented aides, to achieve his ends. A quick study, McNutt worked hard, and gained a firm grasp on state issues.[173] The transition from Legion leader to Indiana politician was not always easy—McNutt spoke about "military preparedness" during the early part of the campaign.[174] But he adjusted, aided by a capable staff. Pleas Greenlee oversaw the McNutt clubs and served as campaign secretary; Bowman Elder collected the campaign contributions; and Frank McHale managed the entire enterprise. Other McNutt acolytes performed needed, sometimes thankless, tasks. At Indiana University, Ward G. Biddle, who ran the bookstore, and Herman B Wells, an up-and-coming instructor of economics, jumped into the McNutt campaign headfirst by soliciting contributions from Democratic employees at the university.[175] Wells, who later became president of Indiana University, even shared with McNutt a bit of gossip that he had collected—what it involved remains unclear—to use against the opposition in "a little mudslinging."[176] Utilizing IU employees for partisan purposes underscored McNutt's ruthless side. Yet recruiting and relying on competent subordinates such as Biddle and Wells also was quintessentially McNutt.

McNutt's campaign drew interest beyond Indiana. The *Providence* (RI) *Journal* sent a reporter to Indiana to cover the youthful dean-Legionnaire-Democrat. This correspondent observed that McNutt was engaging in a new manner of campaigning by making the candidate, rather than the party and its symbols, the star attraction. When giving a speech, McNutt arrived at his venue, often at the last moment and accompanied by a Legion band. He spoke and retired immediately afterward, spending no time handshaking or backslapping.[177] It was a style of speaking that McNutt had started to develop as a professor, when he gave his lectures and exited the classroom rather than remain behind to talk with students. It coincided with McNutt's desire to picture himself as above routine party politics, an effort paralleled by the McNutt for Governor clubs, which recruited independents, Republicans, and Democrats. In addition, the atmosphere surrounding a McNutt speech reflected the candidate's habits and persona, or what one aide dubbed his "elegant attitude" and his "remoteness."[178] Such aloofness did not hurt McNutt because "even earthy Hoosiers were convinced that this man was above the average politician in ability."[179]

Meanwhile, Indiana Republicans fought an uphill battle against McNutt. To broaden its base, the GOP adopted a platform with a "wet" plank and then nominated for governor a Legionnaire, Raymond S. Springer—the first commander of the Department of Indiana. But appeals to opponents of Prohibition and to veterans did little to boost the GOP during economic hard times, and McNutt remained upbeat about his chances. Springer "campaigned vigorously but not too effectively" on a program that stressed tax relief and economy in government.[180] Even fair-minded reporters tended to diminish the Republican candidate's importance. As the campaign drew to a close, Feightner, writing in the *New York Times,* contrasted McNutt, a new guard Democrat who hailed from academe and the American Legion, with another statewide candidate, incumbent senator Jim Watson, a partisan wheelhorse and steadfast old guard Republican. Feightner justified his comparison of McNutt with Watson, and not with Springer, on the grounds that both McNutt, a former commander of the Legion, and Watson, the majority leader of the U.S. Senate, were "nationally known figures."[181]

By October, an increasingly desperate GOP went on the offensive against McNutt. Responding to requests from Indiana, two members of President Hoover's staff asked Secretary of War Patrick J. Hurley to furnish a copy of McNutt's military record.[182] The attack went nowhere; the one-page, single-spaced statement produced by Hurley showed that McNutt had served the military in several capacities, from his training activities during World War I to his postwar duties with the reserves. Thereafter, Republicans could only mutter about McNutt's military service—that he was the "soldier who never fired a gun"—and do so in the softest tones, because Springer had not fought in Europe either.[183] The GOP attacked other aspects of McNutt's past as well. Newspaper broadsides recounted the Temple Tours affair from his days leading the Indiana Legion, portrayed him as a spendthrift, and cast him as a flip-flopper for drafting the state's weak statute on public utilities in 1929 and then urging stricter regulation for utilities in 1932. More ominously, some Republicans alleged that he was sympathetic to the Ku Klux Klan. McNutt sometimes answered the attacks. For example, he explained that no candidate in cahoots with the Klan would have selected a Catholic, McHale, to manage his campaign.[184] Otherwise, he simply gave speeches and waited for victory.

Indiana Democrats prevailed in an unprecedented landslide. McNutt won fifty-five percent of the vote—a record for a gubernatorial candidate—and walloped Springer by 192,000 votes, while FDR crushed Hoover by 185,000 votes in the Hoosier State. The Democrats took all twelve of Indiana's congressional seats, and the incumbent senator, Watson, lost to his Democratic challenger, Van Nuys, by 208,000 votes. The results for the Indiana General Assembly were just as lopsided. When the legislature convened in 1933, Democrats would outnumber Republicans in the Senate by a margin of forty-three to seven and in the House by a count of ninety-one to nine. One Republican, writing of the political scene following the election, thought that the "present leadership" of the GOP had "lost, and merited the loss, of the confidence of the country." He did not expect the Democrats "to do much better" but predicted they "can do no worse."[185] McNutt thus received his chance to lead.

# 6

## A NEW DEAL FOR INDIANA
## (1933–1934)

THE INAUGURATION OF PAUL V. McNUTT as governor of Indiana, on January 9, 1933, was an occasion brimming with pomp and circumstance, with promises of change and renewal. The *Indiana Daily Student* dubbed it "the most colorful and elaborate inaugural ceremony" in two decades.[1] Front and center was the American Legion, with a band attired in Kelly green uniforms playing in tribute to its former national commander. Spectators at this inauguration could purchase army-style medallions featuring McNutt's portrait. In a nod, perhaps, to the incoming governor's literary sensibilities, Meredith Nicholson, the best-selling novelist and a lifelong Democrat, officiated at the inaugural ceremony. And, in an apparent swipe against the Ku Klux Klan, a Catholic priest delivered the benediction.[2]

The festivities commenced with a blare of trumpets by the National Guard and a presentation of the colors of Bloomington's Burton Woolery Post, which McNutt once had commanded, and of the 366th Field Artillery Reserves, in which McNutt served as a colonel. A "piercing wind" ripped through decorations as a drum cohort paced along Senate Avenue to keep warm.[3] At noon, spectators saw their governor—tall, slim, erect, and attired in a morning coat and a wing-tipped collar—take his official oath. McNutt's intonation of "I do," at the end of his oath, struck one reporter as "firm."[4] "Picturesque" was how the *Indianapolis News*, a Republican newspaper, described the ceremony.[5] The day impressed former governor James P. Goodrich, a Republican, who wrote: "McNutt inaugurated Governor with a lot of fuss & feathers for a Democrat."[6]

In his inaugural address, McNutt managed to sound both realistic and hopeful. He acknowledged an economic crisis "as grim and as real as any war" and called on the "unselfish service, energy, intelligence and solidarity" of Hoosiers to meet the challenges ahead, as they had during the First World War. Yet the governor was no strong believer in human virtue, or that the people would sacrifice and serve as the state needed them to. He warned of "those among us who are afraid, who listen to the prophets of evil" predicting the end of democracy. McNutt shrugged aside such doubts as he pledged to prove "that government may be a great instrument of human progress." By invoking the analogy of war, admonishing against fear, pledging action, vowing to fight selfishness, and voicing optimism about the capabilities of government, McNutt's speech presaged Franklin D. Roosevelt's inaugural address two months later.

McNutt's address also rang with the Roosevelt-like promise that he had made during his campaign, to effect a new deal for Indiana. To be sure, the governor, like any traditional-minded Democrat, vowed "to lower the cost of government and simplify its operations," "to reduce and redistribute the burden of taxes," and "to remove special privilege from the seats of power." But McNutt went further by promising to restore "economic equilibrium," to maintain "an adequate system of public education," and, "to provide food, clothing, and shelter, for the destitute, the aged, and the infirm." In other words, he would use the powers of the state's government to provide Hoosiers with a greater sense of security—or safety—from economic hardships. McNutt's commitment to such wide-ranging assistance was highly pragmatic. "Hungry people," he noted, "have been in the vanguard of every revolt against the established order."[7] The new governor, for his part, would seek to reform, not to overturn, his state's political and economic system.

The contrast between an enlightened reform agenda on the one hand and hard-headed realism—even cynicism—about human nature on the other marked McNutt's governorship. McNutt became the architect of Indiana's welfare state, proposing far-reaching legislation two months before the New Deal came into existence, and of its modern structure of government, five years before FDR secured a reorganization program of his own. Indiana's version of the "New Deal" consisted of what could be called the "Five Rs": Revenue, Reorganization, Relief, Reform, and, later on, Recovery. Important as these changes were, McNutt also fashioned a political machine around alcohol licenses, patronage jobs, and campaign contributions from state employees for a brand-new organization, the Hoosier Democratic Club. During his first two years in office, he emerged as a leader who was powerful and polarizing.

Preparations for McNutt's governorship began shortly after his election. The weeks following the election of 1932 were a joyous time for the McNutt family. Paul's parents were proud of his triumph, especially his father, John C. McNutt, who was a longtime Democrat and periodic candidate for political office. Louise McNutt was another booster of Paul; in 1932 she had pinned McNutt for Governor buttons on guests visiting her father's house. But the prospect of leaving her school and friends dampened Louise's joy about moving to Indianapolis. Kathleen McNutt, who never embraced the role of political wife, also felt a "very keen regret" at the thought of leaving Bloomington.[8] McNutt exhibited no such thoughts, for his work at Indiana University (IU) was over, morale at the law school was good, and he was ready to move on.[9]

In staffing his inner circle, the new governor looked outside of academe. He tapped veterans of his election campaign, men who had "learned their political ABCs" in the American Legion.[10] Pleas Greenlee, who had run the McNutt for Governor clubs, became his executive secretary and "patronage dispenser."[11] Bowman Elder, who had handled the campaign's finances, served as treasurer the Hoosier Democratic Club, which was headed by Virgil M. Simmons, one of the few non-Legionnaires in McNutt's coterie. The governor's most trusted adviser was Frank McHale, now a lawyer in Indianapolis. While McHale held no formal position in McNutt's administration, he emerged as the governor's "yes and no" man, the one who made sure staff members and legislators carried out the new governor's orders. McNutt's inner circle would contract and expand over time. R. Earl Peters, chair of the state Democratic Party and one of McNutt's earliest political allies, had a falling out with the governor, as did Greenlee later on. As McNutt recruited new advisers, he looked beyond the Legion. For example, Wayne Coy, a former reporter, started out as a secretary in the governor's office and later headed the state's department of public welfare.[12] McNutt led his team most effectively, for he was a "natural executive" who "knew how to delegate authority" and demand "performance" from underlings.[13] McNutt felt entitled to the best possible staff. When Ward Biddle, an incoming state senator from Bloomington, volunteered to do anything to help the new governor, McNutt asked that Biddle's much-valued secretary, Margaret

Buchanan, be allowed to come to work for him in Indianapolis. Biddle voiced no objection. Buchanan later followed McNutt to the Philippines in 1937, where she grew close to the McNutt family.[14]

Late in 1932, the McNutt team huddled in the resort community of French Lick, a traditional gathering place for Democrats, to plan the new administration. The governor-elect's principal aim was to reduce the costs of government without allowing state-run institutions to deteriorate.[15] McNutt had to tackle the fiscal crisis first. Indiana faced a $3.4 million deficit and the state's constitution restricted the government's ability to go into debt. The constitution reinforced a "conservative outlook in Indiana," that is, "a tendency of Hoosiers to prefer limited state government."[16] Moreover, McNutt's own party had a long history of advocating low taxes, localized authority, and economy in government. During the election of 1932, Roosevelt had castigated President Herbert Hoover as a spendthrift and had vowed, if elected, to balance the federal budget.[17]

In this setting, tax reform and government reorganization leaped to the top of McNutt's agenda. With respect to taxes, the governor-elect was inclined to favor a sales tax because, he noted, it was apt to yield a maximum amount of revenue. He did not like the property tax, which hit hardest the people who owned land, such as farmers. McNutt had mixed feelings about the income tax—like most progressive-minded politicians, he believed that "intangible property" had to be taxed but he worried that such a tax would fall heavily on a small group of citizens. McNutt was firmer on the need for government reorganization, specifically a "drastic retrenchment" of existing offices. Reorganization also meshed with McNutt's aim of removing Republicans from the state's government. Regarding the five-member Public Service Commission, which regulated public utilities, McNutt at first considered firing all three Republican commissioners.[18] In the end, he induced one Republican to resign, which pleased Democrats.[19] The *New Albany Ledger* congratulated McNutt on "drawing first blood" in acting to give Indiana its "new deal."[20]

Indiana's new deal, not unlike FDR's, included assistance to institutions and individuals in need. As a former university dean, McNutt was especially adamant about the need to protect Indiana's system of free education by reestablishing the state's solvency.[21] To some extent, his experience in the American Legion had shown him that if the government could help one group of citizens, such as veterans, it could do likewise for the general population. More important, the scale of the Great Depression pushed him in the direction of activist government. Within a month of his inauguration, 200,000 Hoosiers were unemployed, and local governments, the traditional dispensers of relief in Indiana, were overwhelmed by requests for assistance. McNutt received a delegation from Gary that told him of worsening conditions for indigent families. The governor replied that he was preparing legislation that would allow him to remove any local official who "did not take care of the poor."[22]

That response suggested the sort of governor McNutt intended to be—a strong one who would centralize power in his office and lead the legislature. McNutt asserted as much during his first address to the General Assembly, declaring that the constitutional doctrine of "separation of powers," in Indiana and in the nation as a whole, had developed "many exceptions and modifications" over the years.[23] To be sure, the governorship of Indiana was "a weak institution" in which the executive did little more than select state employees, submit an annual budget to the General Assembly, and veto bills.[24] Yet, a governor could emerge as something other than a "caretaker" if his personality allowed it or the times demanded it.[25] During the Civil War, for example, Governor Oliver P. Morton raised troops for the Union armies, supported President Abraham Lincoln's war policies, and neutralized the opposition Democrats by governing, for two years, without convening the legislature. Morton had gathered revenue via extralegal means and was able to do so because the war represented the gravest crisis that the United States had faced since the ratification of its Constitution.[26]

Unlike Morton, McNutt acted with the sanction of his legislature as he sought to remedy the suffering caused by the depression. McNutt was determined to propose measures that would provide relief and greater security to Hoosiers in need. During discussions with his closest aides, the governor-elect went further by suggesting names of possible floor leaders in the House of Representatives, where the Democrats held a 91-to-9 advantage over the Grand Old Party (GOP), and in Senate, where the margin was a lopsided 43 to 7. McNutt wanted committee chairs and leaders in both houses who would work with his administration.[27] Although the McNutt team did not always get its way, it insisted on having a say in the selection process.[28]

McNutt had more trouble leading his party's state organization, where Peters was an entrenched power. The incoming governor insisted that Peters would neither "make his appointments" nor "outline his legislative program."[29] Yet McNutt declined to sack Peters as the party's chairman. Indeed, he recoiled from taking any steps that would widen the divide between older, more tradition-bound Democrats, such as Peters, and the Legionnaires, or "boy scouts," who had run McNutt's 1932 campaign. McNutt at times used his appointive powers to smooth over these differences. For example, he named an old guard Democrat to Indiana's public utilities commission, but then selected Sherman Minton—a college chum and member of the American Legion—to be the commission's counselor.[30] By so doing, he gave Minton the authority to represent consumers in lawsuits involving public utility rates.

The governor-elect proved equally clever in his dealings with the press. In this area, McNutt faced an overwhelming number of Republican newspapers in the state and in Indianapolis, where the endorsement of McNutt's gubernatorial campaign by Roy W. Howard's *Indianapolis Times* meant little since the paper was not reliably Democratic. Accordingly, McNutt decided to make overtures to the Republican press. As he planned his administration, he gave "tips in advance" to reporters for the *Indianapolis News,* which was owned by Warren C. Fairbanks, the son of Theodore Roosevelt's vice president.[31] The gesture was more than an olive branch. It stemmed from McNutt's background as a journalist and his belief "that a reporter could write a better story if he understood the underlying facts."[32] It also allowed McNutt to give a break to a fallen foe. By the end of 1932, when the economy and Republican fortunes were at their lowest, the *News* had lost readers. It needed any boost—including leaked information from the governor—that might improve its reportage and increase its circulation.[33] McNutt's truce with the *News,* as we will see, was not to last.

Aided by such tactical dexterity, the McNutt administration implemented its agenda. The governor assembled a "brain trust" that included members of the General Assembly, college professors, and assorted confidants "The governor and his advisors," recalled Claude R. Wickard, an incoming state senator, "started out immediately after the election to write the legislation for the state."[34] They gathered secretly at the Indianapolis Athletic Club, soon known as the "bill factory."[35] McNutt strategized with lawmakers, guided their efforts by reading drafts of their legislation, and selected which versions to submit to the General Assembly. McHale also met with members of the legislature to make certain the governor's wishes were carried out.[36]

Meanwhile, McNutt remained the public face of the administration. One day after his inauguration, the governor addressed the General Assembly to introduce his proposals. "Relief is our first problem," he averred. "We must make every resource available." But since resources were limited, McNutt also stressed the need to erase the state's deficit via tax reform and government reorganization. He also wanted revision of banking laws; licensing the sale of alcohol; reform of local elections; assistance to Hoosiers in need; and a law assuring workers the right to organize unions. McNutt called for protecting public education, enactment of old-age pensions, and "co-ordination of un-employment relief activities." To emphasize his point, he declared: "It is the business of government to make those adjustments which guarantee to every man the right to live as a normal human being."[37] Although the governor did not use the terms "liberalism" or "security," these concepts were making their way into Indiana politics.

The Indiana General Assembly produced a legislative avalanche in 1933. Lawmakers convened on January 10, the day after McNutt's inauguration, and adjourned on March 6, two days after FDR took office. They considered path-breaking measures in a range of areas, and the pace of their work was relentless, even frantic. A few legislators—even Democratic ones—compared McNutt's tactics and some aspects of his agenda to those of a dictator. There was praise as well. In March 1933, the *Indianapolis Star,* a Republican newspaper, summarized that year's session with a front-page headline that read: "M'Nutt Program in Entirety Goes into State Laws."[38]

Without doubt the most divisive measure considered by the General Assembly was the new governor's plan to levy a gross income tax. Here the problem facing the administration was twofold: rates of taxation had skyrocketed and the state had been too dependent on the property tax as a means to raise revenue. A law passed in 1932 had set a maximum rate of $1.50 on every $100 of taxable property. But in "emergency situations" Indiana counties could exceed that limitation, which they often did during the Great Depression. More impor-tant, the state and local property tax snared owners of tangible property, such as farms and other real estate, more often than those whose wealth was in the form of paper, such as stocks and bonds.[39] And as the value of property in Indiana fell during the depression, so did the revenue derived from property taxes.[40]

As McNutt and his staff wrestled with the problem of revenue, they accepted the hard reality that "some kind of a sales tax bill" had to be adopted.[41] In his message to the legislature, McNutt prepared lawmakers for what was to come; while "unalterably opposed" to the idea of a sales tax, he acknowledged the fiscal crisis was forcing its consideration.[42] The governor saw such a tax as the best way to raise revenue, even though it would affect all Hoosiers. To soften the blow, the new administration packaged its proposal as a "gross receipts tax" rather than a sales tax. The difference between the two was the means of collection. A sales tax is a surcharge, collected by the seller on behalf of the government, while a gross receipts tax fell on the income (or receipts) of a business. McNutt's plan imposed specific rates of taxation on sales of gas, oil, coal, limestone, and brick; automobiles and tractors; and soft drinks. Electric utilities, contractors, transportation and telephone companies, and professional trades were also taxed. Sponsors of the law asserted that it would broaden Indiana's tax base and increase state revenues by as much as $12 million.[43]

The proposed gross receipts tax won powerful allies and fierce critics. Teachers, teachers' associations, and people associated with higher education favored enactment of the tax as a way to infuse needed cash into the state's educational institutions. Property owners also supported the passage of a gross receipts tax, which they saw as prologue to reducing the taxes on homes and farms. Yet working people and labor unions rejected the tax; businesses, they argued, would pass their costs on to consumers, through higher-priced goods. Big businesses and chambers of commerce fought the gross receipts tax, as did retailers, who argued that the tax would strangle them. Many Hoosiers insisted that the state government tighten its belt before asking average people to adjust theirs.[44] One taxpayer association even threatened a "tax strike" if McNutt signed such a bill.[45]

Egging on these dissenters was the Indianapolis News, which almost daily assailed McNutt's "sales tax."[46] The paper's cartoonist compared the proposed tax to a delectable dessert, irresistible to salivating spendthrifts in the General Assembly; to a pickpocket, lifting millions from the unsuspecting taxpayer; and to a huge roadblock for businesses on the path to good times.[47] Former governor James P. Goodrich read these arguments and privately predicted that both "Big Business" and the News "will look ridiculous a year from now" if people reread their bombastic talk of the "ruin."[48] Yet his was a lonely voice in Republican circles. Even the Indianapolis Times, the most Democratic-inclined paper in the state capital, was cool to the idea of a gross receipts tax.[49]

In response to the opposition, the McNutt administration became more flexible in its goals. The governor might have backed down altogether and accepted a proposal from merchants to use the funds for highways to meet the state's revenue shortfall. But he insisted that highway construction created jobs and boosted purchasing power, which was "the only way out of the depression."[50] Instead, the "best minds" in the governor's office decided that the best way to extinguish the "fire" fanned by the News was to propose a new tax bill that joined the gross receipts tax to an income tax in a "gross income tax."[51] Mc-Nutt's proposed gross income tax imposed a levy of one percent on the income of retailers and individuals and one-quarter of one percent on the income of manufacturers, farmers, and wholesalers.[52]

To enact the tax, McNutt employed secrecy and acted swiftly. Draftsmen at the "bill factory" worked overtime and behind the scenes.[53] After the administration presented the measure, its leaders in the General Assembly decided to suspend the rule that a bill had to be read three times in each chamber before it could be voted on. According to the state constitution, either the House or the Senate could dispense with this rule if two-thirds of its members so decided.[54] The administration had the numbers to do just that. McNutt asked McHale to submit the bill and explain it to lawmakers—an unprecedented request since McHale was not a member of the General Assembly.[55] Then, McNutt's team—McHale, Peters, Lieutenant Governor M. Clifford Townsend, and Senate Majority Leader Anderson Ketchum—rounded up the needed votes.[56] On February 23, both the House and the Senate suspended the rules and passed the tax, a scant three days after it had been introduced.[57]

The tactics employed by the McNutt administration to enact the gross income tax sparked anger and awe among Hoosiers. "This bill," one senator fumed, "is the rock on which the newly created autocracy will wreck itself."[58] Terms such as "steam roller," "roughshod," "lash," and "goose-step" were invoked by the *News* to attack the manner by which the governor had secured passage of his proposal.[59] Even the more independent-minded *Times* reported how the administration's "henchmen" had "jammed through" the legislature a far-reaching and controversial measure.[60] Yet the *Star* which, like the other newspapers, had opposed the tax, still praised the governor's "nerve," "courage," and "consistency" in sticking with a "determined program."[61]

The gross income tax turned out to be a success for McNutt, politically and in terms of policy. Its passage established that this governor could adjust to grassroots pressures and master the legislature. The tax proved effective in at least three ways. First, it increased revenues and allowed the state government to shift the source of revenue away from the property tax. Second, it centralized power in Indianapolis, for the gross income tax was administered by a division within the Indiana Department of the Treasury.[62] Third, the gross income tax helped produce an $11 million budget surplus by 1937. Although opposition to the tax lingered, Hoosiers by and large accepted it while Democrats in particular trumpeted its accomplishments. "The gross income tax has kept every school open and helped to pay every teacher," one party pamphlet crowed.[63] McNutt echoed that message. At one point, the governor wrote that he was glad "to demonstrate my belief in education, even in this time of great national stress."[64] Not surprisingly, state and territorial governors from as far away as Hawaii inquired after Indiana's new tax, and "gross income tax clubs" formed in California.[65] "Impartial tax experts here," the *Wall Street Journal* reported from Indiana, in 1936, "credit the Governor with having done a good job."[66]

McNutt prevailed on another tough issue: the reorganization of Indiana's government. By the 1930s, the state's bureaucracy had become a sprawling mess. It had emerged over decades in a piecemeal fashion; as the state government undertook added responsibilities, a specific agency formed to administer each one. Although Governor Goodrich had pushed a wide-ranging reorganization, the only new department established on his watch was one devoted to conservation. McNutt regarded reorganization as an "imperative."[67] Regrouping of offices and streamlining of government promised to save the state and taxpayer millions of dollars. Reorganization also was a forward-looking idea that harkened back to Progressive Era reformers who had sought to boost efficiency and impartiality in municipal government by hiring a nonpartisan "city manager."[68] Such efforts continued during the 1920s, when the nation's best-known governor, Alfred E. Smith of New York, overhauled his state's government by combining 189 offices into "a cabinet-level series of departments."[69] By the early 1930s, a nationwide movement for state-level reorganization was proposing measures to strengthen the executive branch of state governments.[70]

McNutt's reorganization bill aimed to regroup agencies into eight departments: executive; law; state; audit and control; treasury; education; public works; and commerce and industry. The governor alone headed the executive department, which would oversee the state police and the criminal bureau, both of which institutions had been in the hands of the secretary of state, Frank Mayr—McNutt's rival. Each of the other departments was overseen by a board, one of whose members had to be the governor. For example, the board of the Department of State consisted of the secretary of state (who served as administrator), the governor, and the lieutenant governor. The proposal gave the governor the power to reassign state agencies to any of the eight departments. It also empowered the governor, acting in conjunction with the departmental boards, to "change, or curtail, or abolish" any office and to modify the salary of any official covered by this law.[71] The measure matched elected officers—the governor, lieutenant governor, secretary of state, auditor, superintendent of public instruction, and treasurer—with the department closest to their area of responsibility. Mainly, however, the scheme promoted cabinet government by increasing the power of the governor, who gained the authority to hire or fire any appointee to a state agency.[72]

McNutt's reorganization plan sparked a debate that was intense, wide-ranging, and brief. The *Indianapolis News* accused McNutt of trying to become a "czar" through what critics in the legislature dubbed the "Mussolini Bill."[73] Yet the governor defended this large transfer of power to his office on the grounds that reorganization would advance economy and efficiency in state government.[74] Other newspapers in the capital backed the McNutt plan, the *Times* ardently and the *Star* cautiously.[75] Several Republicans followed suit, including former governor Goodrich, who had felt "frustrated" during his term by an "inability to get state government to move."[76] Likewise, James E. Watson, Indiana's outgoing U.S. senator, refused to criticize the "consolidation of departments" at the state level, since he had favored similar powers for President Herbert Hoover at the national level.[77] Many businessmen, who understood the value of consolidation, thrift, and efficiency, also supported McNutt, as did William A. Rawles, the dean of Indiana University's School of Commerce and Finance. "All the howls about this 'dangerous concentration' of power will subside," Rawles assured McNutt, "when the people and the papers see that you are not going to abuse your power."[78]

The most notable part of the reorganization drive was the attention it garnered across the nation. Newspapers from New York to Phoenix, from Kansas City to New Orleans, commented on the Indiana plan.[79] In Michigan, the *Detroit News* opined that Indiana's governor would hold more power than any executive had held in the Americas "since the Montezumas fell amid the ruins of the Aztec empire," and the *Lansing Journal* pondered the possibility of a "Michigan Mussolini" to go along with the one who seemed to be emerging in Indiana.[80] In a sign of the times, an Oregon man dubbed McNutt the "first dictator of an American State"—and then requested a copy of the bill that was making this transformation possible, so that his governor might obtain "the same broad power"![81] The editorial cartoonist for the *Evansville* (Indiana) *Courier* drew McNutt arising from a map of Indiana with his reorganization plan in hand as all the other states—each with a pair of eyes—looked on.[82]

The reorganization plan sailed through the legislature. Although a few old-line party hands remained unyielding in their devotion to decentralized authority, they were no match for McNutt's troops. By January 27, when the governor submitted his proposal to the legislature, a majority of members of the Senate and House had expressed their approval. To ensure that the regrouping scheme passed, McHale sat in the Senate chambers, where he dispensed instructions to Majority Leader Ketchum. Facing "feeble opposition," both houses passed the reorganization plan within a week.[83]

Another measure further reformed Indiana's government. Nicknamed the "skip elections act," it postponed local and city elections in 102 communities from their scheduled date in 1933 to 1934, when they would be held alongside midterm state and congressional elections. McNutt justified the delay on the grounds of fiscal austerity—holding no city elections in 1933 would save the state $500,000. But the bill extended the terms of sitting officials (sixty percent of them Democrats), and it forced county and city party organizations to coordinate their campaigns with state-level candidates every two years. Republicans attacked the bill as evidence that Democrats were "drunk with power." All three major newspapers in Indianapolis opposed it.[84] The Democrats, however, tacked the skip-election plan onto a minor piece of legislation dealing with insanity inquests and then suspended the rules to speed its passage. In the end, the House and Senate approved the bill by wide margins. The *Indianapolis News* thereupon assailed the law and the means by which it was enacted in an editorial titled "Insane Tyranny."[85]

There were shortcomings in McNutt's reorganization plan. The governor's overhaul of the state government was, in its design and political impact, more Jacksonian than Progressive. McNutt had rejected a proposal to establish the position of state manager to handle the administrative duties of the state.[86] Uninterested in dividing his powers, McNutt, not unlike Andrew Jackson, believed that good government involved empowering a single executive who was responsible to the electorate. The Jacksonians also preached "rotation in office," and they practiced a spoils system with respect to filling jobs. Interestingly, the reorganization of Indiana's government also left the state's executive with considerable control over the appointments and patronage jobs, something that McNutt later exploited.[87]

Overall, however, McNutt compiled a strong record on reorganization. In April 1933, he issued an order revamping the executive branch and grouping the state's 169 offices into eight departments. Within his own office, McNutt established the Division of Public Safety, which gave the state police added power. He then used reorganization to eliminate unnecessary positions and to reduce the cost of government. In 1936, McNutt was able to report that the number of state employees had remained "approximately the same" since he took office, even though the government of Indiana had assumed new responsibilities in the field of public welfare.[88] Such accomplishments occurred within the confines of the existing pattern of governance in Indiana. While McNutt tried to lead his bureaucracy by instituting weekly "cabinet meetings" of the eight department heads, state agencies "continued to operate as distinct units" with little supervision.[89] The *Literary Digest,* a weekly general-interest news magazine, thus rightly qualified its claim, that McNutt was America's "first state dictator," by acknowledging that his was a "constitutional dictatorship."[90]

Along with revenue and reorganization, McNutt promoted relief and reform. Relief involved assistance to those hardest hit by the Great Depression, such as the aged and the unemployed. At first, McNutt operated within the traditions of his party by respecting local authority. Moreover, the state's budget deficit limited his ability to spend money on relief. But as McNutt grasped the depth of the crisis facing poor people, the drain on local resources, and the benefits of federal dollars, he committed the government of Indiana to an expansive program of unemployment relief and public welfare.

Older Hoosiers were among the first groups to benefit from McNutt's relief policies. A movement to lobby state governments to enact pensions for older people had been active nationwide for at least a dozen years. By 1933 nineteen states, including Franklin Roosevelt's New York, had enacted such benefits. Indiana's legislature had passed an old-age pension bill in 1932, but Republican governor Harry G. Leslie had vetoed it. The issue surfaced in the fall campaign that year; Indiana Democrats promised to secure pensions for the aged, and candidate McNutt repeatedly stressed the necessity of such legislation. In 1933, an old-age pension bill cleared the House and Senate by lopsided margins, and the governor signed it into law.[91]

Indiana's pension law was less than impressive. It limited benefits to people who were at least seventy years old and had been residents of the state for at least fifteen years. The county paid half of the pensioner's monthly check and the state the other half, which was not to exceed $15. Many Hoosiers protested the maximum monthly allowance as meager, yet few people received the maximum amount; the average payment under this program was $6—the lowest of any state pension system in the nation.[92] Wayne Coy, McNutt's secretary who later served as state relief administrator, conceded the law's defects but he also argued that it asserted a new principle: that the state has a duty to help the aged. It represented, he said, "the best that could be secured" at that time.[93]

McNutt viewed the old-age law pragmatically. Like many Democrats, he no doubt saw it as a way to conserve money and preserve human dignity; institutionalizing old people in poorhouses was "outlandishly expensive" as well as a "cruel" and "spirit-breaking" policy.[94] To McNutt, these pensions also represented a needed first step toward providing some relief to some of Indiana's poorest residents. When in coming years Hoosiers complained about the law's measly benefits, McNutt expressed sympathy and then cited the Social Security Act, passed by Congress in 1935, which, he reckoned, would provide "more liberal allowances."[95] Indeed, McNutt later became a strong proponent of Social Security, deeming it the "most important" measure passed by Congress in 1935.[96]

McNutt's program to help the unemployed began in a similarly modest fashion. Early in 1933 the governor told a delegation of unemployed people that he was devoting "more time and thought" to their plight than to any other matter.[97] But at that point his financially strapped government lacked the means to help the unemployed. Besides, McNutt asserted, "care of the poor rightfully is a function of local government."[98] He thus chose to improve the coordination of the existing system of poor relief in Indiana, which was run by the trustees of each township.[99] As elected politicians, many of these trustees had allowed partisan favoritism to determine who received relief—food, fuel, and clothing. The legislature tried to remedy such problems by passing, with McNutt's blessing, a bill to form the Governor's Commission on Unemployment Relief (GCUR). The panel was to probe charges of misconduct by township trustees and to recommend to the governor the dismissal of any trustee responsible for misconduct.[100] While this change was in tune with the centralizing thrust of McNutt's reorganization and tax policies, the raising and disbursal of relief dollars remained primarily a local prerogative.[101]

As the economic crisis persisted, McNutt's approach to unemployment relief gradually expanded. In 1933 he signed legislation to allow counties to issue bonds and to establish in advance funds to pay for relief. He also funneled tax dollars to the state highway commission to finance a work-relief program under which unemployed people earned paychecks for building and improving roads. Lastly, McNutt cooperated with the relief programs inaugurated by the Roosevelt administration. Especially important was the Federal Emergency Relief Administration (FERA), led by Harry L. Hopkins, which channeled $500 million to state and county agencies to fund relief. In Indiana, local officials began "stampeding" for FERA dollars and jobs, and they put "a great deal of pressure" on McNutt to defer to their authority.[102] He refused, suspecting that these local officials would behave in a partisan way and thus impede the delivery of relief.[103] Instead, McNutt stated that on all federally funded assistance, the word of the Governor's Commission on Unemployment Relief and that of the FERA was final.[104] As a result, the power of townships over relief slipped in favor of GCUR, which became a virtual branch of FERA. By 1934 Howard O. Hunter, an aide to Hopkins, reported that the dispensing of relief in Indiana was running "about as smoothly as any State."[105]

McNutt was similarly supportive of the Civil Works Administration (CWA), also headed by Hopkins, which provided the unemployed with jobs "on light construction and maintenance projects."[106] The CWA operated for just five months in the winter of 1933–1934, relying on surplus supplies and tools from the U.S. Army. In Indiana, the CWA and GCUR shared the same staff and acted jointly. McNutt, too, worked "wholeheartedly" with the CWA by diverting money earmarked for the state highway fund to underwrite wages and materials for the agency's road construction projects and by urging townships to provide supplies as well.[107] Partly as a result, the CWA in Indiana gained ninety-nine percent of its building materials from local units, a record that Hunter thought "damn good."[108] By December 1933, 100,000 Hoosiers were working for the CWA. Meanwhile, FERA funds continued to flow into Indiana.[109] McNutt thus was able to limit the state's financial commitment to relief, force local units of government to exhaust their resources, and get the federal government to pay the difference. Hunter, in fact, praised the Indiana governor for being an "exceptionally cooperative" partner.[110] And Grace Tully, FDR's secretary, remembered McNutt as "one of the President's most active supporters in the early relief and public works programs."[111]

The concept of security—or protection for economically vulnerable people—began to enter into McNutt's thoughts about the obligations of the state. "The federal and state governments," he stated, "are determined that needy people shall not suffer." After the CWA ceased operations in 1934, McNutt committed himself anew to achieving "*just* and *decent* treatment" for poor people.[112] He decided that state and local governments should care for the permanently disadvantaged "unemployables" while the federal government gave relief to those who were out of work temporarily.[113] McNutt's program included work relief for the unemployed in cities; the distribution of livestock and seed to people in rural areas; and the appointment of county-level relief officers over-seen by GCUR. It was conservative in that it subjected the poor to means tests but liberal in that it pumped money into the economy through work relief, as the CWA had. In 1935, however, the federal government assumed greater re-sponsibility for relief via the Works Progress Administration (WPA), the work relief agency administered by Hopkins, which subsidized artists, actors, writ-ers, and musicians while also building playgrounds, parks, airports, roads, and public buildings. The WPA replaced the FERA and GCUR, although the WPA maintained a state-level office headed by Wayne Coy, who "quickly became a protégé of Harry Hopkins."[114]

During the 1933 session, McNutt also insisted that the General Assembly enact legislation to effect permanent reforms. Two laws stand out, the first of which involved regulation of the banking system. The problem originated with the depressed state of agriculture in Indiana. After the end of World War I, the demand for agricultural products fell, prices declined, and farmers found it dif-ficult to pay their debts. As a result, the banks, which had loaned the farmers money, began to fail. To address the crisis, the Indiana Bankers Association persuaded the state legislature to form a study commission. Herman B Wells, a young economics instructor at Indiana University, did much of the legwork for the twelve-member panel. The commission found that inept management and improper loans, as much as the onslaught of the Depression, had made the state-chartered banks financially unsound. As a solution, it recommended forming a nonpartisan department of financial institutions to oversee all banks, building and loan firms, trust companies, and small-scale lenders.[115]

Banking experts heralded the commission's recommendations as the most comprehensive proposed by any American state. The commission's bill estab-lished a four-member Department of Financial Institutions and gave it discre-tionary power to charter banks and liquidate those that had failed. The pro-posed law regulated banks tightly.[116] The measure had its limitations; it did not insure deposits, as legislation passed at the federal level soon would. Neverthe-less, bankers protested this bill as a first step toward enactment of even more "radical" legislation.[117] A "scrap" ensued when the banking industry "flooded the legislature with telegrams" attacking the bill.[118]

Three things eased the banking bill through the legislature. First, McNutt was inclined from the start to back the measure. The governor knew Wells, had asked him about the commission's work, and had read an early draft of the banking law. But Wells also rewrote the bill to make it even more attractive to

McNutt. Rather than divide the Department of Financial Institutions equally between Democratic and Republican commissioners—as originally planned—Wells's draft empowered the governor to appoint all four commissioners as well as the officials and examiners needed to carry out the law. Second, a nationwide banking panic, which accelerated the passage of banking legislation at the national level and encouraged FDR's decision to declare a bank holiday (which McNutt backed), forced Indiana lawmakers to act. Finally, the Democratic majorities in the House and Senate facilitated this bill's passage. Wells, for his part, "got quite a thrill" as he watched McNutt sign the banking bill into law.[119]

More dramatically, the General Assembly, with McNutt's strong support, enacted legislation to repeal Prohibition and to regulate the sale of alcohol. Prohibition in Indiana dated to 1917, when the General Assembly banned alcohol statewide. Two years later, the legislature endorsed the Eighteenth Amendment, which outlawed the manufacture, sale, and transportation of alcohol nationwide. The Volstead Act, approved by Congress in 1919, defined as intoxicating any beverage containing as much as one-half of one percent alcohol. Yet Hoosiers, particularly those in cities, continued to drink alcohol. In response, the Anti-Saloon League secured legislation to tighten enforcement. Known as the bone-dry law, it imposed fines and jail terms on anyone convicted of being found in possession of alcohol. Despite the law's intention, Indiana never became the "most arid state in the Union."[120] To the contrary, support for Prohibition waned with the death, in 1929, of the Reverend Edward S. Shumaker, leader of the Anti-Saloon League in Indiana, and with the onset of the depression, as Hoosiers began to focus on economic concerns. In 1932, both parties in Indiana put "wet" planks in their platforms. The Democrats, with their urban, immigrant, and Catholic constituencies, were adamant, demanding repeal of the bone-dry law as well as the Eighteenth Amendment. After a fierce internal debate, the Republicans, too, renounced their past support of Prohibition and the bone-dry law.[121]

Despite an emerging "wet" consensus, repeal did not sail through the legislature. The obstacles began with the administration, which introduced two bills. One, to rescind the bone-dry law, had widespread support, but the other, to regulate the sale of beer, wine, and hard liquor, ignited a battle. The control bill proposed a centralized system in which a state excise director, named by the governor, would collect the taxes on alcohol and issue permits relating to its sale. All manufacturers, wholesale distributors, and retail sellers of alcohol would have to be licensed by the state, and there could be no more than one wholesaler in each county for every twenty thousand people. The importation of alcohol also came under close supervision; Indiana would be divided into ten sections, each headed by a state-appointed importer. Under this measure, alcohol licenses would become political plums. Knowing that, a few wets lambasted the proposed setup as a "racket."[122] The dissenters joined with drys to prevent administration forces from suspending the rules and ramming the alcohol bill through the legislature.[123]

The debate on alcohol control lasted two months. McNutt, however, insisted that the bill be passed. The bone-dry law was going to be repealed, he warned, and lawmakers would bear responsibility if no regulation followed. To ease the measure's passage, McNutt and his allies agreed to slash state taxes on alcohol, and they assured lawmakers that the act would take effect only after Congress revised the Volstead Act to permit the sale of beer and wine. The McNutt forces then defeated a host of unfriendly amendments and pushed the alcohol control act and repeal of the bone-dry law through the legislature.[124] After McNutt signed both bills, the *Indianapolis Star* headlined: "Prohibition Era in Indiana Ended after 15 Years."[125]

With the end of Prohibition came joy—and sobering political realities. When Congress, in March 1933, passed the Beer Act, authorizing the sale of beverages with no more than 3.2 percent alcohol, Hoosiers were ready to hoist their steins. In the summer of 1933, a state convention voted to repeal the Eighteenth Amendment. In December 1933, after thirty-five state conventions had decided likewise, the Eighteenth Amendment was repealed by the ratification of the Twenty-First. In the meantime, McNutt exploited the alcohol control act to enhance his power. The governor appointed Paul Fry as excise director, but Frank McHale, as the state's unofficial "beer czar," determined who received licenses.[126] "Hoosier politics being what it was," the journalist Harold Feightner observed, "nearly all of these favors were bestowed on 'deserving' Democrats and McNutt Republicans."[127] The *Indianapolis Times,* a newspaper often friendly toward McNutt, predicted that on April 7 beer with "3.2 per cent alcoholic content and about 96 per cent political 'content'" would go on sale in Indiana.[128] "McNutt has done some excellent things in his administration," the *Times* observed, "but his handling of beer is not one of them."[129]

Such commentary underscored how divisive the McNutt administration was becoming. One Democrat likened the manner in which the governor won approval of the Beer Act to a parent forcing castor oil down a child's throat.[130] According to Claude Wickard, a first-year Democratic senator, any lawmaker who expected "to have some voice" in drafting legislation "didn't." Clerks read drafts of bills in the House and Senate, as the constitution required, but they sometimes read dozens of them simultaneously. As a result, Wickard explained, legislators did not always know what measures were under consideration, and they seldom debated bills intelligently. And then there was McHale, roaming around and pressuring Democrats to remain "ball players" on the governor's team. McHale insisted that all Democrats vote "according to the dictates of the machine."[131] Most did.

Nevertheless, the list of laws enacted by the legislature was, as the *Indianapolis Times* observed, "imposing." The General Assembly imposed new taxes on chain stores and license fees for automobiles. It overhauled the state highway commission and public utilities board, and it established uniform salaries for city, county, and state officials. According to Pleas Greenlee, McNutt squeezed six months of lawmaking into sixty days.[132] And all this legislation had an effect; reduction in utility rates, won by a revamped Public Service Commission, exceeded $1 million in 1933.[133] Emphasizing ends over means, the author George Ade praised the record of the McNutt administration as "salutary and much needed." "We came to the point," he confided to the governor, "where we simply could not get along without some benevolent dictating."[134] From the neighboring states came fond glances. "Indiana Shows a Way," declared the *Cincinnati Enquirer*, as it hailed Indiana's "remarkable" legislature. And in West Virginia, the *Charleston Gazette* applauded McNutt as a "man of action" who was flashing "across the national horizon" in a "spectacular fashion." Perhaps for those reasons, Wickard conceded that McNutt was a "dynamic figure" and, ultimately, a "good governor."[135]

McNutt was unquestionably energetic, and he worked hard at being governor. "While others sleep, he is awake, carefully plotting his course," one politician said. "He outworks his secretaries," a journalist noted, "and is daisy-fresh."[136] During the first months of 1933, McNutt spent his days in conferences, working at his desk, and visiting the Indianapolis Athletic Club for talks with his troops. Often he would stay at the club into the evening hours, when a chauffeur would return him to the governor's mansion. Paul liked to have the evening meal "on time," and he ate "heartily." Dinner-table conversation would have been light, with Kathleen being the "chatterbox" and he remaining the "quiet one." Kathleen performed the roles that convention assigned to women of her class. She made their home a "haven" for Paul, knowing that at the end of a long day, "he's fed up with talking to people about the state." That suited Kathleen, whose interest in politics did not go beyond reading drafts of her husband's speeches and offering the mildest of criticism. Paul, in turn, was "not a bit domestic." Kathleen spent the spring of 1933 replanting around the mansion. But when she showed Paul her garden, he "just walked through it" without noticing "a thing." The couple inhabited different worlds and appeared to drift apart, as politics consumed Paul's life. When a reporter asked Kathleen what her husband's hobbies were, she replied: "I'd say work."[137]

McNutt so loved his job that it was difficult for him to separate work from play. Early in 1933, he sat for a portrait by the artist Thomas Hart Benton, which would be part of Benton's mural *A Social History of the State of Indiana* and was to be exhibited at the Chicago World's Fair. Sitting for it proved a release, for McNutt enjoyed artistic endeavor. As a boy, Paul had won prizes for his art, and as a man he drew a self-portrait that was stunningly realistic.[138] With respect to Benton's project, he saw a chance to impress viewers, if not voters. McNutt hoped that the inclusion of his image would mark a "convincing ending" to Indiana's "cultural and social evolution" as depicted in the mural. Benton obliged, painting a leader who points toward a set of leaflets proclaiming the issues of the day: "reorganization," "unemployment," "banking," "schools," and "sales tax." One observer noted that the mural embodied the "spirit of optimism" that accompanied Roosevelt's New Deal.[139]

McNutt wanted to be a leading man, not a bit player, in that unfolding drama. He met with Roosevelt late in 1932 and, three months later, went to Washington, D.C., for the new president's inauguration. People in the nation's capital caught their first glimpse of the governor, and many were impressed. One photograph showed McNutt in formal morning attire, standing erect, and staring into the camera—while a man turns his head to eyeball him. At a party, a member of McNutt's fraternity, Byron K. Elliott, was chatting with Senator J. Hamilton Lewis, an old, "pink-whiskered" Democrat from Illinois, when there appeared near the doorway "a God-like figure," a "perfect Adonis" wearing a silk hat and an opera cape and carrying an ebony cane. "Good heavens, who is that?" Lewis asked. Elliott told him. As McNutt approached, they both stepped back. Lewis then declared: "Governor McNutt, if I had your commanding physique to couple with my natural audacity, oh what hell I would raise in certain circles I have long wished to disturb!"[140]

Back in Indiana, McNutt's purpose was to calm and to inspire, not to disturb. He warned Hoosiers of the nation's peril and of a possible dark future.[141] But McNutt saw salvation in two values: change and courage. "The functions of government change," he proclaimed. "Government is not in itself something. It is for something. Just now it is for the economic rehabilitation of our people and for the preservation of certain fundamental institutions."[142] Such rhetoric was associated with higher-ranking leaders in the 1930s; in 1936 the journalist Ruby Black wrote Eleanor Roosevelt: "Your husband and you have saved democracy and made it work by bringing the government home to the people."[143] By emphasizing that government must serve the needs of its people, McNutt was able to justify the work of the last session of the General Assembly, identify himself with safe, evolutionary progress (rather than sudden, violent revolution), and endorse the programs begun by President Roosevelt. Indeed, McNutt praised FDR's National Recovery Administration, which promoted industrial planning as a means to tame the unruly cycles of competition, boom, and bust. And like FDR, he employed the analogy of war, emphasizing that people must persevere like soldiers under fire. Even in hard times, McNutt insisted, "we can order a charge and can move forward with courage."[144] The governor could so speak because he had been a soldier and he projected soldierly virtues. After a meeting with McNutt, former governor James Goodrich departed unsure which traits this Democrat possessed. Of one characteristic, however, he was certain: "He has courage."[145]

McNutt was unafraid to punish enemies and reward friends, a trait which became apparent in his complex relationship with the press. In many ways, McNutt personified the reporter's ideal of the approachable executive. During the 1933 session of the General Assembly, he held press conferences twice a day and bantered with journalists off the record. "Many a time his boisterous laugh rang out at some reporter's quip," Harold Feightner remembered.[146] "Some of the questions angered him to the point where he would shout his answers," another correspondent, Tubby Toms, recalled, "but he never carried the grudge."[147] That was not entirely accurate. After one reporter had asked a question that the governor thought embarrassing, McNutt arrived fifty minutes late for his next press conference. When he kept correspondents waiting a day later, they walked out in protest. The next day, he saw the newshounds—at the appointed time.[148]

The vindictive side of McNutt's personality had surfaced most clearly a year earlier. He and Walter D. Myers, the speaker of the Indiana House, were campaigning together—the former for the Democratic nomination for governor and the latter to be the party's choice for U.S. senator. On the stump, McNutt spoke first, and Myers followed. One day, McNutt suggested they reverse the order, and Myers agreed. Alas, when Myers spoke, he delivered McNutt's remarks, which he had heard again and again. Chagrined, McNutt, who now had nothing to say, resolved to take revenge at the party's convention. Instead of supporting Myers, McNutt's allies cast their votes for Frederick Van Nuys, who won the nomination and effectively ended Myers's career. Many years later, Myers tried to return the favor by publishing a novel, *The Guv,* that featured an ambitious, self-seeking, young governor—"Mack Boob"—intended to represent McNutt.[149]

It was in the area of patronage where McNutt's power and ruthlessness shone through. The seeking and the distribution of jobs had been a central part of Hoosier politics since the rise of the Second Party System during the 1830s. Such practices continued into the twentieth century, for Indiana had no counterpart to the Pendleton Act, the law passed by Congress in 1883 to inaugurate merit-based hiring in the federal civil service. The competition for state jobs only intensified in 1933. The Democrats had spent sixteen years in exile, and many longtime party hands expected to be rewarded. Also, with the onset of the depression, more people became desperate for state jobs. Yet the budget crisis left the new administration with little patronage to give out.[150]

To deal with the job seekers, McNutt and Greenlee, his point man on patronage, established criteria for recruiting personnel. They insisted that each job candidate be both well qualified and loyal "to the Democratic cause."[151] And they declined to hire anyone who had offered money to the party before applying for a position. "We have no jobs for sale in this administration," Greenlee averred.[152] He and McNutt believed in a system of governance whereby the party in power shouldered the responsibilities and then rewarded its faithful workers. They also preached sacrifice and party unity—when it was in their interest to do so. "Let's shake ourselves together and present one solid front," Greenlee advised one man, because "the one great fault in the Democratic party is that we fight against ourselves instead of fighting the enemy."[153]

On the patronage front, McNutt and Greenlee engaged multiple enemies, with Greenlee leading the attack. The reorganization bill empowered the governor to dismiss any state employee, and McNutt was determined to exercise this authority. Greenlee did everything possible "to oust Republicans and replace them with deserving Democrats."[154] (He even arranged for the replacement of a "crippled" police officer with a party loyalist.)[155] Furthermore, any Democrat who had donated money to the GOP was excluded from having a state job. To be sure, the administration fired Democrats who were liabilities, and Greenlee excluded from state jobs any Democrat who had backed Frank Mayr, McNutt's rival for the nomination for governor in 1932. Yet Republicans remained the principal targets. The GOP's best-known casualty was Richard Lieber, who had headed the Department of Conservation since 1919 and had done much to establish Indiana's parks system.[156] McNutt first demoted Lieber to director of the division of state parks in a revamped Department of Public Works headed by Virgil Simmons, an intimate of the governor. Apparently pressured to give jobs to Democrats, Lieber resigned his post.[157] His departure prompted one conservationist to exclaim: "'Politics,' what crimes have been committed in thy name!"[158]

The most heinous crime, in the view of many observers, was McNutt's dismissal of six librarians from the Indiana State Library. Letters of condemnation poured in from Democrats and Republicans alike, from prominent citizens—including the suffragist Grace Julian Clarke and the novelist Booth Tarkington—from libraries and universities across Indiana, from learned institutions in other states, and from a librarian at Yale University who denounced the firings as characteristic of a spoils system.[159] The critics stressed the long experience of those being let go and the need to maintain "high grade non-partisan professional service" at the state library.[160] They argued that the governor had injected partisanship into an institution that had been free of such influence. McNutt responded to such charges by claiming that his Republican predecessors had through their appointments infused politics into the state library, and he was simply restoring some balance. The governor assailed the library profession for its "despicable" attacks against the incoming staff at the state library.[161] To be sure, McNutt reappointed one of the librarians slated for removal. But he never admitted that this episode was, as Tarkington rightly noted, a "mistake."[162]

There was a coarseness in McNutt's handling of patronage. Part of the problem involved what one observer has called the mathematics of the dismissals.[163] In 1933 the governor replaced thirty-one part-time Republican oil inspectors with twenty-seven full-time Democratic inspectors. Administration pressure forced the resignation, after thirty-six years of service, of the head of the Indiana School for the Blind. By the end of 1933, the number of employees at a state hospital in Richmond who were Republicans had shrunk from 181 to 34. Tactless and defensive, Greenlee was ill equipped to assuage any hurt feelings. Nevertheless McNutt stood by—and to some extent hid behind—his patronage dispenser, for he relied on Greenlee to sign the dismissal letters.[164] After the *Indianapolis Times* decried the administration's "Tammany methods" and insisted that "Greenlee must go," McNutt brushed aside rumors of his departure as "a fairy tale."[165]

Greenlee stayed on and pushed another controversial initiative: the Hoosier Democratic Club. The aim of this organization was to raise money for the party, place those funds in the hands of the governor, cement party solidarity among state employees, and help the Democrats overwhelm the GOP at election time. Greenlee got the idea for such the club from an old army buddy, who had explained that Republican dominance in Pennsylvania rested on a political machine that required state employees to give three percent of their annual salaries to the GOP. The McNutt administration in 1933 began a similar effort with the Hoosier Democratic Club, which was led by Virgil Simmons, its president; Bo Elder, its treasurer; and Greenlee, its secretary. The outfit became known as the "Two Percent Club" because under it Democratic state workers gave two percent of their annual salaries to the club. In theory, these contributions were "voluntary" because Indiana law prohibited the solicitation of political donations from state employees.[166] In practice, however, the club's leadership applied pressure. "I am really surprised," Greenlee told one man, "that as good a Democrat as yourself should encourage your daughters, who are working for the state, not to pay their dues."[167] The means of collection proved flexible. Managers at state units gathered the money, though not all employees gave the suggested amount, and some people outside of state government also contributed.[168] The Hoosier Democratic Club raised a lot of cash—thousands of dollars every month—because no state job was secure if a worker declined to participate.[169]

The Hoosier Democratic Club lacked neither detractors nor defenders. "Purists held their noses at the tactic," reported Ernest K. Lindley, a columnist who was favorable to McNutt.[170] The *Nation* likened the activities of the Two Percent Club to extortion.[171] And James Albert Woodburn, a retired history professor at Indiana University and former Bull Moose Progressive, thought the club reflected poorly on Indiana. Sherman Minton, a McNutt protégé, disagreed, asserting that people employed by the state had a duty to help "the Party that gave them their job." Besides, he reasoned, this method of fundraising—in small amounts and among a mass of people—was superior to that of the GOP, which collected cash from a few wealthy contributors and then rewarded them with favors, such as tax breaks.[172] (Minton failed to mention that the Hoosier Democratic Club did not refuse money from large donors either.) Jack New, a political operative in Indiana, liked the Two Percent Club because it let Democrats know what was expected of them.[173]

The Hoosier Democratic Club was not unique in North American politics during the 1930s. Canadian prime minister William Lyon Mackenzie King "half-expected wealthy senators to contribute [to the Liberal Party's coffers] as payback for their patronage appointments." And Governor Huey P. Long of

Louisiana had withheld money from the paychecks of state workers and stashed the proceeds in his "deduct box." Louisiana's system, however, involved a naked reach for cold, hard cash, which Long kept in a container that disappeared after his assassination in 1935. Such goings-on made McNutt's Two Percent Club, which advertised itself as voluntary and deposited its money in a bank, seem almost genteel by comparison. Similarly, Martin L. Davey, the Democratic governor of Ohio from 1935 to 1939, strove to enhance his power through the disbursal of liquor licenses and mandatory assessments of five percent on the income of every state worker. But unlike McNutt, Davey was pugnaciously venal. Critics accused his administration of selling liquor licenses outright, and Davey used the money extracted from state employees to try to save his own skin during a primary challenge in 1938, rather than to lift the fortunes of his party, something that the Hoosier Democratic Club claimed to be doing. Davey's shakedowns drew fire from leaders in both parties, and accusations of machine tactics contributed to his defeat in the Democratic primary and the election of Republican John Bricker in 1938.[174]

McNutt's machine was clear about its ends and unapologetic toward its critics. From the time McNutt took office, Greenlee resolved to develop methods that "would keep the Democrats in power."[175] Beer licenses, patronage, and fundraising all advanced that aim. Moreover, McHale, Greenlee, Simmons, and Elder, together, built a political machine openly and honestly and justified it as a necessary evil.[176] Although McNutt said that "Good Government is the best Politics," he knew that compiling a fine record was no assurance of victory at the polls.[177] In urging Indiana Democrats to contribute to the Two Percent Club, McNutt reminded them that the GOP had collected $100,000 for the purpose of defeating the Democratic program. Greenlee, who had resented his party's "inferiority complex," proved more visceral in his rhetoric, vowing to give the GOP "two socks for every one that they give the Democrats."[178] In the long run, the controversy over the Hoosier Democratic Club would hinder McNutt's ambitions for national office. In the short run, however, it provided a means for rallying supporters and defeating foes.

The élan and endeavors of McNutt's "boy scouts"—the governor's supporters from the Legion now embraced this once-patronizing label—cut two ways. Many Democrats praised them. Carleton McCulloch, the Democratic nominee for governor in 1920 and 1924, expressed awe that his party was outpacing the GOP in fundraising. "Paul is the absolute Boss of the Party," he beamed.[179] But not everyone rejoiced. Older party hands hated McNutt's for leading the

Democratic Party away from its core principles: low taxes, limited government, and decentralized authority. They also fumed at the "haughty and arrogant" attitude of McNutt and his aides.[180] Earl Peters became upset over the Two Percent Club, which emerged outside the regular party organization, and resigned his position as chair of the Indiana Democratic Party in 1933. By that point, Democrats appeared to be dividing between those who were "deserving"—the McNutt loyalists—and the "disgruntled," meaning everyone else.[181] According to anecdotes (for few polls existed), something similar was happening statewide. "I'll reckon my cattle and hogs would be for the Governor if they could think," a Republican supporter of McNutt said.[182] At the same time, another man slaughtered his chickens because, he said, all day long they cackled: "McNutt, McNutt, McNutt."[183]

As the 1934 elections approached, a sequence of events lifted the spirits of Republicans. McNutt was embarrassed when the press revealed that his friend Paul Feltus had received a contract to supply the state with textbooks and that his father-in-law's factory had received a contract to sell the state $6,000 worth of wax products.[184] But it was in the area of public safety that the governor came under heaviest fire. In May 1933 McNutt replaced the warden of the prison in Michigan City with a lawyer who had supported his gubernatorial campaign. Weeks later, five members of John Dillinger's gang escaped from that prison. Republicans blamed the break on McNutt's patronage policies. To make matters worse, a year later, Dillinger, brandishing a wooden "gun" blackened with shoe polish, escaped from a jail in Crown Point, Indiana. After that episode, members of McNutt's team began to bicker openly; state safety director Al Feeney insisted that politics had interfered with efforts to improve the state police while Greenlee attacked Feeney as incompetent. McNutt, meanwhile, received abuse from Republicans, some of whom spread the false charge that he and Dillinger were related.[185]

McNutt responded by burying his mistakes and trumpeting his successes. To shore up his record on crime, the governor asked Wayne Coy to investigate the break at Michigan City and propose improvements to the state's prison system. Later, in an action that would have pleased old-style Democrats, McNutt announced that his various policies had saved taxpayers $3.3 million during the first eight months of 1933. At the same time, however, he also identified himself with the New Deal, which was popular in Indiana.[186] Like Roosevelt, McNutt exercised strong leadership, mastered his legislature, and signed bills to end Prohibition and reform banking. Although the governor was more concerned than the president with fiscal discipline and government reorganization, both men were promoting strong, active, and humane government. In dispensing relief, each leader started out by respecting lower-level units of government— McNutt the townships and FDR the states. Indeed, the Indiana governor cooperated closely with the Roosevelt administration on relief, as he later would on economic recovery and social security.

McNutt remained the driving, almost indispensable, force within the Hoosier Democratic Party who was able to vanquish almost any rival, including R. Earl Peters. After resigning as state chairman, Peters announced his candidacy for the Democratic nomination for the U.S. Senate. He had powerful backers, including FDR, White House aide Louis Howe, and Postmaster General James A. Farley, who chaired the Democratic National Committee and who appreciated Peters's support of Roosevelt at the 1932 Democratic National Convention. But the contest for the Senate nomination became a test of McNutt's leadership. He passed. At the state convention in 1934, McNutt's lieutenants nominated, in place of Peters, one of their own: Sherman Minton.[187]

The state GOP decided to "take off [the] gloves" and make the 1934 election a referendum on McNutt rather than on the popular Roosevelt.[188] The Republican State Committee denounced Minton as "McNutt's hand-picked nominee" and assailed "McNuttism," which it defined as a tethering of "Tammany dictatorship and bureaucratic tyranny" capped by an "imperial" governor guilty of "blundering," "riotous spending," and "demoralization of the state police."[189] One GOP tract suggested that McNutt's middle initial could stand for "Vanity," "Vandal," "Vainglorious," "Vindictive," "Vacuous," "Vaudeville," "Voodoo," or "Vomit."[190] Republican senator Arthur Robinson, whom Minton was trying to unseat, entered the fray with attacks on the governor's "dictatorial policies," "notorious" Two Percent Club, and "stupidity" with respect to prison breaks.[191] The Republican campaign slogan eventually encompassed two words: "Stop McNutt."[192]

The Democrats returned fire. In a slap at past GOP governors McCray and Jackson, one Democrat wisecracked: "Why stop McNutt? He hasn't been indicted for anything."[193] Republicans aided the Democratic strategy by emphasizing the governor's more sensational missteps—on Dillinger, for instance—at the expense of discussing bread-and-butter issues related to the economy. McNutt had anticipated as much during his address to the Democratic state convention, when he criticized the GOP's platform for ignoring relief, unemployment, and old-age pensions and the opposition party for singing a "hymn of hate and misrepresentation."[194] Minton, in turn, defended Roosevelt, the New Deal, and McNutt—in that order.[195] Neither he nor any other Indiana Democrat, however, answered "Stop McNutt" with an appeal to "Stand by McNutt."[196]

By October, the canvass had reached a "fever heat" with assorted "spellbinders" haranguing audiences "every night in all corners of the State."[197] One of those speakers was McNutt, who decided to answer his critics. At an event in Indianapolis, the governor ascended the stage, removed his jacket, and announced: "Let's drag the backyard gossip out in the open. I'll answer any question any one wants to ask. Shoot."[198] He proceeded to defend his Two Percent Club, arguing that soliciting contributions from the party's rank-and-file was superior to accepting donations from a few bigwigs. Responding to questions about state contracts, he replied that those always went to the lowest bidders—and anyone knowing otherwise should provide proof. The crowd applauded, and McNutt's advisers believed that the governor had triumphed in this "open forum" format.[199]

As the campaign drew to a close, neither side was certain of the outcome. Many Democrats, thinking that FDR's popularity would trump all else, anticipated victory. Others believed that Republican attacks, amplified by the press, would lift the GOP over the Democrats. Jim Goodrich was "confident" that Robinson would be reelected.[200] Moreover, the *Indianapolis News* reported a poll by the *Literary Digest* showing fifty-five percent of Hoosiers opposed to the New Deal.[201] The *Indianapolis Star* went so far as to exhort voters to "Stop McNutt" by adding more Republicans to the Indiana House and Senate.[202]

The election results left both papers chagrined. Although the GOP gained twenty-six seats in the Indiana House, it still trailed the Democrats 65 to 35. Republicans picked up five seats in the Senate, giving them just 12 to the 38 held by the Democrats. Of the dozen congressmen Indiana was to send to Washington, eleven would be Democrats. And Robinson lost to Minton. McNutt, the *News* acknowledged, had shown much "sagacity" in "rallying" his "organization." "The result speaks for itself. His prestige among Democrats is considerably enhanced."[203] The outcome, the *Star* opined, enabled the state administration "to continue the program it has inaugurated."[204] To McNutt, the election outcome was "most gratifying."[205]

The election left McNutt in a strong position. He held huge majorities in the legislature, and his candidate was off to the U.S. Senate. Minton, of course, had the order correct when he described his election as "a vindication for the New

Deal" and "for McNutt."[206] In an off-year election, when the party in power generally loses ground, the Democrats gained thirteen seats in the U.S. House, for a margin of 322 to 103, and nine in the U.S. Senate, for a 69 to 25 advantage. "The people of the country," Robinson admitted, "continue to endorse the New Deal."[207] Another Indiana Republican attributed his defeat to "too much NRA, AAA, CWA, FERA," combined with "a strong Democratic political machine with plenty of money."[208] When asked about the reasons behind the election results, former Indiana senator Jim Watson quipped: "Too many Democrats."[209]

Nevertheless, there were, for McNutt, hints of trouble ahead. His policies were stirring controversy, and perhaps needlessly so. It is not clear whether his machine was required for victory, since the Republican Party was in such tatters. Moreover, the Two Percent Club left some Democrats uneasy. The author and diplomat Claude G. Bowers, a friend of Farley, at one point accused McNutt of being "unnecessarily ruthless," of taking a "sledge hammer" to his critics, and of developing a "fascist organization" in Indiana.[210] Factional differences between older leaders such as Bowers and younger ones such as McNutt plagued the Hoosier Democratic Party. The 1934 elections confirmed the governor as a commanding, albeit polarizing, figure in Indiana politics.

Paul V. McNutt as an infant, being held by his maternal grandfather,
Jacob M. Neely. In the second row are Paul's father, John C. McNutt (center),
and mother, Ruth Neely McNutt (right). *Courtesy of the Lilly Library,
Indiana University, Bloomington, Indiana.*

McNutt ca. age nine. *Courtesy of the Lilly Library, Indiana University, Bloomington, Indiana.*

McNutt as a student at Indiana University, 1909–1913.
*Courtesy of the Lilly Library, Indiana University, Bloomington, Indiana.*

McNutt as an officer during the First World War.
*Courtesy of the Lilly Library, Indiana University, Bloomington, Indiana.*

Kathleen McNutt, January 1929. *Courtesy of the Library of Congress, Prints & Photographs Division, photograph by Underwood & Underwood* [66612RU].

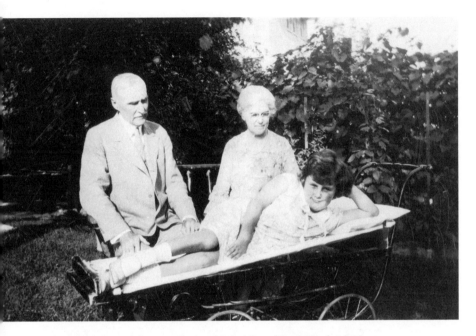

Louise McNutt with her grandparents John C. and Ruth Neely McNutt, ca. 1930. Stricken with tuberculosis of the spine, Louise had to remain in bed. To gain fresh air, she was strapped to a large wooden board and placed on a buggy (pictured) which then was wheeled around the neighborhood. *Courtesy of the Lilly Library, Indiana University, Bloomington, Indiana.*

# NATIONAL OFFICERS

[ *October 11, 1928*
*To*
*October 3, 1929* ]

BOWMAN ELDER
NATIONAL TREASURER
INDIANA

SCOTT W. LUCAS
NATIONAL JUDGE ADVOCATE
ILLINOIS

JAMES F. BARTON
NATIONAL ADJUTANT
IOWA

RABBI LEE J. LEVINGER
NATIONAL CHAPLAIN
OHIO

EBEN PUTNAM
NATIONAL HISTORIAN
MASSACHUSETTS

PAUL V. McNUTT
NATIONAL COMMANDER
INDIANA

LAWRENCE E. McGANN
NATIONAL VICE COMMANDER
ILLINOIS

EDWARD L. WHITE
NATIONAL VICE COMMANDER
CONNECTICUT

MILLER C. FOSTER
NATIONAL VICE COMMANDER
SOUTH CAROLINA

WALTON D. HOOD
NATIONAL VICE COMMANDER
TEXAS

GEORGE MALONE
NATIONAL VICE COMMANDER
NEVADA

*Above.* McNutt (third from the right) and members of the
American Legion meet Benito Mussolini (center) in Rome, 1929.
*Courtesy of the Lilly Library, Indiana University, Bloomington, Indiana.*

*Facing.* National officers of the American Legion, 1928–1929. National Commander Paul
V. McNutt is at the center, and the organization's national treasurer, future McNutt
aide Bowman Elder, is in the top left corner. Below Elder is the national chaplain,
Rabbi Lee J. Levinger. The Legion's version of "Americanism" stressed patriotic service
and welcomed veterans of World War I regardless of their race, ethnicity, or religion.
McNutt's empathy for Jews became further evident when, as high commissioner to
the Philippines (1937–1939), he helped 1,300 refugees flee Nazi Germany and resettle
in Manila. *Courtesy of the Lilly Library, Indiana University, Bloomington, Indiana.*

McNutt and Roosevelt at the Indiana State Fair, 1936.
*Courtesy of the Indiana Historical Society.*

*Facing top.* Democrats on the campaign trail in Indianapolis, 1932. Left to
right: U.S. Senate candidate Frederick Van Nuys, McNutt, Thomas Taggart
Jr., Indianapolis mayor Reginald Sullivan, and Franklin D. Roosevelt.
*Courtesy of Bass Photo Co. Collection, Indiana Historical Society.*

*Facing bottom.* McNutt being fingerprinted by the state police at the Indiana State Fair,
1935. As governor, McNutt reformed the state police but he also endured criticism when
John Dillinger escaped from an Indiana prison. *Courtesy of the Indiana Historical Society.*

*Above.* Louise (left), Kathleen (center), and Paul McNutt
at the high commissioner's residence in Manila, ca. 1937.
*Courtesy of the Lilly Library, Indiana University, Bloomington, Indiana.*

*Facing top.* McNutt and President Manuel L. Quezon of the Philippines share a light
moment, 1938. McNutt wrote: "Ours has been a most happy association based on
confidence and understanding. May our sense of humor grow and last as has our
friendship. With affectionate regards and every good wish, Paul V. McNutt."
*Courtesy of the Filipinas Heritage Library.*

*Facing bottom.* McNutt addresses a welcome-home rally in Indianapolis, June 1939.
*Courtesy of the Lilly Library, Indiana University, Bloomington, Indiana.*

*Above*. Roosevelt greets his newly appointed head
of the Federal Security Agency, August 1939.
*Courtesy of the Library of Congress, Prints &*
*Photographs Division, photograph by*
*Harris & Ewing* (LC-H21-C-1024).

*Right*. Frank M. McHale, McNutt's
confidant and political strategist, 1951.
*Courtesy of AP Photo/ Charles Gorry.*

Wayne Coy, one of McNutt's most capable assistants from 1933 to 1941. *Courtesy of the Library of Congress, Prints & Photographs Division* (D-929).

*Below.* Presidential hopefuls Thomas E. Dewey and Paul V. McNutt arrive by train in Washington, December 1939. *Courtesy of the Library of Congress, Prints & Photographs Division, photograph by Harris & Ewing* (LC-H22-D-7989).

for
President

Paul V. McNutt

OF INDIANA

Lawyer ▪ Educator ▪ Statesman

Trained in Leadership and Government

Experienced in World Affairs

Presidential campaign literature, 1939 or 1940.
*Courtesy of the Lilly Library, Indiana University, Bloomington, Indiana.*

A cartoon in the *Washington Evening Star* comments on McNutt's
presidential prospects, July 1939. *Courtesy of the U.S. Senate Collection,
Center for Legislative Archives, National Archives* (ARC 6012196).

McNutt in October 1941, seven months before his appointment as chair of the War Manpower Commission. *Courtesy of the Library of Congress, Prints & Photographs Division* (LC-USE6-D-000559).

Cartoonist Jim Berryman of the *Washington Evening Star* editorializes on the race for vice president in 1944. Unlike in 1940, McNutt did not receive serious consideration from either the convention delegates or FDR. On the cartoon, Berryman wrote: "With Good Wishes to 'My Favorite Bridesmaid,' the Hon. Paul McNutt!" *Courtesy of the Lilly Library, Indiana University, Bloomington, Indiana.*

MOST RECENTLY LIBERATED PRISONER OF WAR

Cartoonist Clifford K. Berryman of the *Washington Evening Star*
commenting on McNutt's return to the Philippines as high commissioner,
1945. On the cartoon, Berryman wrote: "Governor—I hate to see you go,
but I'm really greatly distressed *to see Mrs. McNutt* go so far away!!!!"
*Courtesy of the Lilly Library, Indiana University, Bloomington, Indiana.*

Participants in the ceremony inaugurating the Republic of the
Philippines, July 4, 1946. Left to right: President Manuel A. Roxas, McNutt,
Vice President Elpidio Quirino, and General Douglas A. MacArthur.
*Courtesy of the American Historical Collection, Rizal Library, Ateneo de Manila University.*

McNutt congratulating Mary E. Switzer of the Federal Security
Agency on receiving the Medal of Merit, December 1946.
*Courtesy of the Schlesinger Library, Radcliffe Institute, Harvard University.*

# 7

## "HOOSIER HITLER"
## (1935–1936)

BY THE MID-1930S, PAUL V. McNUTT had emerged as a nationally known politician who was capable of inspiring awe as well as angst. In 1935 a Hoosier traveling through Ohio and Kentucky claimed that everyone had heard of "Indiana's wonderful Governor."[1] Yet not everyone was enamored of McNutt. Louis Howe, Franklin D. Roosevelt's oldest political adviser, heard complaints about McNutt's reorganization and patronage policies. "Various" Democrats in Indiana, he warned the governor, "do not love you as much as they might."[2] Looking ahead to Roosevelt's reelection campaign, Howe worried about factionalism in Indiana politics, which he characterized as peculiarly "complicated," "impossible" to fathom, and, generally speaking, "a mess."[3] To encourage the Hoosier Democrats to become more united, Howe held "several talks" with the governor.[4] But McNutt never reconciled with his former ally, R. Earl Peters.

In 1935 and 1936, the formula of McNutt's life was two parts Indiana and one part national politics. He had a legislature to lead, a machine to tend, and a strike in Terre Haute to resolve. McNutt's handling of the last of these proved controversial, providing fodder to critics and earning the governor a nickname—"Hoosier Hitler"—that was as unfortunate as it was alliterative. Yet McNutt was looking beyond Indiana. He had to, for his state's governors were prohibited from serving a second consecutive term. And he wanted to, because his ambition for national office, so evident in 1932, remained strong.

In 1935 and 1936 McNutt continued his mastery of the General Assembly. To be sure, the 1934 elections had reduced the Democratic majorities in the House and Senate, and the crisis atmosphere that had prevailed two years earlier had eased. Furthermore, McNutt, stung, no doubt, by charges of being a "dictator," assumed a more laissez-faire posture toward the legislature. Partly as a result, the House and Senate lagged behind the record pace of 1933 in passing administration-sponsored bills. Nevertheless, McNutt again huddled with Democrats before the legislature convened, helped to select the party's floor leaders, and addressed the General Assembly in January. Aided by a special session in 1936, he won passage of almost all of his proposed legislation.[5]

On January 10, McNutt stood before the legislature and outlined his agenda, voicing what would become, over time, an increasingly holistic vision of state-sponsored security for average folks. Insisting that "the first obligation of government is to the humanity it serves," he championed "the security of livelihood through the better use of the natural resources," "security against the major hazards and vicissitudes of life," and "the security of decent homes."[6] To be sure, McNutt was echoing earlier remarks by President Roosevelt. But as a governor, with authority over a specific geographic area with a sizable population, he saw security as central to liberal thought and practice as early as FDR and, perhaps, earlier than his fellow liberals in Roosevelt's administration. The governorship also allowed McNutt to put his ideas into effect. When the General Assembly convened in 1935, McNutt "rang the bell" and commanded lawmakers to begin their work.[7]

McNutt recommended legislation to make the lives of Hoosiers more predictable, safe, and secure. The governor proposed laws to ease the sale of bonds used to finance relief measures for the unemployed; to clarify the responsibilities of county and township officials regarding the disbursement of relief; and to help townships to assist the poor with more dollars from the state and its counties. He urged support of the Social Security Act being considered by Congress; approval of a state recovery act to enforce the codes sanctioned by the National Recovery Administration (NRA); establishment of a statewide department of public welfare; and enactment of a "connected and constructive conservation program." He advocated free textbooks for schoolchildren; laws to reform taxes and regulate installment buying; expansion and professionalizing of the state police; and a permanent system to control alcohol.[8] The governor's address was notable for three reasons. First, McNutt sought to revise and improve laws that the General Assembly had passed two years earlier. Second, he had accented his liberal side, asserting that average people must be "served instead of starved" by their government.[9] Third, McNutt's support for the NRA and Social Security revealed a widening perspective, one designed, in part, to enhance his reputation nationally.[10]

The laws passed by the General Assembly during McNutt's final two years as governor reflected essential aspects of his character. McNutt had long been achievement-oriented, and the legislature presented him with an array of progressive measures to sign. These included a law permitting school boards to buy textbooks and loan them to parents; legislation to tighten safety in mines; annual pensions for blind people; and a requirement that employees working on public works projects receive the prevailing private-sector wage. The General Assembly also reformed the state police. With McNutt's support, it established a four-member board, appointed by the governor, to assist the superintendent of state police; a merit system for the recruitment of police; and a training school for police officers—all signs that the governor wanted no more controversies involving patronage employees and prison breaks. While signing these bills, McNutt insisted on, and received, a balanced budget. Interestingly, FDR shared McNutt's instinct to balance his government's budget, although Roosevelt, who governed on a much larger stage and with much wider responsibilities, never succeeded in doing so.[11]

The 1935 session illustrated that at one level McNutt remained a reformer with the public interest at heart. One example was the regulation of installment buying, which Herman B Wells had been studying since 1934. Wells found that credit firms in Indiana, operating with scant oversight, often charged their customers exorbitant rates of interest. He wanted the governor to back legislation to correct the problem. Wells told McNutt that "the automobile industry, the appliance industry, and the big financial concerns" were against regulation of installment buying. "I'm also realistic to know," he continued, "that if you want to run for president you probably are going to have to look to these interests for campaign funds." So, Wells volunteered, if the governor wanted this bill scuttled he would oblige. McNutt asked: "Is this right? Is it in the public interest?" "Yes, it certainly is," Wells said. McNutt replied: "Very well, I'll tell the boys to put it through."[12] The General Assembly responded by passing six measures to oversee consumer credit. To Wells, these laws represented a "second peak" in the four-year-long effort to overhaul Indiana's financial institutions.[13] McNutt praised them as a "Magna Charta" for consumers.[14]

McNutt was almost as effusive about the General Assembly's record in the area of conservation. In 1935 the legislature passed nearly two dozen laws to regulate the hunting of deer, squirrels, rabbits, pheasants, and wild turkeys. Fish received additional protections—indiscriminate sportsmen no longer could net, pitchfork, or dynamite them, and motorized boats were forbidden to skirt over their spawning areas. But not all the new laws were about prevention. Conservation clubs were allowed to breed fish and game, and the federal government was encouraged to establish national forests in the state. This legislation also gave wide latitude to the Department of Conservation, headed by Virgil M. Simmons, and to the state's director of fish and game, Kenneth M. Kunkel.[15]

It is hard to link McNutt closely to this program, for he was neither an outdoor sportsman nor a member of any conservation club. Nonetheless, the conservation drive underscored several things about his leadership style and persona. The first was McNutt's ability to respond to grassroots pressure. During the 1920s and into the 1930s, conservation organizations such as the Izaak Walton League had urged Indiana's legislature to protect waterways and wildlife, which it did in 1935. At the same time, McNutt's conservation department launched an educational campaign—including speeches, talks, exhibits, and a new monthly publication, *Outdoor Indiana*—to promote responsible hunting and fishing. Simmons and Kunkel prodded Hoosiers to join conservation clubs in their communities. These clubs, in turn, offered advice to game wardens, who became "assistants in the conservation effort" rather than "unforgiving law enforcers." The conservation clubs also worked in tandem with the Walton League and the American Legion, many of whose members were sportsmen—a shrewd way for McNutt to cement and expand his political base.[16] By 1936 over 150,000 Hoosiers had joined such clubs, and Indiana, almost alone among the states, had implemented a conservation program that was both "coordinated" and "popular."[17] McNutt, again, had exploited the talents of his lieutenants, Simmons and Kunkel, and claimed credit for their accomplishments. Once a year, the governor appeared in *Outdoor Indiana* to praise the successes of his Department of Conservation.[18]

The 1935 session showed that McNutt was capable of modifying past policies, such as liquor control. In his message to the legislature, the governor dubbed the 1933 alcohol act "provisional and flexible," coming as it did before the repeal of Prohibition nationwide. A new law, he argued, was needed to prevent the return of the open saloon; to regulate where, when, and how old a person had to be to buy alcohol; to maintain state, not local, control; and to replace the state's single excise director (or "beer czar") with a nonpartisan board.[19] These proposals revealed McNutt's willingness to accommodate complaints about rising drunkenness and about the partisan nature of the 1933 law. They also underscored his consistency. McNutt continued to exalt state over local authority and to use taxes, such as those on alcohol, to keep his state solvent. In drafting the liquor law, he continued to rely on trusted lieutenants such as Frank M. McHale. But this time, the bill only inched through the legislature, for it was "long," "involved," and not well "understood" by most lawmakers. Yet McNutt pressed for immediate action. In the end, Democrats marshaled enough votes in the House and Senate to enact the law.[20]

The alcohol control act proved detailed and durable. The law banned roadhouses, night clubs, and the sale of alcohol on Sundays and holidays. It set opening and closing hours for taverns and penalties for selling alcohol to minors. It established a system for licensing manufacturers, wholesalers, and retailers of beer, wine, and liquor and replaced the excise director with a nonpartisan board whose four members were appointed by the governor. Nevertheless, the 1935 act continued to restrict the number of wholesalers and importers. Furthermore, McNutt placed a partisan stamp on the new commission by naming to it his old excise director, Paul Fry. This system of alcohol control lasted until 1945, when the Grand Old Party (GOP) recaptured the governorship and revamped the excise commission, giving it a Republican cast—proof that the 1935 act had failed to remove politics from the regulation of alcohol. Throughout the 1930s, licenses continued to go to Democrats. It was not unusual to hear a beer seller described as an "efficient party worker," and, significantly, McHale reviewed all applications from wholesalers.[21] Nevertheless, the 1935 law, with its taxes and fees, boosted state revenues. The most fair-minded assessment of the act came from the journalist Harold C. Feightner, who considered it "a model law, or at least one peculiarly fitted to Indiana, with the exception of the political wholesale features."[22]

If conservation and alcohol control illustrated McNutt's pragmatism, industrial recovery highlighted his national ambition. Following in FDR's footsteps, the governor recommended enactment of a state version of the president's National Recovery Administration. The NRA sought to restrict output, raise prices and wages, and restore the industrial sector of the economy. The NRA promoted a partnership between business and government under which companies negotiated codes of competition. These codes set standards for the quality of goods, curbed price slashing and other cutthroat practices, and allowed workers to form unions—a right guaranteed by Section 7(a) of the National Industrial Recovery Act (NIRA), the NRA's parent law. Firms participating in the NRA displayed the agency's emblem, the blue eagle, with its motto, "We do our part." Yet the NRA, according to the historian William E. Leuchtenburg, had "a formidable aggregation of critics" by 1935. "Housewives complained about high prices, businessmen about government edicts, and workers about the inadequacy of 7(a)."[23] The personality of the NRA's director, General Hugh S. Johnson, did not help. Johnson managed to offend industrial leaders with "his trademark mix of bluster, bravado, and baloney."[24]

Why, with all these difficulties, did McNutt recommend a state NRA? On a practical level, McNutt was simply catching up with national policy; since Congress passed the NIRA in June 1933, two months after his legislature adjourned, McNutt had offered no specific recovery program for his state. He also was keen on having Indiana participate in the Public Works Administration (PWA), the part of NIRA that provided dollars for public works projects. On a philosophical level, backing the NRA was a logical outgrowth of McNutt's expansion of the authority of his government. By 1934 the Indiana governor was praising the NRA for ending child labor, curtailing sweatshops, protecting the rights of workers, and spurring business expansion. He also identified himself with the planning aspect of NRA, asserting that his program of taxation and reorganization represented "planning for better state government."[25] But the urgency in McNutt's support for a state NRA stemmed from his ambition. He was thinking about national office—of running for vice president in 1936—and wanted to show loyalty to the Roosevelt administration. McNutt gushed that cooperation with FDR's recovery effort would be a "privilege" and should be the "first duty" of state governments.[26]

On the issue of a state NRA, McNutt's sense of timing deserted him. The bill he proposed ratified all codes approved at the national level. It called for a four-member panel to negotiate new state codes; mandated that codes recognize the right of workers to organize; and set penalties for anyone who violated the act. The *Indianapolis News* immediately led the charge against this expansion of the state government's authority. Under the caption "Next?" the paper's cartoonist drew the "Federal NRA" as a father walking with his five tots—"State NRA," "County NRA," "City NRA," "Township NRA," and "Ward NRA."[27] Opponents of a state-level NRA also benefitted from missteps by McNutt and Roosevelt. Assuming that the president wanted a state NRA, the governor pushed his bill at a time when FDR's recovery program was under fire and when Congress was debating the renewal of the NIRA. In this setting, the president shifted gears, declaring that he preferred state cooperation with a revised NRA instead of new state laws based on the old framework. Roosevelt's switcheroo allowed the *News* and the *Star* to plead for caution. Although the Indiana House passed McNutt's NRA bill, the Senate, three weeks later, approved a weakened version of the measure.[28]

The fight over a state NRA marked a sorry chapter in McNutt's stewardship of Indiana. The governor in this instance had allowed his ambitions, for a state NRA and for higher office, to cloud his judgment. He proved too confident and too trusting—of the drafters of the bill; of his own instincts as to what Roosevelt wanted; and, perhaps, of the president's word as well. When FDR rejected plans for a state NRA, the columnist Raymond Clapper observed, it "appeared to saw off the limb on which Governor McNutt was perched." The prospect of an Indiana NRA vanished in May 1935, when the U.S. Supreme Court, by unanimous vote, declared the president's NRA unconstitutional.[29]

The NRA issue taught McNutt a lesson about the hazards of getting ahead of national policies. With the Social Security Act of 1935, the governor made no sudden moves until after this landmark measure became law. Social Security had its roots in the paucity of private relief available to poor people and the inadequacy of state-level pensions for the elderly. During the 1930s, a grass-roots movement, led by the physician Francis Townsend, emerged to demand that all Americans aged sixty or older receive a monthly federal allowance. Although dismissed by experts and an array of interest groups as fiscally unsound, Townsend "helped keep the issue of old age insecurity at the center of the national policy agenda."[30] The Roosevelt administration answered with the Social Security Act, which inaugurated a system of old-age pensions financed by taxes on payrolls and employers. The law also provided federal grants to states to help elderly people in need and encouraged a federal-state partnership to provide unemployment insurance, assist the blind and the handicapped, and support dependent children. Like Roosevelt, McNutt had practical and political reasons for supporting Social Security—the "Townsend Plan" had gained a following in Indiana. Seven months after FDR signed the Social Security Act, McNutt summoned the General Assembly into special session and proposed three social welfare measures to bring Indiana into compliance with the new law.[31]

Before the General Assembly convened in March 1936, McNutt formed a committee of House and Senate members to draft the three bills. The first, a public health bill, enabled Indiana to claim $120,000 under the Social Security Act in exchange for the state's accepting federal oversight of its health care services. The second inaugurated, in accordance with the Social Security Act, unemployment compensation for workers at firms having eight or more employees. The most important law was the Public Welfare Act, which provided for a state-level department of public welfare with a director and five-member nonpartisan board, named by the governor, as well as county welfare boards, appointed by circuit court judges. Under this law, when Hoosiers turned seventy, they became eligible for monthly pensions up to $30—twice the maximum amount under the state's old-age pension law. Until the first checks went out under Social Security in 1940, the federal government provided half the dollars for Indiana's system of old-age pensions, while the state contributed thirty percent and counties twenty percent. The Public Welfare Act also provided payments for dependent children, pensions for blind people, and medical care and vocational training for the disabled.[32]

The unemployment compensation act, public health act, and public welfare act passed by overwhelming margins. There was some opposition to the public welfare bill by lawmakers who wanted county and township officials to retain control over old-age pensions. Yet the administration's bill won approval in the form McNutt sought. The governor and his advisers again showed their mastery of the legislature—they still could "crack the whip" over lawmakers.[33] The result was enactment of three "far-reaching" laws.[34] Counties in Indiana continued to determine eligibility requirements and assistance for public welfare recipients, and the townships retained their control over poor relief. But the Department of Public Welfare, infused with federal dollars, issued guidelines and heard appeals. The new department thus made the administration of social services in Indiana "more centralized, more progressive, more modern" than ever before.[35]

McNutt's actions highlighted his commitment to New Deal–style security. He was willing to be generous on social welfare programs partly because his state's finances had improved and partly because the federal government would pay nearly half the cost of the Social Security system in Indiana. But he did not have to forge ahead. Social Security encouraged—but did not require—states to participate in such programs as unemployment insurance. McNutt insisted that Indiana do so since state resources, he stated, had proven "tragically" inadequate to "safeguard" Hoosiers against "the major hazards and vicissitudes of life." Social Security, in contrast, represented a "sane and practical" strike against the "destitution and dependency" which often ignited "destructive political and social changes."[36] It was an outlook consistent with McNutt's inaugural address, which warned of "hungry people" revolting against the "established order."[37] It also coincided with his relief policy, whereby Indiana cooperated closely with the administration in Washington, and his core beliefs. An early biographer noted that McNutt "wholeheartedly approved of the entire social security-welfare system."[38] Just before Indiana lawmakers debated the state's participation in Social Security, McNutt urged representatives of FDR's Social Security Board "to sell the legislature the most liberal bill [they] could devise."[39]

McNutt boasted that the three acts passed by the General Assembly would bring "considerable security" to "thousands" of Hoosiers.[40] His thoughts on how to provide security were turning away from local authority. In the debate over the Public Welfare Act, McNutt fought against advocates of "home rule" who wanted to retain township control over poor relief.[41] He also became more explicit in justifying the larger aim of the Public Welfare Act: "We actually have made, for the first time in our national history, the welfare of the workingman, the farmer, the aged, the home, and the child a real concern of the Government." Federal oversight and dollars were, McNutt asserted, in tune with the idea preached by Abraham Lincoln that "the purpose of government" was to "better accomplish those things for the people [that] they could not do so well for themselves."[42] It was an argument that liberals in Lincoln's own party would later voice in defense of other New Deal–like policies.[43]

Throughout 1935 and 1936, McNutt kept up a furious pace. The demands on his time were "unending," he said, and they left him "little opportunity to write or visit old friends."[44] Carleton B. McCulloch, a friend and a past Democratic nominee for governor, considered McNutt "the hardest-working individual" he had ever seen.[45] McNutt's speaking schedule supported that claim.[46] To make his many engagements, the governor continued to travel via airplane. McCulloch recalled a Sunday in 1935 when McNutt "left at noon by plane, flew clear across the State to Portland, where he made a speech, then stopped at South Bend and made another, then dedicated a church at Michigan City, came back for supper and then ran over to Gary to do some broadcasting."[47] Travel of that sort proved risky; twice in one week, McNutt's aircraft had to make unscheduled landings. But he refused to slow down, for he remained "in great demand everywhere."[48]

At times, McNutt tried to relax. Although he was neither a raconteur nor a wit, he enjoyed a good joke and amusing commentary. Like many Americans of his era, he appreciated the "keen analysis" expressed by Will Rogers, a fellow midwesterner, in a "homey," "straightforward," and "humorous" style.[49] Early in 1935, McNutt sat onstage as Rogers entertained an audience at the Indianapolis Armory. Rogers was in fine form as he made light of his visit to the Indiana General Assembly: "It was a joint session—and what a joint!"[50] He teased McNutt as well. "I guess I done about everything there is," Rogers admitted, "except break out of an Indiana jail with a wooden pistol." The crowd laughed—as did McNutt.[51] After Rogers had finished, McNutt put his arm around the speaker and raved: "You are as funny as our leading humorist, Mr. Bryan, President of Indiana University."[52]

For extended rests, McNutt and his wife retired to the dunes of Lake Michigan, in northwestern Indiana. The McNutts probably learned of this area from Tom and Lucy Taggart, the children of Indiana's late political boss, Thomas Taggart Sr., who had pressed for development of a state park at the dunes. Tom and Lucy often joined the McNutts there, as did the ever-gossipy McCulloch. According to McCulloch, days at Lake Michigan passed without a care: "We lolled in the water and loafed on the sand, getting gloriously and painfully sunburned." One time, Paul borrowed a speedboat, and the quintet sped across the lake by moonlight. "We went sophomoric completely," McCulloch remembered, "and sang and yodeled and trilled and altoed and tenored and basso-profundoed for weird and witching hours."[53] After 1934, however, Paul's speaking schedule either prevented or cut short his vacations at the dunes. Nevertheless, Kathleen continued to holiday there herself, along with Tom, Lucy, and Carleton, as she sought "seclusion" from the "maddening" crowds.[54]

Kathleen never reconciled herself to life in the governor's mansion. On the surface, she remained "characteristically witty" and "as charming as ever."[55] She participated in philanthropic enterprises to improve hospitals and social services, and she attended concerts in Indianapolis with Louise. "I'll go to hear anyone play anything," Kathleen admitted.[56] Yet she longed to escape the public eye. After the Indiana author Meredith Nicholson received, with Paul's assistance, a ministerial posting to Paraguay, Kathleen asked him: "When can Lucy and I come and spend a couple of years with you?"[57] Increasingly, she withdrew into a world of her own. The press attributed Kathleen's absences to domestic

obligations. Late in 1934, she apparently fell ill and spent weeks incommuni-
cado. Kathleen had a trained nurse, but as a Christian Scientist she saw no doctor. McCulloch suspected that she had suffered a nervous breakdown. "The heat
of the campaign got on her nerves," he reckoned.[58] That was possible because
the 1934 contest had featured fierce attacks on her husband. By 1935 Kathleen
had pulled herself out of this "retirement," appearing, "becomingly gowned,"
at the opening of the General Assembly.[59] And she also accompanied Paul on
trips outside of Indiana. But she continued to spend long stretches of summer
up at the dunes.[60]

Louise McNutt, in contrast, grew to love politics. As one might expect, she
showed signs of homesickness after her family moved to Indianapolis. But the
pageantry of politics captivated her. On the day of her father's inauguration,
eleven-year-old Louise exclaimed: "It seemed like my birthday."[61] Four years
later, she "couldn't help crying" as Paul prepared to leave office.[62] If Louise
had inherited her mother's charm, she was acquiring her father's taste for public service. Yet she still suffered health problems. A 1934 x-ray disclosed that
Louise's spinal column had weakened, and she had to spend some time back
"on the board." According to Wayne Coy, both the governor and his wife were
"heartbroken" at the news.[63] Louise's relapse may have had prompted Kathleen's withdrawal and her own breakdown later that year.

Paul could find refuge from Kathleen's unhappiness and Louise's illnesses
in his work. McNutt relished nearly everything about politics: the camarade-
rie, the contests for office, the exercise of power, and the Two Percent Club.
Club members met periodically to elect officers and to have fun. In 1937, three
thousand of them convened at the state fairgrounds where they chose leaders,
danced to an orchestra, and watched wrestling bouts and a vaudeville show. Mc-
Nutt also attended these gatherings. Among friends and supporters, he would
take a drink or two—or more, in the first signs of a problem that became pronounced later in his life. At this point, members of the Two Percent Club, like
Hoosiers in general, only saw a polished leader in top form. At a meeting in 1935,
McNutt defended the club as furthering the Democratic agenda and the party's
electoral prospects. "The finger of scorn has been pointed to us," the governor
declared, "but after all results count." The Hoosier Democrats would carry into
battle "a record of which the people of Indiana can well be proud."[64]

That "us-versus-them" mindset increasingly governed McNutt's dealings
with the press. Pleas E. Greenlee, the governor's executive secretary, identified
the challenge for the Hoosier Democratic Party: "We are in power now, but the

Republicans have the press."[65] Greenlee complained that too many Republican newspapers were "on us" regardless of "what we do." "If the Savior were here himself and was a Democrat," he continued, "they would crucify him."[66] To try to remedy the problem, the state party committee enhanced its publicity efforts, issuing news releases touting the administration's achievements.[67] Indiana Democrats started their own organ, the *Hoosier Sentinel*. Yet the McNutt forces resented any whiff of press criticism. Early in his term, the governor had found an ally in Talcott Powell, the editor of the *Indianapolis Times*. When a new editor, Ludwell Denny, took over the *Times* in 1935 and tried to drain the paper of its Democratic "bias," the governor and his friends rebelled. Roy W. Howard, the *Times* publisher, sensed "frostiness" from McNutt when the two men met at a party.[68] The governor was more than cold. In 1936 he had the state insurance commissioner remind the *Times* editors that the government of Indiana owned "several thousand dollars worth of legal advertising" and their paper would see none of that money "until the governor knows The Times' policy" with respect to the upcoming political campaign. The editors of the *Times* ignored the threat, though they thought it "more than a little crude."[69] Democrats in Indiana later decided it made more sense to court the Republican press, as McNutt had done in 1933, rather than fight with editors or use advertising as a way to encourage favorable coverage.[70]

McNutt's threats to the *Indianapolis Times* suggested that his arrogance had not abetted and was, if anything, growing. Many Hoosiers commented on the governor's ego. There was talk of "taking the dome off the State Capitol" in order to "make room for Paul McNutt's head." Assemble McNutt's top advisers, one man observed, and "you'd have some of the biggest snobs in the state."[71] In a way, such conceit was not surprising. McNutt had come far and fast in a short period of time. His unbroken string of successes separated him from many Americans who were still suffering through the depression. Although McNutt had experience in grassroots organizations—the American Legion—and his policies sought to enhance the economic station of average people, he governed from the top down, aided by a tiny coterie of aides who were not in contact with the workers and farmers of Indiana. Such a style of leadership put him at a disadvantage when it confronted social unrest, as McNutt's handling of Terre Haute general strike revealed.

McNutt might have anticipated the events that transpired in Terre Haute, for strikes were a sign of the times in the 1930s. As the economy experienced the first pangs of recovery, in 1934 and 1935, workers, particularly the unskilled,

renewed their decades-long campaign for higher wages, fair work rules, job security, and recognition of unions. The labor movement also had tools in hand
and friends in high places. Section 7(a) of the National Industrial Recovery Act
assured workers the right to organize and bargain collectively. After the Supreme Court declared the NRA unconstitutional in 1935, Congress passed and
FDR signed the National Labor Relations Act, or Wagner Act, which "threw
the weight of government behind the right of labor to bargain collectively."[72]
In this setting, labor leaders organized strikes across the country, including a
general strike in San Francisco. Many employers resisted unionization, at times
violently. Watching from afar was President Roosevelt, who was more comfortable providing workers with relief, pensions, and unemployment insurance than
with guaranteeing them the right to bargain collectively. Although Roosevelt's
private thoughts about the labor movement were at times "patronizing," he did
nothing to impede the organization of unions.[73]

McNutt's record on the rights of workers proved mixed. During the 1933
and 1935 sessions, the Indiana General Assembly passed and McNutt signed
legislation to enhance safety in mines, discourage the employment of under-
age miners, and restrict issuance of injunctions in labor disputes. Nevertheless,
there was no evidence that McNutt had developed warm feelings for labor, since
he hailed from the middle class and his early contacts with the working-class
lads in his hometown had been troubled. Trained as a lawyer, McNutt had developed a great respect for settling disputes in the courts, not in the streets. As
a Legionnaire, he had denounced radical ideologies, making him ill disposed
toward grassroots leaders of leftist persuasion. (In 1935 he signed legislation that
barred from state elections any political party that advocated the forceful over-
throw of the U.S. government.) As a former soldier, McNutt was familiar with
the uses of American troops, and as governor he saw it as his duty "to preserve
order and to protect life and property."[74] McNutt thus was open to deploying
the National Guard to restore order in the face of labor unrest. When violence
between union and non-union miners in Indiana's Sullivan County peaked at
the end of 1933, McNutt dispatched two companies of National Guard troops
and placed the county under martial law until 1936.[75]

Terre Haute proved a much bigger crisis. The showdown began over union
recognition. Workers at the city's Columbian Enameling and Stamping Company had organized a union under the auspices of the NRA and with the assistance of the American Federation of Labor (AFL). But labor leaders suspected
that management was favoring unorganized workers and was trying to form

a company union. In March 1935, they insisted that management institute a closed shop and employ unionized labor only. When the company refused, the workers, nearly five hundred strong, went on strike. Rumors that scab labor would be used to break the strike prompted workers from across the region to express solidarity with the strikers. The bitterness on both sides intensified in July, when the company began to station armed guards at the plant. Thereafter, union leaders called a general strike. Workers in Terre Haute's other major industries walked out, and people in Terre Haute immediately felt the effects. Bus and streetcar service ceased, as did deliveries of milk, bread, and ice. Although the lives of city residents were "severely interrupted," they were not imperiled, for people still had access to groceries and filling stations in nearby communities.[76]

McNutt saw the situation as dire. On July 22, Mayor Sam Beecher informed the governor that services in Terre Haute had stopped and that his city's police were unable to maintain "law and order."[77] He urged McNutt to send the state militia to Terre Haute at once. The governor obliged by dispatching over one thousand troops and placing all of Vigo County under martial law. He signed an order forbidding anyone in the county from carrying weapons or assembling in public. McNutt defended his action by pointing to the mayor's appeal for assistance, the closing of businesses, the disruption of food supplies, and the need to maintain law and order.[78] McNutt's action, which quelled the strike, drew support from many Hoosiers, including company managers, professional people, and workers at the Columbian Company, who were quick to blame the strike on radicals.[79] One woman reported that "a feeling of security" had returned to Terre Haute "since the entrance of the militia."[80] Letters to the statehouse ran almost five to one in favor of what McNutt had done.[81]

Labor leaders and prominent members of the Socialist Party criticized McNutt—harshly. During the summer of 1935, many of them made pilgrimages to Terre Haute, also coincidentally the former home of Eugene V. Debs, a four-time Socialist Party candidate for the White House. The general strike and McNutt's sending of the National Guard stoked the fires. Powers Hapgood, the Socialist Party's candidate for governor of Indiana in 1932, went to Terre Haute, where he condemned martial law and found himself in jail. Hapgood's arrest so outraged Norman Thomas, the Socialist Party candidate for president in 1932, that he headed to Terre Haute, where he accused the governor of instituting "military tyranny" and predicted the emergence of other "Hoosier Hitlers."[82] Even though Thomas did not hang that moniker specifically on McNutt, it became associated with the governor. Charges of "Fascist Terror" appeared in

Socialist and Communist tracts, and one left-leaning union branded McNutt the "Hoosier Hitler."[83]

Such criticism hurt McNutt with labor unions and liberal organizations, which were becoming important constituencies in the Democratic Party. The AFL condemned McNutt as a strikebreaker, while the leaders of the American Civil Liberties Union railed against the "unwarranted interference" of National Guard troops in Terre Haute with the right of citizens to express themselves.[84] Unions from Milwaukee to New York City joined in condemnation. To make matters worse, McNutt did not withdraw National Guardsmen from Terre Haute until February 1936, over a month after Mayor Beecher had requested that he do so. Such actions suggested that the Indiana governor was hostile to workers who supported the strike.[85]

McNutt saw things differently. He distinguished between using the National Guardsmen to uphold public order and deploying them simply to break strikes. During the crisis in Terre Haute, McNutt insisted that he was "very much in sympathy with organized labor" and that he had sent the National Guard only "to maintain law and order."[86] The governor's first assertion was credible, for he had compiled a respectable legislative record on labor issues. Furthermore, when a delegation from Bloomington urged him to send the National Guard "to quell a minor labor dispute," he refused, arguing that to do so in this case would represent strike-breaking.[87] Yet McNutt also used troops to put down labor unrest in Floyd and Clark counties, in southern Indiana, where garment workers had struck to secure recognition of their union. Meanwhile, Terre Haute remained under military rule for over six months, a sign of just how much the general strike had shaken a governor who had long been leery of the underside of human nature. McNutt's action separated him from other Democratic governors of the 1930s who were sympathetic to labor—Herbert Lehman of New York, Pennsylvania's George Earle, and Michigan's Frank Murphy—as well as from the Roosevelt administration, which was perceived as favoring unionization. McNutt's use of the National Guard may have earned kudos among many Hoosiers, but it aroused suspicion among New Dealers that he was not one of them.[88]

While McNutt's actions in Terre Haute were drawing national attention, his eyes were firmly fixed on national office. McNutt's ambition for the White House, aroused in 1932, had never abetted, thanks in part to a collection of friends and advisers who urged him to think beyond the governorship. One devotee was Oscar R. Ewing, a graduate of Indiana University who lived in New York City. Shortly after the Democratic National Convention in 1932, Ewing offered to talk with McNutt "about the future." "Whether we plan for 1936 or 1940," he explained, "depends upon whether or not Roosevelt is elected."[89] FDR's election in 1932 clarified which office the Indiana governor might aspire to. It would not be a seat in the U.S. Senate, which McNutt had declined to run for in 1932 and again in 1934. The presidency and vice presidency were more alluring possibilities. McNutt's advisers seemed uncertain whether Roosevelt would be a one- or a two-term president, and they wondered whether John Nance Garner would be renominated as vice president in 1936. With that in mind, McNutt in 1933 authorized Ewing and Douglas I. McKay, another friend from New York, to form an organization, raise money, and assemble likely campaign managers in the eastern states.[90] McNutt also agreed to choose carefully his public speaking engagements outside Indiana while Ewing and Wayne Coy worked to promote the governor's name in the press. Since McNutt wanted this enterprise kept hush-hush, correspondence among Coy, Ewing, and McKay took on a secretive tone, with references to meetings in New York, to having had "a good talk," and to discussing "this and that."[91] At times, they revealed more than they perhaps intended. Coy wrote Ewing that if his organization required cash it was "quite possible" that the governor and his friends could "assist" since the Hoosier Democratic Club was receiving "several thousand dollars" each month.[92]

Word reached the White House that the McNutt forces were up to something. Postmaster General James A. Farley, who headed the Democratic National Committee (DNC) and who had no use for McNutt, heard from one Hoosier Democrat that McNutt had organized a campaign for the presidency and was claiming control of "eight states at the next convention." Farley relayed this tidbit to Roosevelt, adding: "It is quite evident that our friend Paul is very ambitious!"[93] He was, but not for the presidency—not in 1936, at least. By 1935, Ewing had recognized that no Democrat other than FDR would be nominated in 1936. But the 1940 election was "a different story," and Ewing wanted to see McNutt succeed Roosevelt.[94] To gain the party's nomination in 1940, McNutt began to position himself as FDR's heir. In 1934 he delivered a strong defense of the New Deal that Mary W. Dewson, the head of the women's division of the Democratic National Committee, deemed "excellent."[95] By 1935, the governor was praising Roosevelt as the nation's "greatest peace-time President."[96] One month later, the Indiana Democratic Editorial Association endorsed FDR for president and McNutt for vice president in 1936.[97]

That resolution was part of a boom within Indiana to nominate McNutt for vice president. The campaign was partly spontaneous as Democrats in several counties formed "Roosevelt-McNutt" clubs. When one man sketched a poster of the would-be Democratic ticket, McNutt told him that it was "too early to be making any definite commitments concerning the 1936 campaign" but said he was "very glad to have the poster."[98] Such coyness had characterized the start of McNutt's earlier campaigns, and it continued throughout the winter months of 1935. With respect to the Roosevelt-McNutt clubs, the governor insisted he was in "no sense" a candidate for vice president. But he also voiced "no objection" to such clubs if they promoted "harmony and good feeling."[99] This time, such veiled ambition got him nowhere. The publisher of the *Memphis Press-Scimitar*, who was open to replacing Garner with another candidate, thought that McNutt and his friends had acted "too soon" and "too frequently" in pushing for the vice presidency.[100] FDR in turn gave no hint that Garner, who was serving as a bridge between the administration and conservative Democrats, would be replaced in 1936.[101]

The relationship between Roosevelt and McNutt was complicated, with each man trying to use the other to advance his aims. The president, of course, needed the governor less than the governor needed him. Although FDR had courted McNutt before the Democratic National Convention in 1932 and had hosted him at Hyde Park following the election, he thereafter treated McNutt like any other governor, communicating with him through form letters. The Hoosier met sporadically with the president—on four occasions in 1934, an election year, and twice in 1935. Most of these sessions came at McNutt's request; just three were one-on-one encounters; and many were arranged by intermediaries such Coy, who had worked with Harry Hopkins; Marvin H. McIntyre, one of FDR's secretaries; and Indiana's U.S. senator Sherman Minton.[102] Roosevelt only solicited McNutt's help after the Hoosier showed himself to be an effective partisan speaker. McNutt's defense of the administration during an address at Rushville, Indiana, impressed one listener, who sent word to the president. FDR congratulated McNutt, requested a copy of the address, and urged him to "let me know if you come east" so that they might talk.[103] To cement the governor's loyalty, Roosevelt pledged to go along "with the State administration in Indiana" on the critical question of who would succeed McNutt as governor in 1936.[104]

The succession issue vexed McNutt throughout 1935. Since the state constitution prohibited a governor from serving two consecutive terms, McNutt had to leave office in 1937. He understood that nominating and electing a candidate of his choosing would help solidify his policy agenda, demonstrate his command of the Hoosier Democratic Party, and strengthen his bid for the White House in 1940. Yet two things stood in McNutt's way. First, his foes within the party, led by R. Earl Peters and conservative senator Frederick Van Nuys, had rallied behind the candidacy of E. Kirk McKinney, the head of the Home Owners Loan Corporation in Indiana. More ominously, divisions had surfaced within the McNutt faction over the candidacy of Pleas Greenlee, the governor's executive secretary. Greenlee had been an effective dispenser of patronage, a fact which had won him friends across Indiana in a manner not unlike Jim Farley's distribution of postal appointments at the national level. But McNutt deemed Greenlee ill qualified for the governorship—as FDR later dismissed Farley as ill suited for the presidency. By 1935 Greenlee was campaigning for governor quietly, lining up the support of some McNutt Democrats, such as Paul Fry and Sherman Minton, while offending others, such as Coy, Simmons, and McHale.[105] His actions left McNutt in "a hot spot." If he did nothing, Greenlee would be free to build a machine of his own. If McNutt removed his secretary, however, he "would be accused of ingratitude" by Greenlee and his followers.[106] So rather than take a stand, McNutt let the succession question "ride along" for most of 1935.[107]

Nineteen thirty-six brought clarity to the governor's race. Greenlee began boasting to supporters that he was influential enough to "name the candidate" of the Democratic Party.[108] When such braggadocio reached McNutt's ears, late in 1935, he sat silently, "burning inside." A few days later, he announced Greenlee's "retirement" as executive secretary.[109] Greenlee then launched his gubernatorial bid openly and broke with the statehouse in March 1936, when he promised to rid the Hoosier Democratic Party of "McHale-ism," his term for the rule of "self-appointed bosses and so-called advisors" over the party's traditional rank-and-file membership.[110] McNutt responded by discreetly supporting the candidacy of Lieutenant Governor M. Clifford Townsend, even though he was a "dry" Democrat, a non-veteran, and a politician not closely identified with the governor's inner circle.[111] As in 1934, the McNutt Democrats controlled the state convention, and they nominated Townsend over both Greenlee and McKinney.[112]

The 1936 campaign in Indiana echoed those of 1932 and 1934. As in 1932, the state GOP was, in the words of former governor James P. Goodrich, "drifting."[113] The party renominated Raymond S. Springer, who had lost to McNutt four years earlier, and then campaigned, as it had in 1934, against the sitting governor. Springer rapped McNutt for establishing a "dictatorship" that threatened "the American way of life" [114] The Republican nominee tagged Townsend, like Minton, a mere "proxy" for McNutt.[115] He tried to re-ignite controversies over John Dillinger's prison break, the Two Percent Club, and the gross income tax. Moreover, in a bid to capitalize on McNutt's troubles with labor, the Republican State Committee claimed that the governor had used convict rather than unionized labor to perform state tasks. But while the GOP was wooing workers, Springer was pushing them away by vowing to reconsider the "so-called social security law" endorsed by the Indiana legislature.[116] Such rhetoric led one Republican to lament that his party seemed to be doing everything possible to reinforce FDR's charge that the GOP was led by "economic royalists."[117]

McNutt emphasized that theme as well. In the race for governor, Townsend ran on the record of McNutt, who once again leaped headfirst into the fray. McNutt cast the Democratic Party's campaign as a "crusade" on behalf of Hoosiers requiring "protection against entrenched greed."[118] In Martinsville, he cited his accomplishments—a budget surplus and greater expenditures on schools, old-age pensions, and relief—and warned that Springer's pledge to "cut costs" would take from students, old folks, and the poor "what the Democratic administration has promised and is now giving."[119] McNutt later took a page from the 1934 contest by making his points in question-and-answer sessions with voters. The "versatility and daring" exhibited by McNutt at these "open forums" impressed even the *Indianapolis Star:* "He has gone on week after week defying critics and coming out victorious at each session."[120]

During the election campaign of 1936, Roosevelt sought to use McNutt's oratory to his advantage—and on his own terms. The governor's friends in Washington, D.C., led by Minton, had lobbied for him to be named keynote speaker at the Democratic National Convention in Philadelphia. But FDR assigned McNutt a lesser task, to second his renomination. A month after the convention, McNutt, at Roosevelt's behest, played the part of hatchet man, assailing the publisher William Randolph Hearst, a fierce critic of the Roosevelt administration, in a nationally broadcast address. The governor denounced Hearst and his "enormous fortune," his conservatism and isolationism, and his connections to the now-unpopular Republican administrations of the 1920s.[121] McNutt's "indictment" was, the *New York Post* opined, "devastating," in part because it came from "a prominent Legionnaire" whose patriotism Hearst would have been hard-pressed to question.[122] Even Farley acknowledged that McNutt's speech had gone over "very well," and he told Roosevelt so.[123] Thereafter, the

White House tapped McNutt as a surrogate campaigner, sending him to speak in Ohio, Texas, and Maine. And when FDR went to Indiana to campaign in person, the governor greeted him and rode alongside him in an open car.[124]

Association with Roosevelt carried advantages for McNutt. The governor knew that the president was going to win by a landslide in 1936. McNutt's speeches on behalf of the national ticket, and his occasional visits with FDR, had boosted his prestige among Democrats in Indiana. Carleton McCulloch claimed that "Paul sits very close to the throne" and was becoming "one of the big guns" in the party nationally.[125] The press outside Indiana took notice. In 1936 the *New York Times, Washington Post,* and *Chicago Tribune* all ran articles or features on the Indiana governor. McNutt's speechmaking fed speculation that he would join Roosevelt's cabinet during the president's second term. But it was FDR who would, if reelected, determine which—if any—position McNutt would receive. The election of 1936 marked a watershed for McNutt. Before it, he had been able to act independently, as head of an organization (the American Legion) or unit of government (the state of Indiana). Afterward, McNutt's political advancement grew increasingly dependent on Roosevelt's will. Whether by design or not, FDR was drawing the Hoosier "into a one-sided political relationship." Years later, McNutt boasted that he had resolved to work with Roosevelt until he had attained his prize and then "tell that S.O.B. where to go."[126] Perhaps, but, having defied the Roosevelt forces in 1932 and lost, McNutt now believed that the wiser course of action was to cooperate with the president.

The disparity in the McNutt-Roosevelt relationship became evident in how the two men approached the election in Indiana. Believing that a Democratic triumph would earn him points with the president, McNutt campaigned aggressively. While Roosevelt ignored his opponent, Governor Alf Landon of Kansas, McNutt flailed the Republican nominee as a heartless budget balancer, reactionary, and nonentity. Meanwhile, the McNutt administration pressed state employees to contribute an additional one percent of their annual incomes to the Hoosier Democratic Club, prodded those with automobiles to transport Democratic voters to polling places, and compelled state workers to complete a questionnaire documenting their "election service."[127] FDR, for his part, became so confident of the outcome in Indiana that he canceled a visit to the state in October. Farley, the president's campaign manager, was in contact with party leaders across the nation and liked what he was hearing. He predicted a Roosevelt landslide.[128]

Nineteen thirty-six proved to be another banner year for Democrats. Roosevelt captured 523 electoral votes against just 8 for Landon. The president received sixty-one percent of the popular vote nationwide and almost fifty-seven percent in Indiana. In the congressional contests, Democrats won extravagant margins over Republicans—331 to 89 in the House and 76 to 19 in the Senate— and eleven of the twelve members of Indiana's House delegation would be Democrats. In the state legislature, the Democrats took 23 of the 26 senate seats up for election and increased its membership in the house from 65 to 67. Moreover, Townsend beat Springer—as Farley also had predicted—with almost fifty-five percent of the vote. The *Indianapolis Star* pronounced the Democrats' victory an endorsement of "the generally satisfactory service they have given."[129]

As McNutt prepared to leave the statehouse, the *Star* offered a surprisingly balanced assessment of his record: "Governor McNutt's administration has been one of unusual initiative and accomplishment."[130] What proved "unusual" about its initiatives was they came from the governor's office and were passed by a compliant legislature. With assistance from such capable subordinates as McHale, Simmons, Coy, and Greenlee, McNutt defeated the Republicans in the halls of the capitol and at the ballot box as the Democratic Party prevailed in the elections of 1932, 1934, and 1936. Such triumphs reinforced McNutt's ambition and lifted his prestige.

McNutt was buoyed by his administration's long list of accomplishments. The gross income tax, his most important and controversial initiative, stabilized Indiana's revenues during the 1930s and for years afterward. And it showed that a party could raise taxes and still retain the governorship—as Democratic governor Matthew E. Welsh, who replaced the gross income tax with an income tax and enacted a state sales tax, proved again in the 1960s. McNutt also reorganized Indiana's government so thoroughly that the GOP failed to reverse it during the 1940s. Here, he set the precedent that expansion of state government must yield to periodic streamlining and regrouping, as later occurred under Governor Welsh in the 1960s and Democratic governor Evan Bayh in the 1990s.[131] Reform, another aspect of the McNutt administration, was notable for its breadth, from liquor control to conservation, and depth, by placing banks under stricter supervision than ever before. If McNutt at first was cautious in deferring to local authority on relief, he quickly adjusted, cooperating with the Roosevelt administration and securing millions of federal dollars for public works projects. Work relief put money in people's pockets, increased purchasing power, and bolstered recovery while providing visible markers—public housing units, schools, roads, and other infrastructure—of the state administration.

In 1936 Senator Minton was able to report that the first sign of "recovery" had "definitely come to Indiana" and that the "average man in the factory and on the farm" was grateful to the Democratic Party.[132]

With such achievements, McNutt towered over Indiana politics in a manner not seen since the Civil War. In the 1930s, a time of bland governors nationally—"moderate, un-dramatic, yawn-inspiring men"—Indiana's executive stood out.[133] He was attractive, magnetic, and effective on the stump. He made good newspaper copy, mainly because he always seemed to be doing something. Furthermore, the dire economic circumstances that McNutt inherited, the large Democratic majorities that he commanded, and the energy with which he rallied his supporters invited comparisons to the sitting occupant of the White House. A constituent wrote McNutt in 1933: "With the exception of President Roosevelt and Vice-President Garner you have more well-wishers than any other man elected to public office in the last election."[134] And an early biographer asserted: "Two names resounded from the lips of most Americans during the depression decade of the 1930s—Franklin D. Roosevelt and Paul V. McNutt."[135] That claim was exaggerated, although not wildly so. The names Roosevelt and McNutt could be heard so often in part because many people were either hailing or condemning these leaders.

Both FDR and McNutt used government to afford Americans a greater sense of security from life's hazards. Late in 1936 Roosevelt summarized the aim of his first term as removing some of the "chances" from American life and substituting in their place "security for people so that they would not individually worry" about losing their home, job or business.[136] McNutt speeches also stressed the importance of providing "security" for Hoosiers.[137] He emerged as the architect of Indiana's welfare state, proposing state-sponsored old-age pensions two months before FDR took office, and he was one of the first governors to "get in line" with the Social Security Act in 1935. On such issues, the *Indianapolis Star* editorialized, McNutt "has been alert and aggressive at all times."[138] Thus, he, like FDR, helped to shift debate away from the cultural and ethnic issues that had dominated the 1920s—Prohibition, immigration restriction, and revival of the Ku Klux Klan—and toward redress of economic problems. Hoosiers who had endured corruption in their state's government during the 1920s were satisfied with the results.[139] The editor of the *Anderson Herald* raved: "McNutt Redeems Indiana."[140]

A fair amount of hissing accompanied the cheers, most of it involving tactics. The governor built, almost from scratch, a machine around an unapologetic system of patronage, privileged access to liquor licenses, and the Two Percent Club—McNutt's most enduring "contribution" to state politics. The organization lasted into the 1970s, when Republican governor Edgar D. Whitcomb made participation in it voluntary, and survived the 1980s, after which Governor Bayh ended it once and for all.[141] In the interim, the Two Percent Club remained a curiosity, something unique to a state whose style of partisan activity seemed straight out of the nineteenth century. During the 1970s, it was not unusual for state and local government employees to feel pressure to campaign at election time—an echo of the 1936 contest—for, as one Indiana Democrat put it, "working for the party" was just a part of holding office.[142]

Overall, McNutt's record positioned him to run as the New Deal candidate for president in 1940. To be certain, some observers questioned his commitment to FDR's policies. In 1938, one man dubbed McNutt's governorship an "admixture of political liberalism and machine orthodoxy," as if the two things were separate—a perspective that overlooked the Roosevelt's administration own cooperation with local bosses and their organizations.[143] Two years earlier, a journalist had suggested that McNutt might have been too conservative, that is, he might have "overbalanced" his state's budget, which was nearly $12 million in the black.[144] Yet the governor's fiscal practices were in accordance with the aims, if not the outcomes, of Roosevelt's policies. After all, FDR, during the election campaign of 1932, had promised to balance the federal budget. Attempts to separate McNutt from Roosevelt were strongest in the area of labor policy, where the governor seemed less apt than the president to tolerate strikes. They collapse, however, when one reviews McNutt's strong record on social welfare in general and Social Security in particular. The Indiana governor's ambitions for the White House served to amplify, not to determine, his support of the New Deal.

McNutt was one of only a handful of governors to back with gusto New Deal–style security. "Some cooperated enthusiastically with Roosevelt," the historian James T. Patterson has noted, "others tolerated him, [and] others were stubbornly independent."[145] This variety reflected many factors, such as the alignment of political parties in each state; the degree of factionalism within the local Democratic Party; the ideology, persona, aims, and political skills of the governor; and the state's resources and finances. Some states, like Wisconsin and Minnesota in the early 1930s, pressed ahead with reforms of their own. Others, such as Michigan and Georgia, adopted New Deal–like measures later in the decade, at a time when a backlash against liberalism limited their reach.

A number of conservative states in the South and West resisted the New Deal while wealthy, urban states with strong reform traditions, such as New York, remained at the vanguard of depression-era liberalism. And others still, such as Pennsylvania and Indiana, developed liberal reputations, at least until the GOP resurgence of late 1930s and early 1940s.[146] Governor George Earle of Pennsylvania pushed a "Little New Deal" because, as he explained, "life must be made more secure" for those "at the mercy of economic forces."[147] McNutt's successor, M. Clifford Townsend, continued his agenda. Stated Townsend in 1938, "The issue of the campaign . . . shall be security." He then emphasized: "The people shall be fed. The unemployed must have work. The farmer and the laborer and the businessman must have a fair share of the wealth they produce. The old must have security."[148] Such aims did not meet universal approval; regarding Social Security, "state cooperation was often reluctantly given."[149] Indiana was an exception.

McNutt was more than a mere supporter of the New Deal; he was a part of a generation, an era, and an outlook, about the role of the state and the nature of humans, which made the New Deal possible. The men and women of Roosevelt's administration differed from Progressive Era reformers in that they exuded less optimism about the perfectibility of man (Prohibition, a cause of many Progressives, was an early casualty of the New Deal) and greater faith in the ability of the state to manage the economy and to check human impulses.[150] New Dealers placed less emphasis on expanding opportunity, which in the hands of reckless, unrestrained individuals had helped cause the Great Depression, and more on affording safety, or security, to as many Americans as possible. McNutt, with his military background and global perspective, looked at a world struggling through a "long crisis" that included the Great War, the rise of dictatorships, and the depression. To him, the "heart of the crisis" lay neither in "laws" nor "institutions of government" but in "the will and the purpose of men." People in Russia, Italy, and Germany, McNutt said, had become insecure—"frightened," "hysterical," and "demoralized"—and such fear had overturned the existing social order in those lands. Under Roosevelt, however, America had taken a different path, under which the government engaged in a bold experiment to marshal the nation's "untold resources" and make Americans "confident of our power to provide for own security."[151] Such words meshed with his comment, that government was a "great instrument" waiting to be used to advance a larger purpose.[152] And his belief that reform could dampen the appeal of radicalism and forestall revolution was held by other depression-era liberals, particularly Franklin and Eleanor Roosevelt.[153] Realism about human nature and idealism about the possibilities of a skillfully led democratic state placed McNutt within the intellectual and policy mindset of the New Deal.

McNutt differed from most New Dealers in FDR's White House in that he had been highly successful running a state government. In fact, among Indiana's governors, McNutt deserves to be ranked at the very top.[154] His only real competitor is Oliver P. Morton, who served during the Civil War and who governed for much of his term without a sitting legislature and with direct financial assistance from the Lincoln administration. McNutt, in contrast, led and mastered the General Assembly and was far less dependent on the president of his era. Furthermore, McNutt's policies in the areas of taxation, reorganization, public welfare, and patronage would be felt by Hoosiers for decades. According to Jack New, a longtime Democratic Party operative and frequent critic of McNutt, a person could not travel about Indiana in the twenty-first century without seeing some trace of McNutt's influence. At the same time, none of the state's succeeding governors were able to match "his enormous power."[155] Warts and all, Paul V. McNutt was the greatest governor Indiana ever knew.

# 8

## BREAKING AWAY
## (1937–1938)

AS 1937 OPENED, PAUL V. McNUTT found himself in a strange but not entirely unique position. Like many Americans, he was out of a job, a victim of Indiana's constitution rather than the forces of market capitalism. So, for the first time in a decade, he was free to contemplate what he might do next. There was talk of his opening a law office in Indianapolis. But what he really wanted was a spot in the cabinet of Franklin D. Roosevelt, and he thought that his record, his support for the president in the election of 1936, and the victory of the Hoosier Democratic Party that fall merited such a reward.[1] Some observers speculated that McNutt, because of his leadership of the American Legion, would be named secretary of war.[2] When a fellow governor asked about the rumor, McNutt "waved his cigar" and declared: "It depends on me and only on me."[3] In truth, McNutt had to wait for his assignment from President Roosevelt, and it would not be the War Department. In the meantime, Louise McNutt came up with a tart reply to queries about her father's future: "I think he is going on relief."[4]

In February 1937, FDR came through, nominating McNutt to be United States high commissioner to the Philippines. This was, on the surface, an unusual appointment, for McNutt had never been to East Asia and he was no expert on the Philippines. The post also transferred this aspiring presidential candidate away from his native state and kept him away from the politics of the nation's capital. Yet going to the Philippines allowed McNutt to enhance his foreign policy credentials in anticipation of the election of 1940. In fact, while in Manila. McNutt defended American sovereignty and interests, established a smooth relationship with Philippine leaders, and raised his standing in the archipelago and in the United States. After living almost all of his adult life in Indiana and after considering offers to leave his native state in the 1920s, Mc-Nutt at last got the chance to break away from his parents and oldest friends. That did not mean that he was entirely happy with this break or that he was breaking with his political advisers in Indiana. Between 1937 and 1939, McNutt kept one eye on his duties in the Philippines while focusing the other on the opportunities awaiting him back home.

Why send McNutt to the Philippines? FDR's move was clever, for it settled a campaign debt and exiled a potential competitor at the same time. In 1940 the president, while in the company of close associates, explained allegorically why McNutt had been posted to Manila. A governor of Arizona, he related, once had requested a diplomatic appointment for a "political rival." When asked where his rival might be sent, the governor pointed to a spot on the globe "exactly opposite" Arizona. The man, Roosevelt recounted, was appointed "Minister to Siam."[5] Frank M. McHale, McNutt's political strategist and confidant, heard such talk and concluded the worst—that FDR and his inner circle had sent the inexperienced McNutt to the Philippines expecting him to be "shelled" by controversy and his political career to wilt in the tropical heat.[6] That did not happen.

FDR's decision to name McNutt high commissioner was less malevolent and more spontaneous than McHale thought. By the end of 1936, the president was receiving conflicting advice about what to do about McNutt. Marvin H. McIntyre, FDR's appointments secretary, recommended him for a cabinet post, albeit over the vehement opposition of James A. Farley, postmaster general and chair of the Democratic National Committee (DNC). Farley almost begged the president to keep McNutt out of the cabinet, reminding him of the Hoosier's reluctance to endorse FDR at the Democratic National Convention in 1932. Farley predicted that, as a member of the administration, McNutt would place his presidential ambitions ahead of his departmental duties.[7] But FDR knew that political ambition fueled Farley because Farley, no less than the Hoosier, hoped to win the White House in 1940.[8] The president, who was not above playing opportunistic underlings against one another, repeatedly told Farley that he wished to bring McNutt into the administration, perhaps as chair of the United States Maritime Commission. Farley raised "no objection" to McNutt occupying that position, which was neither high profile nor obviously suited to a former governor from the Midwest. Accordingly, Farley pressed for immediate announcement of the appointment.[9]

A vacant post in Manila helped clarify McNutt's future. In 1936 Frank Murphy resigned as Philippine high commissioner to run, successfully, for governor of Michigan. The president considered several candidates to replace Murphy, but had trouble finding one.[10] Complicating matters was an upcoming visit of Philippine president Manuel L. Quezon to Washington, D.C.; some members of the administration wanted Roosevelt to announce Murphy's successor before Quezon arrived, to prevent the Philippine president from claiming that he had influenced FDR's choice.[11] Finally, at a cabinet meeting in February 1937, Vice President John Nance Garner proposed McNutt as a possible high commissioner. With his own eyes set on a presidential run in 1940, Garner lamented that the former Indiana governor appeared to be campaigning for president already. Therefore, "it might not be a bad idea to send him to the Philippines." Roosevelt smiled. When Farley asked whether that was "far enough," the president laughed.[12] FDR had his nominee.

McNutt's selection as high commissioner came as a "considerable surprise" to members of the foreign policy establishment and, no doubt, to the nominee as well.[13] The former governor of Indiana knew little of the Philippines, though he was not unfamiliar with the wider world thanks, in part, to his leadership of the American Legion. And had expert knowledge of the Philippines been a prerequisite for serving there, Frank Murphy, a former mayor of Detroit, never would have left Michigan. Indeed, McNutt would join a long list of U.S. administrators, few of them authorities on the Philippines. During the first third of the twentieth century, the U.S. president selected the governor-general, the top executive post in the Philippines. These men, and the presidents and political parties they served, had ideas on how the Philippines ought to be governed, rather than expertise. The Republicans, the nation's majority party, possessed a clear vision for the islands: to occupy, pacify, and Americanize them, both politically and economically. President William McKinley, who launched the war against Spain in 1898 and then made the decision to retain the Philippines as a U.S. colony, cast his policy for the country as one of "benevolent assimilation," rather than selfish imperialism, under which the American sense of "justice and right" would replace the "arbitrary rule" of Spain.[14] In contrast, the

Democrats saw imperialism as an exercise in exploitation and betrayal of their nation's democratic ideals. When under Woodrow Wilson the party regained the White House in 1912, it rejected close supervision of the Philippines.[15] In 1916, Wilson signed the Jones Act, which allowed Filipinos to elect a bicameral legislature, consisting of a Senate and House of Representatives, and promised them eventual independence.

Before agreeing to go to Manila, McNutt had to weigh whether doing so would advance his political career. Between 1901 and 1921, the office of governor-general became a "stepping-stone to high office" for Republicans and a place of "banishment" for Democrats.[16] That was true for the first Republican to serve as governor-general, William Howard Taft, and the first Democrat to occupy the office, Francis Burton Harrison. Taft, who was governor-general between 1901 and 1903, proved an "effective administrator." He helped to quell armed Philippine resistance to American rule, promote education and public health, and redistribute church lands.[17] Such a record enabled him to ascend to higher office and become president in 1909. Harrison, a former congressman from New York who became governor-general under Wilson, also proved effective, albeit with a different agenda. In line with Wilson's policy, Harrison increased Filipino participation in the colonial government, cooperated with the Filipino-elected Senate and House, and favored "ultimate independence" for the country.[18] In so doing, Harrison became popular in the Philippines, where streets still bear his name, as others do for Taft. Unlike Taft's, however, Harrison's political career ended in Manila.

As the Wilson administration granted the Philippines greater autonomy, the capacity of the governor-general to project leadership and shape policy diminished. Quezon, who was president of the Philippine Senate from 1916 to 1935, understood that he could "ruin" the administrations of governors-general and "hurt them politically at home" by "opposing their policies."[19] General Leonard Wood, whom President Warren G. Harding named as governor-general, soon discovered this reality. Wood reasserted the prerogatives of his office, halted moves toward further autonomy, and confronted the Philippine legislature, which was dominated by Quezon's pro-independence Nacionalista Party.[20] Interestingly, Wood, a onetime political rival of Harding, had wanted serve as governor-general for a year but wound up remaining in Manila until his death in 1927. By the 1920s, the office of governor-general had thus become less a stepping-stone to higher office and more of a graveyard—politically and even physically.[21] Quezon, too, bore scars from his fights with Wood. "I am afraid

Independence is a dream never to be realized by me," he lamented, as he dubbed the Democrats "our last hope."[22]

FDR's Philippine policy reopened opportunities, for Filipinos to gain their independence and for U.S. officials who backed such an aim to advance politically. During his first campaign for the White House, Roosevelt endorsed his party's long-standing commitment to Philippine independence, as did Frank Murphy, whom the president named governor-general in 1933. Murphy had been an early booster of FDR's presidential campaign in 1932 as well as a successful mayor of Detroit. Roosevelt thus sent Murphy to Manila as a reward for faithful political service.[23] Otherwise, the new governor-general had little knowledge of the islands, just executive experience and Roman Catholic faith, which most Filipinos shared. Generally speaking, Murphy and FDR followed the lead of Congress regarding the Philippines. In 1934 Congress passed the Tydings-McDuffie Act, which granted the country autonomy as a "commonwealth," allowed Filipinos to write their own constitution, and promised them complete independence in 1946.[24] The constitution adopted by Filipinos in 1935 replaced the bicameral legislature with a unicameral National Assembly and vested broad powers in the country's presidency, which Quezon won in a national election. In the interim, the United States remained the sovereign power, with control over Philippine foreign and military affairs. The Tydings-McDuffie Act also replaced the governor-general with a high commissioner. Yet Roosevelt expended little effort outlining the duties of the new office, which Murphy was the first person to occupy. After serving as high commissioner for two years, Murphy went on to become governor of Michigan, U.S. attorney general, and an associate justice on the U.S. Supreme Court.

In this setting, McNutt and his friends debated whether becoming high commissioner would promote his political ambitions. Carleton B. McCulloch, a friend and a former Democratic candidate for governor, considered the appointment "fortunate," for it removed McNutt from the United States at a time when labor unrest was gripping the automobile industry. While in Manila, he reasoned, McNutt could refrain from taking a stand that would alienate either workers or management.[25] Meredith Nicholson, an author who was serving as U.S. minister to Venezuela, disagreed. Nicholson wanted McNutt to take a holiday from public life, open a law office in Indianapolis, and wait for a summons from the party in the tradition of Benjamin Harrison—the last Hoosier to become president.[26] McNutt, too, had mixed thoughts about the job of high commissioner. On the one hand, his heart had been set on a cabinet position, and the Manila assignment seemed a letdown. On the other hand, he knew that serving overseas would raise his profile in the area of foreign policy as he eyed the White House in 1940.[27] FDR, for his part, understood McNutt's desire for higher office and agreed to let him serve as high commissioner for a year or two. He also hinted that the Hoosier could expect a spot in the cabinet after he returned.[28]

Before accepting the president's offer, McNutt had to overcome two obstacles. The first was a tempting invitation to become the first chairman of the New York Stock Exchange. McNutt learned of the opportunity from Frank McHale and Bowman Elder, another longtime adviser, but his friends in New York, Oscar Ewing and Douglas I. McKay, probably played some role in arranging it. Thinking that McNutt "could use the money," McHale was "almost certain" that his friend would jump at the chance to go to New York. But McNutt's mind was set on politics. He asked McHale for the odds on his becoming the next president of the United States. McHale replied: "100 to 1 against." Grinning, McNutt replied that it was "pretty good odds to be 1 out of 100 out of 140,000,000." Besides, he added, "money never made anyone satisfied or happy."[29]

Kathleen, however, did not share Paul's ambitions, and McNutt was reluctant to broach the Philippine assignment with her. After Roosevelt invited him to go to Manila, McNutt telephoned the Indianapolis Athletic Club and asked McHale and Elder to tell his wife and gain her consent. Kathleen again played the "loving, loyal and devoted wife." She set aside her "unpleasant" thoughts about politics and, with tears running down her cheeks, promised to go to the Philippines. She even told Paul "to throw his arms around FDR and give him a big hug" of thanks.[30] Louise exuded more genuine enthusiasm for her father's new assignment. "We are going to the Philippines!" she exclaimed. "It sort of takes your breath away."[31] Louise looked forward to the trip. She treasured her first passport, issued in 1937—over her father's signature as high commissioner.[32]

Like Louise, Paul came to see his new post as something special. At first, though, he, like Kathleen, merely reconciled himself to it. McNutt told reporters that he had no desire to remain in the Philippines "forever." Yet he also knew that there was "a job to be done" and stood "ready to do it."[33] As high commissioner, McNutt would have to prepare the islands, economically and militarily, for independence, at a time when Japan, which had occupied Manchuria in 1931, was poised to plunge into the rest of China. He called the situation in East Asia "so delicate" that "our actions in the Philippines may be of tremendous consequence not only to ourselves but also to the entire world."[34] Agreeing, the *Manila Bulletin* observed that McNutt was being thrust "into the center of the stage in a historical drama in which the problems are internationally involved and the whole plot most intricate."[35] The leading man of Indiana politics thus departed for Manila in "a spirit of high adventure and deep interest."[36]

Filipinos showed deep interest in the high commissioner-to-be, partly because so few of them had ever heard of McNutt.[37] One who had was José P. Laurel, a judge and later a senator. In the mid-1930s, Laurel had drafted a lecture on dictators and dictatorially inclined leaders that included, in the latter category, Franklin D. Roosevelt of the United States and Paul V. McNutt of the state of Indiana.[38] In 1937, some Filipinos expressed disappointment that McNutt had little background on their problems and had been named high commissioner for politically motivated reasons.[39] Quezon mustered a lukewarm endorsement of the choice, stating Roosevelt had made it and he would support it.[40] In the end, however, Philippine politicians and journalists reconciled themselves to McNutt on grounds that he was a "national figure" with a "brilliant record" as a governor as well as a man of "broad education" capable of learning about their country.[41] McNutt also carried the backing of three advocates of Philippine independence: Senator Millard Tydings of Maryland, the co-author of the Tydings-McDuffie Act; Frank Murphy; and FDR.[42] One Philippine paper compared McNutt to Murphy, since both men were midwesterners and Democratic politicians with "a progressive record of public service."[43]

Filipino newspapers quickly embraced McNutt's nomination. When a Republican senator tried to stall McNutt's confirmation by attacking his labor record, the *Manila Bulletin* condemned such "mud-slinging."[44] Similarly, when an old adversary, the pacifist leader Frederick J. Libby, argued that McNutt would support plans to build up the Philippine Army and to militarize the islands, the *Philippines Herald* defended both the plans and the nominee.[45] In words that would have pleased McNutt, the *Herald* insisted that Filipinos "are organizing an army purely for self-defense."[46] In the end, McNutt's nomination won swift confirmation by the U.S. Senate.[47]

By going to Manila, McNutt seemed to have gained an advantage over some of his rivals for the Democratic presidential nomination. A friend of Pennsylvania governor George H. Earle advised Earle to remain in the public's eye as "Governor McNutt is trying to do . . . by going to the Philippines." Politics aside, McNutt worked hard to prepare for the tasks awaiting him in Manila. He conferred with both Murphy and Joseph Ralston Hayden, a Philippine specialist at the University of Michigan who had been vice governor of the islands. After meeting McNutt, Hayden praised him for expressing a willingness to uphold American sovereignty in the Philippines even if it risked a "row" with Quezon.

Yet Hayden also worried that Filipinos would find McNutt a much "colder" character than Murphy, for he viewed the Philippines "strictly from the standpoint of our interests."[48] That provincialism became further evident in the staff that the new high commissioner assembled. It included Wayne Coy, who had overseen relief during McNutt's governorship and would be his administrative assistant, and Leo Gardner, a law professor from Indiana University, who became his legal adviser.[49] McNutt also relied on the experience and advice of J. Weldon Jones, who had been Murphy's assistant and was the acting high commissioner after Murphy returned to Michigan.[50]

The voyage to Manila was long but exciting. Paul, Kathleen, and Louise left San Francisco on April 3, on the SS *President Hoover* and arrived in Manila on April 26, following stops in Hawaii and Japan.[51] Aboard the ship, Kathleen felt as though she had arrived in "the Orient already" since so many passengers were Chinese dressed in "native" garb. Comparing this voyage with those she and Paul had taken to Europe, Kathleen found that passengers crossing the Pacific to be "less sporty" and more "quiet" than those who had sailed the Atlantic. A self-described "rotten" sailor, Kathleen conceded that her husband "loves the sea."[52] The journey afforded Paul "a needed rest."[53]

The period of relaxation ended once the *President Hoover* docked in Tokyo. The U.S. ambassador to Japan, Joseph C. Grew, had planned a luncheon to introduce McNutt to officials of the imperial government. But McNutt's party missed the event, for an alleged case of smallpox on the ship delayed their arrival on Japanese soil. According to Grew, "they were all disgruntled and furious with the Japanese quarantine doctor who had diagnosed smallpox" when all it had been "was a simple case of chickenpox." Their spirits did not lift that evening, even though Grew had arranged a sight-seeing tour. And McNutt's mood soured when the ambassador and his friends invited him to a poker game at which they "robbed McNutt . . . of his shirt." The high commissioner never thanked the embassy for the courtesies it had extended him, and he departed without bidding Grew good-bye. The ambassador to Japan deemed McNutt to be a "big, surly, conceited stuffed shirt" and predicted that he would achieve little in the Philippines, where "a reasonable degree of manners and personal consideration towards the inhabitants" was essential.[54]

McNutt was in danger of being out of his depth for other reasons: what he was to do, and would be allowed to do, in Manila remained somewhat vague. One Filipino newspaper predicted that the high commissioner would be "the real mystery role" in the country, since he lacked the powers of the governor-general, that is, to sign or veto bills passed by the Philippine legislature, to appoint officials, and to take part in the daily process of governance.[55] Instead, he enjoyed access to all records of the Philippine government and had the power to monitor its external relations, for the Tydings-McDuffie Act had placed "foreign affairs" under the "direct supervision and control of the United States." Moreover, the U.S. president had the right to delegate to the high commissioner any power granted him under Tydings-McDuffie. The most significant of these was the authority to suspend any law, contract, or executive order of the Philippine government on grounds that the action would violate an existing contract or impair the country's finances.[56]

Roosevelt saw the role of the high commissioner as limited. He had advised Murphy to refrain from meddling in the affairs of the Philippine government and to function instead as an ambassador who would represent the president and report back to Washington.[57] Murphy became frustrated over so narrow a mandate and by the ease with which Quezon eclipsed him in matters of both protocol and policy.[58] More important, the high commissioner was not to oppose actions taken by the Philippine president, lest he impair relations between their two countries. Partly as a result, questions about the status of the ranking American in Manila persisted. As late as 1939, one Philippine official noted that the duties of the high commissioner had been "only partially determined."[59]

After departing Manila, Murphy prodded Secretary of War Harry H. Woodring to draft detailed instructions for McNutt.[60] But the end product, signed by FDR, remained a study in ambiguity. Roosevelt declined to "burden" McNutt with "specific rules" for his assignment. Instead, the president urged the high commissioner to avoid "unnecessary interference" in Philippine internal affairs, to lend "helpful encouragement" to Quezon's government, and to exercise "sound judgment" in handling U.S.-Philippine relations. Looming on the horizon, Roosevelt warned, were problems involving American bases and trade relations with the Philippines after independence, though he did not request McNutt to find solutions to them. In his instructions, FDR was definite about only two things: that the United States "exercises sovereignty over the Islands" and that McNutt had "precedence over all other officials" there.[61]

McNutt took those two points so seriously that he ignited a diplomatic brouhaha that captured headlines. Three days before McNutt set foot in Manila, the Japanese consul, at a reception to honor Emperor Hirohito, offered a toast his emperor, then one to Presidents Roosevelt and Quezon, jointly, and lastly, a toast to the high commissioner. Shortly thereafter, McNutt sent a communiqué to foreign consuls in Manila stating that at formal occasions, the head of state being honored was to be toasted first, followed by the president of the United States, then the high commissioner, and, finally, the president of the Philippines.[62] The circular aimed to remind the international community, and the Philippine president—who was on a tour of America, Mexico, and Europe—that the United States remained sovereign in the islands. In a further reminder, McNutt sent another letter, affirming that the United States retained "supervision over Philippine foreign affairs" and thus "all communications between foreign officials and the Philippine Government" must be routed through his office.[63]

McNutt's circulars unleashed a firestorm in the United States, where journalists expressed shock that a novice diplomat would go "high-hat" on a matter of protocol.[64] The *Washington Daily News* compared McNutt unfavorably with Dwight Morrow and Frank Murphy, a pair of non-career diplomats who had served capably but humbly in tough assignments—Morrow in Mexico under Calvin Coolidge and Murphy in the Philippines under FDR.[65] In Murphy's home state, the *Lansing State Journal* jested that this fellow McNutt "is acting as if he had dropped the 'Mc' part of his name."[66] The *New York Sun* mocked the Hoosier in Gilbert and Sullivan–style verse:

I am the High Commissioner—
My name is Paul McNutt;
For form I am a stickler, and
I will not stand a cut;
All letters to officials of
The Isles I must see first,
And glasses must be raised to me
By all men with a thirst.

Oh, form is form and dignity
Must not get in a rut,
For right is right and fair is fair
And Paul McNutt's McNutt!
So three loud cheers for Uncle Sam
From palace, home and hut.
And four loud cheers for Franklin D.—
And five for Paul McNutt![67]

Such coverage promoted an unflattering image of McNutt.[68] The conservative columnist Westbrook Pegler likened the Hoosier to a "show horse" who, despite having "grace" and "a big bold stride," still managed to fall flat on his face.[69] On the international stage, the *San Francisco News* opined, McNutt was "all thumbs."[70]

Official Washington was embarrassed by such coverage. Members of the diplomatic corps wondered why the high commissioner had decided to "stick his chin out" when he was supposed to "make friends with the Filipinos."[71] Marvin McIntyre, FDR's appointments secretary, thought that McNutt had "finished himself" politically.[72] Garner conceded: "I'm afraid we've sent a trouble maker there." "I wouldn't say that," replied Roosevelt, "but he seems to be indiscreet."[73] In public, the president withheld comment on the affair, as did Secretary of War Woodring.[74] But Hugh S. Johnson, a newspaper columnist and the former head of the National Recovery Administration, lampooned McNutt with a mock toast: "Hic, hic, hooray, for the U.S.A.!"[75]

The toasting imbroglio was serious in four respects. First, it offers a window into McNutt's instincts about the Philippines, in particular his desire to uphold American sovereignty. Second, he received some praise in the American press for taking a stand that helped the United States avoid "losing face" before Japan.[76] (Hayden, too, applauded him for defending America's position on "a distant and exposed front.")[77] Third, McNutt made a political point: that he was no pushover. Indeed, the new high commissioner would exercise the powers of his office with great confidence and to the "maximum" extent permitted under the law.[78] And fourth, McNutt worked hard to avoid any permanent rupture in U.S.-Philippine relations. He thus accepted a revised State Department circular on consular correspondence. It required that only outgoing "official" communiqués from the Philippine government to American diplomatic and consular officials "be sent to the High Commissioner" for signature. Under the new rules, countries wishing to communicate with the Philippines on issues of war, peace, trade, and transportation were to work through their embassies in Washington, D.C. Less important matters were to be handled by "local authorities" in the Philippines and, as the court of last resort, by the high commissioner.[79] Otherwise, McNutt dismissed the criticism his earlier orders had generated by noting that he was "quite used to newspaper comments, favorable and unfavorable."[80] Behind the scenes, however, the high commissioner fumed that some journalists had tried to provoke a "fight" between him and Quezon.[81]

Fortunately for McNutt, the reaction in Manila was calm. Generally speaking, Filipinos value the importance of social gestures and recoil from acts that might cause guests to lose "face."[82] Moreover, many Filipinos exuded a "colonial mentality"—"an extreme liking for things American"—that had formed over four decades of U.S. rule. As the Filipino historian Teodoro Agoncillo observed: "While the Spaniards almost killed the Filipinos by maltreatment, the Americans, on the other hand, almost smothered the Filipinos with 'kindness.'" Agoncillo lamented the fact that many Filipinos thought it "blasphemous" to "criticize the United States or any American."[83] Accordingly, the press in Manila responded circumspectly to the toasting imbroglio. In an editorial, "Calmly Respectful," the *Manila Bulletin* questioned the need for McNutt's office while conceding that the tone of his circulars had been quite "temperate."[84] The outcome of this "tempest," the *Philippines Free Press* predicted, would be a redefinition of the high commissioner's powers on a basis satisfactory to all.[85] The pro-independence *Philippines Herald* advised Filipinos to respect the "forms" of protocol while guarding "the substance of their autonomy."[86] While dismissing the issue of toasts as "trivial," the *Herald* could not resist hoisting its glass "to the people of the Philippines, truly free."[87]

More than anyone else, it was Quezon who calmed the waters. Instead of commenting on the toasting letters, the president told reporters that he had seen McNutt earlier, in New York, where they had cocktails together. When asked "Who was toasted first?" Quezon quipped: "Nobody. We just had a drink together. I never refuse a drink."[88] A few months later, in August 1937, the president publicly affirmed that the United States was "sovereign" in the islands, that Filipinos would never defy the Americans, and that there was no quarrel between himself and the high commissioner. A month later, he went further. In an unusually deferential gesture for an Asian nationalist leader, Quezon offered McNutt a cigarette from his case and, with press cameras clicking, lit it for him.[89] Nevertheless, the president continued to enhance his own standing—in his own way. He apparently did not object when, at a reception for an Italian mission, a diplomat toasted him and FDR at the same time, leaving out the high commissioner, who was absent.[90]

Quezon's response to the toasting incident underscored his multifaceted persona. At one level, the president liked pomp and ceremony, which, as the head of an emerging state, he deemed important.[91] He dressed for success, donning the best in western-style clothing—a topcoat, gloves, spats, and derby hat—when he visited the U.S. Congress.[92] Offsetting Quezon's formal, public side was a warm, private man who enjoyed a drink, a smoke, and a good joke. Quezon's political dexterity, evident in how he calmed the crisis over toasting, enabled him to adjust his tactics and advance his aims.[93] He had used nationalism and the force of his personality to become a charismatic figure.[94] At the same time, the president's fluency in English, gift for flattery, and skill at playing by the "American rules of the political game" won over officials in the United States.[95] FDR described Quezon as "first and last a politician."[96] His "genius" lay in an "ability to appear all things to nearly all people."[97] That, along with an admixture of warmth and imperiousness, enabled Quezon to become familiar with "strangers."[98]

McNutt and Quezon became quite friendly. To be certain, their competing duties had the potential to breed ill will. Quezon had resented the presence of a high commissioner, even Murphy.[99] He worried that FDR would send to Manila some "green American" who would lecture Filipinos on good government while trampling on the authority of the country's president.[100] And the toasting controversy led Quezon to view McNutt as "bellicose" and "unreasonable," and he braced for "another Wood-Quezon fight."[101] But that first impression faded, as Quezon and McNutt became acquainted informally, over poker. "For us Filipinos, it's the informal talks that count for a lot," Quezon's grandson has stressed.[102] In the masculine world of poker games, with the attendant alcohol, tobacco, and off-color tales—of which Quezon had a large stock—McNutt, a onetime fraternity member and Legionnaire, was at ease. Their senses of humor also matched up quite well.[103] One photograph showed the two men seated on a sofa, with the high commissioner laughing. On the picture, McNutt scrawled a note to Quezon: "Ours has been a most happy association based on confidence and understanding. May our sense of humor grow and last as has our friendship."[104] In fact, within six months of McNutt's arrival, Quezon was hailing him as a straight-shooter and "regular fellow."[105] The high commissioner, in turn, described his dealings with the president as being based on "absolute frankness" and "genuine affection."[106]

There was a political dimension to such conviviality. Establishing a cordial relationship with Quezon would enhance McNutt's reputation as a diplomat and, perhaps, his White House hopes. And it was wise of Quezon to placate McNutt, who was being discussed as a possible successor to FDR. Once, after completing a round of poker, the high commissioner discovered that he had lost 10,000 pesos to Quezon. He wrote out a check and then handed it to the president—who promptly refused it. McNutt protested: "Don't ever think I am not a good sport. Keep it. It's yours." Quezon replied that the money was indeed his, and so he was "giving it" to the high commissioner as a "contribution" to his "presidential campaign fund."[107]

McNutt and Quezon were united by a love of power as well as poker. While McNutt was reorganizing Indiana's government, strengthening the office of governor, and building a powerful Democratic machine, Filipinos had ratified a constitution that placed broad authority in the hands of their president.[108] Quezon even employed McNutt-style tactics, winning passage of a bill to postpone elections set for 1937.[109] Furthermore, Quezon's "authoritarianism" encompassed an extensive system of patronage, close ties to wealthy Filipinos, a propensity to interfere in local politics, huge majorities for the Nacionalista Party in the Philippine National Assembly, and the securing of emergency powers for the presidency.[110] George A. Malcolm, an American jurist in Manila, warned McNutt that the Philippine government appeared "designed to consolidate unlimited . . . power in the hands of one man."[111] This was too much for the high commissioner, who, despite his often heavy-handed rule in Indiana, had been schooled in a political system based on two competitive parties. Following his arrival in Manila, McNutt lamented that "democracy" in the Philippines was more "form" than "substance."[112] Quezon answered such criticism with an argument of his own: Filipinos had achieved a democracy without two "well-balanced parties" because they agreed with the program of the Nacionalista Party—autonomy and "immediate independence"—and had rewarded it at the polls.[113]

While Quezon and McNutt differed over the features of democracy, both men, on a visceral level, understood the exercise of power—and each other. In fact, the high commissioner, over time, eased his objections to the president's political tactics. McNutt endorsed an administration-backed five-million-peso appropriation bill that the *Philippines Herald* dismissed as "Pork Barrel" expenditure but which the high commissioner saw as a way to fund schools and public works.[114] McNutt also welcomed Quezon's plan to revamp the Nacionalista Party after it had divided into two factions. In so doing, the high commissioner argued, somewhat paradoxically, that establishing one huge party would spur other parties to sprout up in opposition to it.[115] The *Herald* predicted the opposite, that the dominant party was apt to become a machine—something with which the Hoosier was familiar.[116] McNutt's accommodating tone on Philippine-style democracy reflected his realism. Just as Quezon adjusted to McNutt's demands for diplomatic precedence, the high commissioner was now adjusting to how the president ran the country politically. In so doing, however, McNutt gave tacit approval to an unhealthy blend of authoritarianism and patronage-based politics that would plague the Philippines for decades.

The relationship between McNutt and Quezon involved many layers. Quezon had used persuasion and charm to win over his American counterparts, though McNutt was not so easily swayed.[117] The high commissioner recognized the president's weaknesses, especially his "impulsiveness."[118] McNutt thus confronted Quezon on matters he thought important. In 1936, for example, the Philippine National Assembly had voted to reduce the pensions of two thousand Americans, many of them teachers, who had retired from the Philippine civil service. In response, Secretary of War Woodring considered suspending the pension act, and the U.S. Senate weighed passing legislation to nullify it.[119] After arriving in Manila, McNutt and his aides settled the dispute. They sent Quezon a legal brief arguing that the action of the National Assembly had breached a contract. When the president continued to oppose the reinstatement of the pensions, McNutt appealed to him as a lawyer: "I want you to read this brief. Then let me know your decision." Quezon did so—and changed his mind. The president endorsed the restoration of the pensions and pledged that the National Assembly would pass it "unanimously." One-party dominance of the Philippine government, which the high commissioner had once condemned, now served one of his aims.[120] In the aftermath of the toasting incident, McNutt relished his triumph on the pension law. "We could not ask for more," he informed Woodring.[121]

The most important matter with which McNutt and Quezon dealt was Philippine independence. Here, they acted—the high commissioner loudly, the president softly—to encourage Filipinos to reconsider the date of independence and the degree of sovereignty they were to receive. The question of trade relations between the United States and the Philippines following independence was another vexing problem. At the outset, McNutt sounded like a firm advocate of Philippine independence. Before he left the United States, the high commissioner, like any good Democrat, lauded the Tydings-McDuffie Act as "wise" and vowed to respect the "large measure of autonomy" the law had granted to Filipinos.[122] He also talked like an "average mid-westerner" when he warned friends that retention of the Philippines could involve the United States in a war with Japan. In so warning, however, he was not joining hands with isolationists, who were strong in his part of the country and who deemed the Philippines "militarily indefensible."[123] McNutt believed that America had to be wary of aggressors, but thought that its natural line of defense in the Pacific lay closer to home, in Hawaii and the Aleutian Islands.[124]

After McNutt arrived in Manila, his focus shifted. He received a memorandum from Admiral H. E. Yarnell, commander of the United States Navy's Asiatic fleet, which portrayed grimly the prospects for an independent Philippines. Yarnell believed the success of the Philippines as a separate nation rested on its ability to achieve economic "stability" and military "security." Neither condition existed in 1937. Mainly, though, Yarnell analyzed the external menace that the Philippines faced: Japanese officials had stated that the islands fell within their nation's "sphere of influence"; leaders in Japan's navy favored an "advance" southward; and Filipinos could not repel an invasion by Japan. "Security is best maintained by policies which are *just* to other nations, and backed by adequate force," Yarnell wrote in depicting Japan as a threat to both the United States and the Philippines. "It is not maintained by a supine withdrawal from areas where trouble may happen."[125] Japan's aggressive intentions became evident in August 1937, when its army marched into China. McNutt, as high commissioner, assisted efforts to evacuate Americans and Filipinos from Shanghai.[126] A few months later, the sinking of the U.S. gunboat *Panay* by the Japanese coupled with a weak American response—accepting an official apology—hardened his resolve.[127] "All of us have watched the developments in China with the greatest interest," McNutt wrote Yarnell, as he urged "a stiffening of our backbone in dealing with foreign affairs."[128]

With that in mind, McNutt had come to some "definite" conclusions by the close of 1937. He wrote the newspaper publisher Roy W. Howard, an advocate of retaining the Philippines, that the United States could not leave "the Orient" without "serious loss of prestige" and "endangering world peace." If America was to remain a power in East Asia, McNutt argued, "she must stay in the Philippines *as the sovereign*."[129] In so arguing, he was not defying public opinion; a Gallup poll showed seventy-six percent of Americans opposed to Philippine independence.[130] But McNutt was breaking with his president in two respects. First, the high commissioner had rebelled against an article of faith for Democrats, that is, Philippine independence. Second, he was forsaking plans favored by Roosevelt, to negotiate an international treaty to guarantee the neutrality of the Philippines after the United States departed.[131] McNutt wanted instead an "understanding" among "Great Britain, America, France and Holland" to protect their possessions "in the Orient."[132] The man who in the 1920s had preferred an enforceable peace based on preparedness to well-meaning but toothless pacts, such as Kellogg-Briand, had resurfaced. Early in 1938 McNutt informed FDR of his opposition to Philippine independence.[133] A month later, he returned to Washington and told the president that the "interests of both countries would be best served by an indefinite continuation of the Commonwealth." Roosevelt's response was masterfully evasive: "If that is what the Filipinos want, let them say so."[134]

Did Filipinos wish to remain under the American flag? And if they did, would their leaders be willing to say so? With respect to the first question, Yarnell believed that only "a small percentage" of Filipinos wanted independence.[135] Roy Howard, who visited the Philippines in 1935, reached a similar conclusion. He correctly termed independence the "one and only issue" in Philippine politics for thirty-five years, asserting that "everyone in public life had to be for it." But, he went on, "every man" with whom he had talked in the Manila government thought that conditions in Asia made Philippine independence an "utter impossibility." Since any sharp "reversal" of "previous teachings" would represent political "suicide" for these men, they would have to wean Filipinos from the idea of independence.[136]

Philippine sugar producers were amenable to delaying independence.[137] With the inauguration of free trade between the United States and its colony in 1913, the volume of Philippine-American trade had increased, skewing the archipelago's economy toward the development of sugar and other products for sale in the United States.[138] In 1937 Placidio Mapa, president of the Philippine Sugar Association, warned that independence and a sudden end to free trade with the United States would be, at this time, suicidal.[139] The Philippines remained heavily dependent on the United States for its livelihood. By 1938 America "consumed four-fifths of the goods leaving Philippine ports" and the largest export commodity, sugar, "went entirely to the United States." The sugar industry represented both a blessing and a curse to the islands, for it provided "the bulk of the national income while subjecting labor to intolerable conditions."[140] A good deal of Quezon's power rested on his link to the landed elite, which, in turn, derived its wealth from the exploitation of tenant farmers. Such a socially combustible set of circumstances threatened to explode following restriction of access to the American market and disruption of the sugar industry.

Other Filipinos who backed a continuation of American sovereignty organized at the grass roots. The Manila-based Commonwealth Association campaigned through its organ, the *Commonwealth Advocate*, for "security, liberty, prosperity and peace" via a "continued political partnership with the United States."[141] From 1935, when the *Advocate* began its crusade, to 1938, the paper noticed a "radical change of attitude" among the residents of the islands.

The latest Sino-Japanese war had aroused "fear of aggression from without" and reinforced sentiments for "a united front" with America.[142] A poll by the *Philippines Free Press* found fifty-five percent of Filipinos opposed to independence before 1946. The survey was, to be sure, unscientific; the paper had sent ballots to a pretty exclusive group—12,500 "responsible, property holding citizens" across the provinces.[143] But the fact that the *Free Press* was willing to ask the question, and that the propertied class had voted as they did, suggested that there was anxiety, in some quarters, over independence. Veterans of the Philippine Revolution, who had yearned for an independent nation, now shuddered at the strength of this nascent movement to remain under the U.S. flag.[144] McNutt observed that the "thrill" of independence was giving way to "anxiety."[145]

Quezon quietly agreed with those who had become uneasy about independence. By mid-1937 he had concluded that separation from the United States would mean "a complete wrecking" of the Philippine economy and the islands' "absorption by Japan."[146] McNutt, who spoke often with the president, thought him adamant: "In his heart, Quezon does not want independence." Instead, he wanted his country to have "dominion status" in the fashion of Canada's relationship with Great Britain.[147] The Philippines, like Canada, would exercise control over its internal affairs while the United States supervised its foreign policy. Dominion status did not mean for Quezon a continuation of the present commonwealth setup. Although the islands would remain under the Stars and Stripes, he wanted no interference in Philippine domestic affairs and for the U.S. State Department, not the high commissioner, to have the final say over its foreign relations. This model of postcolonial relations had been attractive to Quezon for some time; he once confided that if the United States abandoned the Philippines, he would "appeal to Great Britain" to grant his country "territorial status under the British flag."[148] Quezon found it difficult to express such sentiments publicly for three reasons: one, the U.S. Congress and State Department opposed any revisiting of the political aspect of independence; two, if a move to revise the terms of independence was tendered and then rejected by the Americans, Quezon would lose "all political power in the Islands," and three, such a defeat would cost him the respect of nationalist leaders across Asia.[149] So when asked in 1937 to comment on the possibility of "dominion status," for the Philippines, Quezon sidestepped the question.[150]

Quezon pressed indirectly for dominion status. To foment opposition to independence among business leaders, who were petrified of losing preferential access to the American market, Quezon recommended moving the date of independence from 1946 to either 1938 or 1939. The president's recommendation could be, and was, defended as an attempt to educate both Americans and Filipinos so that they might choose "the least onerous" path toward separation.[151] But since no postindependence trade deal existed in 1938, any American withdrawal that year was, as McNutt put it, apt to "murder" the islands economically.[152] The proposal for earlier independence left many Filipinos "bewildered" and sparked a "semi-crash" in Manila's stock market.[153]

McNutt advised the president to proceed cautiously, lest he achieve independence in 1938 and without the trade deal desired by Filipinos. In fact, Quezon deserved some blame for the absence of a trade agreement. In 1937 Roosevelt had formed the Joint Preparatory Committee on Philippine Affairs to examine conditions in the Philippines and to report on the need for legislation in areas such as trade. But Quezon wanted no report that might lead to "immediate legislative action" by the U.S. Congress.[154] When the Joint Preparatory Committee held hearings in Manila, he did nothing to mend differences between its American members, who wanted U.S. tariffs on Philippine goods to increase gradually to one hundred percent of duties, and its Filipino members, who wanted the maximum tariff on goods from their country to reach no more than fifty percent of prevailing U.S. duties.[155] Although Quezon was angling for the best possible deal, his "stalling tactics" denied the U.S. Tariff Commission data on Philippine trade, discouraged Congress from moving ahead with legislation, and disrupted preparations for independence in 1946—all while he was advocating independence in 1938![156] McNutt likened Quezon to "a nervous woman who threatened to commit suicide in order to get something from her husband."[157]

With FDR unwilling and Quezon unable, apparently, to request modification of the date set for independence, McNutt did so. In his first report as high commissioner, he advised the Philippine government to consider continuation of the commonwealth if a majority of Filipinos desired it.[158] More dramatically, in March 1938, he delivered a radio address, broadcast in both the U.S. and the Philippines, on Philippine independence. Speaking like an American-style imperialist, McNutt began by characterizing his nation's "enterprise" in the Philippines as more "altruistic" than the colonialism practiced by Europeans. Unlike Spain, America had improved the Philippines' health care and sanitation, educational system, and capacity for self-government. Far more problematic, he admitted, was U.S. economic policy. The inauguration of free trade between the United States and its colony, in 1913, had increased the volume of Philippine-American trade and had transformed the archipelago's economy in a way that emphasized the development of sugar and other products for sale in the U.S. This growing economic dependence contrasted with the gradual political autonomy granted the Philippines by the United States. "On one hand," McNutt observed, "we sought to sever the ties; on the other we chained them ever closer to us." But the high commissioner was only willing to offer the islands "the best trade deal" that his country could "afford"—Philippine goods would be allowed into the United States, duty-free, as long as doing so did not injure American competitors.[159] By insisting that Filipinos not receive independence on trade terms entirely favorable to them, McNutt was trying, in part, to force them to choose between independence and a continuation of the commonwealth.[160]

McNutt was also interested in protecting America's position in Asia. He warned that his country had a "responsibility" to remain engaged in the world: Abandoning the Philippines would impair America's security and its economy, leaving a "barrier reef of islands from Kamchatka to Borneo" in hostile hands and inhibiting trade with China. McNutt, who was never one to back down from fights, resolved that the United States must not "run away" from the Philippines. So he urged a "realistic re-examination" of independence, aiming for "a permanent political and economic relationship" between the two countries. "Our flag and sovereignty should remain," he insisted, "allowing the Philippines every ounce of domestic autonomy they can absorb—holding in our own hands foreign affairs, tariffs, immigration, currency and public debt."[161]

McNutt's speech looked simultaneously backward and forward. At one level, his talk about defending U.S. interests in Asia mirrored the imperialist rhetoric of such earlier figures as Theodore Roosevelt and Alfred Thayer Mahan. The beginning of McNutt's address, which defended U.S. imperialism as altruistic, sounded downright stodgy—more in line with the rhetoric of William McKinley than that of Franklin D. Roosevelt. On another level, however, McNutt's focus remained on the present state of Asian politics and the threat of Japan. Events on the colonial periphery can circulate back to policies—and to people—in the metropole (or mother country) in what the historian Alfred W. McCoy has labeled the "capillaries of empire."[162] So it was with McNutt, whose experience in the Philippines led him to reaffirm his core principles about the need to restrain aggressive dictatorships. His call for a reexamination of Philippine independence also foreshadowed the geopolitical thinking that came into vogue among U.S. policymakers following World War II. According to this mindset, defending American territory alone would not assure the nation's security; as Harry S. Truman noted at the end of his presidency: "If Communism is allowed to absorb the free nations, then we would be isolated from our sources of supply and detached from our friends."[163] To be certain, McNutt was focusing on a more localized threat (from Japan) in one region (East Asia). Yet he was expressing a geopolitical perspective earlier than Truman and relating it to the Philippines in a manner that separated him from the isolationists, some of whom were willing to abandon the Philippines to Japan if doing so would avert war.[164]

The thoughts McNutt expressed sprang from conviction; the amplification of them was, however, political. McNutt delivered his speech while he was in the United States on a brief trip home whose purpose was blatantly political.[165] McNutt's supporters feted him at a series of formal dinners, the most elaborate of which was in Washington, that were intended to boost his presidential prospects in 1940.[166] McNutt generally made a good impression, shaking hands, discussing the Philippines, vowing to stay at his post, and dodging queries about Roosevelt's interest in a third term.[167] In this setting, McNutt's speech must be read, at least in part, as an effort to present himself as a statesman—thoughtful about the fate of a subject people (and U.S. interests) in Asia and forceful in his willingness to challenge conventional wisdom on Philippine independence.

Quezon considered McNutt's offer to reexamine Philippine independence— and then rejected it. The president glanced at the high commissioner's address and issued a statement that reporters interpreted as a "blanket endorsement" of "McNutt's stand."[168] The next day, however, Quezon, after further study, clarified his position. He informed the press that he had "no objection" to a "realistic reexamination" of independence but not one based on the Tydings-McDuffie Act or the terms expounded by McNutt—and not with any postponement of the date of separation in 1946.[169] Quezon had wanted to reduce the authority of the United States and to expand that of his government. Ceding control over tariffs, immigration, currency, and debt to Washington would not advance that end and would leave the commonwealth with less authority than that "exercised by the Dominions of Great Britain." By rejecting McNutt's proposal, he might have been angling to gain better trade terms from the Joint Preparatory Committee. Quezon thought McNutt's proposals unacceptably preferential for U.S. goods entering the Philippines, and he favored instead "reciprocal advantages" for both nations.[170] Put another way, if Quezon were unable to secure dominion status, he wanted to make sure that independence occurred under the most favorable conditions for his country.

Quezon's sudden reversal on McNutt's speech also was politically motivated. Although Quezon often distinguished between continuing the commonwealth, which he opposed, and Canadian-style dominion status, which he liked, he still sounded, in public, like a fervent nationalist who was opposed to postponement of independence. The president reckoned that middle-class Filipinos were "against independence" while the more populous lower classes "want it as much as ever."[171] With that in mind, and with most Philippine politicians opposing "anything short of complete independence," Quezon repudiated the McNutt speech.[172] "At no time," he told the high commissioner, "did I presume that what I might agree upon and advocate will be accepted by my people."[173] It was an admission that Quezon's hands were tied by public opinion and that any wishes he may have expressed privately to McNutt could be renounced publicly.

McNutt remained convinced that "upon independence" the Philippines would "fall prey" to the "might" of Japan.[174] Partly for that reason, he sought to slow progress toward independence by attacking the report of the Joint Preparatory Committee. The committee recommended a gradual, twenty-year transition toward nonpreferential trade between the two countries. Beginning in 1941, Philippine products, such as sugar, which were expected to survive without preferential trade, would pay gradually rising duties. They would reach twenty-five percent of U.S. tariffs in 1946 and an additional five percent each year until they attained one hundred percent in 1961. American products, in turn, would pay twenty-five percent of Philippine tariffs in 1946 and an additional five percent each year until one hundred percent was reached, again, in 1961.[175] McNutt, in a memorandum to FDR, attacked this plan as "not sufficiently protective of American trade interests."[176] He was so harsh, in part, because he had reservations about committing the United States to specific commercial ties with one country so far into the future.[177]

McNutt's stand on Philippine-American trade cannot be separated from his opposition to independence. In his memorandum to Roosevelt, McNutt warned that the present state of "world politics" precluded any "long term commitments" to American withdrawal from the islands.[178] FDR understood McNutt's bias and rejected his advice. He reminded his fellow Democrat of their party's "uninterrupted" support for Philippine independence and warned that any effort by Washington to reassert "direct control" over the islands would impair relations between the two countries.[179] With that said, McNutt and Quezon fell into line behind Roosevelt's policy. They endorsed the proposals of the Joint Preparatory Committee that covered trade for the period 1941 to 1946 only. In the end, Roosevelt sent the recommendations of the Joint Preparatory Committee to Congress, which in 1939 passed a U.S.-Philippine trade law covering the years 1941 to 1946.[180]

While the trade deal was being finalized, last-ditch moves to reexamine the political side of independence failed to gain traction. In Manila, McNutt's speech had given some lawmakers pause. Manuel A. Roxas, a member of the National Assembly, a rising star in the Nacionalista Party, and a future president of the Philippines, was open to dominion status—if the Philippines received the same powers exercised by Canada.[181] Even the *Philippines Herald,* a strong proponent of independence, opined that a "postponement" was "not inadmissible" since "the Orient was at war," the Philippines was unprepared economically for independence, and McNutt had spoken so "realistically" in appealing for reexamination.[182] But the paper opposed continuation of the commonwealth. Instead, it pleaded for a specific proposal, or "impetus," from the key players in Washington and Manila to move the discussion along.[183] Quezon again said little, and frustration set in. "If the Filipino leaders will advise us what they really want," Key Pittman, chair of the Senate Foreign Relations Committee, declared. "We will give it."[184] In the meantime, McNutt's call for reexamination had sowed doubts among the members of the Joint Preparatory Committee about the Philippines' future political status.[185] Such confusion encouraged isolationists in the U.S. Senate to delay passing the trade bill until Filipino leaders affirmed their desire for independence in 1946, which Quezon and Vice President Sergio Osmeña promptly did.[186]

Reexamination of independence received a second and more public hearing, in Manila, in September 1939—following the outbreak of war in Europe. Quezon, at that point, reiterated his desire for independence in 1946 but invited a "free" discussion of the subject.[187] José E. Romero, a member of the Philippine National Assembly, accepted the invitation and spoke out against "untimely freedom" for the archipelago.[188] His plea went nowhere. Nacionalista Party leaders opposed reexamination, as did the Philippine National Assembly which voted 53 to 6 to uphold 1946 as the date of independence.[189] The old truism, that no politician wanted to be against independence, remained valid.[190]

There was another reason why Romero's bid for reexamination fell flat. By the time Romero made his address, McNutt, a potential ally, had returned to America, and his successor, Assistant Secretary of State Francis B. Sayre, had no interest in reopening the question of independence.[191] Accordingly, Quezon announced that he was preparing the Philippines for independence in 1946, as mandated by the Tydings-McDuffie Act.[192] Any effort to reconsider indepen-

dence clearly required a confluence of factors, beginning with a favorable international setting; vocal support from the high commissioner, the president of the
commonwealth, and more than a few Philippine politicians; and an American
president and Congress willing to reconsider a matter they deemed settled.
None of those conditions ever existed at the same time. After Romero "blasted
away" on behalf of "realistic re-examination," Weldon Jones, McNutt's former
deputy, who sympathized with McNutt's position on independence, lamented:
"Why did he not make this speech in 1938?"[193]

The debate over Philippine independence showed Quezon and McNutt to
be realists as each man defended what he considered his nation's best interests.
Quezon fought for a trade bill favorable to his country, and McNutt did likewise
for the United States—while challenging a plank in his party's platform: Philippine independence. But they went only so far. Regarding dominion status,
Quezon knew that he could not abruptly forsake Philippine independence and
openly ask for the country to remain under the American flag. McNutt could request that, but given his hopes for the Democratic nomination in 1940, he could
not push too hard for it after Roosevelt had ruled otherwise. McNutt understood that if he wanted to succeed FDR, he had to adapt to what FDR wanted.

McNutt was adjusting to something more than new issues, personalities, and
configurations of power in Asia; he was learning to live in what was, to him
and his family, a new land. The change began once McNutt arrived in Manila.
His reception was simple, a consequence, no doubt, of the fact that Quezon
had not returned from Europe.[194] McNutt's office space was nothing special.
Since the Malacanang Palace, the former home of the governors-general, was
now occupied by Quezon, the high commissioner had to rent part of the Elks
Club, "a rambling, draughty, barn-like building" with paper-thin partitions and
swinging doors, "reminiscent of a barroom," that separated McNutt's office
from those of his staff.[195] The McNutts' home, which they rented from a Manila
lawyer, was more comfortable. Called El Nido, it was "swank," well-furnished,
fully staffed, and located on Dewey Boulevard, which ran along Manila Bay.[196]
Kathleen and Louise liked the place—until passersby started to peer in the
front windows. To escape their gazes, mother and daughter went up to the roof
every evening to enjoy Manila's sunsets and the "sweeping view of the water
and the distant islands."[197] Venturing outside during the daytime was trickier.
Weldon Jones had warned McNutt that he was arriving in the hot season when

"torrid" temperatures persisted for weeks.[198] Paul found the warnings about heat and humidity "grossly exaggerated." "We have had some hot weather," he told a friend, "but it is no worse than mid-summer in Indiana."[199]

Baguio, a city nestled in Luzon's Cordillera Mountains, provided a refuge from the climate—and grind—of Manila. Baguio had been founded early in the twentieth century as a center for administration and recreation where U.S. officials "could preside over their precious tropical colony without working up too much of a sweat."[200] Rising five thousand feet above sea level, the city boasted cool, dry air scented by pine trees and flowers. It became the Philippines' summer capital and later a tourist spot. "Up in its pine-crested heights," a Filipino politician wrote, "one feels nearer to God."[201] McNutt agreed, pronouncing Baguio's climate "delightful" and expressing surprise "that such a place could exist in the tropics."[202] In Manila, however, their surroundings remained less than ideal. When the owner of El Nido returned, McNutt had to locate a new abode. He then found himself haggling with the U.S. Congress over a housing allowance. Partly because of such headaches, the McNutts retreated to Baguio "as much as possible."[203]

Kathleen enjoyed the Philippines, up to a point. She remained a charming hostess, who participated in the "social, charitable, and welfare activities" of Manila.[204] Kathleen and Paul took part in the social whirl, and they made quite an impression on the dance floor. Once, during a ball at the Army and Navy Club, a young ensign went over to the McNutts and asked to cut in. Paul yielded. The man took Kathleen's hand and told her: "You didn't want to dance with that old man anyway, did you?" When the ensign learned the identity of his partner, he apologized, but Paul and Kathleen found the mix-up "amusing."[205] Humor helped them to navigate cultural differences. When Quezon invited the McNutts to a picnic, Kathleen, in "good Hoosier spirit," offered to bring a dish. The president said no. When they arrived at the picnic, she knew why. "We found," Kathleen reported, "two trucks waiting for us—one containing tents, tables and benches—the other containing a seven course meal from The Manila Hotel with many waiters resplendent in uniform waiting to serve us." Paul could not resist teasing her about Filipino hospitality, Quezon-style: "Too bad, honey, you didn't bring a bottle of olives."[206]

As time passed, Kathleen grew unhappy in the Philippines. Living there did little to elevate her view of politics. To be certain, Kathleen did express her opinion on one notable, public issue—her endorsement of suffrage for Philippine women provided a "boost" to a plebiscite campaign that ended with Filipinas gaining the vote.[207] But she urged women to exercise this right "gradually" without forsaking their homes for political careers. The women that Kathleen thought best suited for public service were the younger ones such as Louise, who, she reported, was receiving "training in politics and government."[208] In the long run, politics served to separate mother from daughter.[209] In the short run, other problems weighed on Kathleen's mind. While in the Philippines, her father died, and she was unable to return home for the funeral. The tropical climate also left Kathleen in "bad shape," and her health worsened with the onset of menopause.[210] Often bedridden, she spent weeks up in Baguio.[211]

Louise helped by acting as her mother's stand-in. In contrast to Kathleen, she loved the Philippines. "Each day," Louise wrote, "isn't nearly long enough for me to get the full enjoyment."[212] She seemed to blossom under the warm tropical sun. And she "got her first taste of night life" when she attended a dance and did the rumba with a Filipino partner who spoke little English. The press described the youngest McNutt as "poised" and "quiet spoken," much like her father, and as "a comely lass with charm," after her mother. Although Louise enjoyed life in the islands, she was happy when her family returned to the United States in 1939.[213]

While in the Philippines, Paul and Kathleen made some interesting friends. McNutt got along well with Dwight David Eisenhower, a lieutenant colonel who was serving as an aide to General Douglas A. MacArthur. Eisenhower and his wife, Mamie, liked the McNutts.[214] Mamie and Kathleen were both warm, convivial personalities while Ike and Paul were about the same age, had backgrounds in the military, and enjoyed playing golf.[215] They were striving men from the Midwest who, having reached middle age, were experiencing their share of frustration. While McNutt's eyes were fixed on the White House, Eisenhower just "wanted to go back on duty with the U.S. Army." Both men had complex relationships with MacArthur, who had become, in 1935, the chief military adviser to Quezon. While MacArthur spoke in glittering generalities about the promise of the emerging Philippine Army and of the islands following independence, Eisenhower, like McNutt, was more skeptical about the ability of Filipinos to defend themselves and to build an economically robust nation.[216] Partly as a result, Eisenhower's relations with MacArthur deteriorated over time. "Probably no one," Ike later admitted, "has had more, tougher fights with a senior than I had with MacArthur."[217]

Since McNutt was MacArthur's superior, his dealings with the general ran smoothly, at least on the surface. Before McNutt arrived in Manila, reporters in America anticipated "fireworks" between him and MacArthur.[218] A clash seemed likely since both men were "tall, handsome, dynamic, able, extremely ambitious," and accustomed to the limelight.[219] But McNutt and MacArthur carefully avoided a public spat. In an interview, MacArthur hailed McNutt as "an old and valued friend" who understood the need to strengthen American defenses.[220] The high commissioner, in turn, lauded the general's "virtues as a soldier and as a gentleman."[221] With respect to turf—and policy—it was a different story. MacArthur guarded his relationship with Quezon from encroachment by McNutt.[222] More important, MacArthur, unlike McNutt, championed Philippine independence, predicting in 1939 "that the Islands would be independent in 2 years."[223] That same year, he "pooh-poohed" the talk that Japan posed a threat to the Philippines. According to Eisenhower, MacArthur contradicted McNutt's position in such an overt manner because he wished to raise his standing among Filipino nationalists and because he thought that McNutt, who was heading home, "was not going anywhere" politically. But, in 1939, after McNutt landed a new job in the Roosevelt administration as head of the Federal Security Agency, MacArthur immediately sent him "a flowery letter of congratulations."[224]

While in Manila, McNutt worked hard to win over Filipinos. He held press conferences, made speeches, met with Quezon, and traveled about the islands, often by airplane.[225] In addition to relentless energy, McNutt projected tact and drive. Before leaving America, he acknowledged his lack of experience with Philippine affairs, but averred that he had "no axe to grind" and would serve as long as FDR wanted him to.[226] Upon arriving in Manila, McNutt scored a triumph with an impromptu visit to the Luneta, a large park, where he laid flowers at the base of the monument to José Rizal, a symbol of Filipinos' revolt against Spain and the country's greatest hero.[227] Then, on June 12, 1937, McNutt joined General Emilio Aguinaldo, a leader of the revolt against Spain in 1898 and the subsequent war against the United States, to mark the thirty-ninth anniversary of the Philippines' declaration of independence from Spain. That day, McNutt reviewed an assembly of ten thousand Filipinos, many of them veterans of the Philippine-American War.[228] It was a gracious act from someone who opposed Philippine independence.

McNutt comported himself as a gentleman and became well-liked in the Philippines, according to observers and press reports, Ambassador Grew's prediction notwithstanding.[229] The high commissioner praised Quezon for his "courageous" and "statesmanlike" action in restoring pensions to the American teachers.[230] And a few months after Quezon lit McNutt's cigarette, the high commissioner returned the favor, again with photographers recording the event.[231] McNutt's physical appearance also made him popular, for Filipinos often saw handsome politicians as being "approachable, liberal, kind and honest."[232] Whatever the reason or reasons, McNutt gained his share of admirers, accolades, and awards, including admission to the Philippine bar and an honorary doctorate from the University of the Philippines.[233]

Filipinos followed McNutt's presidential prospects intently.[234] The *Philippines Free Press* and the *Philippines Herald* crowed that McNutt, along with Murphy, another rising political star, was making them proud.[235] Filipinos wanted their land to be seen as a "training ground" for American statesmen rather than a place of exile for overly ambitious politicians. They also wished McNutt well because, as the *Herald* editorialized, the high commissioner had been "tactful and thoughtful" and had "won the respect and admiration of everyone."[236] Such praise contained a slice of self-interest. Although the *Herald* disagreed with McNutt's stand on independence, the paper's editor believed that his experience in the islands would make him a "potentially valuable friend" in the White House.[237] Commentary like that signaled that memories of the toasting affair had faded—in the Philippines, at least—and that McNutt's presidential boom was off to a strong start.

Talk of the White House stimulated McNutt's desire to return to America. Until the toasting incident, he had been rising in the polls. An early Gallup survey of possible Democratic nominees had McNutt seventh in a field of eight. By May 1937 he placed fourth, behind James Farley, Governor George Earle of Pennsylvania, and Frank Murphy.[238] Although McNutt ducked questions about the presidency, he kept in touch with "friends" in Indiana about the condition of their organization and the doings of other candidates.[239] The news from home was not always good. Indiana newspapers had "exercised themselves" over the toasting affair to the point that Senator Sherman Minton became concerned over all the unfavorable publicity.[240] Even worse, M. Clifford Townsend, the Democrat who had succeeded McNutt as governor, had settled a steel strike without using troops—a stark contrast with the actions of his predecessor. At a time when sit-down strikes were rocking the automobile industry (and Murphy's governorship) in Michigan, Townsend seemed a political comer. Farley, McNutt's nemesis, seized this opportunity to talk up the sitting Indiana governor as a possible vice-presidential nominee in 1940.[241] Raising Townsend as a rival spelled trouble for McNutt, whose old enemies—Pleas E. Greenlee and R. Earl Peters—were plotting to seize control of the state party.[242] Even though both Townsend and Minton swore allegiance to the former governor, McNutt knew that party factionalism made it risky for him to remain outside Indiana for any length of time.[243]

McNutt had other reasons for returning. After a year in the Philippines, he was growing "homesick."[244] Late in 1937 McNutt sounded both wistful and florid when he radioed greetings to fans attending the annual Indiana-Purdue football game: "From the shores of the Manila Bay to the banks of the Wabash and the Jordan we, exiled by fate from our Hoosier Homeland, echo from the distance [your] loyal cheers."[245] A few months later, he privately described his job in Manila as "done" and his work "routine" and "uninteresting." He was willing to stay in the Philippines only if there was a "change of policy" on independence.[246] Otherwise, McNutt assumed that the Joint Preparatory Committee would finish its report by early 1938, freeing him to return to America.[247] Kathleen's health was pushing Paul to leave the Philippines as well. He thus planned to leave Manila in June 1938, taking a "leisurely" voyage home by way of Europe. Then, that fall, Paul would probably assume the presidency of Indiana University, where he would be able to make occasional speeches and oversee his budding campaign for the White House.[248]

McNutt's plans, although carefully laid, went awry. The trip through Europe, to which FDR had agreed, never took place—a casualty of Kathleen's worsening condition.[249] And McNutt's expectation of swift action by the Joint Preparatory Committee fell victim to Quezon's stalling and to the Hoosier's own call for a reexamination of independence. The presidency of IU, in contrast, seemed to be a sure thing. In 1937 President William Lowe Bryan announced his retirement, and McNutt was the likeliest successor. Half of the university's board of trustees, which would name the next IU president, had been chosen by Governor McNutt. McNutt also had long-standing ties to IU and had worked to maintain state funding for the university during the leanest years of the depression.[250] McNutt's candidacy to succeed Bryan enjoyed the support of Governor Townsend, who agreed "to let the University matter rest" and not to push for the appointment of a new president until McNutt returned in 1938.[251] And fortune smiled when McNutt's protégé, Herman B Wells, became IU's acting president. Wells, who was just thirty-five, pledged not to be a candidate for the presidency, and that seemed a wise decision.[252] Ora L. Wildermuth, a member of the IU board of trustees, was insisting the next president be no younger than forty but no older than fifty-five.[253] That criterion excluded Wells but not McNutt.

By the end of 1937 press reports speculated that McNutt would be selected as the university's next president.[254] Wells even wrote McNutt that everyone at IU was just waiting "to dump all of our troubles" on him, confident that they would be "ironed out."[255]

It never happened. The prospect of McNutt becoming president of IU sparked opposition. Some people protested that McNutt would use the presidency "as a stepping stone to higher political office."[256] Others complained that he was too polarizing, had generated too much "ill feeling," to head an institution designed for "*all* the people."[257] Meredith Nicholson agreed: "If Paul donned the academic robes at Bloomington there would be a howl from the Republican alumni (about two thirds of the total) every time he flew up to Oshkosh to make a speech."[258] Wildermuth, who headed the search for the new president, heard such criticism.[259] He wrote Townsend about having "some very well-defined ideas" about a McNutt presidency which he was willing to share but not on paper.[260] As the only trustee selected by the alumni, not the governor, Wildermuth was free to voice his views. After he became president of the board of trustees, in 1938, he acted on them by conducting a thorough national search for a new president.[261] Even so, by the opening months of 1938, there appeared to be only two candidates for the job: McNutt—and Wells.[262] At a special meeting of the board in March, the trustees voted unanimously in favor of Wells.[263]

How this came about remains unclear. A few things are certain: Wells was a viable candidate for the presidency, despite his age and disavowals of interest, because he had experience and savvy that belied his years. Wells had served on the panel that had recommended reform of Indiana's financial institutions and later became dean of the IU school of business. And during the time he was acting president, he "acted like a president," inaugurating a major self-study of the university.[264] Wells later denied that his behavior in 1937 and 1938 was part of a concerted effort to remain in the top job on a permanent basis.[265] Perhaps, but it proved more effective than the actions of McNutt, who kept quiet in public and allowed friends to boost him in the press.[266] In the meantime, Wildermuth had warmed to Wells, whom he thought would make a "good president" after "a little seasoning" as an acting president.[267] So, while Wells continued to advise McNutt to take the position if it was offered, the trustees increasingly looked toward Wells.[268] On February 8, 1938, the board rejected McNutt's candidacy; four trustees—all of them McNutt appointees—supported the former governor, but the other four board members did not. Having failed to secure a majority, McNutt withdrew from consideration. A month later, the trustees settled on Wells.

McNutt bore Wells no ill will. Wells remained deferential toward his mentor, and McNutt hailed Wells's elevation to the presidency as a "source of great pride."[269] It was much more than that. From 1938 to 1962, Wells served as president of Indiana University and emerged as a kind of educational genius who transformed IU into a "sophisticated modern academic institution."[270] It is unlikely that McNutt would have led the school with such sustained focus. By early 1938, his interest in the IU presidency had waned. Kathleen's illness had grown so serious that a return trip to the United States by autumn was impossible.[271] McNutt thus resolved to spend the balance of 1938 in the Philippines.[272] Having broken away from Indiana in 1937, he appeared, a year later, to be stuck in the very place he had broken away to.

# 9

## HUMANITARIAN—AND HOME
## (1937–1939)

THE CIRCUMSTANCES THAT BROUGHT Paul V. McNutt to, and kept him in, the Philippines wound up saving lives. Between 1937 and 1939, the United States high commissioner helped approximately 1,300 Jews secure visas to flee Nazi Germany and resettle in Manila. The story, including McNutt's part in it, is important, for it revises the argument that the United States government used "paper walls," that is, bureaucratic rules, regulations, and various decrees, to prevent Jewish refugees from reaching American shores in the 1930s, and then "abandoned" European Jewry to Hitler's Holocaust during World War II.[1] It also reveals another dimension of the career of the powerful governor reviled by organized labor as the "Hoosier Hitler."[2]

The portrait of McNutt that emerges is one of a practical politician who, for a variety of reasons, became the instrumental force behind making Manila a haven for refugees. McNutt had developed sympathy for the persecuted. He then reacted to the pleas for assistance from Jewish leaders and exploited unique circumstances to open the Philippines to refugees. McNutt, on one level, was idealistic—someone who believed in a tolerant America, where citizens were defined by their patriotic service rather than their national origin, religion, race, or creed. Yet, on another, more realistic level, he was aware of sinister forces that threatened this vision, at home and abroad. McNutt believed in meeting and mastering the purveyors of hatred, sometimes directly and sometimes not. In the end, he helped over a thousand Jews find refuge from Hitler's tyranny.

At its core, the story of McNutt and Jewish refugees to the Philippines is one of possibility and limitation. McNutt exercised his powers as high commissioner creatively, opportunistically, and pragmatically, that is, in accordance with conditions in the Philippines and with U.S. immigration law. The result was a program that, however praiseworthy, was restricted to refugees of means and depended on McNutt's leadership and the assistance of his allies. Following McNutt's departure from Manila in 1939, this rescue effort was cut short, and the Philippines joined almost all other nations in no longer providing a refuge for the oppressed.

There is no easy answer to the question of why McNutt was willing to help Jewish refugees. Suffice it to say that by the late 1930s, he had developed, or was developing, motivations for resisting Nazism and assisting Jews. On the surface, there was little in McNutt's background to suggest that this would happen. After all, his native state was not known for its racial, ethnic, and religious tolerance. In the 1920s, the Ku Klux Klan (KKK), the avowed opponent of Jews, Catholics, and immigrants as well as of African Americans, attracted widespread support among Indiana's white, native-born, Protestant majority, and for a time it controlled the state's Republican Party. And Martinsville, where McNutt had grown up, later earned an unsavory reputation as a center of race hatred and Klan activity.[3] Yet he was "from" Martinsville, not "of" Martinsville—a fact underscored by his struggles against schoolyard bullies. That harassment had taught McNutt how cruel people can be. It follows that he might have gained sympathy for victims of persecution and for underdogs who fight back despite the odds.

In addition, McNutt later joined an organization that had experienced persecution over the course of American history: the Masonic Order. McNutt's decision to become a Mason proved personal; his maternal grandfather, Jacob M. Neely, with whom Paul was close, was a lifelong Mason who held leadership offices in the order. McNutt was aware of the anti-Masonic movements of the past, and he spoke movingly on behalf of universal brotherhood and against intolerance in addresses before his fellow Masons. In 1939 McNutt told a Masonic gathering that the forces of racial hatred, be they Nazis or the KKK, always sought a kind of "solidarity" by "finding an enemy within" their nations. Anti-Masonic campaigns signified one type of scapegoating, as did anti-Semitism:

"The Jews, an old, historical group, surviving through the centuries, represent an ideal object for that purpose." McNutt condemned "anti-semitism, anti-Masonry, anti-Catholicism, anti-this or anti-that." "If there is anything in the world I hate," he emphasized, "it is a hater."[4]

Other factors reinforced his inclination toward tolerance. McNutt was both an educated man and a college educator and, while such things guaranteed neither open-mindedness nor freedom from anti-Semitism or any other prejudice, they exposed him to a rich body of thought and prepared him for dealing with a variety of people. McNutt's upbringing, in a middle-class home in the middle section of the country, and his training, at a public school and at a state university, shielded him from the social snobbishness and anti-Semitism that permeated upper-crust society in the East, including the Ivy League universities which trained many white Anglo-Saxon males for the foreign service.[5] Until McNutt went to Harvard, he would have known almost nothing of such schools.

Politics fueled, and later tempered, McNutt's opposition to ethnic bigotry and race hatred. McNutt and his father, both Democrats, opposed the power of the Klan in Indiana. During the 1920s, McNutt demonstrated his "Americanism" by joining the American Legion, not the Ku Klux Klan. As mentioned earlier, the Legion, unlike the Klan, remained racially, ethnically, and religiously inclusive, for it was open to all veterans of the Great War. McNutt worked to keep it that way, especially when he helped to arrange the election of Frank McHale, a Catholic, to succeed him as commander of the Indiana Legion in 1927. At that year's state convention, McNutt jabbed at the Klan when he proclaimed that the Legion was not captive to "ancient prejudices and hatreds." "It is not concerned with questions of color, or of race, or of creed," he asserted. "It is concerned with the protection and the betterment of the homeland."[6] After McNutt became national commander of the Legion in 1928, he articulated a vision of Americanism different from that of the Klan. Instead of upholding the power of the nation's white, native-born Protestant majority, McNutt insisted that all U.S. residents, regardless of background, must become citizens, enjoy the same rights, and shoulder the same responsibilities. On an elemental level, he had absorbed the nation's founding creed that "all men are created equal," that is, "equal in rights, privileges and immunities." There were practical reasons for his stand as well. Establishing "domicile" as the requisite for citizenship was "the only tolerable rule" for the United States, where so many people were of "foreign" birth.[7]

McNutt's belief in racial and religious tolerance was never intense or heartfelt enough to lead him to undertake serious political risks. His remarks against the Klan occurred in private, at least until McHale's election as state Legion commander in 1927—when the appeal of the KKK had ebbed in Indiana. McNutt also showed little interest in the plight of African Americans, either as a young man or as a rising politician. His strongest denunciation of discrimination against blacks occurred later in his career, during World War II, when he extolled "Negro workers" as pivotal parts of the nation's war effort and, following the war's end, when he assailed bias in the United States as "the one worm in the shining apple of our international prestige."[8] In both cases, McNutt identified pragmatic, rather than moral, reasons for ending bias, as America struggled to rally all of its citizens in the war against fascism and then appeal to the peoples of Africa and Asia in the Cold War against Communism. Similarly, he did not challenge religious bigotry in an overt way. McNutt never questioned America's restrictive immigration policy, established during the 1920s, which set annual quotas based on one's national origin and applied those quotas in a manner that discriminated against immigrants from Jewish, Eastern Orthodox, and Roman Catholic backgrounds. In 1928, moreover, he allowed the specter of anti-Catholic bias against the Democratic nominee for president, Al Smith, to dissuade him from running for governor of Indiana.[9]

As time went on, McNutt recognized that his own party was coming to include a growing number of racial and religious minorities. By the 1920s, the Democratic Party had proved more welcoming of immigrants than its Republican counterpart, and, partly as a result, voters in the nation's largest cities—the centers of ethnic diversity—had moved into the Democratic camp. Moreover, because of the state GOP's ties to the Ku Klux Klan, African Americans in Indiana began to vote Democratic in statewide and municipal elections a decade before the New Deal. Although most blacks returned to the GOP in national elections during the 1920s, they were becoming a presence within the Indiana Democratic Party by the time McNutt entered the governor's mansion in 1933. Furthermore, Indiana's Jews, who numbered twenty-five thousand and were concentrated in urban centers, also found the Republicans increasingly odious.[10] McNutt, as a Democratic leader, had to know that his party was growing ever more diverse.

As governor, McNutt, handled issues related to race and ethnicity in an opportunistic fashion. He dispensed patronage jobs to African Americans, doubling the number of blacks employed at the statehouse. Yet by 1935 no African Americans had received positions of a supervisory or administrative nature, and McNutt and his staff respected the tradition of racial segregation in state offices.[11] Similar to the administration in Washington, the government in Indianapolis relied on a policy of providing relief to the unemployed regardless of color, rather than a vigorous civil rights program, to woo and win black support. With respect to Jews, McNutt, like Franklin D. Roosevelt, accepted Jewish leaders as partners in his administration. In 1934 the Indiana governor remained neutral when Jacob Weiss, a Jew from Indianapolis, sought election as president pro tem of the Indiana State Senate. Weiss prevailed and emerged as "a close political ally" of McNutt's.[12] The governor's office often solicited Weiss's advice when communicating with Jewish leaders.[13]

McNutt's relationship with Weiss, which would figure into the effort to establish Manila as a haven for refugees, reflected his capacity to learn and to adapt on matters involving Jews. The governor had plenty of opportunity for such growth. He could not help noticing that, three weeks after his inauguration, Adolf Hitler became the chancellor of Germany. McNutt received almost daily reminders of the nature of the Nazi regime in the *Indianapolis Times,* Roy W. Howard's newspaper, which had earned a Pulitzer Prize for exposing the power of the Klan in Indiana and had backed McNutt's election to the statehouse. Throughout 1933, the *Times* publicized the Nazi assault on Jews through photographs and stories bearing such headlines as "Terror Revival Faces Jews in Middle Europe" and "Jews Beset by Hate and Ruin in Germany."[14] Moreover, the editor of the *Times* called for boycotts of German goods as he extended "our profound sympathy to all the racial and political victims of Hitler barbarism."[15]

McNutt also received and read memoranda from Jewish groups detailing Nazi atrocities. He thanked the president of the American Jewish Congress for sending a copy of *Swastika: The Nazi Terror,* for he was interested in reading "an authentic report of the repressions, discriminations, and persecutions visited upon the Jews of Germany."[16] At the end of another report, McNutt jotted: "Are we to join the traitors to the human brotherhood who prey upon the lives and souls of other men, or are we to enlist in the war for justice, a war which is never done!" His disdain for the villain was matched by his respect for the victim. "The plain fact is," he stressed, "that the faith of the Israelites has made them a people, whom forty centuries have not been able to destroy."[17] McNutt, ever respectful of toughness, resiliency, and success, later praised the "thrift, chastity, [and] vision" of Jews—traits that, in his opinion, had braced them to withstand a centuries-long "reign of terror."[18]

McNutt advertised his solidarity with Jews. In March 1933 he addressed a nonsectarian gathering in Chicago, organized by a local rabbi, which McNutt hailed as "one of the first anti-Nazi meetings in the country."[19] There, the governor characterized the Nazi assault on Jews as an "injustice," one that was "outrageous against morality and humanity." "For the second time in my life," this veteran of World War I declared, "I rise to protest against the acts of the German government."[20] McNutt, the "principal speaker," urged the audience to join in his condemnation of Nazism and to "enlist" in a "war" for "justice."[21] Later on in 1933, McNutt, prodded by Jewish editors and Weiss, issued greetings to Indiana's Jews on Rosh Hashanah. His statement prayed for the "continued prosperity and well being of the Jews" and demanded an end to all "intolerance, bigotry, and injustice."[22] A year later, in a similar message, he hoped that Jews at last would receive "their God-given right to carry on untrammeled as men and women without the weight of prejudice, bigotry and slander."[23] McNutt's public criticism contrasted with the silence of the White House. FDR insisted that Germany's treatment of its Jews was "not a governmental affair" and that he could "do nothing" to stop the persecution.[24]

McNutt had a different response to anti-Semites: He favored a Jewish homeland in Palestine. In 1935 he cooperated with Zionist groups in Indiana to celebrate the first ever "Palestine Day." In an official proclamation, McNutt linked the "re-establishment" of a Jewish homeland there to the "ideals of justice" that "animated" democratic nations, including America.[25] For his effort, he won a place in the "Golden Book of the Jewish National Fund." The president of the Indianapolis Zionist District, in tribute, explained that Governor McNutt had "acted courageously and sincerely," had demonstrated "an understanding of our people's worth and dignity," and, significantly, had expressed "continued protests against any injustices heaped upon our people here and abroad."[26] The governor, in response, wrote that he "deeply" appreciated this "signal honor."[27] It may be tempting to dismiss McNutt's private correspondence on such matters as the sort of routine, constituency- and ethnic-based appeals in which all politicians engage. Such an analysis slights the unique conditions under which McNutt governed, during a time when anti-Semitism was on the upsurge and when disparaging comments against Jews were commonplace, even within the Roosevelt administration (Postmaster General James A. Farley once joked that "a Nazi is a person who hates a Jew more than is necessary").[28] Moreover, the fact that McNutt not only read reports of Nazi atrocities—scarcely the domain of the governor of Indiana—but wrote about them, suggests that his missives to Jewish groups were not ordinary form letters. And there were McNutt's words themselves, which strongly condemned Nazi-style bigotry.

In the 1930s, McNutt began to associate Jewish traditions, and Jews themselves, with his political ideology. As governor, McNutt not only secured greater relief for his state's unemployed and pensions for aged Hoosiers. He also argued, more broadly, that it was the "business" of government to assure "every man the right to live as a normal human being."[29] Interestingly, he used that same language two months later when, in Chicago, he chastised the Nazis for their persecution of Jews: "No government can long endure that fails to guarantee to its people the right to live as normal human beings. The present government of Germany thus writes its own destruction."[30] In McNutt's mind, existing as a "normal human being" involved enjoying safety—or security, one of his favorite words—from persecution as well as from privation. As the decade wore on, McNutt was able to broaden his thinking on the aims of the welfare state. In a speech in Boston entitled "Cultural Pluralism in America," he saluted Jewish humanitarianism—philanthropists, relief agencies, social workers, settlement houses—as one progenitor of "security," New Deal–style.[31] McNutt thus expressed an inclusive perspective, that Jews and Jewish contributions toward building America demanded respect.

In the international arena, McNutt believed that the Jews were a central protagonist in the battle between democratic government and fascist tyranny. "Wherever liberalism is well-established," he told a Masonic audience in 1939, "there is little or no anti-semitism. Wherever liberalism weakens and an opportunity is offered to a would-be dictator, anti-semitism is used to create a 'group will' to serve the dictator's ambition."[32] Although as governor McNutt drew attacks from opponents for being himself a dictator, he abhorred dictatorship. He had long favored a program of military preparedness to protect America from anti-democratic regimes. While in Manila, he developed a fear of Japanese militarism and revulsion against the "outrageous brutality" perpetrated by Japanese troops against civilians in China. "McNutt has [a] strong anti-dictator slant," the journalist Raymond Clapper wrote in 1938, "and is echoing current clichés about [how] democracies must stand up to dictators."[33] As the need for collective security became ever more important to McNutt, he sought Jewish allies. "One cannot quarantine a land against tyranny and persecution," he reminded one Zionist. "The world is one. If aggression stalks the peoples of the earth, no land, no person is immune."[34]

Looking ahead, one has to ask: Did McNutt's ambition to succeed FDR in the White House affect his decision, as high commissioner to the Philippines, to allow Jews to settle in Manila? Possibly. There was a political angle to almost all his endeavors. Like other New Dealers, he recognized the strength of group identity in U.S. politics. With an eye toward Jewish voters, McNutt's presidential campaign later drafted a narrative of his service in the Philippines that dis-

cussed his efforts on behalf of refugees and distributed it to the Jewish-American press.[35] McNutt also learned that helping refugees brought benefits from
their sponsors. In August 1939, he pressed the American consul in Budapest to
admit into the United States two brothers of Michael Curtiz, a Hungarian-born
Jew and film director with Democratic-leaning Warner Brothers, later known
for his masterpiece *Casablanca*. McNutt's campaign considered Curtiz "very
influential" in California and "inclined to be liberal with his contributions."
Indeed, Curtiz, in thanking McNutt, cabled: "You will have my wholehearted
support in anything you undertake."[36]

At the same time, political motivation should not be exaggerated in this case.
The events discussed above occurred after McNutt had returned to the United
States from Manila in 1939. While McNutt was in the Philippines, and as he
heard pleas for help from Jewish refugees, there is no evidence that electoral
considerations dictated his decisions. Having seen how the Klan won the allegiance of thousands of his fellow Hoosiers in the 1920s and knowing of the
anti-Semitism of many Americans, he doubtless understood that any push to
help Jews was politically risky. In aiding refugees, McNutt acted from an array
of different experiences, thoughts, and motivations, including, perhaps, a political one. Then, after returning to America, he and his staff packaged his record in
the Philippines into a campaign narrative designed to appeal to a wide variety
of groups, including Jews.

The question of how McNutt helped to bring German Jews to Manila is as
intriguing as why he did so. In a way, his willingness to help Jewish refugees
originated with his determination to protect American prestige in Asia, to reas-
sert U.S. sovereignty over the Philippines, and to stand up to the dictatorships.
For example, McNutt clashed with the German consul in Manila, Gustav Adolf
Sakowski, when Sakowski tried to raise his nation's profile in the Philippines.
In March 1938, the German consul sought to arrange a plebiscite among Ger-
man and Austrian nationals in order to ratify Hitler's *Anschluss* with Austria.
McNutt objected, whereupon Sakowski staged a shipboard meeting, beyond
Philippine waters, at which three hundred Germans and Austrians pledged
allegiance to their enlarged Fatherland. McNutt replied "more sharply" when
Sakowski urged the German Club of Manila to expel its Jewish members. "The
American government," he emphasized, "guarantees religious tolerance and
freedom from persecution to all persons living under its flag."[37] The German

consul again backed down by allowing the club to determine its membership.[38] Although standing up to the Nazis in this context carried no risk, the high commissioner made clear that the Philippines remained U.S. soil and that the rights of its people could not be abridged by any foreign power.

McNutt also demonstrated his concern by allowing Jewish refugees to settle in Manila. The high commissioner's efforts here were compassionate; they responded to events and respected U.S. immigration law. The project originated in September 1937, when twenty-eight German Jews fled Shanghai, China, where Japanese troops were advancing, and came to Manila, where Jewish leaders received them. After learning of the refugees' plight, McNutt waived visa requirements and allowed the refugees into the Philippines. Under the Tydings-McDuffie Act, which granted the Philippines autonomous status as a commonwealth, the U.S. government retained the final say over immigration. In 1935, FDR granted the high commissioner the authority to waive visa requirements for aliens seeking "temporary admission" to the Philippines in "emergency" situations.[39] McNutt did so. The arrival of the twenty-eight Jews from Shanghai "set a precedent for a later immigration program that would involve the High Commissioner and the Jewish community leadership in Manila."[40]

That any refugees made it to Manila may seem surprising, for people seeking entrance to U.S. territory faced obstacles during the 1930s. These included a restrictive immigration policy of quotas based on national origins; anti-immigrant sentiment in Congress and among the larger public during the Great Depression; bureaucratic inertia and anti-Semitism at the Department of State; and a president who only showed fleeting interest in the issue. Another hurdle was a section of the Immigration Act of 1917 that forbade aliens from entering the United States if they were unable to support themselves financially and thus "likely to become a public charge." When enforced strictly, the rule demanded that immigrants prove, not that they possessed the minimal "physical or mental skills required for constructive employment," but that they were likely "to obtain a job under current market conditions"—a daunting task during a worldwide slump.[41] Such a restrictive policy has been criticized by scholars. They emphasize that the annual quota for Germany "was rarely filled" and that immigration to America from the entire world never surpassed fifty-four percent of the overall annual quota of 153,774.[42] The historian David Wyman has been especially harsh, criticizing U.S. policy as "not generous" and the Department of State's overseas consuls for their anti-alien and anti-Semitic bias that "influenced their decisions in visa cases."[43]

In the Philippines, in contrast, policymakers, both American and Filipino, had greater leeway with respect to immigration. After seizing Manila in 1898, the United States imposed its exclusionary immigration laws to the Philippines, but colonial officials permitted Chinese nationals to enter the archipelago illegally, confident that they never would reach the U.S. mainland without the necessary papers. The growth of the Chinese population, in terms of wealth and size, fueled anti-Chinese sentiment and rioting by Filipinos. Similar resentment surfaced regarding the Japanese, who had acquired chunks of land in Davao, on the Muslim-populated southernmost island of Mindanao. To develop Mindanao economically—and to increase his government's control over it—Manuel Quezon encouraged Christian Filipino farmers to settle on the island. It is important to remember that the Philippine constitution said nothing about immigration. This oversight was intentional, for neither Quezon nor U.S. officials wanted to offend Japan by reopening a debate over limiting the influx of Japanese into the Philippines. Furthermore, U.S. immigration law was not being strictly enforced by the Filipinos.[44]

Although McNutt was able to let a small number of Jewish refugees into Manila, he realized that any long-term effort to admit Jews to the Philippines had to be systematic, planned, and based on U.S. statutes, not merely on the high commissioner's authority. The thought of a more extensive venture, using the Philippines as a haven, originated with Julius Weiss—an officer of the American Jewish Joint Distribution Committee (JDC); a member of the Refugee Economic Corporation (REC), which helped to resettle Jewish refugees; and the brother of Jacob Weiss, McNutt's political ally in Indiana. The high commissioner learned of this idea from Jacob Weiss in February 1938, while McNutt was visiting the United States, and he pledged to examine the matter. By May 1938, McNutt had conferred with commonwealth officials, who were receptive to the proposal, and with Jewish leaders in Manila, who began devising a plan to absorb another hundred refugee families. "McNutt felt that the settlement of Jewish refugees could be handled most sympathetically by the Jews themselves," one of his aides noted.[45] Such a method also served to distance the politically ambitious high commissioner from a venture that, at any point, could go awry or spark controversy.

The leadership of Manila's Jews played a key role in determining which refugees would gain entry into the Philippines. The origins of a Jewish community in the Philippines dated back to the days of Spanish colonial rule, when a few Marranos arrived seeking refuge from the Inquisition. The Spanish-American

War and the subsequent suppression of the Filipinos by U.S. troops brought to the Philippines a small number of Jewish American soldiers and tradesmen. Merchants and shopkeepers were among the earliest Jewish entrepreneurs in the Philippines; manufacturers, of embroidery and cigars, came later. These Jewish businessmen prospered, at least to the point where they were able to raise sufficient funds to build Temple Emil, Manila's first synagogue, which opened its doors in 1925. And yet the congregation, numbering about two hundred, lacked the means to maintain the temple's Sunday school, keep its cantor, and hire a rabbi of its own. These difficulties were related to the limited size, and the ample needs, of Manila's Jewish community, which numbered between four and five hundred people by the late 1930s.[46]

Nevertheless, McNutt asked this Jewish community to help resettle the refugees. He approached Philip Frieder, a Jewish American cigar manufacturer, about the REC's plan, explaining that "if the Jewish community could assume responsibility for these families, he would be glad to allow them to enter." Frieder agreed, provided that he and other Jewish leaders in Manila "could select the type of people who were to come." If that sounded exclusionary in its own way, one must remember that only six Jewish families, including Frieder and his brothers Morris and Alex, possessed the means to support refugees; that the cost of sustaining each refugee was fifty cents per day; and that the REC had allocated only $5,000 for the venture. Moreover, the Frieders knew that the long-term success of any resettlement program required the sympathy of Filipinos. It had to be handled "right," that is, the refugees had to be absorbed into the Jewish community, had to secure employment, and had to avoid becoming public charges.[47]

The plan that Frieder and his cohorts developed, and that McNutt presented to Julius Weiss, was, on one level, limited and legalistic. The high commissioner stressed the need to respect the Immigration Act of 1917, which applied to the Philippines, by excluding any alien "likely to become a public charge"—a clause that he deemed "most important." As a former lawyer, law professor, and law school dean, McNutt naturally had developed a great respect for the law in general. He also knew that the Philippine economy left "much to be desired" and that a number of recent émigrés from White Russia had failed to find employment and had become stateless since no other nation would accept them. To prevent another tragedy, Jewish leaders in Manila compiled fourteen categories of needed occupations as well as the number of people to be admitted in each category. Most needed were medical specialists, mechanics, farmers, barbers, accountants, engineers—and one rabbi. McNutt believed in acting "cautiously in accordance with the plan above outlined" because he wanted it to succeed. "The character and conduct of the first groups," McNutt explained to Julius Weiss, "will have much to do in determining the number of those who are permitted to follow."[48]

On another level, the plan outlined by McNutt allowed him and his allies to use laws enacted to restrict immigration to bring Jewish professionals out of Germany. They were able to do this for two reasons. First, the Immigration Act of 1924, which set quotas based on national origins for those seeking to enter the United States, did not cover immigration into the Philippines. (The reason why the 1917 act covered the Philippines, while the 1924 law did not, was that the 1917 act defined the Philippines as part of the United States while the 1924 law did not.)[49] Second, with FDR showing a measure of interest in Jewish immigration (to Palestine) during his reelection campaign in 1936, officials at the Department of State acted to liberalize the "likely to become a public charge" proviso.[50] Even Assistant Secretary of State Wilbur J. Carr—who favored immigration restrictions—conceded, early in 1937, that U.S. consular officers, in issuing visas to aliens, must interpret "likely" to mean that an immigrant would "probably," and not "possibly," become a public charge.[51] McNutt's sympathy was plain. He wrote that he was "deeply interested in the solution of the problem of caring for political refugees" and "very glad to do anything in my power to assist."[52]

Quezon also backed this venture. As a "non-Aryan," he had no affinity with Nazi-style racial policies. During a visit to Europe in 1937, Quezon, his wife, and their son were troubled by a parade in Berlin. The specter of storm troopers, goose-stepping in formation, "shook" the president's wife so that "she shivered in her seat," according to Quezon's grandson, Manuel L. Quezon III. At the same time, back in Manila, Quezon had made some "very good" friends within the Jewish-American community. One reason for these relationships was that Jews, familiar with persecution, "would go out of their way to show friendship and equality with Filipinos" at a time when other Americans would not. The Frieders themselves socialized with Quezon over poker and bridge. As Manuel Quezon III stressed, "That's when the Frieders got close to my grandfather and that's how they were able to approach him if they had any problems."[53] Alice Weston, a daughter of Alex Frieder, recalled that Quezon came to the Frieder home to play cards and that McNutt, another close friend of the president, was part of this group. There, the topic of Jewish refugees came up, and Quezon agreed to allow them to enter Manila. His endorsement proved significant, for although the Department of State issued visas to Jews and the Frieders helped to ease their resettlement, it was the commonwealth officials who determined who disembarked from ships and set foot on Philippine soil.[54] Overall, Quezon's chief contribution to the refugee project was that he agreed to initiatives originated by McNutt and Jewish leaders without impeding them.

McNutt and Jewish leaders strove to ensure that the right sort of refugees reached Manila. The REC worked with the Reich Representation of Jews in Germany (later known as the Reich Association of Jews in Germany), the chief Jewish organization in Germany, to determine who should have the first chance to leave. Applicants sent a dossier, including photographs, curriculum vitae, educational data, and letters of recommendation, to the REC and to the Jewish Refugee Committee in Manila, which McNutt had organized. The members of the latter committee studied applications and forwarded names to the Philippine government for approval. Alex Frieder pored over lists of would-be refugees to the point that he neglected his own business. The committee required each refugee to deposit $1,200 in a Manila bank, a sum sufficient to support the person for two years. Having proven that he or she was unlikely to become a public charge, the State Department then issued a visa from the appropriate consular office. State forbade consular officials from granting visas to any refugee except those accepted by the Jewish Refugee Committee and the commonwealth government. In order to prevent a flood of "more refugees than can be cared for," McNutt advised the Department of War, which oversaw the Philippines, to refrain from publicizing the project. "If this experiment is successful," he stressed, "it may be possible to absorb others."[55]

McNutt remained cautious through the summer and autumn of 1938, as the first wave of a hundred families arrived and settled in Manila. The rather strict process of selection simultaneously handcuffed and shielded the venture. When Secretary of State Cordell Hull asked whether the Philippines would accept five hundred Jews then residing in Italy, McNutt said no. "If and when local situation justifies admission of others," he replied, "visas should be only given to those selected from lists submitted in advance to Commonwealth officials and committee." "With such safeguards," McNutt maintained, "experiment will be successful and maximum number of refugees will be absorbed."[56] Even though the year 1938 witnessed the German Anschluss with Austria, an intensified Nazi assault on Jews, and Roosevelt's renewed interest in the refugee crisis exemplified by his calling of a conference, at Evian, France, to examine the question, any move to revise U.S. immigration laws, the head of the visa division at the State

Department warned, would yield more, not fewer, restrictions. In messages regarding the Philippine effort, officials at State, including Hull, emphasized the need to uphold the "likely to become a public charge" proviso in the 1917 Act.[57]

McNutt's program faced pressure from officials who were inclined to issue visas liberally and from those who wanted to limit immigration. When the U.S. consul in Singapore granted visas to twenty-two Manila-bound refugees, "all of them destitute," the high commissioner reiterated that "visas [must] be given only to those on approved lists" or "hitherto successful efforts to place deserving refugees in the Philippines will fail."[58] Policymakers at the State Department, meanwhile, complained that the amount of cash the refugees were required to possess on arrival—$125 for individuals and $235 for families—was small and that there was an "absence of information" about how they were being placed in jobs.[59] The high commissioner's response was to urge U.S. consulates in Europe to "expedite" the processing of visas approved by Philippine authorities.[60] In June 1939 the Jewish Refugee Committee had applications on file for 2,500 Jewish refugee families and had forwarded to the Department of State lists of 313 people approved for visas.[61]

By the close of 1938, McNutt and Quezon envisioned a larger effort, to resettle ten thousand Jewish refugees, over ten years, on the island of Mindanao. The "Mindanao Plan" emerged in the aftermath of *Kristallnacht* ("Night of Broken Glass"), when Nazi storm troopers attacked Jews and Jewish-owned property during the night of November 9–10, 1938. The pogrom shook Americans and Filipinos alike. The Philippine representative in Washington reported: "There is strong pro-Jewish sentiment all over country in view of recent developments in Europe."[62] In Manila, Filipinos staged an "indignation" rally to protest this example of Nazi brutality.[63] "It is small wonder," the *Philippines Free Press* opined, "that other countries are making unprecedented efforts to find new homes for the Jews."[64] Although not present at the rally, the high commissioner that same evening assailed the Nazi regime during a speech at Manila's Masonic Temple:

> Within the past few months we have seen the reign of law replaced by the sanctification of force, the threat of war adopted as an instrument of national policy, humble men and women denied the freedom to think their own thoughts and to worship God according to their own conscience, and the dispersion all over the world of millions of helpless wanderers with no place to lay their heads.

He contrasted the Germans, who under Hitler had shattered all norms of decency, with the Jews, who had received both "manna" and "the law" from Moses.

"Faith in the law," McNutt proclaimed, "has made the Israelites a people whom forty centuries have not been able to destroy, and forty centuries more will see a virile people."[65] To ensure that kind of future, he began to consider a more extensive resettlement program.

The Mindanao Plan originated in December 1938, when the Department of State asked McNutt how many refugees the Philippines could absorb. He discussed the matter with Quezon, who agreed to open Mindanao to Jewish settlement.[66] McNutt's leadership was not surprising, for Quezon remained cautious on the refugee issue. Although Quezon refused "to close our doors to oppressed people," he rejected "the influx of large numbers of immigrants," which "will create problem[s]."[67] Quezon agreed to Jewish settlement on Mindanao for strategic and economic, more than humanitarian, reasons. He wanted to use Jewish refugees "to obstruct Japanese penetration" of Mindanao.[68] That, combined with the need for people—meaning non-Muslims—and development in this area, led Quezon to consider colonizing Mindanao with Jewish labor. McNutt perhaps thought likewise, for he later praised the economic vitality of a Jewish refugee colony in the Dominican Republic and he also flew to Mindanao to "investigate" reports of Japanese "infiltration" there.[69] In this setting, McNutt forwarded the Mindanao Plan to the State Department and recommended its approval.[70] Undersecretary of State Sumner Welles, in turn, voiced "no objection" to the proposal and characterized it as "an important contribution toward the solution of the refugee problem."[71]

Welles's comment requires further explanation. By the end of 1938, the U.S. government was showing interest both in the plight of Jewish refugees and in work of the Intergovernmental Committee on Refugees (ICR), the product of the Evian Conference, which was directed by an American, George Rublee. Welles, moreover, favored their resettlement in undeveloped parts of the globe. The problem was that the efforts of the ICR failed—badly. Many countries refused to accept any refugees or promised to take in only a small number. The idea of settling Jews in such places as British Guiana, Rhodesia, Madagascar, Cameroon, and Angola never progressed very far. Jay Pierrepont Moffat, head of the Western European desk at State, saw no "visible" willingness on the part of British officials "to admit any Jews at all" into their African colonies.[72] And President Roosevelt showed only passing interest in establishing such havens.[73] FDR, in backing away from them, may have been swayed by Myron C. Taylor, his representative to the ICR, who dismissed talk of Jewish migration to undeveloped areas as impracticable.[74] Or the president may have decided that Palestine had to be the haven for Europe's Jews. He pressed his point with the government of Great Britain, which held a mandate over Palestine, and he reaffirmed his sympathy for the Zionist cause.[75]

In this setting, the Mindanao Plan came under increasing scrutiny, even criticism, in the United States. Jewish leaders were divided over resettlement projects. While some Jews supported them, many American Zionists argued that "a [Jewish] national homeland in Palestine was so clearly the answer" that settlement elsewhere was a waste of precious resources.[76] Meanwhile, in Washington, Welles and Rublee still supported the Mindanao Plan, as did the ICR. But the committee's position may have represented an act of desperation since only two countries, the Dominican Republic and the Philippines, had offered to accept refugees and develop any resettlement plans.[77] Meanwhile, Moffat reported that experts on the Philippines thought that putting refugees in this virgin territory was "suicidal."[78] More worrisome, Francis B. Sayre, assistant secretary of state, dismissed the Mindanao Plan as "utterly impractical."[79] Sayre adjudged the scheme flawed on the grounds that the Jewish refugees were urban dwellers and thus ill suited to become agricultural workers, as called for in the plan. Although this was a reasonable concern, Sayre was not favorable to immigrants or to immigration.[80]

Sayre's opposition proved most significant, for he was the official who replaced McNutt as high commissioner in July 1939. McNutt's decision to leave the Philippines will be addressed later in this chapter. Suffice it to say, his departure dealt a severe blow to the Mindanao Plan. In 1940, Alex Frieder prodded Sayre "to show some interest in the scheme," but his pleas had almost no effect.[81] But with unpleasant memories of the Chinese, who had been materially successful in the Philippines, and of the Japanese, who had designs on the country, the prospect of accepting more immigrants troubled many Filipinos.[82] Just as unsettling were rumors "that Mindanao was to be turned over to the Jewish refugees."[83] After the outrage generated by *Kristallnacht* had died down, one informant for the Refugee Economic Corporation sensed an "anti-Jewish feeling" among Filipinos that was "deep, quite extensive, silent but powerful."[84] To be sure, some refugees decades later remembered the generosity of Filipinos. Moreover, newcomers with needed, or highly unusual, skills became absorbed into the economic and cultural life of Manila. Yet others struggled. Several Viennese physicians who came to Manila were reduced to working as anesthesiologists, pharmacists, or aides to Filipino doctors, who did not look kindly on competition from foreigners.[85]

McNutt understood such sentiments and had opposed as "unwise" any statements that focused "public attention" on "the refugees' entry."[86] Sayre, skeptical

of the venture from the outset, was loath to "create any nasty minority situation" in the Philippines—a reference to the challenge of assimilating European
Jews into this Pacific archipelago.[87] Jewish refugees, he maintained, tend to
"congregate in Manila" and compete with Filipinos economically.[88] The press
in Manila echoed such sentiments. "The problem is to keep immigration within
bounds, to preserve the Philippines for the Filipinos," the *Philippines Free Press*
editorialized. "It's simply a case of charity beginning at home."[89]

This shift became evident as the Philippine Congress considered immigration legislation. The idea for such a law originated in 1938 with the U.S. State
Department, which informed McNutt that the Philippine Assembly might need
to pass special immigration legislation if it intended to proceed with the Mindanao Plan. The first draft of the act featured a quota permitting no more than
one thousand immigrants from each nation to enter the Philippines annually.
Through such uniformity, the law sought to restrict the influx of Chinese and
Japanese immigrants, who exceeded that number each year. The quotas did not
contradict the Mindanao Plan, which permitted one thousand Jews, presumably from one nation—Germany—to enter the Philippines annually. But a year
later, the Philippine Assembly reduced the annual quota of immigrants from
each nation by half, and Sayre advised Quezon to accept the change. Responding to protests by Japan's foreign minister, Sayre defended the revised law as
an attempt "to limit immigration so as to prevent the creation of racial difficulties" which might arise "if unlimited numbers of immigrants should pour into
the country."[90] Sayre's emphasis on the need to prevent "racial difficulties"
was consistent with his earlier warnings, was in line with nativist arguments
inside the United States, and contrasted with McNutt's priorities with respect
to immigration.[91]

Under these circumstances, Quezon's ardor for the Mindanao Plan "cooled
off."[92] When the president agreed to the plan, as one informant for the Refugee Economic Corporation observed, he had acted "impulsively" and without
sufficiently consulting other members of the government." By early 1940 his
cabinet, swayed by the changing mood in the country, voiced concern about the
Mindanao Plan.[93] Accordingly, Quezon, like Sayre, now thought the proposal
was "impractical" and that if implemented it would be a harbinger of "troubles
in the future"—a reference to the "nasty minority situation" Sayre had warned
of. "Some of [Quezon's] advisers suggested that he let the scheme bog down,
practice delay and obstructions," an aide to Sayre explained. "He is following
this advice to a certain extent. His decision to secure legislative action on the
venture was a part of this program."[94] In 1940 Quezon signed the revised im-

migration bill mandating that no more than five hundred people from each nation be admitted the Philippines each year. Although the law allowed him to admit non-quota immigrants, such as political refugees or those with needed skills, without the political will to invoke these provisions the Mindanao Plan faced an uncertain future.[95] Thereafter, various problems, such as the selection of land, training of "pioneer types," and securing of ships, arose to thwart what remained of the project.[96] The outbreak of war in Europe and Germany's conquest of the continent killed it.

The passage of the immigration act illustrated just how much sentiment in the Philippines had shifted in favor of restriction. The unique circumstances that McNutt had exploited to help bring Jewish refugees to Manila between 1937 and 1939 had vanished. Events such as the *Anschluss* and *Kristallnacht*, which had spurred greater concern for refugee issues by the U.S. government and a slightly less restrictive stance by the State Department, at least with respect to the Philippines, had given way to World War II, when "the decline in the issuance of American visas was dramatic."[97] Fear of spies and saboteurs entering a rearming America paralleled Philippine concerns about refugees inundating their country. To make matters worse, the high commissioner who had favored the Mindanao Plan had departed, replaced by a career diplomat whose wariness about the project was plain. With McNutt gone, Quezon, whose empathy for Jewish refugees was never wholehearted, wearied of the Mindanao Plan and signed a restrictive immigration law.

The Philippine venture highlights the challenges facing American and Filipino policymakers as they wrestled with Jewish immigration. Operating in an international environment that was overwhelmingly hostile to refugees, McNutt and leaders of the Jewish community in Manila made a series of difficult choices—of what they could do to save Jewish lives; of how many could be saved; and of who specifically would be saved. Their decision was to follow the law and to admit Jews of a certain socioeconomic class—professionals or those with training that would bolster the Jewish community of Manila and abet the development of the Philippines economically. To justify it, they contended that the only resettlement project likely to be accepted and to continue—or to "succeed," in McNutt's words—was one in which the refugees were seen as boons, not burdens, to the local population and its leadership. Considering how easily Quezon later distanced himself from the refugee issue, especially the Mindanao Plan; how no politician wanted to run for the White House as an advocate of unfettered immigration to U.S. shores; and how the world as a whole did almost nothing to provide havens elsewhere, one can understand their decision.

Nevertheless, given the world's reluctance to help refugees, what went on in the Philippines was remarkable. If Mindanao between 1939 and 1941 was an illusionary haven, then Manila from 1937 to 1939 was a real one—for some. The exact number of Jews who came to Manila remains uncertain, but most accounts place it at over one thousand. The number of those coming to Manila exceeded the population of the largest and best-known refugee colony of Sosúa, in the Dominican Republic. Frank Ephraim, a historian and one of the Manila refugees, stressed the significance of what was occurring: "Between the leadership of the Frieder brothers and McNutt, Jewish lives were being saved."[98] McNutt pushed the project forward, and after his departure he was missed. "We were very upset when Sayre came in," one of the Manila refugees later recalled.[99]

Political ambition lured McNutt away from the Philippines. His trip to America, in February and March of 1938, was a case in point. During the visit, McNutt discussed Philippine independence with Roosevelt and learned from Jacob Weiss about plans to resettle additional refugees in Manila. But the trip also revealed his desire to become president. McNutt left the Philippines in an airplane, which suggested that his business in Washington was pressing. It was not, for FDR had not "summoned" him home.[100]

The political angle to the trip became apparent when McNutt's supporters feted him at a series of dinners. In Washington, over three thousand political leaders jammed the Mayflower Hotel for what one White House secretary dubbed "the big blowout for Paul McNutt."[101] Guests feasted on caviar, smoked salmon, and pâté de foie gras as well as ice cream and three kinds of doughnuts—"the only plebeian touch."[102] They conversed with the high commissioner in the "presidential dining room" over martinis, scotch, bourbon, and whiskey.[103] The affair was the brainchild of Frank M. McHale, McNutt's political confidant, who had become a Democratic national committeeman. McHale thought it important to give McNutt's campaign some publicity, whether favorable or not.[104]

Such words were prescient, for the dinner generated nationwide publicity, much of it negative. Many reporters described the affair as amusingly amateurish and gaudy. The harshest accounts stressed the exotic grub, including a cake that bore the great seal of the United States, and the fact that few senior members of the Roosevelt administration had attended. Booth Tarkington, the Indiana novelist, snickered sarcastically at the "small-but-unselect tea [party]."[105] Seasoned party hands also mocked McNutt's "audacity" and wondered why a candidate would rear his head two years before an election and invite rivals to "hurl bricks" at him.[106] But not all accounts were negative. Some journalists were amazed that McNutt had drawn such a large crowd. Moreover, the openness of his ambition and his willingness to fight for the nomination early on defied politics-as-usual. And McNutt did make a favorable impression, discussing domestic and international politics with those assembled. As the *Washington Evening Star* headlined: "McNutt Passes Political Screen Test." He thus returned to the Philippines with a "greatly enhanced" profile.[107]

Such praise annoyed some members of the administration. Postmaster General James A. Farley, with his eyes fixed on the White House, thought that the McNutt party "created quite a stir."[108] To thwart his rival, Farley continued to warn FDR not to bring him into the cabinet. Roosevelt, though, was still toying with the idea, partly because he liked to hassle Farley; partly because he thought McNutt "a good campaigner" who might be helpful to the administration; and partly because he had hinted to McNutt in 1937 that he would find a place for him in the cabinet.[109] By 1938, however, Roosevelt seemed uneasy about McNutt. He considered the Hoosier a "hot" presidential possibility.[110] He also knew that McNutt was used to marching to his own drum. The president claimed that he had had no "advance" warning that McNutt was planning to publicly recommend reexamination of Philippine independence, though the two men had discussed the topic in private.[111] Farley wondered how FDR would react to McNutt's reception. Roosevelt privately averred he was "not at all disturbed" by it, and in public, he buried whatever concerns he may have had beneath humor.[112] At a press conference, FDR deadpanned: "I guess the Governor will be in to see me." The follow-up query, "Will you go to see the Governor," sparked "laughter."[113]

McNutt wanted to come back to America for good, but needed something to do once he returned. There was talk about him running for the U.S. Senate from Indiana in 1938. FDR hoped that he would, for the Democratic incumbent, Frederick Van Nuys, had opposed the president's bills to add justices to the Supreme Court and to reorganize the executive branch. By 1938, FDR was seeking to rid his party of lawmakers, such as Van Nuys, who had resisted his second-term agenda. Back in Indiana, McNutt's followers also disliked Van Nuys for his display of independence. The resentments of the McNutt forces and those of the White House dovetailed in 1937, when Indiana's governor, M.

Clifford Townsend, announced, after a meeting with Roosevelt, that it would be "impossible" to renominate Van Nuys.[114] That statement paved the way for Indiana Democrats to nominate a liberal, perhaps even McNutt.

McNutt never made it to the Senate for two reasons. First, he had shown little interest in the body, having passed up the opportunity to run for a Senate seat in 1932 and again in 1934. Second, Van Nuys proved a more wily and tenacious adversary than the McNutt forces had anticipated. Late in 1937 he made an overture to the machine by endorsing McNutt for president in 1940. Furthermore, Van Nuys threatened to run as an independent in 1938 if the Democrats failed to renominate him. In this setting, McHale, with McNutt back in the Philippines, decided to work for party unity. At the state convention in July 1938, McNutt's supporters secured Van Nuys's renomination and then endorsed McNutt for president in 1940, if FDR did not run. Even the Republican press was impressed with this shrewd compromise. "Good political strategy has marked the recent leadership of the Democratic party in Indiana," the *Indianapolis News* editorialized.[115] The spirit of harmony that prevailed at the Indiana convention rested, as one columnist noted, on a tethering of "the Van Nuys Thistle" to "the New Deal Rose."[116] McNutt accepted the compromise. He reasoned that a three-way senatorial contest in 1938 would risk the "loss of Indiana" to the Republicans and deliver a "greater blow" to the president's prestige than the renomination of an "opposition senator." But he also knew that FDR's advisers would not like the fact that Van Nuys had managed to remain alive politically.[117]

McNutt was right on both counts. Making peace with Van Nuys no doubt spared the machine an embarrassing defeat, for Roosevelt's so-called purge campaign backfired, badly. Then, in the fall contests, the GOP gained eighty-one seats in the House of Representatives and eight in the Senate. In Indiana, the results were a tad better for Democrats. Although the GOP had captured a majority in the state's House of Representatives for the first time since 1930, Van Nuys won reelection by five thousand votes. At the same time, the senator's triumph offered cold comfort to New Dealers. Senator Sherman Minton, a McNutt protégé but a Roosevelt loyalist, had denounced the "sordid deal" which led to Van Nuys's renomination as "surrender" to the party's conservatives.[118] The president agreed. Roosevelt fumed that, because of "what happened in Indiana," he owed McNutt "nothing" and would give him no position higher than assistant secretary of state after he departed his post in Manila.[119]

Although FDR held grudges, he was not governed by them. Booth Tarkington was probably correct when he asserted that FDR "abhors *all*" who opposed both his court reform and reorganization bills and that the McNutt machine had committed treason by renominating a senator whom Roosevelt "hates."[120] Farley crowed that the action of the Indiana convention had swung the president around to his attitude on McNutt.[121] Yet the president had not ruled out naming McNutt to an office in the administration; he only mentioned giving McNutt a lesser one after he returned to the United States—which McNutt planned to do by summer 1939. The high commissioner had considered his work in Manila done since early 1938. With his wife in better health, he was now free to travel home and to prepare for the 1940 election, among other things.

For his part, McNutt continued to cultivate FDR's favor. He went out of his way to secure presidential approval for a trip that he, Kathleen, and Louise took, early in 1939, to Saigon, Bangkok, and Singapore. He also volunteered to return to America earlier than planned, if Roosevelt wished. FDR abruptly declined the offer: "Get here June 22nd ... as scheduled."[122] McNutt thus would depart the Philippines in May, travel to Washington, D.C., file a final report, and resign his office.[123] He would have to wait for his next assignment and hope that it was an important one.

As McNutt departed Manila, Filipinos bade him a fond farewell. A crowd of ten thousand people made their way to see the high commissioner off. All the expected dignitaries were in attendance, including Quezon and his wife, members of the National Assembly and the cabinet, prominent business leaders, and General Douglas MacArthur. McNutt accepted a nineteen-gun salute, as protocol—the subject of controversy early in his tenure—demanded. Paul, Kathleen, and Louise then said good-bye to the well-wishers. The ceremonies were a stark contrast to the cool welcome that McNutt had received in 1937.[124]

McNutt had won over the Filipinos. At the departure event, there were many moist eyes and a banner that proclaimed "With Deep Gratitude and Appreciation of Your Good Work. The Filipino People Bid You Godspeed."[125] Newspaper retrospectives on his tenure were "rapturous."[126] Editors praised McNutt's knowledge of government, his patriotism, and his future as a rising political star in America. The press hailed McNutt for his diligence and the calm, judicious way in which he discussed such burning issues as Philippine democracy and independence. In large part because of him, U.S.-Philippine relations had remained harmonious. The *Manila Bulletin* called McNutt a statesman of the highest caliber.[127] McNutt thus had succeeded in the fundamental task of any good diplomat, to be well liked in the country where he or she serves.[128]

The gratitude Filipinos expressed toward McNutt will, and should, be viewed skeptically by the generations that came of age during and after the 1960s, when Filipino nationalists and American leftists challenged the benign character of U.S. imperialism. In 1939, however, criticism of that type was a long way off. The *Philippines Herald,* which was committed to independence, dismissed the Philippine-American War of 1899–1902 as a "tragic misunderstanding" and praised subsequent decades as a time, not of colonial rule, but of "reconstruction" and "association" between the two countries.[129] Months later, the *Herald* asserted that "no other subject race has ever before been so completely won over by a subjugating race."[130] The "winning over" comment reinforces a vision— shared by McNutt—of empire, American-style, as distinctively benevolent. Yet the *Herald* also mentioned the concept of "subjugation," endemic to all imperial designs.[131]

As high commissioner during the late 1930s, McNutt failed to achieve his principal aim, to force a reconsideration of Philippine independence. In his final report as high commissioner, he advised the U.S. Congress to provide "sympathetic attention" to a "possible reconsideration" of its Philippine policy if a "majority" of Filipinos wished to remain under U.S. sovereignty.[132] After returning to America, McNutt reiterated that the Philippines, for the sake of its economy and its security, should be granted dominion status.[133] Philippine papers politely rejected the proposal. The *Herald* could not bring itself to condemn McNutt outright, since he had argued his point "so feelingly and sincerely."[134] They could afford to be generous, knowing that few policymakers in Washington and Manila wished to revisit the issue of Philippine independence. But the press also appreciated McNutt's willingness to speak plainly to Filipinos as equals. That was in contrast to the American isolationists who advocated Philippine independence but did so for selfish reasons and in an abrasive manner. When Senator Bennett Clark, Democrat of Missouri, argued for a prompt U.S. withdrawal on the grounds that the Philippines was a curse on America's defenses, the press in Manila reprimanded him more sternly than it ever had McNutt.[135]

McNutt also drew kudos for being an "Apostle of Democracy" who preached his message in and out of season.[136] That was true, up to a point. The high commissioner had insisted in 1937 that democratic governance in the Philippines had to be substantive as well as symbolic. Prodding of that sort perhaps helped to make Filipinos "democracy conscious."[137] Yet McNutt also acquiesced in Quezon's scheme to reunite the two major political factions into one dominant

Nacionalista Party, led by the president, and in the passage of a sizable appropriations bill that gave Quezon additional patronage projects to dispense to clients. In so doing, McNutt continued a tradition in Philippine politics, whereby U.S. officials cooperated with the country's elite-based leadership in ways that perpetuated an emerging "cacique democracy" and inhibited the strengthening of genuine democratic institutions.[138] A viable two-party system never took hold during the McNutt years.

The gap between McNutt's words and deeds is easily explained. He was realistic enough to work with the Philippines' established leadership and political traditions, which bore a resemblance to political machines in the United States, but sufficiently idealistic to take offense at the rise of aggressive dictatorships in Europe and Asia during the 1930s. McNutt thus exhorted Filipinos to adhere to democratic ideals and to remain "a peaceful spot in this troubled world."[139] He believed that protecting democracy and maintaining peace rested on a show of strength, that is, on America holding on to the Philippines. "The more he studied the realities of Far Eastern diplomacy," an aide to McNutt explained, "the more convinced he became that our possession of the Philippines actually lessened and not increased our chances of going to war with Japan."[140] Such comments reflected McNutt's willingness to take steps to contain Japan and his belief in a collective security arrangement involving, at minimum, America and the Philippines. Indeed, the *Herald* had characterized his call for a reexamination of independence as "a direct denunciation of the policy of isolation."[141] After returning to the United States in 1939, McNutt insisted that a foreign policy of "absolute isolation" must yield to a "cooperative peace" if America wished to remain safe and "out of war."[142]

From the standpoint of American colonial policy and the upcoming U.S. presidential election, McNutt handled his duties as high commissioner skillfully. He inserted himself into America's imperial edifice and maintained it with little disruption. He was, as Quezon said, a unique colonial administrator, for he had earned the "respect and admiration" of Filipinos, many of whom disliked his stand on independence, *and* Americans, who might have deemed him too chummy with the Philippine leadership.[143] Partly as a result, this assignment boosted McNutt's career. He had survived his "political exile" and emerged as an authority on East Asian affairs.[144] Yet, McNutt had proposed no "reexamination" of the purposes for, or assumptions behind, American colonialism in the Philippines. Instead, he situated the country within the worldview that he was forming: Democratic capitalism, tempered by New Deal–like reforms, was far superior to fascism and Communism and required a stable global order, free from aggression, to thrive—as did the Philippines. By keeping its island colony and a strong military, America could put Japan on notice, protect the Philippines, and enhance its own security and commerce.

McNutt's last speech in Manila reflected his certitude—and his chauvinism. Rather than discuss what he had learned of the Philippines and its culture, McNutt described his experience there as a "grand adventure," a word he had used before leaving for Manila and one that conjured up images of white settlers and missionaries migrating to exotic locales and bestowing a Pax Americana on subject peoples. He urged Filipinos not to be "impatient about working out an indigenous economy," which was the only way that they would free themselves, permanently, from the United States. And he encouraged them to "keep faith with democratic principles," which would bind them ideologically closer to America.[145] If McNutt's vision for the Philippines placed him ahead of isolationists on the virtues of making a firm stand against aggression, he also overlooked a long-standing aspiration of many Filipinos—for independence. In that sense, McNutt departed Manila as he had arrived, as an American nationalist looking after American interests.

# 10

## PAUL V. AND FRANKLIN D.
## (1939–1940)

WHEN PAUL V. MCNUTT returned to America in June 1939, his supporters staged a colorful welcome-home rally in Indianapolis. McNutt was glad to
be back in part because Franklin D. Roosevelt had made good on his pledge
to appoint him to a ranking position in the government. Starting in July, he
would head the Federal Security Agency (FSA), a new office that was to oversee
and coordinate such New Deal programs as the Civilian Conservation Corps
(CCC), the National Youth Administration (NYA), and the Social Security
Board. The FSA derived from Roosevelt's two-year struggle to reorganize the
executive branch as the federal government assumed additional responsibilities
in the area of public welfare. Having begun his governorship with a program for
reorganization, McNutt started his career as a federal administrator at a time
when FDR was pushing a similar project.

But what McNutt really looked forward to was his campaign to succeed FDR
in the White House. Here he proved out of his depth. After years of operating
as his own man as head of the American Legion, governor of Indiana, and high
commissioner in the Philippines, McNutt gave himself over to the president
and entered an administration where the disdain for him was palpable. Meanwhile, as McNutt prepared his presidential bid, Roosevelt had by the end of 1939
decided to seek a third term. That decision demands and will receive thorough
treatment, for it rendered McNutt's own campaign moot. (McNutt's steward-

ship of the FSA will be covered in chapter 12.) The Hoosier did not know it, but his return to Indianapolis marked the beginning of the end of his political career.

The selection of McNutt to run the Federal Security Agency bewildered many observers. Most of the confusion was expressed by journalists, who read the choice either as an endorsement by the president of McNutt's ambition, as a Roosevelt-style experiment to determine whether McNutt might make a suitable running mate in 1940, or as a Machiavellian attempt to bury the Hoosier beneath a blizzard of paperwork. Within the administration, the biggest hue and cry came from staunch liberals, who suspected that McNutt was not one of them, and Roosevelt confidants, who distrusted the Hoosier's thirst for higher office. Secretary of the Interior Harold L. Ickes reacted to the appointment by privately denouncing McNutt as "intensely ambitious and hard"; as the architect of a "ruthless political machine in Indiana"; as someone "with no social point of view"; as a conservative who enlisted troops "to suppress a strike at the drop of a hat"; and as a "fascist at heart."[1] Following the announcement of McNutt's appointment, Frank Murphy, now the U.S. attorney general, visited with Ickes, and the two men "bemoaned at length" the choice. It meant, they fretted, that Roosevelt now was backing McNutt for president, and the result would be "difficult, if not evil, days" for the "liberal cause."[2]

Such comments underscore the distrust toward McNutt within FDR's official family. In part, this attitude stemmed from the fact that McNutt had established a base independent of the president and often placed his ambitions ahead of Roosevelt's. Postmaster General James A. Farley, who headed the Democratic National Committee, thought him "untrustworthy," and Secretary of Labor Frances Perkins agreed.[3] Along with Ickes and Murphy, Perkins believed that McNutt had given Indiana "illiberal" government, a reference to his handling of the Terre Haute strike and his founding of the Two Percent Club. But her disdain was also personal. Perkins remembered McNutt as "terribly vain," "extraordinarily self-satisfied," and insufferably ambitious.[4]

Those closest to Roosevelt felt an intense loyalty toward their boss, a trait which the president encouraged; FDR's lieutenants thus could not imagine anyone, least of all an outsider from Indiana, joining their circle and then occupying the presidency. Such loyalty led to errors of judgment. Talk about McNutt being a fascist was "ludicrous," as the historian Bernard Donahoe has observed.[5] And he was no conservative either. Even Perkins, who vented about

McNutt's illiberality, conceded that he had organized a "creditable" program of relief in Indiana.[6] Upon accepting the FSA position, McNutt privately remarked that he was "heartily in sympathy with" the Social Security program, which he had set up in Indiana.[7] Moreover, Harry Hopkins, the president's relief administrator, had worked with Wayne Coy, Governor McNutt's point man on relief, and had found McNutt to be not at all conservative. Indeed, Hopkins may have influenced McNutt's appointment to the FSA, for he and Coy had discussed the matter before McNutt had returned from Manila.[8]

Unlike the administration's liberals, FDR did not think McNutt's labor record should be held against him. Speaking as a former governor, Roosevelt commented that a decision to use troops to settle a strike was a difficult matter to judge and he would not judge McNutt. The president, unlike many of those around him, remained a political realist. Hopkins and Perkins had been social workers; Ickes started out as a Chicago-area reformer; and Secretary of Agriculture Henry A. Wallace had a background on farm issues. Although these advisers had worked with politicians in the past, none of them had run for office before 1940, and they were known more for competence and integrity than for political acumen. As a result, they were ill equipped "to understand and sympathize with the needs and desires of professional politicians."[9]

Roosevelt understood better than his aides that his administration had to marshal all available talent for the battles ahead. The president's second term had been dominated by a succession of crises, including the sit-down strikes, which had cost Murphy his governorship; the recession of 1937 to 1938; and the rapid breakdown of the international order. At the same time, Roosevelt pushed projects—Supreme Court reform, executive branch reorganization, and a "purge" of party conservatives in 1938—that critics regarded as a hunger for greater power. The president's lack of success in pressing this agenda signaled that the New Deal was "stalling out," leaving the nation "wary of the future."[10] "Business isn't getting any better," lamented Mary E. Switzer, a veteran bureaucrat who would join McNutt at the FSA, "and the unemployed aren't getting any less numerous and we don't seem to have figured out any very long range plan to ensure the safety of our democracy."[11] This period of "failure" and "preoccupation with the coming of war" left a mark on Roosevelt.[12] "The President looked tired," wrote Courtney Letts de Espil, the American-born wife of the Argentine ambassador, in January 1939, "with deep circles under his blinking eyes."[13] Months later, Hopkins, perhaps FDR's closest and most liberal adviser, found his boss "bored," "tired," and "cranky."[14] To make matters worse, Vice President John Nance Garner, a conservative with White House ambitions, was showing signs of open rebellion.[15]

FDR tried to regroup by circling the wagons, that is, by bringing reliable, practical liberals into his cabinet. Over the first half of 1939, he appointed Hopkins to be secretary of commerce and Murphy to be attorney general. Such moves challenged conservatives on Capitol Hill and hinted that Roosevelt had regained the "fighting spirit" of his first term.[16] The president asserted that situating McNutt at the FSA would temper the New Deal, leaving its programs slimmer and better able to withstand right-wing assaults. By 1939 Roosevelt regarded McNutt as a fine administrator and budget balancer, qualities that he now stressed. Although FDR had failed to deliver on his 1932 campaign promise to balance the federal budget, the goal of fiscal restraint remained. The president told Secretary of the Treasury Henry T. Morgenthau Jr.: "I am sick and tired of having a lot of long-haired people around here who want a billion dollars for schools, a billion dollars for Public Health." McNutt, he said, would "talk turkey" to Aubrey Williams, head of the National Youth Administration, and say "that just because a boy wants to go to college is no reason [the NYA] should finance it." But Morgenthau remained unconvinced by FDR's explanation, as was Harold Ickes.[17] Roosevelt reiterated to Ickes that "McNutt made a good Governor of Indiana and he is a good administrator. I needed a man who is practical and efficient." Yet Ickes thought the president remained instinctively "uneasy" over the McNutt appointment.[18]

Such skepticism was justified, for Roosevelt had cause not to appoint McNutt to another post. After the Hoosier had declined to contest the U.S. Senate seat held by Frederick Van Nuys, an anti-administration Democrat, FDR resolved that he owed McNutt nothing. The president and McNutt never had formed a close relationship partly because they were too much alike. Both men were handsome, articulate, politically adept, and accustomed to dominating the political stage. Frank C. Walker, who served FDR in many capacities, noticed his boss's aversion to any person who forced him "to share the spotlight."[19] The fact that McNutt projected youthful vigor irritated FDR as well. The journalist Walter Trohan once saw McNutt stride toward the president, who looked at him as if to say "Why can that boob walk while I can't?"[20] And there was no personal chemistry to assuage hurt feelings. According to Louise McNutt, Paul's daughter, Roosevelt "responded to human warmth" and "did not understand those without it." "Daddy," she conceded, "grows cold & austere & pompous when he is ill at ease." The result was a "wall" separating the two men.[21]

In the short run, the FSA nomination was for Roosevelt a compromise and for McNutt an opportunity. "If I don't give [McNutt] something," FDR told Perkins, "he'll be sore and he'll be against us. I would rather have him in my corner than not."[22] In order to get the Hoosier on board, the president had to engage in some persuasion, for McNutt had been offered the presidency of the Indiana-based Studebaker Corporation. Roosevelt counseled McNutt against taking such a job, for it would mark him as too oriented toward business. Instead, McNutt should join his team. FDR stressed that he and McNutt were moderates devoted to maintaining "balance" in government by preventing "radicals" from pushing their party too far to the left. It was an easy sell. The FSA oversaw public health, the Bureau of Education, the CCC, the NYA, and Social Security—programs, McNutt observed, that were "all popular" and would require him "to go out into the field."[23] That meant lots of travel and speechmaking—his forte. As Roosevelt explained, McNutt was about to become the head of the agency that gave Americans "their old age checks, their unemployment checks, [and] money to build a hospital with." All that, FDR emphasized, was going to give him "a lot of very good publicity."[24]

In the long run, though, the FSA nomination showed Roosevelt to be a master chess player, for he would use McNutt to check his other subordinates. Beneath his warm exterior, FDR was cold, calculating, and willing to use people to advance his own ends. Roosevelt assembled a stable of talented advisers of diverse viewpoints and played them against one another, in part, to keep his policies running on multiple tracks. The president also enjoyed springing plans on unsuspecting subordinates and savoring their reaction. Objections by administration officials would not have stopped Roosevelt from naming McNutt to the Federal Security Agency, since one of his "rules of life" was to "be flexible in all dealings with human beings."[25] In 1939 presidential favor shined on McNutt. If he made good at the FSA, Roosevelt told Ickes, all would be well. If not, FDR added, "It will be all right too." Ickes knew what that meant: "McNutt is on the spot."[26]

Roosevelt's cultivation of McNutt represented a blow to Jim Farley. That was because McNutt and Farley were adversaries and because Roosevelt and Farley had been drifting apart.[27] Although Roosevelt had relied on Farley to manage his successful campaigns for governor of New York in 1930 and for president in 1932 and 1936, he regarded him as little more than a party functionary. The two men were often uneasy with one another. Roosevelt "enjoyed Jim's discomfiture," Frank Walker recalled.[28] And their approaches to politics differed. Farley believed in "party regularity, loyalty to one's colleagues, absolute honesty, and the understanding that party work would be rewarded."[29] FDR's more dexterous approach stressed the art of maneuvering, the value of deceptiveness, and the need to look outside the Democratic Party to assemble an electoral coalition. Roosevelt named Republicans like Ickes and Wallace to his cabinet, tried to purge conservative Democrats in 1938 (an effort Farley opposed), and cultivated younger leaders and proven vote-getters such as McNutt, whom the postmaster general deemed a self-seeking "S.O.B."[30]

Both the antagonism between Roosevelt and Farley and the rapprochement between Roosevelt and McNutt were linked to another issue: FDR's plans for 1940. Farley wanted to succeed Roosevelt, but the president thought the election of his postmaster general, a Catholic who had never held a major elected office, impossible. Farley, in contrast, insisted that he was suited for the White House and influential with enough state-level organizations to name the party's presidential nominee if FDR declined to run in 1940. Such arrogance could not have improved Farley's relationship with Roosevelt, nor could the postmaster general's importuning of the president to disavow publicly any interest in a third term. Meanwhile, with the once-prodigal McNutt, Roosevelt assumed the role of mentor. In July 1939 FDR urged McNutt to build bridges to labor if he hoped to secure the Democratic nomination. McNutt, after listening to such advice, became convinced that the president would not run again but would not say so "for a long time."[31] Two weeks later, Farley visited the president and departed with the same impression.[32]

What was happening might be called "mutual assured deception." McNutt and Farley were so eager for the presidency that they accepted at face value FDR's assurances that he was ready to retire. It was convenient for them to do so, since neither man was apt to wrest the party's nomination from the president. Nevertheless, Roosevelt's role in shaping their illusions was large. As we will see, by the middle of 1939 FDR was thinking seriously about a third term—and keeping such thoughts to himself.

For McNutt and Roosevelt, much of 1939 was dominated by presidential politics. McNutt's campaign, tended by his lieutenants, had been organizing for some time; it was open, obvious, and amateurish, at least in comparison to what FDR was doing. Hints that the president was receptive to a third term began to surface midway through his second term. But Roosevelt said nothing of his plans. Instead, he encouraged would-be aspirants, watched them perform, waited for events to lend a hand, and prepared for a possible run. If McNutt's campaign for the White House was loud, overtly ambitious, and ultimately unsuccessful, Roosevelt's proved exactly the opposite.

The noise about McNutt running for president had begun in earnest as his term as governor came to a close. In December 1936, James E. Perry, an Indianapolis real estate man, founded the first "Paul V. McNutt for President in 1940 Club" and started selling memberships at a dollar per year.[33] McNutt's friends at the statehouse soon took control of the club, and under Frank McHale's tutelage, branches of it sprang up across Indiana. The McNutt machine played a role in the club's growth; Hugh A. Barnhart, state excise administrator, peddled memberships in it—an example of the mixing of alcohol and politics for which the McNutt administration had become notorious. By the time McNutt returned from the Philippines, every county in Indiana had a McNutt for President in 1940 Club.[34]

Aside from McNutt, the chief figure in the campaign was its chair, Frank McHale. While McNutt was in Manila, McHale tended the machine, handled factional differences within the Hoosier Democratic Party, and became known as "McNutt's Jim Farley" for his "painstaking plan" to elect McNutt president.[35] McHale operated on two assumptions, that FDR would not be a candidate again and that there would be "at least fifteen favorite sons in the field."[36] To make sure that McNutt prevailed, McHale stressed three imperatives. The first was the need to introduce McNutt to Democrats nationwide. To that end, McHale masterminded that massive dinner for his man in Washington in 1938 and the welcome-home event in Indianapolis a year later. Second, McHale believed that campaigns had a natural rhythm and, with that in mind, he pushed his candidate out front and then drew him back. McHale announced McNutt's candidacy after the elections in 1938; the McNutt for President headquarters opened in 1939; and letters to prominent Democrats went out a few months later. But McHale also withheld thousands of such letters in order to keep the campaign from advancing "too fast."[37] Last and most important, McHale pursued a "second choice strategy" by maintaining friendly relations with rival candidates on the assumption that they eventually would back McNutt.[38]

The McNutt campaign had a cautious tone. McNutt did not possess the national reputation of Roosevelt's three most-often-discussed successors: Secretary of State Cordell Hull, Vice President John Nance Garner, and Postmaster General James Farley. In a survey of newspaper editors conducted in June 1939, McNutt failed to be mentioned alongside Garner, Hull, and Farley on a list of possible Democratic nominees. Since none of the three top contenders was identified with the party's liberals, McNutt took pains not to offend New Dealers. It was shrewd strategy, because there was no obvious liberal candidate. Hopkins was divorced, abrasive, anathema to business, and ill with cancer. Murphy had lost his most recent election, as had Governor George Earle of Pennsylvania. Solicitor General Robert Jackson had never held elected office. And both Ickes and Wallace lacked ties to rank-and-file Democrats.[39]

To enter this vacuum, the McNutt campaign employed publicity and positioning. It published brochures depicting McNutt as friendly toward labor—an effort to remedy a clear deficiency—and as a moderately liberal governor who had backed unemployment relief and Social Security while simultaneously reducing taxes, balancing the budget, and streamlining the state government. In 1938 McHale dubbed McNutt "a middle-of-the-road progressive Jeffersonian Democrat" who will "preserve the great advance in social progress" made under FDR.[40] Such an elastic description could be stretched to placate both conservatives and liberals. "His record appeals to every element in the Party," McHale assured Senator Theodore Francis Green of Rhode Island, a member of the Democratic National Committee.[41]

The campaign, however, needed excitement, so its managers decided to accentuate McNutt's personal qualities. One pamphlet proclaimed him "a born leader" in the fields of law, higher education, veterans' issues, military affairs, foreign policy, and state governance. After assuming the governorship, this brochure attested, McNutt had "met the emergency" and restored "confidence and prosperity" to Indiana. On its cover, as on the others, was McNutt's striking visage, with his silver-gray locks, dark eyebrows, square jaw, and a mere trace of a smile—a confident statesman who both revered tradition and was willing to "adjust policies to change."[42] As one aide put it, McNutt was to be sold as a liberal "heart throb," a "practical man," and a "safe man."[43]

Such a strategy required a calculating candidate, and McNutt fit the bill. His response to the FSA appointment proved revealing. While McNutt was discussing his new job with Coy and the columnist Raymond Clapper, the telephone rang. Coy took the call and returned with the news that Secretary of the Navy Claude Swanson had died. According to Clapper, McNutt "thought a minute and [his] first remark was 'If that had happened yesterday [my] conversation with the President might have taken a different course.'" At that point, the three men debated whether heading FSA or Navy would have been better for McNutt's presidential prospects. McNutt expressed no regret over Swanson's passing. As Clapper observed, the conversation "instantly translated" into a discussion of McNutt's "own future."[44]

McNutt was a consummate politician. To be fair, his support for higher education, veterans' benefits, and welfare programs, as well as a realistic foreign and defense policy, had been consistent. Yet he knew how to adjust his positions in response to events, at least in form, and to massage constituency groups. Several examples stand out. First, while McNutt's stand against Philippine independence reflected his vision of America's position in Asia, he also expressed relief that he had not returned home earlier, when he would have been expected to follow up and fight for retention of the Philippines. Doing so, McNutt noted, would have angered "powerful groups," including farmers who wanted to rid the United States of the Philippines and its duty-free agricultural goods.[45] Similarly, a dash of political calculus informed McNutt's assistance to Jewish refugees. Although he acted from a variety of motivations, his campaign used the refugee issue to court Jewish voters. Jewish periodicals ran pictures of McNutt with Jacob Weiss, who had pressed for Jewish immigration into Manila, and as a result, McNutt enjoyed "quite a run in the Jewish press."[46] Like many New Dealers, he recognized the strength of group identity in politics. His response to a brochure on the "Attitude of Paul V. McNutt toward the Negro Race" showed that he understood the power of white southerners within his party and the importance of black voters in northern cities. "Such a pamphlet," McNutt noted, "would be very useful after the nomination, but it might be a dangerous document to have in circulation before the Convention."[47] Lastly, McNutt struck a moderate note when he pledged to spur investment by small corporations, a position with which no conservative would quarrel, while revising the tax code so as to increase the purchasing power of the masses, an aim embraced by the most liberal of New Dealers.[48]

For all its calculations, the McNutt campaign was not a well-oiled machine. Money was a sore point, for the campaign had promised to use no funds from the Two Percent Club, and contributions were slow to arrive from the East, where Oscar Ewing, McNutt's old college friend, was handling matters. There was a project to get state employees in Indiana to donate a percentage of their annual income to McNutt for President Clubs—a tactic that, if known, would have sparked discussion of a targeted "One Percent Club."[49] Pressed for cash, McHale based the campaign on correspondence, contacts, and publicity, as Farley had done for FDR in 1932, rather than on building McNutt organizations in each state, as Ewing urged. Over time, the campaign achieved a number of things. The candidate made inroads in the West, which McHale visited in August 1939, and in the South, where the governor of Mississippi came out in favor of McNutt and the governor of Alabama seemed friendly toward his candidacy. And Maurice Judd, the campaign's publicity director, reported that news coverage of McNutt had been "favorable" over the first half of 1939.[50] Nevertheless, problems persisted. Ewing thought McHale was inclined "to do everything himself," and that he was lax in building the McNutt organizations and unduly impressed by reports of his own role as would-be kingmaker.[51] McHale, in turn, deemed Ewing a novice, ignorant even of the "political situation" in New York, the state where he lived.[52]

The chief disagreement inside the campaign was over McNutt's relationship to FDR. McHale pressed McNutt to stake out an independent position, and the campaign's literature emphasized McNutt's moderation, particularly his skill at balancing Indiana's budget—an apparent slap at a president who had failed to keep federal spending in line with revenue.[53] Ewing, in contrast, advised McNutt to position himself as far to the left as necessary in order to satisfy Roosevelt and gain his support. Coy, whose ties to Hopkins and to the administration had been growing, also thought that McNutt had to "go along with the President."[54] Senator Sherman Minton of Indiana, who, like Coy, had developed loyalties to both the McNutt forces and the White House, went further. Minton announced that McNutt would not seek the presidency if Roosevelt sought a third term. His statement upset members of McNutt's staff, especially McHale. But McNutt decided that Minton's comments had to be seconded lest McNutt appear to be challenging FDR. Almost by happenstance, then, the Hoosier's presidential campaign became a qualified effort.[55]

In truth, there was little in McNutt's background to suggest that he would confront the president directly. In the past, he had been a dutiful son, mindful of elders, as well as a devoted soldier, obedient to superiors. Although McNutt had challenged older members of his party in Indiana when he ran for governor, he did so only up to a point. He showed a willingness to mend fences with more conservative Democrats and to work for change within the established political order. He had tons of ambition but scarcely an ounce of rebellion. Even McNutt's defiance of Roosevelt at the 1932 convention did not qualify as insubordination, for FDR was at this point only a presidential candidate, not his commander in chief. Having fought Roosevelt and lost, he would not do so again. Coy reinforced such thoughts, for he was convinced "that the President is strong enough to control the next convention for himself or some person that he wants."[56] With respect to Roosevelt and the 1940 campaign, McNutt assured one supporter: "I would not be a candidate in opposition to him. I am loyal to the man who is my chief."[57]

Several observers thought that McNutt was making a mistake. One man asked: "Who would want to tie up with the McNutt candidacy with the knowledge that he might withdraw?"[58] Deferring to Roosevelt undermined one of McNutt's assets, his reputation for leadership. Booth Tarkington, cynical about human nature in general and FDR in particular, grasped what was going on. Tarkington lampooned McNutt's contingent campaign as one of "I'm for the Boss if he wants it; *and* if he'll hand it to me—or just step aside—I'll run the job zackly according to his orders." "It may be foxy," Tarkington asserted, "but it doesn't tingle."[59] The McNutt presidential campaign thus proved long on maneuvering, short on excitement, and heavily dependent on Roosevelt's plans for 1940.

What were FDR's intentions as the next election neared? McNutt's staff was as perplexed as most Americans. Coy was getting insights from Hopkins, who thought that the president "did not want to run for a third term, provided he could find someone who would carry out his program." Yet Coy also heard that FDR's "inner circle"—Ickes, Wallace, Perkins, and others—were urging the president to become a candidate.[60] From his distant perch, Tarkington came close to discerning at least one of Roosevelt's motivations: "He's *bound* to want it again—*he* can't *help* it—his love of power and spot light is now a *seated passion* and it controls him."[61]

For a time, Roosevelt was of two minds on whether to continue in office. On the one hand, FDR wanted to retire to his family's estate at Hyde Park, where he was building a presidential library and a secluded hilltop cottage. There, he could be around his prints, papers, and collections, as well as his trees, released from the pressures of office and free to write his memoirs. "All that is in me," he pronounced, "goes back to the Hudson."[62] On the other hand, one wonders how much he wanted to go back home to his stamps, his adult children with their marital difficulties, and his own relatively loveless marriage. The Roosevelts, moreover, made for restless retirees, as Theodore Roosevelt had shown and Eleanor Roosevelt would prove. With war looming, FDR thought himself the only man capable of leading America through the crisis. He also saw an opportunity to achieve the sort of "presidential greatness" that could only come by rising to a "historic challenge."[63] At a dinner early in 1939, he remarked that Abraham Lincoln had entered politics in part to influence the flow of events during a critical time. "Roosevelt was definitely interested in his subject," observed Courtney Letts de Espil, the wife of Argentina's ambassador to the United States. FDR's own date with destiny appeared to be beckoning; when the conversation turned to the troubles in Europe, Roosevelt reported that his ambassador to Great Britain, Joseph Kennedy, "thinks the chances are 2-to-1 in favor of war by spring."[64]

The president also knew that he was leaving a job unfinished at home. The legacy of the New Deal had not been ratified by all Democrats. Conservatives within the party remained powerful, a consequence of the compromised nature of FDR's first nomination, when he accepted Garner as his running mate. And the course and outcome of the 1938 elections, especially the failed purge, Republican gains, and the defeat of a number of New Dealers, underscored the tenuous hold that liberalism had on the country and the ongoing right-left rift within the Democratic Party. The forces of localism, that is, entrenched leaders at the state level and below, prevented Roosevelt from reshaping the Democratic Party. According to the political scientist James MacGregor Burns, FDR gave his party "glorious victories" and pointed it "in new ideological directions." But he failed to make it a consistent "source of liberal thought and action."[65] And, as the historian Susan Dunn has written, he "knew the New Deal had been only half dealt."[66] Seeing few rising liberal leaders on the horizon, the president began to consider seeking a third term in order to keep the Democratic ship sailing on a New Deal tack. Roosevelt's ego reinforced such thoughts. "I don't think," Ickes reckoned, "that he would be happy ... watching another man playing ducks and drakes with his New Deal."[67]

FDR was not unique among presidents in wanting to stay in power. "I have been in the White House with three presidents," Rear Admiral Cary T. Grayson, Woodrow Wilson's physician, once observed, "and I have yet to see one who wanted to leave."[68] Ulysses S. Grant was the first to test the third-term taboo, when he angled for the Republican nomination in 1880. The two-term tradition came under challenge in the twentieth century, when presidential power grew in a sustained fashion. Four years after leaving the White House, in 1912, Theodore Roosevelt ran on the Progressive Party's ticket. The winner of that election, Wilson, served two terms and then maneuvered for a third nomination, which he might have won had he not suffered a stroke in 1919.[69] Thereafter, Calvin Coolidge, who completed Warren Harding's term and then one of his own, hinted that he was amenable to running again. In 1927 Coolidge declared: "I do not choose to run for President in nineteen twenty-eight." This message puzzled the press and abetted Herbert Hoover's successful campaign for the Republican nomination.[70] But, according to a friend of Coolidge's, the president thought the "choose statement" was the best way to encourage a draft, and he became unhappy when it was interpreted otherwise.[71] Interestingly, whenever the issue of a third term came up, FDR remained more silent than Silent Cal.

There are several things to keep in mind about Roosevelt's pursuit of a third term. First, his interest in running developed gradually, in response to political developments at home. Events overseas reinforced his resolve to run again.[72] Moreover, FDR knew that securing a third consecutive term in the White House was unprecedented and would be resisted. To defy a tradition held sacrosanct, FDR had to tread lightly. He dodged press queries about his intentions with humor and grace, so much so that cartoonists drew the president as the Sphinx. Such silence allowed other presidential aspirants to cling to the belief that FDR would not become a candidate. Farley and McNutt both reasoned that Roosevelt was saying nothing about 1940, not because he would run, but because he would not—and a withdrawal would diminish his political clout.[73] The evidence on when the president decided to seek a third term has been described as "incomplete and unclear"—a fact aided by Roosevelt's self-discipline and reticence.[74] The president was so secretive about the 1940 election that his grandson, Curtis Roosevelt, questioned whether he even admitted to himself that he was seeking a third term. According to Ickes, Roosevelt "subconsciously" disassociated himself from the issue.[75]

Yet it is possible to decipher Roosevelt's decision to seek a third term. He showed scant interest in the issue during 1937, when the Supreme Court fight and the onset of the recession might have strengthened his desire to retire. FDR gave little thought to a successor, save to remark that Ickes lacked the temperament and a proper Democratic pedigree to be nominated by the party, and that Wallace, whom he liked, was too much an "idealist" to be an effective president.[76] Hull was interested in the presidency, but his wife, Frances, was certain that "the President won't want him." "He is going to choose some one much more radical," explained Courtney Letts de Espil, an astute observer of the Washington scene. "Hull is too conservative."[77] By 1938, Roosevelt appeared to be grooming two possible heirs, both of them liberals: Robert Jackson and Harry Hopkins. That year he was urging Jackson to run for governor of New York, and he was giving encouragement to Hopkins, who was telling friends that the president had "given him the green light" to begin his campaign.[78]

But Roosevelt took as much as he gave. When Eleanor Roosevelt pressed her husband to do more to prepare a successor, "Franklin always smiled and said he thought people had to prepare themselves, that all he could do was give them opportunities and see how they worked out."[79] Indeed, when Hopkins asked Thomas Corcoran, one of FDR's closest legislative assistants, for a contribution to his "campaign fund," Corcoran replied that he would help "only if the President says so." FDR said nothing.[80] Jackson's gubernatorial campaign never commenced, and Roosevelt's suggestion of it may have been an attempt to thwart Farley, who headed the New York State Democratic Party, or to secure a liberal delegation from the Empire State at the national convention. Roosevelt, in fact, later remarked that Jackson, although capable, lacked the personal magnetism that "is essential in elective public life."[81] Generally speaking, Jackson and Hopkins proved too dependent on FDR's patronage to make plausible presidents. Eleanor Roosevelt believed that her husband "dominated the people around him" and "so long as he was in the picture, it was very hard for anyone to rise to a position of prominence."[82]

McNutt was no Roosevelt retainer, and for that reason FDR decided that he required no extra boost. After selecting McNutt to head the FSA, the president offered no "apostolic laying on of hands."[83] To the contrary, he told reporters that the Hoosier was just one of "ten or twelve or fifteen" men who aspired to be the Democratic nominee in 1940.[84] By promoting, then abandoning, men such as McNutt, Roosevelt could enlarge "the field so that there would be a host of rivals wrestling for delegate votes" and keep his own options open.[85] Kathleen McNutt said it best when she observed that Roosevelt kept telling Paul "I love you, I love you" without ever asking "Will you marry me?"[86] In private, she used a more risqué analogy: "Franklin takes Paul upstairs but nothing ever happens."[87]

By the fall of 1938, FDR had begun to contemplate the possibility of another term. In September, Europe narrowly averted war when the leaders of Great Britain and France agreed to Hitler's annexation of the German-speaking areas of Czechoslovakia. After the crisis had passed, Corcoran remembered that the debate over foreign policy, between those who favored isolation and those who did not, intensified, and Roosevelt "probably began to think that in order to hold the country together" he would have to run in 1940.[88] With respect to domestic politics, FDR was concerned about Democratic losses in the midterm elections, but in October 1938, he and Farley did discuss the 1940 election. FDR predicted the candidacies of several "favorite sons," a deadlocked convention, and the nomination of a "middle of the roader"—a label he later hung on McNutt.[89]

Was Roosevelt willing to enter this fray? Perhaps, if doing so would keep the conservatives at bay. The right wing of the Democratic Party was not without power or purpose. The conservatives, as Susan Dunn explained, "believed that they were merely leasing out their party on a short-term basis to Roosevelt."[90] But FDR opposed any return to party normalcy. "The President foresees difficulties in dealing with the political situation," Attorney General Homer S. Cummings noted late in 1938, "and feels that a hard struggle is ahead of us to keep the Democratic Party a great Liberal, Progressive Party."[91] One wonders who other than Roosevelt had the guile and stature to prevail against the conservatives. The president was coming to an answer. At a dinner in October 1938, he "held forth" on the history of presidents who could have sought a third term. After hearing this discussion, FDR's niece became convinced "that he has it very much in his mind to run again."[92]

During the early months of 1939, the White House tested the idea of a third term. In January, Robert Jackson drafted a newspaper column that discussed the possibility of Roosevelt's running again. But Steve Early, the president's press secretary, refused to clear the article for publication. Then, just a month later, Jackson received permission to speak in favor of a third term. Jackson noticed that, as 1939 wore on, Roosevelt "became inured to the idea of a third term." He attributed the president's interest in breaking the two-term tradition to a desire to best his enemies. Simply stated, Roosevelt would do what his critics were predicting he would do: run in 1940—and then win the election.[93]

The spring of 1939 brought fresh hints that Roosevelt was considering a third term. Two of his closest advisers—Corcoran and Benjamin Cohen, another legislative draftsman—pushed the idea that he must run again. Around the same time, Edwin M. "Pa" Watson, the president's appointments secretary, began receiving analyses of incoming mail on the issue of a third term and forwarding these reports to FDR. Although White House aides often write memoranda in ways that will shape presidential decisions, they also are courtiers who undertake projects, or bring information, that they think the president will like. Eleanor Roosevelt, for her part, suspected that something was up regarding the election. Although the first lady had no idea what her husband was planning to do, she noticed that he was bored with his job and yet unable to recognize that the New Deal was larger than any individual.[94]

In June 1939, Ruby Black, one of Eleanor Roosevelt's closest friends in the press, suggested that FDR would run again. Black observed that the president's scouts were scavenging the country for convention delegates "instructed to support New Deal policies, and uninstructed as to the candidate." As Black explained, FDR wanted a successor who would continue the New Deal, "get the nomination," and "win the election." But none of the most commonly mentioned contenders—Hull, Garner, and Farley—met these three qualifications. And McNutt did not enjoy "White House favor because of a deep-seated distrust of his alleged 'liberalism'" as well as his "high-handed" leadership in Indiana. In the meantime, third-term advocates on Capitol Hill began insisting that neither George Washington nor Thomas Jefferson had been adamant about the two-term tradition. "It looks now," Black surmised, "as if [President Roosevelt] feels that the New Deal can only be saved by his election."[95] A man from Maryland went further, joking that the New Deal without Roosevelt was like a performance of *Hamlet* "sans le Dane."[96]

Whatever one thinks of Black's forecast—much of which came to pass—she had identified an essential problem: by the middle of 1939, no New Dealer had emerged as a viable alternative to FDR. Robert W. Woolley, an old Democratic Party publicist, and Daniel C. Roper, a former secretary of commerce, thought they had found a successor to FDR in Senator Alben W. Barkley of Kentucky. Barkley was an excellent speaker and a solid liberal. But the president was "rather hesitant" to get behind the senator, whom, at age sixty-two, he thought too old.[97] (Neither Roper nor Woolley mentioned McNutt as a possible nominee.) As a result, the political needle was pointing in Roosevelt's direction. Nebraska senator George W. Norris, a progressive Republican turned Independent, wanted to support a candidate who would continue to attack "privilege and organized monopoly," and he saw only one "possibility"—"Roosevelt himself."[98] "Everyone is becoming more and more firmly convinced," Ickes noted, "that it is either Roosevelt or reaction in 1940."[99] But FDR kept mum. After Ickes wrote Anna Roosevelt Boettiger, the president's daughter, about the prospect of a third term, he forwarded their correspondence to Roosevelt. Determined not to take the bait, FDR replied: "Many thanks for letting me see Anna's letter with enclosure. I am returning them herewith for your files."[100]

In truth, by July 1939, Roosevelt seemed serious about running. During a visit at Hyde Park, Farley had urged the president to declare his intentions publicly. "Of course, I will not run for a third term," Roosevelt vowed, "but the best way to handle that situation is to wait until after the North Dakota primary comes along—and when it is necessary for me to file—not to file, thereby indicating that I am not a candidate." By delaying any announcement, FDR was able to keep Farley on a string and his own options open.[101] It worked. A year later, as the president prepared to accept renomination, he related to Homer Cummings the gist of his conversation with Farley. Roosevelt explained that he had refused to issue any statement of withdrawal until "the time came for the selection of delegates" in the primaries, when he would be asked to be a candidate. But no statement was ever released. "It so happened," FDR continued, "[I] was never asked, and, therefore, did not speak."[102]

For McNutt, FDR's interest in another term was significant for three reasons. First, it reinforced the idea that the president had appointed McNutt to head the FSA in part to thwart, not to promote, his ambitions. Second, the manner in which the president pursued his third term highlighted what McNutt was up against: a truly great, instinctive politician. Knowing that once he declared for another term he would become just another candidate, Roosevelt remained aloof and let subordinates campaign for him. Third, FDR's low-key campaign meant that McNutt's bid for the White House remained a qualified one—contingent on Roosevelt not running. In the interim, the president's silence was proving, as Courtney Letts de Espil noted in her diary, "decidedly upsetting for the would-be candidates such as Hull, Farley, Garner, [Montana senator Burton] Wheeler, McNutt and darker horses."[103]

During the last half of 1939, McNutt's presidential hopes started to slip. His campaign was beset by a succession of problems: the outbreak of war in Europe, clamor from third-term advocates, attacks by New Dealers, an increasingly negative press, and a probe of the Indiana machine conducted by the Treasury Department. Partly as a result, McNutt limped into 1940 while Roosevelt was inching toward renomination.

As autumn approached, it was not all gloom for the McNutt campaign. McHale's political trip west had yielded results: Idaho looked "very good"; Nevada was "in great shape"; and Utah "very friendly."[104] There was good news from California, where Jacob Weiss was rallying his friends in the film industry to contribute to McNutt's campaign. And in New England, McHale and Ewing found several politicians "very friendly" toward McNutt, including Senator Green of Rhode Island.[105] McNutt, at Green's invitation, had delivered a speech in Providence which greatly impressed local Democrats. Even more encouraging was a *Newsweek* poll of the "fifty leading Washington correspondents" that placed McNutt behind only Roosevelt as the likely Democratic nominee.[106] But the campaign's best asset was its candidate, who was eager to stump the country. McNutt planned an extensive speaking schedule during the fall. On August 30, 1939, he called the "progress" of his campaign "most heartening."[107]

Things began to change two days later, when Hitler unleashed his war machine. After signing a non-aggression pact with the Soviet Union, Germany was poised to strike Poland, which it did on September 1, 1939. In response, Great Britain and France declared war. Although FDR announced that the United States would not enter the conflict, he asked Congress to revise the neutrality act to allow the British and French to purchase American war matériel. Under a "methods-short-of-war strategy," the U.S. administration would provide supplies, not troops, to assist the democracies. After two months of wrangling and fierce attacks by isolationists, Roosevelt received most of what he had requested. Great Britain and France were permitted to buy weapons on a "cash-and-carry" basis.[108] At one level, the outbreak of war and debate over neutrality relegated the 1940 campaign to the back pages of the newspapers. "Politics is being entirely forgotten," Farley admitted.[109] "It is amazing," remarked Mary Switzer, one of McNutt's subordinates at the FSA, "how we settle down now to the routine of the war."[110] At another level, however, Americans rallied behind the president. "Before this war," Courtney Letts de Espil noted, "the bets & polls gave the Repubs. a 2 to 1 chance for [winning the 1940] election. Now, it is the other way around."[111]

The war placed McNutt in a bind. He could not deliver campaign speeches during a national emergency, and the federal agency he led had little to do with foreign or military policy. Nevertheless, Roosevelt asked McNutt to stay in Washington, and he complied, canceling several speaking engagements.[112] The president also invited him to attend cabinet sessions, though McNutt made few remarks at his first meeting.[113] He was unable to find his voice on the war until November when, on a tour of Florida, he emphasized the value of preparedness, which he had long advocated.[114] McNutt also took aim at subversives, that is, people who sought to destroy America from within. In these troubled times, he warned, "Apostles of Communism and Fascism peddle their deceptive theories."[115] Politically, this seemed to be an astute ploy for a House panel, headed by Democrat Martin Dies of Texas, had been investigating the influence of subversives—particularly "Reds"—in the U.S. government since 1938.[116] It also reflected McNutt's anti-Communist and anti-pacifist outlook, which dated to his early years in the American Legion. But his speeches failed to make national news; when a Connecticut politician was asked about McNutt's presidential prospects, the man purportedly replied: "Who is McNutt"?[117]

The war also hurt McNutt's presidential hopes by amplifying talk of a third term. "If there were to be [a] European war," Woolley predicted in May 1939, "the President would be renominated and reelected."[118] In September, Rexford G. Tugwell, an original member of FDR's "brains trust," believed "like everyone else" that the war had made a third term "inevitable."[119] Senator Norris thought that the president "ought to run again," and in December he said so publicly—in a statement drafted by Tommy Corcoran.[120] In the interim, Bibb Graves, a former governor of Alabama, said that he favored a third term and vowed to get his state's delegation "sewed up for Roosevelt."[121] And Henry Holt, an assistant to the governor of North Dakota, reported strong support for FDR. When asked if North Dakotans would accept McNutt instead, Holt answered: "No."[122]

Momentum for a third Roosevelt term, and resistance to McNutt, had been gathering before the onset of war. Ickes was the first member of the cabinet to endorse publicly FDR's reelection. By August 1939 several New Dealers had followed suit, including Hopkins, Jackson, Murphy, and Senator Joseph Guffey of Pennsylvania. At the Young Democrats Convention, held a month before the invasion of Poland, the third-term advocates led by Guffey sandbagged McNutt, who was scheduled to speak. The Hoosier had been most solicitous of the White House—he had informed the president beforehand of the contents of his remarks. Yet at the convention, McNutt received just fifteen minutes at the podium, meaning that he had to rush through a long speech praising FDR and Social Security. And speaking afterward was Robert Jackson, one of the most ardent supporters of a third term.[123]

Third-term advocates gained an ally in Henry Wallace. Wallace, who had harbored presidential hopes, planned to enter the Oregon primary and cede his delegates to FDR. In so doing, he subordinated his ambitions to Roosevelt in a more obvious way than McNutt had. He thus exhibited a savvy that belied his reputation for being "cold and aloof and transcendental."[124] At the same time, Wallace, like Ickes, failed to get the president to commit himself to running. In December 1939 Wallace told the president that Oklahoma Democrats were organizing "Draft Roosevelt Clubs." FDR responded that he "found it more difficult to form a mental picture of Oklahoma than any other state."[125] Frances Perkins noticed a similar pattern of evasion: "You couldn't get the President to even mention the fact that there was going to be a Presidential election."[126]

Roosevelt's silence and a lessening of the international crisis, as Europe slid into a "phony war" after the demise of Poland, frustrated third-term advocates and gave McNutt an opening. He exploited it by continuing his middle-of-the-road strategy and proposing to reduce the budget of the FSA in 1940. At the same time, his lieutenants spread the word that Roosevelt wanted McNutt to be the Democratic nominee. Such a tactic made sense, for the New Dealers had no candidate other than FDR and only the archconservative Garner was in the race. In this setting, McNutt emerged as a possible bridge between Democratic conservatives and liberals. In November 1939, Tugwell worried that the Hoosier "was making rapid progress in sewing up delegates."[127] And Courtney Letts de Espil observed that McNutt "looms very large as the favorite Dem. pres. candidate for 1940. Only Cordell Hull is a strong opponent for this handsome virile westerner."[128]

At this point, Ickes acted to slow McNutt's momentum. He and Corcoran invited Robert Kintner, a journalist unfriendly toward McNutt, to attend Ickes's next press conference and inquire about reports that the president was backing McNutt. Kintner complied, whereupon Ickes unloaded by denying that

Roosevelt had settled on any one candidate. Ickes predicted that liberals would never accept McNutt, even if the president endorsed him, for they disliked the Two Percent Club and McNutt's use of troops to quell labor unrest. Ickes later wondered whether he had gone too far in blasting McNutt. But he was reassured when FDR made no reproach and when Farley expressed his delight.[129]

Ickes's salvo had a mixed impact on McNutt's campaign. On the one hand, it shored up McNutt's support among some liberals who thought he might be an acceptable nominee if no one else emerged. Benjamin Cohen advised a group of New Dealers to cease and desist, since McNutt might be nominated and elected. Ickes's assault also drew harsh commentary from newspaper editors. A cartoon in the *Washington Evening Star* portrayed McNutt as a fallen gladiator staring at Ickes who, dressed as Caesar, points his thumb downward and proclaims: "He's No Liberal!"[130] On the other hand, however, Ickes's sally exposed the pitfalls of McHale's strategy of pushing McNutt out in front of his rivals. The result was a "ganging-up" by third-term advocates against this "heir presumptuous."[131] In an understatement, Booth Tarkington remarked, "The race is kind of bitterin' up!"[132]

McNutt reacted skittishly to the attacks. He was sensitive to criticism, especially from the press, and he often asked McHale for strategies on how to woo journalists or offset unfavorable coverage.[133] Members of Roosevelt's cabinet were not so easily swayed. To counteract the hostility of Ickes and Farley, McNutt tried humor. "My office," he joked, "is only an epithet away from the Interior Department and a stone's throw from the Post Office Department." He also denounced Ickes as a "second-stringer" in the game of politics.[134] At a party, McNutt shook Ickes's hand only after the interior secretary extended it. Kathleen McNutt was harsher; she remarked that Ickes should not have been at the same soiree as her husband. Upon hearing that, Wallace warned: "Mrs. McNutt is in for having her feelings hurt quite deeply in Washington."[135] Other members of McNutt's family had trouble adjusting to the roughness of national politics. Back in Indiana, John McNutt became so upset about articles critical of his son that his wife had to screen the morning papers before he read them.[136]

Ickes's attack seemed to knock McNutt off his stride; a few days afterward, he delivered an uninspiring address at the Gridiron Dinner. The entertainment that evening featured a Middle Eastern motif, with the star attraction being an eight-foot-high Sphinx modeled after FDR. Journalists portrayed leading politicians, and later in the show, a Valentino-like figure appeared, singing, to the melody of "The Sheik of Araby":

I'm the Sheik of Terre Hutt
My name is Paul McNutt.
To make me President
Costs only Two Per cent.
Few men you'll ever see
With sex appeal like me.
I'll get the women's vote—
The Sheik of Terre Haute.

It was, the *Indianapolis News* exclaimed, "hilarious."[137] McNutt's speech, in contrast, was anything but. He was more appreciative of wit than witty himself and, that evening, his jokes fell flat. McNutt probably got his heartiest laughs when poking fun at his appearance, remarking that attacks from Indiana's newspapers were "enough to make any man's hair turn white." But his closing sounded preachy and self-referencing: "It's a long, long road with soft shoulders on both sides. The hard surface is in the middle."[138] Homer Cummings thought McNutt "in fair form but not up to his best."[139] "Most of the guests I spoke to," the columnist H. L. Mencken wrote, sensed a "hollowness in his remarks, and that he failed utterly to make any really favorable impression."[140]

A greater setback to the campaign was an investigation of McNutt's political machine by the Department of the Treasury. It began innocently enough, when Senators Minton and Van Nuys asked the president to appoint Pleas Greenlee, McNutt's former secretary, to be collector of internal revenue at Indianapolis.[141] The McNutt forces may have been behind the appointment, for they were keen to unify the Hoosier Democrats after Greenlee turned against the machine. Secretary of the Treasury Morgenthau opposed the appointment, arguing that the current collector had performed adequately. But Roosevelt, pressed by the two senators, insisted that Greenlee's name go forward. Morgenthau's assistants thereupon examined the nominee's background—and something caught their eye: Greenlee, a man of humble origins who had earned $4,800 a year as McNutt's secretary from 1933 to 1937, was worth over $103,000. This fortune derived from contributions to Greenlee's unsuccessful bid to become governor of Indiana in 1936 and from stock he held in a beer importing firm organized under McNutt's alcohol control act. Greenlee had helped this company gain a coveted beer license, and he was rewarded with stock. On top of that, he had gotten away with paying little federal income tax. He also had violated state law by failing to report contributions to his campaign and by using campaign dollars for business ventures. FDR read over these findings and remarked: "Obviously we cannot appoint Greenlee."[142]

The investigation of Greenlee opened the door to a probe of the entire Mc-Nutt organization. The catalyst behind the project was Morgenthau. In July 1939 he read an article in *The New Republic* that mentioned how "people closely associated with McNutt" were active in the Two Percent Club. Morgenthau discussed this report with aides. They, in turn, revealed that McHale, who had owned "nothing" in 1932, had amassed around $80,000 through stock in breweries. The treasury secretary decided to pursue the matter, for three reasons. First, the case had parallels with Greenlee's. Second, it was his responsibility to ensure that Americans were paying taxes. Third, Morgenthau wanted to prevent Roosevelt from getting "too much involved" with McNutt, who might be tainted by scandal.[143] At the time McNutt was assuming his duties at the FSA and launching his presidential campaign, his finances fell under intense scrutiny.

The Treasury Department investigation yielded fascinating data on the workings of the McNutt machine. The involvement of Indiana Democrats in beer importing proved widespread and lucrative: William Kunkel, a publisher in Fort Wayne, was president of one importing firm; Thomas Taggart Jr., son of the party's former boss, owned stock in a another (and had failed to report $50,000 of his income); McHale held fifty percent of the stock in two importing corporations. When several liquor dealers admitted that they had made "substantial contributions" to the Two Percent Club, investigators turned their attention to the club. Treasury department officials learned that from 1933 to 1938 the club had raised $750,000; that over $100,000 of that sum had vanished; and that Bowman Elder, the club's treasurer, had overseen a $125,000 slush fund raised from beer importers. As long as the club received its dollars voluntarily and used them for its stated purpose—to further the interests of the Democratic Party—it was under no obligation to pay taxes. With that in mind, Morgenthau's subordinates examined the operations of the Two Percent Club and the finances of Indiana's leading Democrats. They discovered that McNutt had paid no tax on $47,000 which he had earned from speaking fees and poker winnings.[144]

The investigation ran into problems of its own. Morgenthau's team uncovered activities in Indiana that were ethically questionable, even sleazy. For example, money from Elder—and perhaps the Two Percent Club—was used to reimburse McNutt for his travel expenses. And McNutt consistently won at poker games (once, when he lost to a state official, the man lost his position "a few days thereafter").[145] The difficulty for the investigators, though, was that such activities were not illegal. In other areas, they had trouble substantiating wrongdoing. Although several affidavits had corroborated the gossip that state workers had been forced to contribute to the Two Percent Club, they were not "adequate proof" of coercion.[146] An audit of beer importers bogged down when firms reported that some of their files had been lost or "destroyed by fire."[147] To make matters worse, a backlash soon emerged against what seemed a political vendetta. Frank Murphy privately condemned Treasury's efforts to "club" Mc-Nutt.[148] Even Farley felt sorry for his old enemy.[149] And the publisher Roy W. Howard thought that McNutt was receiving "atrocious" treatment at the hands of an administration prone to abuse its power.[150] Agreeing, Ray Clapper published a column entitled "Crucifying McNutt."[151] McNutt, it must be pointed out, was feeding "criticism of Treasury to these columnists," proving that he was sufficiently wily—and tough—to strike back.[152] In the end, to avoid any hint of "persecution," the agents at Treasury, without telling Morgenthau beforehand, settled the Indiana cases out of court by accepting payment of back taxes.[153]

McNutt had dodged a campaign-ending bullet. He often had been lax about his finances, behaving like a spoiled rich boy who expected others to pay his bills. That had been true of his relationship with his father, and it may have been true regarding the Two Percent Club. According to one journalist, when Paul became governor, he was broke but still able to buy a diamond ring for Kathleen a month after the inauguration. Moreover, the former head of the Democratic speakers bureau in Indiana had characterized McNutt as "corrupt."[154] Yet if he had done anything damning, Treasury would have prosecuted him. Morgenthau's agents were "working closely" with the Republican Party chair in Indiana to get information on the Democratic machine, and any whitewash of McNutt would have handed the GOP a golden issue.[155]

Roosevelt's role in the tax probe was delicate to the point of being passive. It is true that the president had been collecting dirt on McNutt, whom he never trusted. For example, when Farley received an anonymous letter about the amount of campaign money spent in Indiana during the 1938 elections, Roosevelt advised him to consult the U.S. attorney general. And when a congressman complained about McNutt using his franking privilege to distribute campaign literature, the president told Farley to leave the congressman's letter "with me."[156] It is also true that Roosevelt had used the Treasury Department to investigate the finances of administration critics and business leaders. The timing of the McNutt investigation led reasonable people to jump to unwarranted conclusions. FDR, the journalist Arthur Krock recalled, "destroyed Paul McNutt by ordering that income tax investigation."[157]

It did not happen quite that way; with respect to McNutt, Roosevelt stayed above the fray while Treasury investigated. Upon hearing that the department and McNutt had settled out of court, Roosevelt commented: "Well, I guess it's all for the best. . . . *We* have been very dignified . . . about the whole matter and have said nothing."[158] The probe was not entirely dignified, of course. In a memorandum marked "personal and confidential," a special agent of the Federal Bureau of Investigation detailed to J. Edgar Hoover the Treasury Department's investigation of McNutt, predicting that, once released, the probe would cause a scandal.[159] FDR, meanwhile, said nothing that might exonerate McNutt until October 1940—when the Hoosier's presidential campaign was a distant memory.[160]

The Treasury Department's investigation damaged McNutt in two ways. First, it gave his campaign a horrible press. Columnists compared McNutt's organization to that of the late Huey Long, another power-hungry governor, and to Kansas City's Pendergast machine, which was crumbling beneath the weight of another income-tax investigation. Second, Treasury's probe had reminded Roosevelt loyalists of McNutt's flaws, and their contempt for him intensified. When McNutt tried to donate $1,000 to FDR's library, Ickes warned against accepting the money since it might have come from employees at the Federal Security Agency. The thought of shaking down one's workers, Ickes alleged—without evidence—"would naturally occur to the man who organized the Two Percent Club."[161] Others joined in the assault. After Chicago "bested" New York by getting McNutt to be its Armistice Day speaker, Mayor Fiorello La Guardia quipped: "If Chicago is committing larceny it is only petty larceny. I wouldn't have the big bum speak in New York."[162] Most troublesome were the president's jibes. At one cabinet meeting, Roosevelt joked that with McNutt's experience heading the Two Percent Club, he might be able to "organize [federal] employees and clean up [the] deficit."[163]

The death knell to McNutt's presidential hopes came at the end of 1939 and the beginning of 1940, when FDR decided to run again. A hint of Roosevelt's intentions came in December 1939, when he asked former governor O. Max Gardner of North Carolina to line up his state's delegation on behalf of Cordell Hull. The president claimed that Hull would be nominated and elected, whereupon Roosevelt would become secretary of state. Taken at face value, this plan showed that the president was not ready to retire; rather, he and Hull would switch jobs and "work out the peace of the world."[164] The scheme was implausible. Although Hull had stature within the party, he was sixty-eight years old, devoid of charisma, burdened by a speech impediment, and no liberal—which meant that Roosevelt never supported him wholeheartedly. Indeed, FDR dismissed Hull as "interested only in trade matters and foreign affairs," "well advanced in years," and lacking "interest in policies generally," meaning the New Deal.[165] But by delivering North Carolina to Hull, Roosevelt could keep that state out of the hands of McNutt or Farley. Pa Watson, the president's appointments secretary, understood the game his boss was playing. "I know what you have been taking about," Watson told Gardner, "and don't you believe a damn word of it. [Roosevelt] is the only possible candidate."[166]

Roosevelt's discussions with Frank Murphy, in December 1939, were even more revealing. The president that month was trying to convince Murphy to resign as attorney general and accept nomination to the U.S. Supreme Court. FDR emphasized that Murphy could do more to advance the liberal cause from the bench than from the cabinet for neither he nor Murphy would be president in 1941. The attorney general disagreed. In 1940, Murphy explained, Democrats had to nominate "a sound progressive" candidate. "That's the only thing to do," Roosevelt conceded. "But I don't believe a Frank Murphy, a Bob Jackson or a Harry Hopkins is going to get [the nomination]."[167] According to the president's own standard, then, that left only one Democrat sufficiently liberal to be the nominee—himself. Foreign affairs were on Roosevelt's mind as well. The president told Murphy that he would run "only if we are in war or on the verge of it." Yet, he already was talking about forming a government of national unity and, not unlike Abraham Lincoln in 1864, thinking about selecting a running mate from the opposition party.[168]

Just as fascinating was Roosevelt's willingness to tack toward the center while also rallying his New Deal base. The president asked his cabinet to help him slice the annual budget deficit by $1.5 billion. "It ought to be done," he insisted, "and if we do it, it will be a *damn good talking point politically.*" Murphy wondered: "What could he be thinking about for 1940!!"[169] Frances Perkins had a strong inkling. In December 1939, Roosevelt told Perkins that he was concerned about divisions among union leaders. To that, she replied: "It's not politically essential as labor will vote [for] FDR anyway."[170]

The best evidence that FDR had decided to run again came from a lunch that he had in January 1940 with his friend Morgenthau. Roosevelt, at the outset, remarked that with respect to the election "I definitely know what I want to do." He then "veered off" to discuss possible sites for the Democratic National Convention. Farley had wanted the convention in New York, his old stomping ground, but the president preferred the Windy City: "Mayor [Edward J.] Kelly of Chicago is for whomever I want, so it is perfectly safe to have the convention in Chicago."[171] (Ten days later, Roosevelt told Ickes: "I am not overlooking the fact that Kelly could pack the galleries for us.")[172] At that point in the conversation, Morgenthau asked: "What did you mean when you said that you definitely knew what you wanted to do?" FDR reiterated the advice a friend had passed along, "to keep on just as you are but keep your mouth shut." Morgenthau understood: Roosevelt was "anxious" to remain at the helm but unwilling to say so publicly. To be certain, the president expressed reservations about running, as he often did: "I do not want to run unless between now and the convention things get very, very much worse in Europe."[173] But Roosevelt had been ahead of the nation in sensing the danger of Nazism. He surely knew that the "phony war" would not last and that Germany would resume its war of aggression.[174]

Politically, though, FDR's spirits rose as 1940 opened. As the president prepared to address Congress, he was, Murphy observed, "all smiles—what a happy warrior."[175] Robert Woolley, a veteran politico with a knack for prognostication, had predicted in May 1939 what was coming to pass: Roosevelt would run because "no one else is in the picture."[176] Agreeing, Senator Claude D. Pepper of Florida commented that there was no other candidate "on the horizon."[177] "Roosevelt," Krock said, "told all the possible candidates he didn't intend to run again just before he cut them down . . . which is hardly the way you act if you want a successor."[178] On the eve of the 1940 Democratic National Convention, the president admitted to a group of party elders that "he had not built up anyone to take over the leadership of the party."[179] For McNutt, that admission was significant. His presidential hopes were dead before the Nazis set foot in Denmark.

# 11

## AMBITION FRUSTRATED
## (1940)

NINETEEN FORTY WAS THE MOST EXCITING, and frustrating, year in Paul V. McNutt's life. It started out on a sour note. The Treasury Department's investigation of McNutt's finances, and those of his machine, had left scars. Other ghosts haunted McNutt, such as his decision to send troops into Terre Haute, which continued to draw fire from labor leaders. McNutt also was in a state of limbo. He had promised not to run against Franklin D. Roosevelt for the Democratic nomination, but the president had said nothing of his own plans. If being held in check like that upset McNutt, he concealed his feelings. His staff insisted that he remained unflappable, "vigorous," and "rugged," meaning ready to fight.[1]

Fight McNutt did, throughout 1940, against formidable odds. Round one, which took place during the spring, involved the race for the Democratic nomination, the ascent of the third-term forces, and the transformation of McNutt's presidential campaign into a bid for the vice presidency. In round two, spanning the Democratic National Convention, McNutt's pugilism entailed more jabbing than punching. Having made himself available for the vice presidency, McNutt did not press the matter as strongly as he might have after Roosevelt tapped someone else. His loyalty to FDR affirmed, McNutt entered round three—the fall campaign—pounding away against Wendell L. Willkie, his old college chum and the standard-bearer of the Grand Old Party (GOP). On the outside, he sounded like a happy warrior. On the inside, he was anything but. Instead of running on his party's national ticket, McNutt had shrunk to being one of Roosevelt's campaign surrogates, landing a few choice blows on a larger-than-life political newcomer whom he once had overshadowed. For McNutt, 1940 began with pain and possibility. It took a few dramatic turns before culminating in disappointment and diminishment. McNutt would taste failure, and he would never be the same again.

As 1940 began, McNutt found himself under attack from many different angles. Especially disturbing was a spate of critical profiles that ran in such magazines as *Life, Look, Saturday Evening Post, The New Republic, The Nation,* and *American Mercury.* The titles of such pieces stressed the candidate's drive ("I Intend to Be President"), ego ("Great God McNutt"), and arrogance ("It Would Be Kind of Nice to Be President").[2] Taken together, the articles eschewed any discussion of McNutt's family and home life, topics that would have humanized him. They depicted instead a man consumed since boyhood with a burning desire to be president. As governor, he had emerged as alarmingly efficient to the point of being ruthless.[3] In such accounts, McNutt's laudable ends, like securing relief for the needy, were overshadowed by his unsavory methods, such as the Two Percent Club. At the national level, Milton S. Mayer of *The Nation* observed, liberals hated the Hoosier's "combination of New Deal brains and Old Deal morals." And Mayer agreed with them:

> Even if McNutt is only half as bad as the New Dealers say he is, he's bad enough. To look at him is to mistrust him. Every writer who has interviewed him has reacted negatively. He is too smooth; and unlike Roosevelt he isn't smooth enough to look as if he weren't smooth. Roosevelt's laugh seems hearty, even if it isn't; McNutt's seems phony, even if it isn't.[4]

Commentary such as that can devastate a campaign. According to one McNutt supporter, it seemed as though the pundits, all at once, had borne down on the Hoosier.[5]

Why such criticism? In part, this was a case of the political chickens coming home to roost. McNutt was, rightly and deservedly, paying for his excesses as governor. The adverse coverage also derived from the excessively packaged nature of McNutt's campaign. For example, in an appeal to women, McNutt's pamphlets had featured "a soft-focused, idealized, super-refined likeness" of the candidate. But when the end product made the platinum-haired McNutt look like the cross between a less-than-stellar former president (Warren G.

Harding) and a bombshell actress (Jean Harlow), the campaign shifted tactics as well as camera angle.[6] New brochures and buttons showed McNutt's face partly in profile, with an expression conveying sternness, determination, and a "millions-for-defense-but-not-one-cent-for-tribute attitude."[7] Manipulation of that sort reinforced the perception that McNutt was getting by on calculation, posturing, and good looks. He was, thought a writer at the *Saturday Evening Post,* trying "to seep into the White House by osmosis" without taking a firm stand on any issue.[8] The columnists Robert Kintner and Joseph Alsop called McNutt a "creature of conditioned reflexes" who had an "empty generality" for any query.[9] Although McNutt headed the agency that oversaw much of the New Deal, he had no trouble appearing before a local chamber of commerce to extol "private enterprise and individual initiative."[10] One journalist, Joseph H. Friend, recoiled at McNutt's political dexterity and authoritarian impulses.[11]

McNutt was no demagogic dictator-in-waiting, but he projected a personal awkwardness that repelled many reporters. McNutt's long-standing desire to soar above his peers and to remain one of the boys continued during his presidential campaign. Recalling McNutt's political coming-out bash in 1938, Alsop and Kintner dubbed the Hoosier "the all-time record holder for cynical effrontery in seeking the presidency."[12] Agreeing, Drew Pearson and Robert S. Allen opined that he had no qualms being "first" in any "parade."[13] McNutt, in turn, tried hard—too hard, perhaps—to befriend reporters. Once, while on the golf links, he approached a journalist, uttered a hearty "hello," and slapped the man on the shoulder "even though he did not know him very well." The story reinforced the perception that McNutt was too aggressive, too prone to push in "where he should not push." Over time, as a writer for the International News Service observed, the national press came to dislike "the white-haired so and so."[14] Publishers also expressed dismay. Roy W. Howard, who had endorsed McNutt's gubernatorial bid and had shared his outlook on Philippine independence, ultimately decided that he did not want to see the super-ambitious Hoosier nominated for president. Howard candidly admitted: "I am always a little bit suspicious of really handsome men, and certainly he's that."[15]

Howard's comment underscored a degree of arbitrariness, even hypocrisy, in the press's coverage. Journalists who criticized McNutt's campaign for being shallow and packaged perhaps forgot that presidential contests emphasizing personality and publicity dated to the turn of the twentieth century. And reporters abetted such campaigning; Jack Alexander justified his profile of McNutt in *Life* on grounds that the candidate was "in the public eye" and a

"natural target for magazine exploitation."[16] Others could not hide their disdain
for McNutt. Alsop and Kintner dismissed him as an "amateur Huey Long in
the garments of Warren Harding."[17] Alva Johnston of the *Saturday Evening Post*
disliked McNutt so much that one observer predicted it would "color anything"
he wrote (Johnston's piece depicted McNutt as an opportunist and a would-be
dictator).[18] William Allen White, the nationally renowned editor of Kansas's
*Emporia Gazette,* pushed the idea that McNutt represented the forces of reaction in the Democratic Party. "Like his modern prototypes who have grabbed
power," White wrote, "he may walk to power as an advanced liberal. Mussolini
and Hitler were both socialists."[19] There was no evidence that White's comments derived from anything other than personal impression.

The superficial dimension to the press coverage became apparent in the space
given to two side matters: McNutt's surname and his looks. Even a friendly
journalist like Ernest K. Lindley thought the candidate's "unfortunate last
name" and the fact that he was "too handsome" were liabilities.[20] The name
"McNutt" evoked memories of Boob McNutt, a witless character drawn by the
cartoonist Rube Goldberg. At a political dinner in Washington early in 1940, a
speaker "dwelt on the improbability of George McNutt as father of his country,
Abraham McNutt as emancipator, Franklin Delano McNutt as hero of the New
Deal." The speech, one observer recalled, was an ordeal for Paul McNutt.[21] A
man who heard the address sensed "some definite malice" aimed at the Hoosier.[22] But the crowd, another attendee commented, "went crazy" with laughter,
and the event "showed well what a handicap the name would be to McNutt."[23]

McNutt's looks garnered more attention. Reporters repeated the line that Mc-
Nutt was "tall, tan, and terrific."[24] His appearance proved an asset and a liability.
It helped him court female voters, and even some men were impressed by Mc-
Nutt; a schoolteacher who saw his picture on the cover of *Time* pronounced him
"a real he-man" whom he would cross party lines to vote for.[25] Such comments
support the idea that Americans often associate good looks with "intelligence,
sensitivity, sincerity, self-confidence, independence, poise, competence, and
good character."[26] And there was a tradition of fine-looking men occupying the
White House, including the McNutt-like Harding. But during the 1930s, after
Harding's demise (physically and in reputation) and before the advent of television (and the election of John F. Kennedy), Americans often equated handsome looks with vanity, vacuity, and arrogance. McNutt "was handsome and
impressive just to look at," Secretary of Labor Frances Perkins recalled, "but
he was very empty."[27] Senator Styles Bridges, Republican of New Hampshire,

thought McNutt "the most conceited good looking man" he had ever seen.[28] And Robert W. Woolley, a longtime Democratic publicist, thought "lightly" of McNutt "because his pulchritude and imposing mien made him seem a kind of God's gift to women."[29] William Allen White used the Hoosier's physical features to attack him as both effeminate and conservative: "McNutt is merely [John Nance] Garner in a high hat, a white vest, a pongee silk scarf, pumps, and the glamour of a movie hero."[30] A politician possessing too many gifts, such as good looks, was apt to inspire as much acrimony as awe.

McNutt's looks did not impress everyone. David E. Lilienthal, administrator of the Tennessee Valley Authority and a fellow Hoosier, first met McNutt at a party in 1940 and found him an informed conversationalist on Philippine policy. But, Lilienthal went on, "His voice isn't pleasant at all—it runs off quickly into a high register that goes through his nose. And he isn't as good-looking as I had thought."[31] Reports of McNutt's superb speaking ability, as well as photos of him, apparently had raised unrealistic expectations.

The attention Paul received, particularly the discussion of his looks, appeared to unsettle Kathleen. She expressed her unease through humor, which was both cleverly deflective and awkwardly risqué. When one Washingtonian asked if Kathleen kept her handsome husband locked up at night in order to protect "impressionable women," she responded: "It's an absolute fact and I feed him beautiful young girls—nothing else!"[32] At a party hosted by Emily Newell Blair, a well-known advocate of women's rights and a supporter of Paul's presidential campaign, Kathleen cut loose. She discussed life in the Philippines and how her many servants had left her little to do, save one marital duty. Kathleen joked she would have returned to America before Paul, but "she couldn't find him a white mistress." She also told a story about a party that they had hosted in Indiana: Paul, at one point, dashed upstairs and was greeted by a woman who "threw her arms around him." Their daughter, Louise, "saw the situation and retreated back into her room," proving, Kathleen joked, that she was a "perfect diplomat."[33] In making these remarks, Kathleen was not trying to intimate that Paul had engaged in extramarital affairs. She simply was holding court in her inimitably colorful way. But such remarks also may have signaled discomfort about sharing her attractive husband with countless admirers.

Kathleen's distaste for politics had not abated. She suggested that she had no intention of being a first lady in the mold of Eleanor Roosevelt. In March 1940, Kathleen attended an annual event hosted by the National Women's Press Club, where she failed to impress at least one politically minded woman—the wife of the Argentine ambassador thought Kathleen "a handsome largish woman" who was "uninteresting."[34] After Eleanor Roosevelt addressed the gathering, as she had since 1933, a journalist asked if Kathleen could imagine speaking at the same conclave "for eight successive years." "Why," she replied, "it never occurred to me to think I might have to."[35] Her remark could be read as disparagement of the first lady's friendliness toward female journalists, a lack of confidence in Paul's presidential bid, or, most likely, frustration with having to occupy the political stage. Indeed, when asked how it felt to be the wife of a man who might be president, Kathleen shot back: "Ask a woman who owns one."[36]

The McNutt campaign had more pressing problems than the reservations of the candidate's wife. By April 1940, the financial state of the operation had become, McHale admitted, "embarrassing." McNutt had wanted to publish a book setting out his ideas, but there was no money to do so. The cash shortfall threatened another project, McNutt's speaking tour through the West, and reduced the campaign organization to little more than a skeleton in many states.[37] "Little has been accomplished," a McNutt supporter in Wisconsin lamented.[38] Underorganized and underfunded, the campaign was no match for the criticism descending upon McNutt. McNutt's staff issued statements to counter attacks from labor leaders, but voters were too willing to be "guided" by columnists. As a result, the candidate's "prestige" had taken a hit.[39] Fissures emerged among staff members, and rumors circulated that the campaign was "folding up."[40] Such talk supported a prediction by James A. Farley that McNutt's candidacy would make no "headway."[41] Josephus Daniels, U.S. ambassador to Mexico and a former secretary of the navy, went further, remarking that none of FDR's possible successors had "clicked" with voters.[42]

To be fair, McNutt commanded some support outside of Washington. Frank P. Graham, president of the University of North Carolina, praised the "remarkable physical stamina" and "dynamic energy" which made McNutt a "great campaigner." And, as Graham reminded Harry Hopkins, McNutt had "gone all the way for the New Deal."[43] Maury Maverick, a well-known former congressman and a firm liberal, agreed, adding that McNutt had performed well as governor of Indiana and that talk of him being a "Fascist" was "silly."[44] There also was support for the Hoosier around his native region. An attack by Secretary of the Interior Harold L. Ickes on McNutt's liberal credentials did him "no harm" in Minnesota, according to one prominent Democrat there. In the Gopher State, this Democrat insisted, McNutt still had many "friends"—as did Roosevelt.[45]

That remark highlighted the biggest obstacle facing McNutt: the specter of FDR running again. The praise that McNutt won from Graham and Maverick, it must be noted, was in reference to his possible nomination as vice president, not president. Indeed, after members of McNutt's staff visited North Carolina, they found Democrats in that state committed to Roosevelt. In Florida, the McNutt forces negotiated an agreement that gave their candidate virtually nothing. The state's delegation would be for Roosevelt if he ran and for McNutt only if the president did not run and endorsed him. Otherwise, the delegation would either remain neutral or back whomever FDR wanted.[46] In Illinois, McNutt's supporters had wanted to enter his name in the primary but, out of deference to Roosevelt, they elected not to. That meant that the Hoosier missed the chance to harvest delegate votes from a neighboring state.[47] Even in Indiana, McNutt's stock was falling. Lorena Hickok, a former reporter and a friend of Eleanor Roosevelt, visited Indianapolis in March and observed that the sentiment was "all Third Term." Members of McNutt's own organization, she observed, "would much rather have the president run!"[48]

By early April, Roosevelt's intentions were becoming apparent. "There are more and more indications," Wayne Coy informed a friend, "that the President will seek a third term."[49] According to O. Max Gardner, a former governor of North Carolina, "by February it was clear that the President was a candidate."[50] Theodore Roosevelt Jr. agreed: "I have felt all along that Franklin did not intend to run for a third term, but recent indications would seem to prove that I am wrong."[51] Even Farley began to acknowledge the unpleasant reality. "I am still of the opinion that the President will not run," he explained in March 1940, "but I can't find many people who will agree with me."[52] "There is every indication," wrote Breckinridge Long, an FDR confidant at the Department of State, "that [the president] will be requested to run."[53]

What were these indications that Roosevelt was going to run? The first was the president's silence—that is, his failure to withdraw, which suggested openness to a draft—and the second was the absence of a plausible alternative nominee.[54] The best evidence that Roosevelt was running was the third-term boom which FDR did nothing to quell. It was orchestrated by a group of administration officials who wanted to keep their jobs and was backed by Democratic bosses and members of Congress who knew that the best way to increase their vote totals was to run with FDR, rather than a bland standpatter, at the top of their ticket. Roosevelt's supporters worked in state primaries and conventions to garner delegates friendly to the president. In Chicago, Mayor Edward J. Kelly entered FDR's name in the Illinois primary, where Roosevelt trounced Garner by a margin of six to one. The victory came on the heels of earlier triumphs by third-term advocates in New Hampshire, Maine, Alaska, and Wisconsin.

Thomas Corcoran, one of FDR's closest aides, thought the "Draft Roosevelt movement" was "going great."[55] And by April, Josephus Daniels beamed that "every State which has acted has declared for the nomination of Roosevelt."[56] At that point, former California senator William Gibbs McAdoo, a long-standing party statesman, could not see "how the Garner and anti-Roosevelt people can extract any comfort from the primaries so far held."[57]

Success did not always come easily. In California, Garner, the choice of party conservatives, had entered the May primary while the liberals remained divided among three factions, including a pro-Roosevelt contingent headed by the unpopular sitting governor, Culbert Olson. Worried that this schism would lead to a Garner victory, McAdoo hoped that he would receive "some encouragement from Washington."[58] But, instead of a statement of support from FDR, all McAdoo got was a note from Attorney General Robert H. Jackson declaring that every third-term advocate "has to act on his own" and a visit from Ickes, who managed to unite the McAdoo and Olson supporters behind a common third-term slate.[59] In the end, though, the fretting and maneuvering mattered little, for the Roosevelt-Olson forces swept the primary, capturing three-quarters of the popular vote.[60] Again, McNutt was left on the sidelines. After the primary, one of McNutt's aides conceded that California's delegation "will of course be for President Roosevelt."[61]

Deciphering the California victory is not difficult. The Roosevelt brand was so popular among Democrats there that the state party's factional disputes were irrelevant. In Missouri, however, the struggle was more intense and, as a result, one detects greater presidential involvement. In the Show-Me State, FDR enjoyed the backing of Governor Lloyd Stark, who wanted to claim the Senate seat held by Harry S. Truman or to succeed Garner as vice president. Stark worked hard—and with some success—against Senator Bennett Clark, another presidential hopeful, for a delegation to the national convention that was "uninstructed" but "pro-Roosevelt."[62] Roosevelt, in turn, expressed appreciation through his appointments secretary, Edwin M. "Pa" Watson.[63] Coordination between the governor and the White House became close. Roosevelt even helped Stark in his race against Truman, who was cool to talk of a third term, friendly to Clark, and a protégé of the moribund machine of Tom Pendergast.[64] The president ordered the head of the Works Progress Administration in Missouri to "clean house of old Prendergast [sic] crowd" and "not [to] use W.P.A. against Gov. Stark."[65] Roosevelt's order, which sounded like a reward to Stark, was dated April 6—three days before the Nazis marched into Denmark.

Although FDR needed no escalation in hostilities to decide to run for a third term, the worsening situation in Europe boosted his political prospects while diminishing those of McNutt. The aura of crisis intensified when Germany invaded Denmark and Norway and then the Low Countries and France. Many Americans understandably thought this was no time to switch leaders. McAdoo played upon such thinking just days before the California primary when he urged state Democrats to endorse a delegation loyal to "the wise and experienced" Roosevelt.[66] Californians did, along with Democrats elsewhere. FDR ran unopposed in Pennsylvania, and he smiled "broadly" when Georgia's convention selected a slate favoring a third term.[67] In North Carolina, Governor Clyde R. Hoey agreed to give his state's delegates to Roosevelt, if the president's name went before the convention. By mid-May, Iowa, Alabama, South Carolina, and Oklahoma had fallen in line, meaning that FDR had amassed almost a majority of the delegates to the national convention.[68]

In this setting, there was almost nothing McNutt could do to secure his party's nomination for president. Once he had said that he would not run against FDR, he could not turn around and enter primaries against the president. The only course for McNutt was to demonstrate loyalty to the White House, hope Roosevelt would not run, and position himself to inherit FDR's support. With that in mind, McHale proclaimed that the campaign was working alongside Roosevelt's backers to select delegates for the national convention. McNutt, in turn, amplified his support for the New Deal by promising to defend average people against the special interests and praising Roosevelt's policies for their "humanitarian" concern.[69] McNutt also reiterated a line he had used in past campaigns, that FDR was America's "greatest peace-time president."[70] But many of Roosevelt's supporters doubted McNutt's fealty. A coterie of third-term advocates that included Harry Hopkins, Ed Kelly, Mayor Frank Hague of Jersey City, and Senators James F. Byrnes of South Carolina and Claude D. Pepper of Florida watched the Hoosier closely. In March, when the "McNutt Crowd" showed signs of breaking their "agreement to support delegates for Roosevelt or whoever Roosevelt is for," Pepper made moves to put them on notice.[71] Unlike McNutt, FDR had a surplus of devoted supporters.

McNutt had no choice but to seek a presidential endorsement for his ambitions. In April 1940, he sent FDR a draft of a book his staff had been assembling and invited him to suggest improvements. The president refused to take the bait, for the book was not worth his time. It was casually titled ("Using Our Heads"), poorly written, and devoid of much original thought—one McNutt aide thought it a standard defense of the administration.[72] Accordingly, Roosevelt asked his press secretary, Steve Early, to draft a reply. Early's letter, which the president signed, was patronizing. After praising the book as "worthwhile" and resting on "sound democratic political philosophy," it went on to correct errors of style. When the manuscript quoted McNutt as saying that he had been "an American for many generations," Roosevelt joshed him: "Some purist most assuredly will challenge this declaration or at least he will suspect that you are a very old man!"[73] It was a swipe at McNutt's vanity, a jab that FDR could take at a marginalized subordinate.

To break out of his isolation, and to resurrect his candidacy, McNutt made several speeches during April and May. His staff scraped up enough cash for an extended tour of the Midwest and West, with forays into the South, and Roosevelt gave McNutt a leave of absence so that he could "peddle his papers."[74] The talks, to be sure, generated some good publicity for McNutt. Before his speech in Bismarck, the local paper dubbed him the "'Adonis' of American Politics."[75] Following his remarks in Wichita, the press lauded him for speaking "vigorously" on behalf of the New Deal.[76] With respect to the war, McNutt's position reflected his beliefs and the national mood: America must build up its defenses but avoid direct participation in the conflict if at all possible.[77]

In the end, though, larger events overwhelmed McNutt's campaign. His speeches on domestic politics sounded out of place in a world preoccupied with war. On the day McNutt spoke in Bismarck, the headline of the local paper proclaimed "Germans Seize Copenhagen, Oslo."[78] When he arrived in Los Angeles, the *Herald-Express* headlined: "Chamberlain Quits, Churchill Premier; Huge Battles Rage in Holland and Belgium."[79] To make matters worse, the Roosevelt juggernaut dogged McNutt. On the day he spoke to Democrats in Phoenix, the *Arizona Republic* observed that "state after state has joined in the demand for a third term and the resounding cries have become louder."[80] FDR's victory in California, coming on the eve of McNutt's visit, elicited an admission from Garner that the president probably would be renominated. In Los Angeles, McNutt acknowledged that it was "perfectly obvious that the President could be nominated if he would accept."[81] Such comments—candid, honest, and realistic, to be certain—further diminished his shrinking presidential prospects. As McNutt left the Golden State, the *Los Angeles Times* dubbed him a "minor candidate" for the Democratic nomination.[82] That same day, Claude Pepper proposed that one of the leaders of the third-term movement ask McNutt to return to Washington, withdraw from the race, and endorse Roosevelt.[83]

McNutt knew his campaign was over. On May 30 he endorsed the president's renomination, arguing that the nation's "security" and "unity" demanded that FDR continue in office: "The emergency which faces us . . . requires the strong leadership and wealth of experience in world affairs that the President alone can provide."[84] The statement reflected the Hoosier's thoughts about what was in the national interest. It also stemmed from careful political calculation.[85] Realizing that he had no chance to win his party's nomination (and perhaps wishing to answer critics who thought him too ambitious), McNutt cloaked his withdrawal in the rhetoric of sacrifice. Yet, at the same time, McHale assured supporters that McNutt's "organization" would "carry on."[86] He may have been positioning McNutt to inherit the presidential nomination, if FDR chose not to run, or to accept a vice-presidential nod instead.[87]

Although McNutt did not say so, he was angling for the vice presidency. He had been interested in running with FDR since the early years of his governorship, and now, with Garner set to retire, it seemed he might get his chance. Besides, the other prospects before him appeared uninviting. McNutt might have tried to return to Indiana, where the state constitution only forbade governors from serving two consecutive terms. Or he could have waited for appointment to a senior cabinet office. But going back to the statehouse would have been a step backward, and there was no guarantee that FDR would bring him into the cabinet. In contrast, Wayne Coy thought that McNutt was suited for the vice presidency by virtue of his "youth, geography, and ability."[88]

The idea that McNutt might run with Roosevelt was not fanciful. The Treasury Department's probe of the McNutt machine had yielded little and was receding as an issue. Moreover, attacks by administration liberals had left McNutt with an image of moderation, something that party conservatives and machine bosses were apt to like. And McNutt's presidential campaign, for all its shortcomings, had managed to introduce (or reintroduce) him to Democrats across the nation. A friend of Interior Secretary Ickes who had heard McNutt defend the New Deal came away "impressed."[89] Even Ickes softened his stand against McNutt, acknowledging that he possessed "real ability" and had been "graceful" in exiting the presidential race.[90] It thus was not surprising when delegates from Florida, at the behest of McHale and Coy, resolved that McNutt be nominated as vice president.[91]

There were barriers to McNutt's plans. FDR would have a large say in the selection of his running mate, and there is no evidence that he had warmed to

McNutt. In June 1940, Roosevelt told Pepper that the nominee for vice president had to have "his feet on the ground," which McNutt did, and "some knowledge of European conditions," which McNutt really did not.[92] In truth, FDR's opinion of McNutt had slipped. When the president was still toying with possible successors, he told former secretary of commerce Daniel C. Roper that the Democratic nominee in 1940 had to be young and vigorous. When Roper asked if that meant McNutt, Roosevelt said "no."[93] To Ambassador Joseph P. Kennedy, FDR remarked that McNutt was "a go-getter if he has a definite assignment, but he's only good if he has a definite assignment."[94] Roosevelt, at one point, ridiculed McNutt as "a flop as a candidate."[95] And Farley once joked that "the President was getting a great kick out of McNutt's efforts to become the Vice Presidential nominee."[96]

Nevertheless, the McNutt campaign stuck with its strategy and reaffirmed its loyalty to the president. At Indiana's state convention, McHale secured passage of a resolution endorsing FDR's renomination. McNutt then delivered a stirring defense of the policies of the Roosevelt administration. He discussed the threat of war and hailed the record of the Democratic Party in expanding security for Americans, both domestically and internationally. Although McNutt did not promise that the United States would assist embattled nations by joining the fight against Nazism, he dismissed a policy of isolation as impossible in an interconnected world. In the end, the Hoosier Democrats selected a delegation to the national convention that was loyal to McNutt *and* supportive of a third term. And when McNutt declined to serve as a delegate in Chicago, it was a signal that he was available for the vice-presidential nomination.[97]

The biggest boost to McNutt's ambitions was the fluidity of presidential politics in 1940. FDR had exhibited stunning discipline in saying nothing about his plans for 1940; in fact, Roosevelt's secretary—and surrogate wife, some said—Missy LeHand did not know, a month before the convention, whether he was going to run again. But the president was entering uncharted waters as he prepared to break historical precedent. Many older, more conservative Democrats resisted the prospect of a third term. The principal opponent was Farley, FDR's postmaster general and chair of the Democratic National Committee, who was on the verge of breaking with his boss. The president had discouraged Farley's presidential ambitions, and Farley was sore that FDR had reneged on his promise to issue a statement withdrawing from the 1940 contest.[98]

The schism with Farley had ramifications for Roosevelt and for McNutt. To the president, Farley had been a kind of political mechanic whose tending of the Democratic Party had mass-produced a succession of electoral triumphs during the previous decade. Even though Roosevelt had managed to secure enough convention delegates, he still needed someone to the direct the third-term forces at the convention. A draft, after all, required an overwhelming show of support, so that it appeared convincing.[99] Farley could not be relied on to accomplish this, and FDR seemed ill inclined to direct his own renomination. Accordingly, there was a good chance that the Democratic National Convention would turn unruly, perhaps even chaotic. If that happened, would Roosevelt be compelled to enlist rivals, such as McNutt, in order to unite the party?

As the convention neared, FDR tried to smooth the way toward his renomination. Gradually and gently, he confirmed, in meetings with senior party leaders, that he was available for a draft. The president discussed the upcoming convention at length with Cordell Hull; although FDR often bypassed or ignored Hull, the white-haired Tennessean projected experience and commanded respect in Democratic circles. In "halting" cadence, the president informed Hull that many people had been urging him to run and that "circumstances" might force his renomination.[100] Hull acceded to the idea of a third term, but Farley did not. During a meeting at Hyde Park, Roosevelt told Farley that he could not in "these times" refuse a draft. The postmaster general replied that he, too, had a duty to perform and would allow his name "to go before the convention" in defense of the two-term tradition.[101] With a battle looming, FDR rallied his supporters. "He did not say whether he was going to accept the nomination or not and I did not ask him," former attorney general Homer S. Cummings noted, after seeing the president. "I think I know, and I think he knows I know."[102] Before the convention, FDR explained to a group of third-term supporters, including Hopkins, Kelly, Byrnes, Frank Walker, and Tammany Hall's Edward J. Flynn, that he would accept renomination with "misgivings." Roosevelt was worried that voters would resent his challenging the two-term precedent. But the party leaders told him they had no one else to nominate and that he had to run.[103]

A sense of uncertainty and unease afflicted Democrats as they convened at the Chicago Stadium. "Grumpy," "spiritless," and "glum" were among the words invoked by journalists to describe the delegates' mood.[104] Courtney Letts de Espil, the American wife of the Argentine ambassador and a past supporter of Hull, found the convention as "stale as old bread" and as "dreary as a week old newspaper."[105] Frances Perkins compared the opening day to "a prayer meeting rather than a circus."[106] The fall of France had dampened spirits as had the GOP, which had nominated Wendell L. Willkie—a little-known, independent-minded businessman who projected vigor and understanding of the crisis overseas. The Democratic malaise also stemmed from the actions of

Roosevelt and his allies. Although the president had been piling up delegates, he had refrained from announcing his candidacy. There was confusion and an absence of leadership at the convention. Farley was on his way out as party chair, displaced by a coalition of regional bosses and administration insiders. Hopkins, who served as Roosevelt's field general at Chicago, had never run a campaign, and he dealt tactlessly with party leaders. The diplomat Joseph E. Davies accurately described the opening of the convention: "While there is a lot of grousing, the masses of the delegates are all for the Boss."[107]

Roosevelt's renomination was an admixture of stagecraft and enthusiasm. The orchestration began as the convention opened. Bob Jackson visited the Chicago Stadium and noticed that microphones had been placed in "very strategic locations" near delegations from states unfriendly to Roosevelt. He informed Mayor Kelly, who had the microphones moved.[108] Kelly went further to ensure that the draft-FDR forces found their voice. On the second day of the convention, the president announced, via a letter read by Senator Alben W. Barkley of Kentucky, that he had "no desire" to be renominated, but that delegates were "free to vote for any candidate" of their choice.[109] Kelly was ready. He had furnished his "leather-lunged" superintendent of sewers with a microphone and instructions to start a "stampede" once Barkley stopped speaking.[110] At that moment, an "ear-splitting" voice, from an undisclosed location, intoned: "We Want Roosevelt." State delegations joined in, chanting "Illinois wants Roosevelt," "New Jersey wants Roosevelt," and "Montana wants Roosevelt." For nearly an hour, delegates hoisted their standards, paraded about, and cheered the president's name.[111] Although Kelly later credited Jackson with giving him the idea to amplify the sentiments of FDR's supporters, it was Representative Edward Hart of New Jersey who really goaded the delegates.[112] The president won renomination on the first ballot. But critics stressed that this draft was, at bottom, a regimented affair "lathered with pretense."[113]

The McNutt campaign also was guilty of pretense. McHale set up one of the "most splendid" headquarters at the convention.[114] It occupied much of the lobby of the Stevens Hotel and had, as its centerpiece, a huge picture of McNutt that made him look "heroic" and "bigger than life."[115] There were "all kinds of entertainment" and plenty to eat and drink.[116] How McNutt paid for all this remains unknown, for his presidential bid had been short of cash. The signs at the headquarters proclaimed "Indiana-McNutt," a hint that the campaign had not given up on the presidency. Indeed, McHale remained flexible about the ends—he was willing "to jump into the contest either for first or second place."[117] But when the convention broke for the president, so too did the McNutt forces. Indiana became the first delegation to march in support of the president's renomination, with McHale hoisting the state's standard as Paul, Kathleen, and Louise looked on from a front-row box. Thereafter McHale openly discussed his friend's prospects for the vice presidency. He predicted that in a large pool of candidates, McNutt would emerge as a contender on the first ballot and pick up votes thereafter.[118]

In 1940, as in 1932, McHale was unable to recapture the magic of 1928, when he had helped to elect McNutt national commander of the American Legion. FDR, stung by the political attacks and defeats of the past four years, was determined to select a vice president who was reliably liberal and thoroughly loyal. In the end, he tapped Secretary of Agriculture Henry A. Wallace of Iowa. Although Wallace had been a Republican as late as 1932 and was known as a novice politician, he had headed the administration's farm program and "was committed to the New Deal approach to government."[119] Along with being personally and philosophically compatible with the president, Wallace was someone whom Roosevelt believed he could groom as a successor. FDR also reckoned that Wallace would boost the ticket in the farm belt, and that was significant because the Republicans nominee for president, Willkie, was a native of Indiana, and his running mate, Oregon senator Charles McNary, was a proponent of federal aid to farmers.[120]

For the Democratic nomination for vice president, no one other than Wallace was acceptable to Roosevelt. To be sure, FDR thrice had asked Hull to run with him. But these offers may have reflected Roosevelt's concern that his own renomination would only be palatable to traditionalist Democrats and the public at large if someone with Hull's stature joined the ticket. After Hull declined the president's offer and Roosevelt won renomination with relative ease, FDR was free to pick Wallace. Among the other possible candidates, Ickes added little to the ticket and Supreme Court Justice William O. Douglas lacked experience. James Byrnes was anathema to Catholics for having converted from Catholicism to the Episcopal faith. Jesse Jones, the Texas banker who headed the Reconstruction Finance Corporation, was too conservative. And the president considered Missouri's Lloyd Stark an insincere liberal and a humorless bore.[121]

What about McNutt? He had midwestern roots, varied experience, liberal credentials, and name recognition, as well as good looks, presence, youth, and energy. At one point, Roosevelt conceded that McNutt "had political strength."[122] But he also had baggage. FDR told aides that he was concerned about the probe of McNutt's finances and the prospect of a scandal erupting during the cam-

paign. Although the investigation by Treasury was winding up, McNutt's enemies were circulating stories of his tax delinquency and settlement just as the
national convention was about to open. The president had other reasons for not
choosing McNutt. The two men lacked rapport and mutual trust. The bottom
line, for Roosevelt, was that McNutt was too ambitious—was too prone to place
his fortunes ahead of the president's. Thanks in part to Farley, FDR had never
forgotten how McNutt had worked against him at the 1932 convention. And
McNutt's elaborate headquarters only advertised his ambition.[123] Roosevelt,
in contrast, valued modesty in his subordinates. Before the 1940 convention
opened, he hinted to Hopkins that none of the "out and out candidates" for vice
president would get the prize.[124] Unlike McNutt, Wallace had no headquarters
at Chicago, and he said nothing publicly about the vice presidency. Not surprisingly, on July 17, a day before the balloting for vice president, Wallace learned
that Roosevelt wanted him on the ticket. Shortly thereafter, McNutt received
the news from Hopkins and the president.[125]

The reaction of McNutt, and his campaign, to Wallace's selection was mixed.
On one level, McNutt was "crushed" by FDR's decision.[126] Claude Wickard,
who had served in the Indiana State Senate and later worked under Wallace
at the Department of Agriculture, saw McNutt at the convention and noticed
his pain, as did the journalist Walter Trohan. McNutt had grown accustomed
to obtaining nearly anything he sought. Moreover, the president had assured
him, just weeks before the convention, that he was a contender for a spot on
the Democratic ticket. For whatever reason, McNutt chose to believe him.[127]
In a measurement of McNutt's expectations—or hopes—he had assigned his
father's young law partner, John Hurt, the task of transporting John and Ruth
McNutt to Chicago if the vice-presidential nomination came through. When
it didn't, he tried hard to mask his disappointment. After getting the word on
the vice presidency, McNutt entered the room where his staff was working and
announced, grinning: "Boys, the President wants Wallace and we must stand
by the President."[128]

McNutt's aides disagreed about what to do. One faction, led by Wayne Coy
and Fowler Harper, thought that McNutt "should concur in whatever the President wanted" and reap the benefits of a graceful exit. Coy and Harper, along
with Oscar R. Ewing, believed that a bright future lay before McNutt, and that
he must not spoil it by forcing his way onto the ticket. This group was more
liberal, more tied to policy issues, and less associated with the nuts-and-bolts
of politics than were McNutt's other advisers, such as McHale, who was "pretty

bitter" about Roosevelt's decision. McHale urged McNutt to fight for the nomination, thinking that he would prevail over Wallace.[129] For McHale, the 1940 convention marked a golden opportunity which had to be seized. He never forgave "the Wayne Coys and the Oscar Ewings" for suggesting otherwise.[130]

McNutt seemed torn between a sense of duty to the president, his ambition to be vice president, and McHale's determination to help him win the prize. Indeed, when McNutt met privately with Wallace to discuss seconding the latter's nomination, McHale telephoned to urge him not to withdraw, for twenty-six senators were plotting a movement to stop Wallace. "The party," Perkins later explained, "longs to promote its own, and Wallace was not its own."[131] Harper, who accompanied McNutt to the meeting with Wallace, took McHale's call, but did not interrupt the conference. When the door opened, McNutt allowed reporters in to snap pictures of him with Henry Wallace. Wickard, at that point, thanked McNutt for "the position he appeared to be taking."[132]

In truth, McNutt's campaign had not given up entirely. During their discussion, McNutt had imposed a condition on Wallace: He would second his nomination only if Farley did. Otherwise, McNutt simply would issue a statement of withdrawal. Farley, of course, was in no mood to assist Wallace's nomination, as the backers of Wallace well knew. What they did not know was that McNutt's team had plans to pack the galleries. At this point, the campaign's aim was unclear. Perhaps McNutt or, more likely, McHale, who seemed determined to secure the vice-presidential nomination for McNutt, hoped to stampede the delegates as Willkie had done a month earlier at the Republican convention. Perhaps McNutt wanted nothing more than maximum exposure, or accolades, as he dramatically exited the race for vice president. At any rate, the McNutt campaign printed its own entrance tickets and instructed its supporters to go to a specific gate, where a guard admitted them. Ralph McGill of the *Atlanta Constitution* soon noticed "hundreds of McNutt rooters" in different sections of the gallery. As the nominations began, his supporters in the galleries "led the verbal revolt, cheering McNutt, booing Wallace."[133]

What followed was one of the most dramatic moments of the convention. Robert S. Kerr, a national committeeman (and later a governor and senator) from Oklahoma, placed McNutt's name in nomination, declaring that he did so at the behest of the party's "rank and file." The demonstration that followed was "the loudest and most enthusiastic of the session."[134] One heard cries of "Stay with 'em Paul" and "Go get it Paul," as McNutt ascended the stage, his jaw "set firmly" and his mouth "frowning."[135] Senator Barkley begged the delegates to quiet down. "Standing, tall and bronzed, the perspiration streaming over his handsome features," McNutt struggled to be heard. Eleanor Roosevelt, who had been sent by FDR to address the convention and to help out Wallace, "laughed heartily" at the tumult.[136] She may have been nervous about what might transpire. "McNutt received a tremendous and spontaneous applause," Courtney Letts de Espil observed. "He appeared to be the Willkie of the democratic convention."[137] As McNutt implored the delegates to settle down, a solitary voice rang out: "Come on, Paul!" The columnist Raymond Clapper explained the scene to radio listeners: "McNutt is trying to withdraw his name from nomination but the crowd, the delegates won't let him. This is the first time I've ever seen a candidate cheered down. I've seen a good many of 'em howled down or booed down. The noise is simply terrific and it is all over the hall."[138]

When McNutt managed to speak, he did the minimum expected of him. Without hesitation—and in a clear, loud, and strong voice—he proclaimed that the Democratic Party must "be and remain a united party" headed by "proven liberals and proven leaders" during this time of crisis.[139] "We have such a leader in Franklin Delano Roosevelt," he went on. "He is my commander-in-chief. I follow his wishes, and I am here to support his choice for vice president."[140] Since McNutt never mentioned Wallace by name, his remarks did not qualify as a seconding speech. Before going to the stage, McNutt had shown the draft to Wallace and said: "This is as much as I can do, Henry."[141] He was, Wallace remembered, "an intensely disappointed man."[142]

As the convention reached its climax, FDR got his way on the vice-presidential nomination. The delegates had not liked the way in which Wallace was being foisted on them, and Clapper thought the demonstration for McNutt was "a protest against being dictated to."[143] But the first lady's speech reminded delegates of the crisis overseas, stressing that this was "no ordinary time." Like McNutt, she did not mention Wallace, but instead appealed for a nonpartisan spirit (a reference, perhaps, to the Iowan's Republican roots), discussed the "grave responsibility" her husband faced, and emphasized that he could not carry on "alone."[144] Her address was concise, simple, and effective for it facilitated Wallace's nomination—he received a majority, albeit not an overwhelming one. The remaining votes were dispersed among an array of contenders, led by Speaker of the House William B. Bankhead of Alabama.[145] Thereafter, Roosevelt accepted renomination. In private, he had threatened to withdraw if the delegates rejected Wallace.

The convention ultimately was a triumph for Roosevelt. To be sure, delegates left Chicago fearful of reprisals for breaking the third-term taboo, and party conservatives threatened to remain on the sidelines rather than campaign for the Roosevelt-Wallace ticket. "I had never seen a situation quite like it at a national convention," Robert Woolley remembered. "Imprecations, avowals that they were through with Roosevelt, were done with the Democratic Party, came from the lips of many."[146] The author Bernard De Voto, a liberal Democrat, denounced the convention as "a dreary, inept, directionless, and amateurish show."[147] Nevertheless, Roosevelt had accomplished his aim of nominating a ticket that was "100 per cent New Deal."[148] Here he could thank Ed Kelly, who had proven a most effective champion of a third term, and Eleanor Roosevelt, whose speech had bolstered Wallace's prospects by giving the delegates something her husband had denied them: "a sign of appreciation."[149]

FDR also owed his success to McNutt, who might have wrested the nomination from Wallace. Although McNutt's strength had been inflated by the packed galleries, he had several things working in his favor: McHale's efforts to line up delegates; McNutt's appeal as an alternative to Wallace (instead of the bland Bankhead); and exhortations for him to remain in the race which made a stampede of the convention seem possible. Roosevelt speechwriter Samuel I. Rosenman recalled that McNutt was "the man who we feared would have the best chance of stampeding the convention against Wallace."[150] "The delegates were ugly," Jim Farley later explained. "They did not want Wallace." McNutt thought he had the votes to be nominated, and Ickes concurred: "He probably would have had [the nomination] on the second ballot if the President had not turned thumbs down on him."[151] According to Bob Jackson, McNutt enjoyed the support of farm-belt delegates, Legionnaires, and conservatives upset over Roosevelt's renomination. Jackson "never had any doubt" that McNutt "would have beaten Wallace."[152] Of the major players at the convention, only Barkley questioned that assessment. But the man who took home the nomination disagreed. "There were hundreds of delegates pledged to [McNutt]," Wallace remembered. "The galleries were full of McNutt people" and had the president "kept his hands off" the convention, "McNutt or Will Bankhead would have been named."[153]

May Thompson Evans, assistant director of the Women's Division of the Democratic National Committee, was so taken by the possibility of McNutt's nomination that she insisted on relating the story to an interviewer nearly four decades later: "McNutt had the vice presidency sewed-up . . . [and] another kind of person would have tested his strength against Roosevelt's." But the president selected Wallace, and McNutt withdrew. In the end, Evans explained, McNutt did something extraordinary: "He put loyalty to the leader of a party above his own deep ambition."[154]

Praise like that would have helped McNutt accept what obviously was a defeat. Jackson, like Evans, was "so strongly impressed" by McNutt's withdrawal that he wrote him to commend his "very generous" act.[155] FDR seemed to agree; the president told McNutt that he had come out of Chicago "with colors high."[156] The convention, another Democrat averred, had made McNutt "the most popular New Deal figure in America" after Roosevelt.[157] But as Carleton B. McCulloch, McNutt's supporter in Indiana, put it, the president had "slipped a stiletto under his left shoulder blade."[158] The novelist Booth Tarkington went further, telling McCulloch that McNutt had been badly abused, that his backside was "all porcupined up with sticking-out tomahawks and hunting-knives."[159] It could have been otherwise. If McNutt had the support he claimed, and if he was serious about national office in 1940, he might have copied Bankhead, who, believing that FDR had double-crossed him, remained in the race for vice president. The McNutt forces knew that the president might decline renomination if the convention rejected Wallace. If that happened, McCulloch fretted, "then where would we be?"[160] One possible answer: in a position to inherit the top prize, which had been the campaign's original aim.

By acting as a statesman and leaving Chicago as the "noblest Roman of them all," McNutt was able to rebut charges that he was excessively ambitious *and* keep alive his hopes for higher office.[161] Perkins praised his decision to withdraw. "I probably felt more friendly, more sympathetic and more associated with him at that time than at any other," she explained. "That was because he had swallowed hard and done the right thing."[162] At the same time, Frank McHale wrote to leading Democrats after the convention, offering to continue the "many friendships" and "happy contacts" which the campaign had made over the past two years.[163] McHale analyzed responses to these letters in order to assess McNutt's prospects for 1944. But he remained skeptical. After withdrawing from the vice-presidential race, McNutt told his campaign manager that they could try again in four years. McHale shook his head—1940 had been McNutt's best chance.[164]

Following the convention, McNutt shrank as a possible candidate for national office. Disappointment over not being picked to run for vice president gave way to diminishment, as McNutt became more and more an instrument of Roosevelt's ambition and agenda. The process began gradually, so gradually that McNutt and his team did not notice it. It started with the fall campaign in 1940.

On the surface, McNutt had reason to be confident coming out of Chicago, where he had "played the part of a brave soldier."[165] Rank-and-file Democrats considered him the "choice of the convention."[166] There was much talk about his future. One party hand wrote: "The more one sees and hears of Paul, the more one is impressed with his loyalty, sincerity and ability."[167] The afterglow in which McNutt basked was matched by a "hang-over" experienced at the White House. "In every Democratic huddle in every precinct of America," one Democrat told the president, the mood after the convention was "sour."[168] Accordingly, Roosevelt worked to rebuild bridges. At a meeting with members of the Democratic National Committee (DNC), he and Wallace stressed the "unusual situation" facing the country and pleaded for national unity. Roosevelt sought to enlist several party leaders, including Byrnes and McNutt, to help with the fall campaign. Working together, they would make a "happy ship."[169]

If the Roosevelt campaign could be compared to a seagoing vessel, then the president was definitely the captain, Wallace the first mate, and McNutt little more than a reliable deckhand. It is true that the White House reached out to the Hoosier. Both FDR and Wallace thanked him for what he had done in Chicago. Wallace, Coy noted, "has been very insistent on giving Paul the kind of consideration which his action merited," and Roosevelt wanted McNutt to "play a major part" in the campaign.[170] FDR had been receiving pressure to name McNutt to succeed Farley as chair of the DNC. But the president chose instead Ed Flynn, the Democratic Party boss in the Bronx. Coy reasoned that replacing one New Yorker with another may have represented an effort to appease Farley. If so, it suggested that placating McNutt remained a lesser concern. Moreover, the need for goodwill gestures receded as the party's wounds healed. Denunciations of the president by conservative Democrats served to solidify the president's support among other segments of the party. Moreover, FDR later gained endorsements from conservative Democratic senators Millard Tydings of Maryland and Carter Glass of Virginia. "Once the tumult, the shouting and the angry passions subsided," Woolley remembered, "sane thinking began to return."[171]

McNutt and his staff pried little from the president and his team. Flynn offered to put McNutt in charge of the campaign's western headquarters, but McNutt decided that that position was not sufficiently prestigious. Flynn did name Ewing, one of McNutt's managers, to be his assistant. Otherwise, the only McNutt supporter to enhance his profile was Coy, whose ties to Hopkins (and FDR) were tightening. During the convention, Coy informed the Roosevelt campaign about the forged entrance tickets distributed to McNutt supporters. After the convention, he wrote effusively to Hopkins, calling him a friend and "inspiration."[172] Such deeds and words do not prove that Coy had betrayed McNutt. They do suggest that his loyalty was shifting toward the president and his circle. McNutt, for his part, sensed his own isolation. Coming out of Chicago, Harper found his mentor's attitude "not satisfactory," and he worried that McNutt might take "precipitous action" perhaps by resigning from the administration. Yet McNutt quickly adopted "a more moderate view of the situation."[173] His strategy appeared to be one of working from the inside or, as McCulloch explained, "to stick with the Organization and 'bore from within.'"[174]

In the fall, McNutt turned his guns on the Republican Party and its standard-bearer, Wendell L. Willkie. Although Willkie proved to be a bundle of contradictions, he posed a threat to the president's reelection. He was a native Hoosier at ease living in New York; a utility executive and Wall Street lawyer who exuded an everyman civic-mindedness; and a lifelong Democrat who became a Republican in 1940. With respect to that year's campaign, Willkie's rise began with a series of favorable profiles in such magazines as *Life, Look,* and the *Saturday Evening Post*—some of the same periodicals that had portrayed McNutt so adversely. Willkie's appeal within the GOP appeared to come from the grass roots, though his nomination stemmed, in part, from a sudden stampede of the party convention. Regarding foreign affairs, he stood apart from the other Republican candidates who were by and large isolationist. To the general public, Willkie's rugged features, tousled hair, and disheveled wardrobe projected homespun magnetism. Sensing his appeal, FDR sighed: "We are going to have a heck of a fight on our hands."[175]

But Willkie was hardly a perfect candidate. His speeches seemed exercises in straddling. Willkie endorsed collective bargaining, regulation of big business, federal pensions, and programs to assist farmers while at the same time blasting the New Deal for seeking "safety" over "risk" and "growth." In the area of foreign policy, he backed Roosevelt's promise to extend "to the opponents of force the material resources of this nation" while at the same time accusing FDR of making "inflammatory statements" to foreign governments that were "inciting us to war."[176] An inclination toward nuance, a lack of specifics and focus, and an undisciplined manner of speaking combined to weaken Willkie's effectiveness on the stump. Nevertheless, as his biographer Steve Neal pointed out, he "would wage the most aggressive and vigorous campaign since the 1896 crusade of William Jennings Bryan."[177]

Roosevelt, in contrast, focused on affairs of state and left the task of campaigning to subordinates, such as McNutt. At the outset, McNutt attacked Republican isolationism, asserting that the GOP and Willkie were unable to grasp the need for preparedness.[178] The implication evolved into a personal attack, with McNutt asserting that all Willkie knew was "business."[179] With respect to foreign affairs, he was "an unknown quantity" who lacked FDR's experience and steadiness.[180] McNutt accused Willkie of running with Republican conservatives by extolling free enterprise, and then away from them by endorsing both aid to Great Britain and the Selective Service Act. He also attacked his fellow Hoosier for demanding military conscription at a time when most Republicans in Congress opposed it. According to McNutt, Willkie was "a man without a party."[181] This was a tune sung by other Democratic orators who attempted to make a liability of the Republican nominee's independence. But David Lilienthal, administrator of the Tennessee Valley Authority, read one of McNutt's speeches and dubbed it a particularly "good analysis" of Willkie's "amazing inconsistencies."[182]

McNutt's speeches also carried some drama, for he was campaigning against a former college classmate. According to Lilienthal, the two men even resembled one another: "McNutt reminds me of Willkie in his personal mannerisms, the husky voice, heavy features, [and] heartiness."[183] Following graduation, their career paths had diverged as Willkie moved into business while McNutt entered politics. Nevertheless, Willkie held McNutt in "affectionate regard" and expressed "pride and satisfaction" with his political ascent.[184] When McNutt ran for governor, Willkie volunteered to help. The two men were delegates to the 1932 Democratic Convention, when they both backed Newton Baker against FDR. But by the late 1930s their relationship had changed, as Willkie entered national life as a critic of the administration in which McNutt served. In fact, when members of McNutt's presidential campaign tried to enlist Willkie, he demurred.[185] Willkie denied press reports that he had contributed money to the McNutt campaign, and he distanced himself from the Democratic candidate, noting that they only saw each once a year at fraternity or alumni functions. As his disdain for the Roosevelt administration intensified, Willkie vowed to thwart McNutt if he ran for president on a New Deal platform.[186] When Willkie entered the presidential race in 1940, he made a splash, which sparked talk about "an oversupply of boy orators from Indiana" and the prospect of Indiana University being rechristened a "Prep School for Presidents" if Willkie and McNutt won spots on the national tickets of their parties.[187] That did not happen, and the fall campaign saw McNutt striving to prevent the election of Willkie, whom he had long overshadowed politically.

McNutt campaigned extensively for Roosevelt. He spoke in eastern cities, across New England, and in his native Midwest. At FDR's behest, he visited Seattle to campaign for a Democratic U.S. Senate candidate. McNutt's addresses reiterated themes that he had been honing for over a decade, that the GOP was the party of "talk" while the Democrats had provided "prompt, effective action" in the face of depression at home and aggression abroad.[188] Events overseas entered into his narrative as never before. McNutt compared America at the close of the 1920s to France before the Nazi onslaught—crass and selfish, then weak and prostrate after the "economic *blitzkrieg* of 1929." Unlike France, however, America had a great leader in Roosevelt.[189] And when Willkie attacked Roosevelt as power hungry, McNutt responded. The Republican nominee, he asserted, evinced a hatred for the president "unequaled in any place this side of Nazi Germany."[190] He pressed the point, exhorting one crowd to "vote the straight Democratic ticket if you love your country."[191] Linking Willkie to the Nazis was a especially vicious attack, given the Republican nominee's German ancestry.

McNutt's strong efforts stemmed from several considerations. First, he loved the Democratic Party and he wanted it to succeed. He also enjoyed giving speeches and was good at it—McNutt's keynote address to Connecticut's state convention "had the crowd on its toes."[192] Mainly, though, a good performance on the stump in 1940 would improve his prospects for national office in 1944.[193] The White House certainly did nothing to muzzle McNutt. To the contrary, John R. Boettiger, the president's son-in-law and the editor of the *Seattle Post-Intelligencer*, advised giving him more "ammunition" against Willkie.[194] And Jerome N. Frank, the chair of the Securities and Exchange Commission, later praised McNutt's "most effective" speeches on behalf of Roosevelt's reelection.[195]

What McNutt thought about being used in this manner is unknown. Rather than discuss his feelings, he busied himself with campaigning. McNutt spoke in "an easy, often conversational style" that gave "vigor" to his remarks.[196] But he also projected anger. Journalists characterized his attacks on Willkie as "militant," "two-fisted," "slashing," and "bitter."[197] McNutt's harshness probably did not reflect his true feelings toward the Republican nominee; during one soiree, Lilienthal noticed that McNutt had avoided "any cracks about Willkie."[198] Memories of the Chicago convention perhaps fueled McNutt's feistiness on the stump. Regarding his own disappointment, he let down his guard only once. Near the end of the 1940 campaign, a voter asked how it felt "campaigning for the presidency for someone else." McNutt replied: "I have no illusions about politics."[199]

McNutt also had no illusions about his political base in Indiana, which was shrinking. The GOP had been making gains in the Hoosier State, and Republican leaders believed that after seven years of the New Deal, sans economic recovery, they would overwhelm the party of McNutt and Roosevelt. Indeed, in March 1940, Lorena Hickok reported that some Indiana Democrats doubted whether McNutt himself would be able to carry the state that year. Partly for that reason, the Hoosier Democrats drifted away from the liberalism of the past decade. At its convention, the state party nominated for governor Lieutenant Governor Henry F. Schricker, a conservative known for his political acumen, ties to farmers and local party officials, trademark white hat, and distance from the McNutt machine. Opposing him was Republican Glenn R. Hillis of Kokomo. In the U.S. Senate race, Sherman Minton carried the Democratic standard against Raymond Willis, a newspaper publisher who had barely lost to Frederick Van Nuys in 1938.[200]

In many ways, 1940 was a rerun of earlier campaigns in Indiana during the McNutt era. Republicans cast Minton as a "New Deal Yes-man" and a product of the Two Percent Club.[201] The state GOP raged against extravagance, waste, taxation, liquor laws, the reorganization act, and two terms of "boss ridden, machine controlled, racket-infested government."[202] Despite these attacks, Minton and McNutt focused on the presidential contest. Minton was "almost completely devoted to defending Roosevelt and attacking Willkie."[203] The senator feared that if the president failed to carry Indiana, no Hoosier Democrat would win. McNutt seemed to agree with that ordering of priorities; in one of his last speeches of the 1940 campaign, delivered in Indiana, McNutt discussed national and international issues exclusively.[204]

Having McNutt address state issues probably would not have boosted the Hoosier Democrats. To be sure, McNutt's energy might have provided a lift, as it had in 1934 and 1936. But having him stump for the state ticket would have reminded voters of his excesses as governor and, perhaps, the recent brouhaha over his finances. Besides, by the end of the 1930s, the nation was turning against the New Deal—Roosevelt ran in 1940 on foreign, not domestic, issues—and this trend was most evident in the historically Republican farm states, including Indiana. Schricker, whose nomination was neither supported nor opposed by the McNutt forces (they merely accepted him to keep the party united behind McNutt's national ambitions), probably did as well as any Democrat might have. The only thing that could have helped the state ticket was a visit by Roosevelt. Minton, in fact, later lamented the president's failure to visit Indianapolis that autumn.[205]

As the contest drew to a close, foreign affairs assumed center stage, and the verbal sallies intensified. Republican leaders had been accusing Roosevelt of leading the nation into war, and Willkie, in a desperate bid for votes, joined this line of attack. He at one point declared that if Roosevelt's promise to keep America out of war was as good as his pledge to balance the budget then "they're already almost on the transports."[206] These were serious charges, which the president answered in a late-campaign swing. He told a crowd in Boston: "Your boys are not going to be sent into any foreign wars."[207] McNutt, in turn, averred that the Democratic Party "is not a war party" and that the president "has done more to save the peace of the world" than anyone alive.[208] And he again reminded audiences of "the mutual hatred of Willkie and Hitler and Mussolini for the President of the United States."[209] He was not the only Democrat to resort to such attacks. Such rhetoric was a preview of coming partisan attractions—or distractions—during World War II. As the historian Richard Polenberg has explained, "few could resist the temptation, at one time or another, to regard a political enemy as an enemy of the nation, or to claim that an opponent's victory would aid the Axis."[210]

McNutt's assaults can be read in several ways. In the short run, they garnered him modest attention in the back pages of the national press. In the long run, however, he regretted them. After Willkie died in 1944, McNutt visited his widow to say that he was "ashamed" of some of the things he had said about her husband.[211] But McNutt's attacks also illustrated how much he had shrunk politically. The Republican nominee directed his fire at the president rather than at Roosevelt's surrogates. During the campaign, Willkie apparently mentioned McNutt only once, in Indiana, when he ridiculed FDR's decision to seek a third term. To make the point that Roosevelt was not an "indispensable" leader and to remind voters that FDR had bossed the Democratic convention, Willkie jibed: "Why didn't he permit the nomination of Paul McNutt? Heaven knows, Paul wanted it."[212]

At the end of the day, Roosevelt triumphed once again. By vowing to keep America out of war, FDR stopped Willkie's momentum and garnered fifty-five percent of the popular vote against forty-five percent for his opponent. Even though Willkie lost, he gave the president a tough race and the nation its closest presidential election since 1916. And he emerged from 1940 a figure of national renown. By defying Republican isolationists, he earned the respect, even affection, of large segments of the electorate.[213]

In Indiana, which Willkie won, the Republicans had more concrete reasons to celebrate. Willis beat Minton, and although Schricker held on to the governorship for the Democrats, he did so by the barest of margins—just four thousand votes. For the first time since 1928, the GOP captured both houses of the legislature and a majority of Indiana's twelve-member congressional delegation. In the long run, Indiana politics changed following this election.[214] A decade of Democratic dominance gave way to a half century of Republican ascendancy. Between 1940 and 1992, the GOP held the Indiana governorship for thirty-six out of fifty-two years. Even Democratic governors, in this period, were usually conservative or moderate in outlook. McNutt, by running a less ruthless regime, might have achieved a more united party and thus delayed, or lessened, the extent of Republican control. Yet such hindsight neglects the fact that even Roosevelt, after eight years in the White House, was still struggling to realign the national party along liberal lines.

McNutt was one of the biggest losers in the election. He had been used by FDR, eclipsed by Willkie, and largely abandoned by Indiana Democrats. Mc-Nutt's political standing in the state was withering as Minton left office and the incoming governor owed little to McNutt or his supporters. Furthermore, McNutt could expect little solace from Roosevelt's circle, where he had never been popular. To be certain, he hoped for another shot at the presidency in 1944, and he still had a job in the administration. But in 1940 McNutt's ambition for national elected office had been thoroughly frustrated.

# 12

## DIMENSIONS OF SECURITY
### (1939–1945)

BEING PASSED OVER FOR the vice presidency represented the first serious setback in Paul V. McNutt's political career. And yet he had reason to look forward as 1940 turned into 1941. Scuttlebutt around Washington had McNutt replacing Josephus Daniels as ambassador to Mexico. Others thought that he would head a new cabinet department to oversee public welfare.[1] If these were not the most prestigious assignments, rumors of McNutt occupying them suggested that he still was needed in the administration. His public career was hardly over, and he continued to head the Federal Security Agency (FSA), which oversaw much of the New Deal.

The Federal Security Agency both frustrated and challenged McNutt. He was not an enthusiastic bureaucrat and the period that he headed the FSA, from 1939 to 1945, proved to be one of tremendous change. Among other things, World War II caused McNutt to broaden and deepen his conception of what "security" meant for Americans. The FSA took on new responsibilities, using its health and welfare programs to enhance America's fitness for fighting. It also oversaw the beginnings of the U.S. government's research in biological weapons—an early program of homeland security. The goal of "security," so evident in the social and economic realms in the 1930s, had expanded into the military and international spheres by the 1940s.

McNutt did not lead these changes single-handedly. Not unlike his practice as leader of the American Legion, McNutt used capable assistants to run the FSA while he sold the agency's efforts via public speeches. After proposing to expand Social Security in 1940, he offered no significant changes to existing FSA programs. In a way, World War II salvaged McNutt's tenure at the FSA, for it allowed him and his subordinates to focus on defense-related matters. The agency expanded recreation for service personnel and defense workers, fought prostitution and venereal disease, and served as a cover for the early stages of the biological warfare program. When McNutt left the Federal Security Agency in 1945, its internal structure and future, as a possible cabinet department, remained unsettled. But the agency survived, even thrived, during the Second World War.

The FSA's activities during World War II underscored the superficiality of Roosevelt's famous remark that Dr. New Deal had been replaced by Dr. Win-the-War. To be sure, the Republican resurgence in the elections of 1938 and 1942 spawned a congressional counterattack against FDR's domestic agenda. That, along with the exigencies of war, caused the demise of such agencies as the National Youth Administration (NYA) and Civilian Conservation Corps (CCC), both of which fell under McNutt's jurisdiction. But Roosevelt resolved that World War II would be "a New Deal war."[2] The administration sought to consolidate the gains won by unions; boost public-sector spending; broaden access to employment via an "economic bill of rights"; cultivate entrepreneurs who were friendly toward labor and hostile to monopoly; and cast reform in global terms.[3] A survival instinct animated many New Deal agencies, including McNutt's FSA, which contributed to the war effort and lasted into the postwar era. So, by studying the work of McNutt and his subordinates at the FSA, it is possible to trace economic security programs of the 1930s through World War II and toward the establishment of a cabinet-level Department of Health, Education, and Welfare in 1953. "The end of reform scarcely meant the end of social and economic change," the historian David M. Kennedy has asserted, "nor even the end of pursuing those goals the New Deal had championed, especially the goal of security."[4]

By the late 1930s, the Federal Security Agency had emerged as the principal government office responsible for affording Americans a sense of economic safety. The agency was born in 1939, following a two-year-long firestorm over executive-branch reorganization. In 1937 FDR had proposed legislation that would have allowed him wide latitude to reorganize his administration via executive orders. Justified as a means to promote efficiency, the scheme nevertheless sparked cries that the president was seeking dictatorial powers. As a result, Congress approved a mild reorganization bill that permitted Roosevelt to make specific administrative changes, subject to veto by either the House or the Senate. Weeks after the legislation passed, FDR submitted his initial reorganization plan, which included the establishment of the Federal Security Agency to supervise social welfare. The White House chose the name Federal "Security" Agency to link it with Social Security and to placate an increasingly conservative Congress, for which the word "welfare" was anathema.[5] International threats played some role in the new agency's name; Roosevelt asserted that a revamped, revitalized U.S. government featuring the Federal Security Agency would impress upon aggressive dictatorial regimes that America could be "tough as well as tender-hearted," that is, serious about national as well as economic security.[6] In the end, the House upheld both the reorganization plan and the FSA, which Roosevelt invited McNutt to head.

McNutt enjoyed a wide mandate at the Federal Security Agency. In announcing the reorganization plan, Roosevelt explained the purpose behind the FSA in general terms: "to promote social and economic security, educational opportunity and the health of the citizens of this Nation."[7] Its administrator had the authority to issue procedural "orders, rules, and regulations," although McNutt was urged to leave "routine activities" in the hands of the FSA's many component offices, advice that he largely followed.[8] The emphasis on component offices was significant, for the Federal Security Agency was a hodgepodge. To be fair, the establishment of the agency made sense, for it united "the health and welfare activities of the federal government."[9] Yet the FSA brought together such independent entities as the Social Security Board (SSB), the Civilian Conservation Corps, and the National Youth Administration. It also acquired the Office of Education from the Department of the Interior, the Food and Drug Administration from Agriculture, and the Public Health Service (PHS) from Treasury.[10] Welding together these disparate parts made for a "tremendously difficult administrative job." That was the judgment of Oscar Ewing, a McNutt confidant who later headed the FSA.[11] According to Jack B. Tate, general counsel for the Social Security Board, the FSA pulled together "the do-good agencies," but it also aroused resentment from the "strong-minded heads" of these agencies, who resisted any diminishment of their authority.[12] Secretary of Labor Frances Perkins sensed as much when she congratulated McNutt on inheriting one of the "most challenging and difficult jobs in the country."[13]

Complicating matters was the potential for conflict between McNutt and career civil servants. Officials at the Social Security Board saw their work as exceptionally important, valued their autonomy, took pride in their mission, and saw McNutt as an interloper who would use the board to advance his fortunes.[14] For that reason, they distrusted him. There also was concern that McNutt knew little about the FSA's programs and was not inclined to learn about them. "His very presence," the historian John A. Salmond wrote, "was galling to men who for a long time had been used to running their own organization in their own way, responsible only to the President."[15]

One person who enjoyed such a relationship with FDR was Arthur J. Altmeyer, chair of the Social Security Board. The contrast between Altmeyer and McNutt was plain. Altmeyer, with his spectacles, bowtie, and PhD from the University of Wisconsin, was "an intellectual and a scholar who cared deeply about the cause of social insurance."[16] He possessed a "cold, practical, technical plodding nature" exemplified by a love of "figures, tables and charts" and a penchant for "careful, meticulous, and well organized" administration.[17] Altmeyer believed that the ideal administrator was diligent, self-effacing, objective, and as interesting to the public "as cold spinach."[18] McNutt, who arrived at the office in a limousine, did not fit that mold. Although the two men clashed, Altmeyer nevertheless considered McNutt a "kind gentleman" who "never bore any animus" over their disagreements.[19] McNutt in turn valued Altmeyer's expertise and managerial skill. Overall, they complemented each other. Altmeyer was a workhorse who enjoyed access to FDR, largely because the Social Security Board had reported directly to the president. McNutt was a political show horse—and a newcomer in Washington.

In many ways, McNutt was prone to act politically at the FSA. For example, he tangled with John Corson, director of the SSB's Bureau of Old Age and Survivors Insurance, over the hiring of a statistician who had been recommended by Secretary of War Harry Woodring. When Corson opposed the appointment, McNutt tried to have Corson removed for insubordination. In the end, Corson held on to his job, mainly because Altmeyer stood by him. Another example of McNutt's allowing politics to influence his decisions involved old-age assistance grants to Ohio. In October 1938 the Social Security Board had found Ohio's government guilty of misuse of federal funds and the Democratic governor, Martin Davey, responsible for using old-age assistance to court elderly voters.

The board declined to provide the state with any federal dollars until the problem was fixed. It was—quickly. Thereafter, Ohio's congressional delegation pushed legislation to restore the grants their state had lost in the interim. The bill was a small measure, geared to Ohio, and McNutt endorsed it. But Altmeyer did not. The Social Security chief appealed to the president, who vetoed the bill on grounds that, if passed, it would encourage corruption and political favoritism in the disbursal of old-age assistance. So, while McNutt understood party politics—he had informed Ohio's congressional delegation that he backed the bill—Altmeyer prevailed in bureaucratic politics in part by exploiting his close ties to Roosevelt.[20]

McNutt should not be condemned too harshly. A certain amount of political posturing could be expected from him. "A few critics," the historian George Q. Flynn noted, "complained because he was a dedicated politician, as though such a vocation were unique to government and precluded meritorious work."[21] Moreover, McNutt was more committed to the FSA's programs than his detractors claimed. As governor, he had exhorted the Indiana General Assembly to participate in the Social Security program, and he had asked members of Social Security Board to help him "sell the legislature the most liberal [public welfare] bill [they] could devise."[22] He also wanted to compile an outstanding record at the FSA. Sensing as much, Jack Tate, the general counsel at Social Security, told his regional attorneys: "McNutt wants to be President of the United States. In order to be President of the United States he's got to do a good job. In order to do a good job, we've got to help him. Does anybody want any more than that?" They all answered: "No."[23]

McNutt, in turn, expected loyalty from his subordinates. Upon becoming federal security administrator, he appointed liaisons to the various offices within the FSA. McNutt also asserted control over the agencies' information desks, accounts, merit appointments, and counsels. He reassigned the lawyers at the Social Security Board to his own staff and insisted on receiving their strongest support. He once asked Tate if he could count on his loyalty. Tate replied that he could. "All right" was McNutt's reply.[24]

Over time, McNutt developed an administrative style to guide the Federal Security Agency. He more or less functioned as a figurehead. McNutt tapped capable individuals to run the agency, which freed him to give speeches on FSA-related issues. According to Altmeyer, McNutt took a "permissive" approach to "the constituent units of the agency" rather than assert his authority over them.[25] Maurine Mulliner, an official at the SSB, remembered McNutt as "a sweet, kindly man" who "never took hold [of the FSA] at all."[26] On the stump, McNutt projected otherwise. "He could make a magnificent public speech," Tate recalled. "You could hand him a speech and he'd go out and in ten minutes make the speech and it would look as though he'd thought it over all his life."[27] The arrangement worked, largely because of McNutt's superb staff. It included such longtime associates as Fowler Harper, the Indiana University law professor who became general counsel at the FSA, and Wayne Coy, who was deputy administrator. John Corson, who was no unbiased observer, thought Coy's capabilities exceeded McNutt's.[28] Rather than indulge in such comparisons, Mulliner simply praised Coy as "extremely able."[29] He projected "horse sense" as well as a knack for "getting things done."[30]

During McNutt's years at FSA, his relationships with Harper and Coy changed. According to Tate, Harper exuded near-complete "adoration" of McNutt. Yet he also stood up to his boss. Harper once disagreed so fiercely with McNutt that he threatened to resign. After McNutt told him to go ahead, a "surprised" Harper backed off.[31] Coy was another matter, for he and McNutt had been drifting apart for some time. The distance originated during the mid-1930s when Coy headed the Works Progress Administration (WPA) in Indiana and grew acquainted with Harry Hopkins, who ran the WPA nationally. The connection between Coy and Hopkins was evident by the time of the 1940 convention, when Coy seemed almost as loyal to the White House as to the McNutt campaign. In the interim, while Coy was serving under McNutt in the Philippines, he received a glowing press as McNutt's "One-Man Brain Trust."[32] Wayne and his wife, Grace, also began moving in the same social circles as Paul and his wife, and Kathleen McNutt did not like that. At one point, Kathleen reminded Grace that the Coys were not in the same league as she and Paul. In time, the two women ended their quarrel. When Wayne Coy entered the hospital in August 1939 with kidney aliments, Kathleen conveyed her concern. He recovered, but his friendship with Paul did not. Coy continued to receive fawning newspaper profiles, and in 1941 he left the FSA to join the White House staff. At that point, Booth Tarkington reckoned that McNutt could "*barely* bear" the "elevation" of "Coy-Boy."[33]

Coy's illness, which lasted from 1939 to 1940, opened an administrative void at the Federal Security Agency, and Mary Elizabeth Switzer, a career civil servant, helped to fill it. Switzer was a remarkable figure, a graduate of Radcliffe College with a degree in international law who went to work for the Department of the Treasury during the 1920s. She rose to become an assistant to the secretary of the treasury in charge of the Public Health Service (PHS), and, as such, she went with the PHS when it was transferred to the FSA. As a professional, Switzer was poised, confident, diligent, and enthusiastic. Switzer and McNutt shared many things in common—a fondness for the theater, football games, a cocktail, and a good book (Switzer's correspondence revealed a familiarity with Shakespeare, Egyptology, whodunits, and the more cerebral titles on best-seller lists). Mainly, though, she was a warm person whose missives conveyed good cheer at Christmastime, wistful memories of her native New England, and pride over her house in Virginia, where she lived with her partner, Isabella Diamond. The reserved McNutt responded positively to such personalities, as seen in his dealings with Manuel L. Quezon. After McNutt's death, Kathleen told Switzer that "Paul loved, admired and appreciated you."[34]

McNutt's relationship with Switzer said much about him, his administrative style, and key aspects of his character. It revealed McNutt's ability to change and adapt by bringing new people into his official family. As a woman and a lesbian, Switzer represented a departure from the all-male, heterosexual makeup of McNutt's circle, which had stretched back to his leadership of the American Legion. Switzer's intellectual roots also broke sharply with the anti-Communist message that McNutt had peddled to Legion audiences. She described herself as a "radical" in college and, like many idealistic people during the 1930s, had expressed some sympathy for the Soviet Union.[35] McNutt's willingness to take such a person into his confidence can be explained by the fact that Switzer concealed, and later revised and outgrew, her leftist infatuations. Her boss, too, had changed from his days as leader of the Legion.[36]

Switzer and McNutt shared other bonds. They both believed in the welfare state, albeit as practical rather than crusading liberals. Switzer's approach to policy toward disabled Americans was a case in point. She championed federal support for vocation rehabilitation, a program that she headed from 1950 to 1970, in order to prepare disabled Americans for employment rather than place them on welfare rolls. Her approach drew bipartisan praise, for she proved fiscally conservative, respectful of the states' prerogatives (especially regarding public health), and a close associate of doctors and the American Medical Association. Indeed, her allegiance was to the Public Health Service rather than to the Social Security Board, which she often disparaged.[37] Accordingly, McNutt, rather than Altmeyer, became Switzer's ally and benefactor at the FSA.

McNutt's closeness to Switzer underscored his administrative style. Partly because of Coy's illness, Switzer gained added responsibilities.[38] In addition to the Public Health Service, she oversaw St. Elizabeth's Hospital in Washington, the Food and Drug Administration, and the Office of Vocational Rehabilitation. She later inherited Coy's title "assistant to the Federal Security Administrator," and when McNutt chaired the War Manpower Commission during World War II, she helped mobilize doctors and nurses for military service.[39] Switzer found McNutt to be a "very interesting and satisfying person to work for."[40] She was grateful for the opportunities that McNutt had given her, and she kept in touch with Paul and Kathleen after they left Washington. Kathleen, in turn, praised Mary's loyalty "a source of strength" to Paul.[41] Cooperation between a Democratic politician and a reform-minded woman had been unusual but not unique during the interwar years. Belle Moskowitz was the "organizational genius" behind the administration of Governor Alfred E. Smith of New York, and Frances Perkins, who served as secretary of labor from 1933 to 1945, was close to FDR. Although "not many men in that era could accept a woman as an equal," Smith, Roosevelt, and McNutt were exceptions.[42]

Switzer's relationship with McNutt and the opportunities it opened to her, especially during 1939 and 1940, highlighted the Hoosier's ambition to be president. Switzer was amazed by her boss's energy; McNutt reminded her of "the weighted little toy you spun on the floor" for he "always landed head up."[43] She became "very much interested" in McNutt's presidential aspirations and found it "fun" to be close to his campaign.[44] Yet Switzer observed that McNutt's frequent absences from the office created "difficulties" for the staff at the FSA, as they "tried to pull together five [very] big agencies."[45] Her work, she lamented, consumed "28 hours of every 24."[46] Nevertheless, Switzer hoped that McNutt would obtain "what he desires to have so strongly"—the White House.[47]

McNutt's ambition helped to fuel one of his most significant initiatives as federal security administrator: an overhaul of Social Security. Tackling Social Security was a way for McNutt to demonstrate some leadership and, at the same time, build bridges to party liberals. To be sure, his commitment to Social Security always had been firm. By 1940, the program had won wide, though not universal, acclaim. "Old age pensions are here to stay," the radio commentator Raymond Gram Swing noted. "A candidate for public office who is not for bigger and better pensions finds himself relegated to private life."[48] It was a fate McNutt wished to avoid.

From its inception, Social Security was a subject of intense debate. The program had emerged during the 1930s, when the federal government assumed greater control over the American economy, and in response to a grassroots movement, led by Dr. Francis Townsend, to provide Americans aged sixty or older with a monthly federal pension which had to be spent within thirty days. Roosevelt's answer to the Townsend movement was the Social Security Act of 1935, under which workers would contribute to their own annuities which would be held in reserve by the federal government until they retired. Social Security thus began as an "income maintenance program" for those who paid into it (via payroll taxes) rather than a "tool of poverty alleviation"—or income redistribution—for the population at large.[49] The program did provide states with grants to assist elderly people in need, and it formed a federal-state program to insure the unemployed, aid the blind and the handicapped, and support dependent children. But the public assistance aspect of Social Security "was both stingier in its benefits and much more vulnerable to public hostility than its social-insurance partner."[50]

The insurance dimension of Social Security faced several challenges as well. It did not cover all workers, such as those engaged in agriculture or domestic work. Pension checks were based on what contributors had paid into the system, and no pensions would be available until 1942. In the interim, tax dollars from the program went into the general funds of the U.S. Treasury—a fact that aroused FDR's critics. Republican presidential nominee Alf Landon warned in 1936 that once the government began collecting these taxes it would misspend them. In 1939 Raymond Gram Swing urged replacing the Social Security's large reserve fund with an annual contingent fund. Would Social Security be solvent in fifty years under such financing? "That is something for the United States of fifty years hence to figure out," Swing asserted.[51] But the president feared that if Social Security became financially unstable, it would become politically vulnerable as well.

Such concerns signaled something important: that Social Security "did not instantly become a venerated institution" the moment FDR signed it into law. In fact, during its first four years, the program experienced a "crisis" until Congress passed the Social Security amendments of 1939.[52] These amendments sought to close the gap between the huge reserve fund projected to accrue from Social Security taxes and the distant promise that these pensions would be paid out. They did so by raising monthly benefits for married men, adding a benefit for widows and orphans, and advancing the date when the first Social Security checks would be sent from 1942 to 1940. With the 1939 amendments, Social Security departed from its original aim, of providing insurance for its contributors, and emerged instead as a program of "family protection" (for married couples and widows, chiefly) that was "more redistributive" of wealth.[53] Congress enacted these changes by lopsided majorities. During the debate, there was even talk of going further, by establishing "a universal minimum benefit" for all Social Security recipients.[54]

McNutt entered this fray by favoring a reformed system of Social Security based on a uniform minimum benefit. In 1939 Roosevelt had considered adding such a benefit to the contributory pensions that workers would receive under Social Security. But the impact of the flat-rate concept was unclear. Some liberals favored the proposal because it would allow higher payments to be made immediately. Yet social insurance advocates, such as Altmeyer, believed that a flat-rate benefit would become a cap on payments and lead to a less generous system—which was why some conservatives backed the idea. There were two other problems with a uniform pension: it was expensive to finance, and cost-of-living variations among the states made it difficult to determine what the nationwide benefit should be. In the end, Roosevelt rejected the idea as too costly, and Altmeyer concurred. But a few advisers within the White House continued to push for a uniform national pension, including McNutt, who decided to advocate such a program in a major speech in New York on March 28, 1940.[55]

McNutt's original, unrevised address was rather lukewarm toward the existing system of Social Security, which he called "about as good as we can expect at this stage." McNutt wanted something more: a "flat-rate, universal pension" to be financed through graduated income taxes. For McNutt, the beauty of this proposal was its "simplicity." Since a flat-rate pension did not require the federal government to catalog every worker's earnings and contributions, Social Security could be run with fewer bureaucrats and fewer dollars. The uniform pension idea underscored McNutt's pragmatism and liberalism as well as his ambition. He supported it partly for the same reason Roosevelt had instituted Social Security, to quell support for Townsend-like schemes with their promise of "fantastic"-sized benefits. That said, McNutt's pension plan, with its progressive taxes, was unapologetically redistributive; he insisted that transferring wealth would enhance purchasing power nationwide, stimulate the economy, and curtail the power of monopoly. Most important, McNutt, in his speech, wanted Americans to view security for older people in need as something other than "charity." He believed that a flat-rate pension would end means tests for poor people, place everyone on an equal footing, and make security a "right" for all Americans. But if his thinking on this issue was advancing into the area of rights consciousness, his idea of "security" remained holistic, that is, cognizant of national and international trends. McNutt thought that establishing a sound, uniform system of Social Security would put money in the pockets of needy

Americans, decrease discontent at home, and solidify democracy in the United States at a time when other nations had turned to dictatorship.[56] Of course, advocating a uniform pension did McNutt no harm politically. It renewed his liberal credentials and made him appear to be a leader—a believer in big ideas. It also placed him in competition with Roosevelt on the New Deal's signature program.[57]

McNutt's plan to reform Social Security never materialized. Altmeyer read a draft of McNutt's remarks and warned Steve Early, FDR's press secretary, that the FSA chief was about to contradict the policies of the president and the will of the SSB. Roosevelt agreed, whereupon Altmeyer tried to stop McNutt from making his address. The staff at the SSB prepared a substitute draft, and Ellen Woodward, a member of the board, took it to New York. Woodward handed McNutt the revised address before he spoke. He followed orders. Reading from the SSB draft, McNutt advocated greater federal grants to states to assist old people in need and an expansion of Social Security to include self-employed workers. And he praised the existing social insurance framework for launching "a splendid attack upon one of the gravest of our problems."[58]

This episode said a great deal about McNutt as a policymaker. Not unlike his stand against Philippine independence, he was bold enough to reopen debate on a matter that seemed settled, that is, enactment of a flat-rate, universal pension. His draft speech was full of liberal fight, chastising the United States for being "a latecomer to the practice of social security," praising the "evolution of charities into universal public services" as a "sound" trend, and calling access to such services a "right" for all Americans.[59] Roosevelt, in contrast, remained committed to the "social insurance paradigm," that is, a system based on compulsory contributions, payroll taxes, and fiscal responsibility—and thus likely to withstand the attacks of conservatives in years to come.[60] Both FDR and McNutt, it must be stressed, were mixing liberal principles, practical considerations, and a grasp of political realities even as they developed different visions—and versions—of Social Security.

McNutt's speech on Social Security also revealed much about his relationship with FDR. In this instance, Roosevelt had to muzzle McNutt because, unlike Philippine independence, Social Security was no side matter for most Americans. On this showdown, McNutt lost out to Altmeyer and then bowed to Roosevelt's wishes, as he would do months later when he withdrew from the race for vice president. To make matters worse, word leaked that McNutt had revised his remarks under pressure. That should have caused members of the press to question his judgment, integrity, and readiness to be president. Reporters, however, were uninterested in McNutt's presidential prospects, which appeared dim in March 1940.[61]

McNutt nevertheless remained interested in the uniform benefit. In April 1940, he stated that the answer to state-level disparities in old-age pensions might be a flat federal payment.[62] Then, in September 1941, McNutt, Altmeyer, Woodward, Perkins, and Secretary of the Treasury Henry Morgenthau Jr. met with Roosevelt to discuss ways of expanding Social Security. But the session amounted to nothing. Morgenthau objected to any broadening of Social Security as fiscally unwise, and Roosevelt backed him by making no commitment to pursue the matter.[63] At this point, FDR preferred to keep Social Security solvent rather than try to extend its reach. Moreover, the timing of the meeting could not have been worse for the president, who was mourning the death of his mother and coping with the crisis overseas.

World War II reinforced and broadened McNutt's conception of security while giving a new mission to the Federal Security Agency. McNutt tied domestic issues—health care, education, and recreation—to efforts to prepare the United States for possible war and, later, to the nation's campaign against the Axis powers. His efforts were not unique; Franklin and Eleanor Roosevelt, among others, recognized a connection between economic security at home and national security abroad. Nevertheless, McNutt proved resourceful in promoting a holistic vision of security by making the FSA relevant to and supportive of the nation's war machine.

With respect to the war, three themes emerged in McNutt's speeches during 1940. First, McNutt catered to the non-interventionist mindset of the American public, especially during the early part of 1940. He insisted that the United States could "provide for security against military invasion" by investing in the upkeep of its land and people. "The chief element of our security," he proclaimed, "lies at home."[64] Second, McNutt carefully distinguished his position from that of the isolationists. He continued to oppose Philippine independence, and he relished attacking Republican isolationists. During an off-the-record event at the National Press Club, McNutt sang a revised version of the Gilbert and Sullivan ditty "I've Got a Little List" which included the verse: "And all those who purport to be an isolationist—They'd none of 'em be missed—They'd *none* of them be missed."[65] Lastly, McNutt stressed the need for arms expenditures in a dangerous world and parroted Roosevelt by advising Americans to "distinguish between right and wrong" in the European war. Making moral judgments about the war, McNutt knew, would benefit the embattled democracies and leave Hitler with "no illusions about our sympathies."[66]

McNutt's rhetoric against the Axis and for preparedness intensified following the Nazi invasion of western Europe. As German forces plowed through France, McNutt stressed that "indifference to the outcome of this tragic struggle means indifference to the future of the United States." Like FDR, McNutt averred that the United States could avoid war, not via a policy of isolation, but by participation in geopolitics. He backed "extending credits to the democracies," which occurred with the enactment of Lend-Lease in 1941; acquisition of bases in the Western Hemisphere, which Roosevelt accomplished via his destroyers-for-bases deal with Churchill; and meeting "the threat of *total war* with *total preparedness.*" "We will get ready, physically and materially," McNutt resolved. "We will build the greatest military and naval and aerial defenses the world had ever seen."[67] Overall, McNutt strongly defended the president's foreign policy "in tones that belied America's nonbelligerent status."[68] Indeed, letters protesting "the jingoism of Paul McNutt" made their way to the White House.[69]

The role of administration cheerleader carried benefits and drawbacks for McNutt. On the one hand, he found a new and more receptive audience for his long-standing, hard-headed views on foreign and defense policy. McNutt continued to stress that America's security was tied to events in the wider world. And his correspondence betrayed sympathy for the "the peoples of Europe" who had fallen to the "forces of brutal aggression."[70] On the other hand, however, he seemed to be in no position to engage the Axis, and his stewardship of the Federal Security Agency appeared to be floundering. "He's a good administrator," an observer remarked in the fall of 1941. "When does he start?" Supporters as well as detractors noted a lack of initiatives coming from McNutt's agency. "So far," one journalist noted, "the former Indiana Governor has nothing spectacular to his credit as Federal Security Administrator."[71]

Such critics failed to recognize the extent to which the Federal Security Agency had been adjusting to the war effort. The FSA differed from other federal domestic agencies in two ways: "by having a greater concentration of *actual* defense-related activities and by repeatedly emphasizing how even the work it was performing that was *not* explicitly related to defense was nonetheless integral to a broad version of the concept of security."[72] McNutt helped point the way. Two months after the outbreak of war in Europe, he stressed that

America "must retain the offensive" against the "enemies of democracy" and that his Federal Security Agency possessed the "technical facilities for coordinated action" against "insecurity and want."[73] To that end, the FSA's Bureau of Employment Security strove to place job-seekers in defense-related industries while the Office of Education and the NYA worked to train Americans for such employment.[74] The Public Health Service played a key role in promoting sanitation and hygiene for soldiers and defense workers, fighting venereal disease, provisioning hospitals and medical centers, and improving nutrition and physical fitness. The National Defense Advisory Commission (NDAC), the board formed by Roosevelt following the outbreak of war in Europe, added its support by asserting that "health and welfare are an integral part of the national defense program" since "hungry people, undernourished people, ill people are a national liability."[75]

FDR also knew that the Federal Security Agency could be helpful during the crisis. In 1940, the president cast security in international as well as domestic terms. During a fireside chat on national defense, he rejected the "cancellation of any of the great social gains we have made in these past years" and advised that every American had a contribution to make "toward the security of our nation."[76] Following his reelection, Roosevelt affirmed the ties between economic security and national defense by designating, at McNutt's behest, the Federal Security Administrator as the "Coordinator of Health, Welfare, Recreation and Related Activities."[77] In September 1941, FDR placed the program within the White House's Office of Emergency Management and christened it the Office of Defense Health and Welfare Services (ODHWS). Federal bureaucrats dubbed the new agency "Odd House."[78]

The ODHWS had its work cut out for it. As the national government acted to implement selective service and purchase armaments, communities felt the change. Young men departed for military training, factories retooled and churned out war supplies, and people who had been unemployed flocked to industrial centers. Between 1940 and 1941, as David Kennedy has written, the "rising tide of military spending began at last to float the wallowing hulk of the economy out of the slough of depression."[79] Isolated hamlets suddenly became boomtowns. When the U.S. government announced plans to build a shipyard in Seneca, Illinois, the community had just one restaurant and a single hotel to feed and house twenty-seven thousand newcomers. McNutt reminded audiences of such challenges. In one town, defense workers and their families took shelter in empty sewer pipes. Education was another problem; one community, flooded by war workers and their children, had to run a school in a "one-room firetrap." Recreation was another headache. McNutt told of one shipyard town where young boys were charging two dollars to introduce male workers to "local girls." And a remote village barred the entrance of African American soldiers training at a nearby base.[80] McNutt could have cited other examples. In Hampton Roads, Virginia, a sign in front of a public swimming pool warned: "Dogs and Soldiers Not Allowed."[81]

To handle such difficulties, the ODHWS provided limited assistance. Its aim was to help individuals and communities involved in the war effort, as well as servicemen, by promoting "social protection" against prostitution and disease and by improving "health, welfare, and morale." As head of the ODHWS, McNutt coordinated existing federal programs in these areas, many of them located in the FSA—to the point that the work of the ODHWS overlapped with that of FSA.[82] At first, the office responded to requests for assistance from local authorities. But as the need for additional facilities became apparent, the ODHWS pressed for more funding. The Landrum Act of 1940 gave the Federal Works Agency (FWA), sibling of the Federal Security Agency, the power to distribute federal dollars to improve schools, hospitals, waterworks, and other infrastructure in areas affected by the national defense effort. Under this setup, the ODHWS's role was confined to reviewing requests for funding.[83]

In the areas of social protection and recreation, the ODHWS and its successor agency, the Office of Community War Services (CWS), went beyond oversight and coordination. Efforts to fight prostitution and to provide servicemen with healthy recreation attracted McNutt's personal attention. He dubbed the problem of recreation "great," and his office worked alongside local authorities to "take advantage of all available facilities and resources" while pressing the Bureau of the Budget to make additional funds available.[84] McNutt's sense of urgency in part stemmed from his experience during World War I, when he had witnessed the army's efforts to educate recruits on the danger of intercourse with prostitutes.

Like many officials in FDR's government, McNutt and his staff associated venereal disease with prostitution. They identified female sexuality as being "potentially dangerous and diseased" while romanticizing the male soldier as a manly, heroic protector who required protection from promiscuous women.[85] Charles P. Taft, McNutt's assistant at the ODHWS, stated that "prostitutes mean venereal disease, just the way a louse means typhus."[86] McNutt was so steeped in conventional, middle-class thinking about sexual propriety and sexual stereotypes that he could not bring himself to utter the word "prostitution" in public; in testimony before a committee of the House of Representatives, he euphemistically denounced the "less desirable commercialized influences" that tempted "the boys in uniform."[87] The meaning behind these words was plain. "The double standard, which took on new life in this period," the historian Marilyn Hegarty has argued, "served to shield numerous servicemen from charges of promiscuity."[88] Women, in contrast, often faced "the long arm of the State."[89]

McNutt fought prostitution with a repressive program that utilized public and private agencies. Believing that the first step was closing brothels, he chose Eliot Ness, the Prohibition agent immortalized by television and Hollywood in *The Untouchables,* as the head of the ODHWS's Social Protection Division. Ness distributed literature about the ill effects of venereal disease, denounced prostitution, and rallied local law enforcement to shut down red-light districts. The May Act of 1941 sanctioned such efforts by making prostitution around military bases a federal crime. Although the Social Protection Division did not eradicate brothels, it posted some gains. Police who refused to close houses of prostitution often heard the threat: "Well, if it's embarrassing for you or if it creates a problem, what about having Eliot Ness come in?" To that they replied, "Oh, no. We'll take care of it."[90]

The crusade against prostitution had serious consequences, especially for women. Backed by the Social Protection Division and the May Act, local law enforcement arrested many women on morals charges who were "neither prostitutes nor venereally diseased."[91] They often subjected them to incarceration, mandatory testing for venereal disease, and a regimen of punishment, counseling, and rehabilitation. Any women who stepped "outside the traditional boundaries of female space" risked being labeled "promiscuous."[92] Nevertheless, many women continued to make their own sexual choices. For example, "Victory Girls" exchanged sexual favors for "a movie, a dance, a Coke or some stronger drink."[93] In this setting, government claims about achieving significant reduction in prostitution or venereal disease were not credible. The closing of brothels merely made it harder, not impossible, for servicemen to satisfy their sexual urges. "It's getting so that a soldier has a devil of a time getting his 'morale' lifted," lamented one man. "Around Daytona Beach [hotels] tell you flatly, if you plan to bring a woman into the tourist cabins you might as well stop right there."[94] And declines in the rate of venereal disease among servicemen derived from the availability of prophylaxis as much as from government campaigns against prostitution and promiscuity. Nevertheless, McNutt only stressed the results, as he saw them, proclaiming that the Social Protection Division was "destroying venereal disease."[95] He supported the division, for he deemed suppression of prostitution to be "of vital importance" and he was adamant about "directing prostitutes and promiscuous women into more socially acceptable ways of life."[96]

McNutt also regarded improved recreation as important to the national defense program, to the point that he helped establish the United Service Organizations (USO). In 1940 McNutt conferred with five private organizations, all of which had provided recreation for servicemen in World War I: the Salvation Army, the Young Men's Christian Association, the Young Women's Christian Association, National Catholic Community Service, and the Jewish Welfare Board. In 1941 these groups, along with the National Travelers Aid Association, joined forces to form the USO. The recreation effort thus entailed a public-private partnership under which the U.S. government acquired land near a military base (or a defense plant), constructed a community center, and leased the building to the USO. At the outset, almost everyone tied to the ODHWS, including Wayne Coy (who had not yet joined the White House staff), believed that recreation for soldiers was the sole domain of the federal government. McNutt thought otherwise, as did Roosevelt. "At my instigation and under my direction," McNutt remembered, "plans were drawn in 1940 for what became the United Service Organizations."[97]

The USO coincided with McNutt's background and core beliefs. Its organizers and volunteers tended to be white, native-born, and either middle class or wealthy. As such, they promoted such bourgeois ideals as "respectability, public decorum, and 'good character.'"[98] The USO based its efforts on several "common faiths"—in God, the brotherhood of man, individual human dignity, and "ethical standards of right and wrong."[99] Toward that end, the organization provided sports facilities, camp shows, books, and religious brochures as well as food, music, and dances where servicemen could meet nice women. As the historian Meghan K Winchell observed, the USO "reified the assumption that white middle-class women were inherently sexually respectable and feminine, thereby strengthening a good girl/bad girl dichotomy."[100] And while the organization endorsed racial equality and integration, it respected segregation in areas where that practice prevailed. When one recalls that McNutt was reared in a middle-class home in a predominantly white environment, that he had met his wife—a good girl—at a dance during World War I, and that his own sexual life revealed nary a blemish, it is clear that the stated values of the USO reflected his own. He remained committed to providing servicemen with "the best influences of their former homes and communities," which included promoting "normal social contacts with decent girls."[101]

Wartime recreation became something of a family effort, as Kathleen McNutt found a niche helping the USO. During World War II, she gradually began to play a larger role in public affairs, even though her distaste for electoral politics continued. In 1942, Kathleen gave a speech praising the vision, courage, and international leadership of Woodrow Wilson, and she volunteered to raise money for Chinese relief. But it was as a hostess at Washington's Stage Door Canteen where Kathleen shone. She spent hours there, "meeting boys in uniform, talking to them at length, introducing them to dancing partners, and showing them the way to the food bar." Her vivacity, warmth, and wit won over many soldiers. Since the Stage Door Canteen opened its doors, one journalist commented, "Mrs. McNutt has been one of the active, and most effective, workers for it."[102]

Paul McNutt did not run the recreation effort by himself. Charles Taft, who became assistant coordinator at the ODHWS after Coy moved to the White House, handled its day-to-day operations. The appointment of Taft, a member of the Cincinnati city council, the son of President William Howard Taft, and the brother of Senator Robert A. Taft of Ohio, may have been the inspiration of Secretary of War Henry L. Stimson, who had served in President Taft's cabinet. Of course, McNutt had worked with Republicans in the past and did do again with Charles Taft, a fellow Legionnaire who had "long been active in religious and community service"[103] Taft performed an array of tasks at the ODHWS and CWS. He clarified the relationship between public and private agencies, battled the Federal Works Agency over turf, and identified areas in need of recreation facilities. He also helped the USO's national chairperson, Thomas E. Dewey, raise seed money for the organization. Such efforts drew praise from people in and out of government. One recreation official noted that the organization that had been a "bawling, brawling brat" when adopted by Taft in 1941 had "grown into sturdy young manhood" under his guidance.[104]

In running the ODHWS, McNutt relied on other capable assistants, such as Mary Switzer at the FSA. Among other things, Switzer helped organize a conference on the importance of nutrition to national defense, worked with the Public Health Service to recruit and assign physicians and nurses for defense-related work, and dispensed federal grants to study military medicine and hygiene. By war's end, Switzer had become the liaison "with all groups working on medical problems in and out of government."[105] She also prodded Americans to maintain good health for the war effort. Switzer appreciated the opportunities McNutt gave her, and she was not alone in this. An official at the ODHWS called working for McNutt "a great satisfaction because you are free to go ahead and do your own job."[106]

McNutt supported his underlings by speaking tirelessly on behalf of their programs. In November 1941, Carleton McCulloch reported that his fellow Hoosier "had spent six of his last eight nights on the sleeper, carrying the torch here, there, and everywhere."[107] As an experienced orator with a range of life experiences, McNutt made his case for better health and nutrition in a number of ways. As a former professor, he naturally cited "medical authorities" who stressed that "efficiency and stamina depend on proper food."[108] As a midwesterner, he employed homespun analogies: "Your grandmother knew the secret [to good health]. So did mine. An Indiana farm dinner."[109] As a politician, he spoke in aphorisms, declaring that "Food is vigor. And vigor is victory."[110] Although McNutt never found policies related to nutrition, health, and recreation as interesting as electoral politics or foreign and military affairs, he enjoyed giving speeches and saw the need to peg the FSA's mission to the war effort. Along with FDR, McNutt made the case that "a narrow focus on violent, man-made, geostrategic threats is a poor recipe for security" and that a successful program for national defense "depends heavily on the nation's human and regulatory infrastructure." Accordingly, during World War II, "most FSA bureaus experienced marked budget increases, growing administrative responsibilities, and continuity of their organizational lease on life."[111]

The ODHWS, which technically was outside the FSA, and Community War Services, which was under the agency, posted both breakthroughs and setbacks. On the negative side, staff members complained of a lack of hands; of a job "too big"; of regional offices inclined toward "scurry and improvisation"; of fights with the FWA; and of budget cuts as the war drew to a close.[112] Furthermore, a systematic effort to alleviate shortages in housing, water, and other services did not begin until 1943, when the War Production Board intervened. But the campaigns on behalf of nutrition and recreation helped to raise public consciousness of these issues. States organized recreation committees, and there was talk about forming a cabinet-level Department of National Recreation after the war. And the USO, founded with McNutt's assistance, opened new opportunities for entertainers while bringing, as Dwight D. Eisenhower observed, "cheer and laughter" to soldiers on every "fighting front."[113] Such accomplishments gratified those who had served at the ODHWS and CWS. "We had fun didn't we?" one man wrote Charles Taft. "The kind that you can have only in worthy and sincere work."[114]

Child care proved a mixed bag at best. The ODHWS and CWS located sites for day care centers, the FWA eventually approved them, and the federal government built 2,800 such facilities which accommodated a total of 130,000 children. Unfortunately, day care centers often "were not ready when and where they were needed."[115] Part of the problem was the Landrum Act, which spun a "bureaucratic tangle" that delayed the granting of funds for new facilities, and the lukewarm response to legislation sponsored by Senator Elbert D. Thomas, an Oklahoma Democrat, to finance child care specifically. In the end, Thomas's bill succumbed to "agency infighting" over how extensive child care should be and reservations about establishing a federally funded system that might outlast the war.[116] Leaders of the Roman Catholic Church also lobbied against this measure out of fear that it would encourage women to remain in the workforce and shun their child-rearing responsibilities. (And not every working mother was willing to place her children in day care.) Taft, as one might expect, had the chore of trying to shepherd Thomas's bill through Congress, for McNutt showed little interest in child care and never championed the idea.[117]

With respect to physical fitness, McNutt acted in an adroit way that avoided the criticism that had bedeviled Eleanor Roosevelt, who had run the project from the Office of Civilian Defense (OCD). As assistant director of the OCD, the first lady, like McNutt, took an expansive view of national defense. She wanted civilians to prepare for emergencies, upgrade their job skills, and volunteer at a range of community institutions. Mainly she wanted to use civilian defense to lift civilians' morale. The more attention-grabbing aspects of Eleanor Roosevelt's efforts included instituting lunchtime dancing sessions as a way to promote physical activity and enlisting the dancer Maris Chaney to develop a recreational program for children. Such a perceived boondoggle excited a furor in Congress and forced the first lady to resign from the OCD. Upon inheriting the physical fitness program, McNutt slashed its budget and staff. Separating himself from past extravagances was something that McNutt had to do, the diplomat William R. Castle chuckled, lest he too become a laughingstock—"a candidate for President must avoid that at all costs."[118] But, through his actions, McNutt also suggested that exhortation, rather than taxpayer dollars, was what Americans needed to shape up physically.

Through the ODHWS, the CWS, and the wartime efforts of the FSA, Mc-Nutt's thoughts on how to manage the home front began to emerge. He stressed the importance of private action and local entities as America's first line of defense. Here, he cited existing realities as well as historical precedents—communities oversaw the Selective Service boards; states assembled the National Guard; and cities and other localities provided recreation and policed sexual vice. In so arguing, McNutt spoke as an idealistic veteran of the Great War who believed—or hoped—that the current global crisis would spark citizens to volunteer in defense of their country. He also sounded like a practical politician when he acknowledged that the United States comprised different regions, communities, and individuals all inclined to act independently.[119]

McNutt's words partly reflected the fact that American politics was turning in a conservative direction. Republican gains in the midterm elections of 1942, along with the nation's focus on the war, had diminished the possibility of further New Deal enactments. The GOP's resurgence produced what the radio commentator Raymond Gram Swing dubbed "a renewal of factionalism" between congressional conservatives and the president.[120] Roosevelt responded by promoting the goal of economic security rhetorically rather than legislatively. During his State of the Union address in 1943, FDR stressed that Americans wanted "assurance against the evils of all the major economic hazards—assurance that will extend from the cradle to the grave. And this great Government can and must provide this assurance."[121] A year later, Roosevelt renewed the liberal fight by calling for passage of a postwar economic bill of rights. Coming on the heels of FDR's remark about Dr. Win-the-War, this speech surprised some commentators, who quipped that Dr. New Deal "obviously has not taken down his shingle."[122]

During World War II, McNutt also remained a devoted New Dealer who saw a role for the federal government in helping communities finance infrastructure, hospitals, and recreation, as Roosevelt's Works Progress Administration had done. It is true that McNutt, as head of the FSA, accepted the liquidation of the Civilian Conservation Corps and the National Youth Administration, but their demise had been almost certain. A major purpose behind the CCC had been to provide relief via work and that need receded, along with unemployment, as the nation mobilized for war. The NYA was a bit different, for it gave young people vocational training and work-related grants to help them remain in school. As America prepared for possible war, the NYA's director, Aubrey Williams, placed less emphasis on assisting students and more effort into preparing people for defense-related work. Yet Congress, led by a coalition of Republicans and southern Democrats, was determined to prune government expenditures by ending as many New Deal programs as possible, including the CCC and the NYA.[123]

McNutt resisted efforts to terminate the CCC and NYA, arguing that that their activities were "fully justified."[124] As a former soldier, he was drawn to the Civilian Conservation Corps, in which the U.S. Army ran camps for men engaged in forestry and conservation-related work. As the country mobilized and the army withdrew officers from the corps, McNutt, after some prodding by Roosevelt, proposed using CCC camps to train leaders drawn from America's universities. The plan, which sought to imbue young men with a spirit of public service, stirred controversy as columnists and ordinary citizens condemned its doe-eyed idealism and militaristic overtones. Criticism of the staff-college concept, as it came to be called, undermined the once-popular CCC, leading Roosevelt, McNutt, and other administration officials to jettison the proposal. Two years later, in 1942, McNutt defended the CCC in testimony before the Senate Committee on Education and Labor. But his words, braced by a letter of support from FDR, failed to save the CCC. McNutt's argument that the NYA could help train defense workers also had scant effect. Failure to appreciate NYA's job-training efforts, he complained, epitomized Americans' resistance to shouldering the responsibilities of "total war."[125]

For McNutt, total war was reason enough to enlarge the welfare state. Since the troops needed to be fit, better health care and nutrition had to become available via "free school lunches, the food stamp plan, and low-cost milk."[126] Invoking Roosevelt's wartime Four Freedoms, McNutt in 1943 credited Social Security with building "a substantial foundation for freedom from want."[127] Accordingly, he backed the extension of Social Security to all members of the armed services and advocated a national program of unemployment insurance to replace the existing federal-state setup. "The health and welfare of the American people," McNutt told a House panel, "constitute national problems and will have to be dealt with really on a national scale." As head of the War Manpower Commission, McNutt continued to weigh the merits of voluntary versus government action and of utilizing federal, state, or local power. But the New Deal remained central to his political philosophy. In response to a charge that FDR had transformed the American state into the "savior of all of the people," McNutt replied: "Governments exist for servicing the people."[128] "The Federal Government," he once matter-of-factly proclaimed, "has accepted a major responsibility for basic security."[129]

In pursuit of that aim, Roosevelt and McNutt sacrificed vulnerable programs, such as the CCC and NYA, in order to maintain popular ones, like Social Security, during an era of global crisis. While there is no evidence that FDR or McNutt intentionally traded one reform for another—Social Security was never on the chopping block—their pragmatism must be stressed. Roosevelt had selected McNutt to be federal security administrator on the assumption that his accomplishments in Indiana, combining humane governance with fiscal responsibility, could be replicated at the FSA, leaving its programs slimmer, stronger, and better able to survive conservative attacks. And protecting Social Security, the New Deal's most precious reform, from insolvency and criticism was one reason why FDR had squelched McNutt's proposal for a uniform national benefit. At the same time, Roosevelt knew when to bow to reality and accept the end of depression-era work-relief agencies that had lost their political viability and economic utility.[130] McNutt may have been more forceful than the president in defending the CCC and the NYA, which were important offices in his Federal Security Agency, but his protests had little effect. Nevertheless, the goal of economic security endured, for it had been overshadowed, rather than replaced, by the pressing need to promote national and homeland security during World War II.

Through the Federal Security Agency, McNutt entered a field which Americans would come to call "homeland security": he had a hand in developing the nation's biological warfare program. At first glance, dealing with biological weapons would seem a stretch for the FSA. But the agency oversaw the Public Health Service, and the federal security administrator had advocated preparedness and total warfare. Moreover, McNutt wanted to be near the battlefield, and the study of biological warfare brought him closer to the actual fighting. The enemy had used poison gas in World War I, and McNutt, among others, feared that history would repeat itself. Secretary of War Stimson told President Roosevelt that although biological warfare involved "dirty business," the country had to be prepared to deal with it.[131]

McNutt was in step with Stimson. As American participation in World War II became a possibility, Roosevelt asked McNutt to investigate "quietly" the matter of biological warfare.[132] The Public Health Service conducted an initial survey, and McNutt remained interested in the subject. In January 1941 he met and corresponded with Isaac Silverman, a psychiatry professor at Georgetown University, who predicted that Germany would resort to biological warfare.

Silverman's warning aroused little interest at the PHS or from Dr. Vannever Bush, chair of the National Defense Research Committee. Yet McNutt took it seriously, asserting that "we cannot be too alert" about biological attacks.[133] Such concerns intensified after America entered the war. In 1942, FBI director J. Edgar Hoover told McNutt that German doctors had arrived in Tokyo to teach the Japanese "the art of bacterial warfare."[134]

By the time of Hoover's warning, the government's study of biological warfare was well under way. In October 1941 Stimson asked the president of the National Academy of Sciences to form a committee to examine the subject. Six months later, a panel known as the WBC Committee (an empty acronym) advised the U.S. government to study every angle of biological warfare and prepare for any possible attack. Agreeing with this advice, Stimson pressed Roosevelt to establish a research unit within the government. The secretary of war recommended that the project be concealed within a civilian agency. He suggested McNutt's Federal Security Agency, largely because of its association with the PHS. The president concurred and with that the War Research Service (WRS) was born.[135]

The War Research Service worked quietly and effectively for three years. The office received its budget from a special $25 million appropriation that allowed Roosevelt to finance national defense projects "of a confidential nature."[136] Structurally, the WRS consisted of three divisions: research/development, administration, and information/intelligence. In addition to coordinating research by civilian agencies of the federal government, it contracted with scientists at universities and institutes across the nation to study diseases related to biological warfare. The government underwrote salaries, materials, and equipment in order to explore the dangers deriving from anthrax, dysentery, tularemia (rabbit fever), mussel poisoning, and fowl plague. The work was top-secret; scientists with WRS contracts held the title "Medical Consultant" rather than "Research Bacteriologist."[137] This secrecy extended to the National Academy of Sciences, which advised the War Research Service via its ABC Committee (another empty acronym), and paralleled efforts by the government of Great Britain, which situated its biological warfare program within the Ministry of Supply. In fact, the WRS shared information with British and Canadian scientists. It also founded a laboratory at Camp Detrick in Maryland and financed twenty-four projects until 1944, when the War Department took charge of the program. By all accounts, Stimson and his team had been satisfied with the accomplishments of the War Research Service, and McNutt himself initiated the transfer of most of its projects to the War Department. By 1944, the mission of the WRS had advanced beyond laboratory study, and the time had come for the military to assume responsibility for its work.[138]

In the interim, McNutt again relied on capable assistants to run the War Research Service. To serve as director, he tapped another Republican, the pharmaceutical entrepreneur George W. Merck Jr. The selection of Merck settled a knotty problem. FDR wanted the person who headed the biological warfare program to be both experienced and sympathetic to his administration. Although Roosevelt rightly wanted the person in charge to be trustworthy and discreet, the president's stipulation "shocked" Stimson, who apparently did not expect political considerations to be injected into a "purely scientific appointment."[139] When FDR rejected the secretary's first choice for the post, Stimson went to McNutt, who proposed Merck. The secretary of war deemed Merck a "fine fellow" and he credited the selection to McNutt.[140] At a time when Merck's pharmaceutical company was working to manufacture penicillin and develop the first antibiotic capable of controlling tuberculosis, its head went to Washington to oversee the biological warfare program.[141]

As an administrator, Merck proved a superb choice. He worked part-time, without pay, and with the title of "special assistant" to the federal security administrator.[142] He received considerable authority to oversee the agency and, like Switzer, appreciated McNutt's support. McNutt returned the compliment, praising Merck's "executive drive" and "tact."[143] Merck had to be a diplomat, for he coordinated researchers at the Departments of Interior, Agriculture, and War; the armed services; and the National Academy of Sciences. He also was tough. When the army commander in Hawaii dismissed Merck's call to vaccinate Hawaii's population against yellow fever, Merck mobilized a consensus in the government to send a PHS officer to Honolulu and the inoculations proceeded. Merck proved so effective as an administrator that Stimson brought him into the Department of War to serve as special consultant on biological warfare. McNutt was likewise impressed, and he tried to arrange some form of public recognition for Merck after the war.[144]

As one might expect, McNutt continued to lean on Switzer, whose fluency in health policy made her an asset to the War Research Service. Switzer was one of four people in McNutt's office authorized to know anything about the work of the WRS.[145] Among other things, she monitored the expenditure of government funds by scientists holding WRS contracts, acted to smooth relations between researchers and their home institutions, oversaw the transfer of most WRS projects to the War Department in 1944, and served as acting director of the WRS following Merck's departure.[146] When the War Research Service ceased all operations in 1947, Switzer had in her files two of the four copies of the agency's top-secret official history. McNutt trusted Switzer, and Merck praised her as a "grand help."[147]

Overall, McNutt had a modest role in shaping the War Research Service. As with the FSA and the ODHWS, he functioned like a chief executive officer, delegating wide responsibility to subordinates while handling a few essential tasks himself. For example, McNutt approached Roosevelt about the agency's budget and secured the requisite funding for it.[148] McNutt approved all contracts between the WRS and its researchers, and, when necessary, he telephoned university officials to gain the services of their scientists. In such a top-secret endeavor, he had no speeches to give. According to the historian Barton J. Bernstein, McNutt would put nothing in writing about "particular projects or other details."[149] Privately, however, he expressed pride in the biological warfare project. "No one wished to take responsibility for spearheading and directing it," McNutt wrote, as he commended Merck in 1946. "In the early days of the war there was resistance to even thinking about the use of this weapon, even to the extent of establishing defensive measures against it."[150]

Between 1942 and 1944, the War Research Service explored ways to defend America against biological attack. A panel at WRS studied crops susceptible to "new insect pests or plant pathogens" and urged enforcement of plant quarantines at the U.S. border.[151] Another WRS team worked with officials at the Department of Agriculture to examine foot-and-mouth disease, an outbreak of which would force the slaughter of cattle, swine, sheep, and goats. Besides devoting greater attention (and dollars) to preventive measures, the committee studied ways to treat and salvage the meat of exposed animals. Another group of scientists developed defenses against rinderpest or cattle plague, producing the first effective vaccine against the disease.[152]

The War Research Service also examined ways of striking at the enemy. Biologists working for the WRS discovered an agent that, when unleashed, prevented plants from bearing fruit. Scientists at the Department of Agriculture proposed a three-pronged attack on the Axis countries' sugar beet crop. The plan sought to infect plants with "sclerotium rot," caused by a fungus that destroyed stems and roots; with "eelworm disease," in which a worm attacked the plant's roots; and with "curly top disease," transmitted by an insect—the beet leafhopper.[153] The WRS was unimpressed: It decided that sclerotium rot would have limited impact in the cooler climes of Nazi-occupied Europe. Thoughts about attacking Japan's rice fields also went nowhere. The conquest of Southeast Asia had provided Japan with additional farmland, thus diminishing the effect of any biological attack. Tactical concerns overruled the use of chemical agents. "The effort required to do a good job against food," an aide to U.S. Army Air Forces general Henry H. "Hap" Arnold advised, "would be better expended against material objectives having earlier and more certain impact."[154]

As McNutt noted, the thought of using biological weapons gave some officials pause. Admiral William D. Leahy "recoiled from the idea," arguing that a first strike by the United States would stir the Axis powers to respond in kind.[155] In a similar vein, the WBC Committee opposed any unprovoked use of offensive biological warfare.[156] And the surgeon general of the U.S. Army insisted that the "primary function" of his office was to preserve life rather than to unleash a biological attack.[157] At the same time, however, the surgeon generals of the army and navy relied on information, taken from *all* research projects, to prepare preventive measures. And the WBC Committee did not rule out using biological weapons, if the enemy struck first. Neither General George C. Marshall, the army's chief of staff, nor Stimson seemed troubled by the prospect of crop poisoning. The range of perspectives and advice derived, in part, from presidential silence, for Roosevelt "never indicated whether he would launch a biological-warfare attack in retaliation for Axis first-use, or whether he might even countenance first-use against Japan," whose bacterial warfare program was much further along than that of Germany.[158] Overall, the biological warfare program during World War II proved modest in comparison to the Manhattan Project, which produced the atomic bomb. A proposal to engage in biological warfare never reached FDR's desk, and the president remained only tangentially aware of the program's development.[159]

McNutt, for his part, never questioned the need to study biological warfare. His praise of Merck for spearheading the WRS was revealing: Merck, and by extension McNutt himself, had stepped up, made a tough choice, and acted to shield Americans against an emerging threat. Such hardheaded thinking became commonplace following the war. In 1946 the U.S. government released Merck's report about the biological warfare program. While some scientists condemned the government's research efforts, others defended them. Since the Axis powers were studying biological warfare, *Science News Letter* editorialized, "It would have been foolish not to have developed all defensive and offensive angles of this potential weapon."[160] In 1949 Secretary of Defense James V. Forrestal felt compelled to reassure the public that bacteriological agents had not been used by any country during the Second World War and that there was no "biological super-weapon" capable of inflicting mass devastation.[161] Neverthe-less, the specter of biological warfare had been raised. In words that would have resonated with Americans of the twenty-first century, Merck warned Stim-son that "the development of agents for biological warfare is possible in many countries, large and small, without vast expenditure of money."[162] With that danger in mind, McNutt placed the biological warfare program at the top of his accomplishments during World War II.[163]

As World War II drew to a close, McNutt's subordinates took a hard look at the Federal Security Agency, applauded its record, and outlined possible changes. Switzer—no unbiased observer, to be sure—maintained that the FSA had been an invaluable part of wartime efforts to fight venereal disease, expand recreation, improve community facilities, and assign doctors and nurses. The "prestige, standing, and effectiveness" of the Public Health Service, she insisted, had been "greatly enhanced" at the FSA, where it became "the pivot around which war health services were organized." Writing in 1946, Switzer stressed that "most of the life of the Federal Security Agency" had been defined by the war.[164] Watson B. Miller, who succeeded McNutt as federal security adminis-trator in 1945, agreed: "The Federal Security Agency measured up to wartime jobs not contemplated when it was established." Yet Miller admitted that the FSA had not always functioned smoothly and "first task," after the war, had to be "internal 'retooling.'"[165]

McNutt's team began planning a larger, more integrated agency. They also sought additional powers for the federal security administrator, including the authority to make recommendations to the president and to Congress, a power already held by the head of the Social Security Board. In 1945, the staff at the FSA recommended elevating their agency to a cabinet-level Department of Health, Education, and Security that would include the Children's Bureau (taken from the Department of Labor), the Division of Vital Statistics (from the Bureau of the Census), and the U.S. Employment Service (from the War Manpower Commission). The new department would be directed by a secre-tary, an undersecretary, and two assistant secretaries. Officials at the Federal Security Agency drafted the report recommending the reorganization and Mc-Nutt forwarded it to President Harry S. Truman, calling its proposals of "vital importance."[166]

At one level, the fate of the Department of Health, Education, and Security underscored the incremental pace of reform during the postwar era. In this case, the culprits were presidential indecision, congressional wrangling, and administrative outspokenness. Truman, to be fair, made changes by moving the Children's Bureau and Division of Vital Statistics into the Federal Security Agency and by transforming the Social Security Board into the Social Security Administration, thus ending its semi-independent status. Truman also advocated establishing a department to oversee the government's health, education, and social welfare programs.[167] But he failed to specify its structure. In 1947 the Senate considered a bill, drafted by Republican George Aiken of Vermont, to form a Department of Health, Education, and Security along the lines proposed by McNutt. Another measure, authored by Republican senator Robert A. Taft of Ohio and Democratic senator J. William Fulbright of Arkansas, promised a more extensive overhaul in which the department would have divisions for health, education, and security, each headed by an undersecretary trained in that field. Yet a consensus on how to proceed never formed, for Truman failed to endorse either Aiken's measure or Taft and Fulbright's.[168] Thereafter, the discussion became embroiled in heated debates over race relations and the expansion of federal authority. Conservatives on Capitol Hill despised Oscar Ewing, McNutt's associate who served as federal security administrator from 1947 to 1952, for pushing FSA policy "as far toward racial equality and national health insurance as was within his power."[169] The establishment of what became known as the Department of Health, Education, and Welfare did not occur until 1953, when a Republican, Dwight D. Eisenhower, occupied the White House.

At another level, the argument on behalf of making the Federal Security Agency a department revealed how much the country's thinking on security had evolved as a result of the depression, the New Deal, and World War II. Although FSA officials stressed the practical benefits of making their agency a cabinet-level department, they also had philosophical reasons in mind: "An Executive Department affirms the national interest in health, education and security as components of the general welfare." Here, in other words, was a way to consolidate and advance the aims of the New Deal, whose programs had added a "life net" or "a second line of protection" through which a person could "provide for his own security." For example, Social Security required a comprehensive, administrative framework through which it might be expanded.[170] Generally speaking, officials at the Federal Security Agency sought to strengthen the notion that "Government's obligation to stand back of the individual" was "a right rather than a charity."[171] The welfare state in general and a department of health, education, and security in particular would promote what Abraham Lincoln called the "legitimate object of Government," that is, to do "for the people as a whole what they need to have done." Moreover, such a department would help the United States address health and social issues in the global arena.[172] Although McNutt's role in these discussions remains unclear, one can discern many of the ideas he had pushed—security as a "right," Lincoln's conception of government, expansion of Social Security, and even the international aspect of security.

In the end, McNutt's actions at the Federal Security Agency stemmed from long-held beliefs as much as from political posturing or pragmatic adjustment. It is true that he was not always a visible leader of the agency and that the FSA's work was shaped by larger events, such as World War II, and sustained by capable staffers, such as Switzer, Taft, and Merck. That said, McNutt had been—and remained—at the forefront of the effort to provide greater security for Americans. An early supporter of Social Security, he had favored expanding the program in 1940. His concern about national security and patriotic sacrifice stretched back to his early days in the American Legion, meaning that he had good reason, in 1940, 1941, and thereafter, to want Americans to be healthy, fit, and ready for war. Almost as predictable was McNutt's willingness to serve his country in a ranking civilian position during the Second World War as he had in lower-echelon military assignments during World War I. Service, along with ambition and security, remained the brightest threads in the skein of McNutt's life.

McNutt acknowledged the many dimensions of security. Before an audience in Louisville, in 1939, he waxed reflective: "It is difficult to find a single word which more nearly epitomizes the longings of the human spirit than the word 'security.' . . . Implied here are those decencies of civilization which we regard as essential to the good life—economic security, political security, intellectual and spiritual security." He looked forward to a time when "the individual felt himself secure against poverty and want, against the ravages of disease and ill-health, against the violent disruption of the ethical ideals incorporated in his cultural heritage."[173] Such words, voiced following a half-dozen years of domestic reform and in the shadow of the Second World War, illustrate the extent to which McNutt grasped the dangers and possibilities of his era.

# 13

## MOBILIZING MANPOWER
## (1942–1945)

IN ADDITION TO THE Federal Security Agency (FSA), Paul V. McNutt headed another, even more visible office during World War II: the War Manpower Commission (WMC). Manpower represented "the ultimate challenge for the nation's mobilizers" because victory depended on finding enough workers to produce war materials and enough men to vanquish the enemy.[1] As head of the WMC, McNutt became a familiar presence on the home front—"Uncle's Sam's Personnel Boss," commented the *Kansas City Star*.[2] In time, however, the press criticized his stewardship of the commission; cartoonists drew an overwhelmed McNutt fighting with military authorities over human resources, trying to "umpire" the wartime mobilization, and drowning in a "manpower muddle."[3] In many ways, chairing the manpower commission was a more arduous and politically divisive task than McNutt's duties at the wartime Federal Security Agency, when he worked to mobilize the federal government's health, educational, and recreational programs to enhance America's defenses. At one point, President Franklin D. Roosevelt described the manpower problem as "awfully difficult," comparable in many ways to "a jigsaw puzzle."[4]

This puzzle had a large number of pieces, and they seldom interlocked. During World War II, the military brass and civilian leaders competed for human resources. Men were drafted into the armed services and dispatched to distant battlefields. Meanwhile, at home, labor unions struggled to maintain hard-won gains from the 1930s while the farm bloc in Congress worked to shield agricultural workers from the draft. Women entered the workforce and confronted prejudice, as did African Americans. And Americans in general opposed conscription for fathers. Moreover, workers had to be trained, placed, and retained in jobs deemed essential to the war effort—and defining what constituted essential work was no easy task. All of this change occurred within a free-market-oriented economy and at a time when Americans, freed from the constraints of the depression, were eager to migrate, make money, and move on to greener pastures. On the home front, then, channeling these individualistic impulses into a collective effort, rather than further extending the welfare state, became the focus of the United States government. Political wrangling ensued, for the so-called Good War quelled neither selfishness nor partisanship.[5]

McNutt struggled as head of the War Manpower Commission. He had entered electoral politics during the 1930s, an era defined by economic limitations, state building, and debates over security at home and abroad. World War II, which brought together boom times, makeshift government agencies, and a cause that few Americans questioned, inaugurated a different set of challenges. By 1942, unemployment had receded and "the issue of economic security had lost much of its appeal."[6] Thus, on the home front, McNutt needed to do more than extol the promise of the welfare state and call for military preparedness; he had to deflect, diminish, or deny the demands of unions, farmers, women, minorities, the public at large, and even the military. To accomplish that, he required unstinting support from the president and Congress, which he did not receive. Furthermore, his approach to mobilizing manpower—an admixture of volunteerism, localism, and coercion—sowed confusion and sparked criticism. To be sure, McNutt's tenure at the WMC was not a complete failure. Had it been, he would have been dismissed, or the country might have turned to compulsory service to fulfill its labor needs. In the end, America produced enough war material and marshaled enough human power to prevail over its enemies. McNutt survived as chair of the WMC, but his reputation as a rising political star did not.

The War Manpower Commission, and McNutt's appointment to chair it, derived from the reactive and gradual manner in which Roosevelt mobilized the home front. After the outbreak of war in Europe, FDR established the Office of Emergency Management in the White House and, after the Nazis invaded western Europe, he formed the National Defense Advisory Committee

(NDAC). Comprising seven commissioners, each responsible for an aspect of the defense program, the NDAC included the industrialist William S. Knudsen as well as the labor leader Sidney Hillman. Yet 1940 was a year of "partial mobilization," for the U.S. public, "in its distaste for war," supported defense measures reluctantly.[7] The enactment of selective service, the announcement of production goals for war supplies, and the fall of France signaled a worsening crisis and prompted further mobilization. The Office of Production Management (OPM), headed by Knudsen and Hillman, replaced the NDAC early in 1941; the Supply, Priorities and Allocation Board (SPAB) followed in August 1941; and a month after the attack on Pearl Harbor, the SPAB was revamped as the War Production Board (WPB).

A number of impulses shaped the mobilization effort. In 1940 the president proceeded cautiously because it was not until the middle of 1941 that Americans saw the necessity of "all-out preparedness."[8] FDR decided to place labor as well as industrial leaders in agencies like the NDAC in order to prevent business executives ("Morgan and Dupont men") from attaining unchecked power—another example of his determination to wage a New Deal war.[9] Moreover, FDR's establishment of several new agencies with overlapping jurisdictions enabled him to arbitrate among them. The onset of economic recovery in 1940 and 1941, along with America's ongoing status as a nonbelligerent, allowed Roosevelt to continue his improvisational approach to home-front mobilization. "I do not believe that there is an awful lot of Government action that is needed at the present time," the president explained. "We have got surpluses in almost everything."[10] Prior to Pearl Harbor, there was no shortage of labor, for there were plenty of unemployed people eager to work.

The manpower situation was not without troubles, even before Pearl Harbor. Since the skills of many workers had eroded during the decade-long depression, the NDAC took charge by coordinating the job-finding and training activities of a dozen federal offices.[11] Later, Hillman, from his position at the OPM, inaugurated an industrial training program which saw 1.5 million workers pass through it by December 1941. To help Hillman "register, recruit, and place workers in war jobs," Roosevelt gave him control of the United States Employment Service (USES), which oversaw 1,500 local branches.[12] But the USES, which had been formed in 1933 to direct the unemployed to relief and public works projects, struggled to find its footing in a nation preparing for possible war. And the demand for workers, many of them newly unionized, grew throughout 1941. That led to strikes—the most since 1937—and a loss of production.[13]

After America entered the war, administration officials, led by Budget Director Harold D. Smith, thought that the government needed to get a firmer handle on manpower. Smith was an influential figure in FDR's government, an efficiency expert who was "doctrinaire" about the value of rational organization.[14] In the fall of 1941, Smith proposed a commission to coordinate manpower among the federal agencies. But Roosevelt hesitated, believing that the problem had not become urgent. Another obstacle was Secretary of Labor Frances Perkins, who saw a manpower commission as encroachment on her domain. But Smith persisted and FDR relented, whereupon the debate shifted to who should chair the panel. The president ruled out appointing a labor leader such as Hillman. Perkins, for her part, preferred a "calm, practical operator" who was uninvolved in politics, and Smith agreed.[15]

Into this mix stepped McNutt. As federal security administrator, he oversaw the USES and, as the head of the Office of Defense Health and Welfare Services (ODHWS), he had observed how the migration of workers to defense-related jobs had raised challenges concerning housing, schools, and infrastructure in locales across the country. McNutt supported Smith's call for a manpower board and expressed interest in heading the panel himself. At one point, FDR asked if he was planning to do so in addition to serving as federal security administrator. McNutt responded by citing the example of Jesse Jones, who simultaneously had served as secretary of commerce and federal loan administrator.[16]

With respect to manpower, McNutt again perceived an opportunity to serve his country—and himself. The United States was being swept up by the war, and McNutt's own family was no exception. Kathleen was singled out by the *Washington Post* as a "model shopper" who planned her purchases in relation to the war effort.[17] She also used her sense of humor to comment on impending shortages—when the War Production Board proposed to conserve cloth by reducing hemlines, the statuesque Kathleen quipped: "Imagine me in a 27-inch skirt! I'd be locked up!"[18] Louise sounded almost as risqué when she suggested a formula for conserving gasoline: people should "drive less and park more."[19] Paul certainly wanted to do his part for the war, albeit in a high-profile, politically visible office. "He had come to the point," Perkins believed, "where he didn't think that being head of the Federal Security Agency was important enough."[20]

McNutt's ambition may have given Roosevelt pause. In February 1942, FDR hinted that he was amenable to naming McNutt to chair the manpower commission. But a week later, he considered asking Wendell Willkie, since co-opting one of the most prominent leaders in the Grand Old Party (GOP) would bolster the administration politically. Moreover, the president respected Willkie as a liberal-minded politician and fellow internationalist. The idea of tapping Willkie aroused little comment from FDR's aides, until Wayne Coy weighed in. Coy asserted that the selection of Willkie would force McNutt, whose Federal Security Agency was "already hooked up" with the manpower issue, into reporting to his old fraternity brother.[21] Roosevelt's advisers needed little persuading; they liked the idea of appointing McNutt, as did many union leaders who either overlooked (or had forgotten) his earlier quelling of labor unrest.[22] In the end, the president took the easiest route and chose McNutt to chair the commission.

On April 18, 1942 Roosevelt signed an executive order establishing the War Manpower Commission and named McNutt as its chair. The panel brought together representatives of the Departments of War, Navy, Agriculture, and Labor; the War Production Board; the Selective Service System; and the U.S. Civil Service Commission. On paper, the chair of the WMC received large authority—to develop policies "to assure the most effective mobilization" of manpower, review civilian and military needs, and direct federal agencies on the allocation of labor.[23] (In announcing the order, the White House stressed that "man power" included "woman power" as well.)[24] Yet the commission "could not prescribe Selective Service policy regarding deferments, had no voice over labor relations, and had no power to enforce its decisions."[25] Since the WMC lacked a legislative sanction, it was a creature of presidential will—and Roosevelt's support for it would ebb and flow. Furthermore, the commission-style setup forced McNutt to consult with some of the strongest personalities in the administration before acting. He had to deal with Perkins at Labor; Secretary of War Henry Stimson and his undersecretary, Robert Patterson; Secretary of the Navy Frank Knox; and Lewis B. Hershey at Selective Service. At the same time, the War Manpower Commission also included figures such as Donald Nelson at WPB and Secretary of Agriculture Claude R. Wickard who would prove less than effective at home-front mobilization.[26]

Appointment to the manpower post placed McNutt in the spotlight once again. The *New York Mirror* dubbed him "America's Super-Manpowerman," a politician of "enormous abilities" and a "master showman" ever prepared to promote himself.[27] The new job, the *Indianapolis Star* proclaimed, restored McNutt to "page 1, top position" in the country's newspapers.[28] But others insisted that accepting the manpower assignment involved political risk. The *Indianapolis*

*Times* stressed the difficulties in directing manpower, noting that this "may be the make-or-break point in the career of Paul V. McNutt."[29]

McNutt's tenure at the War Manpower Commission began with good intentions and lofty rhetoric. At his first press conference, he declared that the WMC would act as a "great clearing house for all wartime labor needs."[30] McNutt maintained that the apportionment of human resources between the military and civilian sectors could be accomplished through the existing labor market without government coercion, though he did not rule out the use of compulsory methods. "If and when national service becomes necessary," he later told a House panel, "it will be the province of the Commander in Chief to say that it is necessary."[31] McNutt believed that a "continuous flow of information," circulated via the WMC, would allow job seekers to adjust to a changing economy. Moved by pragmatism, idealism, and political expediency, he stressed that the allocation of labor was not a job government can do by itself. McNutt argued that relying on "democratic methods" to mobilize manpower would distinguish the United States from its foes.[32] And, like Roosevelt, he had no intention of telling Americans where they had to work. McNutt believed that the British model, of drafting all men and women, would not work in America where civilians had not been "subjected to the dangers of war."[33] Others agreed. The columnist Arthur Krock praised efforts to mobilize workers by the "voluntary method" rather than through regimentation.[34] Senator Theodore F. Green, Democrat of Rhode Island, rejected calls to draft workers as "applying a totalitarian form of government to our democracy."[35]

McNutt and Roosevelt might have explored the benefits of the British model, which represented a compromise between voluntarism and compulsion. The radio commentator Raymond Gram Swing championed Britain's policy, which had been pushed by Minister of Labour Ernest Bevin, a "lifelong labor union leader." Parliament passed legislation placing all Britons and their property at the disposal of the state, which was free to move workers and resources as needed. The power to compel action rested with an undersecretary at the Ministry of Labour and National Service, but he seldom took that step. Swing applauded the British for implementing "a compact policy, under a single man, responsible for distributing all manpower in accordance with an agreed national policy."[36] Implicit in his praise was a critique of the American political economy with its celebration of individual liberty and diffuse centers of power.[37]

The emphasis that McNutt and Roosevelt placed on voluntary cooperation and limited government was not surprising. Although both men had worked to build the welfare state, they had done so in piecemeal fashion, with respect for local authority (at least at first), and within the parameters of capitalism. FDR's efforts to regulate business, his appeals to class hostility, and his seeming about-face in using business leaders to help mobilize the home front, belied the ongoing cooperation between the administration and business exemplified by the work of the Reconstruction Finance Corporation, which loaned money to financial institutions. Likewise, McNutt had addressed business leaders during his run for the presidency, and he had extolled the promise of economic recovery driven by individual initiative.[38] As the head of the ODHWS, he had worked with private organizations to provide recreation for servicemen. McNutt's embrace of voluntary action no doubt derived from overly fond memories of the patriotic spirit that had animated Americans during World War I. He either believed or hoped that once the government roused the public to act during wartime, people would sacrifice for the sake of achieving victory.

With respect to manpower, McNutt's optimism about the capacity of the free market, guided by the gentle hand of government, proved misplaced. His first seven months at the WMC proved hectic, as 1942 saw the threat of labor shortages, worker absenteeism, and high turnover in factories. To make matters worse, the U.S. government failed to specify several needs: the size of the armed forces required to achieve victory; the volume of war material (and how it was to be produced); the number of workers required to run factories, mines, and farms; and the distribution of labor between the military and civilian sectors. The only government offices that had an idea about production and manpower needs were the procurement agencies—the army and navy—and they "either could not or would not provide the required information" to such offices as the WMC and the War Production Board.[39]

As a result of the confusion, no comprehensive policy on manpower emerged. The Selective Service System continued to draft skilled workers, and McNutt's instrument for deferring such workers, the U.S. Employment Service, only advised draft boards on what constituted essential war work. Even when McNutt specified 138 occupations as essential, the final word on deferments remained with local branches of Selective Service. The result was a mad scramble for workers. By August 1942, labor shortages afflicted thirty-five industrial areas. As the historian Paul A. C. Koistinen observed, the WMC "got under way inauspiciously."[40]

McNutt understood the need to assert control over manpower, and he spent considerable time developing a proper organization at the WMC to do so. Among other things, McNutt assembled a staff responsible to him while minimizing the influence of other departments. And for the remainder of 1942, McNutt proved acquisitive—he sought additional power, and FDR gave it to him. In September 1942, the president signed an executive order giving the WMC charge over the USES, National Youth Administration (NYA), and most federal job-training programs. Yet such activities were invisible to a restless public. According to Representative Clarence M. Cannon, Democrat of Missouri, "the Manpower Commission had made some excellent statements but did not seem to be doing anything to carry them out."[41] "Who is supposed to do something about [manpower]?" one constituent asked Harry S. Truman, the Missouri Democrat who chaired a Senate committee monitoring the national defense program.[42] Truman replied that he recently had "a row with McNutt and with the Army over the manpower program," which he deemed in "worse turmoil than it has ever been."[43] The lack of a strategy for manpower and McNutt's willingness to address labor shortages as they emerged—such as when he proposed a mass deferment for dairy workers—suggested that he was "content to treat serious functional disorders with policy Band-aids."[44] Accordingly, the drumbeat for decisive action grew ever louder. The *Washington Evening Star* urged the federal government to "take complete control" of labor, "assign a man to a particular job," and "forbid him to leave it."[45]

McNutt reacted skittishly to talk of compulsion. "I will do everything within my power . . . to make the voluntary method work," he averred.[46] Yet he did employ the threat of coercion. In May 1942 McNutt issued the first in a series of "work or fight" orders; men who refused to work in war industries risked being inducted into the army.[47] He seemed to retreat when he advised the governor of Maryland to refrain from invoking his state's 1917 "Work-or-Fight" law because he saw no "deliberate unwillingness" by Marylanders to work in defense-related industries.[48] But in September 1942, McNutt changed course again when he revealed that the WMC was considering a universal service act that would allow the government to place Americans in essential jobs. The reversal stemmed from congressional pressures and a realization that the free market might be unable to meet America's manpower needs. "Persuasion is not enough and there is not sufficient patriotic urge," McNutt admitted in raising the possibility of a national service act.[49]

By floating this idea, McNutt entered the realm of politics, both interest group and partisan. McNutt understood both the clout of big business and the growing power of labor. Between 1940 and 1945, the number of Americans who were members of unions grew from 8.7 million to 14.3 million. Having been branded a strike-busting governor, McNutt was reluctant to offend organized labor; his correspondence with union leaders during the war proved friendly and full of praise for labor's "unselfish and patriotic" spirit.[50] Partly to appease workers and partly to ascertain the widest possible advice on manpower, McNutt established the Management-Labor Policy Committee (MLPC) within the WMC. The work of the WMC, he insisted, "could be done only with the active participation of management and labor."[51] But by promising to consult with labor and management "on all our major policies," McNutt hindered his ability to set manpower priorities in a forceful way.[52] He soon discovered that both employers, who hated any move toward bigger government, and union leaders opposed national service legislation. President William Green of the American Federation of Labor (AFL) and Philip Murray, head of the Congress of Industrial Organizations (CIO), stressed that "compulsory action now is premature."[53] "The best interests of the labor movement will be served, and any trend toward compulsory legislation avoided," Murray declared, "if local initiative and activity are developed as much as possible."[54]

Manpower became an issue in the elections of 1942. Republicans accused the administration of simultaneously doing too little and too much. The Republican National Committee charged the White House with procrastination and negligence in developing a manpower policy. Accordingly, Senator Robert A. Taft, Republican of Ohio, proposed replacing the War Manpower Commission with a single "War Manpower Director" with authority to plan the nation's manpower needs without resorting to compulsion. "I do not believe," Taft remarked, "the time has yet come when we can adopt a system of forced labor in the factories and on the farms."[55] The Hearst press trumpeted that theme, warning that "forced labor appears inevitable if the Administration wins a vote of confidence." After the GOP gained forty-four seats in the House and nine in the Senate, the Hearst papers crowed that the people had spoken and that there would be "no regimentation of the American worker." Shortly thereafter, an emboldened Taft co-sponsored legislation to abolish the manpower commission altogether.[56]

Such maneuvering was to be expected. Congress and the White House were at odds because the home front remained "an open field for politics as usual."[57] Taft disliked the WMC with its New Dealers, amorphous mandate, and executive-branch origins. And GOP conservatives did not trust talk about voluntarism and limited government from a former governor of Indiana who had "out-New Deal[ed] the New Deal."[58] Others suspected that McNutt would use the commission to curry favor with organized groups and seek the White House in 1944. With that in mind, Harold Smith warned McNutt that he would be blamed "for every false move in the manpower field." McNutt replied that "he had not made a political speech since the war began." Smith held his ground: "The fact that you have made speeches is interpreted as political."[59]

McNutt's reputation as a political animal gained him few friends in the wartime administration. Perkins despised him. And Smith, who believed the WMC needed a nonpolitical chair, had opposed his appointment. So, too, had Frank C. Walker, the head of the Democratic National Committee; after FDR selected the Hoosier, Walker told Ickes that "McNutt is not one of our crowd." Ickes found the choice mystifying, and he wondered "whether the President was laying his hands on Paul as his possible successor" by giving him "a position of extraordinary political possibilities."[60] Even Harry Hopkins, who was not always unfavorable toward McNutt, thought that he should not head the WMC "since he was running for office."[61] Stimson viewed McNutt as a politician in the broadest sense, that is, someone who was angling to accumulate power. "McNutt," he lamented, "is rather anxious to get his clutches on the Selective Service Commission."[62] According to Isaiah Berlin, who worked at the British Embassy in Washington, McNutt was unpopular with FDR intimates, who feared him as a potential presidential nominee in 1944, and with the military, which saw him as angling to take over Selective Service.[63]

McNutt and the military also differed over policy. McNutt insisted that the civilian and military sectors were equally important and that the services must not draft men at will. But Stimson and the nation's military brass believed that the manpower needs of the armed services deserved top priority. In this debate, Taft sided with McNutt: "Stimson and Patterson are more military than the generals and have no appreciation of the part which a civilian population plays in the war."[64] Such arguments failed to move military leaders, who pressed their claim for manpower by citing battlefield needs. War Department officials also exuded contempt for the managers of the civilian economy. Patterson dismissed McNutt and Nelson as "second line men," and Stimson disparaged McNutt's staff as "a lot of callow New Dealers with more ambition than brains."[65]

McNutt's staff was part of his trouble at the WMC. The commission had a vice chairman, Fowler V. Harper, McNutt's protégé from Indiana; an executive director, Arthur J. Altmeyer, who also headed the Social Security Board; and a director of operations, Brigadier General Frank McSherry, who ran job training programs at the FSA. Almost inevitably, there was a "clash of personalities" between Harper, a McNutt loyalist, and Altmeyer, who was accustomed to running his own fiefdom at Social Security.[66] The commission also lacked a clear chain of command, and it was staffed by people who were "temperamentally incompatible."[67] In this setting, other members of the government had their favorites at the commission. Stimson considered General McSherry the "one sensible man" at the WMC.[68] Perkins thought that no one ran the commission effectively until Lawrence Appley became its executive director. In 1942, substandard staff work, and McNutt's tolerance of it, helped keep the WMC at "dead center."[69] Jonathan Daniels, an aide to FDR, sensed "a general feeling of weakness" at the War Manpower Commission.[70] And the president himself complained "that McNutt hasn't done anything with manpower except to make speeches."[71]

Why McNutt was so lenient toward his subordinates is not easily explained. He had been the beneficiary of good staff work in the past and perhaps thought that once he located people with the requisite mixture of loyalty, competence, and experience, his troubles at the WMC would recede. As a boss, McNutt had long been supportive of underlings. At the WMC, he had declined to clean house during the fall of 1942 partly because Frank McSherry, the director of operations, was up for promotion to major general, and McNutt did not want to undermine him. Harold Smith thought such generosity was misplaced. "I told McNutt," he reported to FDR, "that this sort of thing would not do and was the seat of much of his administrative difficulty."[72]

Smith accurately identified other shortcomings in the commission's chair. McNutt was "shy," possessed "something of an inferiority complex," and seemed uneasy with others in the administration, including the president. "This, in part," Smith informed Roosevelt, "accounts for the fact that when he is in your office talking to you, he tends to lecture rather than to discuss an issue." At the same time, some of McNutt's weaknesses were related to his strengths—the sincerity and loyalty he showed toward his staff extended upward, to the president. As the manpower panel began its work, Smith averred, McNutt took "a beating for the Administration" and had done so "like a gentleman."[73] That did not solve the problem of how to allocate human resources. Vice President Henry A. Wallace saw the debate over manpower "getting hotter every day."[74] Representative Warren G. Magnuson, Democrat of Washington, lamented that the WMC was getting "grief" because it "can't seem to arrive at any conclusions."[75]

Some of the criticism of the commission was overdrawn. The War Production Board, in many respects a rival to the WMC, concluded that "potential reserves of manpower were more than adequate to meet the requirements of the war production program through 1943." In the sectors of the economy that had experienced labor shortages during 1942, swift action had stemmed the problem. After the army furloughed soldiers to work in mines, the manpower situation there improved. By the end of 1942, the War Production Board concluded, "manpower requirements of war industries and the Armed Forces had been met." Yet two challenges loomed on the horizon. The first was the "increasing tightness in the labor market." And the second was the inability of the War Manpower Commission to enforce its edicts. Before the army sent soldiers to work in the mines, McNutt had issued an order freezing miners in their jobs. "This order," the War Production Board emphasized, "proved completely ineffective."[76]

As 1942 came to a close, administration officials continued to express frustration. Stimson complained of shortages of soldiers; Wickard warned about a lack of farm workers; and General Lewis B. Hershey, who oversaw Selective Service, admitted that the draft was draining workers from factories. McNutt, in turn, continued to float the idea of compulsory legislation. Roosevelt remained coy, suggesting that he would propose legislation to expand the powers of the WMC only if necessary. "The President," recalled James F. Byrnes, head of the Office of Economic Stabilization, "was loath to delegate powers in this field."[77] But members of Congress were not hesitant to offer solutions of their own. For example, the Truman Committee proposed improvements to the existing WMC: ending army recruitments (so as to prevent interference with the draft); allowing Selective Service boards to order workers to remain in essential occupations; extending the workweek; and placing Selective Service under the charge of the War Manpower Commission. Greater effort within the current voluntary system, rather than "any drastic *compulsory* legislation," was what was needed, the committee concluded.[78]

With all these proposals flying about, Roosevelt almost inevitably had to rethink the manpower program and McNutt's role in it. In a memorandum to the president, McNutt echoed the conclusions of the Truman Committee: The WMC must attain control over Selective Service in order to protect workers in essential occupations, and the commission's reach must extend to the nation at large rather than simply to other federal agencies. McNutt argued that a strengthened WMC was one way to forestall "consideration of a National Service Act."[79] That was the thinking of the financier Bernard M. Baruch, who had headed the War Industries Board during World War I and who was reviewing manpower issues for the White House. But Stimson, along with Hershey, opposed a revamped WMC with control over Selective Service. The secretary of war asserted that the Selective Service System had become "one of our greatest national assets" and must be kept away from civilian officials whose concern was with "our ordinary civil life and its social theories, differences and interests."[80] The argument smacked of military snobbery—and disdain for the New Deal—and Roosevelt would have none of it. "I like B.M.B.'s conclusions," the president affirmed: "No further laws," "Voluntary cooperation," "Central authority," "No further enlistments," and "Improved administration."[81]

After deciding to bolster the existing WMC, Roosevelt tried to find someone other than McNutt to run it. He became attracted to a grand strategy, advanced by James Byrnes, to shift responsibility for manpower to the Department of Labor, which Ickes then would head. Perkins would move to the Federal Security Agency and McNutt would surrender his posts at the FSA and WMC in exchange for Ickes's job at Interior. Upon hearing of this shift, the president quipped: "Jimmie, that sounds like Tinker to Evers to Chance," a reference to three Chicago Cubs known for their skill at turning double plays.[82] But Ickes rejected the swap. He saw running manpower as a thankless chore—a real "man-killer." Besides, Ickes "loved" Interior with its parks and forests, and he worried that McNutt would exploit the nation's resources for his own political gain.[83] Eventually, Ickes decided that he would take over the War Manpower Commission only if he could run it from Interior. By that point, however, the president had changed his mind, and "Perkins, McNutt and Ickes held their bases."[84]

McNutt clung to his job, despite the fact that Roosevelt declined to see him for several weeks in the fall of 1942. McNutt had defenders, such as Harold Smith, who came to believe that McNutt was receiving too much blame for problems at the WMC.[85] Smith informed Roosevelt that McNutt would perform better with a more rational organization at the commission. "I would not guarantee that he can recover the fumble," Smith admitted, but "McNutt will probably do a better job of recovering the ball than will any new person."[86] FDR agreed. "Your memorandum seemed to have had a great effect upon the President," Samuel I. Rosenman, a White House speechwriter, told Smith. "I hope you are right about Paul McNutt, but I have some doubts."[87]

After the president decided to retain McNutt, Smith and Rosenman prepared an executive order to expand the powers of the War Manpower Commission. Issued on December 5, 1942, the order placed Selective Service under the charge of the WMC; required the secretaries of war and the navy to consult with Mc-Nutt before making requests for manpower; ended all voluntary enlistments; mandated that the hiring of defense workers be done through the U.S. Employment Service, which formally came under the WMC; prohibited employers in nonessential fields from holding on to any worker needed in defense industries; and empowered McNutt to issue "policies, rules, regulations, and general or special orders" as needed.[88] By signing this executive order, FDR delivered "the carrot of deferment and the stick of induction into one pair of hands."[89] The *Philadelphia Inquirer* called it "one of the biggest jobs" ever entrusted to a single official.[90] With respect to manpower, the *Boston Globe* editorialized that the period of experimentation was giving way to a time for action. Carleton B. McCulloch, McNutt's supporter in Indiana, sighed that his friend was at last receiving "a little more favorable coverage from the 'typewriter generals.'" But McCulloch fretted: "I don't know how long it will last. His job is terrible."[91] Indeed, one labor advocate predicted that McNutt's commission was bound "to make enemies" and commit errors which "will be remembered."[92] Even Smith remarked that Ickes was "very lucky to have the opportunity of staying where he is."[93]

At that moment, perhaps the most sensible advice came from McNutt's old confidant, Frank McHale. McHale advised McNutt to clean house at the commission; reduce his staff and curtail red-tape; publicize such efforts; and eliminate unnecessary (and unpopular) agencies, like the NYA. He also counseled vigilance: "The wolves have feared you for a long while . . . [Y]ou must protect yourself." McHale's suggestion, that forces within the White House were out to get McNutt, was overdrawn.[94] Yet there was little love for his friend within the administration. Despite vows to remain on "good terms" with McNutt and to help him, Stimson wanted to retain his own influence over manpower, and Hershey wished to do likewise.[95] Meanwhile, Smith, who had helped to save McNutt's job, soon regretted doing so. "McNutt," he complained early in 1943, "could not make decisions."[96] More worrisome was Roosevelt's fickleness. On the one hand, FDR supported McNutt's decision to remove Goldthwaite Dorr as the Department of War's representative on the WMC—a move that offended Stimson. On the other hand, however, when a senator protested McNutt's statement that America would be unable to maintain an armed force of nine million men, the president responded: "Frankly, I think he is wrong."[97] Roosevelt's contradiction of McNutt's assertion came shortly after he had revamped the War Manpower Commission.

Nineteen forty-three was McNutt's best year at the War Manpower Commission, although that is not saying much. His powers peaked as he controlled

Selective Service for twelve months "and the WMC reached an apogee of activity."[98] The commission reorganized itself and worked to keep workers in essential jobs in order to stabilize the employment market. At the same time, McNutt accepted new sources of labor beyond the white male worker. The WMC thus became involved in issues of race and gender, injustice and discrimination, and the use of non-American workers. The commission's policies also sparked a showdown with Congress, which sought to protect both agricultural workers and fathers from the draft. These were large problems, and McNutt received so much criticism that the economist Eliot Janeway deemed him "the most harassed of the Washington czars."[99] McNutt's control over manpower policy diminished, and by the end of 1943 his mandate had withered away.

McNutt used various methods to control the supply of labor. Late in 1942, he divided the nation's labor market into four categories; regions in Category 1 faced a severe shortage of labor while areas in the opposite end, Category 4, had a surplus. To prevent the movement of workers, McNutt and the WMC, also in 1942, had developed Employment Stabilization Plans, under which management agreed not to hire workers unless they had a certificate of availability given by the USES. In 1943 McNutt went further by issuing a new list of essential jobs. But he allowed regional WMC directors to expand that list. As a result, all sorts of occupations only tangentially related to the war effort became identified as essential, from fashioning jewelry to tailoring academic robes to performing in dance studios. Meanwhile, people working in the professions not designated as essential were puzzled. Reporters chimed in as well, asking McNutt to explain why horse racing, but not baseball or football, had been classified as a non-deferrable sport. Such issues sparked banter at press conferences. When one correspondent asked if Frank Sinatra's singing represented essential wartime activity, McNutt evaded the question. And when asked whether laundry work was essential to the war effort, McNutt answered that it depended on local circumstances. He then joked: "I was wondering whether I had enough shirts to get through these days . . . Long live linen." "Did he say Lenin?" a reporter wisecracked.[100]

Not everyone was laughing; the struggle to define essential activity raised friction between the War Department and the WMC. Robert Patterson, undersecretary of war, emphasized that the armed services needed the men most suited for fighting and that jobs in war-related industries could be filled by people unfit for military service. Knowing that the fittest men usually were between the ages of eighteen and thirty, he objected to proposals to defer men attending college. Although McNutt promised to review job classifications (and they were revised throughout the war), Patterson was never satisfied.[101] He remained livid about "over-liberal deferments" that allowed young men to continue civilian pursuits.[102] If McNutt at times seemed too soft, at other times he appeared too tough. In February 1943, he issued a work-or-fight order, telling men in nondeferrable jobs that they could avoid induction into the army only by transferring into essential war work. But the order excited a panic in New York City where 21,000 workers registered with the USES for essential occupations only to discover that 16,000 of them were already in such jobs! Newspapers such as the *Washington Evening Star* complained of a WMC chair disposed to issue dictates on the one hand and of a muddled manpower program on the other.[103]

Congress displayed little confidence in McNutt, his commission, or his work-or-fight threat. During February 1943 the Senate Committee on Appropriations investigated manpower, a problem that Theodore Green called "all-important" to the war effort.[104] That same month, a bipartisan group of senators proposed forming a superagency to oversee offices specializing in economic stabilization, science and technology, production, and manpower. The plan represented a slap at Roosevelt and his underlings, including McNutt, for it promised to rationalize home-front mobilization and allow Americans "to understand exactly where they fit into the total picture."[105] The debate over manpower intensified as Senator Warren R. Austin of Vermont and Representative James Wadsworth of New York, both Republicans, drafted a national service bill empowering the president to place men and women in defense industries.[106]

In 1942 and 1943, Roosevelt declined to support national service—at least in public. Grenville Clark, a lawyer and longtime acquaintance of the president's, pressed hard for such a law. But Roosevelt kept his options open. On the one hand, he told McNutt to prepare a national service act. On the other hand, he evaded the issue until the end of 1942, when he informed Clark that the administration's present approach to manpower was both effective and democratic. Austin and Wadsworth remained unconvinced. The Austin-Wadsworth bill provided "for the selection and assignment of every man between the ages of 18 and 65 and every woman between the ages of 18 and 50." It empowered local boards to draft workers for essential industries if voluntary methods failed.[107] Labor unions "bitterly" opposed Austin-Wadsworth.[108] But Stimson and Patterson backed it. Meanwhile, McNutt remained tied to the president's whims. "I never thought there was the slightest chance of really getting McNutt [in] back of this legislation," Clark reckoned, "unless and until he followed along behind F.D.R."[109]

The president eventually asked Rosenman to reexamine the matter of national service. Assisting Rosenman was a group of advisers that included Harry Hopkins; Admiral William D. Leahy; James Byrnes, who now headed the Office of War Mobilization; and Bernard Baruch, who was Byrnes's ombudsman on manpower. Byrnes's role was pivotal, for he had wide experience in government, was close to the president, and possessed, as Truman later observed, an appetite for "personal aggrandizement."[110] The veteran *New York Times* reporter Turner Catledge called Byrnes "the smartest politician I knew in Washington," a man whose "intelligence and shrewdness carried him to a remarkable career."[111] Although this set of policymakers declined to endorse national service legislation, they did not rule out using more forceful measures to allocate manpower.[112]

The appeal of national service waned by the summer of 1943 as the administration found a "partial solution" to the manpower problem.[113] The WMC allowed local committees to set priorities on where manpower was needed most. Such a plan went into effect in Buffalo and a similar setup took root in the major cities on the West Coast, where high turnover rates had imperiled the production of aircraft. In Buffalo, representatives from the War Production Board, the WMC, and the procurement agencies developed "a priority system for referring workers."[114] Labor and management held seats on Buffalo's priority committee, which worked with the U.S. Employment Service to place workers in essential industries. The West Coast Plan established two committees (one for production issues, the other for manpower), set employment ceilings at plants engaged in nonessential activity, and threatened to withhold war contracts from companies which failed to use their labor supply effectively. According to the historian Paul Koistinen, the plan preserved a subpar system of voluntary cooperation. But it also curtailed worker turnover and absenteeism and forced procurers "to examine more critically their requirements."[115] West Coast–style plans were extended to other cities, such as Washington.[116]

If America had turned a corner in stabilizing its labor supply, McNutt neither received nor deserved praise for the accomplishment. Anna Rosenberg, a former aide to Mayor Fiorello La Guardia of New York and a regional director of the WMC, had fashioned the Buffalo Plan, while Byrnes and Baruch developed the West Coast Plan. To be sure, McNutt participated in meetings on the West Coast Plan, and the program reflected his belief in mobilizing manpower through localism, voluntarism, and some coercion. But McNutt lost ground as a policymaker. John M. Hancock, an assistant to Baruch, found McNutt's draft of the West Coast Plan "sketchy."[117] And when McNutt asserted that his commission would assume responsibility for "all phases of the West Coast Manpower

Program," Byrnes told him that the WMC would run the plan "in collaboration with with the other interested agencies."[118] Not surprisingly, when the
West Coast Plan became public, McNutt received no credit for it. "The Baruch-
Hancock Report," one columnist emphasized, was "so straightforward and
sensible . . . that one wonders why something like it was not prepared and made
available long ago."[119] Others in the press rightly lauded Byrnes for "attacking
this problem of manpower."[120] McNutt, in contrast, had to accept his setbacks
gracefully. Upon hearing that Rosenman was to review job deferments, McNutt
told reporters: "If we can relieve our commission of some of their problems, all
well and good."[121]

Some manpower problems were relieved by bringing women and racial minorities into the workforce. In these areas, McNutt again was more follower
than leader. With respect to women workers, he was too steeped in traditional
roles to challenge them, at least at the start of the war. "All of us want normal
family life to be preserved," he proclaimed.[122] McNutt was no advocate of child
care, which was critically important to the two million married women who
entered the labor force from 1940 to 1944. In 1942 he announced that government policy was "to urge housewives who have no young children to be the first
to enroll [for employment,]" and he advised that "no mother of small children
apply for a full time position until she is satisfied that the children's welfare has
been adequately cared for."[123] Like many people in the early 1940s, McNutt
believed that women lacked the physical strength to do some of the jobs associated with men. But the demand for workers caused men to adapt their thinking
about women's abilities. Stimson dubbed womanpower "the finest single source
of labor available today." "Women," a Department of War brochure advised,
"can be trained to do almost any job."[124]

As women proved their mettle, and as the need for workers persisted, Mc-
Nutt's views evolved. To be fair, he had, in 1942, acknowledged that were only
a few occupations "for which women cannot qualify," and he predicted that
the war would bring "great numbers of women" into the labor market. For that
reason, McNutt saw no need to inaugurate a nationwide campaign to recruit
women for war work—a position with which Frances Perkins agreed.[125] He
was sufficiently respectful of women's abilities, or mindful of their role in the
war effort, to form the Women's Advisory Committee (WAC) within the War
Manpower Commission. The WAC brought together prominent women in the
fields of education, publishing, business, and labor and provided them a forum
from which they pressed for job training, child care, and, interestingly, a form
of national service inclusive of all workers, both female and male. McNutt did

not envision the WAC as a major policymaking organ, but between 1943 and 1945 he did gradually become a cheerleader for working women. In a radio interview, he hailed women workers, the welders of ships and the riveters of warplanes, for "doing jobs as well as men" and emerging as "the real heroines of this war."[126]

The wartime emergency forced McNutt to challenge traditional gender roles. "Any woman, not now employed, should make this a time for a soul searching," he exhorted in 1943. "She should ask herself 'Can I help?'"[127] To husbands who were "not enthusiastic about their wives taking jobs," McNutt gave a familiar retort: "Don't you know there's a war on?"[128] By war's end, he sounded more progressive than practical on the fate of female workers. In 1945 McNutt, in a speech entitled "Women in War and Peace," asserted that "Rosie the Riveter" no less than "Joe the Riveter" had earned the right to a job in the postwar economy. "What about the women who want to work in the factories," he asked. "Shall they all go back to the home? Or into the so-called 'women's industries'? There are many Americans who urge such a road—a blind road of economic discrimination."[129]

Such comments were noteworthy in light of postwar trends, when popular culture often celebrated traditional gender roles and when the percentage of women working outside the home dropped from wartime levels. One could attribute McNutt's remarks about the rights of Rosie the Riveters to expediency— a bid for female votes—but such appeals risked alienating traditionally minded males and females. Besides, when McNutt expressed them, his political career was in eclipse. One could trace McNutt's end-of-the-war defense of women workers to the influence of strong, capable females in his life, such as Mary Switzer at the FSA, although their presence had not led him to give unfettered support to women workers at the beginning of the war. McNutt's patriotism and pragmatism were the likeliest cause of his rather enlightened views. "Women war workers have truly served their country," McNutt wrote in 1945; "mothers became aircraft assemblers and soldiers' wives became ship welders."[130] Even in jobs usually occupied by males, McNutt admitted, "Women proved the equal of men."[131] Had such thoughts been prevalent among America's leadership, the choices available to women might have expanded during the 1940s and 1950s. Instead, as the historian Elaine Tyler May has observed, "Traditional gender roles revived just when they might have died a natural death."[132]

McNutt was less progressive on matters related to race. That was not surprising. Like many liberal politicians of his generation, McNutt approached civil rights with a blend of reluctance and realism coated, at times, with idealistic rhetoric. His record as governor, when black employment at the statehouse increased marginally, revealed as much, as did his presidential campaign, when he weighed the merits of wooing white southerners versus African Americans. As federal security administrator, McNutt offended the National Association for the Advancement of Colored People (NAACP) by trusting state officials to eradicate bias in Social Security benefits. This decision, the NAACP pointed out, placed African Americans at the mercy of lily-white administrations in the South. Yet McNutt complied with a presidential order to improve the government's hiring of minorities, directed underlings at the FSA to review their personnel policies so as to end discrimination, and over time compiled a creditable record hiring African Americans. Under pressure from Eleanor Roosevelt and Walter White, executive secretary of the NAACP, McNutt moved to eradicate discrimination in the U.S. Employment Service, whose branches in the southern states had favored whites over blacks in job referrals. The FSA also developed job-training and morale-boosting programs for African Americans seeking employment in war industries. Such actions reflected McNutt's realization that African Americans represented a valuable supply of industrial labor. "The Negro mechanic or lathe-operator who is pushing a broom," he declared, "is a disgrace to his employer."[133] McNutt went much further when he attacked "the color line in industry" as "a line against democracy." "The only lines that counted in making a ship, a plane, a jeep, or a rifle," he reminded his fellow citizens, "were the lines on the blueprints."[134]

Too often, however, McNutt's deeds—and words—lacked bite. The troubles began in July 1942, when the War Manpower Commission acquired control over the Fair Employment Practices Committee (FEPC), the agency formed by FDR under Executive Order 8802, which prohibited bias in defense industries. The order (and the FEPC) raised expectations and fanned "a rising mood of militancy," according to the historian David M. Kennedy.[135] McNutt admitted that "Negroes and other groups are being discriminated against" and that remedying the problem was one of the WMC's "most important responsibilities."[136] But he struggled. Civil rights leaders criticized the transfer of the FEPC to the WMC, asserting that it undercut the FEPC's autonomy. McNutt lived down to expectations when he postponed hearings, scheduled by the FEPC, to investigate discrimination in railroads. Although it is tempting to attribute the delay to McNutt's political antennae—to his deference to white southerners—Attorney General Francis G. Biddle, acting at FDR's behest, orchestrated the retreat to assuage southern concerns about the growth of federal power. Again, McNutt followed orders—and took a beating for doing so. Letters of protest poured in from leaders of the AFL, the United Automobile Workers (UAW), and a citizen's advocacy committee for African American railway workers, co-chaired by Eleanor Roosevelt and Fiorello La Guardia. In a "warning that prejudice reigns supreme," a columnist for the *Chicago Defender*, a leading African American paper, declared the FEPC "crucified," "dead," and rotting.[137] McNutt made amends by discussing with black leaders ways to strengthen the FEPC. The controversy ended in May 1943, when Roosevelt removed the FEPC from the WMC's authority.[138]

McNutt was happy to surrender the FEPC, which had troubled him "from the very first day."[139] The same could be said for his approach to race relations in general. McNutt knew that a lax response to discrimination would offend African American leaders while a stronger effort risked alienating whites. He dealt with this dilemma in three ways. First, he often walked a thin line in his public statements. While hailing America's racially diverse "team of workers," he acknowledged the "opposition to Negro manpower" and conceded that "prejudice cannot be swept away by fiat, by wishful thinking, by rhetoric."[140] Second, he fought behind the scenes for expanded opportunities for minority groups. He sought to end discriminatory draft calls, which favored the induction of whites over blacks, but failed due to opposition from the military. Finally, McNutt kept a low profile on disputes between blacks and whites; when the promotion of African American workers in Mobile, Alabama, sparked rioting, McNutt remained silent. To be sure, between 1940 and 1945, African Americans migrated to urban areas and secured jobs in war industries. They improved their skills, upgraded themselves economically, and laid the basis for the postwar assault on Jim Crow. But McNutt's manpower commission neither initiated nor forced these changes. At best, it simply accepted them.[141]

Two other groups, farmers and fathers, did more than bedevil McNutt; the debate over their role in the wartime economy led to further diminishment of his authority. In 1942 rural areas began to experience labor shortages. McNutt responded by proposing a mass deferment for fifty thousand dairy workers and suggesting that soldiers be used to harvest crops.[142] He also backed plans by Agriculture Secretary Wickard to transport farm workers to areas where they were needed most. McNutt's most important step was to cede responsibility for farm workers to Wickard.[143] But these efforts represented either half measures or evasions, and it soon became clear that the administration had "a whale of a problem" with respect to agricultural workers.[144]

A number of possible solutions to the shortage of farm labor emerged, few of them practicable. Roosevelt avoided the issue until 1943, when he considered endorsing a national service act to mobilize all workers. At other points, the president suggested that children take in the crops after school—an idea that overlooked the difficulty of harvesting a major staple such as wheat. FDR proposed inducting farmers into the army and then sending them home, but McNutt and Patterson objected that such a ploy "would fool no one."[145] Stimson, who according to Vice President Henry A. Wallace had not "the remotest glimmering of the farm situation," wanted farmers to conserve labor by using more machinery, even though such machinery was in short supply.[146] The War Department rejected a blanket deferment for all agricultural workers, as did the War Manpower Commission. But the farm bloc in Congress thought otherwise. In 1942 Congress asserted itself by deferring farmers engaged in essential war work. A year later, it considered legislation to exempt all agricultural workers.[147]

Faced with such pressures, the administration eventually found enough farm workers. In March 1943, McNutt, Wickard, and General Hershey at Selective Service cobbled together a program to manage agricultural deferments. The policy translated farm labor into "work units"—yardsticks to measure essential agricultural activity—and deferred only the workers who had amassed enough units.[148] Otherwise, the government located reserve sources of labor among rural women and children as well as people from outside the continental United States. Proposals to bring workers from Puerto Rico never got very far because it was difficult to transport these workers and they could not be forced to return home, since Puerto Rico was part of the United States.[149] Nevertheless, fifty thousand workers, mainly from Mexico, entered the United States under the braceros program. Union leaders, fearful of competition from foreign workers, were uneasy about this scheme, although politicians in such states as California found Mexican labor to be "of immense help."[150] McNutt agreed with them, and he urged Secretary of State Cordell Hull to continue the policy. Nevertheless, it was Wickard who really pushed the braceros program.[151]

McNutt took the lead on a separate matter, the drafting of fathers—and it caused him grief. As David Kennedy has explained, married males "had enjoyed exemption from the first draft calls," and "fathers proved even more untouchable, especially those with children born before Pearl Harbor."[152] McNutt's 1943 "work or fight" order ended the blanket deferment for fathers.[153] In so doing, "he invoked the quite defensible rationale that occupational status should be a stronger determinant of manpower disposition than family status."[154] But the decision to end the deferment of fathers betrayed a blend of brashness, indecision, and fumbling. McNutt seemed to attack traditional family values when he asserted "Fatherhood does not excuse any man from making his contribution to victory."[155] Then, sensing that he had gone too far, he postponed drafting fathers until October 1943 and recommended compensation for the dependents of draftees. But the damage was done. Polls showed that Americans preferred to draft single women for noncombat military jobs rather than force fathers into the armed services. Congress entered the picture in December 1943 when it passed a bill to restrict the government's power to induct fathers, end deferments for single men in essential jobs, and restore Selective Service's complete authority over the draft. McNutt "fought the bill" knowing that its passage would "sabotage" his entire manpower program. Thus, when FDR signed the measure, he delivered "a staggering blow to the man who gave up his almost-sure nomination as the 1940 Vice-Presidential candidate."[156]

Why did McNutt experience this setback? Two things stand out. First, his relations with Congress often were poor. McNutt's job performance drew criticism from Truman and Taft in 1942, and the complaints intensified in 1943 and 1944. The manpower commissioner's "work or fight" order offended conservative members of Congress, who dismissed him as a bureaucrat beset by a "'crackdown' complex."[157] "Demands for Paul McNutt's head grow in and out of Congress," William Hassett, an aide to FDR, noted in 1943.[158] Ickes observed that "McNutt has little, if any, standing before Congress," a point proven when a House committee turned down his request to raise the salaries of employees at the USES.[159] Representative Clarence Cannon griped that McNutt had been unable to translate his "practically autocratic" powers into an effective manpower program.[160] At a hearing in 1944, McNutt's evasiveness on whether the WMC required additional legislation to do its job prompted Representative John J. Sparkman, Democrat of Alabama, to snap: "You are the War Manpower Chief."[161] And when McNutt told the Senate Committee on Military Affairs that procurement agencies had "the real power" to stop to labor hoarding, Senator Burton K. Wheeler responded: "Everybody passes the buck."[162] Although McNutt spent considerable time before congressional committees and answered his inquisitors respectfully, his testimony did little to boost his reputation or political standing.[163]

In addition to troubles with Congress, there was a general lack of confidence in McNutt. Eliot Janeway doubted that he would "make good" with the powers the president had given him at the end of 1942, and Biddle deemed him an inferior executive, someone who "hates to make decisions."[164] The *Detroit Free Press*, in a scathing editorial, accused McNutt of caving in to the demands of unions and called him "totally unfit" to head the War Manpower Commission.[165] As McNutt's position in the administration weakened, stronger (and shrewder) personalities filled the void, such as Hershey. The man who went on to run Selective Service for over three decades was a fellow Hoosier and a skilled bureaucratic infighter. Hershey had advocated drafting fathers, but when McNutt took up the cause, he allowed the WMC chair to bear the brunt of the congressional assault. In the end, Hershey reaped the windfall when Congress passed a law to afford protection to fathers *and* restore the independence of the Selective Service System.[166]

Roosevelt's signing of the fathers bill seemed jarring, but his action was unsurprising. It was another stab in McNutt's back, something the president could do with impunity. Even Ickes noted that the original decision to draft fathers had been made by the cabinet and that "McNutt was only carrying out the policy of the President."[167] To be sure, FDR knew that the law did not prohibit the drafting of fathers and that men with children "will have to be inducted."[168] But the part of the act that separated Selective Service from the War Manpower Commission represented a vote of no-confidence in McNutt. As 1943 drew to a close, rumors circulated that Ickes would replace him as chair of the commission. And *Time* compared the ongoing manpower problem to "a vast, sticky pudding which the Administration stirred and stirred, hoping that something in the way of a solution would come to the top. None did."[169]

Between 1942 and 1943, McNutt faced pressures and endured defeats with little complaint and few flashes of anger. He had assumed his duties at the WMC without illusions, telling one supporter that the assignment represented his "most challenging task" to date.[170] Family as well as friends sustained him in wartime Washington. Paul lived at the Shoreham Hotel with Kathleen and Louise, and there was no sign that his love for them had lessened.[171] Paul also enjoyed the companionship of a Doberman pinscher named Skipper. He remained a sports fan, and the fortunes of the Washington Senators provided brief diversions from work. McNutt had another means of escape as well: a 1939 Cadillac sedan that the family used for quick holidays. Paul, Kathleen, and Louise sometimes sought respite from Washington's summers at the Virginia estate of Edward R. Stettinius Jr., a steel executive who worked for the Office of Production Management and later served as secretary of state. If anyone resembled a younger version of Paul, it was the tanned, gray-haired Stettinius. Together, the two men and their families swam, ate fried chicken, and enjoyed country life.[172]

The McNutts also visited the cottage of Joseph E. Davies and his wife, Marjorie Merriwether Post, in the Adirondacks. The couples clicked. Like Paul, Joe had served overseas, as ambassador to the Soviet Union, and Marjorie, like Kathleen, was a Christian Scientist. For Kathleen, time spent in the Adirondacks was "paradise." Years later, she recalled the companionship of friends, the "giggling of the girls," and her attempts to knit a pair of socks for "Paul's big feet." "Paul," she wrote, "loved being there so much."[173] In August 1942, McNutt spent ten days in upstate New York with Davies and his wife. The manpower commissioner would have seen no conflict between minding his duties and taking a holiday. In fact, he insisted that vacations allowed wartime workers to regroup and increase their productive output.[174]

These excursions raise the question: Did McNutt personally sacrifice during the war? Like the country at large, he did, but not as much as people in countries that had faced the Axis onslaught directly. McNutt did not serve in the military, and he had no son, brother, or nephew who might have been drafted and killed on the battlefield. Instead, he resided in Washington in an apartment one reporter described as "swanky."[175] Financially, his wartime jobs involved some degree of sacrifice. McNutt waived the annual salary of $15,000 that he was to receive as chair of the War Manpower Commission. He accepted instead his salary as head of the Federal Security Agency, which was $12,000. Although other administrators worked for less, many of them had amassed fortunes in business. McNutt, in contrast, soon discovered that the cost of living in Washington was consuming half his annual earnings.[176]

McNutt must have wondered whether the personal sacrifices and frequent criticism were worth it. On the surface, he remained stoic. "The going gets pretty tough here," McNutt admitted, "but I can take it."[177] As the journalist George Creel observed, "He himself keeps a tight mouth and, in public at least, carries on as beamingly as though he had never known a kick or a cuff."[178] Old friends offered their support. When McNutt was being "panned in the public press," Carleton McCulloch directed him to the gospel of St. Matthew: "Blessed are you when they revile and persecute you, and say all kinds of evil against you falsely for My sake. Rejoice and be exceedingly glad, for great is your reward in heaven."[179] Kathleen responded that while the family loved the sermon Paul was drawing his inspiration from *Reveille in Washington,* Margaret Leech's Pulitzer Prize–winning study of life in the capital during the Civil War.[180]

McNutt might have drawn more solace from McCulloch's suggested reading, for he gradually began to lose his cool. A 1943 exchange with Ickes at a cabinet meeting was a case in point. Before the president arrived, Ickes noticed that McNutt was "hot under the collar about the criticism that he had been getting from Biddle and me about deferments. He opened the subject and we were going at each other in some heat."[181] McNutt's composure had returned by the time Roosevelt entered the room. At the end of the year, he stayed calm and did not resign when FDR signed the fathers bill. McNutt endured because he believed "that he has been called to the colors by the Commander in Chief."[182] "He won't quit," McCulloch explained, "because it's cowardly to quit under fire."[183] Yet the criticism and humiliations left scars. "Never think that Paul hasn't minded," McNutt's associates informed Creel. "He's as sensitive as proud, and if you took his heart out, you'd find that every hobnail has left its mark."[184]

In 1944 McNutt's standing eroded further when FDR decided to back national service legislation. The catalyst for the change was Grenville Clark, who told Byrnes that the public now supported national service. Clark found allies in Stimson, Knox, and their undersecretaries, who urged the president to give "careful consideration" to national service.[185] Clark made his case to Roosevelt in part by decrying McNutt's handling of manpower as a "misfortune."[186] Harold Smith responded that the war production had been adequate under the existing manpower setup, that workers would view national service as a slap at their contribution to the war effort, and that enactment of such a law would enable the Axis to crow that "a great democratic nation believes it necessary to regiment labor."[187] In the end, Roosevelt split the difference. He endorsed a national service act in his State of the Union address in 1944 and then watched as Wadsworth and Austin introduced a revised version of their bill—which he did little to push.[188]

FDR's endorsement of national service demands further explanation. He may have been tossing a bone to the measure's conservative supporters as a way of offsetting his advocacy of an "economic bill of rights," something that liberals lauded. By backing national service, Roosevelt signaled that winning this war would require greater exertion and cooperation on the home front. The president recently had returned from visiting American forces in the Mediterranean theater, where the selfless sacrifice of U.S. troops belied the "selfish preoccupations of civilians" at home.[189] Yet, understanding that national service was anathema to business leaders, unions, and their representatives on Capitol

Hill, FDR kept his advocacy to a minimum. Roosevelt's decision to endorse national service marked another humiliation for McNutt, who had not been consulted about the change and "was taken by surprise at what was being done in his own 'shop.'"[190]

In 1944, McNutt was on the defensive on another much-discussed matter: occupational deferments. Since Congress had restricted the government's ability to draft fathers, additional servicemen had to be found among the five million men who held agricultural or industrial deferments. That was Hershey's plan, and it had the support of Stimson, Patterson, and General George C. Marshall but the opposition of McNutt and Nelson of the War Production Board. Roosevelt sided with the plan's proponents, telling Hershey and McNutt to review occupational deferments. During a cabinet meeting on March 3, McNutt exploded, arguing that the president's order threatened to disrupt the production of war material. Roosevelt responded by pleading ignorance: "What order? I don't know what order you are talking about." "Why," McNutt said, "you signed one." "I don't know what you are talking about," FDR replied. At that point, the president's men ran for cover. Byrnes denied any involvement in drafting the order, and Stimson told Roosevelt: "All I know is, you told me you wanted something like this done." Throughout the meeting, FDR demanded that McNutt "find out where the order came from." Secretary of the Treasury Henry Morgenthau Jr. thought the scene surreal: "I have never seen a performance like it."[191]

The reason behind Roosevelt's disavowal is not easily identified. He might have signed the order and then either changed his mind or retreated following McNutt's protest. Wallace blamed Stimson and Knox, thinking that "one or the other or both had slipped something over [on the president]."[192] Roosevelt's disengagement may have been the product of declining health. Late in 1943, FDR had returned from the Tehran Conference with a bronchial ailment from which he never fully recovered. In February 1944, when he ordered a review of occupational deferments, he continued to feel the aftereffects of an operation to remove a cyst. Roosevelt's larger problem was advanced cardiovascular disease, which taxed his ability to concentrate. Early in 1945 Stimson cringed over his willingness to "sign any paper."[193] FDR's approval of, and apparent forgetfulness about, the occupational deferments order perhaps exemplified this flaw.

McNutt's behavior is more easily understood: He was frustrated over his loss of power. According to Morgenthau, "McNutt wants to have the sole authority to tell Hershey what classes and what groups [should be inducted]."[194] McNutt took his case to Roosevelt, advising that no men under the age of twenty-six be taken from essential jobs until replacements were found and that the WMC must guide Selective Service on deferments. But Stimson and Patterson, backed by Byrnes and the president, affirmed that "by law" Hershey now had control over deferments.[195] "McNutt," Stimson warned Hershey, "is trying to fight for his own little bailiwick."[196] To be sure, McNutt won a few victories, such as the chance to chair an interagency committee on occupational deferments. But the Selective Service System "remained as independent as ever." And the "manpower crunch" persisted, especially following the Normandy invasion, when the ranks of American fighting men needed to be replenished with fresh troops.[197]

McNutt's conduct at cabinet meetings won him no allies. On March 17, 1944, he held forth, "bellowing for about an hour on the war manpower situation."[198] He was even louder on April 7. After FDR asked about the deferment of miners, McNutt attacked the policies of the army, navy, and Selective Service. "McNutt broke in," Ickes recorded. "His voice and manner when he talks about deferments are contentious. I could see that he was making a bad impression on the President. As a matter of fact, the President snapped back at him as he has never done at any Cabinet meeting."[199] Such outbursts delighted McNutt's critics. "Francis [Biddle] feels, as I do," Ickes wrote, "that a man who talks in a loud insistent voice, is not a strong man."[200] "The whole manpower problem and evil," Stimson reflected, "centers around the personality of McNutt."[201] But the attitude of the president should have been the war manpower chief's greatest concern. "He was pretty mad at McNutt," Ickes stressed.[202]

By alienating Roosevelt, McNutt had eliminated any chance of securing a spot on the party's national ticket. In 1944, the Democratic nomination for vice president would become available again for Wallace remained unpopular among party leaders who thought him too liberal and idealistic in his politics, eclectic in his intellectual pursuits, and standoffish in his manners. Roosevelt recognized Wallace's shortcomings and agreed to consider alternatives. Among the frontrunners were Supreme Court Justice William O. Douglas, a favorite of liberals; Byrnes, whose experience had earned him the nickname "assistant president"; and Truman, who had won renown as head of the Senate committee to end waste in the nation's war effort. As possible vice presidents (or presidents, given FDR's health), each of these men carried baggage: Douglas was young and a sitting member of the Court; Byrnes was anathema to Catholics for having converted from that religion to the Episcopal faith; and Truman was not close to FDR.[203]

McNutt's vice-presidential prospects advanced no farther than a passing mention in the press. He failed to place in a Gallup poll of vice-presidential possibilities. And McNutt's name never came up during a critical preconvention meeting between FDR and party leaders on the vice-presidential nomination. When the president playfully mentioned McNutt's vice-presidential prospects to Morgenthau, the treasury secretary vowed: "I will crawl from here to the Capitol on my stomach and back again if it will keep you from taking McNutt . . . Don't forget about his 2% Club and how he used to win money [at poker]. The man's record is very bad."[204] The criticism McNutt received at the War Manpower Commission contrasted sharply with popular perceptions of Byrnes as a skilled administrator and Truman as watchdog of the public purse.

McNutt watched his political prospects slip away. He claimed to have known from the outset that running the manpower commission would be "political suicide."[205] In truth, he not only sought the job but had fought to keep it. The Indiana novelist Booth Tarkington sensed McNutt's disappointment about the choices he had made. "Wonder what P. V. McN. thinks about Henery W. these days," Tarkington speculated, "and if he ever wonders [d]id he play the right card at the '40 Convention?"[206] In May 1944, McNutt bowed to reality and renounced interest in the vice presidency. Instead, he resolved to settle scores with Roosevelt by thwarting Wallace's renomination. As the balloting for vice president commenced, Frank McHale placed McNutt's name in nomination presumably to exorcize past demons, give his friend a chance at the second spot, or deny votes to Wallace. Little came of the endeavor. After hearing McNutt's vow, that "the President can't lead me in to Wallace," Senator Joseph Guffey of Pennsylvania warned that "when McNutt is through he will have no state delegation, not even Indiana."[207] Fowler Harper conceded that McNutt "has very little influence in Indiana," and Ickes gloated that McNutt "could hardly be elected constable."[208] On the first ballot, McNutt received just thirty-one votes, with twenty-one of them from Indiana.[209] By that point, party leaders had settled on Truman, Roosevelt had accepted their advice, and the convention ratified the choice.[210] A cartoon in the *Washington Evening Star* captured the moment by depicting FDR as the waiting groom, Truman as his latest bride, and McNutt as one of many bridesmaids reaching for the coveted bouquet. Interestingly, the woman whom McNutt had wed nearly three decades earlier expressed relief over the outcome. Kathleen's distaste for politics had not abated.

McNutt's reaction to Truman's nomination remains elusive. Yet there is one clue buried in his private papers. A supporter, Joseph J. Lowry, prepared a retrospective on two Democratic conventions, separated by four years. At the earlier one, in 1940, McNutt had withdrawn from the race for vice president so that Roosevelt could have the running mate of his choice. In the interim, McNutt had proven his loyalty to the president by serving in a "thankless" position at the War Manpower Commission. At the later convention, McNutt's name was hardly mentioned. Lowry titled his piece, "The Forgotten Man"—a depression-era phrase used by Roosevelt.[211] The fact that McNutt saved the piece suggests that it must have carried some meaning for him.

Following the convention, McNutt's authority over manpower continued to erode. Between August and December 1944, it was Byrnes, not McNutt, who signed a series of directives to squeeze workers into essential industries.[212] And in December 1944, Byrnes issued the latest work-or-fight order requiring men in their late thirties either to take jobs in war industries or face the draft.[213] A month later, Byrnes told Hershey to review the deferments of farm workers between the ages of eighteen and twenty. In a further effort to conserve labor, Byrnes imposed a curfew on places of entertainment and assigned enforcement of the curfew to the WMC. The decline in McNutt's clout was plain. In 1942 the *Houston Post* had dubbed him the "boss of U.S. manpower."[214] By the end of 1944 Byrnes held that power, if not the title.

McNutt had less and less to do. To be sure, he tried to help soldiers who would soon become veterans. He took an interest in men who had been disabled by war, and he pressed for a program of vocational rehabilitation for wounded veterans and civilians injured in war plants. His aim was to rehabilitate, retrain, and place the disabled in war work. Unfortunately, he was hampered again by poor relations with Congress and a maladroit handling of bureaucratic (and interest-group) politics. The Veterans Administration (VA), supported by the American Legion, rejected FSA control over vocational rehabilitation. Ultimately, Congress passed a bill giving the VA charge over vocational rehabilitation for soldiers, and the president signed it.[215]

McNutt lost other battles. He tried to use the U.S. Employment Service and the newly established Veterans Employment Service Center to reintegrate veterans into the economy. But FDR assigned responsibility over discharged soldiers to the Re-training and Re-employment Administration, headed by Frank T. Hines—a Republican who had run the VA since the mid-1920s. McNutt spoke out on reconversion to a peacetime economy, and he hoped to use the USES to place Americans in jobs and prevent the return of unemployment. Yet two things inhibited him. The German offensive into the Ardennes in December 1944 had reminded Americans that the war was not over. And Byrnes, who had acquired control over reconversion as well as mobilization, insisted that the economy remain on a wartime footing.[216]

As the setbacks mounted, McNutt began to crack. "I have been hearing for some time," White House aide Jonathan Daniels wrote early in 1945, "that Paul McNutt has been drinking pretty heavily in the daytime." Kathleen became so worried that she often telephoned Mary Switzer at the office to inquire after Paul. McNutt's alcohol abuse may have stemmed, in part, from his latest disappointment, his inability to leave government work for a position in the private sector. If so, it was a case of Catch-22; according to Daniels, when would-be employers learned about McNutt's drinking, they withdrew their job offers.[217] For McNutt, booze became a means of escape. In January 1945 he joined representatives of the WMC and the War Production Board on an inspection tour of Europe. On the surface, McNutt appeared fine as he ad-libbed with reporters. But the trip bored him, and he often stayed in his hotel rooms to drink. It is possible that McNutt had been abusing alcohol for years, for he never had been a teetotaler. Moreover, political life often involved heavy drinking. Jack New, a longtime Democratic Party operative, recalled an "It's party time" attitude among Indiana politicians.[218] In the nation's capital, there was a "culture of alcoholism" in the Senate which took its toll in the form of "health problems," "diminished judgment," and "erratic behavior."[219]

In 1944 and 1945 McNutt exhibited erratic behavior by making extreme statements which may or may not have stemmed from his drinking. His outbursts during cabinet meetings were one manifestation of such conduct (at one session, McNutt shook his fist in the face of Frank Knox). An even more unsettling episode took place in April 1945 when McNutt, speaking in Chattanooga, departed from his text and declared: "As far as the Japanese are concerned, I'm for extermination—in toto!"[220] Such a remark might be attributed to the brutalizing impact of war in general or the racial aspects of the Pacific War in particular. The U.S. government had interned Japanese Americans, a project which McNutt's Federal Security Agency assisted by providing health care services in the relocation camps. Even during wartime, however, his crack about wiping out the Japanese people provoked protests from average citizens and from Eleanor Roosevelt. In response, McNutt claimed that he was trying to exhort Americans to go "all-out in the war against Japan." Yet he could not disguise his contempt for "an enemy whose fanatic disregard for human values" he had noticed during his years in the Philippines.[221]

There was an ideological dimension to McNutt's remark about exterminating the Japanese. McNutt's mindset proved holistic; just as he sought to provide for America's security through a wide-ranging program of domestic reform, military preparedness, and international engagement, he was averse to separate the peoples of the Axis nations from the policies of their governments. McNutt's harshness toward the Germans and Japanese stiffened as he became aware of the Holocaust. Three days after his speech in Chattanooga, McNutt, addressing a Jewish audience in Miami, denounced "the German apparatus of terror, the concentration camps, the murder-factories, the torture rooms, the crematories." "No man living today, Jew or Christian," he averred, "can dare forget the crimes committed against world civilization by the German 'Herrenvolk.' And the 'Herrenvolk' of Asia, the Japanese." As someone who had helped bring Jewish refugees to the Philippines, McNutt's fury was understandable. And his larger argument, that all "points of prejudice and hate" had to be extinguished, was commendable. Nevertheless, he had entered the rhetorical, if not the moral, domain of the enemy. His prepared remarks at Miami, in which he assailed "the decimation of Europe's Jews," had been preceded by his extemporaneous advocacy, in Chattanooga, of extermination for the Japanese (but not for the Germans). Even the title of McNutt's Miami address, in which he offered prescriptions for shaping the postwar world, derived from a familiar Nazi refrain: "Towards a Thousand Year Democracy."[222]

McNutt's attempt to rally Americans against the Japanese proved needless, for the war was about to end. In March and April of 1945, the WMC's area and regional directors began to relax their restrictions on manpower. Congress restored the USES to state control, and Harry Truman, who became president following FDR's death in April 1945, accepted cuts in the budget of the War Manpower Commission before shifting its functions over to the Department of Labor. By that point, Japan had surrendered and McNutt was more than ready to move on.[223]

The record of the War Manpower Commission and its chairman was a mixed bag. Overall, the United States found enough human resources to build its armed forces, run its industries, and produce sufficient war material to defeat its enemies. In testimony before the Truman Committee at the close of 1944, Charles M. Hay, McNutt's deputy at the WMC, reported that sixty-five million men and women were working, ten million had been added to the labor force since 1940, and twelve million were in uniform. Yet Hay admitted progress had been messy, confused, and slow.[224] Part of the problem was the task of mobilizing a decentralized, free-market economy. Another difficulty lay in Roosevelt's disjointed administrative style.[225] "There have been created a vast number of new agencies," Henry Stimson complained, "that head up nowhere except [to] the President, and he is too busy to keep them in order."[226] The emergence of James Byrnes as FDR's most trusted assistant brought a semblance of coherence to policymaking. "In the end," argued the journalist David Brinkley, "the preparations for war succeeded only because the country had manpower, skills, resources and industrial capacity to succeed in spite of itself."[227] The historian Paul Koistinen similarly concluded that "America's plenty allowed the nation to harness its system for hostilities without altering in any basic way peacetime power operations."[228]

McNutt admitted that his handling of manpower had involved trial and error. At one point, he observed that the country would have better off had the War Manpower Commission been formed earlier, even before Pearl Harbor.[229] "Ours is not a program which sprang full blown at one time," he informed a Senate committee in 1945. "It is a program which developed gradually, as the needs of our manpower situation required."[230] In this instance, McNutt's pragmatism came to be seen as weakness—an incremental approach to a pressing problem that demanded focused, determined leadership.

McNutt's contribution to the war often was disparaged, fairly and otherwise. One heard two common criticisms, that McNutt was reluctant to act and that he remained a politician—and thus a prisoner to organized groups. During 1942, McNutt was indeed more inclined to acquire power than to exercise it, and by 1944 he had lost control of deferments to Hershey. Yet, when McNutt's powers crested during 1943, he did act decisively, on drafting fathers, for instance, where he paid a price. His reputation as one "who nursed presidential ambitions and who showed a marked disinclination to . . . offend any potential constituency" proved misleading as well.[231] McNutt's stewardship of the FEPC had offended African Americans, and he was not under the thumb of unions, which disliked the braceros program. In many ways, McNutt seemed hesitant when he should have pressed ahead (in 1942) or proved intrepid (on drafting fathers) when he might have exercised caution or worked harder to build coalitions. For much of the war, then, this veteran politician exhibited a knack for alienating supporters and opponents alike.

Why did McNutt falter at the War Manpower Commission? In part, it was a matter of circumstance. For the first time, McNutt held a high-profile position that was critically important to the war effort and directly responsible to the president. In part, it was due to flagging support from FDR and Congress.

In part, it was because McNutt's ambition lay in electoral politics rather than in bureaucratic aggrandizement. In contrast to his mobilization of the government's health, educational, and recreational programs as head of the wartime Federal Security Agency—an effort so suited to the FSA that it aroused little opposition within the administration—McNutt faced an on-going, fierce struggle over manpower policy. Within the Roosevelt administration, where he was disliked, he appeared tentative and fell victim to such sharp-elbowed competitors as Stimson, Hershey, and Byrnes. Moreover, McNutt's style of leadership, in which he assumed the role of public salesman while his staff handled the details of policy, worked best in offices, such as high commissioner in the Philippines or federal security administrator, which were under the radar of FDR and the public. At the War Manpower Commission, McNutt was at the center of events, and he failed to master them fully. The methods employed by the WMC were, as Koistinen has argued, "flawed but adequate."[232] Adequacy was not enough to sustain McNutt's political appeal. "The triumphal advance of the beautiful Paul," Jonathan Daniels pronounced, was at an end. He was "a man in anticlimax."[233]

# 14

## RETURNING TO THE PHILIPPINES
## (1945–1947)

NINETEEN FORTY-FIVE WAS ANOTHER year of change, for the United States and for Paul V. McNutt. World War II ended, a new president entered the White House, and McNutt returned to the Philippines as high commissioner and then as ambassador. "There is nothing complicated or devious about the McNutt appointment," one correspondent noted. "War Manpower is obviously due to fold . . . McNutt, a good and loyal Democrat but a little too ambitious to have around in peacetime, needs a job. He made a good record during his former service in the Philippines."[1] By going to Manila, McNutt was returning to the scene of past triumphs rather than attempting to revive his political career. Indeed, he accepted the post of high commissioner reluctantly, at President Harry S. Truman's insistence. "I thought I was beyond draft age," McNutt joked. "However, this was a draft."[2] McNutt no doubt sought to forsake the firing line of Washington politics for distant—and familiar—shores.[3] A reporter noticed the toll that the manpower job had taken on McNutt: "His working day stretches to 18 hours. He looks a little tired . . . One senses a restlessness about him."[4] But McNutt retained a strong attachment to the Philippines, and he wanted to help Filipinos "return to normal life" following the war.[5] And since he had firsthand knowledge of the Philippines, his recommendations with respect to U.S.-Philippine relations were likely to receive serious attention from officials in Washington in marked contrast to his experience at the War Manpower Commission.

McNutt planned to go to Manila for no more than a year and then return to America to enter private life. On November 1, 1945, he established residency in New York, where he could begin practicing law after six months. McNutt's years in public life had been unprofitable, and he wanted to bring a measure of financial security to his family, who would not be joining him in the Philippines, at least not initially.[6] Kathleen remained in Washington, while Louise, who had taken a master of arts degree from George Washington University, prepared to enter the Foreign Service. After seeing conditions in the Philippines, Paul was in no hurry to bring them to Manila.

In 1945 the Philippines faced an uncertain future and an array of problems. Japan had conquered the Philippines during World War II. A puppet regime had taken the place of the U.S.-backed commonwealth, and President Manuel L. Quezon had fled to Washington, where he had formed a government in exile. American forces landed in the Philippines in 1944 and liberated Manila in 1945, at the cost of tens of thousands of lives. With peace came freedom from Japan but not from the United States, which retained sovereignty over the Philippines until July 4, 1946, when, according to the Tydings-McDuffie Act of 1934, the semi-autonomous Philippine Commonwealth was to become independent. In the interim, Filipinos and Americans had to address such issues as the fate of Filipino collaborators; the transition from U.S. rule to Philippine sovereignty; and shape of American-Philippine relations, economic and military—all at a time when the Philippines was struggling to rebuild from the ravages of war. McNutt recognized the enormity of his assignment and vowed to "give it all I have."[7]

McNutt's actions between 1945 and 1947 influenced the course of U.S.-Philippine relations for decades. He negotiated a treaty under which the United States secured military bases in its former colony. He helped to secure parity rights for American firms investing in the Philippines and a continuation of preferential trade between the two countries—policies which later generations of scholars would attack as "neocolonialism."[8] McNutt displayed an imperial mentality, that is, a sense that the Philippines, even after independence, must remain close to America—ideologically, economically, and militarily. During the 1930s, he had maneuvered to retain the Philippines as an outpost of America power in order to check the ambitions of Japan. After World War II, he and other U.S. officials sought to use the Philippines to contain new threats. McNutt thus had a part in fashioning America's defense perimeter in East Asia during the Cold

War, and he did so with the consent of a Filipino leadership that was generally favorable toward the United States. Philippine president Ramón Magsaysay later hailed McNutt "as one of the ablest architects" of the "steadfast" relationship between America and the Philippines.[9]

McNutt did not operate in a vacuum, for a number of realities shaped U.S.-Philippine relations between 1945 and 1947. The end of World War II, coupled with the onset of the Cold War, reinforced demands for cooperation between the two countries. U.S.-Philippines ties remained close, but the argument that the Truman administration imposed "onerous trade and defense arrangements on a prostrate ally" is only partially correct for "Philippine leaders bargained more skillfully than their critics admit."[10] The result was a series of compromise agreements in which Filipinos won some of what they wanted, such as a period of preferential trade with the United States, while Americans gained even more, such as investment rights and military installations in a strategically located country. McNutt proved the man in the middle, expressing sympathy for Filipinos, working to cement ties between the two countries, and serving the interests of the United States more than those of its former colony.

The story of American-Philippine relations from 1945 to 1947, and McNutt's impact on them, illustrates what was distinctive and not so distinctive about U.S. imperialism. America's "calibrated colonialism," under which it granted ever-widening autonomy to the Philippines and set a date for independence, combined with the impact of World War II, meant that the United States practiced decolonization in an atmosphere of deadlines and devastation.[11] Thus, as July 4, 1946, neared, U.S. policymakers struggled to transfer sovereignty to the Philippines, rebuild the economy, and reestablish the archipelago as a bastion of American values and power. The United States was not alone in trying to try to maintain influence over a onetime colony. Following World War II, the historian William Roger Louis has observed, "It was hoped that the former colonies would align themselves in foreign affairs and in defence treaties with the United States, Britain, and the other western powers, that the new nations would have stable political regimes, and moreover that they would be democratic."[12] McNutt hoped to effect such an outcome in Manila, as the Philippines lurched from Japanese occupation to U.S. client state.

Conditions in the Philippines after World War II left a void which U.S. officials and Filipino politicians acted to fill. McNutt stepped into this mix, as he influenced debates on such issues as the punishment of Philippine collaborators, the timing of elections, and the structure of postwar trade relations with the United States. At the same time, however, he faced a host of political pressures and constraints as the Philippines confronted the aftereffects of war.

In 1945 the Philippines was in a sorry state. Senator Millard E. Tydings of Maryland, chair of the Senate Committee on Territories and Insular Affairs and co-author with Representative John McDuffie of the 1934 Philippine Independence Act, visited the Philippines in June and reported the grim realities: "The whole Philippine economy has been laid flat. People are without food, clothing, housing and medicine." Sugar, the chief export, had been devastated and "the great cities of the Islands are in ruins." "The visitor to Manila is met by a strange sight," Tydings reported. "Everywhere one looks, thousands of Filipinos are digging in the debris to try to recover a piece of lumber." The only source of order and economic activity in Manila was the United States Army, which was feeding 600,000 people daily.[13] Philippine economists estimated that the archipelago had suffered losses amounting to $860 million during World War II.[14] The surrender of Japan brought little relief. The economy remained stagnant, and people purchased food at unbearably high prices. Inflation, coupled with the perceived "filth and primitiveness of Filipino life," offended U.S. soldiers, who often disparaged the Filipinos as "Flips" or "Gooks."[15] Many GIs judged Filipinos unsuited for independence. Their women, however, were suitable for sexual liaisons. Manila's nightclubs did a brisk trade, and the rate of venereal disease jumped to one of "the highest in the Army's history."[16] McNutt, who as federal security administrator had worked to stamp out prostitution and VD, was returning to an area plagued by both.

Along with the economy, Philippine politics had been shattered by the war. Before the Japanese occupation, a rough consensus had prevailed in the Philippines centered on (1) a demand for independence, (2) concern about an invasion from without or an economic collapse from within following independence, and (3) the need to be aligned with a stronger power such as the United States. Promoting this agenda was Manuel L. Quezon, the first president of the autonomous Commonwealth of the Philippines, and Quezon's Nacionalista Party. Buttressing it was the president's mastery of machine politics, in which money, patronage, and other favors flowed downward to local elites, planters, and sugar manufacturers while votes ascended upward to Nacionalista candidates at election time. The Japanese invasion undermined this stable, semi-authoritarian system. When Quezon departed the Philippines in 1942, he left behind a sizable portion of his government which became the nucleus of a pro-Japanese republic headed by José P. Laurel. After Quezon died in 1944, leadership of the government in exile passed to its vice president, Sergio Osmeña—an aging, less-than-charismatic figure whom Quezon had supplanted as leader of the Nacionalista Party more than two decades earlier.[17]

As World War II came to an end, Philippine politics became fluid. On the surface, the commonwealth regained nominal control over areas liberated by U.S. troops. Osmeña landed with General Douglas A. MacArthur at Leyte in 1944 and reestablished the commonwealth government at Manila in 1945. But the country was divided among those who had remained loyal to Quezon's government, including guerrillas who had fought the Japanese; officials of the Laurel regime, who had cooperated with the occupiers; and the many Filipinos who had accommodated or resisted the enemy as circumstances warranted. Moreover, an anti-landlord insurgency, the Hukbalahap or "Huks," won control of the countryside in central Luzon. The Huks, the Communist Party, and the trade unions united to form the Democratic Alliance, a popular-front-style movement.[18] The restored commonwealth thus experienced something Quezon seldom had: a serious, sustained challenge to its authority by dispossessed people.[19]

The end of the war brought another headache for the Nacionalistas: a leadership contest between Osmeña, who refused to name anyone to his cabinet who had cooperated with the enemy, and Manuel A. Roxas, a rising star in the 1930s who had served in the Japanese-backed government while secretly assisting anti-Japanese rebels. Few ideological issues separated Osmeña and Roxas as each man drew support from both former collaborators and guerrillas. But Osmeña failed to set standards for what constituted collaboration and prosecute suspected collaborators. Overall, the Nacionalista Party, according to one observer, was both "hopelessly corrupt" and "dominated by collaborators, appeasers, and reactionaries."[20] Osmeña, moreover, lacked the leadership skill and financial resources to rebuild Quezon's one-party state.[21]

In this setting, authority in the Philippines rested with the U.S. Army, led by MacArthur. The general was familiar with the Philippines, having served as military adviser to Quezon during the 1930s. Consequently, he interfered in Philippine politics and set occupation policy with little concern for the preferences of the government in Washington. MacArthur took steps to repress the Huks, censor the press, and reestablish the old economic order which had been led by such conservative, wealthy Filipinos as Roxas. The general's policy on collaborators also favored Roxas, widely considered to be "the dynamo behind Laurel."[22] MacArthur, who had known Roxas since the 1930s, absolved his friend of treason and allowed him to reenter politics. After the prewar Philippine Congress reconvened, the Senate elected Roxas as its president. (A constitutional amendment had restored the bicameral Philippine Congress in December 1941. It was this Congress, consisting of a House of Representatives and a Senate, that reconvened in 1945.) When MacArthur left Manila to oversee the occupation of Japan, he "released the remainder of the imprisoned collaborators, an act widely interpreted as a blanket amnesty."[23]

MacArthur's stand on collaborators requires further comment, for it shaped Philippine politics in the immediate postwar period and was one of the first issues with which McNutt had to deal. There had been ambiguity over how Filipinos were to behave under the Japanese. Before Quezon departed the Philippines in 1942, he told the government officials who were staying behind to act as a buffer between the occupiers and the population. Accordingly, basic services continued to function under the Laurel regime. Meanwhile, Filipinos, who were no strangers to foreign rule, did not see Laurel as a puppet leader but as someone who "fooled the Japs" and ran the country.[24] The administration in Washington took a different view. In 1944 President Franklin D. Roosevelt insisted that Filipinos who had collaborated with the Japanese be removed from positions of power. Secretary of the Interior Harold L. Ickes, who oversaw U.S. territories, agreed. After the war, Ickes demanded punishment of collaborators, and he privately attacked Osmeña for timidity on the issue, Roxas for double-dealing, and MacArthur for promoting the ambitions of Roxas. The issue of Filipino collaboration was complicated, but Ickes, along with officials at the Department of State, correctly identified MacArthur's partiality toward Roxas.[25]

Ickes and MacArthur clashed over another matter: whether to send a high commissioner back to Manila. The office had been vacant since 1942, when Francis Sayre had resigned as high commissioner. During the war, there was no reason to replace Sayre, since Quezon and Osmeña lived in Washington and could transact business with the Americans directly. Between 1942 and 1945, two officials at the Interior Department's division of territories, Richard R. Ely and Evett D. Hester, ran what remained of the high commissioner's office.[26] As the war came to an end, however, Ickes advised Roosevelt to name a new high commissioner, preferably someone with experience in the Philippines, such as McNutt, or a person with executive skill.[27] While these discussions went on, the State Department saw no need for another high commissioner, since the Philippines would receive independence in 1946. Eager to protect their authority over the islands, MacArthur and Osmeña also opposed restoring the post. When Truman delayed naming a high commissioner, and instead dispatched Tydings to Manila on a fact-finding mission, MacArthur and Osmeña celebrated their apparent victory.[28]

Time and events, however, were on the side of reinstating a high commissioner. MacArthur's obstructionism ended when he departed for Tokyo following the surrender of Japan. Moreover, with the devastation of the Philippines apparent and independence looming, Truman knew that he needed an experienced high commissioner. McNutt fit the bill. Even Ickes admitted that the Hoosier "had done a pretty good job as High Commissioner" during the 1930s.[29] McNutt renewed his credentials by undertaking, at Truman's request, a survey of the Philippines in July 1945. Two months later, he agreed to serve as high commissioner, having been granted wide authority over all U.S. government offices in the Philippines as well as the right to recommend, in tandem with the Secretary of Interior, policies to assist the Philippines.[30]

There was a strong sense in the United States and the Philippines that McNutt was an excellent choice. One American observer recalled that McNutt, during his first stint in Manila, had balanced the interests of Americans and Filipinos better than any previous high commissioner or governor-general. The publisher Roy W. Howard, who had an abiding interest in the Philippines but little personal regard for McNutt, admitted that his fellow Indianan was a "real friend" to the Filipinos and likely to be of "great assistance" to them.[31] In Manila, there were concerns, perhaps driven by memories of the toasting incident eight years earlier, that McNutt would be "officious and offensive" toward the Philippine government.[32] And a few people speculated that he would revive his earlier project, of trying to reexamine Philippine independence. But that was not the conventional wisdom among the Filipino elite. President Osmeña praised McNutt for having "a sympathetic understanding of our problems."[33] And Carlos P. Rómulo, the Philippines' resident commissioner (representative in the U.S. Congress), characterized McNutt as "most friendly to us."[34] Roxas proved more effusive. During McNutt's visit in July, Roxas "begged him to accept this assignment."[35] "He is a friend of the Filipinos and commands their confidence," Roxas later wrote of McNutt. "He is also my personal friend and I have implicit faith that his policies and attitude will be motivated always by what he believes is to the enduring interest of both the Philippines and the United States."[36]

On a personal and political level, the high commissioner was indeed Roxas's friend. Like MacArthur, McNutt had known Roxas during the 1930s and thought him "the best brain" in the Philippines.[37] Furthermore, McNutt generally backed MacArthur's policy on collaboration, which had allowed Roxas to regain the political spotlight.[38] McNutt saw Roxas as "very popular" and likely to defeat Osmeña in any election. Accordingly, he abetted Roxas's ambitions by pressing Osmeña to hold a presidential canvass in 1946.[39] During that contest, the challenger campaigned vigorously, exploiting "racial animosity" by labeling Osmeña, who was part Chinese, a "Chinese puppet."[40] In public, McNutt remained above the fray, but in private, he preferred the energetic Roxas to the aging Osmeña. After Roxas prevailed, the issue of collaboration faded when the new president declared a general amnesty. While Roxas went on to govern an economically crippled land, he could thank, in part, McNutt and MacArthur for his political revival.[41]

Roxas's faith in McNutt was both unblinkingly realistic and idealistic to the point of naïveté. The Philippine leader had a political, as well as a personal, reason for remaining close to McNutt. Roxas had appraised his country's place in the world and determined that it must remain aligned with the United States. Roxas's intelligence and his capacity to be both pro-American and nationalistic reminded many Americans of Quezon. He shared his predecessor's concerns about the fate of the Philippines after independence, fearing either an economic collapse following the end of the Philippines' privileged access to the U.S. market or invasion by a stronger nation. World War II had confirmed the latter fear, and Filipinos remained conscious of future threats, seeing China, with its vast size, as poised to become Asia's next great power.[42] The developing Cold War was another consideration. As the world began to divide between the West and the Communist states, smaller nations felt pressed to pick a side, and the choice, the *Manila Post* noted, was plain: We "cannot escape dependence on America."[43] In this setting, Roxas championed "frank, open and wholehearted cooperation with the United States."[44]

Roxas was less shrewd in extolling McNutt's friendship for his country because, as the *Manila Post* noted, "McNutt is primarily bound to uphold American interests."[45] During his earlier stint in Manila, McNutt had proven to be an American nationalist and, in many respects, an old-fashioned imperialist. In 1938, his call for a reexamination of Philippine independence envisioned a continuation of U.S. sovereignty over the Philippines in an arrangement resembling the one between Great Britain and Canada. And he believed that maintaining a U.S. military presence in Asia would protect American shores by discouraging potential aggressors, such as Japan. The war years did little to alter his thinking. In 1941 McNutt spoke of the Philippines as an American "outpost" in the "new frontier" of the Pacific, one which enhanced America's security and access to "strategic materials" in Southeast Asia. Withdrawal would benefit neither Americans nor Filipinos. "Shorn of the Philippines and Guam," McNutt argued, "American sea power ebbs," and the result for the United States would be a fortress-like mentality, with a navy confined to defending the North American coastline. For the Philippines, the consequences would be much worse—"a mere trade of sovereignties," with Japan taking over from America.[46] Japan's invasion of the archipelago confirmed McNutt's fears.[47] As the war drew to a close, McNutt again expressed reservations about giving the Philippines independence. The country, he claimed, was unprepared for independence following the devastation of World War II, and it "should not be thrown to the wolves."[48]

The postwar period changed McNutt's thinking about the Philippines in three respects. First, he recognized that the Soviet Union had replaced Japan as the chief threat to America and the Philippines. "The world," he wrote, "... is watching the Philippines. You can be sure Russia is watching the Philippines." McNutt's concern about Soviet intentions stemmed from a number of factors, including his anti-Communism, antipathy toward totalitarian regimes, and willingness to confront bullies—in 1945, he emphasized that in Asia the United States "faces a major test of its stature as a world power."[49]

Second, McNutt by the end of 1945 had accepted the inevitability of Philippine independence, that is, political—if not military or economic—separation from the United States. Talk about revisiting the issue of independence seldom rose above a whisper because, as in the 1930s, Filipinos were unwilling to forsake forty years of "pro-Independence agitation." Moreover, after voicing objections to European colonialism throughout World War II, the U.S. government found it "hard to back down" on Philippine independence.[50] Accordingly, McNutt disavowed any effort to reexamine the question as politically unthinkable.[51]

McNutt also believed that a smooth transition to Philippine sovereignty represented an "opportunity to demonstrate democracy in action to all the peoples of the Orient."[52] And that represented the third change in his thinking. Restoring the Philippine economy and then granting the colony independence would underscore American goodwill and serve a larger U.S. interest, of establishing a bastion of democratic capitalism in Asia. It might even gain for America the "respect of the colonial peoples of the Far East."[53] To be sure, McNutt knew that neither Osmeña nor Roxas was likely to "establish the kind of Philippine Government that...the United States Government would like to see."[54] But, in order to emerge as "the standard-bearer of democracy," the Philippines simply had to establish political system that was more stable, fair, and egalitarian than that of defeated Japan, totalitarian Russia, strife-torn China, and the colonial regimes in India, Burma, and Indochina. "To help the Filipinos achieve their great destiny," McNutt explained, "is one of the most urgent tasks of the United States."[55]

Fueling McNutt's urgency was his revulsion over the devastation of the Philippines. In July 1945, McNutt found conditions almost "indescribable." Manila, he observed, "is a city of missing faces and missing places, and the same thing may be said for the rest of the islands."[56] He acquired a wider frame of reference at the end of 1945, following a visit to Japan. McNutt was shaken by what he saw. "At Osaka," he wrote his wife, "we flew very low in order to see the details of the destruction. This Chicago of Japan is no more." Hiroshima and Nagasaki were worse. "What hath man wrought from atomic energy?" McNutt wondered. "Great cities and their populations completely wiped out—an eraser over a blackboard."[57] Yet he believed that the Philippines had suffered even "greater damage."[58] Roy Howard agreed: "Manila is even worse flattened than Tokyo."[59] The devastation of the Philippines had to be alleviated—fast.

McNutt's ability to affect change proved limited. The Philippines required U.S. assistance and only Congress could appropriate the necessary funds. But McNutt lacked a strong relationship with the House and Senate, and his political clout had diminished. "Aside from close personal friends," an adviser to the Philippine government reported in 1945, "McNutt's prestige in Washington is very low . . . [T]here are few government or Congressional leaders with whom I have talked who have anything complimentary to say about him."[60] Accordingly, McNutt's second stint as high commissioner differed from his earlier go-round in Manila. Between 1937 and 1939, he had been an ascending star whose talents and reputation had made a favorable impression in the Philippines, where he passed most of his time as high commissioner. Between 1945 and 1946, his situation was almost reversed. McNutt was a fading figure, with no prospect of becoming president, who became mired in drafting legislation for the Philippines while in Washington, where he spent a considerable portion of his tenure as high commissioner.

McNutt knew that getting the Philippine economy "off dead center" was his "first big job."[61] Trade and rehabilitation aid were crucial issues, and the U.S. government was divided over how to proceed. The problem originated in the Philippines' prewar economy, which was dependent on selling agricultural products, such as sugar, in the United States duty-free. Any restriction of access to the American market threatened to disrupt the sugar industry and the entire Philippine economy. That was one reason why Quezon sought to reexamine the matter of independence during the 1930s, with the goal of transforming the Philippines into a self-governing dominion that could sell its products duty-free in the United States. Although the effort to reexamine independence failed, Quezon resumed his fight for preferential trade during World War II. After Quezon's death, Osmeña recommended that the Philippines and the United States maintain free trade for twenty years following independence.[62]

Such proposals spawned a debate, principally between the Department of the Interior and the Department of State, over the shape of the postwar, post-independence Philippine economy. Officials at Interior, led by Ickes, Evett Hester, and Undersecretary Abe Fortas, feared that the Philippines could not withstand a sudden stifling of access to the U.S. market. The Philippines, in Interior's view, required a prolonged transition to nonpreferential trade with the United States and protection for American investors in the Philippines. Such policies would give Filipinos the time and means to diversify their economy and lessen their dependence on agricultural exports. Interior's policy was preferential and bilateral, that is, exclusive to relations between the United States and the Philippines. Officials at State, in contrast, held a multilateral perspective that sought to reduce trade barriers across the globe. The State Department also believed that since the Philippines had been separated from the United States by war, the postwar period represented a unique opportunity to redesign the Philippine economy. But that idea failed to gain traction, as policymakers in Washington narrowed their focus to issues of rehabilitation aid and trade. The State Department favored granting the Philippines postwar reconstruction aid and a fifteen-year transition period with gradually increasing duties on Philippine goods and few American-imposed constraints on the Philippine economy. Interior, in contrast, was inclined to be more generous in granting free trade with the United States in lieu of providing direct financial assistance to the Philippines—in exchange for the protection of American investments there.[63]

During these discussions, all sides pursued their own interests. As the end of World War II neared, officials at State were imbued with the notion that expanded trade across the globe would solidify America's economic strength, protect its security, and avert another war. FDR concurred with that sentiment, as did policymakers at the Departments of Treasury and Commerce the latter of which was headed, by McNutt's old bête noire, Henry A. Wallace. Among the Filipino elite, Osmeña, Roxas, and Rómulo all agreed that a continuation of free trade with the United States was in the best interest of the Philippines—if they could obtain it without any strings. But Americans who offered free trade to the Philippines had ulterior motives. For example, Undersecretary of War Robert P. Patterson wanted to establish a stable Philippines tied to America via mutual free trade because he wanted the U.S. Army to retain installations in the archipelago. Ickes shared this outlook. "Bases," Ickes asserted, "would not be of full utility if the Filipinos themselves were not bound to the United States by a feeling of loyalty and by economic interdependence."[64]

McNutt's appointment as high commissioner tilted the debate in favor of Interior's position. Along with Fortas, Ickes, and Hester, McNutt favored a prolonged period of free trade between the United States and the Philippines, and he delayed leaving for Manila until he had "something definite" to offer Filipinos in this area.[65] McNutt felt a strong sense of duty toward the Philippines, and he did not want the devastation of war to afford the Philippines' competitors an advantage in the global sugar market. McNutt thus averred that the "Philippines have a claim on [the] United States superior to [that] of any country or any economic group."[66]

In the fall of 1945, McNutt, Hester, and Rómulo worked closely with Representative C. Jasper Bell, Democrat of Missouri and chair of the House Committee on Insular Affairs, to fashion a Philippine trade act. Under their bill, the Philippines would receive twenty years of free trade with the United States, but Americans would gain a number of benefits as well. Quotas were to be placed on export products entering the United States; when the volume of Philippine exports exceeded the quota, they became subject to full duty. To protect U.S. investments from currency fluctuations, the Philippines was required to maintain the existing ratio between the peso and the dollar. The Bell bill also granted Americans the same rights as Filipinos to own resources and land in the Philippines. To give Americans such equality—or parity—the government in Manila would have to amend its constitution.[67]

The Bell bill sparked controversy. Rómulo was not at all happy with the currency and parity clauses.[68] Filipinos had long been wary of foreign acquisition of their land, and the government in Manila had taken steps to restrict foreign ownership of Philippine property.[69] Accordingly, a number of organized groups protested the parity and currency clauses as "derogatory" to Philippine's sovereignty.[70] Complaints also surfaced from such Philippine industrialists as

Salvador Araneta.[71] "Accept the Bell Act," Araneta warned, "and all efforts to industrialize our economy are bound to fail."[72] Tydings voiced a similar sentiment; if America gave the Philippines twenty years of free trade, the archipelago would be "exactly in the same position" two decades later and would request another extension of free trade.[73]

Tydings complicated matters by introducing an alternative to Bell's bill. Drafted by the Tariff Commission and approved by State, it had "no absolute quotas, no restrictions on economic sovereignty, and no special breaks for Americans." Tydings's measure proposed a "22-year adjustment period during which duties on Philippine exports entering the United States would rise by 5 percent a year to reach the full duty by 1968."[74] Competition between the two bills ended with a White House meeting in November 1945, at which representatives of State and Interior, along with Truman, Tydings, Bell, and McNutt, struck a compromise. The result—the revised Bell bill—contained several changes, the most important of which provided for eight years of mutual free trade followed by a twenty-five-year period in which duties would rise four percent annually, until 1979. This change did not satisfy everyone. Osmeña preferred the first Bell bill, despite its restrictions on Philippine sovereignty, because his country stood to gain twenty, rather than merely eight, years of free trade with the United States.[75]

McNutt understood the shortcomings of the revised Bell bill but supported it as the best deal possible. To be certain, when McNutt resumed the post of high commissioner, he sounded an idealistic note, arguing that "democracy-in-action" in the Philippines had to involve economic as well as political change: "Serfdom" must end; peasants had to own the land they tilled; and the Philippines had to diversify its economy, industrialize, and allow Filipinos to "share in the benefits of the modern age."[76] In making such comments, McNutt had returned to his New Deal roots—to the idea that enhancing the economic station (and security) of average people serves to stabilize the existing political order and strengthen the nation as a whole. But, to a large extent, McNutt was discussing a long-term transformation of the Philippines. In the short term, he spoke of giving Filipinos "a *breathing space* during which they can adjust themselves to an independent economy."[77] According to the high commissioner, the revised Bell bill represented "a step in that direction."[78] McNutt had preferred to give the Philippines twenty years of mutual free trade rather than a period of escalating tariffs. And he did not care for the restrictions on Philippine sovereignty or the extension of property-ownership rights to Americans. In the end, however, he dubbed the Bell measure "the best possible bill which can be gotten through Congress."[79]

Why was Congress unwilling to go further and either be more generous toward the Philippines or simply cut them loose? Lawmakers had experienced pressure from agricultural interests who opposed free trade with the Philippines as a threat to American farmers. There also was a reluctance to spend additional dollars on the Philippines and a sense that, having liberated the country from Japan, "America has done its duty."[80] And in 1945 Congress acted to curtail foreign aid, as did President Truman, who halted Lend-Lease assistance to Great Britain and the Soviet Union following the end of World War II. Policies to extend military and economic assistance to nations threatened by Communist aggression had not yet been developed, for the Cold War did not become a reality to most Americans until 1947 and, even then, Congress had to be prodded to approve military assistance to Greece and Turkey and Marshall Plan aid to western Europe. In the interim, Americans, according to polls, rejected the idea that postwar rehabilitation assistance was a legitimate expense arising from World War II.[81]

Others, both outside and inside of Congress, backed the Bell bill because they had no qualms about keeping the Philippines appended to the United States. The *Washington Post* endorsed the Bell bill on the grounds that "the United States and the Philippines have mutual interests" and after 1946 they would be bound together economically and diplomatically as "associate nations."[82] The Bell bill thus reflected, in part, an imperial mindset, a perspective that the sponsor of the legislation shared. Bell referred to Filipinos as a "generous, kindly, religious, patriotic people who believe in our kind of democracy" and to the Philippines as "the great Christian outpost of Western civilization in the Orient."[83]

McNutt, for his part, showed no interest in further revising the bill. Along with Bell, Patterson, and Ickes, he saw America and the Philippines united by common values, interests, and history, and close trade and defense relations fit that pattern. McNutt praised America's benevolent form of colonialism and Filipinos for resisting Japan, cherishing democracy, and absorbing American culture.[84] No matter that the United States had crushed the first Philippine Republic in 1898, that many Filipinos had collaborated with the Japanese, that Philippine democracy was far from sturdy, and that Filipinos clung to traditional ways. McNutt had constructed his own vision of the Philippines, linked the country to America, and resisted giving it up entirely. He even compared the Philippines to a foster child on the verge of maturity and the United States to its guardian. Such sentimental rhetoric was grounded in a hard reality: America's need for bases in the Philippines—something McNutt stressed in his speeches. Armed might was not the sole source of security, of course. "For many years there will be a special relationship between the two countries," McNutt explained in an address on U.S.-Philippine relations. "We will be obliged to help the Philippines regain their economic health."[85] The Bell bill marked the starting point.

The Bell bill faced a number of hurdles in Congress. Philippine policy was low on the national agenda, as Congress focused on America's reconversion to a peacetime economy. Moreover, Cuban sugar interests lobbied against the Bell bill for giving Philippine competitors special access to the U.S. market, and Secretary of Agriculture Clinton P. Anderson, a proponent of multilateral free trade, took up their cause, persuading the House Ways and Means Committee to delay hearings on it. Representative Robert Doughton, Democrat of North Carolina, the chair of Ways and Means and a supporter of multilateral free trade, declined to move the Bell bill until President Truman assured him that it represented administration policy. In February 1946, after meetings with the secretaries of state, interior, commerce, and agriculture as well as with McNutt, Truman told Doughton that it did, whereupon Ways and Means began its hearings.[86]

McNutt had a hand in breaking the deadlock over the bill. In January 1946, McNutt focused Truman's attention on Philippine trade by defending the Bell bill and responding to Anderson's critique of it. A month later, McNutt visited Washington where he conferred with Truman and "laid the groundwork for broad Administration support of the entire Philippine program."[87] Among other things, McNutt pressed the State Department to give the Bell bill "its unqualified support."[88] "McNutt's arguments," the historian Nick Cullather noted, "bolstered by the consensus among administration officials on the strategic importance of the Philippines, strongly influenced Truman's decision [to back the Bell bill]."[89] Supporters of the measure thereupon spared no effort. "We buttonholed senators and congressmen," McNutt remembered. "We had, perhaps, the most active and persistent lobby any bill has ever attracted."[90] The high commissioner may not have had warm relations with individual members of Congress, but he was able to secure passage of a bill that was born in the House and endorsed by the administration.

McNutt also pleaded publicly for passage of both the Bell bill and a separate rehabilitation act drafted by Tydings. The rehabilitation act, which provided up to $400 million to compensate war-related damage in the Philippines, seemed generous but it was tied tightly to the trade law. Bell had refused to move the rehabilitation bill until the U.S. Congress passed his trade act. Moreover, a provision in the rehabilitation measure, inserted by McNutt, required the Philippines to approve parity rights for Americans before the U.S. government released rehabilitation dollars. In making the case for both bills, McNutt stressed familiar themes: Filipinos, by fighting for the United States in World War II, had earned postwar assistance; their economy was desperate for relief; and passage of the trade and rehabilitation bills represented a test of whether America could keep its promises to a subject people, develop the Philippines into a stable democracy, and remain a power in Asia. He also raised the specter of the Communist menace: "We are not the only ones interested in the Philippines."[91]

Congress ultimately passed the trade bill and rehabilitation measures. The Bell bill went through two rounds of revision. The final version provided for eight years of mutual free trade but reduced the period of declining trade preference from twenty-five to twenty years. The provision pegging the peso to the dollar remained, though the U.S. president now had the power to suspend it. And the final bill guaranteed parity rights for Americans investing in the Philippines, but only in the areas of natural resources and public utilities. The Philippines, which had aspired to twenty years of mutual free trade with the United States, clearly lost a good deal in the bargaining, and that reality, in part, helped the Bell bill sail through the House and Senate without recorded votes. When the measure went to the president, members of the administration acknowledged its imperfections, particularly the infringements on Philippine sovereignty. In the end, however, Secretary of State James F. Byrnes advised Truman to sign it in order to formalize trade relations between the two countries. The president did so, on April 30, 1946.[92]

The Bell bill sparked a heated debate in Manila. There was talk in the press that the act would prevent the Philippines from controlling its natural resources and threats that Filipinos might fight the influence of Americans with the same tenacity with which they had battled the Japanese. A cartoon in the *Philippines Free Press* portrayed Bell leering at a Philippine maid and exclaiming: "Darling I love you so much I could squeeze you to death."[93] Reporters accused McNutt of plotting to postpone independence and chided him as "Paul The Vulture."[94] One paper urged his dismissal—a demand that never had appeared in the Manila press during his first stint as high commissioner.[95] McNutt characterized such attacks as "violent."[96] But the high commissioner's allies disparaged him as well. Rómulo wrote that McNutt had "complicated rather than helped our situation. His ideas of what the Philippine bills should contain do not exactly correspond with ours, but a frontal attack on his position would hurt rather than help our cause."[97] By declining to renounce the Bell bill in its entirety, Rómulo, President Osmeña, and Roxas also came under heavy criticism in the Philippines.[98]

In the end, economic realities trumped nationalist revulsion since, as the *Manila Daily News* conceded, "Beggars can't be choosers."[99] Understanding that the Philippines needed U.S. support, Rómulo, Osmeña, and Roxas all backed the trade act. "We have to make our advances by the slow steps of negotiation and persuasion rather than by outright objection," Rómulo admitted.[100] Following his election as president, Roxas addressed the Philippine Congress and defended the Bell bill on grounds that parity rights for U.S. businesses would lead to greater U.S. investment, that export quotas guaranteed the Philippines a market for its goods, and that the country had to accept the trade bill if it expected to get any rehabilitation dollars.[101]

Ratification of the trade deal proved messy, and McNutt was tangentially involved in the sordid details. First, Roxas's followers in the Philippine House of Representatives "expelled seven members of the Democratic Alliance on trumped-up charges of voter fraud."[102] Their expulsion weakened the opposition to parity rights and allowed the Philippine House to authorize Roxas to conclude an executive agreement with the U.S. government on the basis of the Bell Trade Act. The Senate followed suit. The struggle to approve a constitutional amendment extending parity rights to Americans proved as tricky. To secure a sufficient number of votes in the Philippine House and Senate, Roxas used persuasion and dangled pork-barrel projects before wavering members. After the constitutional amendment cleared the House and Senate, the measure went to the voters, who ratified it in a plebiscite, following an intense campaign organized by Roxas's allies in the provinces.[103] McNutt backed such efforts while reminding Roxas that the U.S. president had the authority to nullify the Bell Act if any American experienced discrimination in the Philippines. Acceptance of the parity clause would remove any such discrimination.[104]

The long-term impact of the Bell Act proved mixed. "The compromise satisfied neither party," the historian Milton Walter Meyer argued. "Filipinos wanted more free trade; Americans disliked preferential economic policies."[105] The Philippines found that free trade was no panacea for its economic ills. By 1950, Cullather observed, "the 1946 trade act had succeeded in increasing export income, but had failed to distribute it equitably, diversify the economy, or increase government revenue."[106] A United States mission found conditions in the Philippines unsatisfactory because of inefficient production, political corruption, and disparities in income.[107] In 1953 Adlai E. Stevenson, the Democratic nominee for president in 1952, visited Manila and pronounced the average Filipino between "20 to 25 per cent worse off than before the war." Squalor lay "behind the façade of fine new buildings," Stevenson reported, and the shaky economy had been steadied only marginally by "American expenditures and the duty-free entry of Philippine products into the United States."[108] In this setting, Huk rebels gained strength, in part by seizing the mantle of nationalism and denouncing leaders like Roxas as American puppets.[109]

There was considerable evidence to support that critique because, on the issue of trade, Roxas was more than willing to follow the Americans' lead. A concern expressed by McNutt in 1945, that Roxas's dynamic personality would lead him to be "chauvinistic" toward the United States, proved unfounded.[110] To the contrary, McNutt, by the close of 1946, was applauding him: "Under the leadership of President Roxas, the Philippines has thrown its lot with the United States."[111] Starting with U.S. policy on collaborators and then continuing with the Bell Act, the Philippines was, with McNutt's strong encouragement, moving "from colony to client state."[112]

After the formalizing of trade relations between the United States and the Philippines, McNutt had two other major tasks to complete: overseeing the transfer of U.S. sovereignty to the Philippine Republic and negotiating a treaty giving America bases in the archipelago. The ceremony signaling the end of direct U.S. rule went off smoothly. On the morning of July 4, 1946, a crowd of more than 200,000 gathered in the Luneta, the principal park in Manila, to watch events unfold. The weather was rainy as the dignitaries assumed their places on the grandstand. Senator Tydings spoke, as did General MacArthur. High Commissioner McNutt delivered a speech and read a proclamation from President Truman just as the rain stopped. At 9:20 AM, McNutt stepped forward to lower the Stars and Stripes while Roxas raised the Sun and Stars. "As the new flag passed the American on its way to the masthead," a member of McNutt's staff recalled, "a mighty cheer went up from the crowd."[113] Roxas and his vice president, Elpidio Quirino, then took their official oaths as leaders of the new government.[114]

On July 4, McNutt presented his credentials to Roxas as the first U.S. ambassador to the Philippines. To many people, he was the obvious candidate for the position.[115] It made sense for McNutt to stay in Manila, where he was in the process of negotiating several treaties, the most important of which dealt with securing U.S. bases in the Philippines. And he expected to conclude that agreement "shortly."[116] He was in for a surprise, for he now was bargaining with representatives of a foreign country rather than dictating policy to leaders of a U.S. territory.

Philippine independence was both a bit less and a bit more than it appeared. "There will be those who will cavil at the realness of the Republic's independence," the *Manila Post*—one of the skeptics—editorialized. "They will point to ... the closeness of relationship with America as [being among the] factors nullifying independence."[117] Speeches on July 4 reinforced the concept of dependency. Roxas devoted much of his address "to a eulogy of America." He argued the "safest course" for the Philippines was to "cleave" to the United States.[118] McNutt agreed. "We are ready to help defend this land against aggression, to maintain its security, and to preserve the right of the people to work out their destiny," he asserted. "America is not withdrawing from the Orient."[119]

Nevertheless, the Philippines achieved political sovereignty on July 4, 1946. After reading Truman's proclamation, McNutt intoned: "A nation is born! Long live the Republic of the Philippines!"[120] Observers from outside the Philippines knew that something significant had occurred that morning on the Luneta. The reestablishment of the Philippine Republic unsettled the governments of France and the Netherlands, which were determined to retain their possessions in Asia. Many Filipinos focused on the change, rather than the continuity, in their dealings with the United States. There were tears as the U.S. flag came down, a recognition that an era had ended. Months later, Thanksgiving passed without official sanction. "Its being stricken off from the statute books, along with other American holidays," the *Manila Post* noted, "is one of those minor manifestations signifying that the Philippines is a republic distinct and independent from the Republic originally colonized by the Pilgrim Fathers."[121] There were further signs of the Philippines asserting its sovereignty. In 1946 Roxas ordered a probe of abuses by U.S. soldiers on the westernmost island of Palawan. He also protested the unauthorized entry of Americans into the Philippines, and demanded that U.S. servicemen secure the permission of his government before arriving in the country. In so doing, Roxas revealed a capacity to "stand up to the Americans if the rights of the Republic are violated."[122]

Philippine officials exhibited similar firmness with respect to military bases. The Tydings-McDuffie Act permitted the United States to negotiate for access to bases, and allowing American forces to remain made sense, for World War II had exposed the vulnerability of the Philippines. Nevertheless, some Filipinos worried that U.S. troops would enjoy special privileges and behave in ways that would offend Philippine sovereignty. In response to such concerns, the Philippine governing elite—Osmeña, Roxas, and Rómulo—trod cautiously; they wanted U.S. forces to stay in order to deter would-be aggressors but were adverse to ceding vast tracts of territory to the Americans. Quirino, whom Roxas entrusted to negotiate the bases treaty, agreed with this perspective. In negotiating with the Americans, Roxas and Quirino reached "a private understanding." "I was to hold firm," Quirino remembered, "while [Roxas] remained the picture of sweet amenability."[123] Through such posturing the two leaders hoped to secure the best deal possible while dampening criticism by Philippine nationalists.

On the American side, nearly everyone dealing with the Philippines accepted the need for bases, from McNutt and MacArthur to Fortas and Ickes to Patterson and his superior, Secretary of War Henry Stimson. McNutt had long urged the United States to maintain a strong military as well as its installations and influence in the Philippines. "It is the interest of America to keep the Philippines safe and secure," he averred in 1946. "There is no more strategic area in the world."[124] Even Tydings, a staunch proponent of "complete and absolute independence" for the Philippines, sounded imperialistic on military matters.[125] Tydings spoke of the United States and Philippines walking "side by side" in pursuit of "security in an ordered world," and he had wanted the United States to conclude a bases treaty before July 4, 1946, after which time Filipinos would have greater leverage.[126] Following talks in Washington, Truman and President Osmeña signed a preliminary statement on bases in May 1945.[127] The next step was to settle on the details.

As negotiations got under way, several concerns emerged for the Philippine government, including joint use of the bases, their size and location, and jurisdiction over U.S. troops. The Departments of State, War, and Navy all agreed that the armed forces of the United States and the Philippines should be permitted to serve on the bases whenever both countries deemed it beneficial. And State had no qualms about reducing the size of the bases. But Roxas and Quirino wanted no bases in urban areas where they would remind Filipinos of the U.S. presence and occupy "commercially and industrially essential areas."[128] The U.S. Army, however, wanted to keep its Manila bases, Fort McKinley and Nichols Field. On another matter, Roxas rejected any effort to exempt U.S.

service personnel from the reach of Philippine courts—a right that, if extended to Americans, would revive the practice of extraterritoriality. In response, the Departments of War and the Navy (but not State) insisted on U.S. jurisdiction "over offenses committed by [Americans] *outside the bases.*"[129]

After the Philippines gained independence, negotiations moved to Manila. During these talks, McNutt grew frustrated, for Quirino was determined to achieve a treaty that also upheld his nation's sovereignty.[130] Moreover, the Philippine delegation leaked accounts of their sessions to the press, which praised Filipino resolve and demanded American concessions.[131] Meanwhile the on-going debate over the Bell Act and parity rights put the U.S. ambassador on the defensive. At one point, McNutt had to suspend the negotiations so that Roxas could campaign for a favorable vote on parity without facing charges that he was ceding military installations to Uncle Sam. While that went on, reports of American troops behaving like "brash, ill-mannered, slovenly and contemptuous children" prompted General Dwight D. Eisenhower, the army's chief of staff, to order an inquiry.[132] Such problems played into the hands of Filipino nationalists, weakened the standing of Roxas and Quirino, and limited McNutt's ability to extract concessions from the Philippine government. Accordingly, Dean Acheson, acting secretary of state, advised McNutt not to "impose conditions which Phil Congress cannot accept."[133]

Faced with such pressures, McNutt responded in three ways. First, in talks with Quirino, he engaged in blustering. After Quirino refused to allow the United States to keep its bases in Manila, McNutt threatened to return to Washington. But the Philippine vice president was unperturbed by such displays of bellicosity: "I found it quite a stimulating exercise to thump the table, too."[134] Accommodation was McNutt's second negotiating tactic, and it allowed him to end the impasse on jurisdiction. The ambassador agreed to restrict U.S. authority only to offenses committed on American bases and incidents between U.S. servicemen. All other jurisdiction would be exercised by the Philippines. The matter of surrendering sites in Manila proved tougher to settle, and McNutt, trapped by the intransigence of both Quirino and officials at the War Department, decided to treat the matter delicately—his third strategy as a negotiator. Late in 1946, General Eisenhower concluded that the United States must not foist a bases treaty on the Philippines and that withdrawal of U.S. troops from the archipelago would be the best course for an overextended American military. McNutt knew of the plan to remove U.S. forces from the Philippines, though there is no evidence he used it to bully Quirino or Roxas. He did not

have to, for the U.S. Army, in December 1946, suspended its construction contracts in the Philippines, and American troops prepared to depart within sixty
days.[135]

The impending withdrawal of American troops broke the impasse. Roxas
stated that removal of all U.S. troops "is not my wish," and McNutt urged the
State Department to prevent the termination of the construction contracts.[136]
Faced with either a complete American pullout or accepting a token U.S. force,
Roxas chose the latter. In so doing, he helped lessen the army's pressure for
bases in Manila. American forces slated to be withdrawn from the Philippines
could be extracted from the capital, and the few that remained could be sta-
tioned elsewhere—on new bases specifically established under the treaty. That
became the Philippine position. McNutt embraced it, the Department of War
accepted it, and President Truman approved it.[137] Perhaps McNutt's most important role in fashioning this consensus was to reassure Secretary of State
Byrnes that average Filipinos were not troubled by the presence of American
troops, that keeping U.S. bases would not damage U.S.-Philippine relations,
and that these installations would enhance the defenses of both countries.[138]

When Roxas and McNutt signed the bases treaty on March 14, 1947, both
men had reason to smile. Under the treaty, the United States gained access to
twenty-three sites, none of them in Manila, for ninety-nine years. The government in Washington acceded to joint use of the bases; accepted limitations on
its jurisdiction over off-base troops; assumed liability for damage, destruction,
and death caused by U.S. servicemen; and relinquished any minerals found on
or near the bases to the government and people of the Philippines. "The Philippines," Cullather has argued, "obtained more latitude in the area of criminal
jurisdiction than other U.S. allies then enjoyed."[139] Roxas hailed the treaty as
assuring the security of the Philippine Republic and the negotiations as affirming Philippine sovereignty. The years to come brought added good news
for Filipinos such as Roxas who favored a small American presence. Because
of budgetary constraints, the United States kept just two major bases in the
Philippines, Subic Naval Base and Clark Air Force Base. Furthermore, under
a military assistance pact—also negotiated by McNutt—the United States
agreed to train and supply the Philippine Army. But because American aid
proved paltry, the government in Manila looked to the U.S. bases and "regional
security arrangements," such as the South East Asia Treaty Organization, to
maintain its defenses.[140]

The bases treaty was one of the most significant—and hard-won—accomplishments in McNutt's career. The Philippine negotiators proved tough, and

some Americans welcomed their intransigence as confirmation that the talks were "being conducted on the basis of give and take between two sovereign nations."[141] After signing the treaty, Roxas could afford to be gracious. He praised McNutt's efforts, noting that he "acted not only as representative of his Government in this negotiation, but, on a number of vital occasions, as our spokesman as well."[142] Did such a compliment mean the ambassador had surrendered his nation's interests to the Philippines? No, because he had secured a larger, long-standing aim—retaining an outpost of American power in the Pacific.

If the bases treaty involved considerable give-and-take, the United States had the final word on two other issues: a loan to the Philippine government and the extension of benefits for Filipino veterans. On both matters, the U.S. government was free to respond generously to Filipino appeals. It failed to do so. With respect to the loan, Roxas wanted $400 million over four years, but he knew that the Congress was ill disposed to extend credit to the Philippines. With that in mind, Roxas worked behind the scenes with McNutt, who lobbied lawmakers and top administration officials to support the Philippine request.[143] The final bill, fashioned by Representative Bell, proved modest—it covered one year and allowed the Reconstruction Finance Corporation (RFC) to lend up to $75 million to the Philippines. Bell told McNutt that this measure was the best that could be had. The House and Senate passed it, and President Truman, working though the RFC, approved $25 million for the Philippines.[144] The Philippines thus had gained a very small loan.[145]

The issue of extending benefits to Filipino veterans proved more complicated and engaged more of McNutt's attention than the loan request. Philippine leaders asserted that Filipinos who had served in the U.S. armed forces were entitled to the same postwar benefits as American veterans, including participation in the programs of the GI Bill. The case for equal treatment originated in 1941, when FDR incorporated the Philippine Army into the United States Armed Forces in the Far East, and it gathered strength when MacArthur and Osmeña promised that Filipino veterans would receive the same benefits as their American counterparts. But it remained unclear whether the government in Washington would provide such compensation to veterans who would become foreign nationals on July 4, 1946. The issue caught Truman's attention in February 1946, when he signed an appropriations bill that gave the Philippines $200 million to compensate its soldiers. Under this measure, Filipino veterans received access to life insurance and disability pensions but were excluded from hospital care and the other programs of the GI Bill. Truman approved the bill reluctantly, believing that America had failed to uphold its "moral obligation" to the Filipino soldiers. Accordingly, he directed McNutt, Patterson, and General Omar N. Bradley, who headed the Veterans Administration, to develop a plan to bring Philippine veterans under the GI Bill.[146]

McNutt's advocacy helped shape the president's empathy for the Philippine veterans for the Hoosier proved forceful on this issue. Truman admitted as much.[147] McNutt recognized that not all veterans' benefits, such as tuition assistance, could be extended to foreign nationals. Yet he argued that excluding Filipinos from the GI Bill had been a "grave error."[148] And he asserted that America had a responsibility to help Philippine veterans, especially "the sick, the disabled, the widows, and the orphans."[149] Ever the realist, McNutt also insisted that the failure to do so would inflame anti-American sentiment in the Philippines. The *Manila Post* agreed, and Roxas himself demanded an end to disparities among veterans.[150]

In the end, however, the Filipinos gained little. The committee assembled by Truman found that the question of including Philippine veterans under the GI Bill required further study. In the interim, McNutt advised the president to propose legislation which would, among other things, expand hospitalization privileges for Philippine veterans and provide a burial gratuity and death benefits to the families of those killed in battle.[151] Not unlike his stand on the Bell bill, McNutt argued that this proposal, however imperfect, provided an immediate remedy. Truman concurred and submitted the measure to the Senate, which passed it in June 1946. Although the bill died in the House, the moral imperative of helping Philippine veterans remained, and Roxas pressed the issue.[152] In 1948 Congress authorized grants to help the Philippine government provide medical care to its veterans. And the burial gratuity, proposed by McNutt, became law in 1951. But plans to bring Filipinos under the GI Bill floundered.[153] Unlike the bases issue, the Philippine government had little leverage on the issue of veterans' benefits.

That said, it is worth noting the idealism and realism of Truman and McNutt—two former soldiers who were determined, in their own minds, to do right by the Filipino veterans. Both men expressed empathy for these veterans *and* linked this issue to geopolitics. In 1950, Truman told the head of the Veterans Administration: "I don't think the Philippine Army, which served with our Forces in the last war, has been fairly treated." He also believed that a policy of magnanimity "will cement the Philippines more closely to us than they are now."[154] McNutt, similarly, complained that the "mishandling" of the veterans issue by Congress had weakened America's standing among Filipinos.[155] The imperial mindset, of trying to keep the Philippines close to the United States, was at work in the attitude of McNutt, Truman, and Roxas regarding veterans' benefits. At the same time, the less-than-generous approach of Congress coincided with that body's imposition of some harsh terms on the Philippines in the Bell Trade Act. All sides were nothing if not consistent.

In his daily duties as high commissioner and ambassador, McNutt was busy. His shuttling between Washington and Manila underscored that fact, and even the *Manila Post,* which often disparaged McNutt's proposals, conceded that he was working hard for what he deemed beneficial to Filipinos. McNutt's diligence came at some cost to his family. For example, Paul's mother died while he was in Manila. Finding it impossible to return home, he directed John E. Hurt, his father's youthful law partner, to arrange the funeral and to care for John C. McNutt. The loss of a parent sparks reflection as well as sadness, and that held true for Paul. "She gave no thought to herself but spent her whole life doing for others," he remembered. "Father and I were the chief beneficiaries." Paul observed that, in the end, "Mother wore herself out."[156] It was a telling remark from a man who was maintaining a grueling pace and looking the worse for it. When Louise joined her father in Manila, she noticed that he was experiencing throat troubles and had struggled to deliver a speech with "his usual vim."[157]

Unlike most residents of Manila, McNutt was able to work, rest, and recuperate in comfortable surroundings. While the high commissioner and his staff worked in a hastily rebuilt apartment building, McNutt resided in a relatively undamaged home used by a U.S. admiral following the liberation of Manila.[158] His domestic space consisted of "a big, white Georgian-Colonial-Tropical structure, with a tiled patio, wide green lawns, luxuriant foliage, and a high white stucco wall surrounding the grounds."[159] Recreational activities included bridge, poker, movies, and baseball games with McNutt and staff. Paul's bachelor life ended in April 1946, when Kathleen and Louise arrived in the Philippines. With Kathleen came the start of a social whirl, while Louise, an official in the State Department's Far Eastern division, brought her interest in international relations to the Philippines. Kathleen bridged the divide between her life choices and those of her daughter by stressing the importance of education for the next generation of women. At the same time, however, she coached her daughter on proper etiquette, to the point that Louise complained: "I have absolutely no confidence in my ability or thoughts."[160] Paul no doubt avoided involvement in such disputes for he continued to spend much, albeit not all, of his time with male associates, leaving Louise, Kathleen, and Grace Woody, his cousin who joined them in Manila, to their own amusements.[161]

While living in Manila, McNutt remained a complex person whose private conduct did not always match his public image. On the surface, he handled official duties adeptly. Cameron Forbes, a former governor-general of the Philippines, visited Manila in 1946 and found McNutt to be "a gentleman of great suavity and pleasing manners" who exuded "good sense."[162] A columnist for the *Indianapolis Times* noticed a commendable shift in McNutt's demeanor. His work in Manila had transformed him from the "ebullient glamour boy" of American politics to an "international figure" of some renown who was "infinitely more serious and less full of conscious charm." The headline of this column—"McNutt Has Sobered during Absence"—was cruelly ironic for, despite McNutt's best efforts, his abuse of alcohol persisted.[163] On New Year's Day 1946, Louise jotted in her diary that a family gathering "would have been fun if Daddy hadn't scared us all by having a drink of egg-nog. I'm afraid he hasn't put temptation entirely behind him."[164] A year later, she lamented that he "seems to have really started drinking again—quite openly now." Louise's "heart sank" when her father, in a drunken state, berated a subordinate over a trivial matter.[165]

Louise was the person who best understood Paul. During an after-dinner conversation in 1947, she reflected on her father's good and bad qualities. "Daddy spoke quite brilliantly this evening," Louise wrote in her diary. "When he is as he was during [the] last p[ar]t of [the] evening I see [the] brilliance, earnestness & searching for truth which must have characterized him. I do not see it very often." The topic of discussion that evening was human nature, with Paul arguing that "all of man's motivations were selfish ones." Grace Woody was "horrified by this philosophy," but Louise defended it by distinguishing between a narrow, materialistic form of selfishness on the one hand and the propensity of humans to pursue their own self-interest on the other. An observer of the exchange remarked that Louise, like Grace, had been able to ignite a spark in Paul, and Louise agreed. But she worried that her own contribution to that evening's seminar had fallen flat. Her father, she lamented, had taken issue with her even though "we were supposed to be arguing on the same side." Louise's explanation for this was that the two of them were "so much alike" that they were "more apt to fight than have a quiet discussion." There was nothing to suggest that Paul grasped the extent to which Louise craved his approval. Instead, he stated his argument in a direct, analytical manner, as though he were fielding questions from the press, talking with his staff, or speaking in public. Following the discussion, a subdued Louise went off by herself to play records and gaze out the window.[166]

Filipinos understood the complexities of McNutt, for they witnessed them firsthand and lived with his legacy for decades. McNutt, as his daughter's diary shows, remained a realist who believed that nations, no less than individuals, acted out of self-interest. He, along with others in the Truman administration and in Congress, had helped the Philippines achieve political sovereignty while allowing the United States to retain influence over its former colony economically, militarily, and diplomatically. McNutt presided at the independence ceremony in 1946, pushed the Bell Act through Congress, pressed for Philippine ratification of parity rights, negotiated the bases treaty, and forged a close relationship with Manila's elite, particularly Manuel Roxas. "Roxas is a man of parts," McNutt wrote, "and, if he is permitted to live, will provide the necessary sound leadership."[167] The allusion, to the president being "permitted to live," was prophetic, for Roxas died in 1948. Nevertheless, wealthy Filipinos continued to exercise power for decades in a system that was more or less democratic until the imposition of martial law in 1972. Such concerns about the stability of the Philippine Republic had surfaced as early as 1946 when the radio commentator Raymond Gram Swing lamented that the government in Manila rested "in the hands of a ruling class not now inclined to lay, or capable of laying, the foundations of true democracy."[168]

American-style decolonization, in which McNutt played an important role, proved efficient in maintaining U.S. interests in the Philippines. America retained its installations at Clark and Subic until 1991, when the Philippine Senate voted against renewal of the bases treaty. Such successes, from a U.S. perspective, dated to McNutt's second stint in Manila. According to the historian D. A. Low, the government in Washington shifted authority to leaders in Manila "with remarkable smoothness" and "Americans reaped their reward in the special commercial and military privileges which they continued to enjoy in the Philippines for decades." The results were plain. With respect to the Philippines, Low, writing in 1982, observed: "There has been a modicum of land reform; but power is still held by those who have owned large estates, and so far all attempts to break their position have been abortive."[169] Nevertheless, the United States appeared to have found a way of reconciling decolonization with its own economic and military interests. As the historian William Roger Louis has explained, U.S. officials pressed their European allies to follow America's example and exchange formal control for "informal association" with their Asian possessions. Such a policy would allow the western nations to "keep out of the limelight" and "pull the strings when necessary" in order to thwart Soviet influence.[170]

McNutt was criticized for ongoing U.S. influence in the Philippines. In 1946 the *Manila Post* accused him—and the United States—of having "imperialistic designs."[171] Although McNutt is not widely known today, Filipinos conversant with his record find much to dislike. Manuel L. Quezon III, the grandson of the former president and a popular historian-pundit, remembered McNutt as the architect of the "unfair trade deals" foisted on the Philippines.[172] Similar complaints can be heard among scholars in the United States. Frank Golay ended his massive history of United States–Philippine relations by asserting that Philippine independence had been betrayed by Bell, MacArthur, and Mc-Nutt.[173] Yet such criticism must be qualified. Close ties between the Philippines and the United States were not imposed on Filipinos entirely against their will, and relations between the two countries were not a one-way street.[174] Although the United States retained economic rights and military installations in the Philippines, keeping such privileges rested upon maintaining good relations with the government in Manila. Rather than being supplicants to the Americans, Philippine leaders, in the 1940s and 1950s, "harassed American businesses, diverted aid, restricted trade, and made military bases the targets of nationalist attacks."[175] Determined to hold on to the bases, American officials accepted the decision of the Philippine Central Bank, in 1949, to nullify the currency restrictions of the Bell Act. Furthermore, the Eisenhower administration acted to reduce friction over the parity clause by extending the same rights to Filipino investors in the United States under the Laurel-Langley Agreement of 1955, which modified the Bell Act in ways favorable to the Philippines.[176]

Nevertheless, the United States paid a price for its neocolonialism in the Philippines. Raymond Gram Swing, whose radio commentaries were hardly radical, bemoaned the hypocrisy of American officials who pressed for bases in the Philippines while attacking Soviet efforts to secure similar military installations in Turkey. "We can have whatever we want, militarily and economically, from the Filipinos," Swing explained in July 1946. "They are helpless without us. But we cannot go about getting it the way we are doing it without sacrificing our reputation as liberators. We need that reputation more than we do bases, trade and profits."[177]

McNutt was incapable of allaying such concerns. Although McNutt proved realistic in retaining U.S. influence in the Philippines and in accepting the compromises embedded in the Bell Act, he never questioned the idea that the United States and the Philippines must remain close. After departing Manila, McNutt journeyed home through India, Iraq, and Egypt, where U.S. policy in the Philippines was "being held up as a horrible example of false independence." Sounding like an innocent, he "was astounded" to find "suspicions of imperialism and self-interest" by peoples in Asia and Africa about American foreign policy. Perhaps he should have reviewed his own comments on the universality of selfishness. But McNutt did not engage in such self-reflection. Instead, he advised Truman to begin "a concerted program of information" to spread word of America's good work in the Philippines.[178] The answer to charges of neoimperialism was improved public diplomacy rather than a shift in public policy.

As in the 1930s, McNutt saw the Philippines through the prism of his own ideology as well as his conception of U.S. interests. The vision that he had expressed in the 1930s, of the Philippines as a self-governing dominion under American influence, more or less came to pass following World War II. This was one of McNutt's most important legacies, and attacks on it baffled him. By 1947 McNutt had more diplomatic experience and had traveled more widely than he had eight years earlier. But in many ways, he was no more worldly.

# 15

---

## FADING AWAY
## (1947–1955)

---

WHEN PAUL V. McNUTT RETURNED to the United States in 1947, there was little sense of anticipation, few crowds, and scant press coverage. Martinsville did organize a "gigantic" welcome-home rally, and McNutt spoke, as he often had, in an unapologetically partisan fashion.[1] But McNutt was not the sole attraction that day, for the event almost doubled as a Democratic Party powwow—and it took place three months after his return. Organizers had no need to hurry. McNutt had no presidential campaign to launch or government job to assume. After submitting a final memorandum on Philippine policy to President Harry S. Truman, McNutt resigned as ambassador, calling it "my last public office."[2]

Politically, McNutt faded away during the final decade of his life. He relocated to New York, opened a law office, undertook an array of business-related ventures, and made money so that Kathleen and Louise might enjoy financial security.[3] If familial responsibilities dissuaded him from considering another run for office, reality—the fact that he was more has-been than rising star—closed the door on any candidacy. McNutt's departure, however, was only as a full-time politician, for he missed the partisan and ideological engagement that characterized public life. McNutt kept mementoes of past triumphs and reminisced about Indiana. He commented on burning issues, even appearing before the U.S. House of Representatives during the second Red Scare. And he continued to campaign for Democratic candidates. It was as if McNutt were fighting to retain his voice in the national conversation. Politics proved a tough habit to break.

In one respect, McNutt proved relevant to postwar politics. Many of the ideas with which he had been identified—anti-Communism and anti-totalitarianism, military preparedness, a realistic foreign policy, and security for Americans from privation, invasion, and subversion—emerged in the political consensus known as Cold War liberalism. McNutt, an early proponent of what conservatives would chide as the welfare-warfare state, had long advocated economic security for Americans at home and national security for America abroad. Although liberals stressed different issues after 1945—such as civil rights for racial minorities—"security" lay at the heart of their thinking. Franklin D. Roosevelt had established the parameters by promoting the New Deal and "the concept that American liberal values should be defended and extended in the larger world."[4] From FDR's economic security state, one sensed a logical progression to the national security state of the 1940s. To contain Communism, the Truman administration "unified the armed forces, expanded the defense budget, harnessed science to military purpose, and forged new institutions . . . like the National Security Council and the Central Intelligence Agency."[5] This legacy would be accepted by Republican moderates such as President Dwight D. Eisenhower, whom McNutt had befriended during his first stint in the Philippines.[6] In the shadow of depression, world war, and cold war, then, the federal government evolved into an instrument to protect Americans from economic insecurity, subversives, and predatory dictators.

McNutt's relationship to Cold War liberalism rested on three components. The first was a set of experiences that allowed him to form a holistic perspective on security. Service in the American Legion had taught him to hate Communists, champion a realistic foreign policy, and trumpet preparedness. As governor and federal security administrator, McNutt embraced and defended the welfare state. He demonstrated a strong interest in geopolitics during his years in Manila, stressing that the United States must remain a power in Asia. In addition, by the late 1930s, he abhorred totalitarianism and sought to check its spread.

Second, McNutt's résumé set him apart from many other politicians and policymakers of the Roosevelt-Truman era. In comparison to such New Dealers as Henry A. Wallace, Harold L. Ickes, Frances Perkins, and Harry Hopkins, McNutt enjoyed a wider range of experiences, from elected politics to state-level reform and New Deal administration to foreign and defense policy. None of the aforementioned New Dealers molded the policy of containment that emerged after World War II, and the civilian officials who fashioned containment policy had almost no background in the politics of the New Deal.[7]

Third, undergirding McNutt's thoughts about security was an unblinking realism about politics. He shared Truman's outlook that "'the people' were fundamentally good," that "evil rested in individuals and the systems of power they created for their own aggrandizement," and that "the realities of life often required an accommodation" with the "inescapable fact" that evil existed.[8] Generally speaking, Cold War liberals looked to a strong, well-led democratic state to temper the worst human impulses and dampen the appeal—and threat—of totalitarianism. In 1952, for example, Democrats John F. Kennedy, Stuart Symington, and Henry Jackson won election to the U.S. Senate by stressing "an anti-communist foreign policy" without repudiating the New Deal.[9]

McNutt might have become the leader of these postwar liberals. He had the ideological credentials to do so, and he projected, for the postwar setting, an appropriate mixture of realism and idealism. He had been a national figure since the late 1920s, and he was older than Kennedy but younger than Truman. Unfortunately for McNutt, his political career ended just as the Cold War began. He thus provided a notable link between two phases of American liberalism: the New Deal and the early Cold War.

In 1947 McNutt settled into a new life filled with activity. He kept a law office in New York and another in the nation's capital, which he visited once a week. His clients included such large corporations as the United States Life Insurance Company and American International Underwriters, an insurance house with international branches. McNutt's New York law firm had six associates, as did his Washington office, and it occupied a "lush" twenty-three-room suite in a Lower East Side building.[10] Subordinates never forgot that they worked for a former politician, whom they always addressed as "Governor."[11] In the waiting room of McNutt's Manhattan office hung framed cartoons spanning his years in state, national, and international affairs. A portrait of Abraham Lincoln graced his office, as did "half a dozen gavels McNutt used in various posts." And behind his "big, impressive desk" stood three flags: one was the Stars and Stripes, the second was for the high commissioner to the Philippines, and the last was for the ambassador to the Philippines.[12] Above the mantel, McNutt placed a painting of Harry S. Truman. When reporters first saw it, they asked if he would accept the second spot on the Democratic ticket in 1948, McNutt smiled and responded: "I've been taught by experience that the President is the one who picks his own running mate, not the convention delegates."[13]

McNutt's remark about the selection of vice presidents was revealing, as was his decision to hang a picture of Truman rather than one of Franklin D. Roosevelt. Although McNutt did not discuss Roosevelt's selection of Henry A. Wallace for the vice presidency in 1940, his secretary, Anne Veihmeyer, sensed his disappointment, as did Kathleen. McNutt's displeasure with FDR emerged in a veiled, passive fashion. In public statements and official correspondence, he proved polite, even effusive, hailing Roosevelt as the "key builder" of victory in World War II, the "master craftsman of the United Nations," and "a great man and a great president."[14] Yet McNutt was loath to memorialize FDR. In 1948, Grace Tully, Roosevelt's private secretary, asked McNutt to write down his recollections of the former president for the Franklin D. Roosevelt Library. He did not answer her letter. Five weeks later, she sent a second request. Again, there was no response. Afterward, Tully made a third appeal: "We are very serious in our desire to have your story of your associations with the Roosevelt administration."[15] McNutt ignored her and remained silent. Around McNutt's Washington office, one seldom heard conversation about FDR and the 1940 campaign. "It was almost like a taboo subject," Veihmeyer recalled. "I never heard him say anything."[16]

McNutt was willing to revisit other, more pleasant aspects of his past. He retained a sentimental side, an attachment to belongings and friends. Well into the 1950s, for example, he held on to his 1939 Cadillac. And, in New York, he entertained one of his oldest friends from Bloomington, the newspaper publisher Paul Feltus, whom he had known since his days as a law professor at Indiana University. Old acquaintances would visit McNutt's Washington office to swap stories, or McNutt would chat with them via telephone. "He wasn't garrulous," Veihmeyer remembered, "but he was warm."[17] McNutt kept in touch with Frank McHale, and he reconciled with Wayne Coy. The trouble between McNutt and Coy had begun in the Philippines during the 1930s, when their wives quarreled, and it deepened after McNutt returned to Washington to head the Federal Security Agency, where Coy served as his deputy before departing for a position at the White House. When an aspiring author who wanted to write a novel about McNutt asked Coy for assistance, he declined, explaining: "My personal relationship with Paul changed so rapidly in the days before the second world war that I do not wish to risk . . . accusation of lack of objectivity."[18] The reconciliation began when McNutt found an old check made out to Coy and sent it to him. Around the same time, McNutt encountered Coy at a Washington country club and proposed "a family reunion" the next time he and Kathleen were in the nation's capital.[19]

If McNutt appeared to long for the company of friends, he showed less nostalgia for his hometown. To be fair, he did small things to boost Martinsville. When Manuel A. Roxas visited the United States in 1946, McNutt brought the Philippine president to Indiana to meet his parents and dine on traditional Hoosier fare. (McNutt's own favorite dishes were rather ordinary: roast beef, lamb chops, angel food cake, and maple mousse.) After returning to the United States in 1947, McNutt sometimes campaigned for Democratic candidates in his native state. McNutt, one relative recalled, remained "loyal to Indiana."[20] And Veihmeyer found him to be a midwestern boy at heart.[21] "This is home," McNutt told an Indiana audience during the election of 1952. "Here you have shared my joys and sorrows. Here my roots are and forever will be deep."[22] But he had no intention of living in Indiana year-round. During World War II, McNutt told reporters that he would not follow in the footsteps of Roosevelt, who often returned to Hyde Park, because that would mean relocating to Martinsville. He had less reason to come home after the death of his mother in 1947. Paul's father stayed in Martinsville until 1948, when he went to live with his son in New York. He died a year later. "My father was alert up until the time he entered the hospital," Paul noted. "But age takes its toll and he grew steadily weaker."[23] John McNutt's passing severed Paul's most personal link to his hometown.

McNutt remained tied to his work, which increasingly drew him into the field of international business. He was elected to the board of directors at United States Life Insurance, and he became the chairman of the board of Philippine American Life Insurance Company, a division of American International Group. McNutt's position at Phil-Am Life sent him back to Manila for extended stays, as he sought to rebuild the trust of war-ravaged Filipinos in private insurance. Government officials in the Philippines welcomed the return of Paul and Kathleen; President Elpidio Quirino hailed the couple as "two of our best friends."[24] McNutt dabbled in other ventures, such as growing abaca, a crop associated with the Philippines, and selling stock in a joint U.S.-Canadian uranium company. But his international focus remained Asia. In 1951 McNutt registered as an agent of the South Korean government. With respect to the Philippines, he helped a Filipino firm secure a contract from the government in

Manila, and he chaired the Philippine-American Trade Council. Upon departing the Philippines as ambassador, McNutt had bade Filipinos "farewell but not
good-bye."[25] He was true to his word.

Such wheeling and dealing—and traveling—gave McNutt a platform to
address U.S. policy in Asia. At one level, he continued to promote American
interests there. He noted, as he had during the 1930s, that the largest markets,
sources of raw materials, and economic potential lay in Asia, where the United
States remained a visible presence. "Our Army of occupation today rules Japan," McNutt beamed. "The American flag flies over a series of outposts . . .
that stretch from Hawaii to the west, north and south of the Pacific. We are
committed beyond recall to the Pacific. That is our frontier."[26] Cushioning such
boastful imperialism was McNutt's advocacy of increased American aid to, and
trade with, Asian nations. He argued that financial assistance dispensed by the
U.S. government had to come with few strings attached or else the peoples of
Asia would resent American meddling. It also had to be geared toward specific projects that would allow Asians to industrialize and exploit their own
resources. McNutt touted expanded trade as most effective means to develop
the countries of Asia and to cement their ties with the United States. It was the
sort of rhetoric one might expect from a former ambassador to the Philippines
and current head of a bilateral trade council, and it rang with the optimistic
boosterism heard in chambers of commerce across small-town America. But
McNutt was serious about the need to pump dollars into the Philippines. In his
final report as ambassador, he criticized the glacial pace at which funds were
being distributed under the Tydings Rehabilitation Act.[27]

McNutt saw America's "special relations" with the government in Manila
as part of a larger design.[28] As someone who had lived in East Asia during the
1930s, he remained wary of Japanese intentions and believed that the United
States should concentrate less on rehabilitating a former enemy and more on
boosting traditional allies, including China. As a diplomat, McNutt had conferred several times with Generalissimo Chiang Kai-shek. And as an anti-Communist, he had exhibited sympathy for Chiang's Nationalist Party in its struggle
against the forces of Mao Zedong. In 1948, McNutt urged the U.S. government
to increase its military assistance to Chiang. He also joined the Public Advisory Committee on China and lobbied for the shipment of food and fuel to the
Nationalist-held cities in an Asian version of the Berlin Airlift.[29] He pressed for
providing aid, such as rice and oil, to Chiang's regime until September 1949—
two months before Mao's Communists took control of mainland China.[30] If
McNutt was naïve in thinking that such products would make a difference to

the Nationalists' cause, he was shrewd enough to avoid a close identification with Chiang and his sagging fortunes on the battlefield.

McNutt's connection to Asia helped broaden his vision for America's future. For example, he became more conscious of racism at home as he sensed its impact abroad. "Even in the friendliest lands," McNutt told an audience in Massachusetts, "there were many who asked with a traveled air about our local color barriers and restricted areas. The hundreds of millions of non-Caucasian peoples who inhabit the Orient are especially interested in that subject. They cannot be fully convinced that we are thorough-going apostles of the four freedoms until we show that we mean the four freedoms to be for everybody." McNutt acknowledged the practical problems with maintaining Jim Crow, observing that doing so "gives ammunition to our enemies," rather than emphasizing a moral or even emotional commitment to racial justice.[31] Nevertheless, his stress on the need to support civil rights in order to bolster America's image overseas mirrored the thinking of many postwar liberals.[32]

There were limitations to McNutt's understanding of Asia. His distrust of Japan began to sound outdated. McNutt voiced such concerns in 1951, when the United States signed a peace treaty with the government in Tokyo. A provision in the treaty, stating that Japan was in no condition to make reparations, offended Philippine leaders, who worried that Japan would evade paying an estimated $8 billion in war damages. McNutt sided with the Philippine government and urged the Truman administration to seek revisions, which it did. The final treaty stressed Japan's moral obligation to make reparations and, in so doing, laid the basis for future Filipino claims. McNutt thus placed America's ties to the Philippines ahead of its emerging alliance with Japan, which became the linchpin of U.S. power in Asia during—and following—the Cold War. He missed the mark, again with respect to Japan, when he privately labeled General Douglas A. MacArthur a "fine military man" but "no civilian administrator."[33] That jibe came in 1945, when McNutt was preparing to replace MacArthur as the leading American official in the Philippines. In truth, MacArthur's administration of postwar Japan saw the implementation land reform, the protection of labor rights, and the strengthening of democratic governance.[34]

As his dealings in the East Asia illustrated, McNutt was unable to withdraw completely from public affairs and the emerging anti-Communist crusade. The film industry, where he had clients, was another case in point. This chapter of McNutt's life began early in 1947, when the House Un-American Activities Committee (HUAC), of the Republican-controlled Eightieth Congress, launched an investigation of Hollywood. Many reasons lay behind HUAC's probe. In the opinion of some conservatives, the film industry had long been of doubtful loyalty, with its blend of hedonism, sexually tinged imagery, foreign-born talent, New Deal ideals, and "Jewish money from New York's garment district." World War II, which saw the release of movies that were sympathetic toward the Soviet Union, fed the impression that Communists had infiltrated Hollywood. And they had, at least to a very small extent. In the Screen Writers Guild, there were radicals whose class consciousness had been fueled by the Great Depression and the exploitative conditions at the studios. But the guild also included both conservatives and liberals, and writers seldom engaged in ideological messaging.[35] Furthermore, filmmaking involved so many layers that no single coterie could manipulate the process.[36] Accordingly, the historian Walter Goodman has labeled the probe of Hollywood "asinine."[37] Only within the context of the early Cold War, and the fear it engendered, could such hearings seem defensible.

The search for Communists in the film industry acquired a drama of its own. HUAC, chaired by Representative J. Parnell Thomas of New Jersey, subpoenaed forty-three witnesses, nineteen of them unfriendly. The unfriendly witnesses, who appeared after a group of friendly or neutral ones, included the famed Hollywood Ten—two directors and eight screenwriters who declined to answer questions about their political allegiance, arguing that such inquiries violated the First Amendment to the Constitution. That reasoning failed to hold up in court, and they were found guilty of contempt. The friendly witnesses struggled as well, albeit for different reasons. They included actors, directors, studio heads, and representatives of the film industry who sought to pose as devotees of freedom of speech, patriotism, and anti-Communism simultaneously. In general, however, they wound up endorsing the committee's work, at least at the outset. Before testifying, Eric Johnston, president of the Motion Picture Association of America, welcomed the HUAC inquiry, denied that studios shielded radicals, and denounced Communism.[38] But he made no mention of the First Amendment. In an early closed-door hearing, Jack Warner, the vice president of Warner Brothers, revealed himself to be no civil libertarian. Warner admitted that there were Communists in Hollywood and asserted that he had dismissed screenwriters for un-American sentiments on the basis of hearsay appearing in the *Hollywood Reporter*. Warner also conceded that he would not in 1947 make a pro-Russian film such as *Mission to Moscow,* which his studio released in 1943 to bolster American sympathy for an embattled wartime ally.[39]

In danger of running in verbal circles when they testified publicly, Johnston and Warner tapped McNutt to be their counsel. McNutt would represent the Motion Picture Association of America, which included such large studios as Metro-Goldwyn-Mayer (MGM), Universal, Twentieth-Century Fox, and Warner Brothers. He was a sensible choice. McNutt was nationally known, had experience testifying on Capitol Hill, and, as a former national commander of the American Legion, possessed strong anti-Communist credentials. He also had developed ties to Hollywood during the 1930s through Jacob Weiss, his former political ally in Indiana. There was, however, a strong possibility of skirmishes between McNutt and HUAC. McNutt had been associated with both the welfare state and the Roosevelt administration, and the committee's chair, Parnell Thomas, "hated the New Deal and all of its works."[40] McNutt was averse to Thomas' abrasiveness and ill disposed toward attacks on *Mission to Moscow,* whose protagonist, U.S. Ambassador Joseph E. Davies, was his friend and law partner. Indeed, a scene in the film depicted Davies's rustic cottage where the McNutts had vacationed with Joe and his wife, Marjorie Merriweather Post.

McNutt's political experience and personal associations helped make him a more committed civil libertarian—or a smarter, more practiced anti-Communist—than either Warner or Johnston. Along with Johnston, McNutt welcomed HUAC's investigation. At the same time, he read over Warner's closed-door testimony and lamented that it had made the movie mogul appear "idiotic."[41] When HUAC's public hearings commenced in the fall of 1947, McNutt decided to take the offensive. He proclaimed free speech to be "one of the basic issues in this investigation." If today's attacks on a "free screen" went unchallenged, he continued, "Will it be radio programs tomorrow? Books and magazines the next day? Where will it end?"[42]

Guided by McNutt, Warner performed adequately during HUAC's public hearings. Warner's opening statement started with something absent from his earlier testimony—a strong defense of civil liberty. Freedom, he stressed, "requires careful nurturing, protection, and encouragement. It has flourished under the guaranties of our American Constitution." Warner mixed idealistic talk about the value of "an enlightened public" with realistic, McNutt-style rhetoric hailing the "free American screen" as the nation's "first line of defense" and "American common sense" as the "determining factor" in ascertaining whether a film might be subversive. Influenced no doubt by McNutt, Warner defended one of his releases: "If making Mission to Moscow in 1942 was a subversive activity, then the American Liberty ships which carried food and guns to Russian allies ... were likewise engaged in subversive activities."[43] But when questioned by the committee, Warner lapsed into making controversial remarks. At one point, he endorsed outlawing the Communist Party of the United States.[44]

Johnston was more consistent during his testimony. He accused HUAC of spreading "scare-head stuff" and feeding the misimpression that "Hollywood Communists are astronomical in number and almost irresistible in power." He, too, defended the "freedom to speak, to hear, and to see." He deplored the committee's resort to "intimidation" and promised to "use every influence at my command to keep the screen free." Sounding like a New Deal liberal, Johnston advised that "a positive program is the best antitoxin for the plague of communism." He even used one of McNutt's favorite words—security: "Revolutions ... won't get anywhere if we wipe out the potential causes of communism. The most effective way is to make democracy work for greater opportunity, for greater participation, for greater security for all our people."[45] It was an argument that McNutt had made during the Great Depression and one that, as we will see, he continued to voice during the Cold War. From available sources, there is no way to determine how closely McNutt had scripted Johnston and Warner. But in Johnston's first letter to Thomas, written before McNutt signed on as counsel, there was no discussion of any "positive program" to fight Communism and only a tepid defense of free speech. As lawyer to both Johnston and Warner, McNutt had to have influenced them, especially when some of their concerns (about *Mission to Moscow*) and words (such as "security") reflected his own.

If McNutt helped shape his clients' testimony behind the scenes, he had little impact on the hearings. It was not for lack of effort. Before Warner testified, McNutt asked for permission to cross-examine witnesses. Since no outside counsel had received that right, Thomas refused the request.[46] A week later, McNutt launched a counterattack by demanding that the committee produce a list of films which it had claimed to have been tainted by Communism. Thomas replied by assailing people of "dubious character"—meaning McNutt—who, he insisted, were striving to thwart HUAC's investigation.[47] McNutt denied the charge. But Thomas, determined to have the last word, sought to link him to a man of unsavory reputation. He asked if McNutt knew Morris Rosner, an aide to Louis B. Mayer who had been charged with stock-market fraud. McNutt responded that he had heard of him, mainly because Rosner lived in Washington's Shoreham Hotel, where McNutt had an apartment. At that point, the matter dropped.[48]

Such roughshod methods became further evident in a dossier compiled by HUAC on McNutt's alleged ties to supposed subversives. According to the document, the former national commander of the American Legion had spoken, in 1942, before such Communist Party front organizations as the "American Slav Congress" and the "Negro Victory Committee." The fact that these talks were wartime, morale-boosting endeavors had not registered with the author of the dossier, nor did the source of this intelligence—the *New York Times*. The document continued with innuendoes about members of McNutt's staff at the War Manpower Commission: William Haber, one of his deputies, had been "investigated by Department of Justice"; George Engeman, a press aide, "was a known party-liner in the Baltimore Newspaper Guild"; and May Thompson Evans, an adviser at the commission and former assistant director of the Women's Division of the Democratic National Committee, had been "cited by the Committee on Un-American Activities." Similar comments followed, climaxing in the dossier's revelation that McNutt "was a constant and close associate with Joseph E. Davies, former ambassador to Russia, and author of Mission to Moscow." The report concluded: "It is a matter of record that Mrs. McNutt was active with Washington Committee for Aid to China."[49] To what end HUAC intended to use this information is unknown. A probe by the Federal Bureau of Investigation in 1948 revealed the capriciousness of the allegations. The FBI conceded that some of the groups McNutt had spoken to during the war had been sympathetic to the Soviet Union. It also noted that Paul's and Kathleen's names had appeared, in 1942, among the "Patrons and Patronesses" of the "Congress of American-Soviet Friendship." Yet the FBI found McNutt to be a "well-known public figure" who was "highly reputable" and "of undoubted loyalty."[50]

Many members of the film industry gained no such exoneration. After being found guilty of contempt, the Hollywood Ten received fines and prison time. Following the HUAC hearings, studio heads met in New York City "to frame a policy" to protect their industry from Communist influence and public criticism. They declined to rehire any of the Hollywood Ten on grounds that they were no longer useful employees. "So began the blacklist," Walter Goodman lamented.[51] Thereafter, Hollywood was less inclined to make films addressing racism, anti-Semitism, and other blemishes in American society.[52] The studios themselves proved opportunistic, producing such anti-Communist films as *The Red Menace* and *I Married a Communist* while permitting the more talented members of the Hollywood Ten "to contribute screenplays under assumed names and for reduced wages."[53]

McNutt's role in establishing the blacklist is difficult to pinpoint. At one level, he was lawyer to the heads of the major studios, and he attended a meeting at the end of HUAC's hearings when the moguls decided not to renew the contracts of the Hollywood Ten. At another level, however, the principal ringleaders behind the blacklist appear to have been Eric Johnston and former secretary of state James F. Byrnes, who also advised the studios. Warner, during questioning before HUAC—and while still under McNutt's sway—had denied any intention of depriving a writer "of a livelihood because of his political beliefs" because "it would be a conspiracy, the attorney tells me, and I know that myself."[54] Notwithstanding such assurances, the idea of dismissing workers for having Communist affiliations had circulated before HUAC's hearings—and before McNutt signed on as counsel. In August 1947 Mayer averred that if he received a list of Communists working at MGM, "he will put them out of the studio."[55] As Goodman observed, "The Hollywood hearings brought forward no heroes."[56] The film industry failed to remain united against the onslaught of HUAC's innuendos, with Warner's closed-door testimony signaling the first crack in Hollywood's advance lines. Nevertheless, HUAC's investigation of the film industry generated negative press and Thomas, perhaps for that reason, decided to halt the hearings earlier than he had planned.[57]

McNutt could claim little credit for the probe's demise. He seldom spoke during the hearings, had failed to transform Johnston and Warner into unstinting civil libertarians, and was at best a bystander when the blacklist came into existence. For McNutt, only two things came out of the investigation of Hollywood. First, the hearings illustrated that McNutt's anti-Communism had evolved away from the strident rhetoric he had employed during the 1920s, when he had been a leader in the American Legion. The shift no doubt stemmed from his maturation as a person and his association with people of different backgrounds and interests such as Davies. Moreover, McNutt had no reason to appeal to popular prejudice by overamplifying his anti-Communism, for he had no thoughts of running for office. Instead, McNutt briefly remained a part of the film industry—the second consequence of his work with Warner and Johnston. In 1950 he headed an investment group that purchased financially troubled United Artists (UA). By that time, however, McNutt's business and legal affairs were so varied that the extent of his involvement in running UA remains unclear. United Artists continued to lose money, and McNutt's group sold the company in 1951.[58]

The investigation of Hollywood showed how McNutt remained tangentially involved in politics. Frank McHale did the most to sustain McNutt's interest by sending him updates on political developments in the Midwest. When McNutt became high commissioner to the Philippines in 1945, McHale conferred with a group of politicians in Cleveland. "After a few drinks," he informed McNutt, "[they] wanted to talk politics and particularly about the 1940 convention. You have a lot of friends in that State and all of them are pulling for you on this new job." The thought of a political comeback, perhaps as Truman's vice president, might have briefly crossed McNutt's mind early in 1948, when he told a reporter: "I am a party man. I always do that which is asked of me."[59] But, when asked to address a political luncheon, McNutt declined, explaining that he had little time for speechmaking. A month later, he rejected an overture from Democrats who wanted to revise their party's platform. Rumors that he might run for the Senate in 1948 came to nothing, as did talk that he might join Truman on the party's national ticket. And speculation about McNutt as a possible favorite-son alternative to Truman went nowhere; Pleas Greenlee, chair of the Indiana Democratic Party and a foe of McNutt, announced: "There is no chance of Indiana going for Mr. McNutt."[60]

McNutt's last, faint hurrah as a presidential candidate came at the 1948 Democratic National Convention. During the roll call of states, Byrd Sims, a delegate from Florida, asked to speak and unexpectedly nominated McNutt for president. Sims was acting out of anger at Truman's civil rights program and fear that the Democratic Party, increasingly torn between its right and left wings, would lose the White House to the Republican nominee, Thomas Dewey. In McNutt, Sims saw not a fellow segregationist but an attractive alternative to the "present leadership," someone who had wide experience in government, a gift for oratory, and an ability to unite all regions of the country. In making his appeal, Sims stressed McNutt's appearance—"he certainly looks better than the Republican nominee"—and recounted the events of eight years earlier when McNutt "stepped before you" and spent twenty minutes trying to calm the convention. "You wanted him for your vice president," Sims reminded the delegates, "and he begged and pleaded with you to take his name out because our late President Roosevelt requested it and wanted Mr. Wallace." In 1948, however, mention of McNutt's name drew a mixture of boos from Truman supporters and cheers from the president's opponents. A radio commentator dismissed Sims's "rather strange nominating speech," and the roll call proceeded.[61] At the end of the balloting, Truman received 947½ votes against 263 for Senator Richard B. Russell of Georgia. McNutt finished third, with one-half of one vote. In nominating

McNutt, Sims acknowledged that he had acted on his own. Indeed, McNutt shunned talk of becoming a candidate for any office with the words: "No. Too old now. Haven't got the stamina to do that anymore." Experience had taught him that politics was a "rough, expensive, disheartening game."[62]

But McNutt remained fascinated with aspects of that game. "He made a study of his fellow man," Anne Veihmeyer observed, "and that was politics."[63] He continued to read and keep abreast of current affairs. Old concerns, such as his commitment to Zionism, remained strong. In 1942 McNutt wished success to the national chair of the United Palestine Appeal in the "task of building a homeland in Palestine for the Jews of the world."[64] Three years later, he hailed Jews for making Palestine "an outpost of world democracy"—a phrase that he had applied to the Philippines—and a "miniature of the United States," replete with "power projects, agricultural colonies, labor exchanges and employment security systems."[65] And in 1947 the Indianapolis Zionist District lauded Mc-Nutt—"our great friend"—for lobbying the General Assembly of the United Nations to vote to partition Palestine into Jewish and Arab states.[66]

McNutt's diplomatic experience led to a brief assignment from the Commission on Organization of the Executive Branch of the Government. The Hoover Commission, as it was known, examined possible changes to the executive branch's operations and structure, including the merits of transferring the Visa Division from the Department of State to the Department of Justice. A task force found the Visa Division's present location to be in accordance with the responsibilities of the State Department and the requirements of U.S. immigration law. In 1949, McNutt reviewed their report and, although he might have noted how State's administration of the Visa Division had kept refugees away from American shores in the 1930s, he refrained from doing so. Instead, he endorsed the conclusion of the task force that the "present system has worked efficiently."[67] His position was not surprising. The help he had given to Jewish refugees occurred within the confines of U.S. immigration policy. He had proposed no changes to existing law or State Department practices during the 1930s, and he again declined to do so in 1949.

When McNutt was not working, his mind wandered, often backward. He reminisced about his earlier life in Indiana and the folks he had known there. "He enjoyed these people," Veihmeyer remembered, and was happiest when conversing with someone like McHale.[68] Gradually, McNutt returned to politics, albeit in limited roles. He became an adviser to the Democratic National Committee.[69] And he returned to Indiana to campaign for the party's candidates during the elections of 1948, 1950, and 1952.

What McNutt said in his speeches was in tune with both the postwar milieu and his past rhetoric. It was almost as if the man, message, and moment had merged, just when he had lost his national prominence. McNutt had been at ease discussing security, and he had the opportunity to do so after World War II when national security became the burning issue. Although McNutt did not ignore domestic programs such as Social Security, which he credited with sustaining the postwar prosperity, his focus shifted toward thwarting the spread of Soviet influence.[70] Along with many Americans, he saw Communism as the twin of fascism and the Soviet Union as an aggressor nation not unlike Nazi Germany. In 1948 McNutt warned that if "the world outside America is overrun by Communists" Americans would be in "deadly danger."[71] He defined the international interests of the United States expansively: "The withdrawal of our influence and strength from any quarter of the globe today . . . would soon shake our own western world, with all its fancied security."[72] "Our country's security," he later affirmed, "is synonymous with the security of the whole free world."[73] Accordingly, he backed policies, such as the Marshall Plan, to contain Soviet power in Europe, and military actions, such as the United Nations intervention in Korea, to halt Communist advances in Asia.[74] McNutt's contribution to containment and to America's emerging defense perimeter in Asia had come when he negotiated a treaty by which the United States received military bases in its former colony.

Philippine policy reflected McNutt's idealism as well as his realism. McNutt, of course, had helped maintain U.S. interests in the Philippines. Yet, on a more elevated note, he also extolled America as the model for Asia. The United States, McNutt declared, "means machines, luxuries, mass production, gadgets, a high standard of living, prosperity for all, big business and little business, power, prestige . . . but above all, America means democracy."[75] Such ideals reflected an ethnocentric perspective that U.S. power was exceptionally good and naïveté that American-style capitalism and democracy were naturally compatible. One finds nowhere in his speeches any endorsement of pacifistic talk about the "brotherhood of man" and "one world"—a phrase popularized by the late Wendell Willkie, his former fraternity brother.[76] To the contrary, McNutt declared that "the bloody ordeal of this century is not over and we have a job to do."[77]

McNutt was conscious of the task ahead; he favored a mobilization of American society to meet the dangers of a divided world. He backed expansion of the draft, a position in tune with his past advocacy of military training. And he remained confident that "preponderant power lies within the confines of the free world"—if it were harnessed.[78] Such rhetoric mirrored the mindset of

Truman's State Department, which averred that "preponderant power must be the object of U.S. policy." Achieving that level of power involved, among other things, "creating a world environment hospitable to U.S. interests and values," "developing the capabilities to overcome threats and challenges," "mobilizing the strength to reduce Soviet influence on its own periphery," "undermining the appeal of communism," and "establishing a configuration of power and a military posture so that if war erupted, the United States would prevail."[79] McNutt, for his part, praised the thrust of Truman's foreign policy as "realistic, courageous and sound."[80]

McNutt also addressed the threat of Communism at home. In 1950 he reminded an audience that for the thirty years the American Legion—and by implication himself—had been "a voice crying in the wilderness" about the need to build the nation's defenses and to confront "Communism, Fascism, and Totalitarianism in any form."[81] McNutt asserted that since the Legion had had no illusions about Communism, it (and he) knew best how to root out subversives, by "keeping our heads" and "using established processes of justice"—a jab, perhaps, at HUAC's probe of Hollywood. In a salvo against Senator Joe McCarthy of Wisconsin, he dismissed more recent (and reckless) foes of domestic Communism as "Joe-Come-Latelys."[82] And he defended liberalism—the "positive, constructive program" implemented by Roosevelt and continued by Truman—for transforming American life at home and thus strengthening America abroad. By contrast, Republican "reactionaries," he predicted, would stifle reform, arouse discontent, and make the country "*puppyfood* for Reds."[83] Such comments suggested that had McNutt sought elected office in the late 1940s, he would have been unafraid to return fire on the Grand Old Party (GOP) at a time when right-wing attacks were eroding the "solid advantage on national security" that the Democrats had enjoyed during and immediately after World War II.[84]

One of McNutt's most forceful assaults on the Republican Party—and defenses of the Democrats—took place in Indiana in the fall of 1948. He made his case for President Truman's election by building his argument to a crescendo, in the fashion of offering a summary to a jury. "We cannot escape reality," he proclaimed, in reviewing the previous thirty years. "We of this generation have lived in storm and stress of immense and incalculable events." With a confrontation with the Soviet Union looming, only the Democratic Party could be trusted to lead America through this latest crisis. Democrats had implemented Social Security, minimum wages, stock-market regulation, farm price supports, and government-sponsored protection for bank depositors, the aged, and the unemployed. The party had fought fascism, contained Communism, built the atomic bomb, unveiled the Marshall Plan, and kept America secure at home and abroad. The election of a Republican president, he asserted, would bring that party's isolationists to power and extend to Russia "an invitation to make all of Europe, and then the world, their satellites."[85] McNutt, like other postwar liberals, positioned himself against the extremes of right and left while defending internationalism, the welfare state, and responsible efforts to root out Communism at home. The liberalism that had emerged by the 1940s was "tough-minded," and McNutt remained a fighter.[86] He returned to the rough-and-tumble style that characterized Indiana politics by denouncing the GOP as "the party of privilege" and warning that the Republicans would "lead us back into the dark economic ages of the 1920s."[87]

McNutt could swing so forcefully because he was not on the ballot. Truman, who won the election in 1948 over the predictions of nearly every pundit, may have heard about McNutt's vigorous campaigning, for the president conferred with the Hoosier at the White House at the end of 1948. Their encounter sparked rumors that McNutt would be offered a position in the administration. Yet such talk came to naught, for Truman owed him nothing.[88] The president failed to carry Indiana, meaning that McNutt's attacks had no effect on the election's outcome. He would remain employed in the private sector.

Aside from speculation about what might have been, what is the larger significance of McNutt's postwar speeches and his ongoing emphasis on security? First, they—and it—showed how someone with a unique background—in the American Legion, depression-era politics, and America's colonial empire—had gained a holistic vision of security before World War II and found an ideological home during the onset of the Cold War. Second, it said something about the mentality of those who shaped the postwar policy of containment. Ronald Reagan, a Cold Warrior (but no liberal), once eulogized John F. Kennedy, unquestionably a Cold War liberal, for retaining a "hard, unillusioned understanding of man and his political choices," for eschewing a diplomacy governed by "soft reason and good intentions," and for insisting that America's defenses be "unsurpassed."[89] McNutt evinced such realism as well. Finally, stressing the idea of security allows one to see both continuity and change in twentieth-century liberalism. New Dealers, led by FDR, pushed economic security in 1930s; Pearl Harbor forced the country to pay attention to national security; and postwar liberals, such as Truman, continued that focus. McNutt, who was in the shadow of both presidents, had put elements of security together by the late 1930s. In so doing, he provided one bridge between two eras of liberalism.

McNutt maintained a grueling pace during his final years. He lived in New York in a plush twelve-room apartment on Fifth Avenue that had a Filipino man-servant, a private elevator, a drawing room overlooking Central Park, and a hall-way decorated with flags of the countries he had visited. His favorite room was a paneled den with clocks showing the time at locales around the globe. If the interior decor seemed stuffy, McNutt remained accessible to family and friends. A cousin by marriage recalled a dinner at the McNutts' apartment during which Paul answered all of the young visitor's questions. Despite the commodious surroundings, Paul never took to New York. The city was full of busy people, which forced him and Kathleen to plan ahead whenever they wanted to social-ize. Kathleen did what she could, arranging lunches with Dwight and Mamie Eisenhower and with Douglas and Jean MacArthur. But Kathleen complained that their neighborhood was overpopulated by Republicans, some of whom had "never seen a Democrat."[90] Offsetting such drawbacks were the cultural attrac-tions, such as the concerts and plays which the McNutts enjoyed as often as pos-sible.[91] "New York is a great place," Kathleen told Paul Feltus, their friend from Bloomington. "There is almost everything here that one wants. What we don't have is things like—you coming up on our front porch on Eighth Street!"[92]

McNutt preferred Washington, "a quiet town," over New York.[93] Paul and Kathleen attended parties at the home of Marjorie Merriweather Post and Joe Davies in the nation's capital. The couples remained close. Joe and Paul were law partners while Marjorie and Kathleen were both Christian Scientists. Mar-jorie liked being around "doers" who were engaged in "mental work."[94] That was Paul, a well-read man with a wealth of life experiences. Yet visits to the nation's capital, where McNutt also had a law firm, seldom involved relaxation. When Paul accepted an offer of season tickets to see the Washington Senators, he admitted that he would be too busy to see many games. For McNutt taking a rest meant getting away—far away. In 1950, he and Kathleen embarked on a fifty-five-day cruise around South America.[95]

By the 1950s, McNutt was working, traveling, and speaking. "Paul is in Wash-ington and soon will be going to Indiana to raise his voice for Governor Ste-venson," Kathleen wrote during the presidential campaign of 1952 when Adlai Stevenson, a Democrat, was challenging their friend Eisenhower.[96] During that contest, McNutt was especially hard on the Republican nominee for vice president, Senator Richard Nixon of California, who had survived reports of

amassing a secret political fund by disclosing his finances and his acceptance
of a cocker spaniel as a gift. McNutt derided "Tricky Dicky Nixon" for "telling
a story about his little dog when the audience wanted to hear about his kitty."[97]
He was harsh toward Eisenhower as well, taking as a betrayal the general's association with such conservative senators as McCarthy, Ohio's Robert Taft,
and William Jenner of Indiana. While Paul was pounding away at the Grand
Old Party, Kathleen was substituting for him at events in New York; she sighed
about "having spent half my life at a speaker's table."[98]

Paul had troubles of his own. He continued to drink—alone and at odd hours
of the day. During a campaign swing through Indiana, Jack New, a Democratic
Party operative, transported him from Richmond to Indianapolis. On that
drive, over fifty miles long, McNutt drank a pint of sloe gin—behavior which
led New to label the former governor an alcoholic. Cigarettes posed at least
as great a threat for he smoked heavily. With respect to his health, McNutt,
on the surface, had little cause for alarm. In 1946 a doctor pronounced him
in excellent shape, despite gallstones and bouts with bursitis. McNutt's office
staff noticed nothing wrong with him—until it was too late. The trouble began
in the fall of 1954, when McNutt introduced Adlai Stevenson at a Democratic
Party rally. His voice sounded like "a raspy whisper."[99] He underwent surgery
and remained away from the office for six months. McNutt's convalescence appeared to progress smoothly, and he embarked on an around-the-world cruise
with Kathleen early in 1955.[100]

McNutt's health rapidly deteriorated. He became ill in Manila and was flown
to Honolulu and then to San Francisco, where a military plane transported him
to New York. He looked terrible—worn, thin, and lost in an outsized coat that
once had fit him. After seeing a photograph of McNutt, one Legionnaire jotted:
"You would never recognize this as a picture of our once robust good looking
Commander."[101] Upon arriving in New York, he went to his apartment. Reports
of improvement proved false, for he was suffering from cancer of the esophagus.
He died at home on March 24, 1955, at the age of sixty-three.[102]

McNutt was buried at Arlington National Cemetery in a ceremony marked
by pomp and solemnity. Attending were such Legionnaires as Louis A. Johnson,
a former national commander and onetime secretary of defense. Otherwise, the
dignitaries mainly came from Indiana—a reflection of McNutt's diminished
stature in national politics. They included former governor Henry Schricker,
U.S. senators Homer Capehart and William Jenner, four members of the U.S.
House of Representatives, and Indiana University president Herman B Wells.

After the service, six white horses drew the caisson carrying McNutt's bronze casket into the cemetery. The cortege stopped near the graves of William Gibbs McAdoo, who had been secretary of the treasury during World War I, and Frank Knox, who was secretary of the navy during World War II. The pallbearers—all infantrymen—then lifted the casket as a band played "Nearer My God to Thee." According to one observer, "The command was given to the ceremonial firing squad to load and fire. Three volleys cracked in the cold springtime air. Then from a distance came 'taps.'"[103] The flag on McNutt's casket was folded and handed to his widow.

Perhaps the most memorable moment was the eulogy delivered by Herman Wells. Wells had known McNutt for a quarter century, had been one of McNutt's earliest protégés, and had reached his position at Indiana University partly because McNutt had sought to become president of something larger. He hailed the passing of a life "replete with struggle, triumph, and unselfish devotion to public duty." "Fearless in meeting his responsibilities," McNutt "bore more than his share of the day's work." He was a man who had loomed large over the political landscape. "As it is with mountains, so it is with men," Wells reflected. "Some dominate their scene even though they walk with giants. Such a man was Paul Vories McNutt."[104]

The press echoed Wells. The *Washington Star* called McNutt "a picturesque figure on the American political scene."[105] The *New York World-Telegram* editorialized that "he achieved a personal popularity matched by few Democratic politicians of his day. He was politically astute but also aroused bitter opposition."[106] Obituaries cited four reasons why he sparked antagonism. First, McNutt was willing to act, at times aggressively. "McNutt was a strong governor," the *Fort Wayne Journal-Gazette* noted. "He did not evade responsibility."[107] Second, he embodied an emerging political tradition, often controversial, that viewed expansively the use of federal power at home and U.S. power abroad. According to the *Memphis Commercial Appeal*, McNutt evinced a "consistent and outspoken devotion to the [Democratic] party and for whatever new-thought liberalism the party might stand."[108] "Indiana," a reporter for the United Press observed, "was one of the first states to cooperate fully with the federal government in its social security program."[109] Third, McNutt possessed a multitude of gifts, and he achieved significant success—things which often provoke resentment. The *Indianapolis Star* recalled Governor McNutt as "young, vigorous, handsome and able" and his political career as "brilliant and almost meteoric."[110] Finally, he worked hard to attain ever higher offices. The *Times* of London dubbed McNutt "a man of great drive and enthusiasm" but "also a man of high ambition."[111]

The fact that McNutt's death drew commentary from a London-based newspaper underscored his international significance. Filipinos also marked his passing. The diplomat Carlos Rómulo hailed McNutt as a friend of the Philippines, as did President Ramón Magsaysay. The press in Manila proved polite, praising McNutt's role in effecting Philippine independence in 1946. In the aftermath of World War II, the *Manila Bulletin* opined, "the transition [from American to Philippine sovereignty] was accomplished as smoothly as it could have been."[112] There was little criticism of McNutt's part in tying the Philippines to the foreign and defense policies of the United States and no mention of the Bell Act, parity rights, or American bases. Such tact no doubt derived from respect for someone who had tried to abet the Philippines' economic revival and national security, albeit on terms in accordance with U.S. interests. But the United States–Philippine relationship had matured by the mid-1950s. The Cold War in Asia had intensified, meaning that Filipino leaders had reason to continue an American military presence in their nation. Economic ties were another matter, for Filipinos sought and secured revisions to the Bell Act via the Laurel-Langley Agreement of 1955. According to an official at the Philippine embassy in Washington, "McNutt did a lot of behind the scenes work in behalf of trade revision between the two countries."[113] That fact, had it been more widely known, might have lifted McNutt's standing further in the eyes of Philippine leaders.

Newspapers generally emphasized the most dramatic aspects of McNutt's career, such as his ambition to be president. The *New York World-Telegram* headline noted that "McNutt Longed to Call White House Home."[114] The *Indianapolis Star* and the *Indianapolis Times* both recounted McNutt's drive for the presidency and the events of the Democratic Convention in 1940.[115] "When Roosevelt was renominated, McNutt's presidential chances faded," observed an editor in Greensboro, North Carolina.[116] Thereafter, a United Press reporter noted, FDR's selection of Wallace for vice president "drove McNutt into political eclipse."[117] He accepted the president's decision and, in so doing, showed that selflessness and sacrifice tempered his famed ambition. "McNutt was a patriot of the highest degree," the *Anderson* (Indiana) *Bulletin* reflected.[118] An editor at the *New York Times* emphasized McNutt's personal qualities almost exclusively. "He had friends, and had them everywhere, because he himself was a friend," this editor stressed. "No person was too obscure for his attention. His was no artificial dignity that had to be preserved at the cost of sincerity. He was kind and generous."[119] Yet his failure to gain the White House helped consign him to the margins of American history. "McNutt," the *Manila Bulletin* editorialized, "came very close to being a great man."[120]

The obituaries were notable for both what they did and what they did not say. There was a great deal of emphasis on McNutt's governorship, mainly from papers in Indiana. Harold Feightner, a veteran Hoosier journalist, praised McNutt's "bold and daring administration" by noting that "few, if any" of its laws "ever have been repealed."[121] Among McNutt's legacies were his reorganization of the state government and enactment of the gross income tax, which, according to the *Elkhart* (Indiana) *Truth*, "has as much support among Republicans as Democrats now."[122] Receiving less attention were his efforts to tailor the federal government's health, education, and welfare programs to World War II–era mobilization and his oft-criticized stewardship of the War Manpower Commission (WMC). The press also ignored McNutt's stealthy oversight of the U.S. government's biological warfare program during World War II and his low-key work on behalf of Jewish refugees during the 1930s. The *National Jewish Post* made no mention of McNutt's passing.[123]

Also missing from the retrospectives was an overall assessment of McNutt's leadership during the course of his career. Was he a catalyst for change or a follower of larger trends and greater leaders? He was, in truth, a bit of both. During the earliest part of McNutt's public life, he was an amplifier, rather than an originator, of the preparedness and anti-Communist programs of the American Legion. As McNutt's star ascended in the 1930s, he grew more creative and more forceful. The wide-ranging agenda he had charted as governor—two months before FDR began putting the New Deal in place—gave him immense power, national exposure, and independence from the new president. As high commissioner of the Philippines in the 1930s, he risked stirring controversy in two areas: his effort to resettle 1,300 Jews in Manila, which took place at a time when the United States and most of the world was averse to assisting refugees, and his speech recommending U.S. retention of the Philippines, which defied the wish of many Americans to limit or end their country's overseas commitments. One of McNutt's first acts as federal security administrator also was bold, his proposed overhaul of Social Security. But he soon acceded to Roosevelt's insistence that the existing insurance-based program remain in place. McNutt proved equally compliant when FDR decided to run for a third term and then selected Wallace as his running mate.

Therein lay McNutt's dilemma. As the trajectory of his career pointed upward, he was tempted to take risks in the pursuit of higher offices. Then, when the top prizes he sought—the presidency and vice presidency—came within reach, his outward confidence surrendered to an inner caution, as if he were afraid to make a mistake and lose what seemed destined to fall into his lap. McNutt also was so talented and his early successes in Indiana came so easily that he never learned how to fight people of equal or greater ability (and renown) to achieve his ends. The consequences were plain. Following the election of 1940, McNutt sank into the role of being a mere instrument of presidential policy—of Roosevelt's mobilization efforts at the FSA, where he performed effectively, and at the WMC, where his actions drew criticism. By the postwar era, McNutt's career had come full circle. Not unlike his leadership of the Legion, he was able to weave long-standing ideas about enhancing the security of Americans into his speeches and the tapestry of public policy with respect to the Philippines, which became part of the U.S. defense perimeter during the Cold War. Nevertheless, one wonders whether the electorate was paying much attention to the words and deeds of this fading political actor.

Although McNutt failed to secure his greatest ambition, he nonetheless helped advance the careers of several distinguished Americans. For example, Wayne Coy served as assistant director of the Bureau of the Budget from 1942 to 1944. In 1947 he became chair of the Federal Communications Commission, where he supported the First Amendment rights of broadcasters and the development of standards for color television. Coy resigned in 1952 and died of a heart attack in 1957. Frank McHale was a member of the Democratic National Committee from 1937 to 1952, a position from which he influenced "the nomination of hundreds of candidates for local, state and national offices." He died in 1975.[124] Mary E. Switzer, McNutt's lieutenant at the FSA, became a "frontline bureaucrat" who worked as assistant to the federal security administrator from 1939 to 1950.[125] In 1950, she became director of the federal government's Office of Vocational Rehabilitation. At the time of her retirement in 1970, Switzer headed an office whose budget exceeded $8 billion, making her "the woman executive with the largest responsibility in the Government."[126] One of the buildings presently occupied by the Department of Health and Human Services in Washington is named in her honor. Herman Wells retired as president of Indiana University in 1962 after twenty-five years at the helm. He then served as the university's chancellor, a largely symbolic position, until his death in 2000 at the age of ninety-seven. Wells has been praised as the greatest president the university ever knew and as a statesman in higher education. His national and international assignments are too numerous to discuss or even to list.[127]

McNutt's legacy—and absence—were felt by his family. A few months after Paul's death, Kathleen wrote Marjorie Merriweather Post that she "was learning innumerable things about living alone," especially how "important matters can't be left to others."[128] In the short run, Kathleen sought refuge with friends. In the long run, she found companionship with Roy Garrett Watson of Boston, a treasurer of the Christian Science Church, whom she married in December 1956. Kathleen and Roy shared many things in common, particularly their faith. Roy represented a change from Paul, for his life revolved around religion rather than politics.[129] Yet Paul's career had left a mark on his widow. "I don't take part in any political activities now," Kathleen told an interviewer in 1964, "but I will always have an enduring interest in politics and be an ardent Democrat."[130]

In many ways, Louise McNutt followed in her father's footsteps. After earning a BA and MA from George Washington University, Louise joined the Department of State's Far Eastern Division, becoming an adviser to the United Nations. "She adores her work," Kathleen remarked. "She is so like her father. She would gladly work overtime forever."[131] Louise, who never married, remained devoted to her profession and parents. In 1965 she accompanied her mother to the campus of Indiana University for the dedication of a large quadrangle-shaped dormitory complex named for Paul McNutt.[132] Louise died in 2000 and bequeathed the university $2 million to fund fellowships, bearing the names of both her parents, for postgraduate students in the humanities.

Like many politicians who never attained the White House, Paul V. McNutt became a forgotten figure. To be sure, the dedication of McNutt Quadrangle and, a year later, the publication by an Indiana-based press of a hagiographic biography revived memories of him in the Hoosier State. Even there, however, he had been largely abandoned. One story is illustrative. During the 1930s, the sculptor E. H. Daniels completed a four-foot-high, white marble bust of McNutt. (He earlier had done a bronze bust of McNutt for the Indiana Memorial Union.) Daniels, unfortunately, had amassed debts in the southern Indiana town of Jasper, where he kept his studio. Eventually, he left Jasper—and McNutt. A sign painter later rented Daniels's workspace and moved the sculpture outside, in back of a parking lot. Years passed and there sat the marble man, weathering the periodic flooding of the Patoka River. Attempts to purchase the piece came to nothing. Then, in 1967, the press in Indiana stumbled upon the story. A reporter photographed a boy gazing at the bust—an image evocative of Shelley's sonnet "Ozymandias," about a desert wanderer who encounters the crumbled statue of a once-powerful king.[133] Said one paper's headline: "How the Mighty Have Fallen: Bust of Once-Famous McNutt Is Left to Weeds and Water."[134] Jaycees from Martinsville organized an effort to remove the bust, whereupon Chancellor Wells suggested that it be placed in McNutt Quadrangle.[135] That is where it went and that is where it remains—without any plaque or marker of any sort to explain who this man was or why he should be remembered.

# Notes

**INTRODUCTION**

1. For aspects of McNutt's career, see Thomas D. Clark, *Indiana University: Midwestern Pioneer*, vol. 2, *In Mid-Passage* (Bloomington: Indiana University Press, 1973), 318–321; Nick Cullather, *Illusions of Influence: The Political Economy of United States–Philippine Relations, 1942–1960* (Stanford, CA: Stanford University Press, 1994), 33–40, 44–64; Lewis E. Gleeck Jr., *The American Governors-General and High Commissioners to the Philippines: Proconsuls, Nation-Builders, and Politicians* (Quezon City, Philippines: New Day Publishers, 1986), 319–340; Lewis E. Gleeck Jr., *Dissolving the Colonial Bond: American Ambassadors to the Philippines, 1946–1984* (Quezon City, Philippines: New Day Publishers, 1988), 9–30; George Q. Flynn, *The Mess in Washington: Manpower Mobilization in World War II.* (Westport, CT: Greenwood Press, 1979); James H. Madison, *Indiana through Tradition and Change: A History of the Hoosier State and Its People, 1920–1945* (Indianapolis: Indiana Historical Society, 1982); Benjamin L. Jessup, "The Career of Paul V. McNutt" (PhD diss., Kent State University, 1995); Patricio R. Mamot, "Paul V. McNutt: His Role in the Birth of Philippine Independence" (PhD diss., Ball State University, 1974); Iwan Morgan, "Factional Conflict in Indiana Politics during the Later New Deal Years, 1936–1940," *Indiana Magazine of History* 79 (March 1983): 29–60; Robert R. Neff, "The Early Career and Gov-

ernorship of Paul V. McNutt" (PhD diss., Indiana University, 1963); James T. Patterson, *The New Deal and the States: Federalism in Transition* (Princeton, NJ: Princeton University Press, 1969); Larry D. Purvis, "'Loyalty to the Chief': The 1940 Presidential Campaign of Paul V. McNutt and Its Potential for Success" (MA thesis, Butler University, 1989); Jerry L. Wheeler, "Fish, Pheasants and Politics: Paul McNutt and the Popularization of Conservation in 1930s Indiana" (MA thesis, Indiana University–Purdue University at Indianapolis, 2002).

2. I. George Blake, *Paul V. McNutt: Portrait of a Hoosier Statesman* (Indianapolis, IN: Central Publishing, 1966).

3. Madison, *Indiana through Tradition and Change*, 415.

4. Inga Arvad, "Did You Happen to See—Paul V. McNutt?" *Washington Times-Herald*, May 4, 1942, copy in the Indiana University Archives, Bloomington, Indiana (first quotation); E. H. Daniels to "Mr. Stanley," February 12, 1940, box 10, Paul V. McNutt Papers (PVMP), Lilly Library (LL), Indiana University, Bloomington (second and third quotations); Birch E. Bayh telephone interview with the author, November 8, 2010 (fourth quotation).

5. Irving Leibowitz newspaper column, "Did FDR Copy M'Nutt Theory," no date [ca. March 25, 1955], Paul V. McNutt Obituaries (complied by Grace Woody), John L. Krauss Collection (private), Indianapolis, Indiana.

6. Paul V. McNutt address at Martinsville, Indiana, April 24, 1935, box 15, PVMP.

7. David M. Kennedy, *Freedom from Fear: The American People in Depression and War, 1929–1945* (New York: Oxford University Press, 1999), 365.

8. McNutt address at Louisville, November 24, 1939, box 17, PVMP.

9. Roy W. Howard to G. B. "Deak" Parker, July 25, 1935, folder: Letters & Articles 1935 June–September, Roy W. Howard Archive, Indiana University School of Journalism, Bloomington. See also William E. Leuchtenburg, *The FDR Years: On Roosevelt and His Legacy,* (New York: Columbia University Press, 1995), 3–4.

10. William E. Leuchtenburg, *The New Deal and Global War* (New York: Time Life, 1964), 37.

11. McNutt address at Louisville, November 24, 1939, box 17, PVMP.

12. "Coordination of Health, Welfare, and Related Activities Affect the National Defense," undated paper, box 42, Caroline F. Ware Papers, FDRL.

13. Mary E. Switzer speech at Howard University, March 10, 1941, box 14, Mary E. Switzer Papers, Schlesinger Library (SL), Harvard University, Cambridge, Massachusetts.

14. Barton J. Bernstein, "America's Biological Warfare Program in the Second World War," *Journal of Strategic Studies* 11, no. 3 (1988): 294.

15. Elizabeth Borgwardt, *A New Deal for the World: America's Vision for Human Rights* (Cambridge, MA: Harvard University Press, 2005), 280 (all quotations).

16. McNutt to W. J. Patterson, November 17, 1928, box 4, PVMP.

17. McNutt to Abba Hillel Silver, January 14, 1942, box 11, Records of the Federal Security Administrator: General Classified Files, 1939–1944, Alphabetical Series, Record Group 235, NACP.

18. James H. Madison, *The Indiana Way: A State History* (Bloomington: Indiana University Press, 1986), 296.

19. Kevin Mattson, *When America Was Great: The Fighting Faith of Postwar Liberalism* (New York: Routledge, 2004), 25 (first quotation) and 180 (second quotation).

20. McNutt campaign speech in Indiana, no date [1950], box 23, PVMP.

21. McNutt address to the American Legion, July 24, 1952, box 23, PVMP.

22. Terry H. Anderson, *The Movement and the Sixties* (New York: Oxford University Press, 1995), 15.

23. Gleeck, *Dissolving the Colonial Bond,* 23–28.

24. Meredith Nicholson to Carleton B. McCulloch, July 14, 1939, box 1, Carleton B. McCulloch Papers, IHS Library, Indianapolis.

25. Frances Perkins, *The Roosevelt I Knew* (New York: Viking, 1946), 3.

26. Curtis Roosevelt, *Too Close to the Sun: Growing Up in the Shadow of My Grandparents, Franklin and Eleanor* (New York: PublicAffairs, 2008), 36.

27. Robert H. Ferrell, *Choosing Truman: The Democratic Convention of 1944* (Columbia: University of Missouri Press, 1994), 93.

28. Perkins, *The Roosevelt I Knew,* 71.

29. The journalist Charles Peters says that the scholarly "consensus" places April 1940, the month of Germany's invasion of Denmark and Norway, as the time when FDR decided to seek a third term. See *Five Days in Philadelphia: "The Amazing 'We Want Willkie!" Convention of 1940 and How It Freed FDR to Save the Western World* (New York: PublicAffairs, 2005), 123. George McJimsey, though, thinks the Republican Party's nomination of Wendell Willkie, which occurred in June 1940, was the decisive factor. See *The Presidency of Franklin D. Roosevelt* (Lawrence: University Press of Kansas, 2000), 196–197. The documents I have examined, however, suggest that Roosevelt's decision occurred at the end of 1939 or beginning of 1940.

30. Gleeck, *The American Governors-General and High Commissioners in the Philippines,* 319.

## 1. "I SEE . . . A GREAT FUTURE" (1891–1913)

1. William R. Castle diary, August 6, 1938, vol. 36, 285 (quotation), Houghton Library (HL); Herbert Corey, "Great God McNutt," *American Mercury*, Indiana Biography: Paul V. McNutt and Family—Presidential Chances, Indiana Clipping File, Indiana State Library (ISL); John E. Hurt oral history, September 23, 1985, 136, Center for the Study of History and Memory (CSHM).

2. "Indiana's McNutt," *Louisville Courier-Journal*, no date, box 26, Paul V. McNutt Papers (PVMP).

3. *Indianapolis Times (IT)*, January 4, 1947, 47.

4. *IT*, May 15, 1933, 3; Mrs. Keyes to Ruth N. McNutt, October 31, 1939, and Ruth McNutt to Keyes, November 5, 1939 (quotation), box 1, PVMP.

5. Paul V. McNutt (hereafter "McNutt") to Elizabeth McNutt, September 22, 1939, box 1, PVMP.

6. Henrietta Hamilton McCormick, *Genealogies and Reminiscences* (Chicago: Privately printed, 1897), 54, 56–57; copy in the Newberry Library, Chicago.

7. John C. McNutt to James Barrett, January 26, 1940, reel 12, Indiana Federal Writers' Project Papers (IFWPP).

8. Reata Lacy McNutt, "The Family McNutt (1997)," unpublished manuscript in the Genealogy Department, ISL.

9. John McNutt to Edward Stanley, January 23, 1940, and J. Scott MacNutt to John McNutt, June 23, 1940, box 1, PVMP; John McNutt to Barrett, January 26, 1940, reel 12, IFWPP. "James McNutt" and "John McNutt," in vol. 13, Family Group Sheets for Selected Martinsville and Morgan Co. Indiana Residents (Early Twentieth Century) M—Major to Miller (Peter), Genealogy Department, Morgan County Public Library, Martinsville, Indiana.

10. *History of Johnson County, Indiana* (Chicago: Brant and Fuller, 1888), 323, 334–339 and D. D. Banta, *A Historical Sketch of Johnson County, Indiana* (Chicago: J. H.

Beers & Co., 1881), 49–55; John McNutt to Barrett, January 26, 1940, reel 12, IFWPP; *New York Herald Tribune*, February 11, 1940, II-2 (quotation).

11. "John Crittenden McNutt," January 1934, box 1, PVMP; *New York Herald Tribune*, February 11, 1940, II-2. According to a different, but not necessarily conflicting, account, John C., in 1891, promised Vories, who was on his deathbed, that he would name his first son after him. Vories then recovered and went on to become state superintendent of schools. "Indiana's McNutt," *Louisville Courier-Journal*, no date, box 26, PVMP.

12. Wayne E. Fuller, *One-Room Schools of the Middle West: An Illustrated History* (Lawrence: University Press of Kansas, 1994), 59.

13. Colleen Kristal Pauwels, "Hepburn's Dream: The History of the Indiana Law Journal," *Indiana Law Journal* 75:1 (Winter 2000), iv; John E. Hurt, *My View of the Twentieth Century* (Martinsville, IN: Privately printed, 2005), 45 (quotations).

14. Maurice L. Bluhm oral history, June 8, 1969, 5, CSHM.

15. McNutt to S. E. DeHaven, September 19, 1932, box 9, PVMP. Suspended in 1877, the law program was reinstituted in 1889 as the "school of law." Colleen Kristal Pauwels, "Inferior to None," *Bill of Particulars: Indiana Law School Alumni Magazine* (Fall 2000), 16–18; *Indiana Student*, May 29, 1894, 1; "John Crittenden McNutt," January 1934, box 1, PVMP.

16. Grace Woody to McNutt, no date, Kevin Kent Collection (private), Martinsville, Ind.

17. Hays Haymaker to Margaret M. Neely, December 8, 1924, and unpublished manuscript, "Brown County Pioneer," July 7, 1882 (quotations), box 1, Neely Family Papers, LL.

18. Family tree, folder: McNutt, Genealogy Library, Johnson County Museum of History, Franklin, Ind.; "Jacob M. Neely" in vol. 14, Family Group Sheets for Selected Martinsville and Morgan Co. Indiana Residents (Early Twentieth Century) M—Miller

(Ralph) to Musgrave, N—Nash to Nutter, O—Olds to Overton, Morgan County Public Library.

19. Nina Jo to Grace [Woody], March 28, 1972, box 1, Neely Family Papers, LL; News clipping, "Taps Sounded Sunday Morning for J. M. Neely," no date [March 1921], Vertical File—Correspondence—Neely, Morgan County Public Library; News clippings, "J. M. Neely Died Sunday," no date [March 1921] and "Jacob Neely Dead at Home in Martinsville," no date [March 1921], box 1, Neely Family Papers, LL; Lewis Atherton, *Main Street on the Middle Border* (Bloomington: Indiana University Press, 1954), 306 (quotation).

20. *New York Herald Tribune,* February 11, 1940, II-2.

21. Michael E. McGerr, *The Decline of Popular Politics: The American North, 1865–1928* (New York: Oxford University Press, 1986), 18–21, 179; Clifton J. Phillips, *Indiana in Transition, 1880–1920* (Indianapolis: Indiana Historical Bureau and Indiana Historical Society, 1968), 1–49; Philip R. VanderMeer, *The Hoosier Politician: Officeholding and Political Culture in Indiana* (Urbana: University of Illinois Press, 1985), 24, 27.

22. John Bartlow Martin notes from Edmund C. Gorrell, "Breadfruit and Bittersweet," unpublished manuscript, Winamac, Ind., 1941, box 240, John Bartlow Martin Papers, Manuscript Division, Library of Congress (LC).

23. Jack New, interview with the author, June 23, 2006.

24. Herman B. Wells and Edward E. Edwards oral history, May 24, 1982, 1, CSHM.

25. Hurt, *My View of the Twentieth Century,* 202–203.

26. Douglas I. McKay to Charles L. Wilson, December 15, 1930, box 6, PVMP.

27. Paul Vories McNutt report card, December 15, 1911, box 1, PVMP. He seemed to confuse the migration pattern of the McNutts with that of the Neelys. McNutt to O. E. Ford, March 8, 1928, box 3, PVMP.

28. Andrew R. L. Cayton and Peter S. Onuf, *The Midwest and the Nation: Rethinking the History of an American Region* (Bloomington: Indiana University Press, 1990), 122.

29. "Alumni Notes by Classes," *Indiana University Alumni Quarterly* 22:1 (Winter 1935): 96.

30. Elba L. Branigan, *History of Johnson County, Indiana* (Indianapolis, IN: B. F. Bowen and Co., 1913), 350.

31. McNutt to Mark L. Duncan, May 5, 1932, box 8, PVMP.

32. Jonathan Mitchell, "McNutt: Beauty in Distress," *New Republic,* April 29, 1940, 566; *New York Herald Tribune,* February 11, 1940, II-2 (quotation).

33. "John Crittenden McNutt," January 1934, box 1, PVMP; Melvyn Hammarberg, *The Indiana Voter: The Historical Dynamics of Party Allegiance during the 1870s* (Chicago: University of Chicago Press, 1977), 158; *Counties of Morgan, Monroe, and Brown, Indiana,* ed. Charles Blanchard (Chicago: F. A. Battey and Co., 1884), 28–31, 689–690; John E. Hurt oral history, September 23, 1985, 15, CSHM; "Indiana's McNutt," *Louisville Courier-Journal,* no date, box 26 (quotation), PVMP.

34. *Martinsville Democrat (MD),* October 23, 1914, 1.

35. Hurt, *My View of the Twentieth Century,* 163.

36. Sylvan Tackitt, interview with the author, June 29, 2006.

37. Ralph V. Sollitt oral history, June 23, 1971, 39, CSHM.

38. John Bartlow Martin, *Indiana: An Interpretation* (Bloomington: Indiana University Press, 1992), 203.

39. Blanchard, *Counties of Morgan, Monroe, and Brown, Indiana,* 11; "Martinsville," 14, reel 18, IFWPP.

40. Ralph H. Storm, "Foreign Groups and Settlements in Morgan County," reel 18, IFWPP.

41. Hurt, *My View of the Twentieth Century,* 47.

42. John E. Hurt oral history, September 23, 1985, 17, CSHM.

43. Ruth Neely McNutt Christmas message, no date, Ruth Neely McNutt Remembrance Book (compiled by Grace Woody), John L. Krauss Collection (private), Indianapolis.

44. Hurt, *My View of the Twentieth Century*, 46.

45. "Indiana's McNutt," *Louisville Courier-Journal*, no date, box 26 (quotations), PVMP; *IDS*, May 15, 1917, 4.

46. Claude G. Bowers to James A. Farley, March 6, 1938, box 6, James A. Farley Papers, LC.

47. Grace Woody to McNutt, no date, Kent Collection.

48. "A Tribute to the Memory of Mrs. J. C. McNutt," January 15, 1947, Ruth Neely McNutt Remembrance Book, Krauss Collection.

49. Ruth Neely McNutt handwritten notes, no date, Ruth McNutt Remembrance Book, Krauss Collection.

50. Grace Woody to McNutt, no date, Kent Collection.

51. Ruth McNutt handwritten Christmas message, no date (first quotation), and "A Tribute," January 15, 1947 (second quotation), Ruth McNutt Remembrance Book, Krauss Collection.

52. Grace Woody to McNutt, no date, Kent Collection.

53. Verse written in the hand of Ruth Neely McNutt, no date, Ruth McNutt Remembrance Book, Krauss Collection.

54. Typescript verse, Kent Collection.

55. Grace Woody to McNutt, no date, Kent Collection.

56. Alice L. Mitchell to Ruth McNutt, October 31, 1913, Ruth McNutt Remembrance Book, Krauss Collection; *IT*, January 4, 1947, 47 (quotation).

57. Howard and Shirley Krauss, interview with the author, July 15, 2006.

58. I. George Blake, *Paul V. McNutt: Portrait of a Hoosier Statesman* (Indianapolis, IN: Central Publishing, 1966), 3.

59. McNutt to Santa Claus, no date, and Santa Claus to McNutt, no date, Ruth McNutt Remembrance Book, Krauss Collection.

60. John McNutt to McNutt, May 19, 1925, box 1 (quotation), PVMP; *IT*, May 15, 1933, 3.

61. Booth Tarkington, *The Magnificent Ambersons* (Bloomington: Indiana University Press, 1989), 28.

62. *IT*, May 15, 1933, 3.

63. Alva Johnston, "I Intend to Be President," *Saturday Evening Post*, March 16, 1940, 21.

64. John Bartlow Martin, "Indiana: An Interpretation," draft manuscript, box 237, Martin Papers, LC.

65. Philip Von Blon, "The Hoosier Schoolmaster," *American Legion Monthly* (January 1929), 24. I am grateful to Joanne Stuttgen, who holds a PhD in folklore from Indiana University and is a resident of Martinsville and an historian of the town, for helping me understand its history and class differences.

66. Johnston, "I Intend to Be President," *Saturday Evening Post*, March 16, 1940, 21.

67. "Indiana's McNutt," *Louisville Courier-Journal*, no date, box 26, PVMP; *IT*, May 15, 1933, 3.

68. Memorandum on meeting with Alice Roosevelt Longworth, February 1, 1942, box 1, Eugene Gressman Papers, Bentley Historical Library, University of Michigan, Ann Arbor.

69. Sara Delano Roosevelt, *My Boy Franklin* (New York: R. Long and R. R. Smith, 1933).

70. Sarah Watts, *Rough Rider in the White House: Theodore Roosevelt and the Politics of Desire* (Chicago: University of Chicago Press, 2003), 42 (all quotations).

71. Harold Smith to Franklin D. Roosevelt, November 23, 1942, box 2, Official File 4905, Franklin D. Roosevelt Papers, Franklin D. Roosevelt Library (FDRL).

72. "Indiana's McNutt," *Louisville Courier-Journal*, no date, box 26, PVMP; Jack Alexander column, "Paul McNutt: 'It Would Be Kind of Nice to Be President, Wouldn't It?'" (quotation), box 178, Raymond Clapper Papers, LC.

73. McNutt to R. A. Shirley, November 24, 1928 (quotations) and Shirley to McNutt, October 25, 1928—both in box 4, PVMP.

74. Von Blon, "The Hoosier Schoolmaster," 24.

75. *Martinsville Reporter,* February 1, 1967, Vertical File—Correspondence—McNutt, Morgan County Public Library.

76. Von Blon, "The Hoosier Schoolmaster," 25.

77. *IT,* May 15, 1933, 3; "Indiana's McNutt," *Louisville Courier-Journal,* no date (quotations), box 26, PVMP.

78. *IT,* May 15, 1933, 3.

79. Von Blon, "The Hoosier Schoolmaster," 25.

80. Atherton, *Main Street on the Middle Border,* 70–72; "History of the Martinsville High School," *The Nuisance: A Monthly Publication of the Senior Class,* Senior Number (May 25, 1909), Morgan County Public Library.

81. *IT,* May 15, 1933, 3; *Martinsville Reporter,* February 1, 1967, Vertical File—Correspondence—McNutt, Morgan County Public Library; Alexander, "Paul V. McNutt: 'It Would Be Kind of Nice to Be President, Wouldn't It?'" box 178, Clapper Papers, LC (quotation).

82. Ruth McNutt Christmas message, no date, Kent Collection.

83. Grace Woody to McNutt, no date, Ruth McNutt Remembrance Book, Krauss Collection.

84. *IT,* May 15, 1933, 3, and Martin, *Indiana: An Interpretation,* 282 (quotation).

85. Alexander, "Paul V. McNutt: 'It Would Be Kind of Nice to Be President, Wouldn't It?'"; Johnston, "I Intend to Be President," *Saturday Evening Post,* March 16, 1940, 21; Robert R. Neff, "The Early Career and Governorship of Paul V. McNutt," PhD diss., Indiana University, 1963, 7 (quotation).

86. *IT,* May 16, 1933, 7 and May 15, 1933, 3 (quotations).

87. Harry Barnard, notes of interview with Edith Willkie, August 29, 1972, box 1, Harry Barnard Papers, LL; "Indiana's Mc-

Nutt," *Louisville Courier-Journal,* no date (quotation), box 26, PVMP.

88. "McNutt at 4," *Life Magazine,* no date, folder, box 10, PVMP.

89. *IT,* May 15, 1933, 3.

90. Ibid. (all quotations).

91. McNutt report cards, 1905–1909, box 1, PVMP; *IT,* May 16, 1933, 7.

92. *IT,* May 15, 1933, 3. Alexander, "Paul V. McNutt: 'It Would Be Kind of Nice to Be President, Wouldn't It?'" (quotation).

93. Editorial, *The Nuisance* (May 25, 1909), Morgan County Public Library.

94. "Brown County Gold, That's All," in *The Nuisance* (May 25, 1909), Morgan County Public Library.

95. "Jack Dorste, Varsity Man," May 9, 1907, unpublished manuscript, Kent Collection.

96. Harry Abbott, "Senior Class Poem," in *The Nuisance* (May 25, 1909).

97. Von Blon, "The Hoosier Schoolmaster," 25.

98. "Senior Class Roll," in *The Nuisance* (May 25, 1909).

99. Ruth M. Burkett, "Class Prophecy," in *The Nuisance* (May 25, 1909).

100. Neff, "The Early Career and Governorship of Paul V. McNutt," 9.

101. Von Blon, "The Hoosier Schoolmaster," 25.

102. Abbott, "Senior Class Poem," in *The Nuisance* (May 25, 1909).

103. *IDS,* September 23, 1909, 1.

104. Oscar R. Ewing oral history, June 7, 1970, 2–4, CSHM; Jessie Call oral history, 4–5, August 1, 1977, CSHM; Byron K. Elliott, "Beta's Pi Chapter," 1–2, March 1982, folder: Beta Theta Pi, Reference File, Indiana University Archives (IUA).

105. Floyd MacGriff, "Transportation," in *The Arbutus 1912,* 111, copy in the Herman B Wells Library (WL), Indiana University, Bloomington.

106. Robert C. Wiles oral history, September 8, 1976, 21, Grover Willoughby oral history, October 31, 1975, 18–20, and John Emmert Stempel oral history, February 24, 1976, 11–13,

Oral History Series (OHS), Monroe County Public Library (MCPL); Thomas D. Clark, *Indiana University: Midwestern Pioneer*, vol. 2, *In Mid-Passage* (Bloomington: Indiana University Press, 1973), 33–38; Johnnie Smith oral history, January 13, 1977, 6 (quotation), OHS.

107. Clark, *Indiana University*, vol. 2, 5.

108. Oscar R. Ewing oral history, June 7, 1970, 11, CSHM; Mrs. Albert L. Kohlmeier oral history, November 11, 1968, 9, CSHM; Herman B Wells, *Being Lucky: Reminiscences and Reflections* (Bloomington: Indiana University Press, 1980), 31, 109–112; C. Leonard Lundin oral history, October 10, 1972, 6–7, CSHM.

109. Lundin oral history, October 10, 1972, 6–7 (quotation), CSHM.

110. Wells, *Being Lucky*, 31.

111. Mary Eloise Sipes, interview with the author, February 15, 2006.

112. Robert H. Ferrell to C. Leonard Lundin, December 11, 1997, attached to Robert H. Ferrell oral history, November 3, 1994, CSHM.

113. Clark, *Indiana University*, vol. 2, 386.

114. Elliott, "Beta's Pi Chapter," 2, IUA.

115. Clark, *Indiana University*, vol. 2, 386, xi–xiii, xi (quotation), and xii.

116. Wells, *Being Lucky*, 112; Clark, *Indiana University*, vol. 2, 7 (quotations).

117. Oscar R. Ewing oral history, June 7, 1970, 2, CSHM.

118. Joseph Barnes, "Willkie" (typescript), 39 (both quotations), box 1, Joseph Barnes Papers, LC.

119. Elliott, "Beta's Pi Chapter," 3, IUA.

120. *IT*, May 16, 1933, 7.

121. Interview with Frank Martindale, April 23, 1955, "Private Life—Indiana U.," 1 (first quotation), and Wilbur Gruber interview, May 20, 1955, "Private Life—Indiana U., 2 (second quotation), box 1, Ellsworth Barnard Papers, LL.

122. Ralph V. Sollitt oral history, June 23, 1971, 40 (quotations), CSHM.

123. For the use of these terms to describe IU students, see "Interview with Lillian Gay Berry, Bloomington, August 8," "Willkie Private Life and Character," 6, no date, box 1, Ellsworth Barnard Papers, LL.

124. *IT*, May 16, 1933, 7.

125. McNutt report cards, 1909–1912, box 1, PVMP; *IT*, May 16, 1933, 7 (quotation).

126. *Indiana Daily Student (IDS)*, December 14, 1909, 1.

127. *IDS*, January 20, 1910, 1 (first quotation); *IDS*, January 19, 1910, 1 (second quotation).

128. *IDS*, May 25, 1910, 1.

129. *IDS*, January 20, 1911, 2.

130. *IDS*, March 13, 1912, 1; *IT*, May 16, 1933, 7.

131. John E. Hurt interview with the author, August 20, 2005; Curtis G. Shake oral history, April 10, 1968, 16 (quotation), ISL.

132. "Cranks," in *The Arbutus 1912*, 123, WL.

133. *IDS*, October 18, 1912, 2.

134. *IDS*, January 20, 1912, 2; *IT*, May 16, 1933, 7 (quotation).

135. *IDS*, December 12, 1912, 2.

136. *IDS*, May 28, 1912, 1; *IDS*, March 12, 1912, 1; *IDS*, May 16, 1913, 2 (quotation). See the not-so-veiled veiled criticism of McNutt in *IDS*, October 14, 1911, 2.

137. "Unilluminated Sarcasms: Strut and Fret," in *The Arbutus 1913*, 97, WL.

138. Ralph V. Sollitt oral history, June 23, 1971, 40, CSHM; Clark, *Indiana University*, vol. 2, 151–155; Steve Neal, *Dark Horse: A Biography of Wendell Willkie* (Lawrence: University Press of Kansas, 1984), 8–9; *IDS*, March 10, 1911, 1; Basil L. Walters to Ellsworth Barnard, December 19, 1959, and "Interview with Lillian Gay Berry," "Willkie Private Life and Character," 6, no date (quotation), both in box 1, Ellsworth Barnard Papers, LL.

139. "George De Hority Interview," "Private Life—Indiana U.," 1, no date, box 1, Barnard Papers, LL; News clipping, "Willkie Ex-Bouncer at Tent Hotel," July 3, 1940, box 2, Barnes Papers, LC.

140. Curtis G. Shake oral history, April 10, 1968, 17, ISL.

141. *IDS,* March 10, 1911, 1; Lundin oral history, October 10, 1972, 4 (quotations), CSHM.

142. C. Leonard Lundin oral history, April 18, 1994, 14 (first quotation), 15 (second quotation), CSHM.

143. *IDS,* March 16, 1912, 2.

144. Neal, *Dark Horse,* 9; *IDS,* March 16, 1912, 2; October 6, 1911, 1; September 25, 1911, 1; October 13, 1911, 1; April 26, 1912, 1; October 5, 1911, 2.

145. *IDS,* November 29, 1911, 3.

146. *IDS,* February 28, 1912, 1.

147. McNutt to William Lowe Bryan, August 1, 1910, McNutt File, William Lowe Bryan Papers, IUA.

148. Bryan to "Whom It May Concern," May 1, 1917, McNutt File, Bryan Papers, IUA.

149. *IDS,* October 2, 1912, 1; George Gill oral history, October 23, 1969, 52 (first quotation), ISL; "Indiana's McNutt," *Louisville Courier-Journal,* no date (subsequent quotations), box 26, PVMP.

150. "Indiana's McNutt," *Louisville Courier-Journal,* no date, box 26, PVMP.

151. *IT,* May 16, 1933, 7.

152. McNutt to Douglas I. McKay, October 26, 1929, box 5, PVMP.

153. *IDS,* April 1, 1913, 2.

154. *IDS,* May 23, 1913, 2.

155. Ibid. (all quotations).

156. All editorials come from *IDS:* "The Glee Club," April 3, 1913, 2; "Strut and Fret," May 16, 1913, 2; "Debating" and "The Indiana Union," May 15, 1913, 2; "The University," June 2, 1913, 2 (quotation).

157. *IDS,* April 8, 1912, 2.

158. "Unilluminated Sarcasms: The Daily Student," in *The Arbutus 1913,* 97, WL, IU.

159. "Special to Oscar L. Thomas . . . From the Indiana University News Bureau," no date, Clipping File: Paul Vories McNutt, IUA.

160. *IT,* May 16, 1933, 7.

161. *IDS,* October 23, 1928, 3.

162. Elliott, "Beta's Pi Chapter," 4, IUA.

163. C. M. Piper to McNutt, May 18, 1925, box 1, PVMP.

164. Linda C. Gugin and James E. St. Clair, *Sherman Minton: New Deal Senator, Cold War Justice* (Indianapolis: Indiana Historical Society Press, 1997), 49–51; Oscar R. Ewing oral history, June 7, 1970, 1–13, CSHM.

165. *IDS,* May 26, 1913, 2.

166. Wendell Willkie to Raymond Clapper, March 9, 1938, box 178, Clapper Papers, LC.

167. Harry Barnard, notes of interview with Edith Willkie, August 29, 1972, folder 22, box 1, Harry Barnard Papers, LL.

168. Elliott, "Beta's Pi Chapter," 10, IUA.

169. "Guy Lemon Interview," "Private Life—Indiana U.," 3, no date, box 1, Ellsworth Barnard Papers, LL; Neal, Dark Horse, 9–10; Alden Hatch, *Young Willkie* (New York: Harcourt, Brace, and Company, 1944), 146 (quotation).

170. Willkie to Clapper, March 9, 1938, box 178, Clapper Papers, LC; James Albert Woodburn to Willkie, January 31, 1940 (quotations), folder 31, box 1, Wendell Willkie Papers, LL.

171. *MD,* February 18, 1916, 2.

172. "Indiana's McNutt," *Louisville Courier-Journal,* no date, box 26, PVMP.

173. George W. Henley to Willkie, January 15, 1940, folder 31, box 1, Willkie Papers, LL.

174. "Interview with Maurice L. Bluhm, October 30, 1952," "Willkie Private Life and Character," 14 (quotations), folder: Private Life (General), box 1, Ellsworth Barnard Papers, LL.

175. "Interview with Frank Martindale, April 23, 1955," "Private Life—Indiana U.," 1, box 1, Ellsworth Barnard Papers, LL.

176. "Ye Gods," in *The Arbutus 1914,* 314, WL (all quotations).

177. *Indiana University Graduates and Degrees from 1830 to 1930,* 496, copy in Virgil Devault Alumni Center, IU, Bloomington.

178. *IT,* May 16, 1933, 7; Alice L. Mitchell to Ruth Neely McNutt, October 31, 1913, Ruth McNutt Remembrance Book (quotation), Krauss Collection.

179. "Indiana's McNutt," *Louisville Courier-Journal,* no date, box 26, PVMP.

## 2. NEW DEPARTURES, OLD HAUNTS (1913–1925)

1. Andrew R. L. Cayton and Peter S. Onuf, *The Midwest and the Nation: Rethinking the History of an American Region* (Bloomington: Indiana University Press, 1990), 122.

2. Robert R. Neff, "The Early Career and Governorship of Paul V. McNutt" (PhD diss., Indiana University, 1963), 17; "Indiana's McNutt," *Louisville Courier-Journal*, no date, box 26, Paul V. McNutt Papers (PVMP), Lilly Library (LL), Indiana University (IU).

3. Richard Norton Smith, *The Harvard Century: The Making of a University to a Nation* (New York: Simon and Schuster, 1986), 11.

4. Ibid., 63.

5. Samuel Eliot Morison, *Three Centuries of Harvard, 1636–1936* (Cambridge, MA: Harvard University Press, 1936), 489.

6. Smith, *Harvard Century*, 13 (quotation).

7. Roscoe Pound, "The Law School, 1817–1929," in *The Development of Harvard University since the Inauguration of President Eliot, 1869–1929*, ed. Samuel Eliot Morison (Cambridge, MA: Harvard University Press, 1930), 477.

8. Morison, *Three Centuries of Harvard*, 337.

9. Paul V. McNutt, "Case Books and Their Study," no date, box 13, PVMP.

10. Bainbridge Bunting, *Harvard: An Architectural History* (Cambridge, MA: Belknap Press of Harvard University Press, 1985), 101–103, 107 (all quotations).

11. Jack Alexander column, "Paul McNutt: 'It Would Be Kind of Nice to Be President, Wouldn't It?'" box 178, Raymond Clapper Papers, Library of Congress (LC).

12. McNutt college notebook, no date, box 12 and annual examinations of McNutt, June 1914, box 1, PVMP; "Alumni Notes by Classes," *Indiana University Alumni Quarterly* (October 1914): 477; "Indiana's McNutt," *Louisville Courier-Journal*, no date, box 26, PVMP; *Indianapolis Times* (*IT*), May 16, 1933, 7 (quotation).

13. Oscar Ewing oral history, August 26, 1966, Social Security Project, Oral History Research Office, Columbia University, New York, 5–6.

14. William McBrien, *Cole Porter: A Biography* (New York: Alfred A. Knopf, 1998), 50.

15. Thomas R. Marshall to Paul V. McNutt (hereafter "McNutt"), May 5, 1916, and Alton B. Parker to McNutt, May 10, 1916, box 1, PVMP; "Case Books," no date, box 13, PVMP. McNutt to Roscoe Pound, Dean, Harvard Law School, August 17, 1926, and April 12, 1927, box 1, Paul V. McNutt Papers (Dean's Files), IU School of Law Library, Bloomington; Neff, "Early Career and Governorship," 30.

16. Neff, "Early Career and Governorship," 27.

17. Alva Johnston, "I Intend to Be President," *Saturday Evening Post*, March 16, 1940, 20.

18. *Martinsville Democrat (MD)*, February 11, 1916, 1, and March 10, 1916, 1.

19. *IT*, May 16, 1933, 7.

20. "Alumni Notes by Classes," *Indiana University Alumni Quarterly* (July 1916), 480; *Indiana Daily Student* (*IDS*), May 14, 1916, 3; *MD*, August 25, 1916, 1; *IDS*, September 20, 1916, 3.

21. *MD*, April 7, 1918, 4.

22. *MD*, April 28, 1916, 1.

23. McNutt to Frank A. Knotts, April 27, 1916, folder 95, box 8, Paul V. McNutt Papers, Indiana State Archives, Indianapolis.

24. *Bloomington World*, October 14, 1916, 1 (first quotation); Meredith Nicholson to Carleton B. McCulloch, January 7, 1936, box 1, Carleton B. McCulloch Papers, Indiana Historical Society (IHS) (second and third quotations).

25. Dane Starbuck, "James P. Goodrich," in *The Governors of Indiana*, ed. Linda Gugin and James E. St. Clair (Indianapolis: Indiana Historical Society Press, 2006), 252.

26. Nicholson to McCulloch, January 7, 1936, box 1, McCulloch Papers, IHS.

27. *IDS*, February 15, 1917, 1; Neff, "Early Career and Governorship," 22.

28. William Lowe Bryan to McNutt, January 28, 1916, McNutt File, William Lowe Bryan Papers, Indiana University Archives (IUA).

29. *IT*, May 16, 1933, 7.

30. Daniel M. Smith, *The Great Departure: The United States and World War I* (New York: John Wiley and Sons, 1965), ix (quotations).

31. Thomas J. Knock, *To End All Wars: Woodrow Wilson and the Quest for a New World Order* (New York: Oxford University Press, 1992), x; Arthur S. Link, *Wilson: Campaigns for Progressivism and Peace, 1916–1917* (Princeton, NJ: Princeton University Press, 1965), 431 (quotation).

32. Clifton J. Phillips, *Indiana in Transition, 1880–1920* (Indianapolis: Indiana Historical Bureau and Indiana Historical Society, 1968), 592 (first quotation); David M. Kennedy, *Over Here: The First World War and American Society* (New York: Oxford University Press, 1980), 32 (second quotation).

33. Thomas D. Clark, *Indiana University: Midwestern Pioneer*, vol. 2, *In Mid-Passage* (Bloomington: Indiana University Press, 1973), 201.

34. Ibid., 202–208; Neff, "Early Career and Governorship," 23.

35. Ronald Schaffer, *America in the Great War: The Rise of the War Welfare States* (New York: Oxford University Press, 1991), 126–127 (all quotations).

36. Bryan to "Whom It May Concern," May 1, 1917, McNutt File, Bryan Papers, IUA.

37. Kennedy, *Over Here*, 188; Neff, "Early Career and Governorship," 23; "Paul Vories McNutt, National Commander, October 11, 1928–October 2, 1929," fiche 2, Department of Indiana, Biographical Files—Paul V. McNutt, National Headquarters of the American Legion Library, Indianapolis.

38. Jack Alexander column, "Paul McNutt: 'It Would Be Kind of Nice to Be President, Wouldn't It?,'" box 178, Clapper Papers, LC.

39. Edward M. Coffman, *The War to End All Wars: The American Military Experience in* World War I (Lexington: University Press of Kentucky, 1998), 55 (first quotation)–56 (second and third quotations).

40. *IT*, May 17, 1933, 5.

41. *IDS*, December 6, 1917, 1.

42. Philip Von Blon, "The Hoosier Schoolmaster," *American Legion Monthly* (January 1929), 48.

43. Kennedy, *Over Here*, 186 (all quotations).

44. Nancy K. Bristow, *Making Men Moral: Social Engineering during the Great War* (New York: New York University Press, 1996), 20.

45. Ibid., photograph #4.

46. Kennedy, *Over Here*, 187.

47. "Indiana's McNutt," *Louisville Courier-Journal*, no date, box 26, PVMP.

48. News clipping, no date, Ruth Neely McNutt Remembrance Book (compiled by Grace Woody), John L. Krauss Collection (private), Indianapolis.

49. Bristow, *Making Men Moral*, 20.

50. McNutt to Mrs. Timolat, May 19, 1918, Paul V. McNutt Papers, Krauss Collection.

51. Sam Catanzarito to McNutt, January 1 and 20, 1919, box 1, PVMP.

52. E. P. Parker Jr. to McNutt, March 24, 1919, box 1, PVMP.

53. Coffman, *War to End All Wars*, 57; "Paul Vories McNutt," fiche 2, Department of Indiana, Biographical Files—Paul V. McNutt, American Legion Library; Von Blon, "Hoosier Schoolmaster," 23 (quotation).

54. Kennedy, *Over Here*, 62.

55. Alonzo L. Hamby, *Man of the People: A Life of Harry S. Truman* (New York: Oxford University Press, 1995), 67.

56. *IT*, May 17, 1933, 5.

57. Hamby, *Man of the People*, 66–78.

58. Sarah Watts, *Rough Rider in the White House: Theodore Roosevelt and the Politics of Desire* (Chicago: University of Chicago Press, 2003), 236; Watson B. Miller to William Wolff-Smith, August 22, 1942, box 12, Records of the Federal Security Administrator: General Classified Files, 1939–1944, Alphabetical Series, General Records of the Department of Health, Education, and Welfare,

Record Group (RG) 235, National Archives, College Park, Maryland (NACP).

59. Kennedy, *Over Here*, 180.

60. McNutt speech to War Mothers, 1923, box 14, PVMP.

61. McNutt to Lawrence P. Carr, December 5, 1930, box 6, PVMP.

62. *IT*, May 17, 1933, 5.

63. Hal K. Rothman, *LBJ's Texas White House: "Our Heart's Home"* (College Station: Texas A&M University Press, 2001), 27.

64. *Washington Post (WP)*, March 24, 1940, 2.

65. *Bloomington Telephone*, September 9, 1924, Newspaper Clippings File, Monroe County Public Library (MCPL); Neff, "Early Career and Governorship," 25.

66. McNutt to A. T. Potter, no date, box 12, PVMP; *IT*, May 17, 1933, 5 (quotation).

67. *IT*, May 17, 1933, 5; Neff, "Early Career and Governorship," 25–26.

68. *WP*, March 24, 1940, 2 (all quotations).

69. *IT*, May 17, 1933, 5.

70. *Bloomington Telephone*, September 9, 1924, Newspaper Clippings File, MCPL.

71. Kathleen McNutt to Marjorie Meriwether Post, no date, box 26, Post Family Papers, Bentley Historical Library (BHL).

72. Kathleen McNutt to Homer S. Cummings, no date, box 131, Homer S. Cummings Papers (first quotation), Kathleen McNutt to Virginia and Edward M. Stettinius, no date, box 651, Edward M. Stettinius Papers (second quotation)—both collections in the Albert and Shirley Small Special Collections Library, University of Virginia, Charlottesville (UVA).

73. Kathleen McNutt to Virginia and Edward M. Stettinius, no date, box 651, Stettinius Papers, UVA.

74. *WP*, March 24, 1940, 2 (all quotations).

75. Howard Krauss interview with the author, July 15, 2006; *WP*, July 27, 1939, box 26, PVMP (quotation).

76. *Indianapolis Star (IS)*, November 1, 1964, secs. 5, 15.

77. John E. Hurt, interview with the author, August 20, 2005; "Portrait of a Lady,"

*Manila Sunday Tribune Magazine*, March 5, 1939; *IS*, August 13, 1939, folder: Indiana Biography—McNutt, Paul V. and Family, Indiana Clipping File, Indiana State Library (ISL); Letter to Miss Kinghorn, July 10, 1944, McNutt Clipping File, Martin Luther King Jr. Memorial Library, Washington, D.C.

78. *Washington Daily News (WDN)*, March 27, 1940, 24.

79. *WP*, March 24, 1940, 2.

80. *IT*, May 17, 1933, 5.

81. *IDS*, November 12, 1932, 4; Neff, "Early Career and Governorship," 25; News clipping, no date, Ruth McNutt Remembrance Book, Krauss Collection (quotation).

82. McNutt to Mrs. Timolat, May 19, 1918, McNutt Papers, Krauss Collection (all quotations).

83. McNutt to Kathleen McNutt, no date, McNutt Papers, Krauss Collection.

84. *IT*, May 17, 1933, 5; *Columbia (SC) State*, August 1, 1939, box 26, PVMP (quotations).

85. I. George Blake, *Paul V. McNutt: Portrait of a Hoosier Statesman* (Indianapolis, IN: Central Publishing, 1966), 8–9.

86. *Washington Times-Herald*, November 20, 1939, box 178, Clapper Papers, LC.

87. Neff, "Early Career and Governorship," 27; News clipping, no date, Ruth McNutt Remembrance Book, Krauss Collection; McNutt to Mrs. Timolat, May 19, 1918, McNutt Papers, Krauss Collection (quotation).

88. Neff, "Early Career and Governorship," 27; John E. Hurt, interview with the author, August 20, 2005; Howard Krauss interview with the author, July 15, 2006; typescript profile, "Mrs. Paul V. McNutt," no date, McNutt Clipping File, King Memorial Library.

89. Clark, *Indiana University*, vol. 2, 58 and 312. Paul had three philosophy courses at IU. McNutt report cards, 1909–1912, box 1, PVMP.

90. Ernest H. Lindley to Executive Committee, September 6, 1919, folder 542, box 15, Ernest H. Lindley Papers, University of

Idaho Library, Moscow, Idaho; Ellsworth Barnard, *Wendell Willkie: Fighter for Freedom* (Marquette: Northern Michigan University Press, 1966), 57; Neff, "Early Career and Governorship," 27; Bryan to McNutt, June 11, 1920, box 1, PVMP.

91. Blake, *Paul V. McNutt*, 377.

92. Neff, "Early Career and Governorship," 28.

93. Blake, *Paul V. McNutt*, 13; *Classified Buyers: Guide of the City of Bloomington, Ind., 1922–1923* (Louisville, Ky.: Caron Directory Co., 1922), copy in Monroe County Historical Society, Bloomington, Ind.; *IT*, May 17, 1933, 5; Monroe County, *Deed Record Books*, vol. 71 (May 1922–February 1923), 7; *A Walk through the University Courts Historic District: Historic Tour Guide no. 8*, pamphlet in the Monroe County Historical Society.

94. See boxes 13 and 14, PVMP.

95. McNutt, "Case Books and Their Study," no date, box 13, PVMP.

96. *Philippine Herald (PH)*, February 19, 1937, 2.

97. *Chattanooga Daily Times*, April 6, 1945, 8.

98. Hoagy Carmichael (with Stephen Longstreet), *Sometimes I Wonder* (New York: Farrar, Straus & Giroux, 1965), 118.

99. Sylvan Tackitt, interview with the author, June 29, 2006 (all quotations).

100. Charles A. Halleck oral history, December 15, 1969, 69, Center for the Study of History and Memory (CSHM).

101. Leroy Baker oral history, October 8, 1976, 36, CSHM.

102. *PH*, February 19, 1937, 2.

103. Ted Keisker to McNutt, May 7, 1925, box 1, PVMP.

104. McNutt to Meredith Nicholson, August 15, 1925, box 1, McNutt Papers (Dean's Files), IU Law Library.

105. *IT*, May 18, 1933, 16.

106. Walter E. Treanor to Aline Treanor, July 19, 1920, box 1, Walter E. Treanor Papers, LL.

107. Sylvan Tackitt, interview with the author.

108. James H. Capshew, *Herman B Wells: The Promise of the American University* (Bloomington: Indiana University Press, 2012), 5.

109. Clark, *Indiana University*, vol. 2, 281.

110. Carmichael, *Sometimes I Wonder*, 118.

111. Herman B Wells, *Being Lucky: Reminiscences and Reflections* (Bloomington: Indiana University Press, 1980), 32.

112. Lander MacClintock oral history, December 17, 1968, 13, CSHM.

113. Clark, *Indiana University*, vol. 2, 281.

114. Wells, *Being Lucky*, 32–33.

115. Colleen Kristal Pauwels, "Inferior to None," *Bill of Particulars: Indiana Law School Alumni Magazine* (Fall 2000): 20.

116. Neff, "Early Career and Governorship," 28.

117. Anne Veihmeyer, interview with the author, March 6, 2005.

118. *IT*, May 18, 1933, 16.

119. McNutt to Bryan, March 17, 1925, box 1, PVMP.

120. Pauwels, "Inferior to None," 20; Maurice L. Bluhm oral history, June 8, 1969, 4, CSHM (quotation).

121. Lander MacClintock oral history, December 17, 1968, 13, CSHM.

122. *IT*, May 18, 1933, 16; John G. McNutt to McNutt, August 10, 1926, and McNutt to John G. McNutt, August 11, 1926 (quotation), box 2, PVMP.

123. Howard and Shirley Krauss, interview with the author, July 15, 2006.

124. Lindley to McNutt, June 25, 1921, August 2, 1921, and September 21, 1921, box 1, PVMP.

125. McNutt to A. T. Potter, no date, box 12, PVMP.

126. "Statement of Domestic Corporations, Etc.," no date [ca. 1922] and Stockholders in Cantol Wax Company, no date [ca. August 1923], box 1, PVMP; *WP*, March 24, 1940, 2; Blake, *Paul V. McNutt*, 13; Paul McNutt and John C. McNutt to James T. Voshell, October 24, 1923 (quotation), box 1, PVMP.

127. 1925 Return of Capital Stock Tax, August 19, 1924, box 1, PVMP.

128. McNutt to A. T. Potter, no date, box 12, PVMP.

129. Ibid.

130. James MacGregor Burns, *Roosevelt: The Lion and the Fox, 1882–1940* (New York: Harcourt, 1956), 83–84.

131. John C. McNutt to McNutt, ca. January 9, 1926, box 2, PVMP.

132. "Bill" to McNutt, August 16, 1920, box 1, PVMP.

133. "Paul Vories McNutt, National Commander, October 11, 1928–October 2, 1929," fiche 2, Department of Indiana, Biographical Files—Paul V. McNutt, American Legion Library; Blake, *Paul V. McNutt*, 11.

134. George W. Lee to McNutt, November 26, 1923 (quotation), and McNutt to V. A. Root, August 29, 1924, box 1, PVMP.

135. Fred B. Ryons to McNutt, August 27, 1924, box 1, PVMP.

136. George W. Lee to McNutt, March 5, 1924, box 1, PVMP.

137. Eugene C. Von Tress oral history, December 12, 1972, 5, CSHM.

138. McNutt to Bryan, October 3 and October 11, 1922, McNutt File, Bryan Papers, IUA.

139. Bursar of Indiana University to McNutt, October 5, 1922, box 1, PVMP.

140. Von Tress oral history, December 12, 1972, 5, 28 (quotation), CSHM.

141. Edith Schuman Tackitt, interview with the author, June 29, 2006.

142. Clark, *Indiana University*, vol. 2, 160; Dorothy C. Collins and Cecil K. Byrd, *Indiana University: A Pictorial History* (Bloomington: Indiana University Press, 1992), 68.

143. Bryan to McNutt, October 6, 1922 (first and third quotations) and October 13, 1922 (second quotation), box 1, PVMP.

144. Von Tress oral history, December 12, 1972, 8–9 (quotation), CSHM.

145. Blake, *Paul V. McNutt*, 16–17; McNutt to Harry W. McDowell, October 25, 1924, box 1, PVMP.

146. W. A. Alexander to McNutt, October 3, 1922, box 1, PVMP.

147. Ralph V. Sollitt to McNutt, August 23, 1923, box 1, PVMP.

148. Bryan to McNutt, October 13, 1922, box 1, PVMP.

149. Von Tress oral history, December 12, 1972, 30, CSHM.

150. F. W. Hunnewell to McNutt, January 28, 1924, box 1, PVMP.

151. Bryan to McNutt, February 4, 1924, box 1, PVMP.

152. Roscoe Pound to McNutt, October 10, 1924, box 1, PVMP; Blake, *Paul V. McNutt*, 19–24; Neff, "Early Career and Governorship," 30; *IT*, May 18, 1933, 16.

153. "Portrait of a Lady," *Manila Sunday Tribune Magazine*, March 5, 1939.

## 3. TRIUMPH AND TRAGEDY (1925–1926)

1. Jack Alexander column, "Paul McNutt: 'It Would Be Kind of Nice to Be President, Wouldn't It?,'" box 178, Raymond Clapper Papers, Manuscript Division, Library of Congress (LC).

2. James H. Madison, *Indiana through Tradition and Change: A History of the Hoosier State and Its People, 1920–1945* (Indianapolis: Indiana Historical Society, 1982), 27 (quotation), 58, 72.

3. Alexander, "Paul McNutt: 'It Would Be Kind of Nice to Be President, Wouldn't It?,'" box 178, Clapper Papers, LC; Robert R. Neff, "The Early Career and Governorship of Paul V. McNutt," (PhD diss., Indiana University, 1963), 30.

4. Neff, "Early Career and Governorship," 28.

5. Thomas D. Clark, *Indiana University: Midwestern Pioneer*, vol. 3, *Years of Fulfillment* (Bloomington: Indiana University Press, 1977), xix.

6. I. George Blake, *Paul V. McNutt: Portrait of a Hoosier Statesman* (Indianapolis, IN: Central Publishing, 1966), 17–18; Paul V. McNutt (hereafter "McNutt") to Hugh E. Willis, August 3, 1937, box 3A, and McNutt to Erwin Griswold, no date [ca. March 1927] and McNutt to William L. West, October

9, 1925, box 1, all in Paul V. McNutt Papers (Dean's Files), Indiana University (IU) School of Law Library, Bloomington.

7. Samuel C. Cleland to McNutt, May 9, 1925, and Shitz Simmons to McNutt, May 15, 1925, box 1, Paul V. McNutt Papers (PVMP), LL, IU; *Danville* (Ind.) *Gazette,* November 15, 1928, and "Charles M. Hepburn" in *Who's Who in America 1928–29*—both in Clippings File, IU Archives (IUA); Charles M. Hepburn to William Lowe Bryan ("Bryan"), April 21, 1923, Hepburn File, William Lowe Bryan Papers, IUA.

8. Arthur H. Greenwood to McNutt, May 11, 1925, box 1, PVMP.

9. Alexander, "Paul McNutt: 'It Would Be Kind of Nice to Be President, Wouldn't It?'" box 178, Clapper Papers, LC.

10. Charles M. Hepburn to Bryan, July 23, 1923, November 3, 1923, and October 30, 1925 (quotation), Hepburn File, Bryan Papers, IUA.

11. Fred O. Jeffers ("Jeffers") to Walter E. Treanor ("Treanor"), July 15, 1929, box 1, Walter E. Treanor Papers, LL.

12. Colleen Kristl Pauwels, "Hepburn's Dream: The History of the *Indiana Law Journal,*" *Indiana Law Journal* 75:1 (2000): ix–xiv; "In re The Indiana Law Journal Submitted by Professor Hepburn, February 13, 1925" (quotations), Hepburn File, Bryan Papers, IUA.

13. Untitled, undated resolution beginning "The law faculty believes," box 1, PVMP; Hepburn to Bryan, March 15, 1925, Hepburn File, Bryan Papers, IUA; Pauwels, "Hepburn's Dream," xiii.

14. McNutt to Bryan, March 17, 1925, box 1, PVMP.

15. Ibid.

16. Bryan to McNutt, March 30, 1925, and Bryan to Hepburn, May 5, 1925 (quotation), box 1, PVMP.

17. McNutt to Reeve Chipman, September 1, 1928, box 4, PVMP (quotation). But Hepburn later congratulated his successor "most heartily" when McNutt became national commander of the American Legion in

1928. Charles M. Hepburn to McNutt, October 12, 1928, box 4, PVMP.

18. Andrew H. Hepburn to McNutt, September 11, 1928, box 1, PVMP.

19. Walter L. Moll to McNutt, May 9, 1925, box 1, PVMP.

20. Blake, *Paul V. McNutt,* 30.

21. Wendell L. Willkie to McNutt, May 16, 1925, box 1, PVMP.

22. C. M. Piper to McNutt, May 18, 1925, box 1, PVMP.

23. Philip Von Blon, "The Hoosier Schoolmaster," *American Legion Monthly* (January 1929), 49; Alexander, "Paul McNutt: 'It Would Be Kind of Nice to Be President, Wouldn't It?,'" box 178, Clapper Papers, LC.

24. "Indiana University School of Law 1925," *Indiana University Bulletin (Official Series)* 23:11 (October 1925): 8.

25. "Progress of the Indiana University School of Law 1926," no date (all quotations), box 2, McNutt Papers (Dean's Files), IU Law Library.

26. Alexander, "Paul McNutt: 'It Would Be Kind of Nice to Be President, Wouldn't It?,'" box 178, Clapper Papers, LC.

27. Herman B Wells, *Being Lucky: Reminiscences and Reflections* (Bloomington: Indiana University Press, 1980), 102.

28. McNutt to Paul L. Sayre, May 7, 1925, box 1, PVMP; Pauwels, "Hepburn's Dream," xx, xxii; In the late 1930s, Harper also co-chaired President Wells's university-wide self-study, which was instrumental in launching IU toward international renown. Wells, *Being Lucky,* 96–97, 258–259.

29. McNutt to Bryan and the Board of Trustees, October 19, 1931, McNutt File, Bryan Papers, IUA; Paul V. McNutt, departmental report, May 14, 1929, box 4, PVMP; McNutt to A. L. Green, February 21, 1930, and letters to McNutt from various law school deans, box 3A. McNutt Papers (Dean's Files), IU Law Library.

30. Bryan to McNutt, May 5, 1925, box 1, PVMP; Wells, *Being Lucky,* 72; McNutt to Bryan and the Board of Trustees, July 8,

1930 (quotation), McNutt File, Bryan Papers, IUA.

31. Wells, *Being Lucky*, 154.

32. Madison, *Indiana through Tradition and Change*, 285–287.

33. Thomas D. Clark, *Indiana University: Midwestern Pioneer*, vol. 2, *In Mid-Passage* (Bloomington: Indiana University Press, 1973), xi; Dorothy C. Collins and Cecil K. Byrd, *Indiana University: A Pictorial History* (Bloomington: Indiana University Press, 1992), xvi, 65; McNutt to Bryan, November 15, 1928, and Bryan to McNutt, November 15, 1928, McNutt File, Bryan Papers, IUA; "Notes of Legislative Committee Meeting," December 6, 1926, box 2, McNutt Papers (Dean's Files), IU Law Library.

34. Looking toward the 1926 session of the legislature, law professor Merrill I. Schnebly shuddered, for "we have seen our hopes of previous years disappointed." Merrill I. Schnebly to McNutt, April 12, 1926, box 2, McNutt Papers (Dean's Files), IU Law Library.

35. McNutt to Bryan and the Board of Trustees, July 8, 1930, McNutt File, Bryan Papers, IUA; McNutt to Bryan and the Board of Trustees, June 10, 1928, McNutt File, Bryan Papers, IUA; Colleen Kristal Pauwels, "Inferior to None," *Bill of Particulars: Indiana Law School Alumni Magazine* (Fall 2000): 23; "Progress of the Indiana University School of Law 1926" and "The Needs of the Law School," box 2, Papers (Dean's Files), IU Law Library.

36. McNutt to Bryan and the Board of Trustees, June 10, 1928, August 27, 1932, and October 19, 1931, McNutt File, Bryan Papers, IUA; McNutt, departmental report, May 14, 1929, box 4, PVMP; Pauwels, "Inferior to None," 23; Treanor to Jeffers, October 15, 1928, and Treanor to "Field," October 5, 1928 (quotations), box 1, Treanor Papers, LL.

37. McNutt to Louis Plost, January 11, 1926, box 2, McNutt Paper (Dean's Files), IU Law Library.

38. Pauwels, "Hepburn's Dream," xvii; McNutt to George O. Dix, May 12, 1926, box 1, and McNutt to Merrill I. Schnebly, April 9, 1926 (quotation), box 2, McNutt Papers (Dean's Files), IU Law Library.

39. Pauwels, "Hepburn's Dream," xviii–xix, xxi–xxii, xxxiii (quotation).

40. McNutt to William E. Clapham, January 6, 1927, box 2, PVMP.

41. McNutt to Roscoe Pound, August 17, 1926, box 1, McNutt to Robert C. Brown, June 29, 1926, and Paul L. Sayre to McNutt, November 1, 1929, box 4, McNutt Papers (Dean's Files), IU Law Library; Treanor to Jeffers, September 21, 1929, box 1, Treanor Papers, LL.

42. McNutt to William E. Clapham, January 6, 1927, box 2, PVMP.

43. Pauwels, "Inferior to None," 26–27.

44. Jonathan Gathorne-Hardy, *Kinsey: Sex the Measure of All Things* (Bloomington: Indiana University Press, 1998), 439–442; Clark, *Indiana University*, vol. 2, 252–254; James H. Madison, *The Indiana University Department of History, 1895–1995: A Centennial Year Sketch* (Bloomington: Department of History, Indiana University, 1995), 9–13; Clark, *Indiana University*, vol. 3, 578–580; Kathryn L. Knapp, *The Kickin' Hoosiers: Jerry Yeagley and Championship Soccer at Indiana* (Bloomington: Indiana University Press, 2004); George M. Logan, *The Indiana University School of Music: A History* (Bloomington: Indiana University Press, 2000), 227–228.

45. McNutt address at Indiana University, no date [1922], box 14, PVMP.

46. Paul V. McNutt, "The Duty of the State," no date [1924], box 14, PVMP.

47. Ibid.

48. McNutt address at Cincinnati, September 18, 1933, box 14, PVMP.

49. McNutt to Meredith Nicholson, August 15, 1925, box 1, McNutt Papers (Dean's Files), IU Law Library.

50. Alexander, "Paul McNutt: 'It Would Be Kind of Nice to Be President, Wouldn't It?,'" box 178, Clapper Papers, LC.

51. McNutt to Raymond H. Snyder, July 22, 1930, box 6, PVMP.

52. McNutt to Herbert S. Hadley, July 14, 1926, Hadley to McNutt, July 20, 1926, McNutt to Hadley, July 23, 1926, and Hadley to McNutt, August 3, 1926, box 2, McNutt Papers; McNutt to David H. Jennings, July 28, 1926, and John C. McNutt to McNutt, July 23, 1926, box 2, PVMP.

53. McNutt to David H. Jennings, July 28, 1926, box 2, PVMP.

54. John C. McNutt to McNutt, July 23, 1926, box 2, PVMP.

55. Booth Tarkington to Carleton B. McCulloch, September 6, 1941, box 1, Booth Tarkington Papers, Indiana Historical Society (IHS).

56. Howard and Shirley Krauss, interview with the author, July 15, 2006.

57. Rolfe Swensen, "Pilgrims at the Golden Gate: Christian Scientists on the Pacific Coast, 1880–1915," *Pacific Historical Review* 72 (May 2003): 229.

58. Sydney E. Ahlstrom, *A Religious History of the American People* (New Haven, CT: Yale University Press, 1972), 1024 (first quotation); Elena M. Kondos, "The Law and Christian Science Healing for Children: A Pathfinder," *Legal Reference Services Quarterly* 12, no. 1 (1992): 5 (second quotation).

59. Kondos, "The Law and Christian Science Healing for Children," 6.

60. Ahlstrom, *Religious History of the American People*, 1024–1025.

61. Swensen, "Pilgrims at the Golden Gate," 233; Louise McNutt Diary, June 23, 1946, John L. Krauss Collection (private), Indianapolis (quotation).

62. Swensen, "Pilgrims at the Golden Gate," 244–245. Christian Scientists point to "thousands of testimonies of healing" as "evidence" of their church's "success." Kondos, "The Law and Christian Science Healing for Children," 6.

63. Howard and Shirley Krauss interview with the author.

64. John McNutt to McNutt, May 19, 1925, box 1, PVMP.

65. Menu from Home Lawn Sanitarium, no date, Kevin Kent Collection (private), Martinsville.

66. Howard and Shirley Krauss interview with the author (quotation as well).

67. Kondos, "The Law and Christian Science Healing for Children," 11.

68. Carleton B. McCulloch to Meredith Nicholson, October 15, 1934, box 1, Carleton B. McCulloch Papers, IHS.

69. John McNutt to McNutt, May 19, 1925, box 1, PVMP.

70. The number of Hoosiers dying from tuberculosis dropped from 107.7 per 100,000 in 1920 to 39.1 per 100,000 in 1940. Madison, *Indiana through Tradition and Change*, 316–318, 316 (quotations).

71. Howard and Shirley Krauss, interview with the author; McNutt to Henry B. Walker, August 17, 1926, box 2, PVMP; John McNutt to McNutt, September 14, 1925, box 1, John McNutt to McNutt, February 5, 1926, box 2, all in PVMP; McNutt to John Worth Kern Jr., May 5, 1925, box 1, McNutt Papers (Dean's Files), IU School of Law Library; *Indianapolis Times* (*IT*), May 18, 1933, 16; McNutt to John G. McNutt, February 26, 1926 (quotation), box 2, PVMP.

72. McNutt to Real Courage Association, June 24, 1926, box 2, PVMP; Howard and Shirley Krauss, interview with the author (quotation).

73. McNutt to Scott W. Lucas, February 15, 1930, box 5, and McNutt to John G. McNutt, August 11, 1926 (quotations), box 2, PVMP.

74. John McNutt to McNutt, September 27, 1927, box 2, PVMP.

75. The families included the McFaddens and the Buskirks. Jack New, interview with the author, June 23, 2006.

76. John C. McNutt to McNutt, September 27, 1927, and McNutt to Real Courage Association, June 24, 1926, box 2, PVMP; Edith Schuman Tackitt, interview with the author, June 29, 2006; Leroy Baker oral history, October 8, 1976, 36, Center for the Study of History and Memory (CSHM); Howard and Shirley Krauss, interview with the author; Raymond Clapper diary, July 14, 1939 (quotation), Clapper Papers, LC.

77. Schedule of Personal Property: Paul V. McNutt, no date [ca. March 1927] and McNutt to Claude M. Ewing, January 5, 1927, box 2, PVMP (quotation)

78. John C. McNutt to McNutt, September 13, 1927, box 3, PVMP.

79. McNutt to Claude M. Ewing, January 5, 1927, box 2, PVMP; McNutt to Roscoe Pound, August 17, 1926, box 1, McNutt Papers (Dean's Files), IU Law Library.

80. John E. Hurt, interview with the author, August 20, 2005.

81. McNutt to W. J. Hockett, February 4, 1927, box 1, McNutt Papers (Dean's Files), IU Law Library.

82. McNutt to Roscoe Pound, August 17, 1926, box 1, McNutt Papers (Dean's Files), IU Law Library.

83. Blake, *Paul V. McNutt*, 45–61.

84. Louise McNutt Diary, January 30, 1936, February 17, 1937, May 6, 1937, and June 23, 1946, Krauss Collection.

85. Howard and Shirley Krauss, interview with the author; Louise McNutt Diary, May 27, 1937 (quotation), Krauss Collection.

86. John C. McNutt to McNutt, September 27, 1927, box 2, PVMP.

87. McNutt to John G. McNutt, August 10, 1926, box 2; McNutt to Henry B. Walker, October 23, 1926, box 1—both in PVMP.

88. McNutt to Henry B. Walker, October 23, 1926, box 1, PVMP.

89. "Billy" [William Rose] to McNutt, September 29, 1926, box 2, PVMP.

90. McNutt to James J. Robinson, December 21, 1929, McNutt Papers (Dean's Files), IU Law Library.

91. McNutt to Scott W. Lucas, February 15, 1930, box 5, PVMP.

92. McNutt to Ernest Rowbotham, March 12, 1930, box 5, PVMP.

93. McNutt to Roger C. Holden, March 20, 1931, and McNutt to Herbert R. Mooney, March 16, 1931 (quotation), box 6, PVMP.

94. McNutt to Oscar Red Dillman, March 12, 1930, box 5, PVMP.

95. McNutt to Douglas I. McKay, February 11, 1930, box 5, PVMP.

96. McNutt to Roger C. Holden, March 23, 1932, box 8, PVMP.

97. Howard and Shirley Krauss, interview with the author.

98. *Indianapolis Star*, August 13, 1939, pt. 5, p. 14.

99. Alexander, "Paul McNutt: 'It Would Be Kind of Nice to Be President, Wouldn't It?,'" (quotation), box 178, Clapper Papers, LC.

100. John W. Wheeler to McNutt, no date [ca. March 1928], box 3, PVMP.

101. McNutt to Frank McHale, April 4, 1928, box 3, PVMP.

102. McNutt to Mark A. Brown, November 17, 1928, box 4, PVMP.

103. McNutt to Elmer Sherwood, November 17, 1928, box 4, PVMP.

104. C. Leonard Lundin oral history, October 10, 1972, 6–7, CSHM; Clark, *Indiana University*, vol. 2, 291–296; Paul V. McNutt, "Service and Sacrifice," no date (quotation), box 24, PVMP.

105. McNutt to Kathleen McNutt, December 31, 1945, Paul V. McNutt Papers, Krauss Collection.

106. Carleton B. McCulloch to Meredith Nicholson, December 12, 1934, January 11, 1935, and February 7, 1935, box 1, McCulloch Papers, IHS; McNutt to R. E. Snoberger, February 5, 1932, box 8, and Frank Lahey to McNutt, April 1, 1946, box 11, PVMP.

107. Frank Freidel, *Franklin D. Roosevelt: The Ordeal* (Boston: Little, Brown, 1954), 138–159; Blanche Wiesen Cook, *Eleanor Roosevelt*, vol. 1, 1884–1933 (New York: Penguin Books, 1992), 302–337; Jan Pottker, *Sara and Eleanor: The Story of Sara Delano Roosevelt and Her Daughter-in-Law, Eleanor Roosevelt* (New York: St. Martin's, 2004), 242–246, 338; John E. Hurt, interview with the author.

108. Geoffrey C. Ward, *A First Class Temperament: The Emergence of Franklin Roosevelt* (New York: Harper and Row, 1989), 591 (quotation), 606–607.

109. Freidel, *FDR: The Ordeal*, 113.

110. *IT*, May 18, 1933, 16.

111. Cook, *Eleanor Roosevelt*, vol. 1, 309.

112. Ward, *A First Class Temperament*, 751–752; McNutt to Ralph N. Smith, December 26, 1927 (quotation), box 3, PVMP.

113. James MacGregor Burns, *Roosevelt: The Lion and the Fox, 1882–1940* (New York: Harcourt, 1956), 91.

114. Cook, *Eleanor Roosevelt*, vol. 1, 313 (first quotation); Burns, *Roosevelt*, 89 (second quotation).

115. McNutt address, September 24, 1933, box 14, PVMP.

116. McNutt to Snyder, July 22, 1930, box 6, PVMP.

117. Alexander, "Paul McNutt: 'It Would Be Kind of Nice to Be President, Wouldn't It?,'" box 178, Clapper Papers, LC.

#### 4. THE LEGION AND LEADERSHIP (1926–1928)

1. Thomas A. Rumer, *The American Legion: An Official History, 1919–1989* (New York: M. Evans & Company, 1990), 5; Richard Seelye Jones, *A History of the American Legion* (Indianapolis: Bobbs-Merrill, 1946), 22 (quotation).

2. Rumer, *American Legion*, 7; Jones, *History of the American Legion*, 23–24; David M. Kennedy, *Over Here: The First World War and American Society* (New York: Oxford University Press, 1980), 218 (quotations).

3. William Pencak, *For God and Country: The American Legion, 1919–1941* (Boston: Northeastern University Press, 1989), 89.

4. At its peak, the Legion had fifty-eight departments, one for each of the fifty states, plus one each for the District of Columbia, the Philippines, Puerto Rico, Panama Canal Zone, Canada, France, Italy, and Mexico. Rumer, *American Legion*, 565–581.

5. Pencak, *For God and Country*, 26.

6. James MacGregor Burns, *Roosevelt: The Lion and the Fox, 1882–1940* (New York: Harcourt, 1956), 80, 86; Jones, *History of the American Legion*, 56–57.

7. Group Staff Meeting, March 1, 1938, roll 30, book 113, p. 21, Henry J. Morgenthau Diary, Franklin D. Roosevelt Library (FDRL).

8. Pencak, *For God and Country*, 100.

9. *Collier's*, June 21, 1919, 22.

10. Pencak, *For God and Country*, 176; Thomas B. Littlewood, *Soldiers Back Home: The American Legion in Illinois, 1919–1939* (Carbondale: Southern Illinois University Press, 2004), 106.

11. Theda Skocpol, *Protecting Soldiers and Mothers: The Political Origins of Social Policy in the United States* (Cambridge, MA.: Harvard University Press, 1992), 151.

12. Pencak, *For God and Country*, 176; Stephen R. Ortiz, *Beyond the Bonus March and the GI Bill: How Veterans Politics Shaped the New Deal Era* (New York: New York University Press, 2010), 6; National Publicity Division, American Legion, "Child Welfare," no date (quotations), box 352, Harold Burton Papers, Manuscript Division, Library of Congress (LC).

13. Rumer, *American Legion*, 115.

14. Jones, *History of the American Legion*, 237 (quotation), 238–239.

15. Rumer, *American Legion*, 115.

16. Jones, *History of the American Legion*, 272–275; Rumer, *American Legion*, 167; Pencak, *For God and Country*, 5 (quotation).

17. Theodore Roosevelt Jr. to Clarence D. Randall, December 23, 1919, box 36, Theodore Roosevelt Jr. Papers, LC.

18. Hanford MacNider speech, undated, box 2, Hanford MacNider Papers, Herbert Hoover Presidential Library (HHPL).

19. Melvin M. Johnson speech, box 352, Burton Papers, LC.

20. William E. Leuchtenburg, *The Perils of Prosperity, 1914–1932*, 2nd ed. (Chicago: University of Chicago Press, 1993), 104; Robert H. Ferrell, *Peace in Their Time: The Origins of the Kellogg-Briand Pact* (New York: W. W. Norton, 1969), 26; Robert David Johnson, *The Peace Progressives and American Foreign Relations* (Cambridge, MA: Harvard University Press, 1995), 204–206, 217, and 200 (quotation).

21. Johnson, *Peace Progressives and American Foreign Relations*, 216.

22. Ferrell, *Peace in Their Time*, 28.

23. Johnson, *Peace Progressives and American Foreign Relations*, 216.

24. American Legion, "Military Training in Our Schools and Colleges—What It Does for American Youth," no date, box 352, Burton Papers, LC; Pencak, *For God and Country*, 9 (quotations).

25. *Indianapolis News (IN)*, November 6, 1934, pt. 2, p. 1.

26. Richard Morris Clutter, "The Indiana American Legion, 1919–1960," (PhD diss., Indiana University, 1974), 85; James H. Madison, *Indiana through Tradition and Change: A History of the Hoosier State and Its People 1920–1945* (Indianapolis: Indiana Historical Society, 1982), 45, 46 (quotation).

27. James H. Madison, *A Lynching in the Heartland: Race and Memory in America* (New York: Palgrave, 200), 38; Leonard J. Moore, *Citizen Klansmen: The Ku Klux Klan in Indiana, 1921–1928* (Chapel Hill: University of North Carolina Press, 1991), 36–40; Rumer, *American Legion*, 167–169; Pencak, *For God and Country*, 256–257.

28. William Clayton Wilkinson Jr., "Memories of the Ku Klux Klan in One Indiana Town," *Indiana Magazine of History* 102, no. 4 (2006): 350; Pencak, *For God and Country*, 137–138.

29. Pencak, *For God and Country*, 107–117.

30. Ibid., 25 (quoting the title of an essay by Arthur M. Schlesinger Sr.).

31. Joseph H. Friend, "Watch Paul McNutt," *Nation*, July 23, 1938, 86–87.

32. Walter D. Myers, "A Collection of Recollections," 163–171, unpublished manuscript, Indiana Historical Society (IHS); Madison, *Indiana through Tradition and Change*, 38, 39.

33. Friend, "Watch Paul McNutt," 86.

34. Harold Feightner oral history, February 28, 1968, 61, Manuscript Division, Indiana State Library (ISL).

35. Feightner oral history, October 24, 1968, 84, ISL.

36. Paul V. McNutt (henceforth "McNutt") to A. C. Sandeford, April 7, 1921 (all quotations), box 1, Paul V. McNutt Papers (PVMP), Lilly Library (LL), Indiana University (IU).

37. *Indiana Daily Student (IDS)*, March 9, 1926, box 25, PVMP; Frederick J. Libby Diary, February 28, 1926, box 3, Frederick J. Libby Papers, LC; William Lowe Bryan to James A. Woodburn, March 30, 1926 (quotations), box 3, James A. Woodburn Papers, LL.

38. Libby Diary, March 3, 1926, box 3, Libby Papers, LC; McNutt to Frank H. Streightoff, March 9, 1926, box 2, PVMP (all quotations).

39. McNutt to Mrs. Frank D. Hatfield, March 15, 1926, folder: McNutt Misc. Speaking Engagements, box 2, Paul V. McNutt Papers (Dean's Files), IU School of Law Library, Bloomington.

40. McNutt to Fred B. Ryons, March 15, 1926, box 2, PVMP.

41. Francis Ralston Welsh, "Thomas Que Harrison," March 22, 1926, box 2, PVMP.

42. *IN*, September 30, 1926, box 25, PVMP.

43. Libby Diary, November 9, 1926, box 3, Libby Papers, LC.

44. McNutt to Newman T. Miller, January 5, 1927, box 1, McNutt Papers, IU Law Library.

45. McNutt to Francis Ralston Welsh, March 19, 1926, box 2, PVMP.

46. McNutt to Robert Adams, March 5, 1926, box 2, PVMP.

47. McNutt to Fred B. Ryons, March 15, 1926 (first quotation) and McNutt to Fred R. Marvin, March 19, 1926 (second quotation), box 2, PVMP.

48. McNutt to Mrs. Frank D. Hatfield, March 15, 1926, box 2; Esther Everett Lape to McNutt, February 8, 1927, and May 27, 1927, box 3A—all in McNutt Papers (Dean's Files), IU Law Library.

49. *Kokomo* (Ind.) *Dispatch*, December 3, 1926, box 25, PVMP.

50. *Bloomington Weekly Star (BWS)*, October 18, 1928, box 25, PVMP; Jack Alexander column, "Paul McNutt: 'It Would Be Kind of Nice to Be President, Wouldn't It?'" (quotation), box 178, Raymond Clapper Papers, LC.

51. C. A. Jackson to McNutt, February 11, 1926, box 2, PVMP.

52. Jack Alexander Column, "Paul McNutt: 'It Would Be Kind of Nice to Be Presi-

dent, Wouldn't It?,'" box 178, Clapper Papers, LC.

53. *Indianapolis Times (IT)*, May 18, 1933, 16.

54. McNutt to C. A. Jackson, April 13, 1926, box 2, PVMP; Philip Von Blon, "The Hoosier Schoolmaster," *American Legion Monthly*, January 1929, 49; "The Progress of the American Legion 1926," box 1, McNutt Papers (Dean's Files), IU Law Library.

55. Jackson to McNutt, March 1, 1926, box 2, PVMP; *IT*, May 18, 1933, 16 (quotations).

56. McNutt to Wilbur S. Donner, August 17, 1926, box 2, PVMP.

57. John Bartlow Martin, *Indiana: An Interpretation* (Bloomington: Indiana University Press, 1992), 273. According to the historian Howard Peckham, false modesty about seeking office fooled no one, for Hoosiers "enjoy their politics." Howard H. Peckham, *Indiana: A History* (Urbana: University of Illinois Press, 2003), 130.

58. McNutt to Marcus F. McCaughan, August 2, 1926, and August 16, 1926, McNutt to John M. McFaddin, August 18, 1926, box 2, PVMP.

59. Robert R. Neff, "The Early Career and Governorship of Paul V. McNutt" (PhD diss., Indiana University, 1963), 34; Joe H. Davis to McNutt, August 3, 1926, McNutt to Harry P. Shultz, August 17, 1926, F. H. McIntosh to McNutt, August 20, 1926, box 2, PVMP.

60. Neff, "The Early Career and Governorship of Paul V. McNutt," 35.

61. Clay A. Phillips to McNutt, September 2, 1926, box 2, PVMP.

62. McNutt to Robert R. Batton, August 16, 1926, and Batton to Frank McHale, August 18, 1926, box 2, PVMP.

63. Forrest E. Livengood to McNutt, September 4, 1926, box 2, PVMP; Alexander, "Paul McNutt: 'It Would Be Kind of Nice to Be President, Wouldn't It?,'" box 178, Clapper Papers, LC; Neff, "The Early Career and Governorship of Paul V. McNutt," 35 (quotation).

64. Jack Alexander Column, "Paul McNutt: 'It Would Be Kind of Nice to Be Presi-

dent, Wouldn't It?,'" box 178, Clapper Papers, LC.

65. Clutter, "The Indiana American Legion," 50.

66. Floyd H. Evinger to McNutt, August 16, 1926, box 2, PVMP.

67. McNutt to Frank H. Streightoff, January 25, 1926, box 2, McNutt Papers (Dean's Files), IU Law Library. The Klan also tried to force Indiana University to purchase books through its outlets. Herman B Wells, *Being Lucky: Reminiscences and Reflections* (Bloomington: Indiana University Press, 1980), 22; Thomas D. Clark, *Indiana University: Midwestern Pioneer*, vol. 2, *In Mid-Passage* (Bloomington: Indiana University Press, 1973), 272–273.

68. John E. Hurt, interview with the author, August 20, 2005.

69. John C. McNutt to Paul McNutt, March 3, 1925, box 1, PVMP. The Klan proposed several measures to expunge the alleged influence of Roman Catholics in state education. McNutt was most likely referring to a measure to prohibit the wearing of religious garb in public schools—an attack on the nuns who taught in many rural public schools. Madison, *Indiana through Tradition and Change*, 67.

70. McNutt to Louis Plost, January 11, 1926 (quotations), and Plost to McNutt, January 7, 1926, box 2, McNutt Papers (Dean's Files), IU Law Library.

71. Herman B Wells oral history re: Ku Klux Klan, January 1968, 3–5, Center for the Study of History and Memory (CSHM).

72. *Vincennes* (Ind.) *Commercial*, September 1, 1926, box 2, PVMP.

73. I. George Blake, *Paul V. McNutt: Portrait of a Hoosier Statesman* (Indianapolis, IN: Central Publishing, 966), 45.

74. Orville B. Kilmer to McNutt, September 13, 1926, box 2, PVMP.

75. Neff, "The Early Career and Governorship of Paul V. McNutt," 37–38; Blake, *Paul V. McNutt*, 47–48; McNutt to Joe Reeve, March 14, 1927, box 2, PVMP; Madison,

NOTES TO PAGES 91–95

*Indiana through Tradition and Change,* 186, 196–200.

76. "Lea" to McNutt, September 5, 1927, box 3, PVMP.

77. Von Blon, "The Hoosier Schoolmaster," 50.

78. Blake, *Paul V. McNutt,* 47; McNutt to Ray H. Weisbrod, March 5, 1927, box 2, PVMP; Von Blon, "The Hoosier Schoolmaster," 50 (quotation).

79. Neff, "The Early Career and Governorship of Paul V. McNutt," 37–38; Blake, *Paul V. McNutt,* 47–48.

80. McNutt to Hanford MacNider, March 11, 1927, box 5, MacNider Papers, HHPL.

81. W. Earl Hall to McNutt, March 25, 1927, box 2, PVMP.

82. Ralph Lloyd Jones to McNutt, March 21,1927, box 2, PVMP.

83. McNutt to Sedley Peck, January 3, 1930, box 5; McNutt to William C. Rose, November 30, 1926, box 2; and McNutt to H. C. Pratt, November 30, 1926, box 2—all in PVMP.

84. McNutt to Walter T. Clark, December 3, 1930, box 6, PVMP.

85. McNutt to William C. Rose, November 9, 1926, box 2, PVMP.

86. Blake, *Paul V. McNutt,* 48–49.

87. McNutt to C. C. Chambers, April 14, 1927, box 2, PVMP.

88. Clutter, "The Indiana American Legion," 45–49; Blake, *Paul V. McNutt,* 50–51.

89. Clutter, "The Indiana American Legion," 131–133.

90. McNutt to Otho R. Brewer, March 1, 1927, box 2, and McNutt to Curtis Hodges, box 3, PVMP.

91. Von Blon, "The Hoosier Schoolmaster," 49; Neff, "The Early Career and Governorship of Paul V. McNutt," 37.

92. Letter to Glenn Seiss, March 16, 1928, box 3, PVMP.

93. Tom McConnell to McNutt, July 24, 1928, box 4, PVMP.

94. Neff, "The Early Career and Governorship of Paul V. McNutt," 38, 37 (quotation).

95. James F. Barton to National Executive Committeemen, American Legion, March 19, 1927, box 4, MacNider Papers, HHPL.

96. H. K. Bachelder to McNutt, September 20, 1926, box 2, PVMP; Blake, *Paul V. McNutt,* 46–47.

97. McNutt to Bachelder, September 23, 1926, box 2, PVMP.

98. *Indianapolis Star* (*IS*), January 27, 1975, Frank M. McHale obituaries, Law Offices of Bingham and McHale (Private), Indianapolis.

99. *Logansport* (Ind.) *Pharos-Tribune & Press,* January 27, 1975, 2.

100. *IN,* January 27, 1975, McHale obituaries.

101. *IS,* January 27, 1975, McHale obituaries.

102. *IS,* February 2, 1975, McHale obituaries.

103. *IS,* January 28, 1975, McHale obituaries.

104. McNutt to Robert R. Batton, August 16, 1926, and Batton to Frank M. McHale ("McHale"), August 18, 1926, box 2, PVMP.

105. Alexander, "Paul McNutt: 'It Would Be Kind of Nice to Be President, Wouldn't It?,'" box 178, Clapper Papers, LC.

106. Clutter, "The Indiana American Legion," 92.

107. *IS,* January 27, 1975, McHale obituaries.

108. *IN,* January 27, 1975, McHale obituaries.

109. Frank M. McHale obituary, no date (1975), Department of Indiana Biographical Files—Frank M. McHale, National Headquarters of the American Legion Library, Indianapolis.

110. Blake, *Paul V. McNutt,* 46–47; Clutter, "The Indiana American Legion," 117.

111. Martin, *Indiana: An Interpretation,* 108.

112. "Frank McHale: Elder Statesman of the Indiana Democratic Party," *The Democratic News,* October 8, 1970, 7, Department of Indiana Biographical Files—Frank M.

McHale, National Headquarters of the American Legion Library.

113. Blake, *Paul V. McNutt*, 51.

114. Kennedy, *Over Here*, 146.

115. McNutt to W. H. Johnson, March 19, 1928, box 3, PVMP.

116. McNutt to Harry J. Lantz, January 6, 1928, box 3; McNutt to Ray Weisbrod, January 20, 1928, and McNutt to McHale, June 12, 1928, box 4—all in PVMP.

117. Blake, *Paul V. McNutt*, 50.

118. McNutt to James A. Dilts, January 20, 1928, box 3, PVMP.

119. McNutt to A. J. Dougherty, July 9, 1928, box 4, PVMP.

120. McNutt to Pleas Greenlee, March 17, 1928; McNutt to John W. Wheeler, March 15 and 17, 1928, box 3, PVMP.

121. McNutt to Milt C. Campbell, March 21, 1928 (quotations), box 3, PVMP.

122. Neff, "The Early Career and Governorship of Paul V. McNutt," 44; McHale to McNutt, May 3, 1928, box 3, and McNutt to Reeve Chipman, September 1, 1928, box 4, PVMP.

123. David L. Shillinglaw to McNutt, February 21, 1928, and McNutt to George E. Denny, April 16, 1928, box 3; E. L. Madison to McNutt, late June 1928, box 4; McNutt to Greenlee, March 17, 1928, box 3; and Wendell L. Willkie to McNutt, October 1, 1928, box 4—all in PVMP.

124. McNutt to R. E. Snoberger, September 19, 1928, box 4, PVMP.

125. McNutt to Willis M. Brauer, August 27, 1928, box 4, PVMP.

126. Guy C. Chambers to McNutt, September 5, 1928, box 4, PVMP.

127. McNutt to Herbert Mooney, April 21, 1928, box 3, and McNutt to Gilchrest B. Stockton, August 18, 1928, box 4, PVMP.

128. Andrew H. Hepburn to Special Investigating Committee, September 26, 1928, box 4, PVMP.

129. Reeve Chipman to Bowman Elder, August 28, 1928, box 4, PVMP.

130. Neff, "The Early Career and Governorship of Paul V. McNutt," 49.

131. Hepburn to Special Investigating Committee, September 26, 1928, box 4, PVMP; Neff, "The Early Career and Governorship of Paul V. McNutt," 49.

132. McNutt to McHale, September 27, 1928, box 4, PVMP.

133. McNutt to Reeve Chipman, September 1, 1928, box 4, PVMP.

134. Neff, "The Early Career and Governorship of Paul V. McNutt," 49–53.

135. *BWS*, October 18, 1928, box 25, PVMP (all quotations); Neff, "The Early Career and Governorship of Paul V. McNutt," 50–51.

136. Tom McConnell to McNutt, July 24, 1928, box 4, PVMP.

137. McNutt to O. L. Bodenhamer, April 5, 1928, box 4, PVMP.

138. Bodenhamer begged off meeting with McNutt. O. L. Bodenhamer to McNutt, April 12, 1928, box 3, PVMP.

139. McNutt to John W. Wheeler, September 14, 1928, box 3, PVMP.

140. McNutt to W. W. Ridenour, April 13, 1928, box 3, PVMP.

141. *BWS*, October 18, 1928, box 25, PVMP. His advisers included C. A. Jackson, a past Indiana commander; Frederick Weicking, current state commander; Klinger, editor of the *Hoosier Legionnaire*; Pleas E. Greenlee, adjutant for the Indiana Department; and McHale. McNutt to John W. Wheeler, September 14, 1928, box 4, PVMP; Neff, "The Early Career and Governorship of Paul V. McNutt," 50. McNutt to R. E. Snoberger, September 24, 1928, box 4, PVMP. See also Blake, *Paul V. McNutt*, 58.

142. *IT*, May 18, 1933, 16.

143. *BWS*, October 18, 1928, box 25, PVMP; Neff, "The Early Career and Governorship of Paul V. McNutt," 51 (quotations).

144. Philip Von Blon, "Therefore Be Resolved," *American Legion Monthly*, December 1928, 24 (quotation), 25.

145. Von Blon, "Therefore Be Resolved," 27.

146. Ibid., 26.

147. *BWS*, October 18, 1928, box 25, PVMP; Neff, "The Early Career and Governorship of Paul V. McNutt," 52, 53.

148. Von Blon, "Therefore Be Resolved," 27.

149. BWS, October 18, 1928, box 25, PVMP.

150. McNutt to Perry Faulkner, November 17, 1928, box 4, PVMP.

151. Ralph T. O'Neil to McNutt, October 16, 1928; O. L. Bodenhamer, "A Statement," *Arkansas Legionnaire*, October 10, 1928; E. A. O'Shaughnessy to McNutt, October 12, 1928; John W. Wheeler to McNutt, October 22, 1928; Charles M. Hepburn to McNutt, October 12, 1928—all in box 4, PVMP; McNutt to William Lowe Bryan, November 17, 1928, McNutt File, William Lowe Bryan Papers, IU Archives.

152. Louise McNutt to McNutt, October 11, 1928, box 4, PVMP.

153. BWS, October 18, 1928, box 25, PVMP.

154. IDS, October 19, 1928, 4.

155. IDS, October 19, 1928, 1.

156. BWS, October 18, 1928, box 25, PVMP.

157. IDS, October 19, 1928, 3.

158. Clark, *Indiana University*, vol. 2, 319.

### 5. NATIONAL VISTAS, STATE ELECTIONS (1929–1932)

1. John W. Wheeler to Paul V. McNutt ("McNutt"), March 16, 1928, box 3, Paul V. McNutt Papers (PVMP), Lilly Library (LL), Indiana University (IU).

2. Robert R. Neff, "The Early Career and Governorship of Paul V. McNutt," (PhD diss., Indiana University, 1963), 53.

3. Fred R. Hill to McNutt, October 17, 1928, box 4, PVMP.

4. Tully Nettleton, "McNutt Is Willing," no date, fiche 3, Department of Indiana, Biographical File—Paul V. McNutt, National Headquarters of the American Legion Library, Indianapolis; McNutt to E. Willoughby, November 17, 1928, box 4, PVMP (quotation).

5. *Indiana Daily Student* (*IDS*), October 19, 1928, 3.

6. McNutt, undated speech beginning "The matter of these lines," box 24, PVMP.

7. Paul V. McNutt, "Squared Shoulders vs. Skulking Feet," no date, box 24, PVMP.

8. McNutt, undated speech beginning "The matter of these lines," box 24, PVMP.

9. William F. Book to McNutt, November 4, 1930, box 6, PVMP.

10. McNutt to Douglas I. McKay, June 30, 1930, box 6, PVMP; *Warsaw* (IN) *Union*, October 30, 1930, 6; Allen Drury, *A Senate Journal, 1943–1945* (New York: McGraw-Hill, 1963), 189 (quotation).

11. McNutt to Leist Lenzen, March 12, 1930, box 5, PVMP.

12. McNutt, "Squared Shoulders vs. Skulking Feet," no date, box 24, PVMP (all quotations).

13. Ibid. (all quotations).

14. Paul V. McNutt, "Service and Sacrifice," no date, box 24, PVMP (all quotations).

15. Ibid. I corrected some of McNutt's capitalization and punctuation, but I did not reproduce the full, standard version of the poem, which can be found in Rudyard Kipling, *Kipling Poems* (New York: Alfred A. Knopf, 2007), 129–131.

16. McNutt to J. Frank Lindsey, November 27, 1929, box 5, PVMP.

17. McNutt speeches in Minnesota, August 8, 1927, and at Purdue University (quotation), November 11, 1925, box 14, PVMP.

18. McNutt to W. J. Patterson, November 17, 1928, box 4, PVMP.

19. McNutt to J. Frank Lindsey, November 27, 1929, box 5, PVMP.

20. McNutt to J. Frank Lindsey, October 7, 1926, box 2, PVMP McNutt apparently told Esther Everett Lape, the head of the American Foundation, which was devoted to encouraging American membership in the World Court, that the "question of American adherence to the World Court is not—or at least should not be made—a political question." See Esther Everett Lape to McNutt, January 8, 1927, box 3A, Paul V. McNutt Papers, Indiana University (IU) School of Law Library, Bloomington. McNutt also said that the United States had to respect the "expressed will of the majority" on issues of the League of Nations and World Court. McNutt

to J. Frank Lindsey, November 27, 1929, box 5, PVMP.

21. McNutt to Newman T. Miller, November 2, 1928, box 4, PVMP.

22. *Detroit News,* December 15, 1929, box 25, PVMP.

23. McNutt to J. Frank Lindsey, November 27, 1929, box 5 (quotation); McNutt to J. Frank Lindsey, October 7, 1926, box 2, PVMP.

24. "Legion Head Urges Cruiser Bill Vote," *New York Sun* clipping, no date [January 1929], and "Legion Protests Cruiser Stoppage," *New York Times* clipping, no date [July 1929], box 25, and Herbert Hoover to McNutt, July 30, 1929, box 5, PVMP (quotation).

25. Richard W. Fanning, *Peace and Disarmament: Naval Rivalry and Arms Control, 1922–1933* (Lexington: University Press of Kentucky, 1995), 103–104; Robert H. Ferrell, *American Diplomacy in the Great Depression: Hoover-Stimson Foreign Policy* (New York: W. W. Norton, 1957), 69.

26. McNutt address in Bloomington, Indiana, no date, box 23, PVMP.

27. William Pencak, *For God and Country: The American Legion, 1919–1941* (Boston: Northeastern University Press, 1989), 176; McNutt to Comrades, June 22, 1929, Disabled Veterans Subject File, American Legion Library. McNutt was the grandson of a Civil War soldier whose family had struggled, unsuccessfully, to have his annual veteran's pension increased. Ralph W. Moss to John C. McNutt, January 9 and 17, 1911; Jacob M. Neely, "Claim for Increase of Pension," March 10, 1911; Affidavit, January 2, 1911; William A. Cullop to Jacob M. Neely, December 11 and 12, 1911; Commissioner of Pensions to Neely, November 18, 1913—all in box 1, Neely Family Papers, LL.

28. McNutt, "Merry Christmas, Buddy!" fiche 1, McNutt File, American Legion Library.

29. News clipping, "Western New York Legion Men Greet Their U.S. Leader," February 16, 1929, fiche 1, McNutt File, American Legion Library (quotation).

30. Albert J. Stader to McNutt, January 30, 1930, box 5, PVMP.

31. Paul Dickson and Thomas B. Allen, *The Bonus Army: An American Epic* (New York: Walker and Co., 2004), 25–30; Thomas B. Littlewood, *Soldiers Back Home: The American Legion in Illinois, 1919–1939* (Carbondale: Southern Illinois University Press, 2004), 106; Stephen R. Ortiz, *Beyond the Bonus March and the GI Bill: How Veterans Politics Shaped the New Deal Era* (New York: New York University Press, 2010), 5 (quotation).

32. "The Soldier's Bonus," no date, box 12, PVMP.

33. He wanted the Legion to "confine" itself to matters affecting veterans of the Great War and their families and to avoid such "controversial" issues as passing a constitutional amendment to abolish child labor. McNutt to E. M. Blessing, October 22, 1929, box 5, PVMP.

34. McNutt address in Massachusetts, January 19, 1929, box 14, PVMP.

35. McNutt to Fellow Legionnaires, no date [1941], box 10, PVMP.

36. *IDS,* June 19, 1929, 1, and February 12, 1929, 1 (quotation).

37. McNutt to William C. Rose, February 9, 1929, box 4, PVMP; *IDS,* May 22, 1929, 3.

38. Mileage report, no date [September 1929], box 5, PVMP.

39. Thomas A. Rumer, *The American Legion: An Official History, 1919–1989* (New York: M. Evans & Co., 1990), 164; Richard Seelye Jones, *A History of the American Legion* (Indianapolis, IN: Bobbs-Merrill, 1946), 62–67; Itinerary, no date [September 1929], box 5, PVMP; *Indianapolis Times (IT),* May 19, 1933, 22 (quotation).

40. McNutt to Mrs. Edgar Mendenhall, April 10, 1927, box 2, PVMP; *IDS,* January 5, 1929, 3.

41. Booth Tarkington was one of many who mocked him. Booth Tarkington to Benito Mussolini, March 24, 1937, box 176, Booth Tarkington Papers, Princeton University Library, Princeton, NJ.

42. *New York Sun,* January 25, 1929, box 25, PVMP; *IT,* May 19, 1933, 22 (quotations).

43. McNutt handwritten letter to Honorary President of FIDAC, no date [August 1929], box 5, PVMP.

44. Walter Treanor to "Field," October 15, 1928, box 1, Walter Treanor Papers, LL; William Lowe Bryan to McNutt, November 14, 1928, McNutt File, William Lowe Bryan Papers, Indiana University Archives (IUA).

45. William Lowe Bryan to McNutt, November 5, 1929, McNutt File, Bryan Papers, IUA; Ruth J. McNutt oral history, May 27, 1969, 29, Center for the Study of History and Memory (CSHM).

46. Walter Treanor to O. P. Field, February 8, 1929, box 1, Treanor Papers, LL.

47. McNutt to William C. Rose, February 9, 1929, box 4, PVMP.

48. *IT,* May 19, 1933, 22; Blake, *Paul V. McNutt,* 61 (quotation).

49. Hanford MacNider to Theodore Roosevelt Jr., September 18, 1933, box 29, Theodore Roosevelt Jr. Papers, LC.

50. Keith D. McFarland and David L. Roll, *Louis Johnson and the Arming of America: The Roosevelt and Truman Years* (Bloomington: Indiana University Press, 2005), 24–26.

51. Harry H. Woodring to McNutt, October 15, 1929, box 5, PVMP.

52. Neff, "The Early Career and Governorship of Paul V. McNutt," 63–64, 65 (quotation); Ferre C. Watkins to McNutt, October 4, 1929, box 5, PVMP.

53. Eddie Lee to McNutt, October 5, 1929, box 5, PVMP.

54. News clipping, "McNutt Nominated for Presidency," ca. November 1929, box 25, PVMP.

55. McNutt to Walter T. Clark, November 16, 1929, box 5, PVMP.

56. McNutt to William C. Rose, December 20, 1929, and McNutt to Kathryn McHale, November 26, 1929 (quotation), box 5, PVMP.

57. McNutt to Douglas I. McKay, October 26, 1929, box 5, PVMP.

58. Jack Alexander Column, "Paul McNutt: 'It Would Be Kind of Nice to Be President, Wouldn't It?,'" box 178, Raymond Clapper Papers, Manuscript Division, Library of Congress (LC); Kathryn McHale to Hans Freelicher, November 16, 1929, and McNutt to Kathryn McHale, November 26, 1929, box 5, PVMP.

59. See Frank McHale ("McHale") to McNutt, March 19, 1929, and R. E. Snoberger to McHale, no date [March 1929], box 4, PVMP.

60. William L. Clements to Walter Hume Sawyer, February 14, 1929, box 5, Walter Hume Sawyer Papers, Bentley Historical Library (BHL).

61. See James O. Murphin to James B. Angell, March 14, 1929, box 5, James O. Murphin Papers and Clements to Sawyer et al., July 16, 1929, box 5, Sawyer Papers—both in BHL; Walter Treanor to Howard Clark, December 10, 1929 (quotation), box 1, Treanor Papers, LL.

62. James P. Goodrich to Will H. Hays, February 14, 1922, box 11, James P. Goodrich Papers, Herbert Hoover Presidential Library (HHPL); James H. Madison, *Indiana through Tradition and Change: A History of the Hoosier State and Its People 1920–1945* (Indianapolis: Indiana Historical Society, 1982), 31–33; Tony L. Trimble, "Warren T. McCrary," in *The Governors of Indiana,* ed. Linda Gugin and James E. St. Clair (Indianapolis: Indiana Historical Society Press, 2006), 266, 278; M. William Luftholtz, *Grand Dragon: D. C. Stephenson and the Ku Klux Klan in Indiana* (West Lafayette, IN: Purdue University Press, 1991), 307–309.

63. Harold Feightner oral history, February 28, 1968, 48 (first quotation), Manuscript Division, Indiana State Library (ISL); and James P. Goodrich to George B. Lockwood, October 10, 1927 (second quotation), box 13, Goodrich Papers, HHPL.

64. McNutt to Douglas I. McKay, February 5, 1932, box 8, PVMP.

65. Ralph B. Bradford to Harry S. New, et al., October 7, 1927; Fred A. Miller to James P. Goodrich, August 31, 1927; and A. H. Beard-

sley to James P. Goodrich, November 17, 1927 (quotations), box 12, Goodrich Papers, HHPL.

66. *Indianapolis Star,* May 4, 1927, box 14, Goodrich Papers, HHPL.

67. L. E. Murray to James P. Goodrich, June 9, 1928, box 1, Goodrich Papers, HHPL.

68. Harry S. New to James P. Goodrich, box 28, and James P. Goodrich to George B. Lockwood, October 10, 1927, box 13, Goodrich Papers, HHPL.

69. McNutt to Gilchrist B. Stockton, August 18, 1928, box 4, PVMP.

70. Meredith Nicholson to McNutt, September 28, 1925, box 1, PVMP.

71. Ralph N. Smith to McNutt, September 15, 1927, and McNutt to Smith, December 26, 1927 (quotation), box 3, PVMP.

72. John C. McNutt to McNutt, September 1, 1927, and September 27, 1927 (quotation), box 3, PVMP.

73. McNutt to Gilchrist B. Stockton, August 18, 1928, box 4, PVMP.

74. Robert J. Pritchell, ed., *Indiana Votes: Election Returns for Governor, 1852–1956, and Senator, 1914–1958* (Bloomington: Bureau of Government Research, Indiana University, 1960), 47; McNutt to Gilchrist B. Stockton, August 18, 1928, box 4, PVMP.

75. James Philip Fadely, *Thomas Taggart: Public Servant, Political Boss, 1856–1929* (Indianapolis: Indiana Historical Society, 1997), 179–211; Weak leadership also hurt the Hoosier Democrats. See Madison, *Indiana through Tradition and Change,* 35–36, 43–44, 58–72; James H. Madison, *The Indiana Way: A State History* (Bloomington: Indiana University Press, 1986), 209, 289–290.

76. Claude G. Bowers to Sherman Minton, November 21, 1934, folder 1934, box 1, Sherman Minton Papers, LL.

77. R. Earl Peters to Jouette A. Shouse, November 7, 1930, box 1, R. Earl Peters Papers, Allen County–Fort Wayne Historical Society (ACHS); Ray Boomhower, "Reginald H. Sullivan," in *The Encyclopedia of Indianapolis,* ed. David J. Bodenhamer and Robert G. Barrows (Bloomington: Indiana University Press, 1994), 1308; James E. Watson to James P. Goodrich, June 5, 1930 (quotation), box 28, Goodrich Papers, HHPL.

78. Arthur Capper to James P. Goodrich, July 23, 1930, box 1, Goodrich Papers, HHPL.

79. McNutt to Gilchrist B. Stockton, January 18, 1930, box 5, PVMP.

80. McNutt to Clint Parker, April 8, 1930, box 5, PVMP.

81. McNutt to John E. Osborn, February 17, 1931, box 6, PVMP.

82. McNutt to O. L. Bodenhamer, December 23, 1929, box 5, PVMP.

83. *Goshen Daily* (IN) *News-Times,* April 4, 1930, 4; McNutt to W. A. Kunkel, February 21, 1930, box 5, PVMP.

84. McNutt to Carl G. Wolfin, July 9, 1930, box 6, Joseph M. Cravens to McNutt, February 17, 1930, and McNutt to Kunkel, February 21, 1930 (quotation), box 5, PVMP.

85. McNutt speech, June 10, 1930, box 2, Treanor Papers, LL.

86. Neff, "The Early Career and Governorship of Paul V. McNutt," 73.

87. Douglas I. McKay to McNutt, July 14, 1930; Pleas E. Greenlee to McNutt, June 12, 1930; Wendell L. Willkie to McNutt, July 7, 1930, box 6, PVMP.

88. Wendell L. Willkie to McNutt, July 7, 1930, box 6, PVMP.

89. Neff, "The Early Career and Governorship of Paul V. McNutt," 73–74.

90. R. E. Snoberger to McNutt, June 11, 1930, box 6, PVMP.

91. McNutt speech, June 10, 1930, box 2, Treanor Papers, LL.

92. Feightner oral history, October 24, 1968, 84, ISL.

93. R. E. Snoberger to McNutt, June 11, 1930, box 6, PVMP.

94. Neff, "The Early Career and Governorship of Paul V. McNutt," 73–75; McNutt to Douglas I. McKay, May 23, 1930, box 6, PVMP.

95. R. Earl Peters to McNutt, September 5 and 26, 1930, box 6, PVMP; *Warsaw* (IN) *Union,* October 30, 1930, 6 (quotation).

96. William F. Book to McNutt, November 4, 1930, box 6, PVMP.

97. Reginald Hall Sullivan oral history, March 22, 1976, 10, ISL.

98. Eliza O. Rogers to McNutt, October 24, 1930, box 6, PVMP.

99. *Madison* (IN) *Daily Herald,* October 27, 1930, box 6, PVMP.

100. News clipping, "McNutt's Burning Desire," October 22, 1930, box 25, PVMP.

101. McNutt to C. W. Niezer, October 22, 1930, box 6, PVMP.

102. McNutt to Robert C. Porter, October 27, 1930, box 6, PVMP.

103. Blake, *Paul V. McNutt,* 89; Neff, "The Early Career and Governorship of Paul V. McNutt," 79.

104. McHale to McNutt, November 5, 1930, box 6, PVMP.

105. Roy W. Feik to McNutt, November 10, 1930, box 6, PVMP.

106. Michael L. Fansler to McNutt, November 6, 1930, box 6, PVMP.

107. McNutt to Homer W. Taylor, December 23, 1930, box 6, PVMP; Neff, "The Early Career and Governorship of Paul V. McNutt," 75–76.

108. Douglas I. McKay to McNutt, March 24, 1930, box 5, PVMP.

109. William F. Book to McNutt, November 4, 1930, Jay White to McNutt, September 30, 1930 (first quotation), and Joseph W. Kimmell to McNutt, November 18, 1930 (second quotation), box 6, PVMP.

110. Harvey White to McNutt, July 14, 1930, box 6, PVMP. A North Carolinian asserted that "McNutt was the only fellow . . . who could bring the Solid South to the Democratic Party," after Smith had lost several southern states in 1928. Jos. P. Zimmerman to McNutt, May 7, 1930, box 6, PVMP.

111. Charles L. Wilson to McNutt, November 6, 1930 (first two quotations), and November 24, 1930 (final quotation), box 6, PVMP.

112. McNutt to Douglas I. McKay, November 17, 1930, box 6, PVMP.

113. McHale to McNutt, November 5, 1930, box 6, PVMP.

114. Douglas I. McKay to Charles L. Wilson, December 15, 1930, box 6, PVMP.

115. McNutt to Dick Shepard, November 26, 1930, box 6, PVMP.

116. McNutt to Charles L. Wilson, November 15, 1930, box 5, PVMP.

117. Ralph D. Gray, "Introduction," in *Gentlemen from Indiana: National Party Candidates, 1836–1940,* ed. Ralph D. Gray (Indianapolis: Indiana Historical Bureau, 1977), ix.

118. Madison, *The Indiana Way,* 209.

119. McNutt to Don F. Stiver, April 9, 1931 (first quotation), and McNutt to J. A. Lynch, December 24, 1931 (second quotation), box 7, PVMP.

120. McNutt to Hermann Wenige, January 31, 1931, box 6, and McHale to McNutt, July 21, 1931, box 7, PVMP.

121. News clipping, "State Leaders Sure of Victory in Next Election," no date [late June 1931], and Philip Lutz Jr. to Pleas E. Greenlee, September 12, 1931 (quotation), both in box 7, PVMP.

122. *Gary News,* August 21, 1931, H. L. Myers to "Fellow Democrat," September 30, 1931, and McNutt to Frank E. Lowe, October 3, 1931, box 7, PVMP.

123. Steve Neal, *Happy Days Are Here Again: The 1932 Democratic Convention, the Emergence of FDR—and How America Was Changed Forever* (New York: William Morrow, 2004), 1–64; Douglas B. Craig, *Progressives at War: William G. McAdoo and Newton D. Baker, 1863–1941* (Baltimore: Johns Hopkins University Press, 2013), 308.

124. Douglas I. McKay to McNutt, January 5, 1931, and McNutt to C. G. Brodhecker, April 29, 1931, box 7, PVMP.

125. McNutt to Douglas I. McKay, June 6, 1931, box 7, PVMP.

126. Ibid.

127. R. Earl Peters to Douglas I. McKay, June 12, 1931, box 1, Peters Papers, ACHS.

128. James A. Farley to Louis Howe, July 1, 1931, box 102, Democratic National Com-

mittee (DNC) Papers, Franklin D. Roosevelt Presidential Library (FDRL).

129. J. A. Lynch to McNutt, December 9, 1930, and McNutt to Douglas I. McKay, August 6, 1931 (quotation), box 7, PVMP.

130. Franklin D. Roosevelt to McNutt, October 27, 1931, and McNutt to J. A. Lynch, December 24, 1931 (quotations), box 7, PVMP.

131. Neff, "The Early Political Career and Governorship of Paul V. McNutt," 101–104, 109–110; Wendell L. Willkie to Bowman Elder, March 31, 1932, and Willkie to McNutt, April 13, 1932, box 8, PVMP.

132. Frank P. Douglass to McNutt, February 10, 1932; McNutt to Douglass, February 15, 1932; and McNutt to Charles L. Wilson, March 17, 1932, box 8, PVMP.

133. McNutt to Douglas I. McKay, March 24, 1932, box 8, PVMP.

134. Mary W. Dewson to McNutt, June 2, 1932, box 8, PVMP.

135. H. L. Myers to "Fellow Democrat," September 30, 1931, box 7, and McNutt to John Clerkin, April 29, 1932, box 8, PVMP; James A. Farley to R. Earl Peters, September 23, 1931, and Peters to Farley, November 33, 1931, box 1, Peters Papers, ACHS.

136. James A. Farley to McNutt, June 15, 1932, box 8, PVMP.

137. Roy W. Howard to All Editors, June 17, 1932, folder: Letters and Articles 1932 January thru June, Roy W. Howard Archive, IU School of Journalism, Bloomington.

138. McNutt to Douglas I. McKay, June 15, 1932, box 8, PVMP.

139. Robert E. Proctor, "Memorandum of Activities of Indiana Delegation, Chicago Convention 1932," no date, box 4, Wayne Coy Papers, FDRL.

140. Neff, "The Early Career and Governorship of Paul V. McNutt," 101–103; Madison, *Indiana through Tradition and Change*, 80.

141. Madison, *Indiana through Tradition and Change*, 80.

142. Proctor, "Memorandum," no date, box 4, Coy Papers, FDRL.

143. *Martinsville Democrat (MD)*, June 24, 1932, 1; Neff, "The Early Career and Gover-

norship of Paul V. McNutt," 116–119; Olive Beldon Lewis oral history, October 2, 1969, 5–6, ISL.

144. Claude R. Wickard oral history, February 6, 1953, for the Columbia Oral History Project, p. 467 (quotation), box 54, Claude R. Wickard Papers, FDRL; Proctor, "Memorandum," no date, box 4, Coy Papers, FDRL; McNutt to Douglas I. McKay, June 15, 1932, box 8, PVMP.

145. Wickard oral history, February 14, 1953, p. 529, box 54, Wickard Papers, FDRL.

146. McNutt to Newton D. Baker, July 15, 1932, box 192, Newton D. Baker Papers, LC; Roy Howard preferred Baker, but found either Smith or Baker preferable to Roosevelt. Howard to All Editors, June 17, 1932, folder: Letters and Articles 1932 January thru June, Howard Archive, IU; Howard to Otto Carmichael, June 27, 1932, box 74, Roy W. Howard Papers, LC. Neff, "The Early Career and Governorship of Paul V. McNutt," 126; Feightner oral history, October 24, 1968, 86, ISL.

147. *IT*, June 27, 1932, 2.

148. Proctor, "Memorandum," no date, box 4, Coy Papers, FDRL.

149. *IT*, June 29, 1932, 1 (quotation).

150. Proctor, "Memorandum," no date, box 4, Coy Papers, FDRL.

151. Neal, *Happy Days Are Here Again*, 270.

152. Roy W. Howard to Otto Carmichael, June 27, 1932, box 74, Howard Papers, LC.

153. Neal, *Happy Days Are Here Again*, 271.

154. Ibid., 274–276, 292.

155. Proctor, "Memorandum," no date, box 4, Coy Papers, FDRL.

156. Daniel Scroop, *Mr. Democrat: Jim Farley, the New Deal, and the Making of Modern American Politics* (Ann Arbor: University of Michigan Press, 2006), 73.

157. *IT*, July 1, 1932, 1.

158. Neff, "The Early Career and Governorship of Paul V. McNutt," 127.

159. Scroop, *Mr. Democrat*, 79–122, 173–190.

160. R. Earl Peters to James A. Farley, March 8, 1939, box 1, Peters Papers, ACHS.

161. Neal, *Happy Days Are Here Again*, 289.

162. Proctor, "Memorandum," no date, box 4, Coy Papers, FDRL.

163. Frank C. Walker to James A. Farley, March 19, 1938, box 48, Frank C. Walker Papers, University of Notre Dame Archives, Theodore M. Hesburgh Library, Notre Dame, Indiana.

164. Donald A. Ritchie, *Electing FDR: The New Deal Campaign of 1932* (Lawrence: University Press of Kansas, 2007), 82.

165. Henry A. Wallace Diary, January 12, 1943, Henry A. Wallace Papers, University of Iowa Libraries, Iowa City.

166. McNutt to Charles L. Wilson, August 4, 1932, box 9, PVMP.

167. H. W. McFarland to FDR, September 1, 1932, box 105, DNC Papers, FDRL.

168. James P. Goodrich to James E. Watson, June 10, 1932, box 28, Goodrich Papers, HHPL.

169. James E. Watson to James P. Goodrich, June 24, 1932, box 28, Goodrich Papers, HHPL.

170. *Hancock (IN) Democrat,* August 11, 1932, box 26, PVMP.

171. *MD,* September 2, 1932, 4.

172. *MD,* September 30, 1932, 1.

173. Lewis oral history, October 2, 1969, 4, ISL.

174. George W. Henley to McNutt, January 15, 1932, box 8, PVMP.

175. Blake, *Paul V. McNutt,* 94, 107; Ward G. Biddle to W. S. Bittner, October 19, 1932, box 1, Ward G. Biddle Papers, IUA; Herman B Wells to Biddle, October 12, 1932, box 16, Personal Papers, Herman B Wells Papers, IUA.

176. Herman B Wells to McNutt, December 9, 1931, box 16, Personal Papers, Wells Papers, IUA.

177. "G.O.P. Makes Losing Fight to Hold Indiana in Ranks," *Providence (RI) Journal,* no date [ca. October 11, 1932] attached to E. B. Rowbotham to McNutt, October 14, 1932, box 9, PVMP.

178. McHale and Greenlee, "Important Bulletin for 'McNutt for Governor' Clubs,"

no date [1932], box 30, PVMP; Lewis oral history, October 2, 1969, 11 (quotations), ISL.

179. Neff, "The Early Career and Governorship of Paul V. McNutt," 132.

180. James P. Goodrich to James E. Watson, June 10, 1932, box 28, and Raymond S. Springer to Goodrich, July 20, 1932, box 25, Goodrich Papers, HHPL; McNutt to Scott Lucas, August 25, 1932, and McNutt to Robert F. Gephart, August 30, 1932, box 9, PVMP; Neff, "The Early Career and Governorship of Paul V. McNutt," 132 (quotation).

181. *New York Times,* October 16, 1932, box 26, PVMP.

182. The endeavor came during the thick of the fall campaign, and the two requesters stressed the "CONFIDENTIAL nature" of their entreaty as well as the need to "take up" this matter *"personally"* with Hurley. Memorandum for Mr. Newton, October 4, 1932, box 714, Secretary's File, Hoover Papers, HHPL.

183. "Statement of the Military Service of Paul Vories McNutt," October 10, 1932, box 714, Secretary's File, Hoover Papers, HHPL; *Ohio State Journal* (Columbus), October 20, 1932, box 26, PVMP (quotation).

184. Newspaper broadside, "Does Indiana Want a 'Left-Handed' Governor?" no date [early November 1932], box 9; unsigned letter to Richard White, August 1, 1932, box 9; McNutt to R. M. McCabe, October 31, 1932, box 9; McNutt to Joe Scanlon, June 13, 1932, box 8, PVMP.

185. Madison, *Indiana through Tradition and Change,* 82–83; Pritchell, *Indiana Votes,* 49; Richard B. Scandrett Jr. to Goodrich, January 26, 1933, box 13, Goodrich Papers, HHPL (quotations).

## 6. A NEW DEAL FOR INDIANA (1933–1934)

1. *Indiana Daily Student (IDS)* January 10, 1933, 1.

2. Jack New, interview with the author, June 23, 2006; *IDS,* January 7, 1933, 1, and January 10, 1933, 1; *Indianapolis News (IN),* January 9, 1933, 1.

3. *IDS,* January 10, 1933, 1.

4. *IDS*, January 10, 1933, 1; *Martinsville Democrat (MD)*, January 13, 1933, 1 (quotations).

5. *IN*, January 9, 1933, 1.

6. James P. Goodrich Diary, January 9, 1933, box 3, James P. Goodrich Papers, Herbert Hoover Presidential Library (HHPL).

7. McNutt inaugural address, January 9, 1933 (all previous quotations), box 14, Paul V. McNutt Papers (PVMP), Lilly Library (LL), Indiana University (IU).

8. John C. McNutt to Paul V. McNutt ("McNutt"), November 16, 1932, box 9, and Frank E. Samuel to Louise McNutt, November 9, 1932, box 9, PVMP; *IDS*, January 7, 1933, 1, and November 12, 1932, 4 (quotation).

9. William Lowe Bryan to McNutt, January 4, 1933, box 9, PVMP.

10. James H. Madison, *Indiana through Tradition and Change: A History of the Hoosier State and Its People 1920–1945* (Indianapolis: Indiana Historical Society, 1982), 77.

11. Robert R. Neff, "The Early Career and Governorship of Paul V. McNutt," (PhD diss., Indiana University, 1963), 289.

12. Harold C. Feightner memorandum, November 17, 1932, box 59, Warren C. Fairbanks Papers, LL (quotation); Madison, *Indiana through Tradition and Change*, 142–143; I. George Blake, *Paul V. McNutt: Portrait of a Hoosier Statesman* (Indianapolis, IN: Central Publishing, 1966), 165, 168.

13. *IN*, March 24, 1955, Paul V. McNutt Obituaries, Grace Woody Scrapbooks, John Krauss Collection (private), Indianapolis.

14. Harold Jordan oral history, May 2, 1973, 5, Center for the Study of History and Memory (CSHM); Margaret Buchanan Diary, June 2, 1939, Mary Eloise Sipes Papers (private), Bloomington, Indiana.

15. Feightner memorandum, November 17, 1932, box 59, Fairbanks Papers, LL.

16. James H. Madison, *The Indiana Way: A State History* (Bloomington: Indiana University Press, 1986), 86 (quotations). An unbalanced budget was allowed only "to meet casual deficits or failures in the revenue" and to pay interest on the state debt. Donald F.

Carmony, *Indiana, 1816–1850: The Pioneer Era* (Indianapolis: Indiana Historical Society, 1998), 43.

17. Donald A. Ritchie, *Electing FDR: The New Deal Campaign of 1932* (Lawrence: University Press of Kansas, 2007), 140–142.

18. Feightner memorandum, November 17, 1932 (all quotations), box 59, Fairbanks Papers, LL.

19. "Toms" to "Mr. McCarthy," no date, box 60, Fairbanks Papers, LL.

20. Bruce W. Ulsh to McNutt, November 22, 1932, box 9, PVMP.

21. "Toms" to "Mr. Everson and "Mr. McCarthy," January 6, 1933, box 60, Fairbanks Papers, LL.

22. Memorandum on Poor Relief, February 3, 1933 (quotation), box 60, Fairbanks Papers, LL.

23. McNutt message to General Assembly, January 10, 1933, box 14, PVMP.

24. Linda C. Gugin, James E. St. Clair, and Thomas Wolfe, "Indiana Governors: Powers and Personal Attributes," in *The Governors of Indiana*, ed. Linda Gugin and James E. St. Clair (Indianapolis: Indiana Historical Society Press, 2006), 1.

25. Madison, *Indiana through Tradition and Change*, 83.

26. Ed Runden, "Oliver Morton, January 16, 1861–January 23, 1867," in *The Governors of Indiana*, ed. Gugin and St. Clair, 140–150, 145.

27. McNutt to Claude R. Wickard, November 18, 1932, box 5, Claude R. Wickard Papers, Franklin D. Roosevelt Library (FDRL); McNutt message to General Assembly, January 10, 1933, box 14, PVMP; Feightner memorandum, November 17, 1932, box 59, Fairbanks Papers, LL.

28. Feightner memorandum, November 17, 1932, box 59, Fairbanks Papers, LL; Neff, "The Early Career and Governorship of Paul V. McNutt," 144–144. Before the General Assembly reconvened in 1935, Greenlee asked legislators for their preferred committee assignments, promising to "do the best we can." Pleas E. Greenlee to LeRoy Smith, De-

cember 11, 1934, box A7134, Paul V. McNutt Papers, Indiana State Archives (ISA).

29. Feightner memorandum, November 17, 1932, box 59, Fairbanks Papers, LL.

30. Feightner memorandum, January 4, 1933, box 60, Fairbanks Papers, LL.

31. Everson to Warren C. Fairbanks, no date, box 60, Fairbanks Papers, LL (quotation).

32. *IN*, March 24, 1955, McNutt Obituaries.

33. F. A. Mangold to "Mr. South," November 15, 1932, box 59, Fairbanks Papers, LL.

34. Claude R. Wickard oral history for the Columbia Oral History Project, 506, box 54, Wickard Papers, FDRL.

35. William F. Welch, interview with the author, January 11, 2006.

36. McNutt to Claude R. Wickard, December 2, 1932, box 5, Wickard Papers, FDRL; Neff, "The Early Career and Governorship of Paul V. McNutt," 146–147, 168–170.

37. McNutt message to General Assembly, January 10, 1933, box 14, PVMP.

38. *Indianapolis Star* (*IS*), March 5, 1933, 1.

39. Madison, *Indiana through Tradition and Change*, 86 (quotation) and 87.

40. Neff, "The Early Career and Governorship of Paul V. McNutt," 172.

41. Mr. Everson to Warren C. Fairbanks, no date, box 60, Fairbanks Papers, LL.

42. *IS*, January 20, 1933, 1.

43. Neff, "The Early Career and Governorship of Paul V. McNutt," 172; *IS*, January 20, 1933, 1. Under a gross receipts tax, the transaction is between "the dealer and the state." *IN*, January 21, 1933, 1.

44. Feightner memorandum, January 24, 1933, box 60, Fairbanks Papers, LL; Sylvan A. Yager to McNutt, February 13, 1933; Joseph T. Day to McNutt, February 23, 1933; Robert C. Lamke to McNutt, January 23, 1933, Kentland Chamber of Commerce to McNutt, January 21, 1933; Oscar Laverty to McNutt, January 20, 1933; C. R. Mittag to McNutt, January 24, 1933, all in box A7132, McNutt Papers, ISA.

45. William Jack Latta to McNutt, February 23, 1933, box A7132, McNutt Papers, ISA.

46. *IN:* January 24, 1933, 6; January 25, 1933, 1; January 27, 1933, 6; January 30, 1933, 6; February 2, 1933, 6; February 4, 1933, 1; February 15, 1933, 1; February 18, 1933, 6; February 20, 1933, 6.

47. *IN:* January 27, 1933, 1; January 28, 1933, 1; January 30, 1933, 1.

48. Goodrich Diary, February 24, 1933, box 3, Goodrich Papers, HHPL.

49. *Indianapolis Times* (*IT*) January 20, 1933, 14.

50. *IT*, February 3, 1933, 15.

51. "C. W. Mc.," memorandum, no date, box 60, Fairbanks Papers, LL.

52. Madison, *Indiana through Tradition and Change*, 88; Neff, "The Early Career and Governorship of Paul V. McNutt," 175.

53. *IN*, February 6, 1933, 1; *IS*, February 8, 1933, 4.

54. *IS*, February 21, 1933, 1.

55. Blake, *Paul V. McNutt*, 138; Welch, interview with the author.

56. *IN*, February 23, 1933, II-1.

57. Neff, "The Early Career and Governorship of Paul V. McNutt," 147, 175.

58. *IN*, February 23, 1933, II-1.

59. *IN*, February 23, 1933, I-1, II-1.

60. *IT*, February 23, 1933, 1.

61. *IS*, February 23, 1933, 8.

62. Madison, *Indiana through Tradition and Change*, 88–89.

63. Stemen to McNutt, July 11, 1935, box 107, McNutt Papers, ISA; Indiana Democratic State Central Committee, *Facts! Gross Income Tax, Sales Tax or What?* (Indianapolis, Indiana Democratic State Central Committee, 1936), 9 (quotation), box 5, Hugh A. Barnhart Papers, Indiana Division, Indiana State Library (ISL).

64. McNutt to Ernest H. Lindley, April 24, 1933, box 2, General Correspondence, Ernest H. Lindley Papers—Records of the Chancellor's Office, Kenneth Spencer Research Library, University of Kansas (KU), Lawrence.

65. McNutt to Raymond C. Brown (acting governor of California), May 17, 1934, box 38, McNutt Papers, ISA; Indiana Demo-

cratic State Central Committee, *Facts!,* 6 (quotation).

66. Neff, "The Early Career and Governorship of Paul V. McNutt," 195.

67. Frank G. Bates, "Indiana Joins the Ranks of the Reorganized States," undated, unpublished paper, box 2, and McNutt to Guy Moffett, February 24, 1933 (quotation), box 16, McNutt Papers, ISA.

68. *Kokomo Tribune,* no date, box 8, McNutt Papers, ISA.

69. Robert A. Slayton, *Empire Statesman: The Rise and Redemption of Al Smith* (New York: Free Press, 2001), 161.

70. Madison, *Indiana through Tradition and Change,* 92.

71. *IS,* January 26, 1933, 1, and *IN,* January 27, 1933, 1 (quotation).

72. *IT,* January 28, 1933, 1.

73. *IN:* January 27, 1933, 1 (both quotations).

74. *IT,* January 28, 1933, 1.

75. *IT,* January 28, 1933, 4; *IS,* January 28, 1933, 8.

76. *IS,* January 31, 1933, 11; Herman B Wells interview with Edward E. Edwards and Dottie Collins, August 9, 1974, 8 (quotations), box 25, Personal Papers, Herman B Wells Papers, Indiana University Archives (IUA).

77. James E. Watson to Warren C. Fairbanks, February 6, 1933, box 60, Fairbanks Papers, LL.

78. Oral Glen Miller to McNutt, January 30, 1933, box 10, and William A. Rawles to McNutt, February 9, 1933 (quotation), box 12, McNutt Papers, ISA.

79. Wayne Coy to Arnold B. Hall, May 17, 1933, box 6, McNutt Papers, ISA; Neff, "The Early Career and Governorship of Paul V. McNutt," 236–237; *New York Herald Tribune,* February 12, 1933, II-4; *Kansas City Star,* February 17, 1933, C; *New Orleans States,* April 21, 1933, 6.

80. *Detroit News,* April 13, 1933, 1 (first quotation), and *Lansing Journal,* January 30, 1933 (second quotation), folder 32, box 3, McNutt Papers, ISA.

81. A. R. McKinley to McNutt, February 14, 1933, box 10, McNutt Papers, ISA.

82. "All Eyes on Us," *Evansville (IN) Courier,* February 28, 1933, box 2, McNutt Papers, ISA.

83. *IT,* January 27, 1933, 1; *IN,* February 1, 1933, 1; *IS,* February 3, 1933, 8 (quotation).

84. *IN,* February 27, 1933, 1, and February 28, 1933, 6; *IS,* February 28, 1933, 8; *IT,* February 27, 1933, 3 (quotation), and February 28, 1933, 4.

85. *IT,* March 2, 1933, 1, and *IN,* March 1, 1933, 6 (quotation).

86. *IS,* February 3, 1933, 8; *Kokomo Tribune,* no date, box 8, McNutt Papers, ISA; Neff, "The Early Career and Governorship of Paul V. McNutt," 223–224.

87. Madison, *Indiana through Tradition and Change,* 93.

88. Neff, "The Early Career and Governorship of Paul V. McNutt," 230; Pleas Greenlee to Huber L. Menaugh, May 22, 1933, folder 113, box 10, and McNutt to Claude A. Campbell, October 21, 1936 (quotation), box A7089 (drawer 97, box B), McNutt Papers, ISA.

89. Neff, "The Early Career and Governorship of Paul V. McNutt," 232 (first quotation); Madison, *Indiana through Tradition and Change,* 93 (second quotation).

90. *Literary Digest,* March 4, 1933, 12.

91. Daniel Beland, *Social Security: History and Politics from the New Deal to the Privatization Debate* (Lawrence: University Press of Kansas, 2005), 57; See articles from *The Eagle Magazine* (1930–1931) as well as an undated, unsigned memorandum [ca. 1933] on the statements issued by the governors who signed such laws. Both documents are in box A7131, McNutt Papers, ISA; *IS:* February 24, 1933, 3, and February 22, 1933, 9; *Old Age Security Herald* (March 1933), 1, box A7131, McNutt Papers, ISA; *IT,* February 24, 1933, 12.

92. *IT,* January 30, 1933, 4; two letters by Louise Singler to Wayne Coy, no date [ca. March 1933], box A7131, McNutt Papers, ISA; W. C. Macy to McNutt, February 24, 1934,

box 54, McNutt Papers, ISA; Beland, *Social Security*, 66.

93. Wayne Coy to Louise Singler, March 28 and May 17 (quotation), 1933, box A7131, McNutt Papers, ISA.

94. *IT*, April 18, 1933, 12.

95. McNutt to Charles Bickel, August 21, 1935, box 87, McNutt Papers, ISA.

96. McNutt to M. H. Freeney, April 13, 1936, box A7092 (drawer 98, box C), McNutt Papers, ISA.

97. *IT*, February 15, 1933, 2.

98. *IT*, February 4, 1933, 3; Minutes of Joint Meeting of State Executive Committee and District Chairmen of the Governor's Commission on Unemployment Relief (GCUR), September 15, 1933 (quotation), box 94, Federal Emergency Relief Administration (FERA) State Series, Record Group (RG) 69, Records of the Work Projects Administration, National Archives, College Park (NACP).

99. *IT*, February 4, 1933, 3.

100. Madison, *Indiana through Tradition and Change*, 109–110; Howard O. Hunter to Harry L. Hopkins, August 13, 1934, box 57, Harry L. Hopkins Papers, FDRL; Lee G. Lauck to Mr. Gill, August 10, 1933, box 91, FERA State Series, RG 69, NACP.

101. The power and ability of the state to provide relief remained limited. The new law allowed township trustees to withhold relief from any person who refused to work on public projects. Neff, "The Early Career and Governorship of Paul V. McNutt," 256. And although the legislature appropriated $2 million to help townships fund unemployment relief during 1933 and 1934, the state's budget deficit consumed those dollars. "Summary Data Regarding Unemployment Relief (as of June 25, 1935)," no date, box 90, FERA State Series, RG 69, NACP.

102. David M. Kennedy, *Freedom from Fear: The American People in Depression and War, 1929–1945* (New York: Oxford University Press, 1999), 171; "Financing Public Employment Relief in Indiana," no date, and Howard O. Hunter to Harry L. Hopkins,

October 17, 1933 (quotation), box 57, Hopkins Papers, FDRL.

103. McNutt to Peter F. Hein, November 9, 1933, box 48, McNutt Papers, ISA.

104. Howard O. Hunter, Memorandum on Indiana, October 25, 1933, box 57, Hopkins Papers, FDRL.

105. Madison, *Indiana through Tradition and Change*, 109; Howard O. Hunter to Harry L. Hopkins, January 19, 1934 (quotation), box 57, Hopkins Papers, FDRL.

106. Kennedy, *Freedom from Fear*, 176.

107. Neff, "The Early Career and Governorship of Paul V. McNutt," 260; Howard O. Hunter to Harry L. Hopkins, November 18, 1933, box 57, Hopkins Papers, FDRL (quotation).

108. Howard O. Hunter to Harry L. Hopkins, no date and February 13, 1934 (quotation), box 57, Hopkins Papers, FDRL.

109. Neff, "The Early Career and Governorship of Paul V. McNutt," 260. In 1933 and 1934, $45.5 million was spent on relief in Indiana. Of that amount, $29 million came from federal sources, $16.5 million from townships, and only $33,000 from the state. "Summary Data Regarding Unemployment Relief (as of June 25, 1935)," no date, box 90, FERA State Series, RG 69, NACP.

110. Howard O. Hunter to Harry L. Hopkins, no date, box 57, Hopkins Papers, FDRL.

111. Grace Tully to McNutt, June 28, 1948, box 23, FDR Memorial Foundation Papers, FDRL.

112. McNutt radio talk on "New Poor Relief Plan in Indiana," April 1, 1934, box A7135, McNutt Papers, ISA.

113. McNutt handwritten note to Raymond Moley, no date [December 1934], box 83, McNutt Papers, ISA.

114. Madison, *Indiana through Tradition and Change*, 125; George T. Blakey, *Creating a Hoosier Self-Portrait: The Federal Writers' Project in Indiana, 1935–1942* (Bloomington: Indiana University Press, 2005), 34 (quotation).

115. Herman B Wells, *Being Lucky: Reminiscences and Reflections* (Bloomington: In-

diana University Press, 1980), 49–50; Neff, "The Early Career and Governorship of Paul V. McNutt," 200–201.

116. No bank could lend ten percent of its capital to any single borrower, and no building and loan could lend a sum equaling more than sixty percent of the value of its real estate. *IS*, January 18, 1933, 1.

117. Herman B Wells interview with Edwards, Collins, and Thomas D. Clark, August 5, 1974, 2 and Wells interview, August 9, 1974, 25 (quotation), box 25, Personal Papers, Wells Papers, IUA.

118. Herman B Wells to Lyman D. Eaton, March 1, 1933, box 16, Personal Papers, Wells Papers, IUA.

119. Wells interview, August 9, 1974, 6–8, box 25; Herman B Wells to Walter S. Greenough, April 7, 1932, McNutt to Wells, December 14, 1932, and Herman B Wells to Lyman D. Eaton, March 1, 1933 (quotation), box 16, all in Personal Papers, Wells Papers, IUA.

120. Michael E. Parrish, *Anxious Decades: America in Prosperity and Depression, 1920–1941* (New York: W. W. Norton, 1992), 97; *IS*, February 14, 1933, 1 (quotation).

121. *IS*, March 2, 1933, 1; Madison, *Indiana through Tradition and Change,* 41–43; Harold C. Feightner, "Indiana Liquor Planks," no date, Indiana State Library (ISL).

122. Harold C. Feightner, "150 Years of Brewing in Indiana," 2–7, undated, unpublished manuscript, ISL; *IT*, January 11, 1933, 1 (quotation).

123. *IS*, February 18, 1933, 1.

124. *IS*, February 14, 1933, 1; *IT*, January 16, 1933, 1; *IT*, February 3, 1933, 4; *IT*, February 8, 1933, 1; *IS*, February 24, 1933, 1; *IT*, February 14, 1933, 1.

125. *IS*, March 2, 1933, 1.

126. *IT*, March 30, 1933, 1.

127. Feightner, "150 Years of Brewing in Indiana," 6, ISL.

128. *IT*, March 31, 1933, 1.

129. *IT*, March 30, 1933, 14.

130. *IT*, February 10, 1933, 1.

131. Wickard oral history, 496, 501, box 54, Wickard Papers, FDRL.

132. *IT*, March 7, 1933, 1 (quotation); Pleas Greenlee to John L. Clark, no date, box 19, McNutt Papers, ISA.

133. Public Service Commission press release on rate cuts, October 8, 1933, box 9, PVMP.

134. George Ade to McNutt, March 12, 1933, box 1, McNutt Papers, ISA.

135. *Cincinnati Enquirer,* March 8, 1933, 4; *Charleston Gazette,* March 11, 1933, 4; Wickard oral history, 530, box 54, Wickard Papers, FDRL.

136. *IT*, May 20, 1933, 3 (both quotations).

137. *IS*, September 4, 1933, E4; *IT*, May 20, 1933, 3 (all quotations).

138. Richard Lieber Diary, February 6, 1933, Richard Lieber Papers, LL. The self-portrait, signed by McNutt, is in the Indiana University School of Law Library.

139. Kathleen A. Foster, Nanette Esseck Brewer, and Margaret Contompasis, *Thomas Hart Benton and the Indiana Murals* (Bloomington: Indiana University Press, 2000), 74, 142.

140. Oscar R. Ewing to Will H. Lanham, March 8, 1933, box 4, Oscar R. Ewing Papers, Harry S. Truman Library (HSTL); Photograph #648003, Notable Personalities, 1942–45, box 134, Records of the Office of War Information, RG 208, NACP; Byron K. Elliott, "Beta's Pi Chapter," 10, March 1982 (all quotations), folder: Beta Theta Pi, Reference File, IUA.

141. *IS*, February 14, 1933, 12.

142. McNutt talk on the Ohio School of Air, September 18, 1933, box 14, PVMP.

143. Ruby Black to Eleanor Roosevelt, November 4, 1936, box 2, Ruby A. Black Papers, Manuscript Division, Library of Congress (LC).

144. McNutt talk on the Ohio School of Air, September 18, 1933, box 14, PVMP. See also William E. Leuchtenburg, *The FDR Years: On Roosevelt and His Legacy* (New York: Columbia University Press, 1995), 35–74.

145. Goodrich Diary, March 8, 1933, box 3, Goodrich Papers, HHPL.

146. *IN*, March 24, 1955, McNutt Obituaries.

147. "McNutt Did a Job They All Agreed Couldn't Be Done," *IN*, no date [March 1955], folder: Ind. Biography—McNutt, Paul V. and Family, Indiana Clipping File, ISL.

148. *IT*, May 20, 1933, 3.

149. Walter D. Myers oral history, January 20, 1972, 42–26, ISL; Jack New, interview with the author; Walter D. Myers, *The Guv: A Tale of Midwest Law and Politics* (New York: Frederick Fell, 1947), 279–300.

150. *IS*, December 13, 1970, II-10; Clifton J. Phillips, *Indiana in Transition: The Emergence of an Industrial Commonwealth, 1880–1920* (Indianapolis: Indiana Historical Bureau and Indiana Historical Society, 1968), 24; Olive Beldon Lewis oral history, October 2, 1969, 6, ISL; Pleas Greenlee to W. S. Darneal, March 20, 1933, folder 45, box 4, McNutt Papers, ISA. By May 1933, 30,000 Hoosiers had applied for positions with the state, but McNutt had only 3,000 vacancies to fill. McNutt to J. R. Rayls, May 2, 1933, box 12, McNutt Papers, ISA.

151. Pleas Greenlee to J. Ben Henry, January 26, 1933, box 7, McNutt Papers, ISA.

152. Pleas Greenlee to J. T. Arbuckle, March 14, 1933, box 1, McNutt Papers, ISA.

153. Wayne Coy to Louis Price, May 23, 1933, box 11; Pleas Greenlee to Alma B. Foltz, July 27, 1933, box 22; Greenlee to John L. Clark, no date (quotation), box 19, McNutt Papers, ISA.

154. McNutt to J. R. Rayls, May 2, 1933, box 12, and Pleas Greenlee to Charles A. Webster, June 24, 1933 (quotation), box 34, McNutt Papers, ISA.

155. Pleas Greenlee to Joe Mellon, May 20, 1933, box 10, McNutt Papers, ISA.

156. Pleas Greenlee to Mrs. Ulrey Dorman, November 14, 1933, box 42, and Greenlee to Louis A. Ludlow, December 27, 1933, box 54, McNutt Papers, ISA; Lewis oral history, October 2, 1969, 5, ISL; Madison, *The Indiana Way*, 257–258.

157. R. A. Frederick, "Colonel Richard Lieber: Conservationist and Public Builder: The Indiana Years" (PhD diss., Indiana University, 1960), 337–339. Correspondence between Lieber and his friends, although cryptic, refers to Lieber's troubles under the new administration. Richard Lieber to Gilbert Pearson, July 19, 1933; Lieber to Raymond E. Willis, August 3, 1933; William J. Mooney to Lieber, July 8, 1933, box 6, Richard Lieber Papers, ISL.

158. William E. Carson to Lieber, October 26, 1933, box 6, Lieber Papers, ISL.

159. Grace Julian Clarke to McNutt, June 10, 1933, box 2, Grace Julian Clarke Papers, ISL. Booth Tarkington to McNutt, June 7, 1933, and Jeanette J. Murphy to McNutt, May 8, 1933, box A7132; Ida K. Tannenbaum to McNutt, June 6, 1933, box 33; Harlow Lindley to McNutt, June 19, 1933, box 26; and Charles E. Rush to McNutt, July 7, 1933, box 31—all in McNutt Papers, ISA.

160. Gladys H. Brenneman to President of the State Library Board, June 3, 1933, box A7132, McNutt Papers, ISA.

161. Ira D. Foster to McNutt, June 6, 1933, and McNutt to Charles E. Rush, June 27, 1933 (quotation), box A7132, McNutt Papers, ISA.

162. Hazel Warren to Pleas Greenlee, July 24, 1933, box 34, and Booth Tarkington to McNutt, June 7, 1933 (quotation), box A7132, McNutt Papers, ISA.

163. Booth Tarkington to Carleton B. McCulloch, June 23, 1933, box 176, Booth Tarkington Papers, Princeton University Library, Princeton, N.J.

164. *IT*, March 21, 1933, 2; Neff, "The Early Career and Governorship of Paul V. McNutt," 295; Pleas Greenlee to John L. Clark, no date, box 19, McNutt Papers, ISA; Nellie Shipp oral history, February 14, 1980, 32, CSHM.

165. *IT*, November 20, 1933, 12 (first two quotations), and December 20, 1933, 1 (third quotation).

166. "Statement of Pleas Greenlee," no date, box A7136, McNutt Papers, ISA; Neff,

"The Early Career and Governorship of Paul V. McNutt," 305–312.

167. Pleas Greenlee to C. A. Moore, April 27, 1934, box A7055 (drawer 82, box A), McNutt Papers, ISA.

168. Grace B. Fink to Wayne Coy, April 4, 1934, box A7135; Pleas Greenlee to Paul G. Smiley, September 27, 1933, box 65; Fink to Coy, April 4, 1934, box A7135; Fink to Greenlee, December 26, 1934, box A7053, Secretary's File—General Correspondence 1934, McNutt Papers, ISA.

169. Wayne Coy to Oscar R. Ewing, August 30, 1933, box 22, McNutt Papers, ISA; Neff, "The Early Career and Governorship of Paul V. McNutt," 312–314.

170. Look, February 13, 1940, box 30, PVMP.

171. Milton S. Mayer, "Pretty Boy McNutt," The Nation, March 30, 1940, 416.

172. Sherman Minton to James A. Woodburn, February 3, 1936, box 3, James A. Woodburn Papers, LL.

173. Jack New, interview with the author.

174. Allan Levine, King: William Lyon Mackenzie King, A Life Guided by the Hand of Destiny (Toronto: Douglas & McIntyre, 2011), 209 (first quotation); T. Harry Williams, Huey Long (New York: Knopf, 1969), 821 (second quotation); President, Fidelity Trust Company, to Bowman Elder, August 4, 1933, box 21, McNutt Papers, ISA; Frank Vazzano, Politician Extraordinaire: The Tempestuous Life and Times of Martin L. Davey (Kent, OH: Kent State University Press, 2008), 209, 250; Richard O. Davies, Defender of the Old Guard: John Bricker and American Politics (Columbus: Ohio State University Press, 1993), 35 and 45.

175. Pleas Greenlee to Ruben Molder, January 21, 1933, folder 117, box 10, McNutt Papers, ISA.

176. Mayer, "Pretty Boy McNutt," 416.

177. "On Publicity," attached to Dudley Smith to Pleas Greenlee, December 20, 1934, box 83, McNutt Papers, ISA.

178. IT, September 27, 1933, 1; Pleas Greenlee to Leo T. Mulva, June 19, 1934 (quotation), box A, drawer 82, McNutt Papers, ISA.

179. Wayne Coy to Ben Stern, March 25, 1933, folder 166, box 14, McNutt Papers, ISA (first quotation); Carleton B. McCulloch to Meredith Nicholson, October 9 and November 13 (second quotation), 1934, box 1, Carleton B. McCulloch Papers, Indiana Historical Society (IHS).

180. IT, June 22, 1933, 12; Donald F. Carmony oral history, July 8, 1985, 6 (quotation), CSHM.

181. R. Earl Peters to McNutt, September 18, 1933, box 30, McNutt Papers, ISA; IT, November 14, 1933, 1; IT, October 30, 1933, 1 (quotations).

182. Victor A. Selby to McNutt, February 9, 1933, box 13, McNutt Papers, ISA.

183. Carmony oral history, July 8, 1985, 6, CSHM.

184. IT, April 5, 1934, 1; Richmond (IN) Palladium, no date [August 1934], box 75, McNutt Papers, ISA.

185. IT: May 15, 1933, 1, October 5, 1933, March 3, 1934, 1, March 12, 1934, 1, March 16, 1934, 16.

186. McNutt statement, no date [July 1934], box A7109 (drawer 106, box B), McNutt Papers, ISA; IT, August 22, 1933, 1; Carleton B. McCulloch to Meredith Nicholson, October 15, 1934, box 1, McCulloch Papers, IHS.

187. Wayne Coy to Harry L. Hopkins, February 25, 1935, box 90, FERA State Series, RG 69, NACP. There were nine candidates, and McNutt supported Minton quietly and belatedly. Minton was grateful for the help. Linda C. Gugin and James E. St. Clair, Sherman Minton: New Deal Senator, Cold War Justice (Indianapolis: Indiana Historical Society, 1997), 72–75.

188. James Goodrich to James Showalter, March 10, 1934, box 12, Goodrich Papers, HHPL.

189. Republican State Committee, Laugh This Off, Governor McNutt (Indianapolis: Republican State Committee, 1934), ISL.

190. Jacob S. Miller, *Vs: Vanities and Vagaries of Indiana's Variously Named Governor* (Indianapolis, 1934), box 57, McNutt Papers, ISA.

191. *IN*, September 27, 1934, II-1 (first quotation); October 17, 1934, II-1 (second quotation); October 31, 1934, II-1 (third quotation).

192. Madison, *Indiana through Tradition and Change*, 133.

193. Margaret E. Paddock to McNutt, October 31, 1934, box 81, McNutt Papers, ISA.

194. R. Earl Peters to James A. Farley, October 31, 1934, box 1. R. Earl Peters Papers, Allen County—Fort Wayne Historical Society (ACHS); *Facts for Every Democrat: Address of Governor Paul V. McNutt as Temporary Chairman of the Democratic State Convention, June 12, 1934* (quotation), Pamphlets Collection, ISL.

195. *IN*, October 20, 1934, 2.

196. *IS*, November 4, 1934, pt. 5, 4.

197. Carleton B. McCulloch to Meredith Nicholson, October 9, 1934, box 1, McCulloch Papers, IHS.

198. *IN*, October 25, 1934, pt. 2, 1.

199. McNutt press release, October 24, 1934, box A7141, McNutt Papers, ISA; *IS*, November 18, 1934, 1 (quotation).

200. Carleton B. McCulloch to Meredith Nicholson, October 15, 1934, box 1, McCulloch Papers, IHS; R. Earl Peters to James A. Farley, October 29, 1934, box 1, Peters Papers, ACHS; C. D. Jackson to McNutt, Pleas Greenlee, Omer Jackson, October 17, 1934, box 78, McNutt Papers, ISA; James Goodrich to F. A. Miller, October 24, 1934, box 12, Goodrich Papers, HHPL (quotation).

201. *IN*, October 19, 1934, 1.

202. *IS*, November 3, 1934, 8.

203. Madison, *Indiana through Tradition and Change*, 133–134; *IN*, November 7, 1934, 6 (quotations).

204. *IS*, November 8, 1933, 10.

205. McNutt to Oscar R. Ewing, November 17, 1934, box 4, Ewing Papers, HSTL.

206. Sherman Minton to Meredith Nicholson, January 14, 1935, box 1, Meredith Nicholson Papers, IHS.

207. Arthur R. Robinson to James Goodrich, November 9, 1934, box 15, Goodrich Papers, HHPL.

208. Robert F. Murray to James Goodrich, November 16, 1934, box 12, Goodrich Papers, HHPL.

209. *Washington Evening Star,* November 25, 1934, A-1.

210. Claude G. Bowers to James A. Farley, March 6, 1938, box 6, Farley Papers, LC.

7. "HOOSIER HITLER" (1935–1936)

1. Robert H. Ross to Paul V. McNutt ("McNutt"), December 26, 1935, box 105, Paul V. McNutt Papers, Indiana State Archives (ISA).

2. Louis Howe to McNutt, January 11, 1935, box 47, Louis Howe Papers, Franklin D. Roosevelt Library (FDRL).

3. Louis Howe to Joseph C. Mahoney, December 12, 1933 (first and second quotations), and Howe to James A. Farley, April 11, 1934 (third quotation), box 16, Official File (OF) 300—Democratic National Committee (DNC), FDR Papers, FDRL.

4. Louis Howe to R. Earl Peters, December 16, 1934, box 47, Howe Papers, FDRL.

5. R. Earl Peters to Louis Howe, February 26, 1935, box 47, Howe Papers, FDRL; *Indianapolis Star* (*IS*), November 9, 1934, 1; Pleas E. Greenlee to LeRoy Smith, December 11, 1934, box A7134, McNutt Papers, ISA; Robert R. Neff, "The Early Career and Governorship of Paul V. McNutt," (PhD diss., Indiana University, 1963), 341–342.

6. *IS*, January 11, 1935, 11.

7. Carleton B. McCulloch to Meredith Nicholson, January 11, 1935 (1934 in original), box 1, Carleton B. McCulloch Papers, Indiana Historical Society (IHS).

8. *Indianapolis News* (*IN*), January 10, 1935, I-2 (quotation).

9. *IS*, January 11, 1935, 11.

10. *IS*, November 18, 1934, 1.

11. *IS*, March 8, 1935, 1, and March 12, 1935, 8, 9; Alan Brinkley, *The End of Reform: New Deal Liberalism in Recession and War* (New York: Vintage, 1995), 24.

12. Herman B Wells, *Being Lucky: Reminiscences and Reflections* (Bloomington: Indiana University Press, 1980), 66–67.

13. Neff, "The Early Career and Governorship of Paul V. McNutt," 215–216; Wells, *Being Lucky*, 67 (quotation).

14. McNutt address, March 11, 1935, box 15, Paul V. McNutt Papers (PVMP), Lilly Library (LL), Indiana University (IU).

15. *IN*, March 11, 1935, 1; *IS*, March 12, 1935, 8; Jerry L. Wheeler, "Fish, Pheasants, and Politics: Paul McNutt and the Popularization of Conservation in 1930s Indiana" (MA thesis, Indiana University–Purdue University at Indianapolis, 2002), 50–52; *IS*, March 12, 1935, 8.

16. Wheeler, "Fish, Pheasants, and Politics," 58–81 (quotations on 73).

17. Neff, "The Early Career and Governorship of Paul V. McNutt," 347; Wheeler, "Fish, Pheasants, and Politics," 85 (first quotation) and 130 (second quotation).

18. Neff, "The Early Career and Governorship of Paul V. McNutt," 348; Wheeler, "Fish, Pheasants, and Politics," 83–84.

19. *IS*, January 11, 1935, 11.

20. Neff, "The Early Career and Governorship of Paul V. McNutt," 360–362; Harold C. Feightner, "A History of the Liquor Industry in Indiana since 1914," 280, unpublished manuscript, box 2, Harold C. Feightner Papers, Indiana State Library (ISL); *IS*, February 18, 1935, 1; *IS*, March 11, 1933, 6 (quotations), and March 9, 1935, 11.

21. Neff, "The Early Career and Governorship of Paul V. McNutt," 367–368; Feightner, "History of the Liquor Industry," 281–290, box 2, Feightner Papers, ISL; Feightner, "Prohibition, Repeal, and Regulation: The Rise and Fall of a Deadly Experiment," 25, ISL; Milo R. McConnell to Hugh A. Barnhart, May 13, 1937, box 7 (quotation); V. G. Coplen to Barnhart, August 12, 1937, box 7; Alice Kenefick to Frank McHale, October 21, 1937, box 8, Hugh A. Barnhart Papers, ISL.

22. Feightner, "Prohibition, Repeal, and Regulation," 18, ISL.

23. William E. Leuchtenburg, *Franklin D. Roosevelt and the New Deal, 1932–1940* (New York: Columbia University Press, 1963) 65–67, 67 (quotation).

24. David M. Kennedy, *Freedom from Fear: The American People, 1929–1945* (New York: Oxford University Press, 1999), 182.

25. McNutt to Harold L. Ickes, October 11, 1935, box 50, McNutt Papers, ISA; Wayne Coy to Marvin H. McIntyre, June 14, 1933, President's Personal File (PPF) 8641, FDR Papers, FDRL; *Facts for Every Democrat: Address of Governor Paul V. McNutt as Temporary Chairman of the Democratic State Convention*, June 12, 1934, Pamphlets Collection, ISL; McNutt address at Purdue University, July 21, 1934 (quotation), box 15, PVMP.

26. *Chicago Journal of Commerce*, February 19, 1935, box A7141, McNutt Papers, ISA; *IN*, February 11, 1935, I-3 (quotations).

27. *IS*, February 4, 1935, 1, 3; *IN*: February 6, 1935, I-1; February 14, 1935, I-6; February 19, 1935, I-1; February 28, 1935, I-1 (cartoon).

28. Franklin D. Roosevelt to McNutt, February 14, 1935, box 105, McNutt Papers, ISA; *IN*, February 16, 1935, I-6; *IS*, February 6, 1935, 1, March 2, 1935, 10, and February 28, 1935, 8.

29. *IS*, February 4, 1935, 1; *IN*: February 16, 1935, I-1 (quotation); Leuchtenburg, *Franklin D. Roosevelt and the New Deal*, 145.

30. Daniel Beland, *Social Security: History and Politics from the New Deal to the Privatization Debate* (Lawrence: University Press of Kansas, 2005), 68–70, 71 (quotation).

31. Kennedy, *Freedom from Fear*, 270–272; George T. Blakey, *Creating a Hoosier Self-Portrait: The Federal Writers' Project in Indiana, 1935–1942* (Bloomington: Indiana University Press, 2005), 33; McNutt message to General Assembly, March 5, 1936, box 8, Information Files, Records of the Administrator of the Federal Security Agency (FSA), Record Group (RG) 235, National Archives at College Park (NACP).

32. McNutt message, March 5, 1936, box 8, Information Files, Records of the Administrator of the FSA, RG 235, NACP; *IN*, March

19, 1936, I-1; *IS,* March 18, 1936, 10; Kennedy, *Freedom from Fear,* 272.

33. *IN:* March 4, 1936, I-3, and March 14, 1936, I-1; *IS:* March 14, 1936, 9; March 12, 1936, 11; and March 8, 1936, 1 (quotation).

34. *IN,* March 19, 1936, I-1.

35. *IN,* March 14, 1936, I-1; James H. Madison, *Indiana through Tradition and Change: A History of the Hoosier State and Its People 1920–1945* (Indianapolis: Indiana Historical Society, 1982), 123 (quotation).

36. Neff, "The Early Career and Governorship of Paul V. McNutt," 275–277; McNutt message, March 5, 1936 (quotations), box 8, Information Files, Records of the Administrator of the FSA, RG 235, NACP.

37. McNutt inaugural address, January 9, 1933, box 14, PVMP.

38. Neff, "The Early Career and Governorship of Paul V. McNutt," 281.

39. Bernice Bernstein oral history, March 3, 1965, 34, Oral History Research Office, Columbia University (OHRO-CU), New York.

40. McNutt address, December 12, 1936, box 8, Information Files, Records of the Administrator of the FSA, RG 235, NACP.

41. *IS,* March 15, 1936, 1.

42. McNutt address, December 12, 1936, box 8, Information Files, Records of the Administrator of the FSA, RG 235, NACP.

43. David L. Stebenne, *Modern Republican: Arthur Larson and the Eisenhower Years* (Bloomington: Indiana University Press, 2006), 154.

44. McNutt to L. Kemper Williams, April 22, 1935, box 110, McNutt Papers, ISA.

45. Carleton McCulloch to Meredith Nicholson, October 3, 1935, box 1, McCulloch Papers, IHS.

46. During the 1933 session of the General Assembly, McNutt declined invitations to speak. See Pleas E. Greenlee to Lewis D. Millman, March 2, 1933, folder 116, box 10, McNutt Papers, ISA. Gradually, he ventured across—and beyond—Indiana. Carleton McCulloch to Meredith Nicholson, April 20, 1934, box 1, McCulloch Papers, IHS.

47. Carleton McCulloch to Meredith Nicholson, October 3, 1935 (quotation), box 1, McCulloch Papers, IHS.

48. Carleton McCulloch to Meredith Nicholson, September 4, 1934, and October 3, 1935 (quotation), box 1, McCulloch Papers, IHS.

49. McNutt to Arthur G. Mitten, folder 7, box 1, Arthur G. Mitten Papers, IHS.

50. *IN,* January 19, 1935, I-1.

51. *IS,* January 19, 1935, 1.

52. Josephine Jackson Hubbard oral history, March 13, 1968, 20, ISL.

53. James Philip Fadely, *Thomas Taggart: Public Servant, Political Boss, 1856–1929* (Indianapolis: Indiana Historical Society, 1997), 152; Carleton McCulloch to Meredith Nicholson, August 2, 1934 (quotations), box 1, McCulloch Papers, IHS.

54. Carleton McCulloch to Meredith Nicholson, July 31, 1935, box 1, McCulloch Papers, IHS.

55. Carleton McCulloch to Meredith Nicholson, December 7, 1934 (first quotation) and October 23, 1933 (second quotation), box 1, McCulloch Papers, IHS.

56. *Boston Transcript,* July 21, 1939, 11; "Portrait of a Lady," *Manila Sunday Tribune Magazine,* March 5, 1939 (quotation).

57. Kathleen McNutt to Meredith Nicholson, August 27, 1933, folder 3, box 1, Meredith Nicholson Papers, IHS.

58. *IN,* July 8, 1935, I-3; Carleton McCulloch to Meredith Nicholson, October 15, 1934, December 7, 1934, and November 13, 1934 (quotation), box 1, McCulloch Papers, IHS.

59. Carleton McCulloch to Meredith Nicholson, January 11, 1935 (1934 in original), box 1, McCulloch Papers, IHS.

60. Carleton McCulloch to Meredith Nicholson, January 27, 1936, and August 20, 1936, box 1, McCulloch Papers, IHS.

61. *IS,* January 10, 1933, 1.

62. Louise McNutt Diary, January 11, 1937, John Krauss Collection (private), Indianapolis, Indiana.

63. *IS*, January 10, 1933, 1; Wayne Coy to Mrs. C. H. Geist, January 20, 1934 (quotations), box 46, McNutt Papers, ISA.

64. *IS*, November 7, 1937, I-6; Jack New, interview with the author, June 23, 2006; *IN*, October 21, 1935, II-1 (quotation).

65. Pleas Greenlee to Charles Michaels, February 6, 1935, box A, drawer 82, McNutt Papers, ISA.

66. Pleas Greenlee to Mary Carney, March 26, 1934, box 39, McNutt Papers, ISA.

67. Dudley Smith to Pleas Greenlee, December 20, 1934, box 83, and press releases, Democratic Legislative News Bureau, February 21 and March 8, 1935, box A7056 (drawer 82, box C), McNutt Papers, ISA.

68. A. M. Threewits to Roy W. Howard, December 12, 1933, box 86, "Annual Report by Lud Denny (Sept. 1935–1936)," September 14, 1936 (first quotation), and Roy W. Howard to Ludwell Denny, December 19, 1936 (second quotation), box 111—all in Roy W. Howard Papers, Manuscript Division, Library of Congress (LC).

69. Ludwell Denny to Roy W. Howard, December 24, 1936, box 111, Howard Papers, LC.

70. "Democratic Press Relations," no date, box 8, file A6801, Matthew E. Welsh Papers, ISA.

71. Donald F. Carmony oral history, July 8, 1985, 6, Center for the Study of History and Memory (CSHM).

72. Kennedy, *Freedom from Fear*, 151; Leuchtenburg, *Franklin D. Roosevelt and the New Deal*, 151 (quotation).

73. Kennedy, *Freedom from Fear*, 297.

74. Neff, "The Early Career and Governorship of Paul V. McNutt," 392 and 376; McNutt to W. D. Richards, December 31, 1935 (quotation), box A7143, McNutt Papers, ISA.

75. Neff, "The Early Career and Governorship of Paul V. McNutt," 376–384.

76. News clipping, "Text of Union Statement on the End of the Strike," no date, folder: Strike—General Strike 1935, Community Affairs File, Vigo County Public Library (VCPL), Terre Haute, Indiana; Donald L.

Bush, "The Terre Haute General Strike," (MS thesis, Indiana State Teachers' College, 1958), 5–23 and 23 (quotation).

77. Sam Beecher et al. to McNutt, July 22, 1935, box A7143, McNutt Papers, ISA.

78. McNutt proclamation, July 22, 1935, and McNutt to Jacob F. Yunginger, August 19, 1935, box A7143, McNutt Papers, ISA.

79. R. S. Foster to McNutt, October 17, 1935; A. G. Burry to McNutt, July 30, 1935; Harold D. Skidmore and Anne Skidmore to McNutt, September 12, 1935; Catherine Coggin to McNutt, September 11, 1935, box A7143, McNutt Papers, ISA.

80. Helen M. Fuchs to McNutt, September 11, 1935, box A7143, McNutt Papers, ISA.

81. Neff, "The Early Career and Governorship of Paul V. McNutt," 399.

82. Powers Hapgood to "Alfred," September 1, 1935, box 6, Powers Hapgood Papers, LL; News clipping, "Socialists Defy Militia," no date (first quotation), box A7143, McNutt Papers, ISA, and Gary L. Bailey, "The Terre Haute, Indiana General Strike, 1935," *Indiana Magazine of History* 80, no. 3 (1984): 223 (second quotation).

83. Handbill, "Fight Fascist Terror!" July 30, 1935 (first quotation), box A7143, McNutt Papers, ISA, and pamphlet, "Paul V. McNutt, Hoosier Hitler," no date [1940] (second quotation), box 30, PVMP.

84. Neff, "The Early Career and Governorship of Paul V. McNutt," 399; Arthur Garfield Hays and Roger N. Baldwin to McNutt, August 27, 1935, box A7143, McNutt Papers, ISA (quotation).

85. Neff, "The Early Career and Governorship of Paul V. McNutt," 399; Dental Technicians Equity of New York City to McNutt, October 15, 1935, box A7143, and Sam Beecher to McNutt, January 25, 1936, box A7101 (drawer 102, box A), both in McNutt Papers, ISA; Bailey, "The Terre Haute, Indiana General Strike, 1935," 223.

86. McNutt to Herman Seide, September 21, 1935, box 7143, McNutt Papers, ISA.

87. Neff, "The Early Career and Governorship of Paul V. McNutt," 406.

88. Ibid., 403–407; Kennedy, *Freedom from Fear*, 289.

89. Oscar R. Ewing to McNutt, July 22, 1932, box 4, Oscar R. Ewing Papers, Harry S. Truman Library (HSTL).

90. McNutt to E. W. Aleon, March 14, 1934, box 35, and Wayne Coy to Oscar R. Ewing, August 30, 1933, box 22, McNutt Papers, ISA.

91. Wayne Coy to Douglas I. McKay, August 22, 1933, box 28; Coy to Oscar R. Ewing, July 10, box 22, McNutt Papers, ISA; Ewing to McNutt, December 17, 1935 (first quotation), and McKay to Ewing, April 19, 1935 (second quotation)—both in box 5, Ewing Papers, HSTL.

92. Wayne Coy to Oscar R. Ewing, August 30, 1933, box 22, McNutt Papers, ISA.

93. Ben F. Garland to Emil Hurja, June 26, 1935 (first quotation), and James A. Farley to Franklin D. Roosevelt, July 6, 1935 (second quotation), box 16, OF 300, FDR Papers, FDRL.

94. Oscar R. Ewing to James H. Hawk, July 5, 1935, box 5, Ewing Papers, HSTL.

95. Mary W. Dewson to Mrs. A. Flynn, April 18, 1934, box 27, DNC—Women's Division Papers, FDRL.

96. *IN*, January 9, 1935, II-1.

97. *IS*, February 10, 1935, 1.

98. McNutt to Edward J. Cullen, February 22, 1935, box A7141, McNutt Papers, ISA.

99. McNutt to Itha McFarland, February 13, 1935, box 101, McNutt Papers, ISA.

100. Burdette Lewis to McNutt, April 1, 1936, box A7096 (drawer 99, box F), McNutt Papers, ISA.

101. Neff, "The Early Career and Governorship of Paul V. McNutt," 432.

102. FDR to McNutt, February 6, 1933, box 12, McNutt Papers, ISA; Stephen Early press release, April 12, 1933, PPF 2836, FDR Papers, FDRL; FDR: Day by Day—The Pare Lorentz Chronology," unpublished manuscript, FDRL; Wayne Coy to Oscar R. Ewing, May 1, 1935, box 5, Ewing Papers, HSTL; Marvin H. McIntyre to FDR, September 11, 1933, PPF 2836, FDR Papers, FDRL.

103. Philip Zoercher to FDR, August 28, 1935 and FDR to McNutt, August 31, 1935 (quotation), PPF 2836, FDR Papers, FDRL.

104. Wayne Coy to Oscar R. Ewing, May 1, 1935, box 5, Ewing Papers, HSTL.

105. Neff, "The Early Career and Governorship of Paul V. McNutt," 420–423; Wayne Coy to Oscar R. Ewing, April 18, 1935, box 5, Ewing Papers, HSTL.

106. Carleton McCulloch to Meredith Nicholson, December 27, 1935 (all quotations), box 1, McCulloch Papers, IHS.

107. Wayne Coy to Oscar R. Ewing, June 3, 1935, box 5, Ewing Papers, HSTL.

108. Wayne Coy to Oscar R. Ewing, June 3, 1935, box 5, Ewing Papers, HSTL.

109. Neff, "The Early Career and Governorship of Paul V. McNutt," 422 (first quotation) and 423 (second quotation).

110. News clipping, "Greenlee Cites 'McHale-ism' as Party Blot," no date (ca. 1936), Della Scott Swinehart Scrapbooks, ISL.

111. Neff, "The Early Career and Governorship of Paul V. McNutt," 424.

112. Carleton McCulloch to Meredith Nicholson, July 13, 1936, box 1, McCulloch Papers, IHS.

113. James P. Goodrich to Everett Watkins, February 16, 1936, box 28, James P. Goodrich Papers, Herbert Hoover Presidential Library (HHPL).

114. *IN*, September 2, 1936, I-8.

115. *IN*, October 7, 1936, I-7.

116. *IS*, September 26, 1936, 1; *IN*, October 10, 1936, I-2; *IN*, October 17, 1936, I-3; Indiana Republican State Committee, "Townsend-McNutt Encourage Convict Labor," undated pamphlet (1936), ISL; *IS*, October 31, 1936, 6 (quotations).

117. Richard Scandrett to James Goodrich, December 1, 1936, box 2, Goodrich Papers, HHPL (quotation); Kennedy, *Freedom from Fear*, 282.

118. *IS*, September 10, 1936, 1; McNutt address at French Lick, August 29, 1936 (quotations), box 16, PVMP.

119. *IS*, September 30, 1936, 7.

120. *IS,* October 29, 1936, 10.

121. *New York Times (NYT),* March 18, 1936, 8; Sherman Minton to McNutt, April 2, 1936, box A7097 (drawer 100, box B), McNutt Papers, ISA; McNutt address at Philadelphia, June 26, 1936, box 16, PVMP; "Gov. Landon Challenged to Disown Hearst," *New York Post,* no date [July 1936] (quotation), PPF 2836, FDR Papers, FDRL.

122. *New York Post,* July 23, 1936, box A7099 (drawer 100, box G), McNutt Papers, ISA.

123. James A. Farley to FDR, July 24, 1936, PPF 2836, FDR Papers, FDRL.

124. Carleton McCulloch to Meredith Nicholson, August 20, 1936, and September 26, 1936, box 1, McCulloch Papers, IHS; James Philip Fadely, "Editors, Whistle Stops, and Elephants: The Presidential Campaign of 1936 in Indiana," *Indiana Magazine of History* 85, no. 2 (June 1989): 115–119.

125. *Washington Evening Star,* December 1, 1935, A-22; Carleton McCulloch to Meredith Nicholson, March 16, 1936 (first quotation), and September 26, 1936 (second quotation), box 1, McCulloch Papers, IHS.

126. *NYT,* June 17, 1936, 2; *Chicago Tribune,* March 22, 1936, pt. 7, 5; *Washington Post (WP),* October 1, 1936, box A7092 (drawer B, box 98), McNutt Papers, ISA; *Bloomington (IN) World,* December 2, 1935, folder 1048, box 108, McNutt Papers, ISA. Neff, "The Early Career and Governorship of Paul V. McNutt," 434 (first quotation) and 430 (second quotation).

127. Kennedy, *Freedom from Fear,* 281; *IS,* October 15, 1935, 5; Fadely, "Editors, Whistle Stops, and Elephants," 107 (quotation). See also *IN,* October 1, 1936, II-1, and October 29, 1936, 1.

128. FDR to McNutt, October 26, 1936, PPF 2836, FDR Papers, FDRL; undated report, "Indiana" (plus attached correspondence), box 52, and James A. Farley to FDR, November 2, 1936, box 35, both in James A. Farley Papers, LC.

129. Madison, *Indiana through Tradition and Change,* 135; James A. Farley to FDR, No-

vember 2, 1936, box 35, Farley Papers, LC; *IS,* November 5, 1936, 10 (quotation).

130. *IS,* January 9, 1937, 8.

131. Madison, *Indiana through Tradition and Change,* 398–400; Hugo C. Songer, "George N. Craig," in *The Governors of Indiana,* ed. Linda Gugin and James E. St. Clair (Indianapolis: Indiana Historical Society Press, 2006), 326; Joseph L. Wert, "Harold W. Handley," in *The Governors of Indiana,* 332; James Philip Fadely, "Matthew E. Welsh," in *The Governors of Indiana,* 338–340; Clifford L. Staten, "Birch Evans Bayh III," in *The Governors of Indiana,* 379.

132. Sherman Minton to James A. Farley, August 10, 1936, box 37, OF 300, FDR Papers, FDRL.

133. James T. Patterson, *The New Deal and the States: Federalism in Transition* (Princeton, NJ: Princeton University Press, 1969), 153.

134. Herbert E. Wilson to McNutt, January 5, 1933, box 9, PVMP.

135. Neff, "The Early Career and Governorship of Paul V. McNutt," preface.

136. William E. Leuchtenburg, *The New Deal and Global War* (New York: Time Life, 1964), 37.

137. McNutt address at Martinsville, April 24, 1935, box 15, PVMP.

138. *IS,* January 9, 1937, 8.

139. Madison, *Indiana through Tradition and Change,* 75–76, 152.

140. *Anderson (IN) Herald,* January 28, 1935, box 91, McNutt Papers, ISA.

141. Ronald J. Allman II, "Edgar D. Whitcomb," in Gugin and St. Clair, *The Governors of Indiana,* 357.

142. *IN,* August 26, 1974, 23; *IN,* September 26, 1974, 1; *IS,* September 21, 1975, 1; *IS,* December 11, 1976, 30; *IN,* January 2, 1978, 7 (quotation).

143. Harold Zink, "Paul V. McNutt," in *The American Politician,* ed. J. T. Salter (Chapel Hill: University of North Carolina Press, 1938), 62.

144. *WP,* October 1, 1936, box A7092 (drawer B, box 98), McNutt Papers, ISA.

145. Patterson, *The New Deal and the States*, 129.

146. See ibid., 129–167, 194–207.

147. Ibid., 149.

148. *IS*, July 13, 1938, 14.

149. John Braeman et al., "Introduction," *The New Deal*, vol. 2, *The State and Local Levels*, ed. John Braeman et al. (Columbus: Ohio State University Press, 1975), xiii.

150. Michael E. McGerr, *A Fierce Discontent: The Rise and Fall of the Progressive Movement in America, 1870–1920* (New York: The Free Press, 2003), 317; Leuchtenburg, *Franklin D. Roosevelt and the New Deal*, 339.

151. McNutt speech in Noblesville, no date [ca. September 18, 1935], box 15, PVMP.

152. McNutt inaugural address, January 9, 1933, box 14, PVMP.

153. Joseph Lash, *Eleanor and Franklin: The Story of Their Relationship Based on Eleanor Roosevelt's Private Papers* (New York: W. W. Norton, 1971), 585, 592.

154. There are no scholarly polls of Indiana's best and worst governors. Former governor Otis R. Bowen cited a Corydon, Indiana, historian who compiled his own listing and placed McNutt as the state's second-best governor, behind Morton. Otis R. Bowen with William Du Bois Jr., *Memoirs from a Public Life* (Bloomington: Indiana University Press, 2000), 170.

155. New, interview with the author; Madison, *Indiana through Tradition and Change*, 152 (quotation).

### 8. BREAKING AWAY (1937–1938)

1. *Bloomington (IN) World*, December 2, 1935, folder 1048, box 108, Paul V. McNutt Papers, Indiana State Archives (ISA).

2. John W. Newson to Franklin D. Roosevelt (FDR), December 16, 1936, folder: McNutt, Paul V. 1933–44, President's Personal File (PPF) 2836, Franklin D. Roosevelt Papers, Franklin D. Roosevelt Library (FDRL); Keith D. McFarland and David L. Roll, *Louis Johnson and the Arming of America: The Roosevelt and Truman Years* (Bloomington: Indiana University Press, 2005), 30–31, 32.

3. William R. Castle Diary, May 11, 1937, vol. 33, 205, Houghton Library (HL).

4. *Indianapolis News (IN)*, October 15, 1936, pt. 2, 1.

5. Henry A. Wallace Diary, February 1, 1940, Henry A. Wallace Papers, University of Iowa Libraries, Iowa City.

6. Frank M. McHale to Kathleen Timolat McNutt Watson, January 17, 1958, Paul V. McNutt Papers and Scrapbooks, John L. Krauss Collection (private), Indianapolis, Indiana.

7. James A. Farley memorandum, December 17, 1936, box 41, James A. Farley Papers, Manuscript Division, Library of Congress (LC).

8. According to Farley, a "wide difference of opinion" surfaced between him and the president over McNutt's future. Farley memorandum, January 13, 1937, box 41, Farley Papers, LC.

9. Farley memorandum, December 17, 1936 (quotation), and January 12, 1937, box 41, Farley Papers, LC.

10. FDR thought about naming Frank C. Walker, a political adviser and future postmaster general, but Walker exhibited interest in a diplomatic posting in France, not the Philippines. The president also consider his attorney general, Homer Cummings, but Cummings begged off. See Farley memorandum, January 13, 1937, box 41, Farley Papers, LC. Homer S. Cummings Diary, December 26, 1936, box 235, Albert and Shirley Small Special Collections Library, University of Virginia (UVA).

11. Francis B. Sayre to Frank Murphy, February 3, 1937, box 5, Francis B. Sayre Papers, LC.

12. Farley memorandum, February 15, 1937, box 41, Farley Papers, LC.

13. Francis B. Sayre to Frank Murphy, February 25, 1937, box 5, Sayre Papers, LC.

14. Frank Hindman Golay, *Face of Empire: United States–Philippine Relations, 1898–1946* (Quezon City, Philippines: Ateneo de Manila University Press, 1997), 47 (quotations), 64.

15. In 1914 Wilson pledged "unyielding allegiance" to the idea of "ultimate independence" for the Philippines and to a program to prepare Filipinos for it. Victor Buencamino Jr. to Manuel L. Quezon, no date [ca. 1914], box 28, Papers of Burton Norvell Harrison and Family, LC.

16. Nick Cullather, *Illusions of Influence: The Political Economy of United States–Philippine Relations, 1942–1960* (Stanford, CA: Stanford University Press, 1994), 8.

17. Rene R. Ecalante, *The Bearer of Pax Americana: The Philippine Career of William H. Taft, 1900–1903* (Quezon City, Philippines: New Day Publishers, 2007), 262. Even José P. Laurel, a prominent Filipino nationalist and critic of American policy in the Philippines, admitted to having "fond" memories of the "distinguished" William Howard Taft. José P. Laurel to Robert A. Taft, June 29, 1940, folder 14, box 28, series 1, José P. Laurel Papers, José P. Laurel Memorial Foundation, Manila, Philippines.

18. Golay, *Face of Empire*, 174.

19. Joseph Ralston Hayden to J. Weldon Jones, March 25, 1937, box 6, J. Weldon Jones Papers, Harry S. Truman Library (HSTL).

20. Manuel Quezon to Francis Burton Harrison, no date [ca. 1921], box 28, Burton Harrison Family Papers, LC; Jack K. Lane, *Armed Progressive: General Leonard Wood* (San Rafael, CA: Presidio Press, 1978), 258.

21. Golay, *Face of Empire*, 230–272.

22. Manuel Quezon to Francis Burton Harrison, April 2, 1928, box 28, Burton Harrison Family Papers, LC.

23. Murphy had appointed FDR's brother-in-law as city controller. In asking to be sent to the Philippines, Murphy probably reasoned that being a governor, even of a colony, would represent a promotion from city hall. Golay, *Face of Empire*, 330–331.

24. Cullather, *Illusions of Influence*, 9–14.

25. Carleton B. McCulloch to Meredith Nicholson, March 5, 1937, box 1, Carleton B. McCulloch Papers, Indiana Historical Society Library (IHS).

26. Meredith Nicholson to Carleton B. McCulloch, June 28, 1937, box 1, McCulloch Papers, IHS.

27. "With an Open Mind," *Philippines Free Press (PFP)*, February 27, 1937, 20.

28. Farley memorandum, March 7, 1937, box 41, Farley Papers, LC; Carleton B. McCulloch to Meredith Nicholson, March 5, 1937, box 1, McCulloch Papers, IHS.

29. Frank McHale to Kathleen Timolat McNutt Watson, January 17, 1958, McNutt Papers and Scrapbooks, Krauss Collection.

30. Ibid.

31. Louise McNutt Diary, April 16, 1937, Krauss Collection.

32. Wayne Coy to the Chief, Bureau of Insular Affairs, January 31, 1938, folder: Paul V. McNutt pt. 2, box 412, Personal Name Information File, 1914–45, Record Group (RG) 350, Records of the Bureau of Insular Affairs (BIA), National Archives at College Park (NACP).

33. *PFP*, February 27, 1937, 20.

34. Paul V. McNutt (hereafter "McNutt") to C. S. Johnston, April 16, 1937, box 9, Paul V. McNutt Papers (PVMP), Lilly Library (LL), Indiana University (IU).

35. "The High Commissioner," *Manila Bulletin (MB)*, February 19, 1937, p. 18; folder 21, box 9, Joseph Ralston Hayden Papers, Bentley Historical Library (BHL).

36. McNutt to C. S. Johnston, April 16, 1937, box 9, PVMP.

37. *Philippines Herald (PH)*, February 19, 1937, 1, 2; *MB*, February 19, 1937, 5.

38. "Dictatorial Government—Its Advantages and Disadvantages," no date, folder 5, box 1, series 5, Laurel Papers, Laurel Foundation.

39. *MB*, no date [ca. February 1937], folder 21, box 9, Hayden Papers, BHL.

40. *PH*, February 19, 1937, 1.

41. *Philippine Tribune*, February 19, 1937, folder 21, box 9, Hayden Papers, BHL.

42. *MB*, February 19, 1937, and *MB*, February 20, 1937, folder 21, box 9, Hayden Papers, BHL.

43. *PH*, February 18, 1937, 4.

44. *MB*, February 25, 1937, p. 12.

45. *PH*, February 22, 1937, 1.

46. *PH*, February 23, 1937, 4.

47. *PH*, February 24, 1937, 1.

48. Eddie Dowling to George H. Earle, May 17, 1937, box 31, George H. Earle Papers, Pennsylvania State Archives, Harrisburg (first quotation); Joseph Ralston Hayden to J. Weldon Jones, March 25, 1937, box 6, Jones Papers, HSTL (subsequent quotation).

49. Bureau of Insular Affairs Radiogram no. 240, April 5, 1937, folder: Paul V. McNutt, pt. 1, box 412, Personal Name Information File, 1914–45, RG 350, NACP.

50. Joseph Ralston Hayden to J. Weldon Jones, March 25, 1937, box 6, Jones Papers, HSTL.

51. J. Weldon Jones to Ford Wilkins, April 1, 1939, box 8, Jones Papers, HSTL.

52. "Mrs. Paul McNutt Writes of Trip," *Martinsville Democrat (MD)*, April 30, 1937, 1.

53. McNutt to C. S. Johnston, April 16, 1937, box 9, PVMP.

54. Joseph C. Grew Diary, April 17, 1937, vol. 85, 3146–3149 (all quotations), Joseph C. Grew Papers, HL.

55. Sidney Fine, *Frank Murphy: The New Deal Years* (Chicago: University of Chicago Press, 1979), 156.

56. "The Role of the AHCommissioner," *Commonwealth Advocate* (Manila, Philippines), November (Second Half) 1936, 39–40.

57. Golay, *Face of Empire*, 343–344.

58. Murphy received a nineteen-gun salute, as any ambassador would, while Quezon got twenty-one guns, the traditional greeting for a head of state. "Personal Salutes," no date, box 39, Burton Harrison Family Papers, LC.

59. George A. Malcolm, "Opinion for the United States High Commissioner," January 9, 1939, box 752, Records of the High Commissioner to the Philippines, RG 126, Office of Territories Classified Files 1907–1951, United States Department of the Interior, NACP.

60. Murphy to Harry H. Woodring, December 31, 1936, box 5, Francis B. Sayre Papers, LC.

61. FDR to McNutt, March 1, 1937, box 6, Records of the Manila Office 1935–1946, RG 126, NACP.

62. Jorge B. Vargas to Manuel Quezon, May 25, 1937, box 152, series 7, Manuel L. Quezon Papers, National Library of the Philippines (NLP).

63. Narrative of McNutt's first stint as high commissioner, no date (all previous quotations), folder: Articles for Administrator (personal), box 1, Information Files, Records of the Administrator of the Federal Security Agency, RG 235, NACP.

64. Ibid.

65. "McNutt Stuff," *Washington Daily News*, May 26, 1937, folder: Radiograms Vol. 2 (1937), box 152, series 7, Quezon Papers, NLP.

66. Typescript notes, "Lansing State Journal" and "Detroit News," both dated May 26, 1937, reel 26, series 4, Quezon Papers, NLP.

67. *PFP*, June 12, 1937, 24.

68. Hugh Johnson, "'Face' and Brains," *New York World-Telegram*, May 24, 1937, Revolving Files: Paul V. McNutt, Social Security Administration Archives (SSAA), Baltimore, Maryland.

69. Westbrook Pegler, "Tom Taggart's Entry," *Kansas City Journal*, May 28, 1937, box 26, PVMP.

70. *PFP*, June 6, 1937, 22.

71. *Fort Wayne (IN) News-Sentinel*, May 22, 1937, 2.

72. Raymond Clapper Diary, June 10, 1937, box 8, Raymond Clapper Papers, LC.

73. Francis Burton Harrison, *Origins of the Philippine Republic: Extracts from the Diaries and Records of Francis Harrison Burton*, ed. Michael P. Oronato (Ithaca, NY: Southeast Asia Program, Department of Asian Studies, Cornell University, 1974), 174.

74. *Washington Daily News*, May 22, 1937, 2; "McNutt Stuff," *Washington Daily News*, May 26, 1937, box 152, series 7, Quezon Papers, NLP.

75. Hugh S. Johnson, "'Face' and Brains," *New York World-Telegram*, May 24, 1937, Revolving Files: Paul V. McNutt, SSAA.

76. *Washington Daily News*, May 22, 1937, 2.

77. "Commissioner McNutt's 'Toasting Incident' Actions Proper, but Misunderstood," *Indianapolis Times* (*IT*), August 16, 1937, folder: Ind. Biography—McNutt, Paul V. Philippines, Indiana Clipping File, Indiana State Library (ISL).

78. Lewis E. Gleeck Jr., *The American Governors-General and High Commissioners in the Philippines: Proconsuls, Nation-Builders and Politicians* (Quezon City, Philippines: New Day Publishers, 1986), 330, 365 (quotation).

79. *PH*, July 23, 1937, 16.

80. *PH*, June 1, 1937, 13.

81. McNutt to Harry H. Woodring, September 17, 1937, box 9, PVMP.

82. "Commissioner McNutt's 'Toasting Incident' Actions," *IT*, August 16, 1937, folder: Ind. Biography—McNutt, Paul V. Philippines, Indiana Clipping File, ISL; Johnson, "'Face' and Brains," *New York World-Telegram*, May 24, 1937, Revolving Files: "Paul V. McNutt," SSAA.

83. Teodoro A. Agoncillo, *History of the Filipino People*, 8th ed. (Quezon City, Philippines: Garotech Publishing, 1990), 382 (all quotations).

84. *MB*, May 26, 1937, p. 12.

85. *PFP*, May 29, 1937, 7.

86. *Philippine Herald Mid-Week Magazine*, May 26, 1937, 12.

87. *PH*, May 29, 1937, 4.

88. *PFP*, May 29, 1937, 7.

89. "Quezon Lights Cigarette for McNutt; Expected Fight Becomes Love Fest," *Indianapolis Star* (*IS*), September 8, 1937, folder: Ind. Biography—McNutt, Paul V., Philippines, Indiana Clipping File, ISL.

90. J. Weldon Jones to McNutt, March 13, 1938, box 8, Jones Papers, HSTL.

91. Jorge Vargas, Quezon's secretary, issued instructions on how Filipinos were to behave in the presence of their president. They were to rise whenever Quezon entered a room; at functions, attendees were introduced to him, not the other way around; and, Vargas emphasized, "The President goes only to parties where he is the guest of honor." Jorge Vargas to Jose Luna Castro, August 11, 1938, box 333, series 7, Quezon Papers, NLP.

92. Typescript news story, no date, folder: Quezon, Manuel L., box 50, Bess Furman Papers, LC.

93. Teodoro A. Agoncillo, "No Finer Paladin: Manuel L. Quezon in Profile," *History and Culture, Language and Literature: Selected Essays of Teodoro Agoncillo*, ed. Bernardita Reyes Churchill (Manila: University of Santo Tomas Publishing House, 2003), 299.

94. Manuel Quezon to Sterling Fisher Jr., March 12, 1937, reel 19, Manuel L. Quezon Papers (microfilm), BHL. "They always say that women couldn't resist Quezon," one Filipina noted. "But neither could men." Theodore Friend, *Between Two Empires: The Ordeal of the Philippines, 1929–1946* (New Haven, CT: Yale University Press, 1965), 51.

95. H. W. Brands, *Bound to Empire: The United States and the Philippines* (New York: Oxford University Press, 1992), 147.

96. Cummings Diary, February 2, 1934, box 234, Cummings Papers, UVA.

97. Brands, *Bound to Empire*, 147.

98. Friend, *Between Two Empires*, 50.

99. George A. Malcolm to Edward J. Kemp, November 5, 1936, box 1, Eleanor Bumgardner Papers, BHL.

100. Manuel Quezon to Roy W. Howard, July 23, 1937, reel 19, Quezon Papers, BHL.

101. Manuel Quezon to McNutt, September 16, 1937 (first two quotations), folder 5, box 1, RG 1—Military Advisor to the Philippine Commonwealth, Douglas A. MacArthur Papers, MacArthur Memorial Archives (MMA); Harrison, *Origins of the Philippine Republic*, 174 (third quotation).

102. Videotaped testimony of Manuel L. Quezon III, Center for Holocaust and Humanity Education, Hebrew Union College, Cincinnati, Ohio.

103. Paulino Misa Capitulo, interview with the author, September 29, 2008, Manila, Philippines.

104. Photo no. FP00653, Retrato Photo Archive, Filipinas Heritage Library, Makati City, Philippines.

105. Manuel Quezon to Roy W. Howard, October 24, 1937 box 133; and Quezon to Howard, May 13, 1939, (quotation), folder: 1939 Philippines, box 158—both in Roy W. Howard Papers, LC.

106. McNutt to Roy W. Howard, December 11, 1937, box 133, Howard Papers, LC.

107. Sergio Mistica, *Manuel L. Quezon: A Character Sketch* (Manila: University of Santo Tomas, 1948), 30.

108. Brands, *Bound to Empire*, 161–163.

109. Narrative of McNutt's first stint as high commissioner, no date, folder: Articles for Administrator (personal), box 1, Information Files, Records of the Administrator of the Federal Security Agency, RG 235, NACP.

110. Alfred W. McCoy, "Quezon's Commonwealth: The Emergence of Philippine Authoritarianism," in *Philippine Colonial Democracy*, ed. Ruby R. Paredes (Quezon City, Philippines: Ateneo de Manila University Press, 1989), 114–157.

111. George A. Malcolm to McNutt, July 6, 1937, box 9, PVMP.

112. "As American Editors See Us (Reprinted Editorial from the *New York Herald-Tribune*)," *MB*, August 13, 1937, 12.

113. Manuel L. Quezon, "The Elimination of Partisanship in a Democracy," an address at Far Eastern University, Manila, August 17, 1940, in Manuel L. Quezon, *Addresses of His Excellency Manuel L. Quezon, President of the Philippines on the Theory of Partyless Democracy* (Manila: Bureau of Printing, 1940), 47 (first quotation) and 53 (second quotation), folder 12, box 24, series 12, Laurel Papers, Laurel Foundation.

114. *PH*, September 16, 1937, 4.

115. *PH*, September 24, 1937, 1.

116. *PH*, September 24, 1937, 4.

117. He had helped to secure Harrison's appointment as governor-general, had complimented him, and had offered him advice. Manuel Quezon to Francis Burton Harrison, August 15, 1913, box 42, and Quezon to Harrison, March 4, 1921, box 28—both in Burton Harrison Family Papers, LC.

118. Harrison, *Origins of the Philippine Republic*, 135.

119. Morris Sheppard to FDR, February 23, 1937; Harry H. Woodring to Marvin H. McIntyre, March 4, 1937; and Woodring to FDR, September 14, 1937, box 17, Official File (OF) 400—Appointments, FDRL.

120. Narrative of McNutt's first stint as high commissioner, no date, folder: Articles for Administrator (personal), box 1, Information Files, Records of the Administrator of the Federal Security Agency, RG 235, NACP.

121. McNutt to Harry H. Woodring, September 17, 1937, box 9, PVMP.

122. Address by Paul V. McNutt at the Ohio Society of New York City, March 8, 1937, box 16, PVMP.

123. "Rock of Refuge," *Commonwealth Advocate*, March 1938, 39.

124. Narrative of McNutt's first stint as high commissioner, no date, folder: Articles for Administrator (personal), box 1, Information Files, Records of the Administrator of the Federal Security Agency, RG 235, NACP.

125. H. E. Yarnell to McNutt, April 1, 1937 (all quotations), box 9, PVMP; Golay, *Face of Empire*, 363–364.

126. *PH*, August 23, 1937, 1.

127. *PH*, December 15, 1937, 1.

128. McNutt to H. E. Yarnell, December 24, 1938, box 10, PVMP.

129. McNutt to Roy W. Howard, December 11, 1937 (all quotations), box 133, Howard Papers, LC.

130. *PFP*, March 26, 1938, 44.

131. FDR to McNutt, March 1, 1937, box 6, Records of the Manila Office 1935–1946, RG 126, NACP.

132. McNutt to Roy W. Howard, December 11, 1937, box 133, Howard Papers, LC.

133. McNutt to James Roosevelt, January 12, 1938, box 45, James Roosevelt Papers, FDRL.

134. McNutt to H. E. Yarnell, December 24, 1938, box 10, PVMP.

135. H. E. Yarnell to McNutt, April 1, 1937, box 9, PVMP.

136. Roy W. Howard to G. B. Parker, November 23, 1935, folder: Letters & Articles 1935 October– December, Roy W. Howard Papers, Roy W. Howard Archive, Indiana University (IU) School of Journalism, Bloomington.

137. "Araneta Speaks on Radio Against 'Untimely Independence' for Philippines," *MB*, October 7, 1939, reel 1, Salvador Araneta Papers, BHL.

138. National Broadcasting Company press release, "Philippine-American Relations," a speech by Paul V. McNutt, March 14, 1938, box 146, Howard Papers, LC.

139. *MB*, March 25, 1937, 3.

140. Cullather, *Illusions of Influence*, 24–25 (all quotations).

141. "Filipinos Compatriots!" *Commonwealth Advocate*, March 1938, 48.

142. "A Radical Change of Attitude" and "Realistic Re-examination," *Commonwealth Advocate*, March 1938, 5–6.

143. *PFP*, September 25, 1937, 41.

144. Harrison, *Origins of the Philippine Republic*, 135.

145. McNutt to Maple T. Harl, May 27, 1937, box 9, PVMP.

146. Roy W. Howard to Richard C. Wilson, July 20, 1937, box 133, Howard Papers, LC.

147. McNutt to Roy W. Howard, December 11, 1937, box 133, Howard Papers, LC.

148. Roy W. Howard to G. B. Parker, November 23, 1935, folder: Letters & Articles 1935 October–December, Howard Papers, IU.

149. McNutt to H. E. Yarnell, December 24, 1938, box 10, PVMP.

150. Manuel L. Quezon press conference, November 27, 1937, reel 16, series 3, Quezon Papers, NLP.

151. *PH*, March 13, 1937, 4.

152. Newspaper column by James G. Wingo, "McNutt Visit May Change Our Attitude on Philippines," no date [February 1938], box 178, Clapper Papers, LC.

153. Arsenio N. Luz to Roy W. Howard, April 20, 1937, box 133, Howard Papers, LC.

154. McNutt to Roy W. Howard, December 11, 1937, box 133, Howard Papers, LC.

155. Wingo, "McNutt Visit May Change Our Attitude on Philippines"; Wayne Coy, Memorandum for the File, October 17, 1938, box 10, PVMP.

156. Golay, *Face of Empire*, 365.

157. McNutt to Roy W. Howard, December 11, 1937, box 133, Howard Papers, LC.

158. Golay, *Face of Empire*, 371.

159. National Broadcasting Company press release, "Philippine-American Relations," a speech by Paul V. McNutt.

160. McNutt to James Roosevelt, January 12, 1938, box 45, James Roosevelt Papers, FDRL.

161. National Broadcasting Company press release, "Philippine-American Relations," a speech by Paul V. McNutt.

162. Alfred W. McCoy, *Policing America's Empire: The United States, the Philippines, and the Rise of the Surveillance State* (Madison: University of Wisconsin Press, 2009), 15.

163. Melvyn P. Leffler, *A Preponderance of Power: National Security, the Truman Administration, and the Cold War* (Stanford, CA: Stanford University Press, 1992), 13.

164. *MB*, June 21, 1937, 14.

165. *IN*, February 18, 1938, 7.

166. *IN*, February 18, 1938, 7.

167. "Everyone Goes to McNutt Party but New Dealers," *New York Herald Tribune*, ca. February 23, 1938, 1, 8, box 178, Clapper Papers, LC.

168. *PFP*, March 19, 1938, 43.

169. Quezon press conference, March 16, 1938, 1–2, 33, reel 16, series 3, Quezon Papers, NLP.

170. Quezon radiogram to McNutt, March 16, 1938, box 18, OF 400, FDRL.

171. *PH*, July 1, 1938, 4.

172. Wayne Coy to A. V. H. Hardendorp, March 11, 1940, box 7, Wayne Coy Papers, FDRL.

173. Quezon radiogram to McNutt, March 16, 1938.

174. Dwight D. Eisenhower Diary (quoting McNutt), July 16, 1939, box 24, Miscellaneous File, Dwight D. Eisenhower Pre-presidential Papers, Dwight D. Eisenhower Library (DDEL).

175. Golay, *Face of Empire*, 375–376.

176. McNutt to FDR, June 30, 1938, box 10, PVMP.

177. Coy, Memorandum for the File, October 17, 1938, box 10, PVMP.

178. McNutt to FDR, June 30, 1938, box 10, PVMP.

179. FDR to McNutt, September 29, 1938, box 10, PVMP.

180. Golay, *Face of Empire*, 378–379.

181. *PH*, April 29, 1938, 2.

182. *PH*, March 16, 1938, 4.

183. *PH*, March 25, 1938, 4 (quotation); *PH*, March 23, 1938, 4.

184. *PH*, April 29, 1938, 2.

185. Cordell Hull to FDR, March 19, 1938, box 18, OF 400—Appointments, FDRL.

186. Sergio Osmeña to Manuel Quezon, March 25, 1939 and Quezon to Bennett Clar, April 13, 1939, box 440, Sol Gwekoh Papers, University of the Philippines (UP)—Diliman, Quezon City, Philippines.

187. J. Weldon Jones to McNutt, September 28, 1939, box 8, Jones Papers, HSTL.

188. *PH*, September 26, 1939, 4.

189. *PH*, September 14, 1939, 1; *PH*, September 30, 1939, 1.

190. George A. Malcolm to McNutt, February 7, 1938, box 10, PVMP.

191. Francis B. Sayre to McNutt, November 18, 1938, box 10, PVMP; *PH*, August 2, 1939, 1.

192. *PH*, September 26, 1939, 1.

193. J. Weldon Jones to McNutt, September 28, 1939, box 8, Jones Papers, HSTL.

194. *PH*, April 24, 1937, 1.

195. Narrative of McNutt's first stint as high commissioner, no date, folder: Articles for Administrator (personal), box 1, Information Files, Records of the Administrator of the Federal Security Agency, RG 235, NACP.

196. *PFP*, May 7, 1938, 29; J. Weldon Jones to McNutt, April 16, 1937, box 8, Jones Papers, HSTL.

197. *PFP*, October 9, 1937, 31; *MD*, July 30, 1937, 2 (quotation).

198. J. Weldon Jones to McNutt, April 16, 1937, box 8, Jones Papers, HSTL.

199. McNutt to Maple T. Harl, May 27, 1937, box 9, PVMP.

200. David Dalton, *Rough Guide to the Philippines* (New York: Rough Guides, 2007), 468.

201. José P. Laurel to James M. Langley, May 21, 1956, folder 9, box 5, series 5, Laurel Papers, Laurel Foundation.

202. McNutt to Maple T. Harl, May 27, 1937, box 9, PVMP.

203. *IS*, April 19, 1938, 2; *PFP*, May 7, 1938, 29 (quotation).

204. *MD*, July 30, 1937, 2.

205. *PFP*, November 26, 1938, 27.

206. Carleton B. McCulloch to Meredith Nicholson, November 5, 1937, box 1, McCulloch Papers, IHS.

207. *PH*, April 27, 1937, 2.

208. *MD*, July 30, 1937, 2 (quotations).

209. Louise McNutt Diary, February 16, 1946, Krauss Collection.

210. Clapper Diary, July 14, 1939, box 178, Clapper Papers, LC.

211. *PFP*, February 19, 1938, 29; McNutt to Herman B Wells, May 11, 1938, folder: McN, box 16, Presidential Papers, Herman B Wells Papers, Indiana University Archives (IUA).

212. Louise McNutt Diary, May 15, 1938, Krauss Collection.

213. *MB*, August 30, 1939, 7.

214. See Mamie Doud Eisenhower to Mr. and Mrs. John Doud, May 7, 1937, box 2, Barbara Eisenhower Papers, DDEL.

215. See Leo M. Gardner to Dwight D. Eisenhower, September 6, 1957, box 885, Official File 212, White House Central Files, Eisenhower Papers, DDEL.

216. Stephen E. Ambrose, *Eisenhower,* vol. 1, *Soldier, General of the Army, President-Elect* (New York: Simon and Schuster, 1983), 109–110, 111 (quotation).

217. Peter Lyon, *Eisenhower: Portrait of the Hero* (Boston: Little, Brown, 1974), 81.

218. Undated news clipping, folder 1, box 1, RG 1, MacArthur Papers, MMA.

219. *PFP,* April 17, 1937, 25.

220. "Notes of an interview with General MacArthur on board the *President Coolidge,*" June 18, 1937, folder 4, box 1, RG 1, MacArthur Papers, MMA.

221. News clipping, "McNutt Lauds MacArthur," October 5, 1937, folder 23, box 9, Hayden Papers, BHL.

222. When rumors emerged from the high commissioner's office that American troops were spying on Filipinos, the general took charge and jotted a note of denial to Quezon, stressing that such skulduggery had "no proper place in the Army of Democracy." Douglas A. MacArthur to Manuel Quezon, June 19, 1937, folder 4, box 1, RG 1, MacArthur Papers, MMA.

223. James Ord to Dwight David Eisenhower, July 18, 1937, box 24, Miscellaneous File, Eisenhower Pre-presidential Papers, DDEL.

224. Eisenhower Diary, July 16, 1939 (all quotations), box 24, Miscellaneous File, Eisenhower Pre-presidential Papers, DDEL.

225. *PFP,* May 8, 1937, 22; *PFP,* July 24, 1937, 21; *PFP,* January 15, 1938, 31; *PFP,* December 4, 1937, 26; *PH,* December 23, 1937, 1.

226. *PFP,* April 10, 1937, 24.

227. *PFP,* May 1, 1937, 4.

228. *PFP,* June 19, 1937, 38.

229. "McNutt's Policies Win Respect of Filipinos," *Fort Wayne (IN) Journal-Gazette,* July 11, 1937, box 9, PVMP; Reece A. Oliver to Kenneth F. Oliver, June 29, 1939, folder: Letters 1917–1950, Reece A. Oliver Papers, ISL; *MD,* May 14, 1937, 2; *MD,* August 6, 1937, 2.

230. *PH,* September 10, 1937, 1.

231. *PH* (Gravure Section), October 23, 1937, 1.

232. *PH,* February 23, 1937, 4.

233. *PH,* September 17, 1938, 1; *PFP,* April 8, 1939, 36-A.

234. *PFP,* August 5, 1939, 8.

235. *PFP,* December 16, 1939, 8; *PH,* July 13, 1938, 4.

236. *PH,* September 13, 1938, 4.

237. *PH,* July 13, 1938, 4.

238. Statement attached to Wayne Coy to Roy C. Bennett, May 21, 1937, box 9, PVMP.

239. *PH,* August 27, 1937, 1 (quotation); McNutt to M. Clifford Townsend, September 10, 1937, box A6967 (drawer 112, box C), M. Clifford Townsend Papers, ISA; Maurice Judd to McNutt, September 21, 1937, folder: Paul V. McNutt 1935–39, Personal Papers, Wells Papers, IUA.

240. Eugene B. Crowe to McNutt, May 29, 1937 (quotation), and Frank M. McHale to McNutt, July 2, 1937—both in box 9, PVMP.

241. Clapper Diary, September 2, 1937, box 8, Clapper Papers, LC.

242. Frank McHale to McNutt, July 2, 1937, box 9, PVMP.

243. Newspaper clipping, "Townsend Pledges Support to M'Nutt for Presidency; Minton Boomed by Friends," no date, folder: 1937 July, box 9, PVMP.

244. McNutt to Herman B Wells, August 26, 1937, folder: McN 1937–38, Presidential Papers, Wells Papers, IUA.

245. Radiogram, McNutt to Frank Hockham, November 14, 1937, box 412, Personal Name Information File, 1914–45, RG 350, Records of the Bureau of Insular Affairs (BIA), NACP.

246. Clapper Diary, February 25, 1938, box 8, Clapper Papers, LC.

247. McNutt to M. Clifford Townsend, September 10, 1937, box A6967 (drawer 112, box C), Townsend Papers, ISA.

248. Clapper Diary, February 25, 1938, box 8, Clapper Papers, LC (quotation). Rumors to this effect had circulated for a while. See Roy W. Howard to Manuel Quezon, July 23, 1939, box 133, Howard Papers, LC.

249. McNutt to FDR, July 3, 1938, box 10, PVMP.

250. Thomas D. Clark, *Indiana University: Midwestern Pioneer*, vol. 2, *In Mid-Passage* (Bloomington: Indiana University Press, 1973), 250 (quotation), 251–263, 388.

251. McNutt to M. Clifford Townsend, September 10, 1937, box A6967 (drawer 112, box C), Townsend Papers, ISA.

252. Clark, *Indiana University*, vol. 2, 400.

253. Ora L. Wildermuth to the Trustees of Indiana University, April 12, 1937, folder: Presidential Selection—Judge O. L. Wildermuth Letters to Trustees 1936–37, William Lowe Bryan Papers, IUA.

254. "McNutt Will Be Offered Indiana 'U' Job, Report," *MB*, folder 22, box 9, Hayden Papers, BHL.

255. Herman B Wells to McNutt, January 10, 1938, folder: Paul V. McNutt 1935–39, Personal Papers, Wells Papers, IUA.

256. Margaret H. Kruke to President of the Board of Trustees, March 15, 1938, folder: Kru 1937–1938, Presidential Papers, Wells Papers, IUA.

257. N. L. Benson to Val Nolan, September 21, 1937, box 1, Val Nolan Papers, LL.

258. Meredith Nicholson to Carleton B. McCulloch, December 2, 1937, box 1, McCulloch Papers, IHS.

259. James H. Capshew, *Herman B Wells: The Promise of the American University* (Bloomington: Indiana University Press, 2012), 98.

260. O. L. Wildermuth to M. Clifford Townsend, July 14, 1937, folder: Wil, drawer 114, box D, Townsend Papers, ISA.

261. Board of Trustees minutes, August 9, 1937, IUA; "Wildermuth to Influence McNutt Boom," *Gary (IN) Post-Tribune*, February 25, 1938, Clipping File: Paul Vories McNutt, IUA.

262. Board of Trustees minutes, November 23, 1937, IUA; "Herman Wells, Seen as New I.U. Prexy, Visits in Calumet," no date, Clipping File: Paul Vories McNutt, IUA.

263. Board of Trustees minutes, March 22, 1938, IUA.

264. Clark, *Indiana University*, vol. 2, 405.

265. Herman B Wells, *Being Lucky: Reminiscences and Reflections* (Bloomington: Indiana University Press, 1980), 94–95.

266. With Wells working for the university and McNutt toying with the university, the choice for some trustees was obvious. One trustee ruled out the candidacy of "any political figure." "McNutt As I.U. President 'Out,'" *IS*, January 7, 1938, Clipping File: Paul Vories McNutt, IUA.

267. O. L. Wildermuth to M. Clifford Townsend, July 14, 1937, folder: Wil, drawer 114, box D, Townsend Papers, ISA.

268. Herman B Wells to McNutt, February 24, 1938, folder: Paul V. McNutt 1935–39, Personal Papers, Wells Papers, IUA; Wells, *Being Lucky*, 105.

269. Herman B Wells to McNutt, October 10, 1938, and January 14, 1939, folder: Paul V. McNutt 1935–39, Personal Papers; McNutt to Wells, May 11, 1938, folder: McN 1937–38, Presidential Papers—both in Wells Papers, IUA.

270. Thomas D. Clark, *Indiana University: Midwestern Pioneer*, vol. 3, *Years of Fulfillment* (Bloomington: Indiana University Press, 1977), 644.

271. Mrs. A. J. Calpha to Board of Trustees, March 18, 1938, folder: Cal 1937–38, Presidential Papers, Wells Papers, IUA.

272. McNutt to Herman B Wells, May 11, 1938, folder: McN 1937–38, Presidential Papers, Wells Papers, IUA.

9. HUMANITARIAN—AND HOME (1937–1939)

1. David S. Wyman, *The Abandonment of the Jews: America and the Holocaust, 1941–1945* (New York: New Press, 1998). Wyman does not mention the Philippine venture in his earlier book, *Paper Walls: America and the Refugee Crisis, 1938–1941* (Amherst: University of Massachusetts Press, 1968).

2. Pamphlet, "Paul V. McNutt, Hoosier Hitler," no date [ca. 1940], folder: 1940 Jan.–June 1940, box 30, Paul V. McNutt Papers

(PVMP), Lilly Library (LL), Indiana University (IU).

3. James H. Madison, *Indiana through Tradition and Change: A History of the Hoosier State and Its People 1920–1945* (Indianapolis: Indiana Historical Society, 1982), 49–75; Ralph H. Storm, "Foreign Groups and Settlements in Morgan County," reel 18, Indiana Federal Writers' Project Papers (IFWPP), Indiana State University Library, Terre Haute; Joanne Raetz Stuttgen, *Martinsville: A Pictorial History* (St. Louis: G. Bradley Publishing, 1995), 156–157.

4. News clipping, "J. M. Neely Died Sunday," no date [March 1921], folder: Printed—Clippings, box 1, Neely Family Papers and McNutt address in Manila, March 30, 1939 (quotation), box 17, PVMP, both in LL.

5. Grace Woody to Paul V. McNutt ("McNutt"), no date, Ruth Neely McNutt Remembrance Book, John L. Krauss Collection (private), Indianapolis; Irwin F. Gellman, *Secret Affairs: Franklin Roosevelt, Cordell Hull, and Sumner Welles* (New York: Enigma Books, 2002), 20–21.

6. Richard Morris Clutter, "The Indiana American Legion, 1919–1960" (PhD diss., Indiana University, 1974), 92.

7. McNutt address at Des Moines, Iowa, July 12, 1928 (quotations), box 14, PVMP.

8. "Text of McNutt's Address in Harlem," *New York Times* (*NYT*) January 29, 1942 (first quotation), fiche 2, Department of Indiana, Biographical Files—Paul V. McNutt, National Headquarters of the American Legion Library, Indianapolis; "End Racial Bias, McNutt Urges," *Boston Daily Globe*, June 27, 1947, 17 (second quotation), box 27, PVMP.

9. John C. McNutt to McNutt, September 1, 1927, box 3, PVMP.

10. Emma Lou Thornbrough, *Indiana Blacks in the Twentieth Century* (Bloomington: Indiana University Press, 2000), 88–89; John K. Jennings to Carleton B. McCulloch, August 20, 1924, box 1, John K. Jennings Papers, LL; Mrs. Zorn A. Smith to R. Earl Peters, May 20, 1932, box 1, R. Earl Peters

Papers, Allen County–Fort Wayne Historical Society (ACHS), Fort Wayne, Indiana; Madison, *Indiana through Tradition and Change,* 47, 52.

11. McNutt to Mrs. Alto Griffin, September 26, 1934, box 76; F. B. Ransom to McNutt, March 14, 1936, box 104; Ransom to Pleas E. Greenlee, October 22, 1935, and Greenlee to Ransom, November 4, 1935, box A7064 (drawer 86, box A), Paul V. McNutt Papers, Indiana State Archives (ISA), Indianapolis.

12. Thornbrough, *Indiana Blacks in the Twentieth Century,* 80; Pleas Greenlee to Carroll W. Cannon, Indiana, December 3, 1934, box A7052, Secretary's File—General Correspondence 1934, McNutt Papers, ISA. Frank Ephraim, *Escape to Manila: From Nazi Tyranny to Japanese Terror* (Urbana: University of Illinois Press, 2003) 28 (quotation).

13. Mrs. Margaret B. Headdy to Jacob Weiss, July 13, 1936, folder: Kir, box A7095 (drawer 99, box D), McNutt Papers, ISA.

14. *Indianapolis Times* (*IT*), March 29, 1933, 7, and September 12, 1933, 9.

15. *IT,* March 25, 1933, 4.

16. McNutt to Bernard S. Deutsch, June 7, 1933, box 21, McNutt Papers, ISA.

17. McNutt handwritten notes attached to "Memoranda on Jewish Situation in Germany," no date, box A7136, McNutt Papers, ISA.

18. McNutt address in Manila, February 24, 1939, box 17, PVMP.

19. Handwritten notes, no date [January 1935] and McNutt to Rabbi Louis D. Gross, January 22, 1935 (quotation), box 95, McNutt Papers, ISA.

20. *Indianapolis Star* (*IS*), March 28, 1933, 1.

21. *Indianapolis News* (*IN*), March 28, 1933, 12 (first quotation); and *NYT,* March 28, 1933, 11 (subsequent quotations).

22. Morris Strauss to McNutt, September 5, 1933, and Pleas Greenlee to *Indiana Jewish Chronicle,* September 6, 1933, and McNutt proclamation, no date [1933] (quotations), box A7054, Secretary's File—General Correspondence 1934, McNutt Papers, ISA.

23. McNutt proclamation, no date [1934], box A7054, Secretary's File—General Correspondence 1934, McNutt Papers, ISA.

24. Arnold A. Offner, *American Appeasement: United States Foreign Policy and Germany, 1933–1938* (Cambridge, MA: Belknap Press of Harvard University Press, 1969), 68. Secretary of State Cordell Hull, meanwhile, avoided Jewish issues: Gellman, *Secret Affairs*, 98.

25. *IN*, January 19, 1935, I-6.

26. Cantor Myro Glass to McNutt, January 25, 1935, box 97, McNutt Papers, ISA.

27. McNutt to Cantor Myro Glass, January 28, 1935, box 97, McNutt Papers, ISA.

28. Raymond Clapper Diary, February 25, 1940, box 9, Raymond Clapper Papers, Manuscript Division, Library of Congress (LC).

29. McNutt message to General Assembly, January 10, 1933, box 14, PVMP.

30. *NYT*, March 28, 1933, 11.

31. McNutt speech on "Cultural Pluralism in America," no date, box 23, PVMP.

32. McNutt address in Manila, March 30, 1939, box 17, PVMP.

33. Clapper Diary, February 25, 1938 (quotation), box 8, Clapper Papers, LC.

34. McNutt to Abba Hillel Silver, January 14, 1942, box 11, Records of the Federal Security Administrator: General Classified Files, 1939–1944, Alphabetical Series, Record Group (RG) 235, National Archives at College Park (NACP).

35. Madison, *Indiana through Tradition and Change*, 132; Stanley Karnow, *In Our Image: America's Empire in the Philippines* (New York: Ballantine, 1989), 344; Lewis E. Gleeck Jr., *The American Governors-General and High Commissioners in the Philippines: Proconsuls, Nation-Builders and Politicians* (Quezon City, Philippines: New Day Publishers, 1986), 319–321. As governor, McNutt joined the American Hellenic Educational Progressive Association and became the first governor of Indiana to issue greetings to Greek groups. "A Tribute to the Memory of Paul V. McNutt," Paul V. McNutt Obituaries (compiled by Grace Woody), Krauss Collection; untitled narrative of McNutt's tenure as high commissioner, no date, box 1, Information Files, Records of the Administrator of the Federal Security Agency (FSA), General Records of the Department of Health, Education, and Welfare, RG 235, NACP; Pat Frank, "Speaking Frankly," February 2, 1940, typescript newspaper column, box 30, PVMP.

36. McNutt to Frank M. McHale, August 30, 1939 (all quotations), box 10, PVMP.

37. *Herald Mid-Week Magazine*, September 2, 1936, 5; "Germans, Austrians Here Renew Oath," *Manila Bulletin (MB)*, April 2, 1938, box 27, J. Weldon Jones Papers, Harry S. Truman Library (HSTL); untitled narrative of McNutt's tenure as high commissioner, no date (quotations), box 1, Information Files—FSA, RG 235, NACP.

38. "Washington Reports German Club Row," *MB*, August 31, 1938, box 27, Jones Papers, HSTL.

39. Frank Ephraim, "Draft: Nomination for Righteous among Nations," September 1, 2004, Center for Holocaust and Humanity Education, Hebrew Union College (HUC); untitled narrative of McNutt's tenure as high commissioner, no date, box 1, Information Files—FSA, RG 235, NACP; George A. Malcolm, memorandum on immigration, no date, and executive order attached to Franklin D. Roosevelt to Frank Murphy, October 28, 1935 (quotations), reel 9, George A. Malcolm Papers, National Library of the Philippines (NLP). See also Harry H. Woodring to McNutt, March 1, 1937, box 6, Records of the Manila Office 1935–1946, Records of the High Commissioner to the Philippine Islands, RG 126, NACP.

40. Ephraim, *Escape to Manila*, 23.

41. Jay Pierrepont Moffat Diary, April 13, 1938, volume 40, Jay Pierrepont Moffat Papers, Houghton Library (HL); Richard Breitman and Alan M. Kraut, *American Refugee Policy and European Jewry, 1933–1945* (Bloomington: Indiana University Press, 1987), 7–8 (all quotations).

42. Henry L. Feingold, *The Politics of Rescue: The Roosevelt Administration and the Holocaust, 1938–1945* (New Brunswick, NJ: Rutgers University Press, 1970), 295–307; Breitman and Kraut, *American Refugee Policy and European Jewry*, 9 (quotation).

43. Wyman, *Paper Walls*, xiii, 212.

44. Nick Cullather, *Illusions of Influence: The Political Economy of United States–Philippine Relations, 1942–1960* (Stanford, CA: Stanford University Press, 1994), 14–16; *MB*, April 23, 1936, 1; "Over 11,000 Ask Opportunity to Go to Mindanao," *MB*, April 13, 1939, box 29, Joseph Ralston Hayden Papers, Bentley Historical Library (BHL), University of Michigan; Raul Pertierra and Eduardo F. Ugarte, "American Rule in the Muslim South and the Philippine Hinterlands," in *Mixed Blessing: The Impact of the American Colonial Experience on Politics and Society in the Philippines*, ed. Hazel M. McFerson (Westport, CT: Greenwood Press, 2002), 201. Thomas M. McKenna, *Muslim Rulers and Rebels: Everyday Politics and Armed Separatism in the Southern Philippines* (Berkeley: University of California Press, 1998), 115; Grant K. Goodman, *Four Aspects of Philippine-Japanese Relations, 1930–1940* (New Haven, CT: Southeast Asia Studies, Yale University, 1967), 11–16; George L. Brandt to George S. Messersmith, December 24, 1938, file: 811B.55/237, box 245, General Visa Correspondence 1914–1940, Visa Division, Department of State, General Records of the Department of State, RG 59, National Archives Building (NAB).

45. Ephraim, *Escape to Manila*, 27–28; "Memorandum of Conversation between Hyman and Frieder," November 28, 1938, Joint Distribution Committee Archives #38/44, file #784 (1 of 3), HUC; untitled narrative of McNutt's tenure as high commissioner, no date (quotation), box 1, Information Files—FSA, RG 235, NACP.

46. Lewis E. Gleeck Jr., "The History of the Jewish Community of Manila," ca. 1991, 2–18, copy in LC; Abraham I. Feldbin and Josef Schwarz, "The Jewish Community of Manila," unpublished manuscript, 2–3, U.S.

Holocaust Memorial Museum (USHMM); the figure of five hundred comes from memorandum of conversation between Hyman and Frieder, November 28, 1938, Joint Distribution Committee Archives #38/44, file #784 (1 of 3), HUC. The figure of four hundred comes from the testimony of Ilse May, August 14, 1997, USHMM.

47. Memorandum of conversation between Hyman and Frieder, November 28, 1938 (all quotations), Joint Distribution Committee Archives #38/44, file #784 (1 of 3), HUC.

48. McNutt to Julius Weiss, May 19, 1938 (all quotations), box 1, Wendell L. Willkie Papers, LL.

49. Sumner Welles to George Rublee, December 13, 1938, box 6, Country Files, Records Relating to the Intergovernmental Committee on Refugees (IGR), RG 59, NACP; Malcolm, memorandum on immigration policy, no date, frames 178–180, reel 9, Malcolm Papers, NLP.

50. Breitman and Kraut, *American Refugee Policy and European Jewry*, 48–49.

51. Wilbur J. Carr to Judge Moore, January 21, 1937, box 14, Wilbur J. Carr Papers, LC.

52. McNutt to Julius Weiss, May 19, 1938, box 1, Willkie Papers, LL.

53. Testimony of Manuel L. Quezon III, HUC.

54. Testimonies of Alice Weston and Manuel L. Quezon III, HUC.

55. "Refugee Immigration in the Philippines," no date [ca. 1940], Jewish Joint Distribution Committee Archives #38/44, file #784 (1 of 3), HUC; Testimony of Alice Weston, HUC; "Jewish Refugee Problem," no date, and McNutt radiogram, July 16, 1938 (quotation), folder: 28943 to, box 1338, General Classified Files 1914–1940, Bureau of Insular Affairs (BIA), RG 350, NACP.

56. Cordell Hull to Harry H. Woodring, September 12, 1938, and McNutt radiogram, September 15, 1938 (quotations), folder: 28943 to, box 1338, General Classified Files 1914–1940, BIA, RG 350, NACP.

57. Breitman and Kraut, *American Refugee Policy and European Jewry*, 56–62; George S. Messersmith to Louis D. Brandeis, October 24, 1938, Item #1054, George S. Messersmith Papers, University of Delaware Library, Newark; Cordell Hull to Harry H. Woodring, September 12, 1938, and Assistant Secretary of State to Woodring, October 8, 1938, folder: 28943 to, box 1338, General Classified Files 1914–1940, BIA, RG 350, NACP.

58. McNutt radiogram, November 21, 1938, folder: 28943 to, box 1338, General Classified Files 1914–1940, BIA, RG 350, NACP.

59. Assistant Secretary of State to Harry H. Woodring, October 8, 1938 (quotation), and McNutt radiogram, October 1, 1938, folder: 28943 to, box 1338, General Classified Files 1914–1940, BIA, RG 350, NACP.

60. McNutt radiogram, November 18, 1938, folder: 28943 to, box 1338, General Classified Files 1914–1940, BIA, RG 350, NACP.

61. "Jewish Refugee Problem," no date, folder: 28943 to, box 1338, General Classified Files 1914–1940, BIA, RG 350, NACP.

62. Elizalde radio message at the end of McNutt radiogram, November 21, 1938, folder: 28943 to, box 1338, General Classified Files 1914–1940, BIA, RG 350, NACP.

63. "Righteous Indignation," *MB*, November 21, 1938, box 57, Jones Papers, HSTL.

64. *Philippines Free Press* (*PFP*), November 26, 1938, 32.

65. *MB*, November 21, 1938, 1.

66. McNutt, on December 2, 1938, solicited advice from the State Department on the Mindanao Plan. Interestingly, more than a month later, on January 18, 1939, officials at State claimed credit for taking the initiative. Proposed reply to the High Commissioner's Telegram, No. 903, of December 2 to the Bureau of Insular Affairs, no date, and Memorandum of Conversation Regarding Refugee Colonization in Mindanao, January 18, 1939, box 6, Country Files, IGR Records, RG 59, NACP.

67. "Willing to Aid Refugees, Says Quezon," *Manila Tribune*, December 6, 1938, box 57, Jones Papers, HSTL.

68. George L. Brandt to George S. Messersmith, February 17, 1939, file: 811B.55/40, box 244, General Visa Correspondence 1914–1940, RG 59, NAB.

69. "Mindanao Plan Wins Approval," *MB*, December 9, 1938, box 57, Jones Papers, HSTL; McNutt address at White Sulphur Springs, May 8, 1941, box 19, PVMP; *IN*, January 1, 1938, II-1 (both questions).

70. McNutt radiogram, December 3, 1938, folder: 28943 to, box 1338, General Classified Files 1914–1940, BIA, RG 350, NACP.

71. Sumner Welles to Harry H. Woodring, December 8, 1938, folder: 28943 to, box 1338, General Classified Files 1914–1940, BIA, RG 350, NACP.

72. Henry J. Morgenthau Jr., "Refugees (Up to the Outbreak of War: 1938–39)," May 19, 1946, 5, box 406, Henry J. Morgenthau Jr. Papers, Franklin D. Roosevelt Library (FDRL); Benjamin Welles, *Sumner Welles: FDR's Global Strategist* (New York: St. Martin's Press, 1997), 225; Gellman, *Secret Affairs*, 97, 137, 229; Sumner Welles to FDR, November 28, 1938, *Documentary History of the Franklin D. Roosevelt Presidency*, vol. 12, *FDR's Protest of the Treatment of Jews in Germany*, ed. George McJimsey (Bethesda, MD: University Publications of America, 2003), 463–475; Breitman and Kraut, *American Refugee Policy and European Jewry*, 61–63; Breckinridge Long manuscript, "Refugees 1938–1940," box 202, Breckinridge Long Papers, LC; Moffat Diary, November 15, 1938 (quotations), vol. 41, Moffat Papers, HL.

73. Concerning President Roosevelt and refugees to the Philippines, there exists only one, brief, unconfirmed wire report that FDR had "instructed" McNutt to admit to the Philippines 200 Jewish families totaling 1,000 people. Wilcox to John O'Brien, August 19, 1938, *Documentary History of the Franklin D. Roosevelt Presidency*, vol. 33, *Myron Taylor and the Establishment of the Intergovernmental Committee on Political Refugees, 1938*, ed. George McJimsey (Bethesda, MD: University Publications of America, 2006), 241.

74. "Address of the Honorable Myron C. Taylor," October 3, 1938, *Documentary History of the Franklin D. Roosevelt Presidency*, vol. 12, 272.

75. FDR to Theodore Francis Green, October 19, 1938, box 1123, Theodore Francis Green Papers, LC.

76. Feingold, *The Politics of Rescue*, 300.

77. Sumner Welles to Cordell Hull, January 3, 1939, box 44, Cordell Hull Papers, LC.; "Meeting of the Inter-Governmental Committee," October 17, 1939, *Documentary History of the Franklin D. Roosevelt Presidency*, vol. 33, 616–618, 621, 625, 634, 636, 640–644, 647, 649, 651, 656, 668, 683, 705, 729.

78. Moffat Diary, December 16, 1938, box 211, Sumner Welles Papers, FDRL.

79. Ephraim, *Escape to Manila*, 43.

80. Francis B. Sayre, "Autobiography" (original ms.), Nov. '54–June '55, chapter 18, 379–380, box 23, Francis B. Sayre Papers, LC.

81. J. Weldon Jones to Francis B. Sayre, March 27, 1940, box 6, Jones Papers, HSTL.

82. George L. Brandt to George S. Messersmith, January 30, 1939, file: 811B.55/237, box 245, General Visa Correspondence 1914–1940, RG 59, NAB.

83. George L. Brandt to George S. Messersmith, February 17, 1939, file: 811B.55/40, box 244, General Visa Correspondence 1914–1940, RG 59, NAB.

84. Stanton Youngberg to Charles J. Liebman, February 23, 1940, file: 811B.55 J/397, box 244, General Visa Correspondence 1940–1945, RG 59, NAB.

85. Ilse May testimony, August 14, 1997, USHMM; Gleeck, *The History of the Jewish Community of Manila*, 19–20. In 1946, during his second stint as high commissioner, McNutt tried to help Jewish doctors who had come to Manila in the 1930s but could not practice medicine. McNutt to Manuel Roxas, June 17, 1946, box 9, Records of the Washington Office, 1942–48, Records of the High Commissioner to the Philippines, RG 126, Office of Territories Classified Files 1907–1951, United States Department of the Interior, NACP.

86. George L. Brandt to George S. Messersmith, February 17, 1939, file: 811B.55/40, box 244, General Visa Correspondence 1914–1940, RG 59, NAB.

87. Stanton Youngberg to Charles J. Liebman, February 23, 1940, file: 811B.55 J/397, box 244, General Visa Correspondence 1940–1945, RG 59, NAB.

88. Sayre, "Autobiography," chapter 18, 380.

89. *PFP*, May 4, 1940, 1.

90. Proposed reply to the High Commissioner's Telegram, no date [ca. January 18, 1939], box 6, Country Files, Records Relating to the IGR, RG 59, NACP; George L. Brandt to George S. Messersmith, April 20, 1939, file: 811B.55/237, box 245, General Visa Correspondence 1914–1940, RG 59, NAB; Francis B. Sayre to FDR, April 15, 1940, box 7, and Conversations between Mr. Sayre and the Minister for Foreign Affairs, Mr. Arita, May 1, 1940 (quotation), and May 6, 1940, box 9, Sayre Papers, LC.

91. Sayre explained the reasons for the change to the Japanese foreign minister. The Philippine legislature had acted "allegedly to restrict the Jewish and Chinese quotas." Joseph C. Grew Diary, April 1940 Summary, vol. 100, Joseph C. Grew Papers, HL.

92. J. Weldon Jones to Francis B. Sayre, April 1, 1940, folder: High Commissioner 1936–40, box 6, Jones Papers, HSTL.

93. Stanton Youngberg to Charles J. Liebman, February 23, 1940, file: 811B.55 J/397, box 244, General Visa Correspondence 1940–1945, Visa Division, RG 59, NAB (quotation).

94. J. Weldon Jones to Francis B. Sayre, April 1, 1940, box 6, Jones Papers, HSTL.

95. "Quezon to Sign Bill on Aliens," *MB*, April 16, 1940, box 28, Jones Papers, HSTL; Bill no. 1732 attached to Breckinridge Long to Francis B. Sayre, October 4, 1940, file: 811B.55/514, box 233, General Visa Correspondence 1940–1945, RG 59, NAB.

96. Feingold, *The Politics of Rescue*, 99.

97. Breitman and Kraut, *American Refugee Policy and European Jewry*, 112.

98. "Jewish Refugee Problem," no date, folder: 28943 to, box 1338, General Classified Files 1914–1940, BIA, RG 350, NACP; *NYT,* February 14, 2005, A14 Allen Wells, *Tropical Zion: General Trujillo, FDR, and the Jews of Sosúa* (Durham, NC: Duke University Press, 2009); Ephraim, *Escape to Manila,* 58 (quotation).

99. Lotte Hershfield, interview with the author, February 13, 2005.

100. *IN,* February 18, 1938, 7.

101. *IN,* February 18, 1938, 7; Lela Mae Stiles Diary, February 23, 1938 (quotation), box 22, Lela Mae Stiles Papers, FDRL.

102. News clipping, "McNutt Hailed by Thousands in Lavish Scene," no date, box 178, Clapper Papers, LC.

103. *PFP,* March 26, 1938, 42.

104. Clapper Diary, February 23, 1938, box 8, Clapper Papers, LC.

105. *IN,* February 18, 1938, 7, and *PFP,* March 5, 1938, 30; "Everyone Goes to M'Nutt Party," *New York Herald Tribune (NYHT),* ca. February 23, 1938, 1, 8, box 178, Clapper Papers, LC; Booth Tarkington to Carleton B. McCulloch, February 21, 1938 (quotation), box 176, Booth Tarkington Papers, Princeton University (PU) Library.

106. *Washington Evening Star (WES),* February 23, 1938, A-8.

107. "Party for M'Nutt Draws Thousands," *WES,* February 24, 1938, box 26, PVMP; *WES,* February 23, 1938, A-8, B-1 (first quotation); "Everyone Goes to McNutt Party," *NYHT,* ca. February 23, 1938, 1, 8, box 178, Clapper Papers, LC; Julius C. Edelstein, "McNutt Stock Booms," March 15, 1938 (second quotation), box 9, Hayden Papers, BHL.

108. James A. Farley to Claude G. Bowers, March 21, 1938, box 6, James A. Farley Papers, LC.

109. James A. Farley, memorandum, January 11, 1938, and December 11, 1937 (quotation), box 42; Farley memorandum, August 25, 1938, box 43, Farley Papers, LC.

110. Farley memorandum, February 10, 1938, box 42, Farley Papers, LC.

111. Harold Ickes Diary, March 19, 1938, 2667, LC.

112. Farley memorandum, February 24, 1938, box 42, Farley Papers, LC; "Roosevelt 'Calm' at McNutt Boom," *WES,* February 24, 1938 (quotation), box 26, PVMP.

113. Press Conference Number 434, February 15, 1938, Franklin D. Roosevelt, *Complete Presidential Press Conferences of Franklin D. Roosevelt,* vol. 11, *1938* (New York: Da Capo Press, 1972), 156.

114. Farley memorandum, July 6, 1938, box 43, Farley Papers, LC; Samuel C. Cleland to FDR, July 8, 1938, box 17, Official File (OF) 300—Democratic National Committee, FDRL; Carleton B. McCulloch to Meredith Nicholson, February 28, 1938, box 1, Carleton B. McCulloch Papers, Indiana Historical Society (IHS); "Van Nuys Checks Blow to Position," *IS,* ca. July 16, 1937, box 9, PVMP (quotation).

115. AP clipping, "Backs McNutt in 1940," October 27, 1937, box 9, Hayden Papers, BHL; Frederick Van Nuys newsletter, no date [ca. January 1938], box A6967 (drawer 112, box C), M. Clifford Townsend Papers, ISA; Carleton B. McCulloch to Meredith Nicholson, July 18, 1938, box 1, McCulloch Papers, IHS; *IN,* July 12, 1938, 6 (quotation).

116. *IS,* July 6, 1938, 8; Susan Dunn, *Roosevelt's Purge: How FDR Fought to Change the Democratic Party* (Cambridge, MA: Belknap Press of Harvard University Press, 2010), 139 (quotations).

117. McNutt to Frank M. McHale, July 19, 1938, box 10, PVMP.

118. William E. Leuchtenburg, *Franklin D. Roosevelt and the New Deal, 1932–1940* (New York: Harper and Row, 1963), 267–271; Madison, *Indiana through Tradition and Change,* 78, 147–148; Sherman Minton to FDR, July 9, 1938 (quotations), box 17, OF 300—Democratic National Committee, FDRL.

119. Farley memorandum, August 25, 1938, box 43, Farley Papers, LC.

120. Booth Tarkington to Carleton B. McCulloch, August 24, 1938, box 176, Tarkington Papers, PU.

121. Farley memorandum, August 25, 1938, box 43, Farley Papers, LC.

122. Harry H. Woodring to FDR, January 3, 1939, box 412, Personal Name Information File, 1914–45, BIA, RG 350, NACP; FDR handwritten comment on Edwin M. Watson to FDR, May 9, 1939 (quotation), box 19, OF 400, FDRL.

123. Carleton B. McCulloch to Meredith Nicholson, April 11, 1939, box 1, McCulloch Papers, IHS.

124. *PH,* May 11, 1939, 16; untitled narrative of McNutt's tenure as high commissioner, no date, box 1, Information Files—FSA, RG 235, NACP.

125. "Thousands Join in Farewell," *Manila Bulletin,* May 12, 1939, box 33, Joseph and Stewart Alsop Papers, LC; *PH,* May 11, 1939,1 (quotation).

126. Gleeck, *The American Governors-General and High Commissioners in the Philippines,* 339.

127. "Along the Road," *PH,* May 12, 1939, and "The High Commissioner," *La Vanguardia,* May 11, 1939; "McNutt Still Needed," *MB,* May 11, 1939, box 33, Alsop Papers, LC.

128. Gleeck, *The American Governors-General and High Commissioners in the Philippines,* 340.

129. *PH,* July 4, 1939, 4.

130. *PH,* September 6, 1939, 4.

131. Julian Go, "Introduction," in *The American Colonial State in the Philippines: Global Perspectives,* ed. Julian Go and Anne L. Foster (Pasig City, Philippines: Anvil Publishing, 2005), 13–16.

132. *PH,* January 11, 1939, 4.

133. *IS,* August 23, 1939, 22.

134. "The High Commissioner," *La Vanguardia,* May 11, 1939, box 33, Alsop Papers, LC; and *PH,* May 10, 1939, 4 (quotation).

135. "The High Commissioner," *La Vanguardia,* May 11, 1939, box 33, Alsop Papers, LC; *PH,* May 3, 1938, 1, and May 4, 1938, 4.

136. "Along the Road," *PH,* May 12, 1939 (quotation), box 33, Alsop Papers, LC.

137. Summary of McNutt's service in the Philippines attached to Maurice Judd to Jo-seph Alsop and Robert Kintner, June 12, 1939, box 33, Alsop Papers, LC.

138. Go, "Introduction," 14.

139. "Keep Faith with Democracy—AHC," *PH,* May 10, 1939, 4.

140. Untitled narrative of McNutt's tenure as high commissioner, no date, box 1, Information Files—FSA, RG 235, NACP.

141. *PH,* March 24, 1938, 4.

142. *PH,* August 22, 1939, 1.

143. *Third Annual Report of the President of the Philippines to the President and Congress of the United States . . .* (Manila, 1940), 6, copy in American Historical Collection, Rizal Library, Ateneo de Manila University, Quezon City, Philippines.

144. Untitled narrative of McNutt's tenure as high commissioner, no date, box 1, Information Files—FSA, RG 235, NACP.

145. *PH,* May 10, 1939, 1, 4.

## 10. PAUL V. AND FRANKLIN D. (1939–1940)

1. *Mobile Register,* July 12, 1939, box 26, Paul V. McNutt Papers (PVMP), Lilly Library (LL), Indiana University (IU); *Richmond (IN) Palladium and Sun,* July 14, 1939, Oversize—Federal Security Agency Clippings, PVMP; *New York Herald Tribune* (*NYHT*), July 16, 1939, II-1; AP article, "McNutt Comes to Washington," July 20, 1939, box 178, Raymond Clapper Papers, Manuscript Division, Library of Congress, (LC); Harold L. Ickes Diary, July 15, 1939, 3581 (quotations), box 5, Harold L. Ickes Papers, LC.

2. Ickes Diary, July 24, 1939, 3597, box 5, Ickes Papers, LC.

3. Daniel Scroop, *Mr. Democrat: Jim Farley, the New Deal, and the Making of Modern American Politics* (Ann Arbor: University of Michigan Press, 2006), 158.

4. Frances Perkins oral history, book 7 (1955), 393 (first quotation), 390 (subsequent quotations), Oral History Research Office, Columbia University (OHRO-CU); Perkins oral history, book 7 (1955), 390.

5. Henry Morgenthau Jr. Presidential Diary (microfiche), April 11, 1939, Henry

Morgenthau Jr. Papers, Franklin D. Roosevelt Library (FDRL); Ickes Diary, July 15, 1939, 3580, box 5, Ickes Papers, LC; Bernard Donahoe, *Private Plans and Public Dangers: The Story of FDR's Third Nomination* (Notre Dame, IN: University of Notre Dame Press, 1965), 194 (quotation).

6. Perkins oral history, book 7 (1955), 393.

7. Raymond Clapper Diary, July 7, 1939, box 178, Raymond Clapper Papers, LC.

8. Ickes Diary, July 15, 1939, 3583, box 5, Ickes Papers, LC; Wayne Coy to Paul V. McNutt ("McNutt"), May 19, 1939, box 10, PVMP; Oscar R. Ewing oral history, April 29, 1969, Harry S. Truman Library (HSTL).

9. Ickes Diary, July 15, 1939, 3586, box 5, Ickes Papers, LC; Donahoe, *Private Plans and Public Dangers*, 8 (quotation).

10. Alonzo L. Hamby, *For the Survival of Democracy: Franklin Roosevelt and the World Crisis of the 1930s* (New York: Basic Books, 2004), 366.

11. Mary E. Switzer to Margaret Hunt, April 13, 1939, box 50, Mary E. Switzer Papers, Schlesinger Library (SL).

12. Barry D. Karl, *The Uneasy State: The United States from 1915 to 1945* (Chicago: University of Chicago Press, 1983), 155.

13. Courtney Letts de Espil Diary, January 17, 1939, box 2, Courtney Letts de Espil Papers, LC.

14. Morgenthau Presidential Diary, May 16, 1939, Morgenthau Papers, FDRL.

15. In 1939 Garner failed to follow his custom and greet the president when his train arrived in Washington. Morgenthau Presidential Diary, May 16, 1939, Morgenthau Papers, FDRL.

16. Donahoe, *Private Plans and Public Dangers*, 92.

17. Morgenthau Presidential Diary, July 11, 1939, Morgenthau. Papers, FDRL.

18. Ickes Diary, July 15, 1939, 3586, box 5, Ickes Papers, LC.

19. Donahoe, *Private Plans and Public Dangers*, 195; Robert H. Ferrell, ed., *FDR's Quiet Confidant: The Autobiography of Frank*

*C. Walker* (Niwot: University Press of Colorado, 1997), 152 (quotation).

20. Walter Trohan, *Political Animals: Memoirs of a Sentimental Cynic* (Garden City, NY: Doubleday, 1975), 197.

21. Louise McNutt Diary, February 13, 1947, John L. Krauss Collection (private), Indianapolis.

22. Perkins oral history, book 7 (1955), 391.

23. Clapper Diary, July 7, 1939 (all previous quotations), box 178, Clapper Papers, LC.

24. Perkins oral history, book 7 (1955), 392.

25. Frances Perkins, *The Roosevelt I Knew* (New York: Viking, 1946), 5–6 (quotations). On Roosevelt's operating style, see Ferrell, *FDR's Quiet Confidant*, 153; Robert H. Jackson, *That Man: An Insider's Portrait of Franklin D. Roosevelt*, ed. John Q. Barrett (New York: Oxford University Press, 2003), 111, and Eleanor Roosevelt, *This I Remember* (New York: Harper and Brothers, 1949), 3. For the president's love of surprises see Jeff Shesol, *Supreme Power: Franklin Roosevelt vs. the Supreme Court* (New York: Norton, 2010), 274–275, 291–306.

26. Ickes Diary, July 15, 1939, 3586, box 5, Ickes Papers, LC.

27. Ickes Diary, July 15, 1939, 3583, box 5, Ickes Papers, LC; Scroop, *Mr. Democrat*, 143–164.

28. Jackson, *That Man*, 32–33; Ferrell, *FDR's Quiet Confidant*, 105 (quotation).

29. Scroop, *Mr. Democrat*, 3.

30. Jackson, *That Man*, 17; James A. Farley memorandum, July 23, 1939, box 44, James A. Farley Papers, LC (quotation); Robert W. Woolley to Edward M. House, January 6, 1933, box 8, Robert W. Woolley Papers, LC.

31. Farley memorandums, July 6, 7, and 23, 1939, box 44, Farley Papers, LC; Clapper Diary, July 7, 1939 (quotation), box 178, Clapper Papers, LC.

32. Farley memorandum, July 23, 1939, box 44, Farley Papers, LC.

33. *Indianapolis Times*, December 16, 1936, 5; "By-Law of the Paul V. McNutt for President in 1940 Club," April 24, 1937, box 1, Paul V. McNutt for President in 1940 Club,

Inc. Papers, Manuscript Section, Indiana State Library (ISL).

34. James E. Perry to McNutt, January 14, 1937, and news clipping, "McNutt Club Puts Quietus on Ballyhoo," no date [July 1937], box 9, PVMP; *Indianapolis News* (*IN*), May 18, 1937, 7; news clipping, "First McNutt for President Club Organized," no date, Vertical File—Correspondence—McNutt, Morgan County Public Library, Martinsville, Indiana; J. S. Hruskovich to Hugh A. Barnhart, July 20, 1939, box 13, Hugh A. Barnhart Papers, ISL; *Indianapolis Star* (*IS*), March 14, 1930, 3.

35. Drew Pearson and Robert V. Allen, "Paul V. (No Boob) McNutt," in *What They Say About Paul V. McNutt* (Indianapolis, IN: Paul V. McNutt Headquarters, 1940), 28 (quotations).

36. Frank M. McHale to George W. Rauch, February 14, 1939, box 2, George W. Rauch Papers, LL.

37. Hugh A. Barnhart to Frank M. McHale, January 13, 1939, folder 83, box 12, Barnhart Papers, ISL; Frank M. McHale to George W. Rauch, February 2, 1939, box 2, Rauch Papers, LL; McHale to C. Jasper Bell, June 20, 1939, folder 1329, C. Jasper Bell Papers, Western Historical Manuscripts Collection (WHMC), University of Missouri Library, Columbia, Missouri; McHale to McNutt, April 25, 1939 (quotation), box 10, PVMP.

38. Frank M. McHale to McNutt, June 12, 1939, McHale to John Nance Garner and McHale to James A. Farley, both March 29, 1939, box 10, PVMP.

39. "The Columbia Survey," July 12, 1939, box 2, Theodore Francis Green Papers, John Hay Library, Brown University (BU), Providence, Rhode Island; George McJimsey, *Harry Hopkins: Ally of the Poor, Defender of Democracy* (Cambridge, MA: Harvard University Press, 1987), 124–125; Irwin F. Gellman, *Secret Affairs: FDR, Cordell Hull, and Sumner Welles* (New York: Enigma Books, 1995), 204–212; Donahoe, *Private Plans and Public Dangers*, 8–14, 23–26, 74–76.

40. Pamphlets, *Labor Record of Paul V. McNutt as Governor of Indiana* and *Record of Paul V. McNutt in Government Finance*, no date [ca. 1939]—both in box 178, Clapper Papers, LC; *Manila Bulletin* (*MB*), November 25, 1938, 1 (quotations).

41. Frank M. McHale to Theodore Francis Green, March 29, 1939, box 2, Green Papers, BU.

42. Pamphlet, *For President Paul V. McNutt*, July 15, 1939, box 178, Clapper Papers, LC.

43. Oscar R. Ewing to Frank M. McHale, July 7, 1939, box 10, PVMP.

44. Clapper Diary, July 7, 1939, box 178, Clapper Papers, LC.

45. McNutt to Frank M. McHale, April 20, 1939, box 11, Wayne Coy Papers, FDRL.

46. Maurice Judd to McNutt, July 26, 1939, box 10, PVMP.

47. McNutt to Frank M. McHale, November 8, 1939, box 10, PVMP.

48. "McNutt Would Encourage Sound Investment," *NYHT*, no date, article attached to photograph in folder: McNutt, Paul V., and Mrs. Dead [1 of 2], *New York Telegram and Sun* Collection, Prints and Photographs Division, LC. For the purchasing-power liberals see Landon R. Y. Storrs, *The Second Red Scare and the Unmaking of the New Deal Left* (Princeton, NJ: Princeton University Press, 2013), 53, 107.

49. Herbert Corey, "Great God McNutt," *American Mercury*, January 1940, 32; Frank M. McHale to McNutt, May 2, 1939, box 10, PVMP; Hugh A. Barnhart to "Sir," July 18, 1939 (quotation), folder 89, box 13, Barnhart Papers, ISL.

50. Oscar R. Ewing to Frank M. McHale, June 7, 1939, box 10, PVMP; Carleton B. McCulloch to Booth Tarkington, August 21, 1939, box 202, Booth Tarkington Papers, Princeton University (PU) Library; Frank M. Dixon to McHale, March 28, 1939, box 11, Coy Papers, FDRL; McHale to McNutt, June 12, 1939, and Maurice Judd to McNutt, July 26, 1939 (quotation), box 10, PVMP.

51. Oscar R. Ewing to McNutt, June 21, 1939, box 10, PVMP.

52. Frank M. McHale to McNutt, April 11, 1939, box 11, Coy Papers, FDRL.

53. Alva Johnston, "'I Intend to Be President,'" *Saturday Evening Post,* March 16, 1940, 70; *IS,* May 29, 1939, 2.

54. Oscar R. Ewing to McNutt, June 21, 1939, and Wayne Coy to McNutt, May 19, 1939 (quotation), box 10, PVMP.

55. Maurice Judd to Wayne Coy, June 13, 1939, box 11, and Coy to Virgil Simmons, June 20, 1939, box 13, Coy Papers, FDRL.

56. Wayne Coy to E. M. Grimm, June 12, 1939, box 7, Coy Papers, FDRL.

57. McNutt to Donald Lester, March 5, 1940, box 10, PVMP.

58. *IS,* June 18, 1939, 1.

59. William Ritchie to Harlan Wood, July 5, 1939, box 18, Coy Papers, FDRL, and Booth Tarkington to Carleton B. McCulloch, August 15, 1939 (quotation), box 176, Tarkington Papers, PU.

60. Wayne Coy to McNutt, May 19, 1939, box 10, PVMP.

61. Booth Tarkington to Carleton B. McCulloch, August 7, 1938, box 176, Tarkington Papers, PU.

62. James MacGregor Burns, *Roosevelt: The Lion and the Fox* (New York: Harcourt, 1956), 409; *Washington Evening Star (WES),* November 20, 1939, A-2; Doris Kearns Goodwin, *No Ordinary Time: Franklin and Eleanor Roosevelt: The Home Front in World War II* (New York: Simon and Schuster, 1994), 74 (quotation).

63. H. W. Brands, *Traitor to His Class: The Privileged Life and Radical Presidency of Franklin Delano Roosevelt* (New York: Random House, 2008), 535.

64. Letts de Espil Diary, January 17, 1939, box 2, Letts de Espil Papers, LC.

65. For divisions within the Democratic Party, see Douglas B. Craig, *After Wilson: The Struggle for the Democratic Party, 1920–1934* (Chapel Hill: University of North Carolina Press, 1991), 1–14, 296–305, and Anthony J. Badger, *The New Deal: The Depression Years,*

*1933–1940* (Chicago: Ivan Dee, 1989), 271; Burns, *Roosevelt: The Lion and the Fox,* 380 (quotations).

66. Susan Dunn, *Roosevelt's Purge: How FDR Fought to Change the Democratic Party* (Cambridge, MA: Belknap Press of Harvard University Press, 2010), 92.

67. Badger, *The New Deal,* 246; Harold L. Ickes to Anna Roosevelt Boettiger, June 1, 1939 (quotation), box 233, Ickes Papers, LC.

68. Robert W. Woolley, unpublished autobiography, chapter 42, 1, box 44, Woolley Papers, LC.

69. William S. McFeely, *Grant: A Biography* (New York: Norton, 1981), 482–483; Patricia O'Toole, *When Trumpets Call: Theodore Roosevelt after the White House* (New York: Simon and Schuster, 2005), 152–223; Robert H. Ferrell, *Woodrow Wilson and World War I* (New York: Harper and Row, 1985), 219, 222–223; Woolley, unpublished autobiography, chapter 42, 2, box 44, Woolley Papers, LC.

70. Donald R. McCoy, *Calvin Coolidge: The Quiet President* (Lawrence: University Press of Kansas, 1967), 382–387; Joan Hoff Wilson, *Herbert Hoover: Forgotten Progressive* (Boston: Little, Brown, 1975), 121 (quotation), 122–126.

71. Clapper Diary, July 13, 1933, box 8, Clapper Papers, LC.

72. Works that date Roosevelt's decision to run for a third term to the period before the Nazi invasion of western Europe, in the spring of 1940, and thus emphasize the political motivation, include Donahoe, *Private Plans and Public Dangers,* viii–ix; Badger, *The New Deal,* 246–247; and Roy Jenkins, *Franklin Delano Roosevelt* (New York: Times Books, 2003), 110–111. For the more traditional view, that FDR made his decision following the fall of western Europe to the Nazis, see Robert E. Sherwood, *Roosevelt and Hopkins: An Intimate History* (New York: Harper and Brothers, 1950), 169–170; William E. Leuchtenburg, *Franklin D. Roosevelt and the New Deal, 1932–1940* (New York: Harper and Row, 1963), 315; Herbert S. Parmet and Marie B. Hecht, *Never Again: A President Runs for a*

*Third Term* (New York: Macmillan Company, 1968) 176; Gellman, *Secret Affairs*, 215; and Susan Dunn, *1940: FDR, Willkie, Lindbergh, Hitler—the Election amid the Storm* (New Haven, CT: Yale University Press, 2013), 40. For a revisionist view that holds that FDR had wanted to retire all along and only decided to run for a third term in July 1940, see Richard Moe, *Roosevelt's Second Act: The 1940 Election and the Politics of War* (New York: Oxford University Press, 2013).

73.  Roosevelt press conference, July 11, 1938, *Complete Presidential Press Conferences of Franklin D. Roosevelt*, vol. 14, *August 1939– December 1939* (New York: Da Capo Press, 1972), 257; "Keepers of the Great Secret," *Columbus Dispatch*, no date [ca. July 1940], box 2, S. J. Ray Papers, HSTL; *WES*, January 24, 1940, 1; Farley memorandum, January 19, 1939, box 43, Farley Papers, LC; Clapper Diary, July 7, 1939, box 178, Clapper Papers, LC.

74.  Albert Lepawsky to William O. Douglas, January 8, 1976, folder: ALP—New Dealers Lepawsky Correspondence with, Albert Lepawsky Papers, Center for New Deal Studies, Roosevelt University (RU), Chicago, Illinois.

75.  Curtis Roosevelt interview with the author, March 21, 2005; Harold L. Ickes to Anna Roosevelt Boettiger, June 1, 1939 (quotation), box 233, Ickes Papers, LC.

76.  Jenkins, *Franklin Delano Roosevelt*, 104; Clapper Diary, September 2, 1937, box 8, Clapper Papers, LC; Farley memorandum, March 7, 1937 (quotations), box 41, Farley Papers, LC.

77.  Letts de Espil Diary, September 30, 1938 (quotations), box 2, Letts de Espil Papers, LC. On Hull's ambition, see Gellman, *Secret Affairs*, 207, and A. Walter Burton to Cordell Hull, July 14, 1939, box 44, Cordell Hull Papers, LC.

78.  Jackson, *That Man*, 32; Sherwood, *Roosevelt and Hopkins*, 95 and 98 (quotation).

79.  E. Roosevelt, *This I Remember*, 213.

80.  Albert Lepawsky, interview with Thomas Corcoran, November 18–19, 1971, Lepawsky Papers, RU.

81.  Jackson, *That Man*, 33; Belle Willard Roosevelt Diary, undated [ca. November 1944] (quotation), box 134, Kermit and Belle Roosevelt Papers, LC.

82.  Jenkins, *Franklin Delano Roosevelt*, 104; E. Roosevelt, *This I Remember*, 213 (quotation).

83.  Meredith Nicholson to Carleton B. McCulloch, July 14, 1939, box 1, Carleton B. McCulloch Papers, Indiana Historical Society (IHS).

84.  Roosevelt press conference, July 11, 1938, *Complete Presidential Press Conferences of Franklin D. Roosevelt*, vol. 14, 11.

85.  Burns, *Lion and the Fox*, 411 (quotation). See also "McNutt Relegated by Roosevelt," *New York Times*, no date [July 1939], box 26, PVMP.

86.  *NYHT*, February 11, 1940, sect. II, 2.

87.  Clapper Diary, March 22, 1938, box 178, Clapper Papers, LC.

88.  Albert Lepawsky, interview with Thomas Corcoran, November 18–19, 1971, Lepawsky Papers, RU.

89.  Farley memorandum, October 14, 1938, box 43, Farley Papers, LC.

90.  Dunn, *Roosevelt's Purge*, 82.

91.  Homer S. Cummings Diary, December 18, 1938, box 235, Homer S. Cummings Papers, Albert and Shirley Small Special Collections Library, University of Virginia (UVA).

92.  Helen Roosevelt Robinson Diary, October 8, 1938, box 448, Franklin D. Roosevelt Jr. Papers, FDRL.

93.  Robert H. Jackson, "The Attorney-Generalship of Robert H. Jackson," 5, no date, Box 189, Robert H Jackson Papers, LC; Robert H. Jackson oral history, (1952–53), 750 (quotation), OHRO-CU.

94.  Morgenthau Presidential Diary, May 22, 1939, FDRL; Jonathan Daniels to Josephus Daniels, July 30, 1939, box 32, Josephus Daniels Papers, LC; James H. Rowe to Edwin M. Watson, May 19, 1939, January 4, 1940, March 9, 1940, and April 8, 1940, and Watson to FDR, December 20, 1939, and January 10,

1940, box 10, Edwin M. Watson Papers, UVA; Sherwood, *Roosevelt and Hopkins*, 117–118.

95. Ruby Black typescript columns, November 20, 1939, December 23, 1939, and June 14, 1939 (quotations), box 1, Black Papers, LC.

96. A. W. Lafferty, "New Deal without Roosevelt?" July 11, 1939, box 3, Harry L. Hopkins Papers, Georgetown University Library, Washington, D.C.

97. Woolley memorandum, May 10, 1939, box 18, Woolley Papers, LC.

98. George W. Norris to Claude Pepper, August 28, 1939, box 370, George W. Norris Papers, LC.

99. Harold L. Ickes to Anna Roosevelt Boettiger, June 1, 1939, box 233, Ickes Papers, LC.

100. FDR to Harold L. Ickes, June 6, 1939, box 233, Ickes Papers, LC.

101. Farley memorandum, July 23, 1939, box 44, Farley Papers, LC.

102. Cummings Diary, July 12, 1940, box 235, Cummings Papers, UVA.

103. Letts de Espil Diary, February 28, 1940, box 2, Letts de Espil Papers, LC.

104. Frank M. McHale to McNutt, September 14, 1939, box 10, PVMP.

105. McNutt to Frank M. McHale, August 30, 1939, and "Report of Visit of Frank M. McHale, Oscar R. Ewing, and M. L. Fansler to Rhode Island," December 1, 1939 (quotation), folder: 1939 November, box 10, PVMP. See also reports in the same folder by McHale, Ewing, and Fansler on Connecticut, Maine, Massachusetts, and New Hampshire.

106. Edward J. Higgins to McNutt, August 29, 1939, and Higgins to Oscar R. Ewing, October 4, 1939, box 3, Green Papers, BU; "Memorandum for Governor McNutt," November 17, 1939 (quotation), box 10, PVMP.

107. McNutt to Oscar R. Ewing, August 30, 1939, box 10, PVMP.

108. David M. Kennedy, *Freedom from Fear: The American People in Depression and War, 1929–1945* (New York: Oxford University Press, 1998), 426–433, 434 (both quotations).

109. James A. Farley to John Cudahy, October 5, 1939, box 8, Farley Papers, LC.

110. Mary E. Switzer to Richard R. King, September 25, 1939, box 51, Switzer Papers, SL.

111. Letts de Espil Diary, October 24, 1939, and November 30, 1939 (quotation), box 2, Letts de Espil Papers, LC.

112. McNutt to Fred Cone, September 20, 1939, box 10, McNutt Papers, LC.

113. Ickes Diary, September 9, 1939, 3699, box 5, Ickes Papers, LC.

114. "Nearly 600 Hear Talk," *Florida Times-Union*, no date [November 1939], box 10, PVMP.

115. Editorial, "Danger Lies Within," no date, attached to Dick Habbe to McNutt, November 27, 1939, box 10, PVMP.

116. Badger, *The New Deal*, 225.

117. McHale, Ewing, and Fansler report on Connecticut, December 1, 1939, box 10, PVMP.

118. Woolley memorandum, May 10, 1939, box 18, Woolley Papers, LC.

119. Henry A. Wallace Diary, February 5, 1940, Henry A. Wallace Papers, University of Iowa Libraries (UIL), Iowa City.

120. Wallace Diary, November 21, 1939 (quotation), Wallace Papers, UIL, and Ickes Diary, December 6, 1939, 3974, Ickes Papers, LC.

121. Wallace Diary, November 27, 1939, Wallace Papers, UIL.

122. Wallace Diary, November 17, 1939, Wallace Papers, UIL.

123. *MB*, June 7, 1939, 1; Donahoe, *Private Plans and Public Dangers*, 101; Edwin M. Watson to FDR, July 28, 1939, box 10, Watson Papers, UVA; McNutt speech, August 12, 1939, box 178, Clapper Papers, LC; "Ambush Laid for McNutt at Parley," *IN*, August 12, 1939, folder: Indiana Biography—McNutt, Paul V. and Family—Presidential Chances, Indiana Clipping File, ISL; news clippings, "Nomination Bid Seen in McNutt Talk," no date [July 1939], box 26 and "The Mirror of Washington," no date [ca. September 1939], box 10, PVMP.

124. Donahoe, *Private Plans and Public Dangers*, 116; Wallace Diary, December 20, 1939, and November 16, 1939, Wallace Papers, UIL; Harold L. Ickes to Anna Roosevelt Boettiger, June 1, 1939, box 233, Ickes Papers, LC (quotation).

125. Wallace Diary, December 11, 1939 (all quotations), Wallace Papers, UIL.

126. Perkins oral history, book 7 (1955), 405, OHRO-CU.

127. *Washington Daily News (WDN)*, October 16, 1939, 16; Wallace Diary, December 19, 1939, Wallace Papers, UIL; *Richmond (VA) Times-Dispatch*, November 19, 1939, 2; "Paul Vories McNutt," *Vicksburg (MS) Evening Post*, November 3, 1939, and "McNutt—'Heir Presumptuous,'" *WES*, November 26, 1939, box 178, Clapper Papers, LC. "McNutt a Face Saver for Both Factions," August 20, 1939, box 26, PVMP; Booth Tarkington to Carleton B. McCulloch, August 17, 1939, box 176, Tarkington Papers, PU; Henry A. Wallace oral history (November 28, 1939), 599 (quotation), OHRO-CU.

128. Letts de Espil Diary, November 19, 1939, box 2, Letts de Espil Papers, LC.

129. Harold L. Ickes to James A. Farley, November 18, 1939, box 8, Farley Papers, LC; *IN*, December 8, 1949, I-4; Ickes Diary, December 10, 1939, 3979, 3980–3981, box 5, Ickes Papers, LC.

130. Ray F. Donnan to Harold L. Ickes, December 12, 1939, and F. W. Meyers to Ickes, December 17, 1939, box 233, Ickes Papers, LC; *MB*, August 3, 1939, 1; Wallace Diary, November 27, 1939, Wallace Papers, UIL; Democratic National Committee publicity bureau, "Political Editorial Digest," December 19, 1939, box 233, Ickes Papers, LC; *Philippines Free Press*, December 30, 1939, 22 (quotation).

131. Thomas L. Stokes column, December 1, 1939 (first quotation), and "McNutt—'Heir Presumptuous,'" *WES*, November 26, 1939 (second quotation), box 178, Clapper Papers, LC.

132. Booth Tarkington to Carleton B. McCulloch, December 8, 1939, box 176, Tarkington Papers, PU.

133. McNutt to Frank M. McHale, April 3, 1939, box 11, Coy Papers, FDRL.

134. *WES*, December 16, 1939, A-18.

135. Ickes Diary, December 24, 1939, 4043, and December 30, 1939, 4052, box 5, Ickes Papers, LC; Wallace oral history (January 18, 1940), 691 (quotation), OHRO-CU.

136. Frank M. McHale to McNutt, April 3, 1939, box 10, PVMP.

137. *IN*, December 11, 1939, I-8.

138. "Gridiron," no date [ca. December 10, 1939], box 7, Information Files, Records of the Administrator of the Federal Security Agency, Record Group (RG) 235, National Archives, College Park (NACP).

139. Cummings Diary, December 9, 1929, box 235, Cummings Papers, UVA.

140. H. L. Mencken, *The Diary of H. L. Mencken*, ed. Charles A. Fletcher (New York: Alfred A. Knopf, 1989), 134.

141. Edwin M. Watson to FDR, June 13, 1939, James M. Rowe to Watson, June 16, 1939, and Watson to Henry Morgenthau Jr., June 20, 1939, box 10, Watson Papers, UVA.

142. Ernest H. Vaughn to Chief, Intelligence Unit, Bureau of Internal Revenue, July 12, 1939, and FDR to Morgenthau, July 24, 1939 (quotation), box 518, Morgenthau Papers, FDRL.

143. Summary of meeting between Morgenthau, Foley, and Reynolds, July 26, 1939, Henry Morgenthau Diaries, reel 56, vol. 205, 205, Morgenthau Papers (microfilm), FDRL (all quotations).

144. Jas. N. Sullivan to Chief, Intelligence Unit, Bureau of Internal Revenue, December 2, 1939, Morgenthau Diaries, roll 68, book 252, 6–19, and "Indiana Cases of Tax Evasion 1939–1940," no date (quotation), box 405, both in Morgenthau Papers, FDRL.

145. Sullivan to Elmer L. Irey, December 9, 1939, and Memorandum for the Secretary, December 4, 1939 (quotation), roll 68, book 252, 151–156, 1–4, Morgenthau Papers, FDRL.

146. "Indiana Cases of Tax Evasion 1939–1940," no date, box 405, Morgenthau Papers, FDRL.

147. Memorandum for the Secretary, December 4, 1939, roll 68, book 252, 1–4, Morgenthau Papers, FDRL.

148. Harold Smith Diary, January 17, 1940, box 3, Harold Smith Papers, LC.

149. Wallace Diary, January 30, 1940, Wallace Papers, UIL.

150. Roy W. Howard to Raymond Clapper, April 2, 1940, box 9, Clapper Papers, LC.

151. WDN, no date, box 178, Clapper Papers, LC.

152. Morgenthau Presidential Diary, May 2, 1940, Morgenthau Papers, FDRL.

153. "Indiana Cases of Tax Evasion 1939–1940," no date, box 405, Morgenthau Papers, FDRL.

154. Letter to Roy Howard, June 17, 1933, box 77, Roy W. Howard Papers, LC, and William R. Castle Diary, August 6, 1938, vol. 36, 285 (quotation), Houghton Library (HL).

155. Castle Diary, September 7, 1939, vol. 38, 309, HL.

156. Farley memorandum, December 28, 1938, box 43, Farley Papers, LC, and Wallace Diary, January 18, 1940 (quotation), Wallace Papers, UIL.

157. See Morgenthau Presidential Diary, April 11, 1938, and July 17, 1939, Morgenthau Papers, FDRL; Arthur Krock oral history, 1950, 52 (quotation), OHRO-CU.

158. Morgenthau Presidential Diary, May 2, 1939, Morgenthau Papers, FDRL.

159. B. F. Sackett to J. Edgar Hoover, January 13, 1940, FBI File of Paul V. McNutt, FBI Building, Washington, D.C.

160. FDR to Henry Morgenthau Jr., October 4, 1940, roll 87, book 319, 145, Morgenthau Papers, FDRL. Thomas E. Dewey, a front-runner for the Republican Party's nomination for president, had criticized "the failure to prosecute or exonerate McNutt on the income tax charges." G. Mennen Williams Diary, March 2, 1940, box 1, G. Mennen Williams Non-Gubernatorial Papers, Bentley Historical Library (BHL).

161. Drew Pearson and Robert S. Allen, "The Washington Merry-Go-Round," no date [ca. June 1940], folder: Indiana Biography—McNutt, Paul V. and Family—Presidential Chances, Indiana Clipping File, ISL; Ickes Diary, November 26, 1939, 3939 (quotation), box 5, Ickes Papers, LC.

162. Ickes Diary, December 24, 1939, 4008–4009, box 5, Ickes Papers, LC.

163. Clapper Diary, January 25, 1940, box 9, Clapper Papers, LC.

164. Jonathan Daniels to Josephus Daniels, February 16, 1943, box 3, Daniels Papers, LC.

165. Gellman, Secret Affairs, 23–30, 207–210; William Lyon MacKenzie King Diary, November 17, 1938, 880, and April 23–24, 1940, 439 (all quotations), Library and Archives Canada, Ottawa, Ontario.

166. Jonathan Daniels to Josephus Daniels, February 16, 1943, box 3, Daniels Papers, LC.

167. Frank Murphy, notes of appointment with FDR, December 5, 1939, box 1, Eugene Gressman Papers, BHL.

168. Murphy, notes of appointment with FDR, December 9, 1939, box 1, Gressman Papers, BHL.

169. Murphy, notes of appointment with FDR, December 19, 1939, box 1, Gressman Papers, BHL.

170. Memorandum on conversation with FDR and Frank Murphy, December 5, 1939, box 52, Frances Perkins Papers, Rare Book and Manuscript Library, Columbia University, New York.

171. Morgenthau Presidential Diary, January 24, 1940, Morgenthau Papers, FDRL.

172. Harold Ickes, The Secret Diary of Harold Ickes, vol. 3, The Lowering Clouds, 1939–1941. New York: Simon and Schuster, 1954), 122.

173. Morgenthau Presidential Diary, January 24, 1940, Morgenthau Papers, FDRL.

174. Frances Perkins did not believe his disavowal of interest in a third term. Kirstin Downey, The Life and Legacy of Frances Perkins—Social Security, Unemployment, and the Minimum Wage (New York: Anchor Books, 2009), 305.

175. Murphy notes on the opening of Congress, January 3, 1940, box 1, Gressman Papers, BHL.

176. Robert W. Woolley to FDR, May 31, 1939, box 17, Woolley Papers, LC.

177. Claude D. Pepper Diary, January 17, 1940, box 1, series 439, Claude D. Pepper Papers, Claude D. Pepper Library, Florida State University, Tallahassee.

178. Krock oral history, 1950, 52.

179. James F. Byrnes, chapter "VP 1940," no date, box 9, book materials, James F. Byrnes Papers, Department of Special Collections, Clemson University Libraries, Clemson, South Carolina.

**11. AMBITION FRUSTRATED (1940)**

1. Before Claude R. Wickard, a former Indiana lawmaker, became undersecretary of agriculture, he had to assure his boss, Henry A. Wallace, that he "had never paid a cent into the Two Percent Club." Henry A. Wallace Diary, January 29, 1940, Henry A. Wallace Papers, University of Iowa Libraries (UIL); leaflet, no date [ca. January–June 1940], box 30; press release, September 1, 1939, box 10, Paul V. McNutt Papers (PVMP), Lilly Library (LL), Indiana University (IU). "Perplexities Worry M'Nutt," no date [early 1940] (quotations), *Los Angeles Times (LAT)*, box 178, Raymond Clapper Papers, Manuscript Division, Library of Congress, (LC).

2. Alva Johnston, "'I Intend to Be President,'" *Saturday Evening Post,* March 16, 1940, 20–21, 67–70; Herbert Corey, "Great God McNutt," *American Mercury* (January 1940), 30–36; Jack Alexander, "Paul McNutt: 'It Would Be Kind of Nice to Be President, Wouldn't It?,'" *Life,* Box 178, Clapper Papers, LC; Tully Nettleton, "McNutt Is Willing," box 26, McNutt Papers, LL; Milton S. Mayer, "Men Who Would Be President: Pretty Boy McNutt," *The Nation,* March 30, 1940, 415–418; Ray Millholland, "Magnificent McNutt," *American Magazine* (January 1940), 26–27, 131–132; Jonathan Mitchell, "McNutt: Beauty in Distress," *New Republic,* April 29, 1940,

565–568; Ernest K. Lindley, "Garner Versus McNutt," *Look,* February 13, 1940, 17–21.

3. Mayer, "Pretty Boy McNutt," 415.

4. Mayer, "Pretty Boy McNutt," 415, 418 (quotation).

5. J. Newell to Paul V. McNutt ("McNutt"), February 23, 1940, box 10, PVMP.

6. Johnston, "'I Intend to Be President,'" 70.

7. Carleton B. McCulloch to Booth Tarkington, January 4, 1940, folder 3, box 202, Booth Tarkington Papers, Princeton University (PU) Library.

8. Johnston, "'I Intend to Be President,'" 70.

9. Robert Kintner and Joseph Alsop, "The Capital Parade," *Washington Evening Star (WES),* July 10, 1939, box 178, Clapper Papers, LC.

10. "McNutt Courts Business and Predicts Abundance," *Christian Science Monitor,* January 16, 1940, fiche 3, Department of Indiana, Biographical File—Paul V. McNutt, National Headquarters of the American Legion Library (ALL).

11. Joseph H. Friend, "Watch Paul McNutt," *The Nation,* July 23, 1938, 86–88.

12. "The Capital Parade," *WES,* July 10, 1939, box 178, Clapper Papers, LC.

13. "Washington Merry-Go-Round," *San Francisco Chronicle,* June 26, 1939, box 26, PVMP.

14. Wallace Diary, November 27, 1939, Wallace Papers, UI.

15. Roy W. Howard to Raymond Clapper, April 2, 1940, folder: Letters and Articles 1940 January thru June, Roy W. Howard Archive, IU School of Journalism, Bloomington; Howard to Ludwell Denny, December 24, 1936 (quotation), box 111, Roy W. Howard Papers, LC.

16. Michael E. McGerr, *The Decline of Popular Politics: The American North, 1865–1928* (New York: Oxford University Press, 1986), 138–183; Jack Alexander to Miss Harrison, May 20, 1973 (quotation), folder: McNutt, Genealogy Library, Johnson County Museum of History, Franklin, Indiana.

17. Joseph Alsop to Mr. Thomson, April 24, 1940, folder 665, Champ and Bennett Clark Papers, Western Historical Manuscripts Collection (WHMC).

18. Unsigned letter to Wesley Winans Stout, January 27, 1940, box 10, PVMP (quotation); Johnston, "'I Intend to Be President,'" 20, 68, and 67.

19. William Allen White, "Candidates in the Spring," *Yale Review* (March 1940), 439.

20. Lindley, "Garner Versus McNutt," 21.

21. *Time*, July 10, 1939, 17; Mitchell, "McNutt: Beauty in Distress," 567 (quotation).

22. Jay Pierrepont Moffat Diary, January 20 to 21, 1940, vol. 44, Jay Pierrepont Moffat Papers, Houghton Library (HL).

23. William R. Castle Diary, January 21, 1940, vol. 39, 37, HL.

24. *Chicago Times*, February 11, 1940, 3-M; Mitchell, "McNutt: Beauty in Distress," 565.

25. Millholland, "Magnificent McNutt," 26; Reece A. Oliver to Kenneth F. Oliver, November 1, 1939 (quotation), folder: Letters 1917–1950, Reece A. Oliver Papers, Manuscript Section, Indiana State Library (ISL).

26. Thomas C. Reeves, *A Question of Character: A Life of John F. Kennedy* (New York: Free Press, 1991), 2.

27. Frances Perkins oral history, book 7 (1955), 390, Oral History Research Office, Columbia University (OHRO-CU).

28. Castle Diary, May 20, 1937, vol. 33, 205, HL.

29. Robert W. Woolley, unpublished autobiography, chapter 48, 15, box 44, Robert W. Woolley Papers, LC.

30. White, "Candidates in the Spring," 439.

31. David E. Lilienthal, *The Journals of David E. Lilienthal*, vol. 1, *The TVA Years, 1939–1945* (New York: Harper and Row, 1964), 203.

32. Millholland, "Magnificent McNutt," 132.

33. Raymond Clapper Diary, November 20, 1939, box 178, Clapper Papers, LC.

34. Courtney Letts de Espil Diary, March 10, 1940, 940, box 2, Courtney Letts de Espil Papers, LC.

35. Ruby A. Black to Eleanor Roosevelt, March 13, 1940, box 2, Ruby A. Black Papers, LC.

36. Carleton B. McCulloch to Meredith Nicholson, August 21, 1940, box 1, Carleton B. McCulloch Papers, Indiana Historical Society (IHS).

37. Frank M. McHale to McNutt, April 16, 1940, box 10, PVMP.

38. Ralph M. Immell to O. Robinson, February 14, 1940, box 10, PVMP.

39. McNutt statement, January 23, 1940, and J. Patrick Beacom to Frank M. McHale, January 14, 1940 (quotations), box 10, PVMP.

40. Fowler V. Harper to Oscar R. Ewing, April 25, 1940, Ewing to Harper, April 29, 1940, and J. Patrick Beacom to Frank M. McHale, January 14, 1940 (quotation), box 10, PVMP.

41. James A. Farley to Claude G. Bowers, December 21, 1939, box 5, Claude G. Bowers Papers (II), LL.

42. Josephus Daniels to Claude G. Bowers, April 20, 1940, box 5, Bowers Papers (II), LL.

43. Frank Graham to Harry Hopkins, July 13, 1940, box 2, Harry Hopkins Papers, Georgetown University (GU) Library.

44. Maury Maverick to Harry Hopkins, July 2, 1940, box 3, Hopkins Papers, GU.

45. Edwin Peterson to Franklin D. Roosevelt, December 16, 1939, President's Personal File (PPF) 6356, Franklin D. Roosevelt Library (FDRL).

46. Frank M. McHale, Oscar R. Ewing, and M. L. Fansler report on North Carolina, December 4, 1939, folder: 1939 November, and "Memorandum" by J. N., no date, folder: January 1940, box 10, PVMP.

47. Carleton B. McCulloch to Meredith Nicholson, February 14, 1940, box 1, McCulloch Papers, IHS.

48. Lorena Hickok to Eleanor Roosevelt (ER), March 8, 1940, *Empty without You: The Intimate Letters of Eleanor Roosevelt and Lorena Hickok*, ed. Roger Streimatter (New York: Free Press, 1998), 227.

49. Wayne Coy to Edward D. Hester, March 13, 1940, box 7, Wayne Coy Papers, FDRL.

50. Jonathan Daniels to Josephus Daniels, February 16, 1943, box 33, Josephus Daniels Papers, LC.

51. Theodore Roosevelt Jr. to Alf M. Landon, February 28, 1940, box 29, Theodore Roosevelt Jr. Papers, LC.

52. James A. Farley to William Phillips, March 1, 1940, 1940, box 9, James A. Farley Papers, LC.

53. Breckinridge Long to Claude G. Bowers, April 5, 1940, box 5, Bowers Papers (II), LL.

54. During a meeting with Canadian prime minister William Lyon MacKenzie King in April 1940, FDR declined to rule out running, kept quiet about his intentions, and complained that no New Dealer had emerged as a suitable successor. He dismissed the most likely Democratic nominees as either "inadequate or impossible." William Lyon Mackenzie King Diary, April 23 and 24, 1940, 439–440, Library and Archives Canada, Ottawa, Ontario.

55. "The Political Mill," WES, February 22, 1940, box 10, PVMP; and Robert H. Jackson, "The Attorney Generalship of Robert Jackson," 5, no date, box 189, Robert H. Jackson Papers, LC; William Gibbs McAdoo to Joseph Tumulty, February 9, 1940, box 471, William Gibbs McAdoo Papers, LC; Wallace Diary, February 13, 1940, Wallace Papers, UIL; Carleton B. McCulloch to Meredith Nicholson, February 14, 1940, box 1, McCulloch Papers, IHS; WES, April 10, 1940, A-1, and March 13, 1940, A-5, and March 28, 1940, A-17; Claude D. Pepper Diary, April 3, 1940, and February 20, 1940 (quotation), box 1, series 439, Claude D. Pepper Papers, Claude D. Pepper Library, Florida State University (FSU).

56. Josephus Daniels to Claude G. Bowers, April 20, 1940, box 5, Bowers Papers (II), LC.

57. William Gibbs McAdoo to Harold L. Ickes, April 6, 1940, box 471, McAdoo Papers, LC.

58. William Gibbs McAdoo to Harold L. Ickes, April 6, 1940, box 471; and McAdoo to James E. Murray, January 23, 1940 (quotation), box 470, McAdoo Papers, LC.

59. Robert H. Jackson to William Gibbs McAdoo, February 14, 1940, box 16, Jackson Papers, LC; New York Times, March 15, 1940, 12.

60. William Gibbs McAdoo to Edwin M. Watson, May 9, 1940 (quotation), box 471, McAdoo Papers, LC; LAT, May 8, 1940, 1.

61. "Reports on Western Trip," no date [May 1940], box 10, PVMP.

62. News release, "Governor Lloyd C. Stark Completely Successful in Obtaining Uninstructed, Pro-Roosevelt Delegation," no date [April 1940], box 14, Edwin M. Watson Papers, Albert and Shirley Small Special Collections Library, University of Virginia (UVA).

63. Edwin M. Watson to FDR, December 20, 1939, box 14, Watson Papers, UVA. See also Lloyd C. Stark to Watson, November 17, 1939, December 2, 1939, December 20, 1939, and December 26, 1939; Stark to FDR, January 6, 1940; FDR to Stark, January 11, 1940, all in reel 1, Documents from the White House Files of Franklin D. Roosevelt Pertaining to Harry S. Truman, Harry S. Truman Library (HSTL).

64. When the Clark forces tried to get one of their own appointed as a district attorney, Stark advised that "a word to Bob Jackson will stop this maneuver." To that, FDR jotted: "Pa Tell Jackson." FDR handwritten comment on Edwin M. Watson to FDR, March 29, 1940, box 14, Watson Papers, UVA. Frank McMurray to Harry S. Truman, February 8, 1940; Truman to McMurray, February 14, 1940, box 166, Senatorial and Vice Presidential File, HSTL.

65. FDR handwritten note, April 6, 1940, box 14, Watson Papers, UVA.

66. Pamphlet, "Draft Roosevelt," May 4, 1940, box 166, Senatorial and Vice Presidential File, HSTL.

67. WES, April 21, 1940, A-2, and April 26, 1940, A-3 (quotation).

68. Pepper Diary, April 29, 1940, FSU; *Arizona Republic*, May 9, 1940, 3; *WES*, May 12, 1940, B-2, and May 16, 1940, A-11.

69. *WES*, February 25, 1940, A-5, and February 28, 1940, A-3; McNutt address in Raleigh, January 8, 1940 (quotation), box 6, Information Files, Records of the Administrator of the Federal Security Agency (FSA), Record Group (RG) 235, National Archives, College Park (NACP).

70. *WES*, April 21, 1940, A-2.

71. Pepper Diary, February 3, 1940, and March 26, 1940 (quotation), FSU.

72. "Comments on the Book 'Using Our Heads,'" no date [1940], box 10, PVMP.

73. McNutt to FDR, April 4, 1940, and attached note; FDR to Steve Early, no date; and FDR to McNutt, April 10, 1940 (quotation), PPF 2836, FDRL.

74. Carleton B. McCulloch to Meredith Nicholson, April 27, 1940, box 1, McCulloch Papers, IHS.

75. *Bismarck (ND) Tribune*, April 9, 1940, 1.

76. *Wichita (KS) Eagle*, April 21, 1940, 1.

77. *Los Angeles Herald-Express*, May 11, 1940, A-4.

78. *Bismarck (ND) Tribune*, April 9, 1940, 1.

79. *Los Angeles Herald-Express*, May 10, 1940, 1.

80. *Arizona Republic*, May 11, 1940, II-8.

81. *Albuquerque Journal*, May 9, 1940, 1, and *Los Angeles Herald-Express*, May 11, 1940, A-4 (quotation).

82. *LAT*, May 12, 1940, pt. II, 4.

83. Pepper Diary, May 12, 1940, FSU.

84. Press release, May 30, 1940, box 14, Randolph Carpenter Papers, Department of Special Collections, Wichita State University (WSU) Libraries, Wichita, Kansas.

85. "Friends Ponder M'Nutt's Future," *Indianapolis News (IN)*, no date [ca. May 31, 1940], fiche 3, Department of Indiana, Biographical File: Paul V. McNutt, ALL.

86. Frank M. McHale to Randolph Carpenter, June 13, 1940, box 14, Carpenter Papers, WSU.

87. *Indianapolis Star (IS)*, July 1, 1940, 1.

88. "Friends Ponder," *IN*, no date [ca. May 31, 1940], fiche 3, McNutt Biographical File: Paul V. McNutt, ALL; Wayne Coy to Davis Vandivier, May 31, 1940 (quotation), box 16, Coy Papers, FDRL.

89. Frank M. McHale to Wayne Coy, March 23, 1940, box 11, and Coy to Edward D. Hester, March 13, 1940, box 7, Coy Papers, FDRL; Henry Stuart to Harold L. Ickes, June 17, 1940 (quotation), box 234, Harold L. Ickes Papers, LC.

90. Harold L. Ickes to Henry Stuart, June 25, 1940, box 234 (first quotation), and Harold L. Ickes Diary, June 2, 1940, 4440 (second quotation), box 6—both in Ickes Papers, LC.

91. Wayne Coy to Frank M. McHale, June 4, 1940, box 11, Coy Papers, FDRL.

92. Pepper Diary, June 1, 1940, folder 4, box 1, series 439, Pepper Papers, FSU.

93. Wallace Diary, March 23, 1940, Wallace Papers, UIL.

94. Michael Beschloss, *Kennedy and Roosevelt: The Uneasy Alliance* (New York: W. W. Norton, 1980), 200.

95. Clapper Diary, February 25, 1940, box 9, Clapper Papers, LC.

96. Henry A. Wallace oral history (January 18, 1940), 687, OHRO-CU.

97. Wayne Coy to Harry Hopkins, July 1, 1940, box 4, Hopkins Papers, GU; *IS*, June 28, 1940, 12, and June 27, 1940, 1.

98. Henry Morgenthau Jr. Presidential Diary, June 28, 1940, Henry Morgenthau Jr. Papers, FDRL; *WES*, April 23, 1940, A-10; Wallace Diary, March 6 and 23, 1940, Wallace Papers, UIL. Daniel Scroop, *Mr. Democrat: Jim Farley, the New Deal, and the Making of Modern American Politics* (Ann Arbor: University of Michigan Press, 2006), 181–182.

99. Bernard Donahoe, *Private Plans and Public Dangers: The Story of FDR's Third Nomination* (Notre Dame, IN: University of Notre Dame Press, 1965), 171.

100. Memorandum of conversation, July 3, 1940, box 47, Cordell Hull Papers, LC.

101. Doris Kearns Goodwin, *No Ordinary Time: Franklin and Eleanor Roosevelt, The*

*Home Front in World War II* (New York: Simon and Schuster, 1994), 113.

102. Homer S. Cummings Diary, July 12, 1940, box 235, Homer S. Cummings Papers, UVA.

103. James F. Byrnes, chapter "VP 1940," no date, folder 6, box 9, book materials, James F. Byrnes Papers, Department of Special Collections, Clemson University Libraries, Clemson, South Carolina. At the eleventh hour, FDR disavowed any ambition for a third term no doubt to make the draft that was to come seem all the more spontaneous. Joseph E. Davies to Marjorie Merriwether Post Davies, May 4, 1940, box 11, Post Family Papers, Bentley Historical Library (BHL).

104. *Des Moines Register (DMR)*, July 17, 1940, 6 (first quotation); *Hartford Courant,* July 16, 1940, 1 (second and third quotations).

105. Courtney Letts de Espil Diary, July 17, 1940, box 3, Courtney Letts de Espil Papers, LC.

106. *Birmingham News,* July 16, 1940, 1.

107. *DMR,* July 1, 1940, 4, July 3, 1940, 1, and July 13, 1940, 1; Eleanor Roosevelt, *This I Remember* (New York: Harper and Brothers, 1949), 214–215; *Cleveland Plain Dealer,* July 15, 1940, 1; Joseph Davies to Marjorie Davies, July 12, 1940 (quotation), box 11, Post Family Papers, BHL.

108. Robert Jackson oral history, 1952–1953, 770, OHRO-CU.

109. *Hartford Courant,* July 17, 1940, 1.

110. Goodwin, *No Ordinary Time,* 126.

111. *DMR,* July 17, 1940, 1 (all previous quotations).

112. Jackson oral history, 1952–1953, 770, OHRO-CU; "Two Men at Last Liven Convention," *Cleveland Plain Dealer,* July 17, 1940, 8.

113. *Buffalo Evening News,* July 17, 1940, 18; *Rocky Mountain News,* July 20, 1940, 8 (quotation).

114. *Chicago Daily News,* July 15, 1940, 4.

115. Perkins oral history, book 7 (1955), 423, OHRO-CU.

116. Claude R. Wickard oral history, 1482, box 55, Wickard Papers, FDRL.

117. *IS,* July 16, 1940, 1, and July 1, 1940, 1 (both quotations).

118. *DMR,* July 17, 1940, 5, and *IS,* July 17, 1940, 1.

119. May Thompson Evans oral history, January 30, 1978, 51, J. Y. Joyner Library, East Carolina University (ECU), Greenville, North Carolina.

120. See Claude R. Wickard Diary, July 11, 1940, box 20, Claude R. Wickard Papers, FDR; Perkins oral history, book 7 (1955), 412, OHRO-CU; Frances Perkins, *The Roosevelt I Knew* (New York: Viking, 1946), 127; Curtis Roosevelt, *Too Close to the Sun: Growing Up in the Shadow of My Grandparents, Franklin and Eleanor* (New York: PublicAffairs, 2008), 173; Jackson oral history, 1952–1953, 754–755, OHRO-CU.

121. Letts de Espil Diary, June 15, 1940, and July 24, 1940, box 3, Letts de Espil Papers, LC; Jackson oral history, 1952–1953, 754–758, OHRO-CU; Ickes Diary, August 4, 1940, 4686–4687, Ickes Papers, LC.

122. Robert H. Jackson, "The Attorney Generalship of Robert H. Jackson," 7 (quotation), box 189, Robert H. Jackson Papers, LC.

123. Ickes Diary, August 4, 1940, 4686, box 6, Ickes Papers, LC; Jackson, "The Attorney Generalship of Robert H. Jackson," 7, box 189, Jackson Papers, LC; *IS,* July 4, 1940, 1; Claude A. Wickard, "The 1940 Convention," no date, *Documentary History of the Franklin D. Roosevelt Presidency,* vol. 13, *The Presidential Campaign of 1940,* ed. George McJimsey (Bethesda, MD: University Publications of America, 2003), 172.

124. Wallace Diary, July 9, 1940, Wallace Papers, UIL.

125. "The McNutt Ticket," unsigned, undated manuscript, in McJimsey, *Documentary History,* vol. 13, 44; Wickard Diary, July 18, 1940, box 20, Wickard Papers, FDRL; Robert W. Woolley, unpublished autobiography, chapter 48, 16, box 44, Robert W. Woolley Papers, LC; James A. Farley memorandum, August 16, 1940, box 45, Farley Papers, LC; FDR to McNutt, August 3, 1940, PPF 2836, FDRL; "History Will Call Him a Great

American," *Bloomington (IN) Star-Courier,* no date [March 1955], Paul V. McNutt Obituaries, John L. Krauss Collection (private), Indianapolis.

126. *IS,* July 19, 1940, 1.

127. Wickard oral history, 1485, box 55, Wickard Papers, FDRL; Walter Trohan, *Political Animals: Memoirs of a Sentimental Cynic* (Garden City, NY: Doubleday, 1975), 121; Wickard Diary, June 27, 1940, box 20, Wickard Papers, FDRL. During a June 1940 meeting, Roosevelt encouraged McNutt's ambitions. Wickard Diary, June 27, 1940, box 20, Wickard Papers, FDRL.

128. John E. Hurt interview with the author, August 20, 2005; Fowler V. Harper to Wayne Coy, July 29, 1940, box 7, Coy Papers, FDRL; Woolley, "Politics Is Hell," chapter 48, 16 (quotation), box 44, Woolley Papers, LC.

129. Wickard, "The 1940 Convention," 184 (quotations). See also Fowler V. Harper to Wayne Coy, August 2, 1940, and Coy to Harper, August 6, 1940, box 7, Coy Papers, FDRL.

130. Frank M. McHale to Kathleen McNutt, January 17, 1958, McNutt Papers, Krauss Collection.

131. Perkins oral history, book 7 (1955), 481.

132. Wickard, "The 1940 Convention," 185 (quotation). *DMR,* July 19, 1940, 1.

133. Wickard, "The 1940 Convention," 186; "The McNutt Ticket," 42; *Atlanta Journal,* July 19, 1940, 3, 15; *Atlanta Constitution,* July 21, 1940, 8 (quotations).

134. *Hartford Courant,* July 19, 1940, 2 (quotations). On Kerr, see "History Will Call Him a Great American," *Bloomington (IN) Star-Courier,* no date [March 1955], McNutt Obituaries, Krauss Collection.

135. *Atlanta Constitution,* July 19, 1940, 3 (first two quotations); *Buffalo Evening News,* July 19, 1940, 5 (second two quotations).

136. *Atlanta Constitution,* July 19, 1940, 3 (all quotations).

137. Courtney Letts de Espil Diary, July 18, 1940, box 3, Letts de Espil Papers, LC.

138. Radio broadcast of McNutt's address to the Democratic National Convention, July 18, 1940, call number LWO5326—R5B3, Title 18844244, Motion Picture, Broadcasting and Record Sound Division, LC.

139. Ibid.

140. *Atlanta Constitution,* July 19, 1940, 3 (quotation).

141. "The McNutt Ticket," 44. McNutt read only the last part of a prepared speech. See speech draft, no date [1940], box 4, Coy Papers, FDRL.

142. Wallace oral history ("The Democratic National Convention"), 1231, OHRO-CU.

143. *Hartford Courant,* July 20, 1940, 6; *St. Paul Pioneer Press,* July 19, 1940, 1; radio broadcast of McNutt's address to the Democratic National Convention, July 18, 1940 (quotation), Call Number LWO5326—R5B3, Title 18844244, LC.

144. *St. Paul (MN) Pioneer Press,* July 19, 1940, 1 (all quotations).

145. Bankhead won 329.26 votes. *Providence Journal,* July 19, 1940, 6.

146. *Chicago Daily News,* July 19, 1940, 1; *Montgomery (AL) Advertiser,* July 20, 1940, 4, and July 21, 1940, 1; Woolley, unpublished autobiography, chapter 48, 17 (quotation), box 44, Woolley Papers, LC.

147. Bernard De Voto to Elmer Davis, July 21, 1940, box 1, Elmer Davis Papers, LC.

148. *Atlanta Constitution,* July 21, 1940, 8.

149. Goodwin, *No Ordinary Time,* 133.

150. *Atlanta Journal,* July 19, 1940, 15; Samuel I. Rosenman, *Working with Roosevelt* (New York: Harper and Brothers, 1952), 215 (quotation).

151. *IS,* July 19, 1940, 1; *IN,* July 11, 1947, pt. 1, p. 10 (first quotation), and Ickes Diary, July 21, 1940, 4624 (second quotation), box 6, Ickes Papers, LC.

152. Jackson oral history, 1952–1953, 762–763 (quotation), OHRO-CU.

153. Alben W. Barkley to Henry A. Wallace, June 12, 1954, reel 50, and Wallace to Barkley, May 21, 1954 (quotation), reel 49, Wallace Papers, UIL.

154. Evans oral history, January 30, 1978, 51–52, ECU.

155. Jackson oral history, 1952–1953, 762–763, OHRO-CU.

156. FDR to McNutt, August 3, 1940, PPF 2836, FDRL.

157. J. F. B. Carruthers to Lowell Mellett, July 26, 1940, box 10, PVMP.

158. Carleton B. McCulloch to Booth Tarkington, July 29, 1940, folder 3, box 202, Tarkington Papers, PU.

159. Booth Tarkington to Carleton B. McCulloch, August 1, 1940, folder 8, box 176, Tarkington Papers, PU.

160. Farley memorandum, August 16, 1940, box 45, Farley Papers, LC, and Carleton B. McCulloch to Booth Tarkington, August 5, 1940 (quotation), folder 3, box 202, Tarkington Papers, PU.

161. Carleton B. McCulloch to Booth Tarkington, July 29, 1940, folder 3, box 202, Tarkington Papers, PU.

162. Perkins oral history, book 7 (1955), 483.

163. Frank M. McHale to Robert F. Wagner, July 27, 1940, box 699, Personal Files, Robert F. Wagner Papers, GU.

164. Frank M. McHale to McNutt, August 6, 1944, box 10, PVMP; William F. Welch interview with the author, January 11, 2006. Welch was a protégé of McHale's.

165. Wickard Diary, July 19, 1940, box 20, Wickard Papers, FDRL.

166. Gustave Breaux to Alben W. Barkley, July 19, 1940, box 12, Political File, Alben W. Barkley Papers, Margaret I. King Library, University of Kentucky, Lexington.

167. Arthur O. Garrett to Frank M. McHale, August 5, 1940, box 10, PVMP.

168. J. F. B. Carruthers to FDR, July 31, 1940, box 10, PVMP.

169. Farley memorandum, August 1, 1940, box 45, Farley Papers, LC.

170. FDR to McNutt, August 3, 1940, PPF 2836, FDRL; Henry A. Wallace to McNutt, August 5, 1940, McNutt Papers, Krauss Collection; Wayne Coy to Harry Hopkins, August 28, 1940, box 8; Coy to Fowler V. Harper, July 31, 1940, box 7; and Coy to Harper, August 6, 1940 (quotations), box 7, Coy Papers, FDRL.

171. J. F. B. Carruthers to FDR, July 31, 1940, box 10, PVMP; Wayne Coy to Fowler V. Harper, August 6, 1940, box 7, Coy Papers, FDRL; Ruby A. Black to Eleanor Roosevelt, July 23, 1940, box 2, Black Papers, LC; Courtney Letts de Espil Diary, September 29, 1940, box 3, Letts de Espil Papers, LC; Woolley, unpublished autobiography, chapter 48, 17–18 (quotation), box 44, Woolley Papers, LC.

172. Carleton B. McCulloch to Meredith Nicholson, August 21, 1940, box 1, McCulloch Papers, IHS; "The McNutt Ticket," 42; Wayne Coy to Harry Hopkins, August 28, 1940 (quotation), box 8, Coy Papers, FDRL.

173. Fowler V. Harper to Wayne Coy, July 29, 1940, box 7, Coy Papers, FDRL.

174. Carleton B. McCulloch to Booth Tarkington, July 29, 1940, folder 3, box 202, Tarkington Papers, PU.

175. Steve Neal, Dark Horse: A Biography of Wendell Willkie (Lawrence: University Press of Kansas, 1984), 25–180, 85 and 122 (quotation).

176. "Acceptance Address of Wendell L. Willkie, Republican Nominee for President," August 17, 1940 (all quotations), box 3, Wendell L. Willkie Papers, LL.

177. Justin H. Libby, "Wendell Willkie and the Election of 1940," Gentlemen from Indiana: National Party Candidates, 1836–1940, ed. Ralph Gray (Indianapolis: Indiana Historical Bureau, 1977), 306–309. See also Willkie speech in South Bend, September 30, 1940, box 3, Willkie Papers, LL, and criticism of his overlong acceptance speech in Neal, Dark Horse, 136, 143 (quotation).

178. McNutt address in Portland, September 6, 1940, folder 2253, George Peek Papers, WHMC.

179. McNutt address in Springfield, September 27, 1940, box 18, PVMP; McNutt address in Buffalo, October 25, 1940, box 6, Information Files—FSA, RG 235, NACP.

180. McNutt address in Marion, November 4, 1940, box 18, PVMP.

181. McNutt address in Baltimore, September 19, 1940, box 18, PVMP.

182. Libby, "Wendell Willkie and the Election of 1940," 306; Lilienthal, *Journals*, vol. 1, 208 (quotation).

183. Lilienthal, *Journals*, vol. 1, 202.

184. Wendell L. Willkie to Clapper, March 9, 1938, box 178, Clapper Papers, LC. See also Willkie to McNutt, May 16, 1925, box 1, and Willkie to McNutt, October 1, 1928, box 4, PVMP.

185. Wendell L. Willkie to McNutt, March 20, 1931, box 5, Paul V. McNutt Papers, Indiana University School of Law Library, Bloomington (quotations); Newton D. Baker to Willkie, July 23, 1932, box 192, Newton D. Baker Papers, LC; Wayne Coy to Willkie, June 10, 1938, box 1, Willkie Papers, LL.

186. Wendell L. Willkie to Clapper, March 8 and 9, 1938, box 178, Clapper Papers, LC; unaddressed Willkie letter, October 5, 1939, box 1, Willkie Papers, LL. In a conversation with Benjamin V. Cohen, one of FDR's lieutenants, Willkie "pooh-poohed" the idea that he and McNutt were "close friends." See Benjamin V. Cohen, "Conversation with Willkie," December 11, 1939, box 4, Harry Barnard Papers, LL. Willkie seemed favorable to McNutt's campaign, but he knew that public endorsement of it by a utility man would have hurt McNutt. Willkie denied making any financial contribution to the campaign. See Clapper Diary, March 8, 1938, box 178, Clapper Papers, LC, and Willkie to Paul E. Fisher, May 27, 1939, box 1, Willkie Papers, LL.

187. Lilienthal, *Journals*, vol. 1, 165 (first quotation); Herman B Wells to John M. Roberts, July 17, 1940 (second quotation), folder: Ro 1940–41, Presidential Papers, Herman B Wells Papers, Indiana University Archives (IUA).

188. Stephen Early to McNutt, October 10, 1940, and John R. Boettiger to FDR, October 10, 1940, box 10, PVMP; McNutt address in Baltimore, September 19, 1940 (quotations), box 18, PVMP.

189. McNutt address in Portland, September 6, 1940, folder 2253, Peek Papers, WHMC.

190. McNutt address in Springfield, September 27, 1940, box 18, PVMP.

191. *Portland (ME) Press Herald*, September 9, 1940, 4.

192. Oscar R. Ewing to McNutt, September 9, 1940, box 10, PVMP.

193. An editor in Philadelphia believed that to be McNutt's aim, and he offered him some sanguine advice: "to lay low" until the next presidential election season arrived. C. William Duncan to McNutt, December 7, 1940, box 10, PVMP.

194. John R. Boettiger to FDR, October 10, 1940, box 10, PVMP.

195. Jerome N. Frank to McNutt, November 7, 1940, box 33, Jerome N. Frank Papers, Manuscripts and Archives, Yale University Library, New Haven, Connecticut.

196. *Buffalo Evening News*, October 26, 1940, 18 (first quotation); *Springfield (MA) Daily Republican*, September 28, 1940, 2 (second quotation).

197. *Springfield (MA) Union*, September 28, 1940, 1 (first quotation); *Springfield Daily Republican*, September 28, 1940, 1-A (second and third quotations); *Bangor (ME) Daily News*, September 6, 1940, 24 (last quotation).

198. Lilienthal, *Journals*, vol. 1, 202.

199. *Sioux City (IA) Journal*, October 15, 1940, 1.

200. Lorena Hickok to ER, March 8, 1940, *Empty without You*, 227; James H. Madison, *Indiana through Tradition and Change: A History of the Hoosier State and Its People, 1920–1945* (Indianapolis: Indiana Historical Society, 1982), 149–151.

201. Randolph H. Mayes to Clyde C. Carlin, July 6, 1940 (quotation); "Minton Boasts He's a Product of a 2 Percent Club," *Chicago Tribune*, March 14, 1940; "Senator Clark Rakes 2% Club as Minton Leaps to Its Defense," *IN*, March 12, 1940, all in box 2, Raymond E. Willis Papers, Manuscript Division, Indiana State Library (ISL).

202. Senator William E. Jenner speech, October 8, 1940, box 8, William Ezra Jenner Papers, Archives of Hanover College, Duggan Library, Hanover, Indiana.

203. Linda C. Gugin and James E. St. Clair, *Sherman Minton: New Deal Senator, Cold War Justice* (Indianapolis: Indiana Historical Society, 1997), 143.

204. McNutt address in Marion, November 4, 1940, box 18, PVMP.

205. James L. MacDowell, "Henry F. Schricker," in *The Governors of Indiana*, ed. Linda Gugin and James E. St. Clair (Indianapolis: Indiana Historical Society Press, 2006), 310–311; Anthony J. Badger, *The New Deal: The Depression Years, 1933–1940* (Chicago: Ivan Dee, 1989), 280–281; Sherman Minton to George W. Norris, November 25, 1940, box 370, George W. Norris Papers, LC.

206. Neal, *Dark Horse*, 159.

207. Goodwin, *No Ordinary Time*, 187.

208. McNutt address in Marion, November 4, 1940, box 18, PVMP.

209. McNutt address in Clayton, Missouri, October 15, 1940, box 18, PVMP.

210. Richard Polenberg, *War and Society: The United States, 1941–1945* (Philadelphia: Lippincott, 1972), 186 (quotation). Governor Herbert Lehman of New York insisted that Hitler, Mussolini, and Stalin were rooting for Roosevelt's defeat, and Wallace declared that the totalitarian powers saw the ill-prepared, error-prone Willkie as "their candidate." Ellsworth Barnard, *Wendell Willkie: Fighter for Freedom* (Marquette: Northern Michigan University Press, 1966), 259.

211. *WES*, September 28, 1940, A-11, October 17, 1940, A-22, and October 26, 1940, A-18; Harry Barnard notes of an interview with Edith Willkie, August 29, 1972 (quotation), folder 22, box 1, Harry Barnard Papers, LL.

212. Willkie address in Hammond, Indiana, October 22, 1940, box 4, Willkie Papers, LL.

213. Robert Dallek, *Franklin D. Roosevelt and American Foreign Policy, 1932–1945* (New York: Oxford University Press, 1979), 250–251. See, for example, Katharine Hepburn to

Harry Barnard, April 29, 1940, box 1, Harry Barnard Papers, LL.

214. McDowell, "Henry F. Schricker,"311; Madison, *Indiana through Tradition and Change*, 151.

## 12. DIMENSIONS OF SECURITY (1939–1945)

1. Carleton B. McCulloch to Meredith Nicholson, December 27, 1940, and November 27, 1941, box 1, Carleton B. McCulloch Papers, Indiana Historical Society (IHS).

2. Richard Polenberg, *War and Society: The United States, 1941–1945* (Philadelphia: Lippincott, 1972), 77; Eric Larrabee, *Commander in Chief: Franklin Delano Roosevelt, His Lieutenants, and Their War* (New York: Harper and Row, 1987), 3 (quotation).

3. Richard Hofstadter, *The American Political Tradition and the Men Who Made It* (New York: Vintage, 1973), 451 (quotation); Stephen B. Adams, *Mr. Kaiser Goes to Washington: The Rise of a Government Entrepreneur* (Chapel Hill: University of North Carolina Press, 1997), 62.

4. David M. Kennedy, *Freedom from Fear: The American People in Depression and War, 1929–1945* (New York: Oxford University Press, 1999), 363.

5. Barry Dean Karl, *Executive Reorganization and Reform in the New Deal: The Genesis of Administrative Management, 1900–1939* (Cambridge, MA: Harvard University Press, 1963), 256; Richard Polenberg, *Reorganizing Roosevelt's Government: The Controversy over Executive Reorganization, 1936–1939* (Cambridge, MA: Harvard University Press, 1966), 187–188; David Brinkley, *Washington Goes to War* (New York: Ballantine Books, 1988), 212 (quotations); Larry DeWitt, "Never a Finished Thing: Arthur J. Altmeyer and the Formative Years of Social Security," unpublished manuscript, no date, 140, Social Security Administration Archives (SSAA).

6. Mariano-Florentino Cuéllar, *Governing Security: The Hidden Origins of American Security Agencies* (Stanford, CA: Stanford Law Books, 2013), 66.

7. Paul V. McNutt interview (quoting FDR), no date [ca. 1939], box 4, Mary E. Switzer Papers, Arthur and Elizabeth Schlesinger Library (SL).

8. This was the opinion of the acting general counsel at the FSA. See John Henry Lewis to Paul V. McNutt ("McNutt"), August 4, 1939, box 4, Switzer Papers, SL.

9. Edward D. Berkowitz, "Rehabilitation: The Federal Government's Response to Disability, 1935–1954," PhD diss., Northwestern University, 1976, xiii.

10. The FSA also oversaw such institutions as St. Elizabeth's Hospital and Howard University. DeWitt, "Never a Finished Thing," 140.

11. Oscar R. Ewing oral history, August 26, 1966, 11 (both quotations), Oral History Research Office, Columbia University (OHRO-CU).

12. Jack B. Tate oral history, June 3, 1965, 55, OHRO-CU. The FSA's unwieldy nature persisted in its successor, the Department of Health, Education, and Welfare (HEW), which Congress established in 1953. Ewing reflected that there were "few departments" tougher to run than HEW. Ewing oral history, August 26, 1966, 11, OHRO-CU.

13. Frances Perkins to McNutt, no date [1939], box 12, PVMP.

14. Maurine Mulliner interview, January 28, 1965, 56, SSAA; Tate oral history, June 3, 1965, 55–56, OHRO-CU, and John J. Corson oral history, March 3, 1967, 52, SSAA.

15. Maurine Mulliner oral history, April 26, 1967, 160–161, OHRO-CU; John A. Salmond, The Civilian Conservation Corps, 1933–1942: A New Deal Case Study (Durham, NC: Duke University Press, 1967), 179 (quotation).

16. DeWitt, "Never a Finished Thing," 143.

17. Bernard Bellush, He Walked Alone: A Biography of John Gilbert Winant (The Hague: Mouton, 1968), 118.

18. Bruce Catton column, "Headline Success in Industrial Legislation—but Altmeyer, of Social Security, Likes Obscurity," August 10, 1939, box 2, Arthur J. Altmeyer Papers Part 1, Wisconsin Historical Society (WHS), Madison.

19. Leonard Lesser oral history, March 16, 1966, 3, and Arthur J. Altmeyer oral history, June 29, 1967, 75 (quotations), both in OHRO-CU.

20. Corson oral history, March 3, 1967, 50, SSAA; Social Security Board press release, September 30, 1938, and "Political Aspects of the Administration of Old-Age Assistance in Ohio," no date [1938], box 6, Altmeyer Papers Part 1, WHS; Arthur J. Altmeyer, The Formative Years of Social Security (Madison: University of Wisconsin Press, 1966), 121–122; Arthur J. Altmeyer, handwritten, undated notes ["1940, c. Mar. 28" and "concerning 1939, July"], box 4, Altmeyer Papers Part 1, WHS; Altmeyer oral history, June 29, 1967, 75–76, OHRO-CU.

21. George Q. Flynn, The Mess in Washington: Manpower Mobilization in World War II. (Westport, CT: Greenwood Press, 1979), 10.

22. Bernice Bernstein oral history, March 3, 1965, 34, OHRO-CU.

23. Tate oral history, June 3, 1965, 56, OHRO-CU.

24. Mulliner oral history, April 26, 1967, 161; Lavinia Engle oral history, April 21, 1967, 131; Tate oral history, June 3, 1965, 94 (quotation), all in OHRO-CU.

25. Altmeyer oral history, June 29, 1967, 77, OHRO-CU.

26. Mulliner oral history, April 26, 1967, 274 (both quotations), OHRO-CU.

27. Tate oral history, June 3, 1965, 96, OHRO-CU.

28. Corson oral history, March 3, 1967, 10, SSAA.

29. Mulliner oral history, April 26, 1967, 274, OHRO-CU.

30. "The Mirror of Washington," Philadelphia Ledger, August 19, 1939, box 4, Wayne Coy Papers, Franklin D. Roosevelt Library (FDRL).

31. Tate oral history, June 3, 1965, 95, OHRO-CU.

32. Newspaper clipping, "McNutt Has One-Man Brain Trust in Coy," July 18, 1938, box 4, Coy Papers, FDRL.

33. Grace Coy to Wayne Coy, "Sunday" and "Saturday" [ca. August 1939], press notice, "Wayne Coy, McNutt's Advisor, Returns to Official Duties," April 29, 1940, Kathleen McNutt to Grace Coy, ca. August 1939, and Federal Communications Commission press release, "Biographical Sketch of Chairman Wayne Coy," July 2, 1951, all in box 4, Coy Papers, FDRL; *Manila Bulletin*, January 17, 1941, 15; Booth Tarkington to Carleton McCulloch, September 6, 1941 (quotations), box 177, Booth Tarkington Papers, Princeton University (PU) Library.

34. "Biographical Sketch of Miss Mary Elizabeth Switzer," no date, box 14; Mary E. Switzer to Elizabeth Brandeis Rauschenbush, August 11, 1943, box 61; newspaper clippings, "Miss Switzer, McNutt Aide, Sidetracks," no date, and "Treasury Aide Loves Work," no date, microfilm reel M-53; Switzer to Lillian Adlow Friedberg, April 11, 1941, and Switzer to Rauschenbush, August 11, 1943, box 61; Switzer to Estelle Warren, December 20, 1939, box 57; Switzer to Leonard Jacobs, December 20, 1948, box 51; Switzer to Richard King, December 9, 1939, box 51; Switzer to Dr. and Mrs. John W. Trask, December 24, 1942, box 56; Switzer to Victor Weybright, September 14, 1942, December 21, 1942, and August 13, 1943, box 63; and Kathleen McNutt to Switzer, no date [1955] (quotation), box 53—all in Switzer Papers, SL.

35. Mary E. Switzer to Maurice Neufeld, August 12, 1937 (quotation), box 54, Switzer Papers, SL. Switzer once tried to see the Moscow purge trials from the point of view of their perpetrator, Joseph Stalin. See Switzer to Pat Powers, no date [ca. 1937], box 54, Switzer Papers, SL.

36. When Fowler Harper faced allegations of being a Communist, Switzer was outraged. Given McNutt's close relationship with Fowler, he no doubt was as well. Mary E. Switzer to Victor Weybright, March 25, 1940, box 63, Switzer Papers, SL.

37. Berkowitz, "Rehabilitation," 219–262, especially 245, 250, and 241.

38. Even before Coy entered the hospital, Switzer was speaking to agency officials on Coy's behalf. See Mary E. Switzer to Tracy Copp, August 2, 1939, box 59, Switzer Papers, SL. Tracy Copp was at the Office of Education, which was not under Switzer's charge, though she admitted that she was able to "push along some things [Tracy and I] have been interested in." Switzer to Estelle Warren, October 27, 1939, box 57, Switzer Papers, SL.

39. "Biographical Sketch of Miss Mary Elizabeth Switzer, Assistant to the Federal Security Administrator," no date, and "Highlights on Experience in Health and Medical Work of Miss Mary E. Switzer," no date, box 14, Switzer Papers, SL.

40. Mary E. Switzer to Richard King, December 9, 1939, box 51, Switzer Papers, SL.

41. Mary E. Switzer to Kathleen McNutt, no date [ca. March 1955] and Kathleen McNutt to Switzer, no date [ca. March 1955] (quotation), box 53, Switzer Papers, SL.

42. Kirstin Downey, *The Life and Legacy of Frances Perkins—Social Security, Unemployment, and the Minimum Wage* (New York: Anchor Books, 2009), 76 (first quotation) and 303 (second quotation).

43. Mary E. Switzer to Victor Weybright, August 13, 1943, box 63, Switzer Papers, SL.

44. Mary E. Switzer to Richard King, December 9, 1939, box 51, Switzer Papers, SL.

45. Mary E. Switzer to Estelle Warren, December 20, 1939, box 57, Switzer Papers, SL.

46. Mary E. Switzer to Estelle Warren, October 27, 1939, box 57, Switzer Papers, SL.

47. Mary E. Switzer to Richard King, December 9, 1939, box 51, Switzer Papers, SL.

48. "Saner Social Security," January 28, 1939, box 3, Raymond Gram Swing Papers, LC.

49. Daniel Beland, *Social Security: History and Politics from the New Deal to the Privatization Debate* (Lawrence: University Press of Kansas, 2005), 68–70, 77 (quotations).

50. Alan Brinkley, "The New Deal Experiments," in *The Achievement of American Liberalism: The New Deal and Its Legacies,* ed. William H. Chafe (New York: Columbia University Press, 2003), 7.

51. Edward Berkowitz, "The First Advisory Council and the 1939 Amendments," in *Social Security after Fifty: Successes and Failures,* ed. Edward D. Berkowitz (New York: Greenwood Press, 1987), 59; "Saner Social Security," January 28, 1939 (quotation), box 3, Swing Papers, LC.

52. Berkowitz, "The First Fiscal Advisory Council and the 1939 Amendments," 56. "The problem of the reserve," Altmeyer recalled, "helped us to get the amendments of 1939." Altmeyer oral history, June 29, 1967, 66, OHRO-CU.

53. Beland, *Social Security,* 104 (both quotations).

54. Mark H. Leff, "Historical Perspectives on Old-Age Insurance," in Berkowitz, *Social Security after Fifty,* 41.

55. DeWitt, "Never a Finished Thing" 145–146; W. R. Williamson to Arthur J. Altmeyer, April 12, 1940; "Mr. Myer" and Williamson, April 12, 1940; "A Possible Plan for a Basic Flat Rate Pension," attached to Altmeyer to Harold Smith, December 30, 1940; and "Revision of the Old Age Security Program," March 19, 1939, all in box 8, Altmeyer Papers Part 1, WHS; Altmeyer to Stephen Early, March 28, 1940, folder: ALJ McNutt Speech Incident, Arthur J. Altmeyer Papers, SSAA; "The Capital Parade," *Washington Evening Star,* July 15, 1939, box 228, Individual File, Herbert Hoover Papers, Herbert Hoover Presidential Library (HHPL).

56. FSA press release, March 28, 1940 (all previous quotations), folder: ALJ McNutt Speech Incident, Altmeyer Papers, SSAA.

57. As McNutt prepared to propose an enlargement of Social Security, White House aide Tommy Corcoran advised FDR to issue a statement upon signing the Social Security amendments of 1939 in order to receive maximum credit for "any future opening up of the old age pension" system. Roosevelt did so.

Tommy G. Corcoran to FDR, August 7, 1939, box 1, Official File (OF) 3700, Franklin D. Roosevelt (FDR) Papers, FDRL.

58. Arthur J. Altmeyer to Stephen Early, March 28, 1940, folder: ALJ McNutt Speech Incident, Altmeyer Papers, SSAA; Telephone call between Early and Altmeyer, March 28, 1940, box 2, Altmeyer Papers Part 1, WHS; Altmeyer, *Formative Years of Social Security,* 122–123; DeWitt, "Never a Finished Thing," 148. McNutt speech, "Major Problems of Social Security," March 28, 1940 (quotation), folder: ALJ McNutt Speech Incident, Altmeyer Papers, SSAA.

59. FSA press release, March 28, 1940, folder: ALJ McNutt Speech Incident, Altmeyer Papers, SSAA.

60. Beland, *Social Security,* 74.

61. Leff, "Historical Perspectives on Old-Age Insurance," 32. The White House advised reporters to destroy all copies of McNutt's original text on grounds that he had chosen to revise his remarks. Undated note to correspondents, folder: ALJ McNutt Speech Incident, Altmeyer Papers, SSAA. McNutt went along with this story, explaining to reporters that he "decided to make some changes. See *New York Times* (*NYT*), March 29, 1940, 15. The only paper to cover the McNutt speech on Social Security was the *New York Times.* See *NYT,* March 29, 1940, 15.

62. Social Security Board *Daily Press Digest,* April 1940, box 4, Altmeyer Papers Part 1, WHS.

63. Harold D. Smith Diary, September 30, 1941, box 3, Harold D. Smith Papers, FDRL.

64. McNutt address, January 17, 1940, box 6, Information Files, Records of the Administrator of the Federal Security Agency, Record Group (RG) 235, National Archives, College Park (NACP).

65. Paul V. McNutt, "Should We Stay in the Philippines?" February 5, 1940, and "National Press Club Off-the Record Party," March 1, 1940 (quotation), both in box 17, PVMP.

66. McNutt address, January 13, 1940, box 17, PVMP.

67. McNutt address at Arlington Cemetery, May 30, 1940, box 1, Information Files, Records of the Administrator of the Federal Security Agency, RG 235, NACP.

68. Flynn, *The Mess in Washington*, 14.

69. Cuéllar, *Governing Security*, 103.

70. McNutt speech to the American Legion, no date, box 4, Information Files— FSA, RG 235, NACP, and McNutt to Chryst Loukas, December 14, 1941 (quotation), box 10, PVMP.

71. "McNutt's Lack of Action Criticized," *Indianapolis Times*, October 4, 1941 (all quotations), folder: Ind.—Biography McNutt, Paul V. and Family, Indiana Clipping File, Indiana State Library, Indianapolis.

72. Cuéllar, *Governing Security*, 109.

73. McNutt address, November 12, 1939, box 18, Richard V. Gilbert Papers, FDRL.

74. Draft article for National Rehabilitation News, "The Federal Security Agency and the National Defense Program," July 23, 1940, box 79, Switzer Papers, SL.

75. *Democratic Digest*, August 1940, 15.

76. "Fireside Chat on National Defense," May 26, 1940, *The Public Papers and Addresses of Franklin D. Roosevelt*, vol. 9 (1940), *War— and Aid to Democracies*, ed. Samuel I. Rosenman (New York: Macmillan, 1941), 237 (first quotation) and 239 (second quotation).

77. McNutt to FDR, November 18, 1940, box 1, OF 3700, FDR Papers, FDRL; Switzer speech, March 10, 1941, box 14, Switzer Papers, SL (quotation).

78. "Office of Defense Health and Welfare Services," no date, book B, box 2, Records of the Federal Security Agency: Dean Atlee Snyder Files, 1940–1958, RG 235, NACP; Charles Schottland oral history, June 4, 1965, 9 (quotation), OHRO-CU.

79. Kennedy, *Freedom from Fear*, 476.

80. Studs Terkel, *"The Good War": An Oral History of World War Two* (New York: Pantheon Books, 1984), 309–312; McNutt address, January 22, 1941 (quotations), box 4, Information Files—FSA, RG 235, NACP.

81. Richard Norton Smith, *Thomas E. Dewey and His Times* (New York: Simon and Schuster, 1982), 337.

82. "Coordination of Health, Welfare, and Related Activities," undated typescript paper [ca. April 1941), box 42, Caroline F. Ware Papers, FDRL. Technically, this paper covered the old post of Coordinator of Health, Welfare, Recreation, and Related Activities but the aims/work of that position and of the ODHWS were almost indistinguishable.

83. "Office of Defense Health and Welfare Services," no date, and "Factual Statement about the Office of Defense Health and Welfare Services," March 1, 1943, book B, box 2, Snyder Files—FSA, RG 235, NACP.

84. McNutt to Harold D. Smith, February 26, 1941, box 91, Records of the Administrator of the Federal Security Agency: General Classified Files, 1939–1944, RG 235, NACP.

85. News clipping, no date, Ruth Neely McNutt Remembrance Book, John L. Krauss Collection (private), Indianapolis; and Marilyn B. Hegarty, *Victory Girls, Khaki-Wackies, and Patriotutes: The Regulation of Female Sexuality during World War II* (New York: New York University Press, 2008), 2 (quotation).

86. Hegarty, *Victory Girls, Khaki-Wackies, and Patriotutes*, 67.

87. McNutt testimony before the House Committee to Investigate the Interstate Migration of Destitute Citizens, March 25, 1941, box 33, FSA General Classified Files, 1939–1944, RG 235, NACP.

88. Hegarty, *Victory Girls, Khaki-Wackies, and Patriotutes*, 16.

89. Ibid., 12–49.

90. McNutt to Mrs. Hereford Smith, March 29, 1943, box 11, FSA General Classified Files, 1939–1944, RG 235, NACP; Eliot Ness to "Sheriff," no date, box 19, William H. McReynolds Papers, FDRL; McNutt address, February 3, 1942, folder 1140, C. Jasper Bell Papers, Western Historical Manuscripts Collection (WHMC); Hegarty, *Victory Girls, Khaki-Wackies, and Patriotutes*, 6; McNutt to Guy Moffatt, June 17, 1942, folder: Federal Security Agency—Public Health Service, box

19, McReynolds Papers, FDRL; Schottland oral history, June 4, 1965, 10 (quotation), OHRO-CU.

91. Hegarty, *Victory Girls, Khaki-Wackies, and Patriotutes*, 28.

92. Karen Anderson, *Wartime Women: Sex Roles, Family Relations, and the Status of Women during World War II* (Westport, CT: Greenwood Press, 1981), 104–111; Hegarty, *Victory Girls, Khaki-Wackies, and Patriotutes*, 60 (quotation).

93. Richard Lingeman, *Don't You Know There's a War On? The American Home Front, 1941–1945* (New York: G. P. Putnam's Sons, 1970), 88.

94. William L. O'Neill, *A Democracy at War: America's Fight at Home and Abroad in World War II* (Cambridge, MA: Harvard University Press, 1995), 264; Arnold J. Sagalyn to Charles Taft, November 7, 1943 (quotation), box I-68, Charles Taft Papers, LC.

95. Hegarty, *Victory Girls, Khaki-Wackies, and Patriotutes*, 28; McNutt statement, March 22, 1945, Committee on Appropriations, United States House of Representatives, Seventy-Ninth Congress, First Session, *Hearings on Department of Labor—Federal Security Agency Appropriation Bill for 1946, Part 2* (Washington, DC: U.S. Government Printing Office, 1945), 19 (quotation).

96. Hegarty, *Victory Girls, Khaki-Wackies, and Patriotutes*, 20 (first quotation) and McNutt to Mrs. Hereford Smith, March 29, 1943, box 11, Records of the Administrator of the Federal Security Agency: General Classified Files, 1939–1944, RG 235, NACP (second quotation).

97. Thomas C. Billig to Jack B. Tate, February 10, 1941, box 91, Records of the Administrator of the Federal Security Agency: General Classified Files, 1939–1944, RG 235, NACP; Charles Taft to Horace D. Taft, April 12, 1941, box I-25, Charles Taft Papers, LC; McNutt to Dwight D. Eisenhower, July 7, 1947 (quotation), box 12, PVMP.

98. Meghan K. Winchell, *Good Girls, Good Food, Good Fun: The Story of USO Host-*

*esses during World War II* (Chapel Hill: University of North Carolina Press, 2008), 3.

99. Julia H. M. Carson, *Home Away from Home: The Story of the USO* (New York: Harper and Brothers, 1946), xii.

100. Carson, *Home Away from Home*, 20–138; Winchell, *Good Girls, Good Food, Good Fun*, 5 (quotation).

101. Winchell, *Good Girls, Good Food, Good Fun*, 9; McNutt to Charles A. Lindbergh, April 10, 1941, box 21, Charles A. Lindbergh Papers, Manuscripts and Archives, Yale University Library, New Haven, Connecticut (first quotation). McNutt testimony before the House Committee to Investigate the Interstate Migration of Destitute Citizens, March 25, 1941 (second quotation), box 33, FSA General Classified Files, 1939–1944, RG 235, NACP.

102. On Kathleen's dislike of politics, see Kathleen McNutt to Herbert Lehman, January 7, 1942, folder 612, Special Correspondence, Herbert Lehman Papers, Herbert Lehman Suite, Columbia University, New York. For her activities during the war, see Kathleen McNutt address, February 25, 1942, box 3, Information Files—FSA, RG 235, NACP; Kathleen McNutt to Frank Murphy, May 1, 1942, reel 73, Frank Murphy Papers, Bentley Historical Library, University of Michigan, Ann Arbor. *Indianapolis News*, September 26, 1945, pt. 2, 4 (quotations).

103. Press release, Office of the Coordinator of Health and Welfare and Related Services, February 10, 1941, box 2, John Punnett Peters Papers, Manuscripts and Archives, Yale University Library (YUL).

104. Charles Taft to Horace Taft, April 12, 1941, box I-25, Charles Taft to Seth Taft, April 29, 1943, and September 25, 1943, box 30, and Charles Taft Diary, May 17, 1941, June 16, 1941, and July 28, 1942, box I-1, all in Charles Taft Papers, LC. Winchell, *Good Girls, Good Food, Good Fun*, 4–5. *USO Bulletin*, June 6, 1941, in Charles Taft Diary, June 9, 1941, box I-1; Jane M. Hoey to Charles Taft, October 27, 1943, box I-51; Frank S. Lloyd to Charles Taft, September 30, 1943, box I-56; Harry J.

Emigh to Charles Taft, September 28, 1943 (quotation), box I-44, all in Charles Taft Papers, LC.

105. M. L. Wilson to Mary E. Switzer, April 7, 1941, box 87, FSA General Classified Files, 1939–1944, RG 235, NACP; "Accomplishments and Objectives of the Office of Defense Health and Welfare Services," undated typescript summary, box 4, and Mary E. Switzer to Erwin Schuller, July 7, 1944 (quotation), box 56, both in Switzer Papers, SL.

106. Mary E. Switzer interview, January 31, 1943, folder 179, box 14, Switzer Papers, SL; newsletter by Sherwood Gates, November 8, 1943, book J, box 5, Snyder Files—FSA, RG 235, NACP (quotation).

107. Carleton McCulloch to Booth Tarkington, November 24, 1941, box 202, Tarkington Papers, PU.

108. "National Nutrition Conference for Defense," *Journal of the American Medical Association*, June 7, 1941, box 17, Martha May Eliot Papers, SL.

109. McNutt radio broadcast, March 5, 1942, box 19, PVMP.

110. McNutt speech, March 13, 1942, box 19, PVMP.

111. Cuéllar, *Governing Security*, 211 (first and second quotations) and 69 (third quotation).

112. Office of Community War Services Final Report attached to Pearce Davies to Dean Atlee Snyder, September 15, 1947, book H, box 4, Snyder Files—FSA, RG 235, NACP (both quotations).

113. "Industrial Mobilization for War: History of the War Production Board," Part 5, 119, box 111, Julius Krug Papers, LC; Diehl to Dean Atlee Snyder, July 10, 1945, and Final Report by Pearce Davies attached to Pearce Davies to Snyder, September 15, 1947, book H, box 4, Snyder Files—FSA, RG 235, NACP; Lingeman, *Don't You Know There's a War On*, 285; Carson, *Home Away from Home*, viii (quotations).

114. Walter Hoving to Charles Taft, October 13, 1943, box I-51, Charles Taft Papers, LC.

115. Final Report by Pearce Davies attached to Davies to Dean Atlee Snyder, September 15, 1947, book H, box 4, Snyder Files—FSA, RG 235, NACP; O'Neill, *A Democracy at War*, 242; Polenberg, *War and Society*, 148–149 (quotation).

116. Anderson, *Wartime Women*, 123 (all quotations).

117. Charles Taft Diary, March 12, March 13, March 17, March 23, April 4, June 8, June 17, July 5, October 14, and November 11—all in 1943, box I-2, Charles Taft Papers, LC. See also O'Neill, *A Democracy at War*, 242.

118. Doris Kearns Goodwin, *No Ordinary Time: Franklin and Eleanor Roosevelt: The Home Front in World War II* (New York: Simon and Schuster, 1994), 280–281, 323–326; *Chicago Tribune*, April 19, 1942, I-16 William R. Castle Diary, March 26, 1942 (quotation), vol. 43, Houghton Library, Harvard University, Cambridge, Massachusetts.

119. McNutt address, November 8, 1941, box 4, Information Files—FSA, RG 235, NACP.

120. Raymond Gram Swing broadcast, February 22, 1943, box 21, Swing Papers, LC.

121. "Address to the Congress on the State of the Union," January 7, 1943, *The Public Papers and Addresses of Franklin D. Roosevelt*, vol. 12 (1943), *The Tide Turns*, ed. Samuel I. Rosenman (New York: Harper and Brothers, 1950), 31.

122. Swing broadcast, January 11, 1944, box 24, Swing Papers, LC.

123. McNutt statement, March 16, 1942, Committee on Appropriations, United States House of Representatives, Seventy-Seventh Congress, Second Session, *Hearings on Department of Labor—Federal Security Agency Appropriation Bill for 1943*, Part 2 (Washington, DC: U.S. Government Printing Office, 1942), 1; Richard A. Reiman, *The New Deal and American Youth: Ideas and Ideals in a Depression Decade* (Athens: University of Georgia Press, 1992), 172–178; John A. Salmond, *A Southern Rebel: The Life and Times of Aubrey Willis Williams, 1890–1965* (Chapel

Hill: University of North Carolina Press, 1983), 160; John A. Salmond, "National Youth Administration," in *Franklin D. Roosevelt, His Life and Times: An Encyclopedic View*, ed. Otis L. Graham and Meghan Robinson Wander (New York: Da Capo Press, 1985), 279.

124. McNutt statement, June 17, 1942, Committee on Appropriations, United States Senate, Seventy-Seventh Congress, Second Session, *Hearings on H.R. 7181 Department of Labor—Federal Security Agency Appropriation Bill for 1943* (Washington, DC: U.S. Government Printing Office, 1942), 291.

125. Salmond, *The Civilian Conservation Corps*, 202–206, 213–214; McNutt to Byron Mitchell, August 13, 1942 (quotation), box 74, FSA General Classified Files, 1939–1944, RG 235, NACP.

126. McNutt address, October 25, 1941, box 19, PVMP.

127. Press release, August 14, 1943, box 4, Altmeyer Papers Part 1, WHS.

128. McNutt statement, March 16, 1942, House Committee on Appropriations, *Hearings on Department of Labor—Federal Security Agency Appropriation Bill for 1943, Part 2*, 13 (first quotation), 20 (second quotation), 21 (third quotation).

129. McNutt statement, August 8, 1941, box 10, PVMP.

130. John Morton Blum, *V Was for Victory: Politics and American Culture during World War II* (New York: Harcourt Brace and Company, 1976), 235.

131. Merck speech, May 16, 1946, box 13, and Gerard Piel, "BW," Life, November 18, 1946, box 12, Records Relating to the War Research Service (WRS), 1942–1947, RG 235, NACP; Henry L. Stimson to FDR, April 29, 1942 (quotation), box 11, War Research Service Records, RG 235, NACP.

132. McNutt to Dwight D. Eisenhower, July 7, 1947, box 12, PVMP.

133. R. E. Dyer to "Dr. Thompson," February 7, 1942, box 11, PVMP; Barton J. Bernstein, "America's Biological Warfare Program in the Second World War," *Journal of Strategic Studies*, 11, no. 3 (1988), 297; Isaac J. Silverman

to McNutt, February 10, 1941, and McNutt to Silverman, February 26, 1941 (quotation), box 11, WRS Records, RG 235, NACP.

134. J. Edgar Hoover to McNutt, January 30, 1942, box 11, PVMP.

135. McNutt to J. Edgar Hoover, February 10, 1942, box 11, PVMP; Memorandum on the "Department of War," no date [ca. 1945], box 1, Committees on Biological Warfare (CBW) Files, Archives of the National Academy of Sciences (NAS), Washington, D.C.; Merck speech, May 16, 1946, box 13; Department of War press release, January 3, 1946, Henry L. Stimson to FDR, April 29, 1942, report marked "Top Secret," March 25, 1944 (attached to Switzer to McNutt, June 30, 1947), box 11, all in WRS Records, RG 235, NACP.

136. Quoted in McNutt to FDR, September 4, 1942, box 10, WRS Records, RG 235, NACP.

137. E. B. Fred to George W. Merck Jr., January 19, 1943, box 4, CBW Files, NAS; Old Contracts," no date, box 10; War Research Project #1, box 5; "Subject for Research: Dysentery," box 7; War Research Projects # 41, 3 and 17, box 8; and War Research Project #12, box 5; Merck to Arthur G. Norman, September 25, 1943 (quotations), box 3, all in WRS Records, RG 235, NACP.

138. "Organization of B.W. in the United Kingdom," November 10, 1942, and "Outline of B.W. Organization in U.K.," no date, box 5, and "Conference of Canadian C-1 Committee, C.W.S. and W.R.S. on B.W.," October 15, 1943, box 4, all in CBW Files, NAS; report marked "Top Secret," March 25, 1944, Henry L. Stimson to McNutt, April 17, 1944 (answering McNutt's memorandum of April 13, 1944); Stimson and McNutt to FDR, May 8, 1944; and FDR to McNutt, June 8, 1944, all in box 11, WRS Records, RG 235, NACP.

139. George W. Merck Jr. to McNutt, September 14, 1942, box 13, WRS Records, RG 235, NACP; Stimson Diary, July 24, 1942 (quotations), Henry L. Stimson Papers, YUL.

140. Stimson Diary, August 27, 1942, Stimson Papers, YUL.

141.  Roy Vagelos and Louis Galambos, *Medicine, Science, and Merck* (New York: Cambridge University Press, 2004), 163.

142.  McNutt to George W. Merck Jr., August 26, 1942, box 12, and Switzer to Taylor H. McCauley, May 9, 1944, box 3, WRS Records, RG 235, NACP.

143.  George W. Merck Jr. to McNutt, no date [June 1944], box 12, WRS Records, RG 235, NACP; and McNutt to Owen J. Roberts, March 8, 1946, box 61, Switzer Papers, SL (quotations).

144.  Robert C. Richardson to John J. McCloy, June 5, 1943, and Memorandum on Assignment of Public Health Service Officer to Hawaii, July 29, 1943, box 10, WRS Records, RG 235, NACP; Karl R. Lundeberg to William Scobey, October 1, 1944, in "Historical Report of War Research Service, November 1944," 118, box 5, CBW Files, NAS; Mary E. Switzer to George W. Merck Jr., March 12, 1946, box 61, Switzer Papers, SL.

145.  George W. Merck Jr. to McNutt, October 29, 1943, box 11, WRS Records, RG 235, NACP.

146.  Mary E. Switzer to Dr. Arthur R. Lack Jr., September 28, 1944, box 3; McNutt to Switzer, June 29, 1944, box 13; Cora M. Downs to Switzer, March 27, 1944, Switzer to Downs, March 10, 1944, E. B. Fred to Chancellor Malott, February 7, 1944, "Telephone Conversation with Dr. Fred and Dr. Baldwin," February 1, 1944, box 13; George W. Merck Jr. to Norman T. Kirk, July 12, 1944, box 11, WRS Records, RG 235, NACP.

147.  Mary E. Switzer to McNutt, June 30, 1947, box 11, and George W. Merck Jr. to McNutt, August 21, 1942 (quotation), box 12, WRS Records, RG 235, NACP.

148.  McNutt to FDR, September 4, 1942, and FDR to Henry Morgenthau, September 26, 1942, box 10; McNutt to FDR, February 9, 1943, FDR to McNutt, February 20, 1943, and April 18, 1943, McNutt to FDR, April 5, 1943, McNutt to Harold D. Smith, July 5, 1943, and FDR to Morgenthau, July 13, 1943, box 11, WRS Records, RG 235, NACP.

149.  Paul V. McNutt–Edmund E. Day contract, no date [1943], box 5, WRS Records, RG 235, NACP; E. B. Fred to George W. Merck Jr., May 14, 1943, box 8, CBW Files, NAS; Bernstein, "America's Biological Warfare Program in the Second World War," 297 (quotation).

150.  McNutt to Owen J. Roberts, March 8, 1946, box 61, Switzer Papers, SL.

151.  George W. Merck Jr. to Frank B. Jewett, December 8, 1942, box 10, WRS Records, RG 235, NACP.

152.  Report on Foot and Mouth Disease, no date [ca. January 1944], box 10, WRS Records, RG 235, NACP; and Report on the "Implications of Biological Warfare," no date [1945], box 6, CBW Files, NAS.

153.  "Oppenheimer Asserts That War, Not Atom, Is Key U.N. Problem," *New York Herald Tribune*, May 17, 1946, box 13, WRS Records, RG 235, NACP. Plan for Attack on the Sugar Beet Crop of the Axis Nations in Europe, attached to William W. Diehl, E. B. Lambert, and Freeman Weiss to William D. Leahy, August 4, 1942 (quotations), box 10, WRS Records, RG 235, NACP.

154.  "Drs. Diehl, Lambert and Weiss Project," September 30, 1942; memorandum on "Conference on Biological Warfare as Related to the Destruction of Crops," April 9, 1943; and "A Summary of the Rice Question," no date [ca. 1943], all in box 4, CBW Files, NAS; Bernstein, "America's Biological Warfare Program in the Second World War," 309 (quotation).

155.  Bernstein, "America's Biological Warfare Program in the Second World War," 304.

156.  "A Thumb-nail Sketch of the Development of Biological Warfare," November 24, 1942, box 5, CBW Files, NAS.

157.  R. C. Jacobs to H. H. Bundy, August 18, 1941, box 1, CBW Files, NAS.

158.  R. C. Jacobs to H. H. Bundy, August 18, 1941, box 1, and "A Thumb-nail Sketch of the Development of Biological Warfare," November 24, 1942, box 5, both in CBW Files, NAS. Bernstein, "America's Biological War-

fare Program in the Second World War," 308, 304 (quotation).

159. Bernstein, "America's Biological Warfare Program in the Second World War," 293 and 297.

160. "Scientists Assail Bacteria Warfare," *NYT*, no date, box 6, Elmer Davis Papers, LC; *Science News Letter*, January 12, 1946, 20–21 (quotation).

161. *NYT*, March 13, 1949, 35.

162. Merck report to the Secretary of War, January 3, 1946, box 6, CBW Files, NAS.

163. McNutt to Dwight D. Eisenhower, July 7, 1947, box 12, PVMP.

164. Mary E. Switzer to Leonard A'Hearn, June 12, 1946, box 1, Switzer Papers, SL.

165. Watson B. Miller to Hugh R. Jackson, January 24, 1947, box 1, Switzer Papers, SL.

166. Jack B. Tate to Watson B. Miller, June 7, 1945, box 1, Switzer Papers, SL; "Reorganization of Federal Programs for Health, Education, and Social Security," July 4, 1945, and McNutt to Harry S. Truman, July 6, 1945 (quotation), box 576, White House Central File (WHCF): Official File (OF), Harry S. Truman Papers, Harry S. Truman Library (HSTL).

167. Harry N. Rosenfeld to Oscar R. Ewing, September 9, 1947, box 1, Switzer Papers, SL.

168. Memorandum on "Legislation to Establish a Department of Health, Education and Security" attached to Ewing to Matthew J. Connelly, March 27, 1947, box 576, WHCF: OF, Truman Papers, HSTL. Dividing the department into three operating units struck many officials at FSA as too rigid; Aiken's committee reported a revised bill, albeit one that retained the tripartite structure. Harry N. Rosenfeld to Oscar R. Ewing, September 9, 1947, box 1, Switzer Papers, SL; memorandum on "Legislation to Establish a Department of Health, Education and Security," attached to Ewing to Connelly, March 27, 1947, and Harry S. Truman to Connelly, April 8, 1947, box 576, WHCF: OF, Truman Papers, HSTL.

169. Karen Kruse Thomas, *Deluxe Jim Crow: Civil Rights and American Health Policy, 1935–1954* (Athens: University of Georgia Press, 2011), 253.

170. "Reorganization of Federal Programs for Health, Education, and Social Security," July 4, 1945, box 576, WHCF: OF, Truman Papers, HSTL.

171. Jack B. Tate to Watson B. Miller, June 7, 1945, folder 8, box 1, Switzer Papers, SL.

172. "Reorganization of Federal Programs for Health, Education, and Social Security," July 4, 1945, box 576, WHCF: OF, Truman Papers, HSTL.

173. McNutt address, November 24, 1939, box 17, PVMP.

### 13. MOBILIZING MANPOWER (1942–1945)

1. Keith E. Elier, *Mobilizing America: Robert Patterson and the War Effort, 1940–1945* (Ithaca, NY: Cornell University Press, 1997), 282.

2. *Kansas City Star*, December 6, 1942, 1.

3. *Washington Evening Star* (*WES*), September 2, 1943, and *Chicago Tribune* (*CT*), April 18, 1944—both in George Q. Flynn, *Lewis B. Hershey, Mr. Selective Service* (Chapel Hill: University of North Carolina Press, 1985); Undated cartoon by Jim Berryman, Paul V. McNutt Papers, John L. Krauss Collection (private), Indianapolis, Indiana.

4. George Q. Flynn, *The Mess in Washington: Manpower Mobilization in World War II* (Westport, CT: Greenwood Press, 1979), 231–232.

5. Richard Polenberg, *War and Society: The United States, 1941–1945* (Philadelphia: Lippincott, 1972), 186.

6. Ibid., 188.

7. U.S. Employment Service, "A Short History of the War Manpower Commission (WMC)" (unpublished manuscript), June 1948, 2 (first quotation) and 1 (second quotation), box 1, Robert Goodwin Papers, Harry S. Truman Library (HSTL).

8. Ibid., 3.

9. Doris Kearns Goodwin, *No Ordinary Time: Franklin and Eleanor Roosevelt: The Home Front in World War II* (New York: Simon and Schuster, 1994), 54–55; Polenberg, *War and Society*, 7 (quotation).

10. Polenberg, *War and Society*, 7.

11. "Short History of the WMC," 13.

12. Flynn, *Mess in Washington*, 6–8, and 9 (quotation).

13. Maury Klein, *A Call to Arms: Mobilizing America for World War II* (New York: Bloomsbury, 2013), 334; "Short History of the WMC," 14; Flynn, *Mess in Washington*, 8.

14. Frances Perkins oral history, book 8 (1955), 122, Oral History Research Office, Columbia University (OHRO-CU). Harry S. Truman thought him an "A 1 conniver." Harry S. Truman to Jonathan Daniels, February 26, 1950, in *Off the Record: The Private Papers of Harry S. Truman*, ed. Robert H. Ferrell (New York: Penguin Books, 1980), 174.

15. Harold D. Smith Diary, February 7, 1942, box 3, Harold D. Smith Papers, Franklin D. Roosevelt Library (FDRL); Perkins oral history, book 8 (1955), 121, OHRO-CU; William D. Hassett, *Off the Record with F.D.R.* (London: George Allen and Unwin, 1960), 36, 38; Perkins oral history, book 8 (1955), 122 (quotation), OHRO-CU.

16. Paul V. McNutt ("McNutt") testimony before the House Committee on Interstate Migration, March 25, 1941, box 33, Records of the Federal Security Administrator: General Classified Files, 1939–1944, Records of the Administrator of the Federal Security Agency, Record Group (RG) 235, National Archives, College Park (NACP); "Short History of the WMC," June 1948, 29; Smith Diary, February 7, 1942, box 3, Smith Papers, FDRL.

17. "Mrs. McNutt Cited as Model Shopper," *Indianapolis Star* (reporting the *Washington Post*'s story) (*IS*), July 5, 1942, pt. 4, 4.

18. "'I'll Suffer in Short Skirts'—Mrs. McNutt," *Indianapolis Times* (*IT*), April 10, 1942, 5.

19. Carleton B. McCulloch to Meredith Nicholson, November 27, 1941, box 1, Car-leton B. McCulloch Papers, Indiana Historical Society (IHS).

20. Perkins oral history, book 8 (1955), 138, OHRO-CU.

21. Frances Perkins, *The Roosevelt I Knew* (New York: Viking, 1946), 119; Smith Diary, February 7 and 14 (quotation), 1942, box 3, Smith Papers, FDRL.

22. Flynn, *Mess in Washington*, 16.

23. "Short History of the WMC," June 1948, 35 (quotation) and 36.

24. *Chicago Tribune* (*CT*), April 19, 1942, pt. 1, 12.

25. Polenberg, *War and Society*, 20.

26. Flynn, *Mess in Washington*, 17.

27. "McNutt: America's Super-Manpowerman," *New York Mirror*, April 26, 1942, fiche 2, Department of Indiana, Biographical Files—Paul V. McNutt, National Headquarters of the American Legion Library (ALL).

28. "McNutt as Man-Power Administrator Seen as Presidential Threat in 1944," *IS*, April 26, 1942, folder: Indiana Biography—McNutt, Paul V. and Family—Presidential Chances, Indiana Clipping File, Indiana State Library (ISL).

29. *IT*, October 6, 1942, folder: Indiana Biography—McNutt, Paul V. and Family, Indiana Clipping File, ISL.

30. Flynn, *Mess in Washington*, 19.

31. *Buffalo Evening News*, April 20, 1942, 1; McNutt statement, October 14, 1943, Committee on Appropriations, United States House of Representatives, Seventy-Eighth Congress, First Session, *Hearings on the First Supplemental National Defense Appropriation Bill for 1944* (Washington, DC: U.S. Government Printing Office, 1943), 1099 (quotation).

32. McNutt address, June 12, 1942, box 19, Frank J. McSherry Papers, United States Military Institute, Army Heritage Education Center, Carlisle Barracks (CB).

33. Polenberg, *War and Society*, 20; Flynn, *Mess in Washington*, 25; McNutt statement, October 21, 1942, Committee on Military Affairs, United States Senate, Seventy-Seventh Congress, Second Session, *Hearings on S. 2397, S. 2479, S. 2788, S. 2805, S. 2815, and S.*

2842 (Washington, DC: U.S. Government Printing Office, 1942), 28 (quotation).

34. Arthur Krock, "In the Nation," *New York Times* (*NYT*), April 20, 1942, fiche 2, Department of Indiana, Biographical Files—McNutt, ALL.

35. Theodore Francis Green to Ernest Richardson, March 29, 1943, box 287, Theodore Francis Green Papers, Manuscript Division, Library of Congress (LC).

36. Raymond Gram Swing radio broadcast, November 4, 1942 (all quotations), folder 4, box 20, Raymond Gram Swing Papers, LC.

37. Swing broadcast, June 22, 1943, folder 4, box 22, Swing Papers, LC.

38. Goodwin, *No Ordinary Time*, 482; David M. Kennedy, *Freedom from Fear: The American People in Depression and War, 1929–1945* (New York: Oxford University Press, 1998), 84–85; William E. Leuchtenburg, *The FDR Years: On Roosevelt and His Legacy* (New York: Columbia University Press, 1995), 245; "McNutt Courts Business," *Christian Science Monitor*, January 16, 1940, fiche 3, Department of Indiana, Biographical File—McNutt, ALL.

39. Frederick F. Stephan to Arthur J. Altmeyer, November 23, 1942, box 18, McSherry Papers, CB; Bernard Baruch to FDR, November 7, 1942, box 2, Official File (OF) 4905, Franklin D. Roosevelt (FDR) Papers, FDRL; Paul A. C. Koistinen, *Arsenal of World War II: The Political Economy of American Warfare, 1940–1945* (Lawrence: University Press of Kansas, 2004), 381 (quotation).

40. *WES*, May 21, 1942, 1-X, July 7, 1942, A-2, and August 20, 1942, B-2; *Baltimore News-Post*, November 2, 1942, 3; *Boston Globe*, December 7, 1942, 14; *Syracuse Post-Standard*, December 7, 1942, 4; Koistinen, *Arsenal of World War II*, 382 (quotation).

41. Harold D. Smith to Franklin D. Roosevelt, November 23, 1942, box 2, OF 4905, FDR Papers, FDRL; Perkins oral history, book 8 (1955), 143, OHRO-CU; Executive Order No. 9139, September 17, 1942, box 1, Verbatim Transcripts of Meetings and Sum-

mary Minutes, Records of the Chairman of the WMC, RG 211, Records of the War Manpower Commission, NACP; McNutt statement, October 1, 1942, Committee on Appropriations, United States House of Representatives, Seventy-Seventh Congress, Second Session, *Hearings on the Second Supplemental National Defense Appropriation Bill for 1943* (Washington, DC: U.S. Government Printing Office, 1942), 468 (quotation).

42. James Doarn to Harry S. Truman ("Truman"), no date [ca. November 1942], box 79, Senatorial and Vice Presidential Papers (SVPP), Harry S. Truman Papers, HSTL.

43. Truman to James Doarn, November 25, 1942, box 79, SVPP, Truman Papers, HSTL.

44. Elier, *Mobilizing America*, 297, 293 (quotation).

45. *WES*, September 17, 1942, A-10.

46. McNutt press conference, March 1, 1943, box 1, Transcripts of Press Conferences, Records of the WMC Chairman, RG 211, NACP.

47. *WES*, May 31, 1942, B-2.

48. *WES*, August 3, 1942, A-1.

49. *WES*, September 7, 1942, A-9, September 16, 1942, 1-X, and September 29, 1942 (quotation), A-3.

50. William L. O'Neill, *A Democracy at War: America's Fight at Home and Abroad in World War II* (Cambridge, MA: Harvard Universuty Press, 1995), 207; McNutt to Walther Reuther, March 27, 1943 (quotation), box 32, United Automobile Workers (UAW) President's Office: Walter Reuther Collection, Archives of Labor and Urban Affairs, Wayne State University (WSU). See also McNutt to William Green, July 4, 1942, box 3, Record Group 1:23, Office Files of the President: William Green Files, 1940–1952, George Meany Memorial Archives (GMMA).

51. Flynn, *Mess in Washington*, 17–19; McNutt statement, February 7, 1945, Committee on Military Affairs, United States Senate, Seventy-Ninth Congress, First Session,

*Hearings on S. 36 and H.R. 1752—Mobiliza-tion of Civilian Manpower* (Washington, DC: U.S. Government Printing Office, 1945), 100 (quotation).

52. McNutt address, June 12, 1942, box 19, McSherry Papers, CB.

53. *WES,* October 6, 1942, A-1; McNutt to FDR, October 28, 1942, box 1, OF 4905, FDR Papers, FDRL; *Chester Wright's Labor Letter,* October 31, 1942, GMMA (quotation; italics in original).

54. Philip Murray to "Sirs and Brothers" in the Congress of Industrial Organizations, November 19, 1943, box 94, Philip Murray Papers, American Catholic History Research Center, Catholic University of America (CUA), Washington, D.C.

55. "The 1942 Campaign Question Box," October 1942, and "Digest of Current National Legislation, October 1942 (quotations), box 42, Harold Burton Papers, LC.

56. *Baltimore News-Post,* November 13, 1942, 3 (all quotations); George C. Hart to FDR, November 13, 1942, box 3, OF 4905, FDR Papers, FDRL.

57. David M. Jordan, *FDR, Dewey, and the Election of 1944* (Bloomington: Indiana University Press, 2011), 65.

58. Robert A. Taft to George Marshall, December 10, 1942, in *The Papers of Robert A. Taft,* vol. 2, *1939–1944,* ed. Clarence E. Wunderlin Jr. (Kent, Ohio: Kent State University Press, 1997), 392; *Nashville Banner,* December 10, 1942, 18 (quotation).

59. *Buffalo Evening News,* December 8, 1942, 18; Harold D. Smith to FDR, November 23, 1942 (quotations), box 2, OF 4905, FDR Papers, FDRL.

60. Perkins oral history, book 8 (1955), 142; Harold L. Ickes Diary, April 26, 1942, 6574 (quotations), box 5, Harold L. Ickes Papers, LC.

61. Henry Morgenthau Jr. Presidential Diary (microfiche), November 6, 1942, Henry Morgenthau, Jr. Papers, FDRL.

62. Henry Stimson Diary, October 15, 1942, Henry L. Stimson Papers, Yale University Library (YUL).

63. H. G. Nicholas, ed., *Washington Despatches, 1941–1945: Weekly Political Reports from the British Embassy* (Chicago: University of Chicago Press, 1981), 96.

64. Robert A. Taft to Herbert Hoover, January 12, 1943, box 1286, Robert A. Taft Papers, LC.

65. Eiler, *Mobilizing America,* 300; Stimson Diary, October 20, 1942 (first quotation), and October 15, 1942 (second quotation), Stimson Papers, YUL.

66. McNutt statement, October 21, 1942, Senate Committee on Military Affairs, *Hearings on S. 2397, S. 2479, S. 2788, S. 2805, S. 2815, and S. 2842,* 34; "Short History of the WMC," June 1948, 41, (quotation).

67. Harold D. Smith to FDR, November 23, 1942, box 2, OF 4905, FDR Papers, FDRL.

68. Stimson Diary, October 15, 1942, Stimson Papers, YUL.

69. Perkins oral history, book 8 (1955), 130, OHRO-CU; Harold D. Smith to FDR, February 19, 1943 (quotation), box 2, OF 4905, FDR Papers, FDRL.

70. Jonathan Daniels, *White House Witness, 1942–1945* (Garden City, NY: Doubleday, 1975), 57.

71. Ickes Diary, November 28, 1942, 7249, box 9, Ickes Papers, LC.

72. Harold D. Smith to FDR, November 23, 1942, box 2, OF 4905, FDR Papers, FDRL.

73. Ibid.

74. Henry A. Wallace oral history ("Oscar Cox"), 1860, October 3, 1942, OHRO-CU.

75. Warren G. Magnuson to G. H. Waterman, February 22, 1943, box 36, Warren G. Magnuson Papers, University of Washington Libraries, Seattle.

76. "Industrial Mobilization for War: History of the War Production Board," Part 3, July 18, 1946, 175 (first quotation), 186 (all subsequent quotations), box 111, Julius Krug Papers, LC.

77. *WES,* October 26, 1942, X-1; October 27, 1942, A-5; October 21, 1942, A-1; October 25, 1942, A-21; October 29, 1942, X-1; and October 13, 1942, A-1; James F. Byrnes, *All in One*

*Lifetime* (New York: Harper and Row, 1958), 175 (quotation).

78. "Preliminary Report on Manpower," October 19, 1942, attached to Truman to FDR, October 23, 1942, box 2, OF 4905, FDR Papers, FDRL. Italics in original.

79. McNutt to FDR, no date (ca. November 1942), box 2, OF 4905, FDR Papers, FDRL.

80. Truman to FDR, October 23, 1942, and Bernard Baruch to FDR, November 7, 1942, box 2, OF 4905, FDR Papers, FDRL; Stimson Diary, October 19 and 20, 1942, Stimson Papers, YUL; Henry L. Stimson to FDR, November 5, 1942, (quotations), box 2, OF 4905, FDR Papers, FDRL.

81. FDR to Bernard Baruch, et al., November 11, 1942, box 2, OF 4905, FDR Papers, FDRL.

82. Byrnes, *All in One Lifetime*, 191.

83. Ickes Diary, November 28, 1942, 7248 (quotations), and November 29, 1942, 7260, box 9, Ickes Papers, LC.

84. Byrnes, *All in One Lifetime*, 192.

85. Ickes Diary, December 6, 1942, 7270–7271, and 7280, box 9, Ickes Papers, LC.

86. Harold D. Smith to FDR, November 23, 1942, box 2, OF 4905, FDR Papers, FDRL.

87. Smith Diary, December 4, 1942, box 3, Smith Papers, FDRL.

88. Executive Order No. 9279, December 5, 1942, folder 100 War Manpower Comm. Misc. 1942–43, Lewis B. Hershey Papers, CB.

89. Kennedy, *Freedom from Fear*, 636.

90. *Philadelphia Inquirer*, December 7, 1942, 14.

91. *Boston Globe*, December 7, 1942, 14; Carleton B. McCulloch to Meredith Nicholson, December 16, 1942 (quotations), box 1, McCulloch Papers, IHS.

92. *Chester Wright's Labor Letter*, December 12, 1942, GMMA.

93. Smith Diary, December 4, 1942, box 3, Smith Papers, FDRL.

94. Frank M. McHale to McNutt, December 23, 1942, box 11, Paul V. McNutt Papers (PVMP), Lilly Library (LL), Indiana University (IU).

95. Stimson Diary, December 10, 1942, Stimson Papers, YUL.

96. Ickes Diary, January 17, 1943, 7382, box 10, Ickes Papers, LC.

97. Eiler, *Mobilizing America*, 305; Chan Gurney to FDR, February 5, 1943, and FDR to Gurney, February 16, 1943 (quotation), President's Personal File (PPF) 8323, FDR Papers, FDRL.

98. Flynn, *Mess in Washington*, 62.

99. Eliot Janeway, *The Struggle for Survival: A Chronicle of Economic Mobilization in World War II* (New Haven, CT: Yale University Press, 1951), 325.

100. Flynn, *Mess in Washington*, 59–64; McNutt press conferences, August 23, 1943, August 30, 1943, and June 28, 1943 (quotation), box 2, Transcripts of Press Conferences, Records of the WMC Chairman, RG 211, NACP.

101. Robert Patterson to McNutt, February 9, 1943, box 4, Correspondence with Government Officials 1942–1945, Records of the WMC Chairman, RG 211, NACP; Patterson to Felix Frankfurter, November 3, 1942, box 182; Patterson to George C. Marshall, March 22, 1944, and McNutt to Patterson, March 22, 1943, box 183, all in Robert Patterson Papers, LC.

102. Robert Patterson to George C. Marshall, March 22, 1944, box 183, Patterson Papers, LC.

103. *WES*, February 8, 1943, A-6, July 29, 1943, A-2, and August 17, 1943, A-3; "Short History of the WMC," June 1948, 47, box 1, Goodwin Papers, HSTL.

104. Theodore Green to Kenneth McKellar, February 27, 1943, box 288. Green Papers, LC.

105. Press release, February 1, 1943, box 288, Green Papers, LC.

106. *WES*, February 8, 1943, A-1.

107. Flynn, *Mess in Washington*, 83. Grenville Clark to FDR, July 3, 1942; Clark to Henry Stimson, December 2, 1942; FDR to Clark, June 13, 1942, and November 6, 1942, all in reel 106, Stimson Papers, YUL; FDR to Clark, December 30, 1942, OF 1413, FDR

Papers, FDRL; James W. Wadsworth to Albert L. Cox, February 12, 1943, and Austin-Wadsworth joint statement on proposed National War Service Act of 1943, no date [ca. February 1944] (quotation), box 21, James W. Wadsworth Jr. Papers, LC; Koistinen, *Arsenal of World War II*, 396.

108. Summary of telephone call from "Mr. McGrady," no date [ca. March 1943], box 182, Patterson Papers, LC.

109. Grenville Clark to James W. Wadsworth, October 9, 1943 (quotation), box 21, Wadsworth Papers, LC. For Stimson's support, see Wadsworth to Clark, July 9, 1943, box 21, Wadsworth Papers, LC. For Patterson's position, see Robert Patterson to McNutt, ca. September 15, 1943, box 183, Patterson Papers, LC.

110. Harry S. Truman Diary, May 6, 1948, in *Off the Record*, 134.

111. Turner Catledge, *My Life and the Times* (New York: Harper and Row, 1971), 70.

112. Koistinen, *Arsenal of World War II*, 384.

113. Polenberg, *War and Society*, 22.

114. Flynn, *Mess in Washington*, 65–67; Koistinen, *Arsenal of World War II*, 384 (quotation).

115. Flynn, *Mess in Washington*, 65; Koistinen, *Arsenal of World War II*, 385, 386, 387 (quotation).

116. *WES*, October 14, 1943, 1.

117. Flynn, *Mess in Washington*, 65, 68, 71; Bernard Baruch to James F. Byrnes, July 29, 1943, box 10, War Mobilization Materials, James F. Byrnes Papers, Department of Special Collections, Clemson University (CU) Libraries, Clemson, South Carolina; Memorandum by John M. Hancock, August 3, 1943 (quotation), box 40, Bernard M. Baruch Papers, Seeley G. Mudd Library, Princeton University (PU).

118. War Manpower Commission press release, August 18, 1943 (first quotation), and James Byrnes to McNutt, August 27, 1943 (second quotation), box 40, Baruch Papers, PU.

119. "The Baruch-Byrnes Report on Manpower," *Washington Post* (typescript), September 26, 1943, box 40, Baruch Papers, PU.

120. *WES*, September 12, 1943, C-1.

121. McNutt press conference, September 13, 1943, box 2, Transcripts of Press Conferences, Records of the WMC Chairman, RG 211, NACP (quotation). The War Manpower Commission had been relieved of a number of responsibilities, including the ability to enforce decisions of the local priorities committees. And one of the most drastic cudgels available to the government, the power to deny raw materials and fuel to firms that violated employment ceilings, remained in the hands of the War Production Board. "Industrial Mobilization for War: History of the War Production Board," Part 5, 1944, August 22, 1946, 121, box 111, Krug Papers, LC.

122. Flynn, *Mess in Washington*, 173; Audio recording, "Washington Reports on Rationing," March 14, 1943 (quotation), box 29, Prentice Marsh Brown Papers, Bentley Historical Library (BHL).

123. McNutt statement for *Ladies' Home Journal*, October 1942, box 11, PVMP.

124. McNutt statement, October 1, 1942, House Committee on Appropriations, *Hearings on the Second Supplemental National Appropriation Defense Bill for 1943*, 470; War Department, *You're Going to Employ Women*, no date [1943] (both quotations), box 4, Subject Series 1942–1945, Records of the Chemical Warfare Service, RG 175, NACP.

125. McNutt to FDR, April 2, 1942 (both quotations), box 19, McSherry Papers, CB; Frances Perkins to FDR, November 2, 1942, box 2, OF 4905, FDR Papers, FDRL.

126. "History of the Women's Advisory Committee, War Manpower Commission," February 1945, box 8, Correspondence with Government Officials, Records of the WMC Chairman, RG 211, NACP; Flynn, *Mess in Washington*, 176; McNutt radio speech on "Womanpower,'" no date (quotations), box 5, Speeches, Radio Addresses, Interviews, and Statements of Chairman McNutt, RG 211, NACP.

127. McNutt draft article for *The Women,* no date [ca. late 1943], box 11, PVMP.

128. McNutt draft article, "Women in the War—1943," for *Cosmopolitan* (April 1943), box 11, PVMP.

129. McNutt speech on "Women in War and Peace," no date [1945], box 5, Speeches, Radio Addresses, Interviews, and Statements of Chairman McNutt, RG 211, NACP.

130. Karen Anderson, *Wartime Women: Sex Roles, Family Relations, and the Status of Women during World War II* (Westport, CT: Greenwood Press, 1981), 7; James T. Patterson, *Grand Expectations: The United States, 1945–1974* (New York: Oxford University Press, 1996), 31–38, 362–369; McNutt to H. A. Koehler, August 31, 1945 (quotation), box 11, PVMP.

131. McNutt, "Women in War and Peace," no date [1945], box 5, Speeches, Radio Addresses, Interviews, and Statements of Chairman McNutt, RG 211, NACP.

132. Elaine Tyler May, "Cold War—Warm Hearth: Politics and the Family in Postwar America," in *The Rise and Fall of the New Deal Order, 1930–1980,* ed. Steve Fraser and Gary Gerstle (Princeton, NJ: Princeton University Press, 1989), 159.

133. O'Neill, *A Democracy at War,* 241; National Association for the Advancement of Colored People (NAACP) press release, no date [ca. December 15, 1939], box 233, Ickes Papers, LC; McNutt to the Heads of the Constituent Organizations of the Federal Security Agency, September 16, 1941, box 60, Records of the Federal Security Administrator: General Classified Files, 1939–1944, RG 235, NACP; Flynn, *Mess in Washington,* 155–157; Paul V. McNutt to Archibald MacLeish, May 15, 1942 (plus attachment), box 15, Archibald MacLeish Papers, LC; McNutt address, June 12, 1942 (quotation), box 19, McSherry Papers, CB.

134. McNutt article, "Negro Manpower," for the *Chicago Defender,* December 21, 1944, box 11, PVMP.

135. Kennedy, *Freedom from Fear,* 768.

136. McNutt to Ewart C. Guinier, April 27, 1942, box 5, Alphabetical Series, Records of the Federal Security Administrator: General Classified Files, RG 235, NACP.

137. Walter White to McNutt, October 13, 1942, frame, reel 30, Part 18: Special Subjects, Series C: General Office Files Justice Department–White Supremacy, NAACP Papers (microfilm), LC; Summary of memorandum, Francis Biddle to FDR, January 29, 1943, box 2, OF 4905, FDR Papers, FDRL; McNutt to William Green, January 22, 1943, folder 2, box 3, RG 1:23, Office Files of the President: William Green, GMMA; Walter Reuther to McNutt, January 14, 1943, and Citizens' Committee to Save Colored Locomotive Fireman's Jobs to "Member," January 12, 1943, box 32, UAW President's Office: Reuther Collection, WSU; David Brinkley, *Washington Goes to War* (New York: Ballantine Books, 1988), 250 (quotations).

138. Flynn, *Mess in Washington,* 162.

139. Ibid., 162, 158 (quotation).

140. McNutt article on "Negro Manpower" for the *Chicago Defender,* December 21, 1944, box 11, PVMP.

141. O'Neill, *A Democracy at War,* 240–241; Kennedy, *Freedom from Fear,* 775–776; Flynn, *Mess in Washington,* 156, 162–168.

142. WMC minutes, June 10, 1942, box 1, Verbatim Transcripts of Meeting and Summary Minutes, RG 211, NACP. For the reluctance of the War Manpower Commission to furlough soldiers see Fowler Harper to Robert Patterson, March 1, 1943, box 183, Patterson Papers, LC, and McNutt statement, February 26, 1943, Committee on Appropriations, United States Senate, Seventy-Eighth Congress, First Session, *Hearings on Investigation of Manpower* (Washington, DC: U.S. Government Printing Office, 1943), 24. Stimson Diary, February 9, 1943, Stimson Papers, YUL.

143. Claude R. Wickard to McNutt, August 17, 1942 (plus attached document), box 1, Verbatim Transcripts of Meeting and Summary Minutes, RG 211, NACP; Flynn, *Mess in Washington,* 137; Henry A. Wallace Diary,

January 12, 1943, Henry A. Wallace Papers, University of Iowa Libraries (UIL). Wickard remembered: "Paul V. McNutt was chairman of the War Manpower Commission. I got along all right with him—nothing special." Claude R. Wickard oral history, 2648, box 56, Claude R. Wickard Papers, FDRL.

144. McNutt Statement, September 28, 1942, Committee on Agriculture, United States House of Representatives, Seventy-Seventh Congress, Second Session, *Hearings on Farm Labor and Production* (Washington, DC: U.S. Government Printing Office, 1942), 94.

145. Wallace Diary, February 19, 1943, Wallace Papers, UIL; Flynn, *Mess in Washington*, 133, 135, 139; Robert Patterson to Henry Stimson, "Notes on Cabinet Meeting, March 4, 1943" (quotation), reel 127, Stimson Papers, YUL.

146. Wallace Diary, March 10, 1944, Wallace Papers, UIL.

147. Robert Patterson to Robert R. Reynolds, March 1, 1943, box 182, Patterson Papers, LC; Wickard Diary, November 2, 1943, box 20, Wickard Papers, FDRL; Millard E. Tydings to Lewis B. Hershey, October 15, 1942, folder: White House Correspondence 1941–1943, Hershey Papers, CB; Flynn, *Mess in Washington*, 136; Patterson to Lister Hill, February 27, 1943, box 182, and Patterson to McNutt, April 1, 1943, box 183, Patterson Papers, LC.

148. Flynn, *Mess in Washington*, 140 (quotation); Lewis B. Hershey to Alexander Fitz Hugh, March 6, 1944, Hershey's Staybacks—1943, 1944, 1946, Hershey Papers, CB.

149. Flynn, *Mess in Washington*, 143–144; McNutt statement, November 26, 1943, Committee on Appropriations, United States Senate, Seventy-Eighth Congress, First Session, *Hearings on First Supplemental National Appropriation Bill for 1944* (Washington, DC: U.S. Government Printing Office, 1943), 514, 520, 523–525.

150. Claude R. Wickard to McNutt, August 17, 1942 (plus attached document), box 1, Ver-

batim Transcripts of Meeting and Summary Minutes, RG 211, NACP; Remarks of Senator Sheridan Downey in McNutt statement, September 16, 1943, Committee on Military Affairs, United States Senate, Seventy-Eighth Congress, First Session, *Hearings on S. 763—Married Men Exemption [Drafting of Fathers]* (Washington, DC: U.S. Government Printing Office, 1943), 161 (quotation).

151. McNutt statement, September 16, 1943, Senate Committee on Military Affairs, *Hearings on S. 763—Married Men Exemption*, 161; McNutt to Cordell Hull, November 4, 1943, January 27, 1944, and September 16, 1944, box 2, Correspondence with Government Officials, Records of the WMC Chairman, RG 211, NACP; Flynn, *Mess in Washington*, 141; WMC Minutes, June 10, 1942, box 1, Verbatim Transcripts of Meeting and Summary Minutes, RG 211, NACP; Wickard Diary, ca. June 3, 1942, box 20, Wickard Papers, FDRL.

152. Kennedy, *Freedom from Fear*, 634–635.

153. *WES*, February 11, 1943, A-1.

154. Kennedy, *Freedom from Fear*, 636.

155. Press clipping, "Father Draft Order Explained by WMC," August 14, 1943, box 14, UAW War Policy Collection, WSU.

156. "New WMC Order Seen Deferring Draft of Fathers," *PM*, June 15, 1943, box 14, UAW War Policy Collection, WSU; Patterson to Stimson, "Notes after Cabinet Meeting, May 7, 1943," reel 127, Stimson Papers, YUL; Flynn, *Mess in Washington*, 200, 202; Kennedy, *Freedom from Fear*, 636; "Manpower," *Time*, December 20, 1943, 16 (quotations).

157. *IS*, February 24, 1943, 1.

158. Hassett, *Off the Record with F.D.R.*, 160.

159. Klein, *A Call to Arms*, 546; Ickes Diary, February 27, 1943, 7499 (quotation), box 10, Ickes Papers, LC.

160. Cannon, Democrat of Missouri, was chair of the House Committee on Appropriations. McNutt statement, June 16, 1942, Committee on Appropriations, United States House of Representatives, Seventy-Seventh Congress, Second Session, *Hearings on the*

First Supplemental National Defense Appropriation Bill for 1943, Part 1 (Washington, DC: U.S. Government Printing Office, 1942), 640.

161. McNutt statement, March 28, 1944, Committee on Military Affairs, United States House of Representatives, Seventy-Eighth Congress, Second Session, Hearings on H. Res. 30 Investigations of the National War Effort (Washington, DC: U.S. Government Printing Office, 1944), 103.

162. McNutt statement, September 16, 1943, Senate Committee on Military Affairs, Hearings on S. 763—Married Men Exemption, 169.

163. Byrnes, All in One Lifetime, 92–93; "M'Nutt Career Faces Big Test," IT, October 6, 1942, folder: Indiana Biography—McNutt, Paul V. and Family, Indiana Clipping File, ISL.

164. Ickes Diary, January 24, 1943, 7395 (first quotation), and March 20, 1943, 7555 (second quotation), box 10, Ickes Papers, LC.

165. Detroit Free Press, November 30, 1945, 6.

166. WES, February 11, 1943, X-1; "Draft-Age Fathers Warned to Expect Call This Year," PM, April 13, 1943, box 14, UAW War Policy Collection, WSU; Kennedy, Freedom from Fear, 636; Time, December 20, 1943, 16.

167. Ickes Diary, December 12, 1943, 8445, box 11, Ickes Papers, LC.

168. FDR to Burton K. Wheeler, December 31, 1943, box 9, OF 1415, FDR Papers, FDRL.

169. Ickes Diary, December 5, 1943, 8414, box 11, Ickes Papers, LC; Klein, A Call to Arms, 692 (quotation).

170. McNutt to James G. McDonald, April 25, 1942, folder 98, drawer 361, James G. McDonald Papers, Herbert Lehman Suite, Columbia University, New York.

171. See news clipping, "Former Teacher Greets McNutt," no date, box 7, Correspondence with Government Officials, Records of the WMC Chairman, RG 211, NACP.

172. Letter to Miss Kinghorn, no date, folder: McNutt Paul V. & Mrs. McNutt, Clipping File, History and Biography Division, Martin Luther King Jr. Memorial Library, Washing-ton, DC; McNutt to Clark Griffin, June 8, 1946, box 11, PVMP; Louise McNutt to Mrs. Virginia Stettinius, no date, and Edward R. Stettinius to McNutt, July 19, 1941; and Kathleen McNutt to Virginia and Edward R. Stettinius, no date, box 651, Edward R. Stettinius Papers, Albert and Shirley Small Special Collections Library, University of Virginia (UVA).

173. Joseph E. Davies to Marjorie Merriwether Post, September 1, 1949, box 12, Post Family Papers, BHL; Kathleen McNutt Watson to Post, September 6, 1971 (quotations), box 26, Post Family Papers, BHL.

174. McNutt to John C. McNutt, July 23, 1942, and McNutt statement, April 12, 1943, box 11, PVMP.

175. Ed Lockett to David Hulburd, November 16, 1945, folder 317, Dispatches from Time Correspondents, 1942–1968, Houghton Library (HL).

176. McNutt statement, June 23, 1943, Committee on Appropriations, United States Senate, Seventy-Eighth Congress, First Session, Hearings on H.R. 2935—Labor-Federal Security Appropriation Bill for 1944 (Washington, DC: U.S. Government Printing Office, 1944), 28; Ed Lockett to David Hulburd, November 16, 1945, folder 317, Dispatches from Time Correspondents, 1942–1968, HL.

177. McNutt to William E. Sawyer, February 15, 1943, box 9, Records of the Federal Security Administrator: General Classified Files—Alphabetical Series, RG 235, NACP.

178. George Creel, "The Strange Case of Paul McNutt," Collier's, July 29, 1944, 58.

179. Carleton B. McCulloch to Booth Tarkington, March 2, 1943 (first quotation), box 202, Booth Tarkington Papers, Rare Books and Special Collections, Princeton University (PU) Library; Holy Bible: The New King James Version (New York: Thomas Nelson, 1982), 601 (second quotation).

180. Carleton B. McCulloch to Booth Tarkington (quoting Kathleen McNutt), March 2, 1943, folder 4, box 202, Tarkington Papers, PU.

181. Ickes Diary, July 25, 1943, 8018, box 10, Ickes Papers, LC.

182. *Time,* December 20, 1943, 16; Creel, "Strange Case of Paul McNutt," 58 (quotation).

183. Carleton B. McCulloch to Booth Tarkington, May 22, 1944, box 202, Tarkington Papers, PU.

184. Creel, "Strange Case of Paul McNutt," 58.

185. Grenville Clark to James Byrnes, December 27, 1943, box 21, Wadsworth Papers, LC; Henry Stimson, Frank Knox, et al. to FDR, December 28, 1943 (quotation), box 8, Book Materials, Byrnes Papers, CU.

186. Grenville Clark to Henry Stimson, December 30, 1943, reel 108, Stimson Papers, YUL.

187. Harold D. Smith to FDR, January 9, 1944, box 9, OF 1413, FDR Papers, FDRL.

188. Grenville Clark, "National Service Legislation," January 15, 1944, reel 108, Stimson Papers, YUL; Clark to James W. Wadsworth, February 4, 1944, box 21, Wadsworth Papers, LC.

189. John Morton Blum, *V Was for Victory: Politics and American Culture during World War II* (New York: Harcourt Brace and Company, 1976), 254.

190. Swing broadcast, January 11, 1944, box 24, Swing Papers, LC; Byrnes, *All in One Lifetime,* 207 (quotation).

191. Hassett, *Off the Record with F.D.R.,* 237; Morgenthau Presidential Diary, March 3, 1944 (quotations), Morgenthau, Papers, FDRL.

192. Wallace Diary, March 3, 1944, Wallace Papers, UIL.

193. Robert H. Ferrell, *The Dying President: Franklin D. Roosevelt, 1944–1945* (Columbia: University of Missouri Press, 1998), 25–27; Grace Tully, *F.D.R.: My Boss* (New York: Charles Scribner's Sons, 1949), 273; Jordan, *FDR, Dewey, and the Election of 1944,* 47; Michael Beschloss, *The Conquerors: Roosevelt, Truman and the Destruction of Hitler's Germany, 1941–1945* (New York: Simon and Schuster, 2002), 200 (quotation).

194. Morgenthau Presidential Diary, March 17, 1944, Morgenthau Papers, FDRL.

195. Flynn, *Mess in Washington,* 21; Stimson Diary, March 23, 1944 (quotation), Stimson Papers, YUL.

196. "Telephone conversation between the Secretary of War and Major General Lewis B. Hershey," March 17, 1944, reel 127, Stimson Papers, YUL.

197. Klein, *A Call to Arms,* 693 (both quotations).

198. Morgenthau Presidential Diary, March 17, 1944, Morgenthau Papers, FDRL.

199. Stimson Diary, April 7, 1944, Stimson Papers, YUL, and Ickes Diary, April 9, 1944, 8784 (quotation), box 11, Ickes Papers, LC.

200. Ickes Diary, April 29, 1944, 8844, box 11, Ickes Papers, LC.

201. Stimson Diary, April 7, 1944, Stimson Papers, YUL.

202. Ickes Diary, April 9, 1944, 8784, box 11, Ickes Papers, LC.

203. Robert H. Ferrell, *Choosing Truman: The Democratic Convention of 1944* (Columbia: University of Missouri Press, 1994), 2–21.

204. Jordan, *FDR, Dewey, and the Election of 1944,* 148, 152, 124; Morgenthau Presidential Diary, July 6, 1944 (quotation), Morgenthau Papers, FDRL.

205. News clipping, "'Political Suicide,' Says McNutt of Manpower Job," no date [ca. December 31 of either 1942 or 1943], box 27, PVMP.

206. Booth Tarkington to Carleton B. McCulloch, July 9, 1943, box 177, Tarkington Papers, PU.

207. *WES,* May 10, 1944, B-12; Wallace Diary, no date [July 1944], Wallace Papers, UIL; Charles Marsh, "The Vice Presidency" in Wallace Diary, July 11, 1944 (quotation), Wallace Papers, UIL.

208. Wallace oral history ("Fowler Harper"), 2680 (first quotation), OHRO-CU, and Ickes Diary, April 29, 1944, 8844 (second quotation), box 11, Ickes Papers, LC.

209. Jordan, *FDR, Dewey, and the Election of 1944,* 174–176.

210. Although Roosevelt thought Truman lacked color and vision, the Missouri senator had shown "integrity," "executive ability," and a knack for picking competent subordinates. Ferrell, *Choosing Truman*, 34–88; Belle Willard Roosevelt Diary, undated [ca. November 1944] (quotations), box 134, Kermit and Belle Roosevelt Papers, LC.

211. Jim Berryman cartoon, no date [1944], McNutt Papers, Krauss Collection; Carleton B. McCulloch to Booth Tarkington, July 28, 1944, folder 4, box 202, Tarkington Papers, PU; Joseph J. Lowry, "The Forgotten Man," no date, box 11, PVMP (quotation).

212. WMC press release, August 4, 1944, box 2, Office Files of D. Thomas Curtin, RG 211, NACP; press release, October 4, 1944, box 2, OF 4905, FDR Papers, FDRL; "WMC to Tighten Flow of Labor," *Washington News*, December 12, 1944, box 40, Baruch Papers, PU; press release, December 23, 1944, box 184, Patterson Papers, LC.

213. David Robertson, *Sly and Able: A Political Biography of James F. Byrnes* (New York: W. W. Norton, 1994), 370.

214. Press release, January 3, 1945, and James Byrnes to McNutt, February 20, 1945, box 7, Correspondence with Government Officials, Records of the WMC Chairman; *Houston Post,* December 17, 1942 (quotation), box 4, Office Files of Lawrence Hammond, all in RG 211, NACP.

215. Kathleen J. Frydl, *The GI Bill* (New York: Cambridge University Press, 2009), 75–99.

216. Flynn, *Mess in Washington*, 240–243; Robertson, *Sly and Able*, 370–378; Byrnes to McNutt, December 21, 1944, box 4, Correspondence with Government Officials, Records of the WMC Chairman, RG 211, NACP.

217. Daniels, *White House Witness,* 253 (quotation).

218. Philip Broughton to Frederic W. Wile Jr., May 17, 1943, box 5, Office Files of Frederic W. Wile, Jr., RG 211, NACP; News clipping, "McNutt Lauds U.S. Workers," no date [ca. January 1945], box 7, Records of the WMC Chairman, RG 211, NACP; Daniels, *White House Witness,* 253; Jack New oral history, July 9, 1985, 9 (quotation), Center for the Study of History and Memory (CSHM).

219. Lewis L. Gould, *The Most Exclusive Club: A History of the Modern United States Senate* (New York: Basic Books, 2005), xii.

220. Carleton B. McCulloch to Booth Tarkington, May 22, 1944, box 202, Tarkington Papers, PU; *Chattanooga Daily Times,* April 6, 1945, 3 (quotation).

221. McNutt to Lex Green, May 29, 1942, box 7, Records of the Federal Security Administrator: General Classified Files—Alphabetical Series, RG 235, NACP; Polenberg, *War and Society,* 83; summaries of letters, Joseph W. Myers (April 26, 1945) and Phoebe Wilson Herrold (April 26, 1945), box 1533, General File, Truman Presidential Papers, HSTL; McNutt to Eleanor Roosevelt, April 18, 1945, box 11, PVMP; McNutt to Earl Thacker, June 19, 1945 (quotations), box 11, PVMP.

222. McNutt speech, April 8, 1945 (all quotations), box 4, Speeches, Radio Addresses, Interviews, and Statements of Chairman McNutt, RG 211, NACP.

223. Flynn, *Mess in Washington,* 92–101, 122–125, 247–249.

224. Hay statement, December 8, 1944, box 2, Correspondence with Government Officials, Records of the WMC Chairman, RG 211, NACP.

225. Flynn, *Mess in Washington,* 256; Felix Frankfurter Diary, January 24, 1943, box 2, Felix Frankfurter Papers, LC.

226. Henry Stimson to Leonard S. Horner, May 7, 1943, reel 107, Stimson Papers, YUL.

227. Brinkley, *Washington Goes to War,* 52.

228. Koistinen, *Arsenal of World War II,* 400–401.

229. McNutt statement, October 14, 1943, House Committee on Appropriations, *Hearings on the First Supplemental National Defense Appropriation Bill for 1944,* 1119.

230. McNutt statement, February 7, 1945, Senate Committee on Military Affairs, *Hear-*

ings on S. 36 and H. R. 1752—Mobilization of Civilian Manpower, 100.

231. Brinkley, Washington Goes to War, 249.

232. Koistinen, Arsenal of World War II, 400.

233. Daniels, White House Witness, 58–59.

## 14. RETURNING TO THE PHILIPPINES (1945–1947)

1. Win Booth to Art Monroe, September 8, 1945, folder 304, Dispatches from Time Correspondents, 1942–1968, Houghton Library (HL).

2. Carlos P. Rómulo to Sergio Osmeña, September 1, 1945, box 1.1, Carlos P. Rómulo Papers, University of the Philippines (UP) Library, Diliman; Paul V. McNutt ("McNutt") to Paul Fagan, September 29, 1945 (quotation), box 7, Records of the Washington Office 1942–1948, Records of the High Commissioner to the Philippine Islands, Record Group (RG) 126, National Archives at College Park (NACP).

3. But he also suggested that he was trading one firing line for another. McNutt to Harry W. Berdie, September 24, 1945, box 7, Records of the Washington Office of the High Commissioner, RG 126, NACP.

4. Atlanta Journal, April 6, 1945, 18.

5. McNutt to Irene Murphy, August 23, 1945, box 44, Mary E. Switzer Papers, Arthur and Elizabeth Schlesinger Library (SL).

6. Ed Lockett to David Hulburd, November 16, 1945, folder 317, Dispatches from Time Correspondents, HL.

7. McNutt to Oscar Cox, September 28, 1945, box 22, Oscar Cox Papers, Franklin D. Roosevelt Library (FDRL).

8. See Stephen Rosskamm Shalom, The United States and the Philippines: A Study of Neocolonialism (Quezon City, Philippines: New Day Publishers, 1986), 1–32; Samuel K. Tan, A History of the Philippines (Quezon City: University of the Philippines Press, 1987), 80–92.

9. Ramon Magsaysay, "Text of Message of Condolence to Mrs. Paul V. McNutt," Correspondence File—1955, Ramon Magsaysay Papers, Ramon Magsaysay Center, Manila, Philippines.

10. Milton Walter Meyer, A Diplomatic History of the Philippine Republic: The First Years, 1946–1961 (Claremont, CA: Regina Books, 2004), 3; Nick Cullather, Illusions of Influence: The Political Economy of United States–Philippine Relations, 1942–1960 (Stanford, CA: Stanford University Press, 1994), 42 (quotations).

11. Paul A. Kramer, The Blood of Government: Race, Empire, the United States, and the Philippines (Quezon City, Philippines: Ateneo de Manila University Press, 2006), 362. The historian William Roger Louis has called the use of timetables "a distinctly American contribution to the process of decolonization." William Roger Louis, Imperialism at Bay: The United States and the Decolonization of the British Empire, 1941–1945 (New York: Oxford University Press, 1978), 9.

12. Louis, Imperialism at Bay, 568–569.

13. Millard E. Tydings, "Conditions in the Philippines," no date [ca. June 1945], folder: Philippine Trip 1945, box 3, series IV, Millard E. Tydings Papers, Hornbake Library, University of Maryland, College Park (UMCP).

14. Walter Wilgus, "Economic Outlook for the Philippines," Foreign Policy Reports, October 1, 1945, 203, box 11, Elmer Davis Papers, Manuscript Division, Library of Congress (LC).

15. Leroy I. Setzoil to Frieda Kirchway, July 26, 1945 (first quotation), folder 5373, and Setzoil to Kirchway, August 3, 1945 (second and third quotations), folder 5374, both in The Nation Records, HL.

16. Leroy I. Setzoil to Frieda Kirchway, July 26, 1945; Kirchway to Mildred Adams, August 27, 1945, folder 5375; and Setzoil to Kirchway, August 3, 1945 (quotation), folder 5374, Nation Records, HL.

17. Cullather, Illusions of Influence, 10–31; Frank Hindman Golay, Face of Empire: United States–Philippine Relations, 1898–1946 (Quezon City, Philippines: Ateneo de Manila

University Press, 1997), 421–428; Teodoro A. Agoncillo, "No Finer Paladin: Manuel L. Quezon in Profile," in *History and Culture, Language and Literature: Selected Essays of Teodoro A. Agoncillo*, ed. Bernardita Reyes Churchill (Manila: University of Santo Tomas Publishing House, 2003), 289–291.

18. Cullather, *Illusions of Influence*, 33, 48, 62–64.

19. It is true that, during the 1930s, Nacionalistas felt pressure from a grassroots insurgency, the Skadalistas, but such popular movements in the 1920s and 1930s were narrow in vision, limited in membership, and local in appeal. Patricio N. Abinales and Donna J. Amoroso, *State and Society in the Philippines* (Pasig City, Philippines: Anvil Publishing, 2005), 148. Vince Boudreau, "Methods of Domination and Modes of Resistance: The U.S. Colonial State and Philippine Mobilization," in *The American Colonial State in the Philippines*, ed. Julian Go and Anne Foster (Pasig City, Philippines: Anvil Publishing, 2005), 270–286.

20. Golay, *Face of Empire*, 448–450; Cullather, *Illusions of Influence*, 49; Paul P. Steindorff to Edward R. Stettinius Jr., September 19, 1945, box 11, Paul V. McNutt Papers (PVMP), Lilly Library (LL), Indiana University (IU); Leroy I. Setzoil to Frieda Kirchway, July 10, 1945 (quotations), folder 5373, *Nation* Records, HL.

21. Cullather, *Illusions of Influence*, 44.

22. Cullather, *Illusions of Influence*, 12; Golay, *Face of Empire*, 450; Leroy I. Setzoil to Frieda Kirchway, August 13, 1945, folder 5373, and D. Day to Editors, August 6, 1945 (quotation), folder 5375, *Nation* Records, HL.

23. Golay, *Face of Empire*, 450; Cullather, *Illusions of Influence*, 45, 46, 47 (quotation).

24. Golay, *Face of Empire*, 440; D. Day to Editors, August 6, 1945 (quotation), folder 5375, *Nation* Records, HL.

25. Harold L. Ickes to Sergio Osmeña, September 11, 1945, box 4, Sergio Osmeña Papers, National Library of the Philippines (NLP); Golay, *Face of Empire*, 451; Harold L.

Ickes Diary, October 20, 1945, and November 4, 1945, 10,074 and 10,100–10,101, box 13, Harold L. Ickes Papers, LC; D. Day to Editors, *The Nation*, August 6, 1945, folder 5375, *The Nation* Records, HL; Paul P. Steintorf to Edward R. Stettinius Jr., August 13, 1945, *Foreign Relations of the United States: Diplomatic Papers, 1945*, vol. 6, *The British Commonwealth, the Far East* (Washington, DC: U.S. Government Printing Office, 1969), 1231–1232 (hereafter "*FRUS, 1945*, vol. 6").

26. McNutt to Office of U.S. High Commissioner in Washington, June 28, 1946, box 2, Radiograms, Records of the High Commissioner to the Philippines, RG 126, NACP.

27. Roosevelt declined to comment on McNutt, but he rejected sending Ickes, who also was interested in the position. (Ickes had young children who would have found life in Manila hard.) Charles P. Taft, who had run the Office of Community War Services under McNutt, was also in the running. Ickes Diary, February 10, 1945, and March 4, 1945, 9548 and 9592, box 12, Ickes Papers, LC.

28. Frank P. Lockhart to Joseph C. Grew, February 26, 1945, and March 7, 1945, *FRUS, 1945*, vol. 6, 1193–1195; Sergio Osmeña to Franklin D. Roosevelt, April 8, 1945, and Osmeña to Harry S. Truman ("Truman"), April 19, 1945, box 8, and Osmeña to Douglas A. MacArthur, May 4, 1945, and MacArthur to Osmeña, May 7, 1945, box 6, all in Osmeña Papers, NLP.

29. Memorandum by Assistant Secretary of State William Phillips, May 9, 1945, *FRUS, 1946*, vol. 6, 1200–2101; Harold Ickes to Truman, July 17, 1945, box 9, Records of the Washington Office of the High Commissioner, RG 126, NACP; Ickes Diary, March 4, 1945 (quotation), 9592, box 12, Ickes Papers, LC.

30. Press release, "Executive Order Relating to the United States High Commissioner," September 14, 1945, box 55, series 4, Manuel A. Roxas Papers, UP.

31. Mrs. M. L. Liddell to Truman, September 7, 1945, box 1090, White House Cen-

tral File (WHCF): Official File (OF) 400, Harry S. Truman Papers, Harry S. Truman Library (HSTL); Roy W. Howard to Manuel A. Roxas, October 8, 1945 (quotations), box 8, series 1(b), Roxas Papers, UP.

32. Vicente G. Sinco to Carlos P. Rómulo, January 3, 1945 [probably 1946], box 1.1, Rómulo Papers, UP.

33. *Manila Daily News (MDN)*, November 6, 1945, 3; Secretary Reyes to Carlos Rómulo, September 7, 1945 (quotation), box 8, Osmeña Papers, NLP.

34. Carlos P. Rómulo to Sergio Osmeña, September 14, 1945, box 1.1, Rómulo Papers, UP.

35. Manuel Roxas to Roy W. Howard, November 1, 1945, box 211, Roy W. Howard Papers, LC.

36. Manuel Roxas to Jacob M. Avery, October 26, 1945, box 1, series 1, Roxas Papers, UP.

37. Francis Burton Harrison, *Origins of the Philippine Republic: Extracts from the Diaries and Records of Francis Harrison Burton,* ed. Michael P. Oronato (Ithaca, NY: Southeast Asia Program, Department of Asian Studies, Cornell University, 1974), 135.

38. Ickes Diary, November 4, 1945, 10,101, box 13, Ickes Papers, LC.

39. Harold Ickes, McNutt, and Sergio Osmeña to Truman, November 6, 1945, box 2, Records of the Washington Office of the High Commissioner, RG 126, NACP; Ed Lockett to David Hulburd, November 16, 1945 (quotation), folder 317, Dispatches from *Time* Correspondents, HL.

40. Cullather, *Illusions of Influence,* 48.

41. David Bernstein to Sergio Osmeña, February 6, 1946, box 2.1, Rómulo Papers. Osmeña privately admitted that "McNutt was turning against him." See "Flying Trip to Manila 1946," W. Cameron Forbes Journals, vol. 5, 1935–1946, 563, LC; Golay, *Face of Empire,* 454; "Upon the triumph of Roxas," the *Manila Post* reported. "McNutt did not repress his exultation." *Manila Post (MP),* May 5, 1946, 2.

42. *MDN,* February 3, 1946, 1, and September 1, 1945, 1; *MP,* April 28, 1946, 1.

43. *MP,* June 1, 1946, 2.

44. *MP,* July 4, 1946, I-1.

45. *MP,* March 2, 1946, 2.

46. McNutt speech, March 12, 1941, box 5, Information Files, Records of the Administrator of the Federal Security Agency (FSA), RG 235, NACP.

47. FSA press release, undated [early 1942], box 3, Information Files, Records of the Administrator of the Federal Security Agency, RG 235, NACP.

48. *Washington Evening Star,* March 24, 1945, A-3, and *Atlanta Journal,* April 6, 1945, 18 (quotation).

49. McNutt typescript comments beginning "I am on my way to the Philippines..." no date [ca. November–December 1945], box 11, PVMP.

50. Benjamin Appel to Merle Colby, July 31, 1945, box 11, PVMP.

51. McNutt press release, December 24, 1945, box 11, PVMP.

52. Ed Lockett to David Hulburd, November 16, 1945, folder 317, Dispatches from *Time* Correspondents, HL.

53. McNutt radio address, January 20, 1946, box 7, Records of the Washington Office of the High Commissioner, RG 126, NACP.

54. David Bernstein to Sergio Osmeña, February 6, 1945, box 1.2, Rómulo Papers, UP.

55. McNutt report on Mission to China and Japan, December 29, 1945, box 11, PVMP.

56. McNutt statement, February 28, 1946, Committee on Appropriations, United States House of Representatives, Seventy-Ninth Congress, Second Session, *Hearings on the Interior Department Appropriation Bill for 1947 Part I* (Washington, DC: U.S. Government Printing Office, 1946), 1048.

57. Typescript notes by Paul V. McNutt to Kathleen McNutt, December 31, 1945, box 11, PVMP.

58. McNutt statement (press release), December 19, 1945, box 11, PVMP.

59. Roy W. Howard to G. B. Parker, May 20, 1946, folder: Letters & Articles 1946 January thru July, Roy W. Howard Papers, Roy W. Howard Archive, Indiana University School of Journalism, Bloomington.

60. David Bernstein to Sergio Osmeña, December 6, 1945, box 1.2, Rómulo Papers, UP.

61. Ed Lockett to David Hulburd, November 16, 1945, folder 317, Dispatches from *Time* Correspondents, HL.

62. Cullather, *Illusions of Influence*, 25; H. W. Brands, *Bound to Empire: The United States and the Philippines* (New York: Oxford University Press, 1992) 172; *Manila Bulletin* (*MB*), March 25, 1937, 3; Golay, *Face of Empire*, 454–455; Acting Secretary of State to FDR, March 20, 1945, *FRUS, 1945, 6,* 1216–1217.

63. Executive Committee on Economic Foreign Policy to Chairman of the Filipino Rehabilitation Commission, June 26, June 4, 1945, box I-184, Charles P. Taft Papers, LC; Cullather, *Illusions of Influence*, 24–30, 32, 37.

64. Golay, *Face of Empire*, 455; Cullather, *Illusions of Influence*, 28–36; "Recommendations of the Department of Commerce Regarding Trade Relations with the Philippines," June 25, 1945, Robert P. Patterson to William L. Clayton, June 4, 1945, and Harold L. Ickes to Clayton, June 3, 1945 (quotation), all in box I-184, Charles Taft Papers, LC.

65. Carlos P. Rómulo to Sergio Osmeña, September 14, 1945, box 1.1, Rómulo Papers, UP.

66. McNutt to Richard R. Ely, January 18, 1946, *Foreign Relations of the United States* in *Foreign Relations of the United States: 1946,* vol. 8, *The Far East* (Washington, DC: U.S. Government Printing Office, 1971), 863 (hereafter "*FRUS, 1946,* vol. 8").

67. Golay, *Face of Empire*, 457–458.

68. Carlos P. Rómulo to David Boguslav, May 2, 1946, box 1.2, Rómulo Papers, UP.

69. Paul P. Steintorf to Edward R. Stettinius Jr., April 17, 1945, August 29, 1945, September 19, 1945, and September 28, 1945; Dean

G. Acheson to Steintorf, September 20, 1945, *FRUS, 1945,* vol. 6, 1220–1221, 1223–1228.

70. "Philippine People Warn That Full Independence May Be Undermined," *United States Congressional Record,* June 14, 1946, folder 8989, C. Jasper Bell Papers, Western Historical Manuscripts Collection (WHMC).

71. Secretary Reyes to Sergio Osmeña, no date [late 1945 or early 1946], box 5, Osmeña Papers, NLP.

72. Salvador Araneta, "The Philippines Independence May Succeed without Free Trade" no date [ca. 1946], reel 1, Salvador Araneta Papers, Bentley Historical Library (BHL).

73. Tydings statement, October 17, 1945, Committee on Ways and Means, United States House of Representatives, Seventy-Ninth Congress, First Session, *Hearings on H.R. 4185, H.R. 4676, H.R. 5185 A Bill to Provide for Future Relations between the United States and the Philippine Islands* (Washington, DC: U.S. Government Printing Office, 1945), 84.

74. Cullather, *Illusions of Influence,* 35 (all quotations). Although he favored the Tydings bill, President Truman, facing a divided administration, was receptive to alternatives. Samuel I. Rosenman to Truman, October 25, 1945, box 1572, OF 1055, WHCF, Truman Papers, HSTL.

75. McNutt to Truman, January 25, 1946, box 1572, OF 1055, WHCF, Truman Papers, HSTL; McNutt statement, February 15, 1946, *House Committee on Ways and Means, Hearings on H.R. 4185, H.R. 4676, H.R. 5185,* 210; Golay, *Face of Empire,* 460–461. Osmeña was reluctant to endorse the revised bill. See McNutt to Truman, January 25, 1946, box 1572, OF 1055, WHCF, Truman Papers, HSTL. It is not clear whether Osmeña was present at the meeting in November because all McNutt noted was that Osmeña had been "invited to participate." Eightieth Congress, First Session, House Document No. 389, *Seventh and Final Report of the United States*

*High Commissioner to the Philippine Islands* (Washington, DC: U.S. Government Printing Office, 1947) 33.

76. McNutt radio interview, January 17, 1946, box 22, PVMP.

77. McNutt radio script, November 14, 1945, box 22, PVMP.

78. McNutt address, January 10, 1946, box 22, PVMP.

79. Statements of Bell, McNutt, and Rómulo, November 14, 1945, *House Committee on Ways and Means, Hearings on H.R. 4185, H.R. 4676, H.R. 5185*, 133–135; McNutt statement (press release), April 2, 1946, box 11, and McNutt speech, December 2, 1945 (quotation), box 22, PVMP.

80. American Rice Growers Cooperative Association to "Colleague," November 16, 1945, folder 8953, Bell Papers, WHMC; Carlos P. Rómulo to Sergio Osmeña, August 28, 1945 (quotation), box 8, Osmeña Papers, UP.

81. John Morton Blum, *V Was for Victory: Politics and American Culture during World War II* (New York: Harcourt Brace and Company, 1976), 312, 323.

82. "Philippine Future," *Washington Post* (*WP*), December 1, 1945, 6.

83. Bell statement before the House Committee on Ways and Means, October 15, 1945, box 1572, OF 1055, WHCF, Truman Papers, HSTL.

84. McNutt speech, October 18, 1945; McNutt radio script, November 14, 1945; McNutt radio interview, January 17, 1946—all in box 22, PVMP; McNutt radio speech, January 20, 1946, box 7, Records of the Washington Office of the High Commissioner, RG 126, NACP.

85. Tydings statement, October 17, 1945, and McNutt statement, February 15, 1946, House Committee on Ways and Means, *Hearings on H.R. 4185, H.R. 4676, H.R. 5185*, 90, 208; McNutt radio broadcast, February 23, 1946 (quotation), box 10, Records of the Washington Office of the High Commissioner, RG 126, NACP.

86. Carlos P. Rómulo to Sergio Osmeña, August 28, 1945, box 8, Osmeña Papers, NLP;

Rómulo to Osmeña, January 2, 1946, box 1.2, Rómulo Papers, UP; Clinton P. Anderson to Truman, January 7, 1946, and Truman to Robert L. Doughton, February 11, 1946, box 1572, OF 1055, WHCF, Truman Papers, HSTL; Cullather, *Illusions of Influence*, 38; Golay, *Face of Empire*, 462.

87. McNutt to Truman, January 18, 1946, box 1572, OF 1055, WHCF, Truman Papers, HSTL; McNutt press release, February 13, 1946 (quotation), box 7, Records of the Washington Office of the High Commissioner, RG 126, NACP. For examples of how the White House relied on McNutt to overcome Doughton's resistance, see Richmond B. Keech to Truman, February 7, 1946, and Vernon E. Moore to McNutt, February 9, 1946, box 1572, OF 1055, WHCF, Truman Papers, HSTL.

88. Memorandum for conference with Byrnes, February 15, 1946, box 11, PVMP.

89. Cullather, *Illusions of Influence*, 40.

90. Shalom, *United States and the Philippines*, 51.

91. Carlos P. Rómulo to Harold Ickes, January 25, 1946, box 1572, OF 1055, WHCF, Truman Papers, HSTL; Golay, *Face of Empire*, 473–474; Cullather, *Illusions of Influence*, 50–51; McNutt address, March 14, 1946, box 10; McNutt press release, February 13, 1946, box 7—both in Records of the Washington Office of the High Commissioner, RG 126, NACP; McNutt statement, February 4, 1946, box 11, Records of the Manila Office 1935–1946, Records of the High Commissioner to the Philippine Islands, RG 126, NACP; McNutt statement, April 12, 1946, Committee on Finance, United States Senate, Seventy-Ninth Congress, Second Session, *Hearings on H.R. 5856 An Act to Provide for Trade Relations Between the United States and the Philippines, and for Other Purposes,* (Washington, DC: U.S. Government Printing Office, 1946), 18 (quotation).

92. Meyer, *Diplomatic History of the Philippine Republic*, 10–13; Golay, *Face of Empire*, 462–464; Shalom, *United States and the Philippines*, 51. Regarding the bill's imperfections,

Secretary of State James F. Byrnes thought that the "special favors" granted to Americans in the legislation were "inconsistent with our promise to grant the Philippines genuine independence" and likely to ignite a reaction against the United States in Asia. Byrnes to Truman, April 18, 1946, *FRUS, 1946*, vol. 8, 873–874. Secretary of Commerce Wallace voiced similar concerns but conceded that the Philippines would have to accept the Bell Act as written in order to gain the assistance contained in the bill. Henry A. Wallace to Truman, April 19, 1946, box 1572, OF 1055, WHCF, Truman Papers, HSTL.

93. Evett Hester to McNutt, April 4, 1946 and Hester to McNutt, April 6, 1946 (quotation), box 1, Radiograms, Records of the High Commissioner to the Philippine Islands, RG 126, NACP.

94. Evett Hester to McNutt, April 6, 1946, and April 9, 1946 (quotation), box 1, Radiograms 1946, Records of the High Commissioner to the Philippines, RG 126, NACP.

95. Evett Hester to McNutt, April 9, 1946, box 1, Radiograms, Records of the High Commissioner to the Philippines, RG 126, NACP.

96. Eightieth Congress, First Session, House Document No. 389, *Seventh and Final Report of the United States High Commissioner to the Philippine Islands*, 39.

97. Carlos P. Rómulo to Renato Constantino, March 20, 1946, folder 23, box 1.2, Rómulo Papers, UP.

98. "Was the Malacanan caught napping?" one editorial writer wondered, in blaming the measure's unfavorable terms on the most recent occupants of the presidential palace. Evett Hester to McNutt, April 6, 1946, box 1, Radiograms, Records of the High Commissioner to the Philippines, RG 126, NACP. During the presidential campaign, Osmeña's supporters attempted to make an issue out of the Bell Act, but they proved unable to do so because they had helped formulate the legislation and recoiled from launching an all-out attack on the United States—as did Roxas

and Rómulo. Eightieth Congress, First Session, House Document No. 389, *Seventh and Final Report of the United States High Commissioner to the Philippine Islands*, 39 and 110.

99. Evett Hester to McNutt, April 4, 1946, box 1, Radiograms, Records of the High Commissioner to the Philippines, RG 126, NACP.

100. Cullather, *Illusions of Influence*, 36, and Carlos P. Rómulo to Renato Constantino, March 20, 1946 (quotation), box 1.2, Rómulo Papers, UP.

101. Meyer, *Diplomatic History of the Philippine Republic*, 13.

102. Cullather, *Illusions of Influence*, 51.

103. Meyer, *Diplomatic History of the Philippine Republic*, 14; Shalom, *United States and the Philippines*, 57; Albert A. Villavery to Jose P. Leon, March 10, 1947, box 34, series 4, Roxas Papers, UP. Box 34 of the Roxas Papers contains other documents illustrating how well organized this campaign was. For Roxas's swing through the provinces, see Meyer, *Diplomatic History of the Philippine Republic*, 52–53. For the irregularities in the campaign, see Shalom, *United States and the Philippines*, 58.

104. Memorandum of conversation re: Philippine Commercial Treaty, December 10, 1946, box 16, Country Files 1929–1953, Records of the Philippine and Southeast Asia Division, General Records of the Department of State, RG 59, NACP.

105. Meyer, *Diplomatic History of the Philippine Republic*, 53.

106. Cullather, *Illusions of Influence*, 85.

107. Report to the President of the United States Economic Survey Mission to the Philippines, October 9, 1950, *Foreign Relations of the United States* in *Foreign Relations of the United States: 1950*, vol. 6, *East Asia and the Pacific* (Washington, DC: U.S. Government Printing Office, 1976), 1497–1502.

108. Adlai Stevenson, "Ballots and Bullets," *Look*, June 2, 1953, in *The Papers of Adlai Stevenson*, vol. 5, *Visit to Asia, the Middle East and Europe, March–August 1953*, ed. Walter

Johnson, et al. (Boston: Little, Brown, 1974), 91.

109. Meyer, *Diplomatic History of the Philippine Republic*, 53, 79–80.

110. David Bernstein to Sergio Osmeña, February 6, 1946, folder 21, box 1.2, Rómulo Papers, UP.

111. Memorandum of conversation, Philippine Commercial Treaty, December 10, 1946, box 16, Country Files—Philippines, RG 59, NACP.

112. Cullather, *Illusions of Influence*, 6–41.

113. Lewis E. Gleeck Jr., *Dissolving the Colonial Bond: American Ambassadors to the Philippines, 1946–1984* (Quezon City, Philippines: New Day Publishers, 1988), 17–18; Nathaniel P. Davis to "Mother," July 7, 1946 (quotation), box 1, Nathaniel P. Davis Papers, HSTL.

114. *MB*, July 5, 1946, 1, 12

115. "As American Editors See Us," *MB*, July 11, 1946, 6. McNutt had told Truman that he would remain in Manila for only a month following independence (see *MP*, April 17, 1946, 1). With that in mind, the president offered the post of ambassador to former senator Harry B. Hawes, a fellow Missourian and co-author of an early version of the Philippine independence act. After Hawes declined the honor, however, the ambassadorship passed to McNutt. See J. S. McDaniel to McNutt, May 21, 1946, Harry B. Hawes to Truman, May 7, 1946, and Truman to Hawes, May 10, 1946, box 11, PVMP.

116. McNutt to Mark A. McCloskey, September 10, 1946, box 11, PVMP.

117. *MP*, July 4, 1946, 7.

118. *MP*, July 5, 1946, 1.

119. *MP*, July 5, 1946, 7.

120. *MB*, July 5, 1946, 1.

121. *MB*, July 4, 1946, Independence Edition, World Reaction sect., 1; *MP*, July 5, 1946, 2; *Evening Herald (Manila)*, July 4, 1946, 1; *MP*, November 28, 1946, 8 (quotation).

122. *MP*, September 18, 1946, 6.

123. Ricardo T. Jose, "Manuel L. Quezon and the Commonwealth, 1935–1944," in *Philippine Presidents: 100 Years*, ed. Rosario

Mendoza Cortes (Quezon City, Philippines: New Day Publishers, 1999), 107; Cullather, *Illusions of Influence*, 52–53; Frank P. Lockhart to Edward Stettinius Jr., "Preliminary Understanding with the Philippine Commonwealth for Acquisition by the United States of Military and Naval Bases," April 18, 1945, *FRUS, 1945*, vol. 6, 1203–1204; Elipidio Quirino, *The Memoirs of Elpidio Quirino* (Manila: National Historical Institute, 1990), 222 (quotations).

124. Cullather, *Illusions of Influence*, 52–53; Joseph C. Grew to Frank P. Lockhart, March 7, 1945, and Lockhart to Edward Stettinius Jr., "Preliminary Understanding with the Philippine Commonwealth," April 18, 1945, *FRUS, 1945*, vol. 6, 1194–1195, 1203–1204; McNutt remarks, November 27, 1946 (quotation), box I-184, Charles Taft Papers, LC.

125. "Statement of Hon. Millard Tydings," October 17, 1945, Committee on Ways and Means, United States House of Representatives, Seventy-Ninth Congress, First Session, *Hearings on H.R. 4185, H.R. 4676, H.R. 5185*, 90.

126. "Memorandum on the Philippines," attached to Tydings to Truman, April 25, 1945 (quotation), box 2, series 4, Tydings Papers, UMCP.

127. Truman and Osmeña, "Preliminary Statement," May 14, 1945, *FRUS, 1945*, vol. 6, 1208–1209.

128. John Carter Vincent to James Byrnes, June 6, 1946, *FRUS, 1946*, vol. 8, 880–881; Manuel Roxas to McNutt, October 30, 1946, box 3, series I (b), Roxas Papers, UP; "Philippines Firm on Limitation of Bases," *New York Times*, October 16, 1946 (quotation), box 11, Elmer Davis Papers, LC.

129. Cullather, *Illusions of Influence*, 54; John Carter Vincent to James Byrnes, June 6, 1946, *FRUS, 1946*, vol. 8, 881 (quotation).

130. Cullather, *Illusions of Influence*, 54–55; Dean Acheson to McNutt, July 2, 1946, *FRUS, 1946*, vol. 8, 895; Minutes of the 24th Meeting of the Cabinet, August 27, 1946, and Minutes of the 28th Meeting of the Cabinet,

September 10, 1946, box 6, series 4, Roxas Papers, UP.

131. *MP*, October 3, 1946, 2; October 19, 1946, 1; and November 21, 1946, 1. To what extent leaks influenced the discussions is impossible to say, though McNutt reported them to Byrnes. McNutt to James Byrnes, September 5, 1946, and September 25, 1946, *FRUS, 1946*, vol. 8, 905, 919.

132. Cullather, *Illusions of Influence*, 55; *MP*, April 11, 1946, 1, and October 23, 1946, 1 (quotation).

133. Manuel Roxas to McNutt, October 30, 1946, box 3, series I (b), Roxas Papers, UP; Dean Acheson to McNutt, October 15, 1946, *FRUS, 1946*, vol. 8, 921 (quotation).

134. *MP*, October 19, 1946, 12; Quirino, *Memoirs*, 225 (quotation).

135. McNutt to James Byrnes, September 7, 1946 and Robert Patterson to Byrnes, November 29, 1946, *FRUS, 1946*, vol. 8, 907, 934–935; John H. Hilldring to McNutt, December 13, 1946, *FRUS, 1946*, vol. 8, 936. Cullather, *Illusions of Influence*, 57.

136. Manuel Roxas to H. E. Beyster, January 10, 1947 (quotation), box 1, series I (b), Roxas Papers, UP, and McNutt to James Byrnes, December 23, 1946, *FRUS, 1946*, vol. 8, 940.

137. Cullather, *Illusions of Influence*, 57, and Robert Patterson to James Byrnes, December 27, 1946, *FRUS, 1946*, vol. 8, 941; Byrnes to the Embassy in the Philippines, January 14, 1947, *Foreign Relations of the United States: 1947, vol. 6, The Far East* (Washington, DC: U.S. Government Printing Office, 1972), 1102–1103 (hereafter "*FRUS, 1947*, vol. 6").

138. McNutt to James Byrnes, January 27, 1947, *FRUS, 1947*, vol. 6, 1104.

139. "Agreement between the Republic of the Philippines and the United States," March 14, 1947, file 1, folder 1, box 21, Elpidio Qurinio Papers, Filipinas Heritage Library, Makati City, Philippines; Cullather, *Illusions of Influence*, 58 (quotation).

140. McNutt to George C. Marshall, March 14, 1947, *FRUS, 1947*, vol. 6, 1108; Meyer,

*Diplomatic History of the Philippine Republic*, 102–103, 43 (quotation).

141. *WP*, September 4, 1946, 6.

142. McNutt to George C. Marshall, March 14, 1947, *FRUS, 1947*, vol. 6, 1109.

143. "Agenda for Discussion with the President," no date, box 9, Records of the Washington Office 1942–1948, and radiogram of joint statement of Roxas and McNutt, May 24, 1946, box 1, Radiograms—both in Records of the High Commissioner to the Philippines, RG 126, NACP; Roxas statement, May 11, 1946, and Roxas remarks, May 15, 1946, box 11, PVMP; Manuel Roxas to C. Jasper Bell, July 5, 1946, folder 8994; McNutt radiogram, June 26, 1946, folder 8992; Roxas to Bell through McNutt, July 22, 1946, folder 8995—all in Bell Papers, WHMC.

144. Officials at the Department of the Treasury thought $75 million would be enough to get the Philippines through the next year, and members of Congress were inclined to accept the loan if it was attached to a bill extending the life of the RFC. Bell accepted such a measure. C. Jasper Bell to McNutt, July 17, 1946, and July 29, 1946, folder 337; Bell to McNutt, July 30, 1946, folder 8996—all in Bell Papers, WHMC; Dean Acheson to U.S. Embassy, Manila, March 5, 1947, *FRUS, 1947*, vol. 6, 1105–1106.

145. Bell was amenable to giving the Philippines a loan less than the $100 million requested by Manila. Richard R. Ely to Frank P. Lockhart, July 17, 1946, box 16, Country Files—the Philippines, RG 59, NACP.

146. Meyer, *Diplomatic History of the Philippine Republic*, 18; Richard R. Ely to Carl Hayden, October 3, 1945, box 14, Records of the Washington Office of the High Commissioner, RG 126, NACP; McNutt, Summary of Memorandum, August 23, 1946, and "Statement by the President," February 20, 1946 (quotation), box 1575, OF 1055-H, WHCF, Truman Papers, HSTL.

147. Truman to Omar N. Bradley, February 12, 1946, box 1575, OF 1055-H, WHCF, Truman Papers, HSTL.

148. McNutt to Truman, February 11, 1946, box 1575, OF 1055-H, WHCF, Truman Papers, HSTL.

149. McNutt press release, May 25, 1946, box 6, Records of the Washington Office of the High Commissioner to the Philippines, RG 126, NACP.

150. McNutt to Truman, February 11, 1946, box 1575, OF 1055-H, WHCF, Truman Papers, HSTL; MP, January 20, 1946, 2; Meyer, Diplomatic History of the Philippine Republic, 18.

151. McNutt to Truman, March 15, 1946, box 1, Records of the Manila Office of the High Commissioner to the Philippines, RG 126, NACP.

152. Richmond B. Keetch to Truman, May 16, 1946. Truman to McNutt, May 18, 1946, Truman to Sam Rayburn, May 18, 1946, Omar Bradley to Truman, August 15, 1946, box 1575, OF 1055-H, WHCF, Truman Papers, HSTL; Meyer, Diplomatic History of the Philippine Republic, 18–20, 43–44, 100–101.

153. Truman to George C. Marshall, August 16, 1948, box 1575, OF 1055-H, WHCF, Truman Papers, HSTL; Meyer, Diplomatic History of the Philippine Republic, 100–101; By 1950 Truman's advisers recognized that the time to extend tuition allowances to Filipino veterans had elapsed. George M. Elsey to Truman, June 9, 1950, box 1575, OF 1055-H, WHCF, Truman Papers, HSTL.

154. Truman to Carl R. Gray Jr., June 13, 1950, box 1575, OF 1055-H, WHCF, Truman Papers, HSTL.

155. McNutt to Truman, August 26, 1946, box 1575, OF 1055-H, WHCF, Truman Papers, HSTL.

156. MP, March 2, 1946, 2; McNutt to John E. Hurt, January 15, 1947 (quotations), box 12, PVMP.

157. Louise McNutt Diary, December 21, 1946, John L. Krauss Collection (private), Indianapolis.

158. House Document No. 389, Seventh and Final Report of the United States High Commissioner to the Philippine Islands, 48.

159. Ed Lockett to David Hulburd, March 7, 1945 (quotations), folder 337, Dispatches from Time Correspondents, HL.

160. MP, September 19, 1946, 4, and April 24, 1946, 4; Louise McNutt Diary, January 29, 1947 (quotation), Krauss Collection.

161. Louise McNutt Diary, June 23, 1946, and January 29, 1947, Krauss Collection.

162. "Flying Trip to Manila 1946," W. Cameron Forbes Journals, vol. 5, 1935–1946, 501, LC.

163. "McNutt Has Sobered," Indianapolis Times, May 21, 1946, Folder: Indiana—Biography-McNutt, Paul V. Philippines, Indiana Clipping File, Indiana State Library (ISL).

164. Louise McNutt Diary, January 1, 1946, Krauss Collection.

165. Louise McNutt Diary, February 19, 1947, Krauss Collection.

166. Louise McNutt Diary, February 16, 1947 (all quotations), Krauss Collection.

167. McNutt to Mark A. McCloskey, September 10, 1946, box 11, PVMP.

168. Raymond Gram Swing broadcast, July 4, 1946, folder 6, box 33, Raymond Gram Swing Papers, LC.

169. D. A. Low, "The Asian Mirror to Tropical Africa's Independence," The Transfer of Power in Africa: Decolonization, ed. Prosser Gifford and William Roger Louis (New Haven, CT: Yale University Press, 1982), 15.

170. William Roger Louis (with Ronald Robinson), "The Imperialism of Decolonization," in Ends of British Imperialism: The Scramble for Empire, Suez and Decolonization, ed. William Roger Louis (New York: I. B. Tauris, 2006), 466 (first quotation), 467 (second and third quotations).

171. MP, June 1, 1946, 2.

172. Manuel L. Quezon III conversation with the author, February 12, 2005.

173. Golay, Face of Empire, 484.

174. When, for example, the Manila Post's editorials against the Bell Act and parity rights grew heated, the paper, under pressure from its readers, had to deny charges of anti-Americanism. MP, September 26, 1946, 6.

175. Cullather, Illusions of Influence, 2.

176. Ibid., 147, 189.

177. Swing broadcast, October 17, 1946, box 34, Swing Papers, LC.

178. McNutt to Truman, May 6, 1947, box 162, President's Secretary's File: Subject File, Truman Papers, HSTL.

### 15. FADING AWAY (1947–1955)

1. "McNutt Urges Democrats to Back Truman," *Manila Times* (*MT*), August 9, 1947, *Manila Times* Library and Morgue (*MTLM*), Lopez Memorial Museum (LMM), Pasig City, Philippines.

2. Paul V. McNutt to Harry S. Truman, May 8, 1947, box 1571, Official File (OF) 1040, White House Central File (WHCF), Harry S. Truman Papers, Harry S. Truman Library (HSTL). "Charges vs. US 'Astound' McNutt," *MT*, March 30, 1947, *MTLM* (quotation).

3. When Thomas E. Dewey retired from politics in 1954, McNutt observed that any officeholder was obliged to give "some consideration to his family and future." News clipping, no date [1954], box 27, Paul V. McNutt Papers (PVMP), Lilly Library (LL), Indiana University (IU).

4. Michael J. Hogan, *A Cross of Iron: Harry S. Truman and the Origins of the National Security State, 1945–1954* (Cambridge: Cambridge University Press, 1998), 8; Gary Gerstle, "The Protean Character of American Liberalism," *American Historical Review* 99 no. 4 (1994), 1070–1072; Alonzo L. Hamby, *Liberalism and Its Challengers: From F.D.R. to Bush*, 2nd ed. (New York: Oxford University Press, 1992), vii (quotation).

5. Hogan, *Cross of Iron*, 3.

6. As Michael Hogan has pointed out, the chief dissenter in national politics from the security-centered postwar consensus was the right wing of the Republican Party. See Hogan, *Cross of Iron*, 5–21, 70.

7. Melvyn P. Leffler, *A Preponderance of Power: National Security, the Truman Administration, and the Cold War* (Stanford, CA: Stanford University Press, 1992), 19.

8. Alonzo L. Hamby, *Man of the People: A Life of Harry S. Truman* (New York: Oxford University Press, 1995), 314.

9. Jonathan Bell, *The Liberal State on Trial: The Cold War and American Politics in the Truman Years* (New York: Columbia University Press, 2004), 269.

10. "Record of Time in Washington for P.V.M," no date [ca. June-July 1951], box 12, PVMP";Paul V. McNutt Enjoys a Lush Law Practice,'" *Indianapolis Times* (*IT*), March 26, 1948 (quotation), folder: Ind. Biography— McNutt, Paul V. and Family—Presidential Chances, Indiana Clipping File, Indiana State Library (ISL).

11. Anne Veihmeyer, interview with the author, March 6, 2005.

12. Associated Press clipping, "McNutt Cut Wide Swath in Business," *Indianapolis News* (*IN*), March 25, 1955, Paul V. McNutt Obituaries (Complied by Grace Woody), John L. Krauss Collection (private), Indianapolis, Indiana.

13. "Paul V. McNutt Enjoys a Lush Law Practice,'" *IT*, March 26, 1948.

14. Veihmeyer interview; Howard Krauss, interview with the author, July 15, 2006; "Statement on Franklin D. Roosevelt by Paul V. McNutt," no date (first and second quotation), box 9, Correspondence with Government Officials, Records of the Chairman of the War Manpower Commission, Record Group (RG) 211, National Archives at College Park (NACP); Paul V. McNutt ("McNutt") to Mrs. Forrest L. Henkel, April 20, 1945 (third quotation), box 11, PVMP.

15. Grace Tully to McNutt, June 28, 1948, August 4, 1948, and September 14, 1948 (quotation), box 23, Franklin D. Roosevelt (FDR) Memorial Foundation Papers, Franklin D. Roosevelt Library (FDRL).

16. Sidney Hyman to McNutt, February 4, 1949, box 23, FDR Memorial Foundation Papers, FDRL; Ann Veihmeyer oral history, June 1, 2001 (quotation), 13, Center for the Study of History and Memory (CSHM), IU, copy in the PVMP.

17. Paul L. Feltus, "History Will Call Him a Great American," *Bloomington* (*IN*) *Star-Courier*, no date [March 1955], McNutt

Obituaries, Krauss Collection; Veihmeyer oral history, June 1, 2001, 6, 13 (quotation).

18. C. R. Black to Anne Veihmeyer, February 14, 1952, and T. G. Proctor to McNutt, October 11, 1948, box 12, PVMP; Wayne Coy to Geoffrey May, November 6, 1956 (quotation), box 4, Wayne Coy Papers, FDRL.

19. McNutt to Wayne Coy, October 31, 1951, box 12, PVMP.

20. "Servants Recall 20 Years with McNutt," IN, no date, folder: Ind. Biography—McNutt, Paul V. and Family, Indiana Clipping File, ISL; Krauss interview (quotation).

21. Veihmeyer interview.

22. 1952 Campaign Speech box 23, PVMP.

23. McNutt press conference, June 28, 1943, box 2, Transcripts of Press Conferences, Records of the Chairman of the War Manpower Commission, RG 211, NACP; news clipping, "Rites Set for Judge J. C. McNutt," December 12, 1949 (quotation), Vertical File—Correspondence—McNutt, Morgan County Public Library, Martinsville, Indiana.

24. Maurice R. Greenberg and Lawrence A. Cunningham, The AIG Story (New York: Wiley, 2013), 112–113; "McNutt Elected US Life Director," MT, February 2, 1948; "McNutt U.S. Life Board Chairman," MT, September 21, 1947; "Insurance Firm Honors McNutt," MT, February 26, 1948; "EQ Fetes the McNutts at Malacanan," MT, May 28, 1952 (quotation), MTLM.

25. McNutt to W. Stuart Symington, August 22, 1951, and October 31, 1951, and McNutt to Corporation Service Company, June 29, 1951, box 12, PVMP; "McNutt Registered as Foreign Agent," MT, June 26, 1951; "McNutt Firm Wins Ammo Bid," MT, February 25, 1948; and "McNutt Boosts US-PI Trade Ties," MT, January 1, 1948, "US Ambassador Pays PI Tribute," MT, March 22, 1947 (quotation), MTLM.

26. "McNutt Affirms US' Orient Role," MT, June 26, 1947, MTLM.

27. "McNutt Cautions US Not to Dictate to Nations," MT, no date, "McNutt Stresses Importance of PI Relations," MT, December 26, 1947, and "McNutt Boosts US-PI Trade Ties," MT, January 1, 1948"; McNutt Report Criticizes US," MT, August 14, 1947, MTLM.

28. "McNutt Urges Expansion of US Trade," MT, December 11, 1947, MTLM.

29. "McNutt Completes Inspection Tour," MT, March 5, 1947, "Warns Against Aid to Japs," MT, April 5, 1948, MTLM. Report on the Sixth Meeting of the Public Advisory Committee on China, March 3, 1949, and McNutt to Paul Hoffman, May 19, 1949, box 12, PVMP.

30. McNutt to Paul Hoffman, September 19, 1949, box 12, PVMP.

31. Boston Globe, June 27, 1947, 17.

32. See Mary Dudziak, Cold War Civil Rights: Race and the Image of American Democracy (Princeton, NJ: Princeton University Press, 2000), 3–17, 152–202.

33. Milton Walter Meyer, A Diplomatic History of the Philippine Republic: The First Years, 1946–1961 (Claremont, CA: Regina Books, 1965), 134–136; McNutt to Matthew J. Connelly (plus attached telegram), July 24, 1951, box 110, President's Secretary's File: General File, Truman Papers, HSTL; Ed Lockett to David Hulbard, November 16, 1945 (quotation), folder 317, Dispatches from Time Correspondents, 1942–1968, Houghton Library (HL).

34. Michael Schaller, Douglas MacArthur: The Far Eastern General (New York: Oxford University Press, 1989), 131.

35. Richard M. Fried, Nightmare in Red: The McCarthy Era in Perspective (New York: Oxford University Press, 1990), 73 (quotation), 74.

36. Louis B. Mayer, the head of Metro-Goldwyn-Mayer (MGM), informed HUAC that because scripts went through so many departments few Communist ideas reached the screen. Memorandum Re: L. B. Mayer, August 28, 1947, box 5, Hollywood Blacklist Names LaCava to Menjou, Committee on Un-American Affairs: Exhibits, Evidence, Etc. Regarding Committee Investigations, Records of the United States House of Representatives, RG 233, National Archives Building (NAB), Washington, D.C.

37. Walter Goodman, *The Committee: The Extraordinary Career of the House Committee on Un-American Activities* (New York: Farrar, Straus and Giroux, 1968), 225.

38. Fried, *Nightmare in Red*, 76–77; Eric Johnston to J. Parnell Thomas, September 29, 1947, box 4, Hollywood Blacklist Names Gassner to Kriegel, Committee on Un-American Affairs: Exhibits, Evidence, Etc., RG 233, NAB.

39. Testimony of Jack Warner, May 15, 1947, folder: HUAC Exec. Session—Hollywood May 15, 1947, (no box number), Hollywood Investigation Exec. Session Transcripts (selected), Committee on Un-American Activities: Committee Minutes, 1947–1950, RG 233, NAB.

40. Robert K. Carr, *The House Committee on Un-American Activities, 1945–1950* (New York: Octagon Books, 1979), 216.

41. "McNutt Film Aide on House Inquiry," *New York Times* (*NYT*), September 17, 1947, box 5, Hollywood Blacklist Names LaCava to Menjou, Committee on Un-American Affairs: Exhibits, Evidence, Etc., RG 233, NAB; Larry Ceplair and Steven Englund, *The Inquisition in Hollywood: Politics in the Film Community, 1930–1960* (Garden City, NY: Anchor Books/Doubleday, 1980), 280 (quotation).

42. McNutt statement, October 24, 1947, box 5, Hollywood Blacklist Names LaCava to Menjou, Committee on Un-American Affairs: Exhibits, Evidence, Etc., RG 233, NAB.

43. Jack L. Warner statement, October 20, 1947, Committee on Un-American Activities, United States House of Representatives, Eightieth Congress, First Session, *Hearings Regarding the Communist Infiltration of the Motion Picture Industry* (Washington, DC: U.S. Government Printing Office, 1947), 9–11 (quotations).

44. Warner testimony, October 20, 1947, in ibid., 19.

45. Eric Allen Johnston testimony, October 27, 1947, in ibid., 306–308 (quotations).

46. Warner testimony, October 20, 1947, in ibid., 7.

47. "McNutt Leads Counterattack," *MT*, October 28, 1947, and "McNutt Rebuked for Statements," *MT*, October 29, 1947 (quotation), *MTLM*.

48. McNutt statement, October 28, 1947, *Hearings Regarding the Communist Infiltration of the Motion Picture Industry*, 362, 362. Memorandum re: Morris Rosner, also known as Mickey Rosner, October 8, 1947, box 7, Hollywood Blacklist Names Richards to Stevenson, Committee on Un-American Affairs: Exhibits, Evidence, Etc., RG 233, NAB.

49. "Paul V. McNutt," no date, box 5, Hollywood Blacklist Names LaCava to Menjou, Committee on Un-American Affairs: Exhibits, Evidence, Etc., RG 233, NAB.

50. M. A. Jones to "Mr. Nichols," March 10, 1954, Federal Bureau of Investigation File of Paul V. McNutt, Washington, D.C.

51. Fried, *Nightmare in Red*, 77; Goodman, *The Committee*, 219 (quotation).

52. Fried, *Nightmare in Red*, 78.

53. Goodman, *The Committee*, 224.

54. Ellen Schrecker, *Many Are the Crimes: McCarthyism in America* (Boston: Little, Brown, 1998), 327; Warner testimony, October 20, 1947, *Hearings Regarding the Communist Infiltration of the Motion Picture Industry*, 53 (quotation).

55. Memorandum re: L. B. Mayer, August 28, 1947, box 5, Hollywood Blacklist Names LaCava to Menjou, Committee on Un-American Affairs: Exhibits, Evidence, Etc., RG 233, NAB.

56. Goodman, *The Committee*, 225.

57. Fried, *Nightmare in Red*, 78; Goodman, *The Committee*, 220; Motion Picture Association of America, "Weekly Digest of Press Opinion," November 29, 1947, box 32, PVMP; Carr, *The House Committee on Un-American Activities, 1945–1950*, 74–75.

58. News clipping, "Under McNutt's Rule: UA Will Continue TV Counterattack," *Washington Post*, July 31, 1950, box 23, FDR Memorial Foundation Papers, FDRL; Tino Balio, *United Artists: The Company That Changed the Film Industry* (Madison: University of Wisconsin Press, 1987), 14–15.

59. Frank McHale to McNutt, October 7, 1948, box 12, PVMP; McHale to McNutt, October 31, 1945 (first quotation), box 7, Records of the Washington Office 1942–1948, Records of the High Commissioner to the Philippine Islands, RG 126, NACP: *Indianapolis News* (*IN*), February 2, 1948, 6 (second quotation).

60. McNutt to Virginia M. Rigby, July 5, 1948, box 12, PVMP; McNutt handwritten comment on "Chris" to McNutt, August 17, 1948, box 12, PVMP; *IN*, February 2, 1948, 6 (quotation).

61. NBC Radio broadcast of the Democratic National Convention, July 14, 1948, Call Number RWB 6465 B1–4, Mavis Number 1721794–1–1, Motion Picture, Broadcasting and Record Sound Division, LC.

62. Zachary Karabell, *The Last Campaign: How Harry Truman Won the 1948 Election* (New York: Alfred A. Knopf, 2000), 159; NBC Radio broadcast of the Democratic National Convention, July 14, 1948, LC; Veihmeyer interview (quotation).

63. Veihmeyer interview.

64. McNutt to Mrs. Harry Allison Goldstein, April 25, 1945, box 11, PVMP; McNutt to Abba Hillel Silver, January 14, 1942 (quotation), box 11, Records of the Federal Security Administrator: General Classified Files, 1939–1944, Alphabetical Series, RG 235, General Records of the Department of Health, Education, and Welfare, NACP.

65. McNutt speech, April 8, 1945 (all quotations), box 4, Speeches, Radio Addresses, Interviews, and Statements of Chairman McNutt, Records of the Chairman of War Manpower Commission, RG 211, NACP.

66. Resolution, Zionist Organization of America, Indianapolis District, November 29, 1947, box 12, PVMP.

67. McNutt to H. J. L'Heureux, April 4, 1949, file #111.662/4–449 and "Report of the Visa Task Force, March 31, 1949, 25 (quotation), file #111.662/4–1249—both in box 470, Decimal File, 1945–1949, General Records of the Department of State, RG 59, NACP.

68. Veihmeyer interview.

69. "Democrats Name McNutt Adviser," *MT*, no date, *MTLM*.

70. McNutt remarks, October 26, 1948, box 22, PVMP.

71. McNutt address, October 25, 1948, box 22, PVMP.

72. McNutt remarks, August 4, 1947, box 22, PVMP.

73. McNutt campaign speech in Indiana, no date [1950], box 23, PVMP.

74. "McNutt Backs Marshall Plan," *MT*, October 10, 1947, and "World Outlook Bright—McNutt," *MT*, May 23, 1952, *MTLM*.

75. McNutt address, November 27, 1946, box I-184, Charles Taft Papers, Manuscript Division, Library of Congress (LC).

76. McNutt campaign speech in Indiana, no date [1950], box 23, PVMP.

77. McNutt address, July 24, 1952, box 23, PVMP.

78. McNutt draft speech, December 22, 1949, and McNutt campaign speech in Indiana, no date [1950] (quotation), box 23, PVMP.

79. Leffler, *A Preponderance of Power*, 19.

80. McNutt campaign speech in Indiana, no date [1950], box 23, PVMP.

81. McNutt speech, August 20, 1950, box 23, PVMP.

82. McNutt address, July 24, 1952, box 23, PVMP.

83. McNutt speech, October 29, 1948, box 22, PVMP.

84. Julian E. Zelizer, *Arsenal of Democracy: The Politics of National Security—from World War II to the War on Terrorism* (New York: Basic Books, 2010), 120.

85. McNutt campaign speech in Indiana, no date [1948], box 12, PVMP.

86. Kevin Mattson, *When America Was Great: The Fighting Faith of Postwar Liberalism* (New York: Routledge, 2004), 25 (quotation).

87. McNutt campaign speech in Indiana, no date [1948], box 12, PVMP.

88. "McNutt Will Confer with Truman Today," *Indianapolis Star* (*IS*), November

30, 1948, folder: McN 1949–49, Presidential Papers, Herman B Wells Papers, Indiana University Archives (IUA).

89. Bernard von Bothmer, *Framing the Sixties: The Use and Abuse of a Decade from Ronald Reagan to George W. Bush* (Amherst: University of Massachusetts Press, 2010), 46.

90. *IN*, February 20, 1954, 3; Krauss interview; Kathleen McNutt to John Mason Brown, no date [1952] (quotation), folder 3509, John Mason Brown Papers, HL.

91. *IN*, February 20, 1954, 3.

92. Paul L. Feltus, "History Will Call Him a Great American," *Bloomington (IN) Star-Courier*, no date [March 1955], McNutt Obituaries, Krauss Collection.

93. Veihmeyer interview.

94. Krauss interview; Veihmeyer interview (quotations).

95. McNutt to Clark C. Griffith, April 19, 1951, box 12, PVMP; Associated Press notice, "McNutt Sails," February 7, 1950, attached to photograph in *New York World-Telegram and Sun* Collection, Prints and Photographs Division, LC.

96. Kathleen McNutt to John Mason Brown, no date [1952], folder 3509, Brown Papers, HL.

97. "1952 Campaign Speech," no date, box 23, PVMP.

98. Press release, October 26, 1952, box 23, PVMP; Kathleen McNutt to John Mason Brown, no date, folder 3509, Brown Papers, HL (quotation).

99. Jack New oral history, July 9, 1985, 8, CSHM; Frank Lahey to McNutt, April 1, 1946, box 11, PVMP; Veihmeyer interview; news clipping, *IN*, March 24, 1955 (quotation), McNutt Obituaries, Krauss Collection.

100. News clippings, "Paul McNutt Dies," no date [March 1955], and "Former Governor Paul V. McNutt Dies," *IS*, March 25, 1955, McNutt Obituaries, Krauss Collection.

101. Press clippings, "McNutt Is 'Much Better,'" "McNutt Blood Plea Cancelled," and "McNutt, Ailing, Stops Here on Flight to Hospital," and handwritten note to "Jack,"

March 9, 1955—all in fiche 2, Department of Indiana, Biographical Files—Paul V. McNutt, National Headquarters of the American Legion Library, Indianapolis, Indiana.

102. Indiana news service clipping, "McNutt's Flag Lies in State Capital Today," no date [March 1955], Vertical File—Correspondence—McNutt, Morgan County Public Library.

103. "Solemn Pomp Marks McNutt Funeral," *IS*, no date, 4, folder: Ind. Biography—McNutt, Paul V. and Family, Indiana Clipping File, ISL.

104. "Eulogy by Herman B Wells," March 28, 1955, box 12, PVMP.

105. "Paul V. McNutt," *Washington Star*, March 25, 1955 (quotation), McNutt Obituaries, Krauss Collection. McNutt's death received less attention in newspapers outside of New York, Washington, D.C., and Indiana. See, for example, *Philadelphia Inquirer*, March 25, 1955, 38; *Baltimore Sun*, March 25, 1955, 21; *Chicago Sun-Times*, March 25, 1955, 9; and *San Francisco Chronicle*, March 25, 1955, 5.

106. "McNutt Longed to Call White House Home," *New York World-Telegram*, March 24, 1955, McNutt Obituaries, Krauss Collection.

107. "Paul V. McNutt," *Fort Wayne (IN) Journal-Gazette*, March 27, 1955, McNutt Obituaries, Krauss Collection.

108. "Two Celebrated Democrats," *Memphis Commercial Appeal*, March 26, 1955, McNutt Obituaries, Krauss Collection.

109. *Philippines Herald (PH)*. March 25, 1955, 2.

110. "Paul V. McNutt," *IS*, March 25, 1955, McNutt Obituaries, Krauss Collection.

111. "Mr. Paul V. McNutt," *Times* (London), March 25, 1955, McNutt Obituaries, Krauss Collection.

112. *PH*, March 25, 1955, 2; *Manila Evening News*, March 26, 1955, 3; *Manila Bulletin (MB)*, March 26, 1955, 12 (quotation).

113. *PH*, March 25, 1955, 2.

114. "McNutt Longed to Call White House Home," *New York World-Telegram*, March 24, 1955.

115. *IS* and *IT*, both March 25, 1955, Mc-Nutt Obituaries, Krauss Collection.

116. News clipping from Greensboro, North Carolina, March 25, 1955, McNutt Obituaries, Krauss Collection.

117. *MT*, March 26, 1955, 11.

118. "Paul Vories McNutt," *Anderson (IN) Daily Bulletin*, March 25, 1955, 4.

119. "A Friend Departs," *NYT*, March 25, 1955, McNutt Obituaries, Krauss Collection.

120. *MB*, March 26, 1955, 12.

121. "McNutt Gained, Kept Respect of Newsmen," *IN*, March 24, 1955, McNutt Obituaries, Krauss Collection.

122. "McNutt and Davis," *Elkhart (IN) Truth*, March 26, 1955, McNutt Obituaries, Krauss Collection.

123. *National Jewish Post*, March 25, 1955, 8.

124. Kimberly A. Zarkin and Michael J. Zarkin, *The Federal Communications Commission: Frontline in the Culture and Regulation Wars* (Westport, CT: Greenwood Press, 2006), 166; "Frank M. McHale, 83, Giant in Indiana Politics," *IS*, January 27, 1975 (quotation), Frank M. McHale Obituaries, Law Offices of Bingham and McHale (Private), Indianapolis, Indiana.

125. Edward D. Berkowitz, "Rehabilitation: The Federal Government's Response to Disability, 1935–1954" (PhD diss., Northwestern University, 1976), 247.

126. Berkowitz, "Rehabilitation: The Federal Government's Response to Disability,

1935–1954," 250; *NYT*, October 17, 1971, 77 (quotation).

127. See James H. Capshew, *Herman B Wells: The Promise of the American University* (Bloomington: Indiana University Press, 2012).

128. Kathleen McNutt to Marjorie Merriweather Post, August 3, 1955, box 26, Post Family Papers, Bentley Historical Library (BHL).

129. *IS*, December 12, 1956, 11. For the suggestion that Marjorie may have played matchmaker, see Roy Garrett Watson to Post, no date [late 1956 or early 1957], box 26, Post Family Papers, BHL.

130. *IS*, November 1, 1964, sect. 5, 15.

131. *IN*, November 28, 1969, 17; *IS*, November 1, 1964, sect. 5, 15 (quotation).

132. *IN*, November 28, 1969, 17.

133. News clipping, *Martinsville (IN) Daily Reporter*, August 1, 1967, Vertical File—Correspondence—McNutt, Morgan County Public Library; news clipping, "McNutt's Bust Abandoned," no date, and E. Ross Bartley to William Espenschied, August 2, 1967, Clipping File: Paul Vories McNutt, IUA.

134. News clipping, no date [1967], Clipping File: Paul Vories McNutt, IUA.

135. "McNutt Bust to Go to Museum," *Martinsville (IN) Daily Reporter*, September 9, 1967, Vertical File—Correspondence—McNutt, Morgan County Public Library; Herman B Wells to John E. Hurt, July 27, 1967, Clipping File: Paul Vories McNutt, IUA.

# Bibliography

ARCHIVAL COLLECTIONS

**Ann Arbor, Michigan**
*Bentley Historical Library,*
*University of Michigan*
Salvador Araneta Papers
Prentice Marsh Brown Papers
Eleanor Margaret Bumgardner Papers
William A. Comstock Papers
Hilmer Gellein Papers
Josephine Gomon Papers
Eugene Gressman Papers
Joseph Ralston Hayden Papers
James O. Murfin Papers
Frank Murphy Papers
George Murphy Papers
Post Family Papers
Manuel L. Quezon Papers (microfilm)
Walter H. Sawyer Papers
G. Mennen Williams Non-gubernatorial
 Papers

**Abilene, Kansas**
*Dwight D. Eisenhower Library*
Barbara Eisenhower Papers
Dwight D. Eisenhower Papers
 Pre-presidential Papers
 White House Central Files
Mamie Doud Eisenhower Papers
Vertical File

**Baltimore, Maryland**
*Social Security Administration Archives*
Arthur J. Altmeyer Papers
Revolving Files

**Bloomington, Indiana**
*Indiana University Archives*
Ward G. Biddle Papers
Margaret Buchanan Papers
Board of Trustees Minutes
William Lowe Bryan Papers
Thomas D. Clark Papers
Clipping File
Reference File
Herman B Wells Papers
Ora L. Wildermuth Papers

*Indiana University School of Journalism*
Roy W. Howard Archive

*Indiana University School of Law Library*
Paul V. McNutt Papers (Dean's Files)
Leon H. Wallace Papers (Dean's Files)

*Lilly Library, Indiana University*
Ellsworth Barnard Papers
Harry Barnard Papers
Claude G. Bowers Papers
Warren C. Fairbanks Papers
Charles A. Halleck Papers
Powers Hapgood Papers
John K. Jennings Papers
Richard Lieber Papers
Paul V. McNutt Papers

Sherman Minton Papers
Neely Family Papers
Val Nolan Papers
Mrs. Samuel M. Ralston Papers
George Washington Rauch Papers
Edward A. Rumley Papers
Walter E. Treanor Papers
Wendell L. Willkie Papers
James A. Woodburn Papers

*Monroe County Historical Society*
Deed Record Books
Newspaper Clippings File

*Monroe County Public Library*
Indiana Room, Vertical File

*Mary Eloise Sipes Collection (Private)*
Margaret Buchanan Diary and Papers

**Cambridge, Massachusetts**
*Harvard Law School Library*
Paul V. McNutt Class Reports

*Houghton Library, Harvard University*
John Mason Brown Papers
William R. Castle Diary
Joseph C. Grew Diary
Jay Pierrepont Moffat Diary
*The Nation* Records
Dispatches from *Time* Inc. Correspondents,
    1942–1968

*Arthur and Elizabeth Schlesinger Library, Radcliffe Institute, Harvard University*
Martha May Eliot Papers
Mary E. Switzer Papers

**Carlisle Barracks, Pennsylvania**
*United States Military History Institute,*
*Army Heritage and Education Center*
Lewis B. Hershey Papers
Frank J. McSherry Papers

**Charlottesville, Virginia**
*Albert and Shirley Small Special Collections Library, University of Virginia*
Homer S. Cummings Diary and Papers
Louis A. Johnson Papers
Edward R. Stettinius Jr. Papers
Edwin M. Watson Papers

**Chicago, Illinois**
*Center for New Deal Studies, Roosevelt University*
Albert Lepawsky Papers

**Cincinnati, Ohio**
*Center for Holocaust and Humanity*
*Education, Hebrew Union College*
American Jewish Joint Distribution Committee Archives Collection (photocopies)
Records of the Bureau of Insular Affairs,
    General Classified Files (photocopies)
"Nomination for Righteous among Nations:
    Paul V. McNutt" by Frank Ephraim

**Clemson, South Carolina**
*Clemson University Libraries*
James F. Byrnes Papers

**College Park, Maryland**
*Hornbake Library, University of Maryland*
Millard E. Tydings Papers

*National Archives at College Park*
General Records of the Department of
    Health, Education, and Welfare—Record
    Group 235
    Records of the Federal Security
        Administrator
    Records Relating to the War Research Service, 1942–1947
    Subject Files of Watson B. Miller
Records of the Bureau of Insular Affairs—
    Record Group 350
    General Classified Files, 1898–1945
Records of the Chemical Warfare Service—
    Record Group 175
    Miscellaneous Series, 1942–1945
    Subject Series, 1942–1945
Records of the Office of Territories—Record
    Group 126
    General Classified Files, 1907–1951
    Records of the High Commissioner to the
        Philippine Islands
Records of the Office of War Information—
    Record Group 208
    Photographs of Notable Personalities,
        1942–1945

General Records of the Department of
State—Record Group 59
Decimal Files, 1930–1939 and 1945–1949
Records Relating to the Intergovernmen-
tal Committee on Refugees
Records of the War Manpower Commis-
sion—Record Group 211
Office Files of D. Thomas Curtin
Office Files of Lawrence Hammond
Office Files of John F. Kinerk
Office Files of Allan M. Wilson
Office Files of Frederick W. Wile Jr.
Records of the Chairman of the War Man-
power Commission
Records of the Work Projects Administra-
tion—Record Group 69
Central Files: States, 1935–1944 (Indiana)
Civil Works Administration State Series
(Indiana)
Federal Emergency Relief Administration
State Series (Indiana)

**Columbia, Missouri**
*Western Historical Manuscripts Col-
lection, University of Missouri*

C. Jasper Bell Papers
Clarence Cannon Papers
Champ and Bennett Clark Papers
George N. Peek Papers
Lloyd Stark Papers

**Columbus, Indiana**
*Cleo Rodgers Memorial County Library*
Indiana Room, "Indiana Governors" Folder

**Detroit, Michigan**
*Archives of Labor and Urban Af-
fairs, Wayne State University*
United Automobile Workers Local 9
Collection
United Automobile Workers President's Of-
fice: Walter P. Reuther Collection
United Automobile Workers Research De-
partment Collection
United Automobile Workers War Policy
Collection
United Automobile Workers Washington Of-
fice: Donald Montgomery Collection

**Fort Wayne, Indiana**
*Allen County–Fort Wayne Historical Society*
R. Earl Peters Papers

**Franklin, Indiana**
*Johnson County Museum of History*
Genealogy Library, McNutt Family File

**Hanover, Indiana**
*Archives of Hanover College, Duggan Library*
William Ezra Jenner Papers

**Harrisburg, Pennsylvania**
*Pennsylvania State Archives*
George H. Earle Papers

**Hyde Park, New York**
*Franklin D. Roosevelt Library*
Francis Biddle Papers
Oscar Cox Papers
Wayne Coy Papers
Democratic National Committee Papers
Democratic National Committee Women's
Division Papers
Mary W. Dewson Papers
FDR Memorial Foundation Papers
Richard V. Gilbert Papers
Harry L. Hopkins Papers
Louis Howe Papers
William H. McReynolds Papers
Lowell Mellett Papers
Henry J. Morganthau Jr. Diaries and Papers
Franklin D. Roosevelt Papers
Official File
President's Personal File
President's Secretary's Files
Franklin D. Roosevelt Jr. Papers
James Roosevelt Papers
Harold Smith Papers
Lela Mae Stiles Papers
Henry A. Wallace Papers
Caroline F. Ware Papers
Sumner Welles Papers
Claude R. Wickard Diary and Papers

**Independence, Missouri**
*Harry S. Truman Library*
Nathaniel P. Davis Papers
Oscar R. Ewing Papers

Robert C. Goodwin Papers
J. Weldon Jones Papers
S. J. Ray Papers
Harry S. Truman Papers
  General File
  Official File
  Post-Presidential Papers
  President's Appointments File
  President's Personal File
  President's Secretary's File
  Senate and Vice Presidential Papers
  White House Files of Franklin D. Roosevelt
    Pertaining to Harry S. Truman

**Indianapolis, Indiana**
*National Headquarters of the
American Legion Library*
Department of Indiana, Biographical File
  (Paul V. McNutt and Frank M. McHale)
Subject File: Disabled Veterans of World War
  (Non-Compensated)

*Irwin Library, Butler University*
Allegra Stewart Papers

*Law Offices of Bingham and McHale (Private)*
Frank M. McHale Obituaries

*Indiana Historical Society Library*
Philip Lutz Jr. Papers
Carleton B. McCulloch Papers
Arthur G. Mitten Papers
Walter D. Myers Recollections
Meredith Nicholson Papers
James A. Stuart Papers
Booth Tarkington Papers

*Indiana State Archives, Indiana Commission
on Public Records*
Dillinger Gang Files
Ralph F. Gates Papers
Records of the Governor's Commission on
  Unemployment Relief
Paul V. McNutt Papers
Henry F. Schricker Papers
M. Clifford Townsend Papers
Matthew E. Welsh Papers

*Indiana Division, Indiana State Library*
Hugh A. Barnhart Papers
Grace Julian Clarke Papers

Harold C. Feightner Papers
Indiana Clipping File
Virginia Ellis Jenckes Papers
Richard Lieber Papers
Paul V. McNutt Papers
Paul V. McNutt for President in 1940 Club,
  Inc., Papers
James H. Meyer Papers
Walter D. Myers Papers
Reece A. Oliver Papers
Della Scott Swinehart Scrapbooks
Raymond E. Willis Papers

*John L. Krauss Collection (Private)*
Louise McNutt Diary and Papers
Paul V. McNutt Obituaries (Compiled by
  Grace Woody)
Paul V. McNutt Papers and Scrapbooks
Ruth Neely McNutt Remembrance Book
  (Compiled by Grace Woody)

**Iowa City, Iowa**
*University of Iowa Libraries*
Henry A. Wallace Diary and Papers

**Lawrence, Kansas**
*Kenneth Spencer Research Library, University of Kansas*
Ernest H. Lindley Papers
Harry H. Woodring Papers

**Lexington, Kentucky**
*Margaret I. King Library, University of Kentucky*
Alben W. Barkley Papers
Jouette Shouse Papers

**Lexington, Virginia**
*George C. Marshall Library*
George C. Marshall Papers

**Madison, Wisconsin**
*Wisconsin Historical Society*
Arthur J. Altmeyer Papers

**Makati City, Philippines**
*Filipinas Heritage Library*
Elpidio Quirino Papers
Retrato Photo Archive

**Manila, Philippines**

*José P. Laurel Memorial Foundation Library*

José P. Laurel Papers

*Ramón Magsaysay Awards Foundation, Ramón Magsaysay Center*

Ramón Magsaysay Papers

*National Library of the Philippines*

Coquingco Collection

George A. Malcolm Papers

President Ferdinand Marcos Documents

Rare Serials Collection

Sergio Osmeña Papers

Manuel L. Quezon Papers

**Martinsville, Indiana**

*Morgan County Public Library*

Genealogy Department, Vertical File

*Kevin Kent Collection (Private)*

**Moscow, Idaho**

*University of Idaho Library*

Ernest H. Lindley Papers

**Newark, Delaware**

*University of Delaware Library*

George S. Messersmith Papers

**New Haven, Connecticut**

*Yale University Library Manuscripts and Archives*

Jerome N. Frank Papers

Charles A. Lindbergh Papers

John Punnett Peters Papers

Henry L. Stimson Diary and Papers

**New York, New York**

*Herbert Lehman Suite, Columbia University*

Herbert Lehman Papers

James G. McDonald Papers

*Rare Book and Manuscript Library, Columbia University*

Frances Perkins Papers

*New York Public Library*

Norman Thomas Papers

**Norfolk, Virginia**

*MacArthur Memorial Archives*

Douglas MacArthur Papers

**Ottawa, Ontario**

*Library and Archives Canada*

Diaries of William Lyon Mackenzie King

**Notre Dame, Indiana**

*University of Notre Dame Archives, Theodore M. Hesburgh Library*

John W. Cavanaugh Papers

Frank C. Walker Papers

**Pasig City, Philippines**

*Lopez Memorial Museum*

*Manila Chronicle Collection*

*Manila Times/Daily Mirror Library and Morgue*

Photo Collection

**Princeton, New Jersey**

*Department of Rare Books and Special Collections, Princeton University Library*

Booth Tarkington Papers

*Seeley G. Mudd Library, Princeton University*

Bernard M. Baruch Papers

James V. Forrestal Diary and Papers

Arthur Krock Papers

**Providence, Rhode Island**

*John Hay Library, Brown University*

Theodore Francis Green Papers

**Quezon City, Philippines**

*Rizal Library, Ateneo de Manila University*

American Historical Collection

*Main Library, University of the Philippines–Diliman*

Sol Gwekoh Papers

Carlos P. Rómulo Papers

Manuel A. Roxas Papers

*Jorge B. Vargas Museum, University of the Philippines–Diliman*

Jorge B. Vargas Papers

**Seattle, Washington**
*University of Washington Libraries*
Henry M. Jackson Papers
Warren G. Magnuson Papers

**Silver Spring, Maryland**
*George Meany Memorial Archives*
American Federation of Labor Records
  Department of Civil Rights—Record
    Group 9
  Office of the President, William Green's
    Files, 1940–1952—Record Group 1
  Secretary-Treasurer's Files, George Mea-
    ny, 1940–1953—Record Group 2

**Terre Haute, Indiana**
*Indiana State University Library*
Indiana Federal Writers' Project Papers
Ross Lockridge Papers

*Vigo County Public Library*
Special Collections, Community Affairs
  Files

**Washington, D.C.**
*American Catholic History Research Cen-
ter, Catholic University of America*
Philip Murray Papers

*Federal Bureau of Investigation*
FBI File of Paul V. McNutt

*Georgetown University Library*
Harry L. Hopkins Papers
Robert F. Wagner Papers

*Martin Luther King Jr. Memorial Library*
Department of History and Biography, Clipping File

*Archives of the National Academy of Sciences*
Committees on Biological Warfare Files

*Library of Congress, Manuscript Division*
Joseph and Stewart Alsop Papers
Newton D. Baker Papers
Joseph Barnes Papers
Ruby A. Black Papers
Brotherhood of Sleeping Car Porter Papers
Harold Burton Papers
Vannevar Bush Papers

Wilbur J. Carr Papers
Raymond Clapper Papers
Thomas G. Corcoran Papers
George Creel Papers
Josephus Daniels Papers
Elmer Davis Papers
James A. Farley Papers
W. Cameron Forbes Journals
Bess Furman Papers
Felix Frankfurter Papers
Theodore Francis Green Papers
Papers of Burton Norvell Harrison and
  Family
Roy W. Howard Papers
Cordell Hull Papers
Harold L. Ickes Diary and Papers
Robert H. Jackson Papers
Jesse H. Jones Papers
Julius Krug Papers
William D. Leahy Diary
Courtney Letts de Espil Diary and Papers
Frederick J. Libby Diary and Papers
Breckinridge Long Diary and Papers
Archibald MacLeish Papers
John Bartlow Martin Papers
William G. McAdoo Papers
National Association for the Advancement of
  Colored People Papers
George W. Norris Papers
Robert P. Patterson Papers
Kermit and Belle Roosevelt Papers
Theodore Roosevelt Jr. Diary and Papers
Francis B. Sayre Papers
Raymond Gram Swing Papers
Charles P. Taft Papers
Robert A. Taft Papers
Irita Van Doren Papers
James W. Wadsworth Jr. Papers
Robert W. Woolley Papers

*Library of Congress, Prints and Photographs
Division*
*New York World-Telegram and Sun* Collection

*National Archives Building*
Publications of the Federal Government—
  Record Group 287
  Congressional Hearings

Records of the United States House of Rep-
resentatives—Record Group 233
Records of the House Committee on Un-
American Activities
General Records of the Department of
State—Record Group 59
Visa Division, General Visa Correspon-
dence, 1914–1945

*Archives of the United States Holocaust Memo-*
*rial Museum*
"The Jewish Community of Manila" by Abraham I. Feldbin and Josef Schwarz

**West Branch, Iowa**
*Herbert Hoover Presidential Library*
James P. Goodrich Diary and Papers
Herbert Hoover Papers
  Post-Presidential Papers
  Presidential Papers
Hanford MacNider Papers
Walter Trohan Papers

**Wichita, Kansas**
*Wichita State University Library*
Randolph Carpenter Papers

**Wilmington, Delaware**
*Historical Society of Delaware*
George S. Messersmith Papers

INTERVIEWS AND
ORAL HISTORIES

**Author's Interviews**
Rick Applegate, March 10, 2006, Indianapo-
lis, Indiana
Birch E. Bayh, November 8, 2010 (telephone)
Paulino Misa Capitulo, September 29, 2008,
Manila, Philippines
Lotte Hershfield, February 13, 2005, Cincin-
nati, Ohio
John E. Hurt, August 20, 2005, Martinsville,
Indiana
Howard and Shirley Krauss, July 15, 2006,
Indianapolis, Indiana
Jack New, June 23, 2006, Greenfield, Indiana
Manuel L. Quezon III, February 12, 2005,
Cincinnati, Ohio (informal conversation)

Curtis Roosevelt, March 21, 2005, Hyde Park,
New York
Mary Eloise Sipes, February 15, 2006, Bloom-
ington, Indiana
Edith Schuman Tackitt and Sylvan Tackitt,
June 29, 2006, Bloomington, Indiana
Ann Veihmeyer, March 6, 2005, Silver
Spring, Maryland
William F. Welch, January 11, 2006, India-
napolis, Indiana

**Frank Murphy Oral History Project,**
**Bentley Historical Library, University of**
**Michigan, Ann Arbor**
James A. Farley, November 11, 1964
Joseph R. Hayden, February 15, 1965
G. Mennen Williams, December 1964

**Center for New Deal Studies, Roosevelt**
**University, Chicago**
Thomas Corcoran interview with Albert
Lepawsky, November 18–19, 1971

**Center for Holocaust and Humanity**
**Education, Hebrew Union College,**
**Cincinnati**
Testimony of Ralph Preiss
Testimony of Manuel Quezon III
Testimony of Alice Weston

**Center for the Study of History**
**and Memory, Indiana University,**
**Bloomington**
Leroy Baker, October 8, 1976
Maurice L. Bluhm, June 8, 1969
Robert F. Byrnes, December 20, 1968
Jessie Call, August 1, 1977
Donald F. Carmony July 8, 1985
Hobart Creighton, July 20, 1971
Clyde G. Culbertson, April 29, 1992
Nellie Stipp Daly, February 14, 1980
Oscar R. Ewing, June 7, 1970
Robert H. Ferrell, November 3, 1994
Charles F. Fleming, February 28, 1974
Hugh Gray, May 19, 1973
Charles A. Halleck, December 15, 1969
John E. Hurt, September 23, 1985
Harold Jordan, May 2, 1973
Mrs. Albert L. Kohlmeier, November 11, 1968

C. Leonard Lundin, October 10, 1972, and April 18, 1994
Lander MacClintock, December 17, 1968
Frank McHale, August 2, 1972
Ruth J. McNutt, May 27, 1969
J. Irwin Miller, March 9, 1982
Jack New, July 9, 1985
Harold Platt, October 14, 1980
Milton Shubert Sebree, June 7, 1980
R. V. Sollitt, June 23, 1971
Edward C. Von Tress, December 12, 1972
Anne Veihmeyer, June 1, 2001
Joseph E. Walther, July 10, 1992
Herman B Wells, January 1968 and March 6, 1971
Herman B Wells and Edward E. Edwards, May 24, 1982

**Oral History Research Office, Columbia University, New York**
Arthur J. Altmeyer, September 14, 1966, and June 29, 1967
Bernice Bernstein, March 3, 1965
Ewan Clague, March 23, 1965
Peter A. Corning, March 16, 1966
Lavinia Engle, April 21, 1967
Oscar Ewing, August 26, 1966
Isidore S. Falk, July 28, 1965
James A. Farley, August–September 1957
Robert H. Jackson, 1952–1953
Arthur Krock, 1950
Maurine Mulliner, April 26, 1967
Frances Perkins, 1955
Samuel I. Rosenman, 1950
Charles Schottland, June 4, 1965
Jack B. Tate, June 3, 1965
Henry A. Wallace, 1952–1953
Claude R. Wickard, February–October 1953 (copy on Wickard's Papers, Franklin D. Roosevelt Library)
Kenneth Williamson, January 27, 1967

**East Carolina Manuscript Collection, J. Y. Joyner Library, East Carolina University, Greenville, North Carolina**
May Thompson Evans, January 30, 1978

**Indiana State Library, Indianapolis**
Edward Beecher Bender Oral History, October 31, 1968

Roger D. Branigan, October 19, 1971
Harold C. Feightner, February 28 and October 24, 1968
George Gill, October 23, 1969
Josephine Jackson Hubbard, March 13, 1968
Virginia Ellis Jenckes, October 11 and 12, 1967
Olive Beldon Lewis, October 2, 1969
Walter D. Myers, January 20, 1971
Curtis G. Shake, April 10, 1968
Reginald Hall Sullivan, March 22, 1976

**Oral History Series, Monroe County Public Library, Bloomington, Indiana**
Elizabeth Bridgewaters, July 1974
Henry Hammond, February 12, 1974
Alice Nelson, November 6, 1974
Hugh Ramsey, July 12, 1974
Johnnie Smith, January 13, 1977
John Emmert Stempel, February 24, 1976
Elma Stevenson, August 20, 1976
Robert C. Wiles, September 8, 1976
Grover Willoughby, October 31, 1975

**Regional Oral History Office, University of California, Berkeley**
Frank Bane, 1965

**Seeley G. Mudd Library, Princeton University, Princeton, New Jersey**
William O. Douglas, 1961–1963

**Social Security Administration Archives, Baltimore**
George E. Bigge, February 25, 1966
Abe Bortz, August 23, 1973
John J. Corson, March 3, 1967
Maurine Mulliner, March 29, 1966

**Harry S. Truman Library, Independence, Missouri**
Lois Bernhardt, September 19, 1989
Laurence H. Bunker, December 14, 1976
Oscar L. Chapman, January 12, 1973
Oscar R. Ewing, April 29, 1969, April 30, 1969, May 1, 1969, May 2, 1969
Arthur S. Flemming, June 19, 1989
Durward R. Gilmore, January 20, 1989
Robert C. Goodwin, October 13, 1977
Paul H. Griffith, March 9, 1971
Richmond B. Keech, July 26, 1967

David L. Lawrence, June 30, 1966
Harry N. Rosenfield, July 23, 1980
Walter Trohan, October 7, 1970

**Shoah Foundation Institute Interviews, United States Holocaust Memorial Museum**
Testimony of Ernest Burger, January 14, 1996
Testimony of Gisela Golombek, January 31, 1995
Testimony of Ilse May, August 14, 1997
Testimony of Fritz Schulman, May 1, 1996

**United States Military History Institute, Carlisle Barracks, Pennsylvania**
Albert C. Wedemeyer, 1984

PUBLISHED GOVERNMENT
DOCUMENTS

Committee on Agriculture, U.S. House of Representatives, 77th Congress, 2nd Session. *Hearings on Farm Labor and Production.* Washington, DC: U.S. Government Printing Office, 1942.

Committee on Appropriations, U.S. House of Representatives, 77th Congress, 2nd Session. *Hearings on Department of Labor—Federal Security Agency Appropriation Bill for 1943, Part 2.* Washington, DC: U.S. Government Printing Office, 1942.

Committee on Appropriations, U.S. House of Representatives, 79th Congress, 1st Session. *Hearings on Department of Labor—Federal Security Agency Appropriation Bill for 1946, Part 2.* Washington, DC: U.S. Government Printing Office, 1945.

Committee on Appropriations, U.S. House of Representatives, 77th Congress, 2nd Session. *Hearings on the First Supplemental National Defense Appropriation Bill for 1943, Part 1.* Washington, DC: U.S. Government Printing Office, 1942.

Committee on Appropriations, U.S. House of Representatives, 78th Congress, 1st Session. *Hearings on the First Supplemental National Defense Appropriation Bill for 1944.* Washington, DC: U.S. Government Printing Office, 1943.

Committee on Appropriations, U.S. House of Representatives, 79th Congress, 2nd Session. *Hearings on the Interior Department Appropriation Bill for 1947 Part I.* Washington, DC: U.S. Government Printing Office, 1946.

Committee on Appropriations, U.S. House of Representatives, 77th Congress, 2nd Session. *Hearings on the Second Supplemental National Defense Appropriation Bill for 1943.* Washington, DC: U.S. Government Printing Office, 1942.

Committee on Appropriations, U.S. Senate, 78th Congress, 1st Session. *Hearings on First Supplemental National Appropriation Bill for 1944.* Washington, DC: U.S. Government Printing Office, 1943.

Committee on Appropriations, U.S. Senate, 78th Congress, 1st Session. *Hearings on H.R. 2935—Labor-Federal Security Appropriation Bill for 1944.* Washington, DC: U.S. Government Printing Office, 1944.

Committee on Appropriations, U.S. Senate, 77th Congress, 2nd Session. *Hearings on H.R. 7181 Department of Labor—Federal Security Agency Appropriation Bill for 1943.* Washington, DC: U.S. Government Printing Office, 1942.

Committee on Appropriations, U.S. Senate, 78th Congress, 1st Session. *Hearings on Investigation of Manpower.* Washington, DC: U.S. Government Printing Office, 1943.

Committee on Finance, U.S. Senate, 79th Congress, 2nd Session. *Hearings on H.R. 5856 An Act to Provide for Trade Relations between the United States and the Philippines, and for Other Purposes.* Washington, DC: U.S. Government Printing Office, 1946.

Committee on Military Affairs, U.S. House of Representatives, 78th Congress, 2nd Session. *Hearings on H. Res. 30 Investigations of the National War Effort.* Washington, DC: U.S. Government Printing Office, 1944.

Committee on Military Affairs, U.S. Senate, 78th Congress, 1st Session. *Hearings on S. 763—Married Men Exemption [Drafting of*

*Fathers*]. Washington, DC: U.S. Government Printing Office, 1943.

Committee on Military Affairs, U.S. Senate, 77th Congress, 2nd Session. *Hearings on S. 2397, S. 2479, S. 2788, S. 2805, S. 2815, and S. 2842*. Washington, DC: U.S. Government Printing Office, 1942.

Committee on Military Affairs, U.S. Senate, 79th Congress, 1st Session. *Hearings on S. 36 and H.R. 1752—Mobilization of Civilian Manpower*. Washington, DC: U.S. Government Printing Office, 1945.

Committee on Un-American Activities, U.S. House of Representatives, 80th Congress, 1st Session. *Hearings Regarding the Communist Infiltration of the Motion Picture Industry*. Washington, DC: U.S. Government Printing Office, 1947.

Committee on Ways and Means, U.S. House of Representatives, 79th Congress, 1st Session. *Hearings on H.R. 4185, H.R. 4676, H.R. 5185 A Bill to Provide for Future Relations Between the United States and the Philippine Islands*. Washington, DC: U.S. Government Printing Office, 1945.

Eightieth Congress, 1st Session. *House Document No. 389, Seventh and Final Report of the United States High Commissioner to the Philippine Islands*. Washington, DC: U.S. Government Printing Office, 1947.

U.S. Department of State. *Foreign Relations of the United States: Diplomatic Papers, 1945, vol. 6, The British Commonwealth, the Far East*. Washington, DC: U.S. Government Printing Office, 1969.

U.S. Department of State. *Foreign Relations of the United States in Foreign Relations of the United States: 1946, vol. 8, The Far East*. Washington, DC: U.S. Government Printing Office, 1971.

U.S. Department of State. *Foreign Relations of the United States: 1947, vol. 6, The Far East*. Washington, DC: U.S. Government Printing Office, 1972.

U.S. Department of State. *Foreign Relations of the United States in Foreign Relations of the United States: 1950, vol. 6, East Asia and the Pacific*. Washington, DC: U.S. Government Printing Office, 1976.

BOOKS, ARTICLES, AND THESES

Abinales, Patricio N., and Donna J. Amoroso. *State and Society in the Philippines*. Pasig City, Philippines: Anvil Publishing, 2005.

Adams, Stephen B. *Mr. Kaiser Goes to Washington: The Rise of a Government Entrepreneur*. Chapel Hill: University of North Carolina Press, 1997.

Agoncillo, Teodoro A. *History of the Filipino People*. 8th ed. Quezon City, Philippines: Garotech Publishing, 1990.

Ahlstrom, Sydney E. *A Religious History of the American People*. New Haven, CT: Yale University Press, 1972.

Altmeyer, Arthur J. *The Formative Years of Social Security*. Madison: University of Wisconsin Press, 1966.

Ambrose, Stephen E. *Eisenhower*. Vol. 1, *Soldier, General of the Army, President-Elect*. New York: Simon and Schuster, 1983.

Anderson, Karen. *Wartime Women: Sex Roles, Family Relations, and the Status of Women during World War II*. Westport, CT: Greenwood Press, 1981.

Anderson, Terry H. *The Movement and the Sixties*. New York: Oxford University Press, 1995.

Atherton, Lewis. *Main Street on the Middle Border*. Bloomington: Indiana University Press, 1954.

Badger, Anthony J. *The New Deal: The Depression Years, 1933–1940*. Chicago: Ivan Dee, 1989.

Bailey, Gary L. "The Terre Haute, Indiana General Strike, 1935." *Indiana Magazine of History* 80, no. 3 (1984): 193–226.

Balio, Tino. *United Artists: The Company That Changed the Film Industry*. Madison: University of Wisconsin Press, 1987.

Banta, D. D. *A Historical Sketch of Johnson County, Indiana*. Chicago: J. H. Beers & Co., 1881.

Barnard, Ellsworth Barnard. *Wendell Willkie: Fighter for Freedom*. Marquette: Northern Michigan University Press, 1966.

Beland, Daniel. *Social Security: History and Politics from the New Deal to the Privatization Debate.* Lawrence: University Press of Kansas, 2005.

Bell, Jonathan. *The Liberal State on Trial: The Cold War and American Politics in the Truman Years.* New York: Columbia University Press, 2004.

Bellush, Bernard. *He Walked Alone: A Biography of John Gilbert Winant.* The Hague, Netherlands: Mouton, 1968.

Berkowitz, Edward D. "Rehabilitation: The Federal Government's Response to Disability, 1935–1954." PhD dissertation, Northwestern University, 1976.

———, ed. *Social Security after Fifty: Successes and Failures.* New York: Greenwood Press, 1987.

Bernstein, Barton J. "America's Biological Warfare Program in the Second World War." *Journal of Strategic Studies* 11, no. 3 (1988): 292–317.

Beschloss, Michael. *The Conquerors: Roosevelt, Truman and the Destruction of Hitler's Germany, 1941–1945.* New York: Simon and Schuster, 2002.

———. *Kennedy and Roosevelt: The Uneasy Alliance.* New York: Norton, 1980.

Blake, I. George. *Paul V. McNutt: Portrait of a Hoosier Statesman.* Indianapolis, IN: Central Publishing, 1966.

Blakey, George T. *Creating a Hoosier Self-Portrait: The Federal Writers' Project in Indiana, 1935–1942.* Bloomington: Indiana University Press, 2005.

Blanchard, Charles, ed. *Counties of Morgan, Monroe, and Brown, Indiana.* Chicago: F. A. Battey and Company, 1884.

Blum, John Morton. *V Was for Victory: Politics and American Culture during World War II.* New York: Harcourt Brace and Company, 1976.

Bodenhamer, David J., and Robert G. Barrows, ed. *The Encyclopedia of Indianapolis.* Bloomington: Indiana University Press, 1994.

Borgwardt, Elizabeth. *A New Deal for the World: America's Vision for Human Rights.* Cambridge, MA: Harvard University Press, 2005.

Bowen, Otis R., with William Du Bois Jr. *Memoirs from a Public Life.* Bloomington: Indiana University Press, 2000.

Branigan, Elba L. *History of Johnson County, Indiana.* Indianapolis: B. F. Bowen and Co., 1913.

Braeman, John, et al. *The New Deal.* Vol. 2, *The State and Local Levels.* Columbus: Ohio State University Press, 1975.

Brands, H. W. *Bound to Empire: The United States and the Philippines.* New York: Oxford University Press, 1992.

———. *Traitor to His Class: The Privileged Life and Radical Presidency of Franklin Delano Roosevelt.* New York: Random House, 2008.

Breitman, Richard, and Alan M. Kraut. *American Refugee Policy and European Jewry, 1933–1945.* Bloomington: Indiana University Press, 1987.

Brinkley, Alan. *The End of Reform: New Deal Liberalism in Recession and War.* New York: Vintage, 1995.

Brinkley, David. *Washington Goes to War.* New York: Ballantine Books, 1988.

Bristow, Nancy K. *Making Men Moral: Social Engineering during the Great War.* New York: New York University Press, 1996.

Bunting, Bainbridge. *Harvard: An Architectural History.* Cambridge, MA: Belknap Press of Harvard University Press, 1985.

Burns, James MacGregor. *Roosevelt: The Lion and the Fox, 1882–1940.* New York: Harcourt, 1956.

Bush, Donald L. "The Terre Haute General Strike." MS thesis, Indiana State Teachers' College, 1958.

Byrnes, James F. *All in One Lifetime.* New York: Harper and Row, 1958.

Capshew, James H. *Herman B Wells: The Promise of the American University.* Bloomington: Indiana University Press, 2012.

Carmichael, Hoagy, with Stephen Longstreet. *Sometimes I Wonder.* New York: Farrar, Straus & Giroux, 1965.

Carmony, Donald F. *Indiana, 1816–1850: The Pioneer Era*. Indianapolis: Indiana Historical Society, 1998.

Carr, Robert K. *The House Committee on Un-American Activities, 1945–1950*. New York: Octagon Books, 1979.

Carson, Julia H. M. *Home Away from Home: The Story of the USO*. New York: Harper and Brothers, 1946.

Catledge, Turner. *My Life and the Times*. New York: Harper and Row, 1971.

Cayton, Andrew R. L., and Peter S. Onuf. *The Midwest and the Nation: Rethinking the History of an American Region*. Bloomington: Indiana University Press, 1990.

Ceplair, Larry, and Steven Englund. *The Inquisition in Hollywood: Politics in the Film Community, 1930–1960*. Garden City, NY: Anchor Books/Doubleday, 1980.

Chafe, William H., ed. *The Achievement of American Liberalism: The New Deal and Its Legacies*. New York: Columbia University Press, 2003.

Churchill, Bernardita Reyes, ed. *History and Culture, Language and Literature: Selected Essays of Teodoro Agoncillo*. Manila: University of Santo Tomas Publishing House, 2003.

Clark, Thomas D. *Indiana University: Midwestern Pioneer*. Vol. 2, *In Mid-Passage*. Bloomington: Indiana University Press, 1973.

———. *Indiana University: Midwestern Pioneer*. Vol. 3, *Years of Fulfillment*. Bloomington: Indiana University Press, 1977.

Clutter, Richard Morris. "The Indiana American Legion, 1919–1960." PhD dissertation, Indiana University, 1974.

Coffman, Edward M. *The War to End All Wars: The American Military Experience in World War I*. Lexington: University Press of Kentucky, 1998.

Collins, Dorothy C., and Cecil K. Byrd. *Indiana University: A Pictorial History*. Bloomington: Indiana University Press, 1992.

Cook, Blanche Wiesen. *Eleanor Roosevelt*. Vol. 1, *1884–1933*. New York: Penguin Books, 1992.

Cortes, Rosario Mendoza, ed. *Philippine Presidents: 100 Years*. Quezon City, Philippines: New Day Publishers, 1999.

Craig, Douglas B. *After Wilson: The Struggle for the Democratic Party, 1920–1934*. Chapel Hill: University of North Carolina Press, 1991.

———. *Progressives at War: William G. McAdoo and Newton D. Baker, 1863–1941*. Baltimore: Johns Hopkins University Press, 2013.

Cuéllar, Mariano-Florentino. *Governing Security: The Hidden Origins of American Security Agencies*. Stanford, CA: Stanford Law Books, 2013.

Cullather, Nick. *Illusions of Influence: The Political Economy of United States-Philippine Relations, 1942–1960*. Stanford, CA: Stanford University Press, 1994.

Dallek, Robert. *Franklin D. Roosevelt and American Foreign Policy, 1932–1945*. New York: Oxford University Press, 1979.

Dalton, Davis. *Rough Guide to the Philippines*. New York: Rough Guides, 2007.

Daniels, Jonathan. *White House Witness, 1942–1945*. Garden City, NY: Doubleday, 1975.

Davies, Richard O. *Defender of the Old Guard: John Bricker and American Politics*. Columbus: Ohio State University Press, 1993.

Dickson, Paul, and Thomas B. Allen. *The Bonus Army: An American Epic*. New York: Walker and Co., 2004.

Donahoe, Bernard. *Private Plans and Public Dangers: The Story of FDR's Third Nomination*. Notre Dame, IN: University of Notre Dame Press, 1965.

Downey, Kirstin. *The Life and Legacy of Frances Perkins—Social Security, Unemployment, and the Minimum Wage*. New York: Anchor Books, 2009.

Drury, Allen. *A Senate Journal, 1943–1945*. New York: McGraw-Hill, 1963.

Dudziak, Mary. *Cold War Civil Rights: Race and the Image of American Democracy*. Princeton, NJ: Princeton University Press, 2000.

Dunn, Susan. *1940: FDR, Willkie, Lndbergh, Hitler—the Election amid the Storm.* New Haven, CT: Yale University Press, 2013.

———. *Roosevelt's Purge: How FDR Fought to Change the Democratic Party.* Cambridge, MA: Belknap Press of Harvard University Press, 2010.

Elier, Keith E. *Mobilizing America: Robert P. Patterson and the War Effort, 1940–1945.* Ithaca, NY: Cornell University Press, 1997.

Ephraim, Frank. *Escape to Manila: From Nazi Tyranny to Japanese Terror.* Urbana: University of Illinois Press, 2003.

Escalante, Rene R. *The Bearer of Pax Americana: The Philippine Career of William H. Taft, 1900–1903.* Quezon City, Philippines: New Day Publishers, 2007.

Fadely, James Philip. "Editors, Whistle Stops, and Elephants: The Presidential Campaign of 1936 in Indiana." *Indiana Magazine of History* 85, no. 2 (June 1989): 101–137.

———. *Thomas Taggart: Public Servant, Political Boss, 1856–1929.* Indianapolis: Indiana Historical Society, 1997.

Fanning, Richard W. *Peace and Disarmament: Naval Rivalry and Arms Control, 1922–1933.* Lexington: University Press of Kentucky, 1995.

Feingold, Henry L. *The Politics of Rescue: The Roosevelt Administration and the Holocaust, 1938–1945.* New Brunswick, NJ: Rutgers University Press, 1970.

Ferrell, Robert H. *American Diplomacy in the Great Depression: Hoover-Stimson Foreign Policy.* New York: W. W. Norton, 1957.

———. *Choosing Truman: The Democratic Convention of 1944.* Columbia: University of Missouri Press, 1994.

———. *The Dying President: Franklin D. Roosevelt, 1944–1945.* Columbia: University of Missouri Press, 1998.

———. *Peace in Their Time: The Origins of the Kellogg-Briand Pact.* New York: W. W. Norton, 1969.

———. *Woodrow Wilson and World War I.* New York: Harper and Row, 1985.

———, ed. *FDR's Quiet Confidant: The Autobiography of Frank C. Walker.* Niwot: University Press of Colorado, 1997.

———. ed. *Off the Record: The Private Papers of Harry S. Truman.* New York: Penguin Books, 1980.

Fine, Sidney. *Frank Murphy: The New Deal Years.* Chicago: University of Chicago Press, 1979.

Flynn, George Q. *Lewis B. Hershey, Mr. Selective Service.* Chapel Hill: University of North Carolina Press, 1985.

———. *The Mess in Washington: Manpower Mobilization in World War II.* Westport, CT: Greenwood Press, 1979.

Foster, Kathleen A., Nanette Esseck Brewer, and Margaret Contompasis. *Thomas Hart Benton and the Indiana Murals.* Bloomington: Indiana University Press, 2000.

Fraser Steve, and Gary Gerstle, eds. *The Rise and Fall of the New Deal Order, 1930–1980.* Princeton, NJ: Princeton University Press, 1989.

Frederick, R. A. "Colonel Richard Lieber: Conservationist and Public Builder: The Indiana Years." PhD dissertation, Indiana University, 1960.

Freidel, Frank. *Franklin D. Roosevelt: The Ordeal.* Boston: Little, Brown, 1954.

Fried, Richard M. *Nightmare in Red: The McCarthy Era in Perspective.* New York: Oxford University Press, 1990.

Friend, Theodore. *Between Two Empires: The Ordeal of the Philippines, 1929–1946.* New Haven, CT: Yale University Press, 1965.

Frydl, Kathleen J. *The GI Bill.* New York: Cambridge University Press, 2009.

Fuller, Wayne E. *One-Room Schools of the Middle West: An Illustrated History.* Lawrence: University Press of Kansas, 1994.

Gathorne-Hardy, Jonathan. *Kinsey: Sex the Measure of All Things.* Bloomington: Indiana University Press, 1998.

Gellman, Irwin F. *Secret Affairs: Franklin Roosevelt, Cordell Hull, and Sumner Welles.* New York: Enigma Books, 2002.

Gerstle, Gary. "The Protean Character of American Liberalism." *American Historical Review* 99, no. 4 (1994): 1043–1073.

Gifford, Prosser, and William Roger Louis, eds. *The Transfer of Power in Africa: Decolo-*

*nization, 1940–1960.* New Haven, CT: Yale University Press, 1982.

Gleeck, Lewis E., Jr. *The American Governors-General and High Commissioners to the Philippines: Proconsuls, Nation-Builders, and Politicians.* Quezon City, Philippines: New Day Publishers, 1986.

———. *Dissolving the Colonial Bond: American Ambassadors to the Philippines, 1946–1984.* Quezon City, Philippines: New Day Publishers, 1988.

Go, Julian, and Anne L. Foster, eds. *The American Colonial State in the Philippines: Global Perspectives.* Pasig City, Philippines: Anvil Publishing, 2005.

Golay, Frank Hindman. *Face of Empire: United States-Philippine Relations, 1898–1946.* Quezon City, Philippines: Ateneo de Manila University Press, 1997.

Goodman, Grant K. *Four Aspects of Philippine-Japanese Relations, 1930–1940.* New Haven, CT: Southeast Asia Studies, Yale University, 1967.

Goodman, Walter. *The Committee: The Extraordinary Career of the House Committee on Un-American Activities.* New York: Farrar, Straus and Giroux, 1968.

Goodwin, Doris Kearns. *No Ordinary Time: Franklin and Eleanor Roosevelt: The Home Front in World War II.* New York: Simon and Schuster, 1994.

Gould, Lewis L. *The Most Exclusive Club: A History of the Modern United States Senate.* New York: Basic Books, 2005.

Graham, Otis L., and Meghan Robinson Wander, eds. *Franklin D. Roosevelt, His Life and Times: An Encyclopedic View.* New York: Da Capo Press, 1985.

Gray, Ralph D., ed. *Gentlemen from Indiana: National Party Candidates, 1836–1940.* Indianapolis: Indiana Historical Bureau, 1977.

Greenberg, Maurice R., and Lawrence A. Cunningham. *The AIG Story.* New York: Wiley, 2013.

Gugin, Linda, and James E. St. Clair, eds. *The Governors of Indiana.* Indianapolis: Indiana Historical Society Press, 2006.

———. *Sherman Minton: New Deal Senator, Cold War Justice.* Indianapolis: Indiana Historical Society, 1997.

Hamby, Alonzo L. *For the Survival of Democracy: Franklin Roosevelt and the World Crisis of the 1930s.* New York: Basic Books, 2004.

———. *Liberalism and Its Challengers: From F.D.R. to Bush.* 2nd ed. New York: Oxford University Press, 1992.

———. *Man of the People: A Life of Harry S. Truman.* New York: Oxford University Press, 1995.

Hammarberg, Melvyn. *The Indiana Voter: The Historical Dynamics of Party Allegiance during the 1870s.* Chicago: University of Chicago Press, 1977.

Harrison, Francis Burton. *Origins of the Philippine Republic: Extracts from the Diaries and Records of Francis Harrison Burton.* Ed. Michael P. Oronato. Ithaca, NY: Southeast Asia Program, Department of Asian Studies, Cornell University, 1974.

Hassett, William D. *Off the Record with F.D.R.* London: George Allen and Unwin, 1960.

Hatch, Alden. *Young Willkie.* New York: Harcourt, Brace, and Company, 1944.

Hegarty, Marilyn B. *Victory Girls, Khaki-Wackies, and Patriotutes: The Regulation of Female Sexuality during World War II.* New York: New York University Press, 2008.

*History of Johnson County, Indiana.* Chicago: Brant & Fuller, 1888.

Hofstadter, Richard. *The American Political Tradition and the Men Who Made It.* New York: Vintage, 1973.

Hogan, Michael J. *A Cross of Iron: Harry S. Truman and the Origins of the National Security State, 1945–1954.* Cambridge: Cambridge University Press, 1998.

Hurt, John E., *My View of the Twentieth Century.* Martinsville, IN: Privately printed, 2005.

Ickes, Harold. *The Secret Diary of Harold Ickes.* Vol. 3, *The Lowering Clouds, 1939–1941.* New York: Simon and Schuster, 1954.

Jackson, Robert H. *That Man: An Insider's Portrait of Franklin D. Roosevelt.* Ed. John Q. Barrett. New York: Oxford University Press, 2003.

Janeway, Eliot. *The Struggle for Survival: A Chronicle of Economic Mobilization in World War II.* New Haven, CT: Yale University Press, 1951.

Jenkins, Roy. *Franklin Delano Roosevelt.* New York: Times Books, 2003.

Jessup, Benjamin L. "The Career of Paul V. McNutt." PhD dissertation, Kent State University, 1995.

Johnson, Robert David. *The Peace Progressives and American Foreign Relations.* Cambridge, MA: Harvard University Press, 1995.

Johnson, Walter, et al., eds. *The Papers of Adlai Stevenson.* Vol. 5, *Visit to Asia, the Middle East and Europe, March–August 1953.* Boston: Little, Brown, 1974.

Jones, Richard Seelye. *A History of the American Legion.* Indianapolis: Bobbs-Merrill, 1946.

Jordan, David M. *FDR, Dewey, and the Election of 1944.* Bloomington: Indiana University Press, 2011.

Karabell, Zachary. *The Last Campaign: How Harry Truman Won the 1948 Election.* New York: Alfred A. Knopf, 2000.

Karl, Barry D. *Executive Reorganization and Reform in the New Deal: The Genesis of Administrative Management, 1900–1939.* Cambridge, MA: Harvard University Press, 1963.

———. *The Uneasy State: The United States from 1915 to 1945.* Chicago: University of Chicago Press, 1983.

Karnow, Stanley. *In Our Image: America's Empire in the Philippines.* New York: Ballantine, 1989.

Kennedy, David M. *Freedom from Fear: The American People in Depression and War, 1929–1945.* New York: Oxford University Press, 1999.

———. *Over Here: The First World War and American Society.* New York: Oxford University Press, 1980.

Kipling, Rudyard. *Kipling Poems.* New York: Alfred A. Knopf, 2007.

Klein, Maury. *A Call to Arms: Mobilizing America for World War II.* New York: Bloomsbury, 2013.

Knapp, Kathryn L. *The Kickin' Hoosiers: Jerry Yeagley and Championship Soccer at Indiana.* Bloomington: Indiana University Press, 2004.

Knock, Thomas J. *To End All Wars: Woodrow Wilson and the Quest for a New World Order.* New York: Oxford University Press, 1992.

Koistinen, Paul A. C. *Arsenal of World War II: The Political Economy of American Warfare, 1940–1945.* Lawrence: University Press of Kansas, 2004.

Kondos, Elena M. "The Law and Christian Science Healing for Children: A Pathfinder," *Legal Reference Services Quarterly* 12, no. 1 (1992): 5–71.

Kotlowski, Dean J. "Breaching the Paper Walls: Paul V. McNutt and Jewish Refugees to the Philippines, 1938–1939," *Diplomatic History* 33, no. 5 (2009): 865–896.

———. "The First Cold War Liberal? Paul V. McNutt and the Idea of Security from the 1920s to the 1940s," *Journal of Policy History* 23, no. 4 (2011): 540–585.

———. "Independence or Not? Paul V. McNutt, Manuel L. Quezon, and the Reexamination of Philippine Independence, 1937–9," *International History Review* 32, no. 3 (2010): 501–531.

———. "Launching a Political Career: Paul V. McNutt and the American Legion, 1919–1932," *Indiana Magazine of History* 106, no. 2 (2010): 119–157.

Kramer, Paul A. *The Blood of Government: Race, Empire, the United States, and the Philippines.* Quezon City, Philippines: Ateneo de Manila University Press, 2006.

Lane, Jack K. *Armed Progressive: General Leonard Wood.* San Rafael, CA: Presidio Press, 1978.

Larrabee, Eric. *Commander in Chief: Franklin Delano Roosevelt, His Lieutenants, and*

*Their War.* New York: Harper and Row, 1987.

Lash, Joseph P. *Eleanor and Franklin: The Story of Their Relationship Based on Eleanor Roosevelt's Private Papers.* New York: W. W. Norton, 1971.

Lasser, William. *Benjamin V. Cohen: Architect of the New Deal.* New Haven. CT: Yale University Press, 2002.

Leffler, Melvyn P. *A Preponderance of Power: National Security, the Truman Administration, and the Cold War.* Stanford, CA: Stanford University Press, 1992.

Leuchtenburg, William E. *The FDR Years: On Roosevelt and His Legacy.* New York: Columbia University Press, 1995.

———. *Franklin D. Roosevelt and the New Deal.* New York: Harper and Row, 1963.

———. *The New Deal and Global War.* New York: Time Life, 1964.

———. *The Perils of Prosperity, 1914–1932.* 2nd ed. Chicago: University of Chicago Press, 1993.

Levine, Allan. *King: William Lyon Mackenzie King, A Life Guided by the Hand of Destiny.* Toronto: Douglas & McIntyre, 2011.

Lilienthal, David E. *The Journals of David E. Lilienthal.* Vol. 1, *The TVA Years, 1939–1945.* New York: Harper and Row, 1964.

Lingeman, Richard. *Don't You Know There's a War On? The American Home Front, 1941–1945.* New York: G. P. Putnam's Sons, 1970.

Link, Arthur S. *Wilson: Campaigns for Progressivism and Peace, 1916–1917.* Princeton, NJ: Princeton University Press, 1965.

Littlewood, Thomas B. *Soldiers Back Home: The American Legion in Illinois, 1919–1939.* Carbondale: Southern Illinois University Press, 2004.

Logan, George M. *The Indiana University School of Music: A History.* Bloomington: Indiana University Press, 2000.

Louis, William Roger, ed. *Ends of British Imperialism: The Scramble for Empire, Suez and Decolonization.* New York: I. B. Tauris, 2006.

———. *Imperialism at Bay: The United States and the Decolonization of the British Em-* pire, *1941–1945.* New York: Oxford University Press, 1978.

Luftholtz, M. William. *Grand Dragon: D. C. Stephenson and the Ku Klux Klan in Indiana.* West Lafayette, IN: Purdue University Press, 1991.

Lyon, Peter. *Eisenhower: Portrait of the Hero.* Boston: Little, Brown, 1974.

Madison, James H. *Indiana through Tradition and Change: A History of the Hoosier State and Its People, 1920–1945.* Indianapolis: Indiana Historical Society, 1982.

———. *The Indiana University Department of History, 1895–1995: A Centennial Year Sketch.* Bloomington: Department of History, Indiana University, 1995.

———. *The Indiana Way: A State History.* Bloomington: Indiana University Press, 1986.

———. *A Lynching in the Heartland: Race and Memory in America.* New York: Palgrave, 2001.

Mamot, Patricio R. "Paul V. McNutt: His Role in the Birth of Philippine Independence." PhD diss., Ball State University, 1974.

Martin, John Bartlow. *Indiana: An Interpretation.* Bloomington: Indiana University Press, 1992.

Mattson, Kevin. *When America Was Great: The Fighting Faith of Postwar Liberalism.* New York: Routledge, 2004.

McBrien, William. *Cole Porter: A Biography.* New York: Alfred A. Knopf, 1998.

McCormick, Henrietta Hamilton. *Genealogies and Reminiscences.* Chicago: Privately printed, 1897.

McCoy, Alfred W. *Policing America's Empire: The United States, the Philippines, and the Rise of the Surveillance State.* Madison: University of Wisconsin Press, 2009.

McCoy, Donald R. *Calvin Coolidge: The Quiet President.* Lawrence: University Press of Kansas, 1967.

McFarland, Keith D., and David L. Roll. *Louis Johnson and the Arming of America: The Roosevelt and Truman Years.* Bloomington: Indiana University Press, 2005.

McFeely, William S. *Grant: A Biography.* New York: W. W. Norton, 1981.

McFerson, Hazel M., ed. *Mixed Blessing: The Impact of the American Colonial Experience on Politics and Society in the Philippines.* Westport, CT: Greenwood Press, 2002.

McGerr, Michael E. *The Decline of Popular Politics: The American North, 1865–1928.* New York: Oxford University Press, 1986.

———. *A Fierce Discontent: The Rise and Fall of the Progressive Movement in America, 1870–1920.* New York: The Free Press, 2003.

McJimsey, George. *Documentary History of the Franklin D. Roosevelt Presidency.* 43 vols. Bethesda, MD: University Publications of America, 2001–2009.

———. *Harry Hopkins: Ally of the Poor, Defender of Democracy.* Cambridge, MA: Harvard University Press, 1987.

———. *The Presidency of Franklin D. Roosevelt.* Lawrence: University Press of Kansas, 2000.

McKenna, Thomas M. *Muslim Rulers and Rebels: Everyday Politics and Armed Separatism in the Southern Philippines.* Berkeley: University of California Press, 1998.

Menken, H. L. *The Diary of H. L. Mencken.* Ed. Charles A. Fletcher. New York: Alfred A. Knopf, 1989.

Meyer, Milton Walter. *A Diplomatic History of the Philippine Republic: The First Years, 1946–1961.* Claremont, CA: Regina Books, 2004.

Mistica, Sergio. *Manuel L. Quezon: A Character Sketch.* Manila: University of Santo Tomas, 1948.

Moe, Richard. *Roosevelt's Second Act: The Election of 1940 and the Politics of War.* New York: Oxford University Press, 2013.

Moore, Leonard J. *Citizen Klansmen: The Ku Klux Klan in Indiana, 1921–1928.* Chapel Hill: University of North Carolina Press, 1991.

Morgan, Iwan. "Factional Conflict in Indiana Politics during the Later New Deal Years, 1936–1940," *Indiana Magazine of History* 79 (March 1983): 29–60.

Morison, Samuel Eliot, ed. *The Development of Harvard University since the Inauguration of President Eliot, 1869–1929.* Cambridge, MA: Harvard University Press, 1930.

———. *Three Centuries of Harvard, 1636–1936.* Cambridge, MA: Harvard University Press, 1936.

Myers, Walter D. *The Guv: A Tale of Midwest Law and Politics.* New York: Frederick Fell, 1947.

Neal, Steve. *Dark Horse: A Biography of Wendell L. Wilkie.* Lawrence: University Press of Kansas, 1984.

———. *Happy Days Are Here Again: The 1932 Democratic Convention, the Emergence of FDR—and How America Was Changed Forever.* New York: William Morrow, 2004.

Neff, Robert R. "The Early Career and Governorship of Paul V. McNutt." PhD diss., Indiana University, 1963.

Nicholas, H. G., ed. *Washington Despatches, 1941–1945: Weekly Political Reports from the British Embassy.* Chicago: University of Chicago Press, 1981.

Offner, Arnold A. *American Appeasement: United States Foreign Policy and Germany, 1933–1938.* Cambridge, MA: Belknap Press of Harvard University Press, 1969.

O'Neill, William L. *A Democracy at War: America's Fight at Home and Abroad in World War II.* Cambridge, MA: Harvard University Press, 1995.

Ortiz, Stephen R. *Beyond the Bonus March and the GI Bill: How Veterans Politics Shaped the New Deal Era.* New York: New York University Press, 2010.

O'Toole, Patricia. *When Trumpets Call: Theodore Roosevelt after the White House.* New York: Simon and Schuster, 2005.

Paredes, Ruby R., ed. *Philippine Colonial Democracy.* Quezon City, Philippines: Ateneo de Manila University Press, 1989.

Parmet, Herbert S., and Marie B. Hecht. *Never Again: A President Runs for a Third Term.* New York: Macmillan Company, 1968.

Parrish, Michael E. *Anxious Decades: America in Prosperity and Depression, 1920–1941.* New York: W. W. Norton, 1992.

Patterson, James T. *Grand Expectations: The United States, 1945–1974.* New York: Oxford University Press, 1996.

———. *The New Deal and the States: Federalism in Transition.* Princeton, NJ: Princeton University Press, 1969.

Pauwels, Colleen Kristal. "Hepburn's Dream: The History of the Indiana Law Journal." *Indiana Law Journal* 75, no. 1 (Winter 2000): i–xxxiii.

———. "Inferior to None." *Bill of Particulars: Indiana Law School Alumni Magazine* (Fall 2000): 15–36.

Peckham, Howard H. *Indiana: A History.* Urbana: University of Illinois Press, 2003.

Pencak, William. *For God and Country: The American Legion, 1919–1941.* Boston: Northeastern University Press, 1989.

Perkins, Frances. *The Roosevelt I Knew.* New York: Viking, 1946.

Peters, Charles. *Five Days in Philadelphia: The Amazing "We Want Willkie!" Convention of 1940 and How It Freed FDR to Save the Western World.* New York: PublicAffairs, 2005.

Phillips, Clifton J. *Indiana in Transition, 1880–1920.* Indianapolis: Indiana Historical Bureau and Indiana Historical Society, 1968.

Polenberg, Richard. *Reorganizing Roosevelt's Government: The Controversy over Executive Reorganization, 1936–1939.* Cambridge, MA: Harvard University Press, 1966.

———. *War and Society: The United States, 1941–1945.* Philadelphia: Lippincott, 1972.

Pottker, Jan. *Sara and Eleanor: The Story of Sara Delano Roosevelt and Her Daughter-in-Law, Eleanor Roosevelt.* New York: St. Martin's, 2004.

Pound, Roscoe. "The Law School, 1817–1929." In *The Development of Harvard University since the Inauguration of President Eliot, 1869–1929.* Ed. Samuel Eliot Morison. Cambridge, MA: Harvard University Press, 1930.

Pritchell, Robert J., ed., *Indiana Votes: Election Returns for Governor, 1852–1956, and Senator, 1914–1958.* Bloomington: Bureau of Government Research, Indiana University, 1960.

Purvis, Larry D. "'Loyalty to the Chief': The 1940 Presidential Campaign of Paul V. McNutt and Its Potential for Success." MA thesis, Butler University, 1989.

Quezon, Manuel L. *Addresses of His Excellency Manuel L. Quezon, President of the Philippines on the Theory of Partyless Democracy.* Manila: Bureau of Printing, 1940.

Quirino, Elipidio. *The Memoirs of Elpidio Quirino.* Manila: National Historical Institute, 1990.

Reeves, Thomas C. *A Question of Character: A Life of John F. Kennedy.* New York: Free Press, 1991.

Reiman, Richard A. *The New Deal and American Youth: Ideas and Ideals in a Depression Decade.* Athens: University of Georgia Press, 1992.

Ritchie, Donald A. *Electing FDR: The New Deal Campaign of 1932.* Lawrence: University Press of Kansas, 2007.

Robertson, David. *Sly and Able: A Political Biography of James F. Byrnes.* New York: W. W. Norton, 1994.

Roosevelt, Curtis. *Too Close to the Sun: Growing Up in the Shadow of My Grandparents, Franklin and Eleanor.* New York: PublicAffairs, 2008.

Roosevelt, Eleanor. *This I Remember.* New York: Harper and Brothers, 1949.

Roosevelt, Franklin D. *Complete Presidential Press Conferences of Franklin D. Roosevelt.* Vol. 11, *1938.* New York: Da Capo Press, 1972.

———. *Complete Presidential Press Conferences of Franklin D. Roosevelt.* Vol. 14, *1939.* New York: Da Capo Press, 1972.

Roosevelt, Sara Delano. *My Boy Franklin.* New York: R. Long and R. R. Smith, 1933.

Rosenman, Samuel I. *Working with Roosevelt.* New York: Harper and Brothers, 1952.

———. ed. *The Public Papers and Addresses of Franklin D. Roosevelt.* Vol. 9 (1940), *War—and Aid to Democracies.* New York: Macmillan, 1941.

———. ed. *The Public Papers and Addresses of Franklin D. Roosevelt.* Vol. 12 (1943), *The Tide Turns.* New York: Harper and Brothers, 1950.

Rothman, Hal K. *LBJ's Texas White House: "Our Heart's Home."* College Station: Texas A&M University Press, 2001.

Rumer, Thomas A. *The American Legion: An Official History, 1919–1989.* New York: M. Evans & Co., 1990.

Salmond, John A. *The Civilian Conservation Corps, 1933–1942: A New Deal Case Study.* Durham, NC: Duke University Press, 1967.

———. *A Southern Rebel: The Life and Times of Aubrey Willis Williams, 1890–1965.* Chapel Hill: University of North Carolina Press, 1983.

Salter, J. T., ed. *The American Politician.* Chapel Hill: University of North Carolina Press, 1938.

Schaffer, Ronald. *America in the Great War: The Rise of the War Welfare States.* New York: Oxford University Press, 1991.

Schaller, Michael. *Douglas MacArthur: The Far Eastern General.* New York: Oxford University Press, 1989.

Schrecker, Ellen. *Many Are the Crimes: McCarthyism in America.* Boston: Little, Brown, 1998.

Scroop, Daniel. *Mr. Democrat: Jim Farley, the New Deal and the Making of Modern American Politics.* Ann Arbor: University of Michigan Press, 2006.

Shalom, Stephen Rosskamm. *The United States and the Philippines: A Study of Neocolonialism.* Quezon City, Philippines: New Day Publishers, 1986.

Sherwood, Robert E. *Roosevelt and Hopkins: An Intimate History.* New York: Harper and Brothers, 1950.

Skocpol, Theda. *Protecting Soldiers and Mothers: The Political Origins of Social Policy in the United States.* Cambridge, MA: Harvard University Press, 1992.

Slayton, Robert A. *Empire Statesman: The Rise and Redemption of Al Smith.* New York: Free Press, 2001.

Smith, Daniel M. *The Great Departure: The United States and World War I.* New York: John Wiley and Sons, 1965.

Smith, Richard Norton. *The Harvard Century: The Making of a University to a Nation.* New York: Simon and Schuster, 1986.

———. *Thomas E. Dewey and His Times.* New York: Simon and Schuster, 1982.

Stebenne, David L. *Modern Republican: Arthur Larson and the Eisenhower Years.* Bloomington: Indiana University Press, 2006.

Storrs, Landon R. Y. *The Second Red Scare and the Unmaking of the New Deal Left.* Princeton, NJ: Princeton University Press, 2013.

Streimatter, Roger, ed. *Empty without You: The Intimate Letters of Eleanor Roosevelt and Lorena Hickok.* New York: Free Press, 1998.

Stuttgen, Joanne Raetz. *Martinsville: A Pictorial History.* St. Louis: G. Bradley Publishing, 1995.

Swensen, Rolfe. "Pilgrims at the Golden Gate: Christian Scientists on the Pacific Coast, 1880–1915. *Pacific Historical Review* 72 (May 2003): 229–263.

Tan, Samuel K. *A History of the Philippines.* Quezon City, Philippines: University of the Philippines Press, 1987.

Tarkington, Booth. *The Magnificent Ambersons.* Bloomington: Indiana University Press, 1989.

Terkel, Studs. *"The Good War": An Oral History of World War Two.* New York: Pantheon Books, 1984.

Thomas, Karen Kruse. *Deluxe Jim Crow: Civil Rights and American Health Policy, 1935–1954.* Athens: University of Georgia Press, 2011.

Thornbrough, Emma Lou. *Indiana Blacks in the Twentieth Century.* Bloomington: Indiana University Press, 2000.

———. *Indiana in the Civil War Era, 1850–1880.* Indianapolis: Indiana Historical Bureau and Indiana Historical Society, 1965.

Trohan, Walter. *Political Animals: Memoirs of a Sentimental Cynic.* Garden City, NY: Doubleday, 1975.

Tully, Grace. *F.D.R.: My Boss*. New York: Charles Scribner's Sons, 1949.

Vagelos, Roy, and Louis Galambos. *Medicine, Science, and Merck*. New York: Cambridge University Press, 2004.

VanderMeer, Philip R. *The Hoosier Politician: Officeholding and Political Culture in Indiana*. Urbana: University of Illinois Press, 1985.

Vazzano, Frank P. *Politician Extraordinaire: The Tempestuous Life and Times of Martin L. Davey*. Kent, OH: Kent State University Press, 2008.

Von Blon, Philip. "The Hoosier Schoolmaster." *American Legion Monthly*. January 1929.

Von Bothmer, Bernard. *Framing the Sixties: The Use and Abuse of a Decade from Ronald Reagan to George W. Bush*. Amherst: University of Massachusetts Press, 2010.

Ward, Geoffrey C. *A First Class Temperament: The Emergence of Franklin Roosevelt*. New York: Harper and Row, 1989.

Watts, Sarah. *Rough Rider in the White House: Theodore Roosevelt and the Politics of Desire*. Chicago: University of Chicago Press, 2003.

Welles, Benjamin. *Sumner Welles: FDR's Global Strategist*. New York: St. Martin's Press, 1997.

Wells, Allen. *Tropical Zion: General Trujillo, FDR, and the Jews of Sosúa*. Durham, NC: Duke University Press, 2009.

Wells, Herman B. *Being Lucky: Reminiscences and Reflections*. Bloomington: Indiana University Press, 1980.

Wheeler, Jerry L. "Fish, Pheasants and Politics: Paul McNutt and the Popularization of Conservation in 1930s Indiana." MA thesis, Indiana University–Purdue University at Indianapolis, 2002.

Wilkinson, William Clayton, Jr. "Memories of the Ku Klux Klan in One Indiana Town," *Indiana Magazine of History* 102, no. 4 (2006): 339–354.

Williams, T. Harry. *Huey Long*. New York: Knopf, 1969.

Wilson, Joan Hoff. *Herbert Hoover: Forgotten Progressive*. Boston: Little, Brown, 1975.

Winchell, Meghan K. *Good Girls, Good Food, Good Fun: The Story of USO Hostesses during World War II*. Chapel Hill: University of North Carolina Press, 2008.

Wunderlin, Clarence E., Jr., ed. *The Papers of Robert A. Taft*. Vol. 2, 1939–1944. Kent, OH: Kent State University Press, 1997.

Wyman, David S. *The Abandonment of the Jews: America and the Holocaust, 1941–1945*. New York: New Press, 1998.

———. *Paper Walls: America and the Refugee Crisis, 1938–1941*. Amherst: University of Massachusetts Press, 1968.

Zarkin, Kimberly A., and Michael J. Zarkin. *The Federal Communications Commission: Frontline in the Culture and Regulation Wars*. Westport, CT: Greenwood Press, 2006.

Zelizer, Julian E. *Arsenal of Democracy: The Politics of National Security—from World War II to the War on Terrorism*. New York: Basic Books, 2010.

# Index

DEAN J. KOTLOWSKI is Professor of History at Salisbury University in Maryland, author of *Nixon's Civil Rights: Politics, Principle, and Policy,* and editor of *The European Union: From Jean Monnet to the Euro.*